Sue Bailey.

November 1986.

TREEN

and other wooden bygones

AN ENCYCLOPAEDIA AND SOCIAL HISTORY

EDWARD H. PINTO

BELL & HYMAN

Published by
BELL & HYMAN LIMITED
Denmark House
37–39 Queen Elizabeth Street
London SE1 2QB

First published in 1969 by
G. Bell & Sons Ltd
Reprinted 1976, 1979, 1985

DEDICATION

TO MY BELOVED WIFE
WHO PARTNERS ME IN EVERYTHING
AND HAS MADE THE LAST TWENTY-THREE YEARS
THE HAPPIEST OF MY LIFE

March, 1968

ISBN 0 7135 1533 3

Printed in Great Britain at the
University Press, Cambridge

Contents

☆   ☆   ☆

Acknowledgments   ix

INTRODUCTION   1
I   The Apothecary   11
II   Costume Accessories   21
III   Drinking   30
IV   Eating   67
V   Farm   90
VI   Fire and Lighting   107
VII   Kitchen   129
VIII   Laundry and Cleaning Devices   147
IX   Love Spoons and Other Love Tokens   158
X   Miscellany   165
XI   Mortars, Grinders and Graters   179
XII   Moulds   183
XIII   Nuts – Gourds – Fruit Stone, Jet and Bog Oak Jewellery – Petrified Wood   191
XIV   Parcelling, Postage, Sealing, and Document Storage   198
XV   Pastimes   204
XVI   Printing (Textile and Wallpaper) and Woodcut and Engraving Blocks   243
XVII   Reading, Writing, Copying, Drawing, Painting and Modelling Ancillaries   248
XVIII   Sailors', Sailmakers' and Fishermen's Devices   265
XIX   Scientific and Reckoning, Measuring, Calculating and Weighing   272
XX   Tea, Coffee and Chocolate-Drinking Accessories   289
XXI   Textile Workers' Devices   299

XXII	Tobacco Accessories	326
XXIII	Toilet and Bedroom Accessories	357
XXIV	Tools, Devices, Techniques and Some Products of Specialized Woodworkers	376
XXV	Trade and Craft Devices, Miscellaneous	393
XXVI	Trade Signs, Ships' Figureheads, Fairground Steeds, etc.	410
XXVII	Tuition	416
XXVIII	Watch Stands	424

Appendix I	Why the Pinto Collection has gone to Birmingham	427
Appendix II	A Selection of Formerly Normal Uses of the Word Treen	430
Appendix III	Rhyming List of Wares Composed by Ashley, Umbrella and Parasol Maker, of Bath—1811	432

For Further Reading — 434

Glossary — 437

Index — 443

Acknowledgments

The title page of this book should read 'By Edward H. and Eva R. Pinto'. The reason why it does not, is that I should then have had to omit the dedication and acknowledgment of my indebtedness to my wife. However, my most grateful thanks are certainly due to her for her great contribution during the past twenty-three years: she has not only shared my enthusiasm in collecting wooden bygones, but also the patient research which has gone into finding out as much as possible about the many curious objects which we have acquired or seen. Additionally, she has undertaken the considerable task of correcting all, and typing nearly all the manuscript for this book, has read the proofs, compiled the comprehensive index, and has arranged the groupings and taken most of the hundreds of photographs of some three and a half thousand objects.

For permission to illustrate objects which are not in the Pinto Collection, my thanks are due to the individuals and authorities to whom acknowledgment is given under the plates concerned.

I am also particularly grateful to the following for kindly allowing me to include articles or extracts from my writings, which have appeared in their issues—*Apollo; Cabinet-Maker; Connoisseur; Country Life; The Times; Wood; Woodworker; Antiques, U.S.A.*

For generous information from their store of knowledge or assistance in research, my thanks are due to all the following— Mr. T. W. Bagshawe; Mr. A. Golding Barrett; Sir Geoffrey Callender, M.A., F.S.A.; Mr. John F. Chalkley; Mrs. C. Cole; Lord Cullen of Ashbourne, M.B.E.; the Dowager Lady Cullen of Ashbourne; Miss Elizabeth David; Messrs. Fribourg and Treyer (Mr. R. H. Bridgman-Evans, M.C.); Mr. John Gloag, F.S.A.; Mr. W. L. Goodman; Miss Sylvia Groves; Commander F. Hart, R.N. (Retd.); Mrs. Kate Havinden; Mr. Jack Hawkins (Green Bros. of Hailsham); the late Commander G. E. P. How, R.N., F.S.A.Scot. and Mrs. How; Mr. F. J. Howe; Mr. G. Bernard Hughes; the late Courtenay Ilbert; Mr. James Laver, C.B.E., B.A., F.R.S.A.; Miss Agnes Lothian; Miss Marian McNeill; Mr. D. R. Matthews; Mrs. Winifred Millar; Sir Alan Moore; Miss Janet Murray; Capt. F. C. P. Naish; Mr. T. R. Nevin, T.D., LL.B., J.P.; Mr. Ian Niall; the late Dr. N. M. Penzer, F.S.A.; Mr. Charles Rattray; Mr. Raph Salaman; the late Rev. C. J. Sharp; Mr. C. Thomas; Mr. F. A. Turner; Mr. G. Bernard Wood.

For much helpful information and assistance, I am also indebted to the officials of the following museums, art galleries, institutions, etc.: Belfast Museum and Art Gallery—Mr. W. A. Seaby, F.S.A., F.M.A.; Birmingham Assay Office—Mr. A. H. Westwood, Assay Master; Birmingham Museum and Art Gallery—Mr. John Lowe, M.A., F.S.A., Mr. N. Thomas, M.A., F.S.A., Mr. P. Klein; Bowes Museum, Barnard Castle—Mr. Frank Atkinson, B.Sc., F.M.A.; Bradford City Art

Gallery and Museum—Mr. John H. Morley, M.A., A.M.A., Miss Anne Ward; British Museum—Mr. R. D. Barnett, M.A., Litt.D., F.S.A., Mr. R. L. S. Bruce-Mitford, M.A., F.S.A., F.M.A., Mr. J. W. Brailsford, M.A., F.S.A., F.M.A., Mr. J. Cherry, B.A.; Burghley House—Mr. A. J. Whitby; Cooper Technical Bureau, Berkhampstead —the late Mr. R. Oliver-Bellasis; Glasgow Art Gallery and Museum—Mr. Andrew Hannah, M.A., D.A., A.T.D., F.M.A., Mr. William Wells, M.A., F.M.A.; Guildhall Library—Mr. A. H. Hall, Mr. Godfrey Thompson; Guildhall Museum—Mr. Norman Cook, B.A., F.S.A., F.M.A.; Haslemere Educational Museum—Mr. A. L. Jewell, A.M.A., F.L.S.; Leeds City Museum—Mr. C. M. Mitchell, F.S.A., F.M.A.; London Museum—Mr. D. B. Harden, O.B.E., M.A., F.S.A., Mrs. Mary Speaight; Luton Museum, the late Mr. Charles Freeman, F.M.A.; Manchester Gallery of English Costume, Miss Anne M. Buck, B.A., F.M.A.; Museum of Childhood, Edinburgh—Mr. Patrick Murray, F.S.A.Scot.; National Maritime Museum, Greenwich—Lt. Commander G. P. B. Naish, R.N.R., B.A., F.S.A.; National Museum of Antiquities of Scotland— Mr. R. B. K. Stevenson, M.A., F.S.A., F.S.A.Scot., F.M.A., Mr. S. Maxwell, M.A., F.S.A.Scot.; National Museum of Ireland—Mr. J. Raftery, M.A., D.Phil.; Norwich Museums—Miss Rachel M. R. Young, M.A.; Public Records Office; Reading Museum of English Rural Life— Mr. C. A. Jewell, B.Sc.; Royal Botanic Gardens, Kew—Sir George Taylor, D.Sc., F.R.S.E., F.L.S., V.M.H., Mr. F. N. Howes, D.Sc., Mr. C. R. Metcalfe, M.A., Ph.D.; Royal College of Surgeons—Mr. John Lambert; Royal Scottish Museum— Mr. Ian Finlay, M.A.; Science Museum— Mr. J. A. Chaldecott, M.Sc., A.Inst.P., Mr. H. R. Calvert, M.A., D.Phil., B.Sc.,

F.R.A.S., F.M.A., Mr. K. R. Gilbert, M.A., D.I.C., Mr. W. T. O'Dea, B.Sc., M.I.E.E., F.M.A.; Victoria and Albert Museum—Mr. P. K. Thornton, M.A., Mr. D. J. V. Fitzgerald, M.A., Miss E. Aslin, Mrs. H. J. Morris; Wallace Collection—Mr. F. J. B. Watson, C.V.O., B.A., F.S.A.; Wellcome Historical Medical Museum—Mr. F. N. L. Poynter, B.A., Ph.D., F.R.S.L., F.L.A.; Welsh Folk Museum— Mr. Iorwerth C. Peate, M.A., D.Sc., D. Litt.Celt, F.S.A., F.M.A., Mr. Ffransis G. Payne, M.A., F.S.A., Mr. J. Geraint Jenkins, M.A., F.S.A.

Finally, friends overseas who I would like to thank, include: In Europe, Copenhagen, Nationalmuseet—Dr. Axel Steensberg; Groningen, the Niemeyer Nederlands Tabacologisch Museum—Mr. Theodorues Niemeyer, Mr. Georg A. Brongers, Mr. Tiemen H. Kimm; Munich, the Bayerisches National Museum—Prof. D. Theodor Müller; Oslo, Mr. Anders Gurhold; Stockholm, Nordiska Museet—Prof. Gösta Berg; Zeszyty Naukowe Univerytetu Jagiellonskiego—Mr. Michal Maśliński. In Canada, Mr. and Mrs. W. Klyn; Mr. and Mrs. E. J. Stone. In the U.S.A., Mr. Dennis Abdalla; Miss Ruth Adomeit; Prof. Schuyler Cammann (University of Pennsylvania); Mr. J. Burley Crane; Mr. Harry Dengler; Mr. Edward Durell; the late Mr. Larry Johnson; Mr. and Mrs. James A. Keillor; Mr. W. Redhed; Miss Alice Winchester.

For permission to reproduce the extracts from 'The Story of San Michele', I also thank John Murray (Publishers) Ltd., London, and E. P. Dutton and Co. Inc., New York.

EDWARD H. PINTO

Introduction

General

Twenty years have elapsed since the appearance of *Treen*, my first book on this subject. It met with much kinder reviews and more enthusiastic welcome than I had ever dared to hope. That it fulfilled a need for collectors and others interested in the way of living of the past, told in terms of the things which our ancestors made and used, cannot be doubted, for it quickly went out of print and secondhand copies of the book, published at 25*s.*, now fetch £10 or more.

Interest in treen and other wooden bygones has grown enormously since 1949; there are today many more collectors and there is now need for a much more comprehensive reference book. As Mrs. Pinto's and my collection grew, during the past 20 years, from some 2,000 objects to approximately 7,000, our knowledge increased commensurately, and now seems to be the time to write this encyclopaedia, particularly as our collecting days are drawing to a close, and our collection has now passed into the safe keeping of the Birmingham Museum and Art Gallery, where it will, we hope, give pleasure to a larger public than has been possible in the past. The reasons why the Pinto Collection of Wooden Bygones has left Oxhey Woods House for Birmingham, are told in Appendix I, at the end of this volume.

I suppose that the publication of *Treen* in 1949 was primarily the reason why we came to put the collection on view in our home in 1955. The history of the collection and the sequence of events are as follows. As a boy, more than fifty years ago, I already had three particular interests which have never abated—history, wood and craftsmanship, particularly craftsmanship in wood. As I also showed early signs of collecting mania, it was, perhaps, inevitable that I should become a collector of wooden bygones.

Most of the Pinto Collection was assembled during the last 30 years, but in a humble way I commenced collecting with schoolboy pennies. The pence were limited; although they grew to shillings soon after I started earning money, it was only about 1930 that the collection began to grow rapidly. When I married, my wife caught the collecting 'disease' and thenceforth our home filled and our pocket emptied twice as fast!

I was fortunate in being able to integrate my work with my hobby and was able to make various aspects of design and craftsmanship in wood my living, until 1964 when I retired. This background, combined with collecting, initiated a sequence of events which finally led to the public opening of the collection: first came requests to write articles for technical and art journals, next followed books (which included *Treen*), lectures, broadcasts, television, and participation in judging for competitions and bursaries in various branches of wood craftsmanship. Naturally, the combination of these activities increased cognisance of and interest in our collection and by 1954 we were receiving between 3,000 and 4,000 letters a year, all connected with wood, craftsmanship, historic research, identification of objects, or requests to view. Between 1954 and 1965, this voluminous correspondence from museums, collectors and wood craftsmanship enthusiasts all over the world grew to some 5,000 letters per annum!

Until 1954, we lived all over our house, with our treasures spread around us, but much as we enjoyed answering questions and showing people round, my wife and I were forced to the conclusion that we must take drastic steps, if we were to have any time left for reading, writing, research, etc. There seemed only two possible alternatives: one was to ignore most of the letters and refuse requests to view; the other was to put the collection on an organized basis. The first was unthinkable: we considered it wrong to refuse to show a collection which was arousing increasing interest from people from almost all parts of the world, so we embarked on the second. The collection occupied roughly half the house, so we decided to divide it horizontally, making ourselves a flat across the first floor and devoting most of the ground floor to the major part of the collection. Had we realized what an immense undertaking it would prove and how many thousands of pounds it would cost, we doubt whether we would have ever embarked on the scheme. But if we had not done so, we, too, would have missed much pleasure, for when my wife and I were at home at weekends, we enjoyed meeting and chatting to charming and interesting people, who came each year in increasing numbers.

As a result of eleven seasons of "Open to View", we have made friends in all parts of the United Kingdom, Eire, the U.S.A., Canada, Australia, Tasmania, New Zealand, South Africa, India, Pakistan, Ghana, Nigeria, Israel, Transvaal, Rhodesia, Uganda, Brazil, Argentine, Syria,

Sweden, Holland, Denmark, France, Switzerland, Italy, Germany, Turkey, Yugoslavia, Norway, Belgium, Spain, Portugal, Finland, etc. That our visitors enjoyed themselves, we know from what they told us, from the nice comments in our "Remarks Books", from visits which ensued through recommendations, and from the many people who took season tickets and came here repeatedly. Having expended so much in putting the collection on view and with its upkeep and continuous expansion costing much more than the income from "Open to View", we hoped that increasing numbers would visit it each year, as indeed they did.

We were often asked if the collection were unique: we believe it is and we are glad that it, its method of presentation, and its five acre garden setting, which was open to visitors and housed some of the larger exhibits in specially designed buildings, elicited so much appreciation. We have enjoyed collecting and, quite apart from the useful contribution which they made to the heavy cost of upkeep, we liked having the general public, collectors, wood craftsmen, art students, historians and schoolchildren come to see the result. It was a great source of satisfaction to us that so many children who first came in school classes, quickly returned on their own, or with friends and relatives, to whom they gave conducted tours. It is pleasing to know that our collection has provided stimulation in design and revived interest in hand craftsmanship. For the reasons given in Appendix I, the "Open to View" at Oxhey Woods House has now unfortunately ended, but it is appropriate to express here our grateful thanks to all those who, in recent years, have made gifts which, in due course, will go on display again in Birmingham as part of the Pinto Collection, with due acknowledgments to their generous donors.

Although this encyclopaedia is planned on a much more lavish scale than *Treen*, with many more headings and much more profusely illustrated, there still have to be some omissions, or only brief references to certain speciality subjects, which require a considerable amount of text and illustration. These omissions will be the subject of another book now being written jointly by Mrs. Pinto and myself. The most important of the omitted subjects are Scottish ware—including pen-and-ink ware, transfer ware, tartan ware, etc.—and Tunbridge wood mosaic. On both these forms of decorative ware, we have carried out long and original research and will, we hope, be able to present a very complete picture, containing some new and interesting facts. In the same book, it is intended to include a chapter on *Bois Durci*. It is then intended to follow on with another book covering those wooden bygones which correctly come under the heading of the smaller work of the cabinet-maker.

In the main, the scope of this book is limited to objects of European origin, including articles made in or exported from Europe to the U.S.A., Canada, Australia, New Zealand, South Africa and other countries where culture derives from Europe. Some few additions are included, such as oriental objects intended largely for export to Europe.

In order to make this work as comprehensive and interesting as possible, not only are some part wood and part metal objects, and a few of other materials, deliberately included, but also there are dissertations on commodities and customs connected with the social history aspect of wooden bygones, which I hope will help to bring the past to life.

In my previous book, I said that the word treen was defined by the *Oxford Dictionary* as "(i) made of tree; wooden (ii) of or belonging to, obtained or made from a tree or trees—1670". I went on to say

'References to treen are numerous in old English literature, particularly to chalices, cups, bowls, platters and "services of treen".

Never, I think has the term been applied to any object larger than, say, a spinning wheel. Moreover, it is not generally interpreted as covering objects designed primarily for ornament, such as carved figures.

In other words, the term "treen" usually described the miscellanea of small wooden objects in daily domestic or farm use and in trades and professions, and only objects within this scope are included in this book'.

Although, over the years, I have discovered many more references to treen, I think that, in the main, the above evaluation of the word remains correct, except, perhaps, to add that nearly all the objects formerly described as treen, were wholly or in part the product of the turner and that most of them were one-piece objects. Where they consisted of more than one piece, their junction was effected by turnery means, such as a lipped bowl and cover, or a stem threaded or dowelled and glued into a base; in other words, they were not cabinet or joiner made.

The best known 16th-century reference to treen is that which occurs in a sermon by John Jewel, the Elizabethan Bishop of Salisbury:

'In old time we had treen chalices and golden priests, but now we have treen priests and golden chalices'.

(a very similar statement has also been attributed to Archbishop Boniface, 1240–1270). A selection of formerly normal uses of the word treen is given in Appendix II. Here are two unusual references. John Evelyn in *Sylva* (1664), extolling the virtues and drink values of the sap of certain trees, refers to them as "Treen Liquors". James I of Scotland, in an Act of 1425, referring to the Queen's Ferry over the Forth, laid down that all the ferries for transporting horses should have for "ilk boate a treene brig (wooden gangway)".

I repeat that objects intended solely for ornament, such as carved figures and panels were never described as treen. Indeed, fitness for purpose may be said to have been the distinguishing feature of treen, but beauty of form and love of craftsmanship were rarely overlooked and great care was taken in selecting suitable timber for purpose, so that it provided the desired strength, colour, grain and sometimes ornament. Probably, treen and other wooden bygones are usually so satisfying because they are, in general, peasant work and, therefore, a natural and unselfconscious form of expression. The objects are nearly always of good form and even where decorated, they are more ornamental construction than constructed ornament. What lapses there are into bad taste, mostly belong to the last three quarters of the 19th century; even then, small objects of wood were among the lesser offenders.

In old turnery, the work left by the English turner varies from the comparatively coarse, suitable for kitchen, farm, etc., to the finest, thinnest and most gracefully formed, largely reserved, at one time, for drinking vessels. For fine work, the English turner probably had no peer; in great part, this was because it was the fashion for the wealthy, in the 17th century, to have their drinking cups, wassail bowls and other vessels turned from costly imported lignum vitae and other choice hard woods.

The English fine carver of small objects did not have the same encouragement. Where the carving itself formed the purpose, as in ornamental kitchen moulds, butter prints, etc., he was very competent, sometimes highly accomplished, but where the carving was merely an embellishment, he was seldom given a chance to show his skill: the wealthy Englishman, when spending his money on fashionable trifles, either preferred objects made of an intrinsically valuable material, such as gold, silver or ivory, rather than wood, or to be modish, he purchased imported trifles of carved box or pearwood. Consequently, most of the fine art carved objects illus-

trated in this book, are of French, Italian, or other western European origin.

There are four things which are sometimes very difficult to state with certainty about treen and other wooden bygones. The first is the wood; the second is the date; the third is the purpose for which made, and the fourth is why a thing was made of wood rather than of some other apparently more suitable material. When I wrote *Treen*, there were supposed to be some 30,000 identified varieties of hardwoods and 75 of softwoods; now, the identified hardwoods have, I believe, doubled and the softwoods have increased to more than 100. Luckily, at the time most of the objects described and illustrated in this book were made, the varieties of woods commonly used in Europe were considerably less. Even so, those most familiar with small objects of wood, can often do no more than hazard a guess, although it will probably be correct. But identification of wood by viewing long grain, figure, colour, etc. and estimating weight, is, at best, equivalent to facial identification of humans and open to grave error. There is only one way of identifying wood with any certainty and that, the equivalent of fingerprinting a human, is by microscopic examination of a carefully prepared cut-off section of end grain; to obtain this, without damaging the specimen, is not usually practicable. Colour, long grain and weight certainly help, but can be misleading, even on large surfaces; on small ones, shaped and sometimes carved all over, discoloured by fats, wines, or other stains, faded or darkened by age and then possibly varnished additionally, naming the wood may be a case of fools stepping in where angels fear to tread. This is the reason why, in many instances, woods used are not named in the various chapters.

The dating of treen and other small wooden objects is difficult because there are no hall-marks, as on silver, touchmarks, as on pewter, design books, as in furniture, nor great names among the makers. Another difficulty is that the simpler objects, having once been designed correctly for purpose, remained unchanged generation after generation; moreover, fashions largely by-passed rural areas. What have we to go on then? The answer is that there are a few original dated pieces, from which we can assume dates for others of similar design. Trade cards, of which the dates are known, sometimes give descriptions and illustrations of the objects made and sold. There are documentary records and descriptions, including some inventories with (although rarely) sketches in the margins, some dated books on turnery, showing pictures of objects then fashionable, and a few dated pictures which include treen in their composition. Most valuable for dating, are objects with names of makers stamped or engraved on them; where these are London makers, I have been able to establish the addresses and, through them, the dates in a number of instances. This is because, over a period of years, Mrs. Pinto and I have been able to build up the finest library of London Directories and related volumes, in private hands. We are continually adding to it and at the present time it totals between 80 and 90 volumes and includes the first London Directory, issued in 1677. Our collection contains the valuable nucleus gathered together and annotated by the late Sir Ambrose Heal.

There are known dates when certain commodities came into vogue and the wooden objects which were then designed for their use or service. There are approximate dates when certain foreign woods were first imported and in the 19th century there are some trade catalogues. Finally, there are the resemblances of certain treen objects to counterparts in silver, pewter, glass, china, etc. It will be readily realized that there is a large margin for error in some of these aids to dating and possibly most of all in the last. This is because treen was sometimes the contemporary, some-times the ancestor and at other times the country cousin of similar objects in other materials, the latter lagging 50 years or more behind its sophisticated city relations. It must be obvious, therefore, that considerable research and experience are the best guides, but even so the word "probably" should really be inserted before dates, just as it should before woods.

Some people believe that many of the aforementioned methods are out-of-date, now that the scientific system of radio carbon dating, or carbon-14 dating, as it is also called, has come into being. This is the last thing that is claimed by the scientists who have developed this revolutionary technique. The subject is too long and complex to describe here, but the position is summarized by H. Barker, in an article entitled *Radio carbon dating: its scope and limitations*, which appeared in *Antiquity* in 1958. His conclusion is '... that the carbon-14 dating method is at its best in fixing the broad outlines of a chronology rather than the fine details'.

The most important thing to understand is that radio carbon dating establishes, within reasonable limits, when a tree died, not when the objects made from the tree were actually made; this obviously underlines the need for experience to augment science. As an instance, after the last war I was presented with a portion of an oak roof beam from the bomb damaged roof of the Middle Temple Hall, which was erected in the reign of Elizabeth I. I had three cigar caskets made from it. Radio carbon dating would have to declare the caskets as at least 400 years old— possibly much more, because roof beams were often re-used timber from other buildings, or from old ships. Taking the other side of the picture, if a faker were careless enough to make a '500 year old object' from a tree cut down during the last 100 years, radio carbon dating would detect it.

Probably the most useful employment

of the technique at present is for the dating of wooden objects found in rock tombs, where a date of within a hundred years or so may be established, instead of a guess, limited to, say, one or two thousand years; but contamination by bog burials, fungal or bacterial growth, and other sources, can upset calculations.

Even assuming, however, the optimum of an accuracy of 100 years and the certainty that the object was made soon after the tree was felled, it is not of value in dating ordinary wooden bygones, as opposed to archaeological specimens. For instance, a period of 100 years or so would mean that (*a*) an object might have been made at the end of Elizabeth I's reign or the beginning of Queen Anne's, or (*b*), it could have been made in the reign of George III or George V.

Whilst the purpose for which an object was made can usually be determined accurately, there are instances where there may be two or even several correct answers. For example, a wooden steak beater or butter maul are one and the same object, made and used for either purpose. Then there are long cylindric boxes, which are sometimes found containing knitting needles, crochet hooks, pens or pencils. The answer is that they were general-purpose, turned storage cylinders, which were bought from a turner and used for whatever purpose you chose; this applies to many boxes and vessels from which you could formerly make your selection at the turner's, cooper's, or whitewood boxmaker's establishment. There are also objects where the original use has been changed and, additionally, there are real 'dunno-whats'. The first are difficult to deal with, for if the owner of a 'cat' remembers her grandmother using it as a bonnet stand, you will never convince her that it was not the original purpose!

When our collection was on view here, we had a 'dunno-what' corner and invited visitors to solve the problems. Some un-doubtedly correct answers were obtained in this way, usually from elderly people, and some solutions have resulted from showing mystery objects on television. Certain ancient objects, however, still hold their secrets and probably some will always do so, because they were made as individual answers to a particular person's requirements, they are unique and have no counterparts. I suspect also that, in some instances, they failed to do their intended jobs, but their creators could not bear to throw away the results of so much labour.

Finally, why were certain objects made of wood when it was obviously unsuitable for the purpose? I think the answer usually is that wood was, and very often still is the cheapest and easiest material in which to make a prototype or try-out for subsequent manufacture in another material. The elaborately carved, 16th-century dish, Plate 2, is an instance. It still retains traces of its original gilding, and was probably made to try out on some handsome Italian buffet, so that the wealthy patron could judge the general effect, before the goldsmith created his golden masterpiece. In the Wallace Collection are some carved, gilded, wood patterns for wall candle brackets and the subsequently made ormolu brackets are in the same collection. The elaborately carved pearwood candlesticks, Plate 123, have been deliberately stained and finished to simulate bronze; as even their prickets are of wood, it is obvious that they were try-outs and never intended for use. That oddity, the wooden moustache cup, Plate 313, *M*, is so crude that either it was a preliminary to a proto-type, or else one must consider that, perhaps, the inventor of the device combined in his person 'the walrus and the carpenter'!

The format of this encyclopaedia is designed, I hope, for easy reference, by arranging it under twenty-eight main subject headings, each commencing with a historic synopsis and then proceeding to describe the objects, as far as possible, alphabetically, and with a good index. The arrangement, however, has resulted in three particular limitations. The first, a lack of description of methods of manufacture, particularly turnery and coopering, is overcome by a brief description in Section XXIV, *Tools of Specialized Woodworkers*. The second, the reason why the introduction of lignum vitae to England, at the beginning of the 17th century was of especial importance to turnery, drink vessels particularly, is described in the introduction to Section III, *Drinking*. The third is the omission of the chapter on the treen of North-west Europe, which was included in *Treen*. As it is both distinctive and interesting, because of its geographic and historic background, it is included here, in revised and expanded form, under the heading of *Background to Folk Art*; the objects which come under this heading are illustrated in their appropriate sections.

Background to Folk Art

No country can attain any reasonable degree of comfort without wood, but countries with vast forests can enjoy a high standard of comfort and be very prosperous without many other commodities.

In Norway, Sweden, Denmark, Finland, Switzerland, Latvia, Estonia and other countries, as well as parts of Germany, Austria and Russia, wood, in the past, was the universal provider. In these countries men, and women too, are born in the tradition of wood craftsmanship, for from time immemorial timber has supplied not only the building material for the houses and churches of the majority of the people, but also most of the articles in everyday, festive and ceremonial use. It is also the fuel which warms them. For those countries with sea coasts, the fishing fleet and merchandise carrying boats, made largely of timber, were primarily the means of living, whilst inland, forestry, cooperage and general woodwork have always provided employment for large percentages of

the population of each nation. The economy of many of these countries has been built largely on wood and its export from some of them, in the form of sawn timber, plywood, furniture, woodware, matches, wood-pulp, etc., still provides, in some instances, a large part of the exchange necessary for the national prosperity.

Those countries lying in northern climes have vast forests, mainly of pine, birch, beech and alder, which provide more of the useful than of the beautifully grained timbers and, consequently, bold carving suitable to the materials and vividly coloured paints are introduced extensively, to make useful articles beautiful. Fitness for purpose is rarely sacrificed to ornament, but the most ordinary domestic articles are invariably attractive in design. The forests of central Europe and the Balkan countries contain more hardwoods and, in consequence, their ornament more often takes the form of fine carving, left unpainted.

Too often the treen of all the northern countries, as well as that of Denmark, Holland and North Germany, is classified as Scandinavian, or even more restrictedly, as Norwegian. Admittedly, there is great similarity in style and ornament of the woodwork employed in the Scandinavian Peninsula and round the shores of the Baltic, as well as in North-west Russia and Iceland and, without definite knowledge of the place of origin, it is often impossible to say from which country an article emanates. Traditional patterns being handed down from father to son, make it equally difficult to date much of the work accurately. But in some countries there are both national and regional differences in design, which can be best studied in their museums.

A good place in England for studying and learning to identify, as far as possible, North-west European treen, from its authentic labels of origin, is the Educational Museum at Haslemere, Surrey. The Museum's comprehensive exhibit of folk arts was mostly collected personally by the Rev. Gerald S. Davies, in North-west Europe. Some of the specimens gathered together date back to the 16th century. Seeing them *en masse*, it is noticeable how all are distinguished by the natural instinct to make design subservient to material and never to attempt more naturalistic portrayals of fruit, flowers, men or beasts, than material and practical purpose of object will allow.

Whilst the peasants of nearly all the countries of North-west Europe use colour and decorate their woodwork with geometrical chip carving, acanthus scrolls, rope moulding and figures of animals, particularly horses, lions, dragons of the sagas and dogs, they nearly all possess some characteristics which help identification. Norway and Sweden seem to have adopted curved and carved outlines and relief carving rather more than the other countries, with an emphasis on bold sweeps, scrolls, lettering and monograms. These features show in harness saddles (see Plate 427, *C*), cake boxes (see Plate 138, *M*), washing bats (see Plate 150) and mangling boards (see Plate 153). A common feature of Norwegian carving is a very square human head. North Germany portrays the human figure and much of the ornament has a distinct Gothic flavour. Swedish treen is often similar to Norwegian and where painted, red, blue, green and yellow comprise the usual colour scheme, but the Swedish peasants, in some of their finest work, have also developed a distinctive carved, fluted pattern, of the type familiar on Sheffield plate. Sometimes the flutes are straight and vertical; at others, they spiral, as in the jug and double drinking cup, Plate 48. The wood of these pieces is almost invariably birch, carefully selected for burr figure, and the flutes are ornamented with bone studs.

Holland, being short of wood, tends to flatness in design and the obvious desire to economize in timber. The ornament consists, almost invariably, of intricate but finely executed small-scale geometrical designs, covering the whole surface, the carved roundel being very much in evidence, as in the Friesland footwarmer, Plate 126, and the mangling boards from the same province, Plate 153. It is a mistake to think that the Dutch taste is generally more sombre than that of the other north-western countries. This impression prevails because oak is particularly favoured for treen and it is usually weathered or stained dark brown or black and not picked out in colour, as is so much of the Scandinavian work. Treen must be considered, however, against the background for which it is or was designed. In Scandinavia, wood is the traditional house building material, inside and out; with a background of wood for floor, walls and ceilings, in large part unpainted, the bright colours of the treen provided a welcome and much needed contrast. In Holland, on the other hand, red brick has been for centuries the normal building material and with the interior walls plastered and whitened, and very often a floor of red quarry tiles, the black oak treen, especially when interspersed with gleaming copper, brass and pewter, forms an effective contrast.

Individual Danish treen at times shows all the features already described, but *en masse* has a distinctive character of daintiness. Much of the 17th-, 18th- and 19th-century Danish treen, like the furniture, wall panelling and ceiling beams, is plain and simple, free from or sparse in carving and relying on paint for its ornament. The favourite subjects for ornament are vases and urns of rather formally arranged but natural flowers, floral wreaths and sprays, all in charming colours and generally against a blue background. Occasionally, scenic panels and figures are introduced; painted dates, initials and love tokens are common. Whilst the carving is probably not finer than that of other North-west

European countries, a lighter feeling is introduced by more piercing and by making the piercings as large as possible, without reducing the tracery below the minimum necessary for strength and purpose. Daintily turned and fretted balusters, too, are introduced wherever continuous surfaces are unnecessary for strength.

Iceland is the greatest puzzle. The island has neither metal nor trees. The main supply of wood, until recently, was driftwood rescued from the sea. The craving to make and beautify has had, therefore, to compete with the instinct to husband every available spar for winter fuel, yet so far has love of beauty triumphed, that Iceland has contributed some of the most satisfying and restrained designs and delicate execution. Geometrical patterns, leaving sufficient plain surface as a contrast, are fairly common, but fine, free scrolls, dragons, horses and runic lettering are other characteristic features. Probably the exceptional value of the timber to the Icelander has played some part in ensuring the care, which is everywhere evident, that design and craftsmanship shall be worthy of material.

Russia is so vast that its treen is naturally most varied. In the East it is Oriental, in the West, European, and the South-west so essentially Slavonic that folk art merges almost imperceptibly into the design idiom of Hungary, Roumania, Bulgaria and Yugoslavia, which, in their turn, have much in common with the folk art of Greece. Of the Russian European, that from latitudes between those of Holland and Iceland follows closely shapes and ornament of its western neighbours. The carved designs are largely geometrical, with the roundel very much to the forefront; often the infilling of the roundel is some variant of a rose design. Plants are largely drawn on for inspiration and are portrayed rather crudely and with sparse detail, but generally more naturalistically than in Scandinavia. Typical Russian motifs are the

'Sirin' and the 'Alconost', the 'Swastika' and figures with raised arms and outstretched hands. The 'Sirin' and 'Alconost' were mythological birds, which had power to assume the shapes of women and they were usually depicted with face, arms and upper part of the body of a woman and the lower part of the body, legs, claws, wings and tail of a bird. The 'Swastika' or 'Fylfot' was a symbol of good luck in Russia, as in Greece and India, from the earliest times. The figures, with raised and outstretched arms, simply signified adoration. Another common motif consists of symbolic animals, such as lions, horses, stags or birds, facing each other and separated by the tree of life.

In Russia, the word *krasny* denotes red or beautiful and where colours are used, red is usually predominant, with a fair sprinkling of brown, blue and white. In Lithuania, green and yellow are the colours second in popularity to red.

Availability of timber varies considerably among the countries of North-west Europe, but certain factors in common have combined to create their virile peasant woodcraft and have caused what, at first sight, appears an almost incomprehensible expenditure of labour on simple articles in daily use. All these countries, to a varying degree, have long, cold, dark winters. They all have, or had, small scattered communities, dependent entirely on themselves for their needs and pastimes. Finally, they all had the peasant custom of making love tokens, more fully described in Section IX, *Love Spoons, etc.* These factors combined, account for the amount of work put into peasant woodcraft, woodsloyd, or *husflid*. Sloyd is an English word derived from the Swedish *slöjd*. It is applied to the making of articles by individuals or families in the home, as opposed to mass production in factories; *husflid* is the Norwegian term for 'home industry'. Both apply particularly to the work of peasants, who were and still largely are their own carpenters, joiners, carvers, turners and painters. During the long winter months, there is little that can be done out of doors and before the coming of electricity and its large family, not least television, woodworking tools provided men with indoor work, while the women sat at their looms, spinning wheels, lace bobbins or needlework. With so many months compulsorily spent indoors, time is often of even less account than material and, in consequence, each man of necessity developed the patience to create for the home, the carriage gear, or the sledge, a wealth of beautiful objects, in accordance with his taste and skill.

The basic reasons for the virile tradition of carving in the mountainous districts of Switzerland, North Italy and Germany, Austrian Tyrol, etc. are the same as those described for North-west Europe.

I have deliberately used the term Folk Art, in preference to Peasant Art, to describe the unselfconscious expression of traditional ornamented craftsmanship, because in the days of sailing, sailors were as great contributors as peasants, particularly in the carving of love tokens. Moreover, it will be understood that Folk Art has a much wider connotation than wood, covering, as

it does, work in metal, horn, leather, basketry, textiles, etc.

Although Folk Art is mostly confined to the beautifying of useful objects, some of them were more ceremonial than practical, being connected with customs and festivals. Under these headings come such objects as ceremonial bowls, marriage spoons, love spoons, various christening presents, special ornamental food moulds, carved vessels used at religious or other festive gatherings, Christmas doves and small Christmas trees, ingeniously made from slivers of wood and curled shavings.

The most important characteristic of Folk Art is its conservativeness. It never made any attempt to be in the fashion. It has its own regional traditions in colours, but in the designs of all the countries discussed here, it keeps to roundels, other geometric shapes, and objects provided by nature. Occasionally, it slowly absorbs some new motif from the upper stratas of its own society. In the second half of the 18th century, the rococo fashion influenced Folk Art considerably in some European countries, but it owes nothing directly to the classical vocabulary of ancient Greece or Rome.

I

The Apothecary

This section heading has been used to cover a selection of the wooden objects formerly used by doctors, surgeons, dentists, opticians, pharmacists, artificial limb makers, etc., and also certain devices used both in hospital and home nursing. Apothecary or medicine cabinets are somewhat briefly discussed here and will be more fully described and illustrated in a subsequent book devoted to the smaller work of the cabinet-maker. The mortar with its pestle, the traditional sign of the apothecary, and the grinder, both indispensable adjuncts of medicine, have a chapter to themselves. Microscopes will be found under Section XIX, *Scientific*. Certain objects such as lemon squeezers, wooden bowls, etc., used by apothecaries, had greater use in the kitchen and will be dealt with under that heading.

Apothecary Cabinets

Apothecary cabinet is an omnibus term covering both large cabinets on stands, formerly used by doctors carrying out their own dispensing and by chemists, and also smaller portable wood cabinets, originally with outer cases of leather, used in households and when travelling, and also carried by doctors when visiting patients. They are almost invariably examples of good cabinet making; a few are superb. Their fittings, too, are usually of excellent quality. Most

18th-century examples are of mahogany, but a few, made *circa* 1700, are of walnut. In the 19th century, mahogany continued its popularity, but examples were also made in rosewood and oak. Constructionally, these cabinets generally fall into two categories. One variety has a hinged lid, which when raised discloses a range of pigeon-holes filled with labelled bottles of various sizes; below, are one or more drawers containing various fitted trays and boxes. The other variety may have fixed or hinged tops, and a pair of doors. The hinge line of the doors is normally set 2 in. to 3 in. from the front, so that each door itself forms a cabinet fitted with small bottles; larger bottles are in compartments in the upper part of the main carcase, with small drawers pulling out below. Both types are usually provided with strong carrying handles.

In the absence of hall-marks on silver fittings, experience is required in dating, because both varieties each had two separate fashionable periods. The first cabinet or box door type was made in the 1680–1720 period, usually as an approximately 8 in. cube, with a slightly convex hinged top. Most of the surviving examples were made in Germany or the Low Countries and were of walnut, with ornamental steel mounts, straps, carrying handles, etc. The lock of the hinged top secures the doors and inside are several shallow drawers, pigeon-holes and fret pierced galleries to the door fitments. They contain pewter phials and glass bottles with pewter caps. The interiors are lined with paper of the patterns found inside book covers of the period. A lidded casket type of cabinet came into vogue about 1720 and held sway generally until about 1770, when a cabinet with box type doors returned to fashion until the end of the century.

This second box door type cabinet, Plate 3, was larger than the first, almost invariably of mahogany, but occasionally of satinwood. It usually stood 12 in. to 15 in. high, by 12 in. to 13 in. wide and 8 in. to 9 in. deep. It was fitted with baize-lined compartments for bottles in the box doors, and in the upper part of the carcase, with fitted drawers below. At the back is commonly found a sliding panel, concealing a row of poison bottles. The example illustrated, which has this feature, is also interesting in having, inside the sliding panel, the original trade label of Ambrose Godfrey, a London chemist, established in 1680. From 1740 until 1777, Godfrey was at The Phoenix Head in Southampton Street, Strand. From 1779, when the street was numbered, the address became 31 Southampton Street. As the address on the label is The Phoenix Head, this cabinet was used or sold by him before 1779.

The hinged lid, box type cabinets returned to favour about 1800 and were made again throughout the 19th century, to a high standard of workmanship.

Apart from their general condition, apothecary cabinets are valued by collectors on the basis of the completeness or paucity of their fittings. Although it is not too difficult to find old glass-stoppered glass bottles, there was no standardization of sizes and chances of finding one to fit an empty pigeon-hole are remote. When used for travelling, the glass stoppers were secured by washleather or parchment, tied with thread and these covers are sometimes found intact. Many of the bottles and boxes still retain their original contents, among which rhubarb, bicarbonate and camphor figure prominently. A drawer containing lignum sawdust may also be found in an old cabinet. A kind of porridge made from the sawdust and water was formerly regarded as a specific for venereal diseases. Few old cabinets seem to have been without glauber salts and the German chemist and physician, Glauber, was quite often honoured by the chemist setting up his shop at the sign of "The Glauber's Head".

Additional to bottles, most of these old cabinets, if complete, contain a silver or brass hand balance and weights, a glass pestle and mortar, mixing bowl, measures (some have double measures), a mixing or pill slab of glass or glazed pottery and a palette knife.

Apothecary Jars

Old drug jars available for collectors are mostly in various forms of glazed pottery. Wooden survivals are very rare and nearly always of continental make. Originally, they were all boldly and attractively labelled and the style of writing and form of labels sometimes give a clue to dates; unfortunately, the labels have often disappeared and then there can be no proof that these, in many instances, very general turnery containers were for drugs and not other dry stores, which were sold by grocers, etc. The name of contents was sometimes sign-written on a shield directly painted on the jar, at others on an applied paper label, which was subsequently varnished over. In the absence of labels and other knowledge both country of origin and actual date are problematical. Out of the 12 jars illustrated, Plate 4, only those designated German or Mallorcan-Spanish are definitely identifiable, although *C* and *F* are probably English.

Artificial Limbs

Rigid peg-legs and other non-mechanical

prostheses have great antiquity, but mechanical aids for amputees go back further than is generally realized. At Croan, near Wadebridge, Cornwall, is preserved a relic known as the black hand of Carew. John Carew lost his right hand at the siege of Ostend in 1601 and used an artificial hand thereafter. This hand, of some dense, dark hardwood, has articulated fingers with brass joints and a thumb which swivels on a brass ratchet. Holes in the stump and grooves in the back of the hand show that the fingers were originally controlled by wires or gut lines. An artificial hand of iron was made about 1504 for the robber knight, Götz von Berlichingen. It had articulated fingers and is said to have permitted him to make a heavier sword cut than he could do with his original hand. The fingers had to be locked on the article which it was desired to grip. In the Royal College of Surgeons, London, is an artificial leg of wood, bronze and iron, excavated from a 300 B.C. tomb at Capua.

It is only since the 1920s that wooden artificial legs have gradually been superseded by light alloys. Even the latest, however, have feet of willow, which is light, strong, springy and prevents jarring. Even although the light alloy possesses no weight advantage over the willow, it is cheaper and quicker to manufacture, because less hand skill is required, and it is easier to alter when the amputee gains or loses weight. It must be admitted, however, that for the above-knee amputee, the metal socket is not as kind as was its predecessor of springy willow.

In Plate 5 are illustrated two "Anglesey" all-willow artificial limbs for above-knee amputees, and two artificial feet of willow, in different stages of manufacture. The "Anglesey" was named after the first Marquis of that name, who lost a leg at Waterloo. In 1851, Frederick Gray of 7 Cork Street, Bond Street, possibly the same Frederick Gray who from 1839 was a bootmaker at 1 Little Ryder Street, St. James's, advertised 'Artificial leg maker by appointment to the Marquis of Anglesea'. Whether Gray invented or perfected the limb, I have been unable to ascertain. In 1866, the firm had become Frederick and Philip Gray, and in 1878, Philip Gray. By 1892, Philip had moved to 19 Maddox Street, Regent Street, but was still advertising the "Anglesea", one of the finest artificial legs ever made. The examples illustrated were produced by Rolph and Hancock of 197 South Lambeth Road, after the First World War; they continued making it until 1964. The unpainted example, shown upright, is interesting as a First World War example of a suction held limb, as opposed to the waist belt attachment with shoulder strap, which is still normal, although experiments in suction fixings have been proceeding actively ever since the last war. The limb shown with knee bent has been made during the last ten years; when complete, it would have a waist belt and shoulder strap. The incomplete foot, not yet hollowed out for the leg joint, shows the toe movement, with one of the two rubber compression 'rods' in position. The other is a completed foot, with the joint plate and the cavity behind it for the rubber heel compression 'rod'.

Bandage Winder
The type of bandage winder and tautener shown in Plate 6, A, adjustable for various widths, is English, mid-19th-century. It is said to have been invented by Florence Nightingale at the time of the Crimean war.

Bleeding Bowls
The majority of survivals are of pewter, silver and glazed earthenware, but some rather crude, pole lathe turned bowls, Plate 6, H and J, usually of sycamore, are found in diameters of 3½ in. to 6 in. Being free of ornament and virtually unchanging in design, they are impossible to date accurately,

but most of the survivors are probably of the 17th or early 18th century; they could be earlier. They are also known as barbers' bowls, but this does not necessarily denote that they were made for shaving, although they may sometimes have served that purpose. The London Company of Barbers was founded in 1461–2 and the barbers also acted as surgeons. In 1540, the position was regularized by the formation of the Company of Barber-Surgeons. Barbers continued to practise as blood-letters until 1745, when a separate Company of Surgeons was formed. The barber's familiar red and white spirally striped pole dates back to those times, when the barber practised phlebotomy. Originally the pole had a practical use: it was portable and designed for the patient to grip, to assist the flow of blood during phlebotomization. As the pole was liable to become blood-stained, it was painted red. When not in use, it was spirally wound with bandage and hung outside the barber's shop as a sign that he practised phlebotomy.

Blood-letting and Cupping, or Phlebotomization Outfit

Blood-letting and cupping, as a remedy for many ills, goes back at least to the third century B.C. in western Europe. In early times, surgeons believed that the human body was affected by the phases of the moon and the direction of the wind, and blood-letting was mainly carried out when the moon was on the increase and never when the south wind blew. Like the moon and the wind, the popularity of phlebotomy waxed and waned. In England, its fashionable heyday was probably the 18th century, due to over-eating and, even more, to excessive drinking. The outfit illustrated, Plate 6, is Anglo-French, *circa* 1740. The mahogany case, with brass lock, escutcheon, and lifting handle, is English. It measures $8\frac{1}{4}$ in. square by $4\frac{1}{2}$ in. high. The fitted interior is lined with cerise velvet. The brass scarificator by Savigny is French,

as are probably also the three remaining circular and one oval of the original four circular and two oval cupping glasses, which have adjustable valves. The lead-lined, lidded compartment in the front of the case (not visible in the photograph), would originally have contained a methylated spirit heater and a container for spirit.

There were two methods of cupping—dry and wet. In the first, the interior of the glass cup was heated over the methylated spirit, or by burning inside it a spirit-saturated piece of cotton wool. The cup was then swiftly applied to the affected part, which had already been damped, in order to create a vacuum or partial vacuum inside the cupping area, which caused the skin to lift and the serum to accumulate. The valve was then adjusted gradually to restore the atmospheric pressure inside the cup and permit its removal.

Wet cupping was a subsequent operation to the dry cupping already described, which had brought the blood to the surface. The scarificator, with its 10 razor-sharp blades, adjustable for depth of cut desired, concealed in the face plate, was pressed against the skin of the area to be treated and the spring released, making 10 simultaneous cuts. The dry cupping glass, having been re-heated, was then applied, the amount of blood desired drawn out, and the valve adjusted, as above.

Bottle Cases, etc.

Protective wooden cases with screw-on lids, Plate 7, for holding bottles, tumblers, various pots, O, syringes, J, K, L and M, thermometers, R and S, etc. and for camphor, and also iodoform and mercury sprinkling, N, were made in large quantities throughout the Victorian period, possibly a little earlier. Many of them are in use today, as good as the day they were made. They were intended for general protection and especially for travelling and were the products of high grade, speciality turners, a few of whom stamped their names on the containers. These include S. Maw & Sons of London from about 1850 to 1875, who became, from 1878 to approximately the end of the century, S. Maw Son & Thomson, and Pearce & Co. of London & Bristol, recorded in 1866 and 1867.

Ninety-nine per cent of the containers are of selected boxwood and french polished; a few, such as *D*, *E*, *F* and *G*, are of lignum vitae or ebony. A minority are labelled or inlaid with the names of their former contents. The dome-topped bottle cases, in many sizes and differing considerably in profile of lids, appear to have been made throughout the Victorian period, the flat-topped examples, with overhanging moulded rims, *A*, *B* and *C*, mostly were made between 1840 and 1870. The very small ones, group *H*, include three ornamental boxwood cases for perfume bottles, which were made up to 1914.

Cachet Machines
Finot's improved cachet machines of 1896, bottom right Plate 8, consists of four components—a spring-loaded, wood-handled cachet holder, shown in front of the wooden board with 12 china-lined circular cavities, a sliding zinc or nickel plate with 12 corresponding holes and a small metal funnel. Its purpose was to fill and seal 12 cachets at a time. The half cachets were arranged in the cavities in the board, the metal plate was then slid over, and the powder poured in through the funnel. The plate was then removed and a moistening roller passed over the lips of the half cachets. The upper halves of the cachets, having been moistened on a damp pad, were then pressed home and sealed by means of the spring-loaded cachet holder. The whole outfit, probably of French manufacture, originally sold for 15*s*.

Camphor Containers
This designation is problematical. Nothing definite appears to be known about these queer-shaped, two-decker (occasionally three-decker) containers, made of various hardwoods, which turn up occasionally, more often than not incomplete. This absence of information is the more peculiar inasmuch as they do not appear to be earlier than 19th-century. The containers, Plate 7, *P* and *Q*, consist of a small top compartment, contained within a cap of nipple shape, and a lower compartment of crown outline, which has two or three small vent holes near the top, and unscrews near the base. Occasionally a third straight-sided cylindric compartment, also drilled with small vents, is screwed between the upper and lower ones. The two-deckers are about 4 in. and the three-deckers 6 in. high.

Dentists' and Anaesthetists' Gags
The boxwood chisel type and screw cone props, Plate 8, *C* and *D*, were used for opening and holding open tensed jaws during mouth operations, throughout the 19th and early part of the 20th century. They are now superseded by plastics. The name S. Maw is found on some wooden props (see *Bottle Cases*).

Dental Instruments
Barbers not only practised surgical bleeding from early times (see *Bleeding Bowls* and *Blood Letting Outfits*), but also extracted teeth. In fact, when Henry IV, in 1399, awarded a London barber 6*d*. a day to draw the teeth of the poor, free of charge, he may be said to have commenced the State dental service. The barber must have been very busy, for toothbrushes, unfortunately, were not made nor used until several hundred years after, although the value of raw fruit and vegetables for cleaning the teeth was realized and mouthwashes, sometimes containing extraordinary ingredients, were used to wash the teeth, and cloths to rub the gums were employed at an early date. The vicious looking tooth extractors, known as dental keys, Plate 8, *A* and *B*, have ebony cross-bar handles. Both the straight and the cranked examples

date from the late 18th or early 19th century and are believed to be English.

Ear Trumpets

The example illustrated, Plate 9, *F*, is early 19th-century, English, made of lignum vitae and measures 4½ in., closed. Folding ear trumpets to fit in a case, now usually lost, were products of hardwood and ivory turners and were generally made in lignum vitae, rosewood or ivory.

Eye Cups

Dr. Ball's Eye Cups, Plate 9, *G*, were claimed to cure nearly every weakness of the eyes. Dr. Ball, an American, protected them in the U.S.A. with patents in 1851, 1865 and 1869. The bulbs were of india-rubber and cups were made both of lignum vitae and ivory. The sole agent in Great Britain was J. Fletcher of Richmond Villa, Chichester, Sussex, who sold—

> The Ivory Cups for cataracts and impaired vision at £2. 12. 6 per set.
> The Ivory Cups with myopic attachments for the near sighted £2. 16. 0 per set.
> The Lignum Vitae Cups for ordinary cases such as weak and watery eyes £1. 6. 0 per set.
> The Lignum Vitae Cups for slight myopia £1. 10. 0 per set.

The original box, shown with the lignum vitae cups, contains directions and sheets of testimonials. Summarizing, the directions say that the cups were to be used for 3 minutes at night, before going to bed. Their object was to cause a proper amount of blood to flow through the eyes and restore the diminished convexity of the cornea. Some of the air was first ejected from the ball, then the cup was placed centrally over the eye, with lids closed; the ball was then allowed to expand, the suction holding on the cup.

Eye Testers

The 19th-century eye tester, Plate 9, *H*, is English and consists of a calibrated, rectangular section, boxwood rod, on one end of which is fixed an eyepiece, provided with a magnifying glass. Mounted on a slide on the rod is a circular brass frame, filled with a white card on which is printed the words MY SIGHT. In use, the disc is slid along the calibrated rod, until the words appear at their clearest to the viewer. Some models have a second eyepiece pivoted and blanked out, to cover the eye not under test.

Funnels and Funnel Cases

Small funnels of glass, silver, pewter and occasionally lignum vitae or boxwood, are part of the normal equipment of old apothecary cabinets. They also occur as separate items with boxwood or ebony cases of their own. In wood, they are the simple sort of items which are impossible to date accurately. A set of silver funnels with an ebony case are illustrated in Plate 9, *J*. The larger wooden funnel, *K*, is of a type used by apothecaries, vintners and in the kitchen. Other examples are illustrated under Section VII, *Kitchen: Funnels*.

Gout Stools—see Section XXIII, *Toilet and Bedroom Accessories*

Iodoform Sprinklers—see *Bottle Cases*

Massage Balls and Massage Roulettes

The massage ball illustrated, Plate 6, *L*, is Chinese; this type of ball, revolving in a block of the same wood, has probably been used for many centuries. How does the ball get in the block? Some people think that the ball is scooped out of the solid, by means of a very thin, curved blade; my view is that the ball is made separately, that the block or outer casing is undercut and swelled by moisture and the ball is carefully smoothed and dried to a rather lower moisture content, before being inserted. As both dry out, sufficient space is left to allow the ball to revolve, but not come out; the ball is then probably well waxed.

The massage roulette, *K*, is English, of mahogany, and was advertised for sale between 1880 and 1890. The three rollers revolve independently.

Measures, Double Cup Type

These turned boxwood measures, Plate 6, *F* and *G*, which also have their counterparts in silver and pewter, were formerly much used by apothecaries and chemists, as well as for domestic purposes (see Section XIX, *Scientific*). Size numbers are sometimes stamped on them. *G*, the smallest, is 1.S.; the largest which I have found is 8.S. The most popular size, *F*, and consequently the one found most frequently, is 5.S. A particular use of this size was for making soda water in a Gasogene: the large cup was used for bicarbonate of soda and the small one for citric acid. Another use for double cup measures was for the powders for the Seidlitz mixture.

Because many people have only seen the 5.S size, *F*, which also happens to be egg cup size, the persistent myth has arisen that these measures are hen and duck egg cups!

Mercury Droppers—see *Bottle Cases*

Operation Pegs

These are tapering, turned pegs of boxwood, 1½ in. to 2 in. long, Plate 9, *M*. They are still used for plugging post-operation tubes.

Pill Boxes

Turned wooden boxes for pills have gradually been superseded, first by cardboard during the 19th century, and later, to a great extent, by glass bottles and plastic containers. Care had to be taken in the selection of wood, to ensure that it was a clean looking variety, free from taste or unpleasant odour. Sycamore met all these requirements and being a good turnery wood and formerly cheap, was the most popular in use by the druggist. The four pill boxes of different diameter, Plate 8, *N*, were made by Robinson & Sons Ltd. of Chesterfield, about 1850. The polished boxwood aperient box, in the form of a miniature chamberpot, *M*, is an amusing, 19th-century trifle. The nest of five pill boxes, *J*, which screw together, belonged to Dr. William Palmer, the Rugeley, Staffs., poisoner. Palmer was executed for his many murders, on June 13, 1856.

An unusual tribute to a vendor of pills is a memorial to Lionel Lockyer, in Southwark Cathedral. Lockyer, a physician of dubious reputation, died in 1672. His tomb is crowned by his sculptured semi-recumbent figure, with legs outstretched but trunk upright and face turned as though about to read an inscription at the back, which extols his pills.

Pill Making Machines

Although varying considerably in size and somewhat in details, the example illustrated, Plate 8, *K*, may be considered a typical 19th-century specimen. It consists of two components. The main board, of mahogany, has one part fitted with a marble rolling slab and the other part with a brass plate, arranged in parallel fluted grooves. A raised brass rim, on three sides, prevents warping, keeps the pill 'mass' from spilling over and acts as a guide to the upper board. The upper board or slide is provided with handles at each end and has a correspondingly fluted brass plate and guides. The pill mass, previously prepared in a mortar, was rolled on the marble slab into a long cylinder of the right length to provide, when cut, the desired number of pills. When placed across the lower grooved plate, the pill mass was cut and divided by pressing downwards on it the upper grooved board and sliding it backwards and forwards.

Pill Rounders

After the pills had been made and cut on the

pill making machine, they were rounded and finished by rotating them, with slight pressure, on a smooth surface, under a pill rounder, Plate 8, *L*, a circular block of dense hardwood, provided with a slight. upstanding rim. Pill rounders are $\frac{5}{8}$ in. to $\frac{3}{4}$ in. thick and from $2\frac{1}{4}$ in. to $3\frac{3}{4}$ in. in diameter, according to the size of pill to be rounded. No difference in design occurs between 18th- and 19th-century rounders.

Pill Silverers

The 18th- or early 19th-century pill silverer illustrated, Plate 8, *H*, is a hollow boxwood sphere on stem and foot. The $2\frac{1}{2}$ in. diameter sphere unscrews into two halves. The pills, when hard, were placed in it, then moistened with mucilage of acacia; some silver leaf was added, the cover replaced and the container shaken with a rotary motion, until a coating of silver was evenly distributed on the pills.

Root Cutters

The traditional type illustrated, Plate 6, *M*, with pivoted knife at one end, was made in a considerable range of hardwoods and in slightly varying shapes, and was used generally, but not exclusively, by apothecaries. Cutting was a necessary preliminary to pounding many tough materials with a pestle in a mortar. Other speciality root cutters are described and illustrated in Section V, *Farm* and Section VII, *Kitchen*.

Sand Glasses (Thirty-second)

Sand glasses in general are described in Section XIX, *Scientific*, but the 30-second sand glass was an essential medical accessory. Before second hands were common on watches, 30-second sand glasses in lignum vitae cases, Plate 9, *O*, or boxwood pocket cases, were carried by all medical men for timing pulses and temperature readings. The specimen illustrated was used by Dr. Woods, surgeon of Llandilo, South Wales, between 1840 and 1860.

Scoops

Wooden scoops were formerly made in great variety of shapes, sizes and qualities, ranging from large and coarse types used on the farm—Section V—and in the kitchen—Section VII—to small and well finished apple scoops—Section IV, *Eating*. In between, are some of high grade and unusual shape, the purpose of which cannot always be classified. Possibly the $6\frac{1}{2}$ in. long scoop illustrated, Plate 8, *F*, may help to classify others of a somewhat similar nature. This graceful and well finished yew-wood specimen is carved on the underside in a leaf pattern and has its handle formed by the twisted tails of two Aesculapian serpents, the heads of which border the scoop and extend downward towards its point. Aesculapius was the Greek god of the medical art, to whom serpents were sacred.

Searces

Searces, Plate 6, *B*, *C* and *D*, are shallow bowls which screw on to hollow stem and foot and together form a sieve and receptacle. In the base of the bowl is inserted a fine brass wire mesh (now often missing). They were used for sieving powders, the fine powder passing into the receptacle, leaving lumps or impurities in the bowl. They are now considerable rarities. Small ones, about 3 in. in diameter, usually of box or maple and with serrated edges, date from the 16th or early 17th century. Also from the 17th century, are some shallower maple or boxwood, serrated edged specimens like *B*, about 4 in. in diameter, burnt in simulation of tortoiseshell. Specimens of similar size to the last, but turned from lignum vitae and with plain edges, as *D*, were made in the late 17th and early 18th centuries.

Stethoscopes

The single ear wooden stethoscope was a modification of René Laennec's paper roll of 1819. Several different vase- or trumpet-shaped designs were made during the remainder of the century, and a selection is illustrated, Plate 9, *A* to *E*. The binaural type commenced to supersede the single ear trumpet about 1886. Commenced, however, is the operative word: War Office Stores managed to dish out some single ear types from somewhere, for issue to army doctors in the 1914–18 War!

Some single ear stethoscopes were turned in one piece, usually from cedar, but box, ebony and lignum vitae were also used; folding ones consisting of two parts, constructed in two different ways, are all shown. *D* has a threaded joint half-way up the stem, so that it reverses and telescopes to fit in a pocket case. The other, *E*, has a detachable stem, threaded into a collar at the base; when not in use, the stem is detached and passes sideways through a hole in the collar, as shown in the picture and the whole device was then wedged inside the doctor's silk hat. My old doctor, in the 1930s, had carried the example illustrated, in this manner, when visiting his patients by horse carriage in the first decade of this century, as had his father before him.

Stoppers

Plain wooden stoppers for apothecary jars are now very rare. The boldly carved example illustrated, Plate 8, *E*, may well be unique. It is of walnut, carved with a hand grasping an Aesculapian serpent; part of the thumb and the head of the serpent are missing. It probably dates from the 17th century.

Surgeons' Instruments

Surgeons' instruments in general are outside the scope of this book, although some of the instrument handles and the outer cases are often interesting examples of wood craftsmanship. The small dissecting case included, Plate 9, *N*, is of mahogany; the facing of the handles of the five scalpels,

made by Laundy, are ebony. The silver blow pipe was for inflating blood vessels in dissection. The outfit was used by William Aston, a surgeon, about 1798.

The pocket instrument case, *circa* 1820–1830, Plate 9, *L*, is believed to have been used for vaccination scarifiers or dental instruments.

It is hard to realize now, how agonizing and utterly insanitary surgery was even 100 years ago. A visit to the unique operating theatre at old St. Thomas' Hospital, in St. Thomas' Street off Borough High Street, Southwark, is an eye-opener.

Syringe Cases—see *Bottle Cases*

Thermometer Cases—see *Bottle Cases*

Trephination Chisels—see Section XXI, *Textile Workers' Devices: Button-hole Cutters.*

Tumbler Cases—see *Bottle Cases*

Witches Brew Bowl

It is difficult to evaluate an object such as the large cup with everted rim, Plate 8, *G*. Its shape and the motifs skilfully carved round it, denote a date before the end of the 17th century, but I think it may be later. The traditional witch ingredients carved round it—vipers, toads, lizards, snails, etc. —were by no means confined, in the 17th century, to concoctions compounded by old women who, at that time, were still being drowned for possessing the 'evil eye'. It was an age when the long tested efficacy of herbal and other remedies were inextricably mixed with mumbo-jumbo, incantations and superstitions, and nullified by inclusion of revolting additions. All the following were frequently included in remedies or cures for ailments or diseases, or as antidotes to poisons: pounded mummy flesh; powdered skulls of new born babies; powder of toads; bellies of lizards; oil of middle aged fox; fat of a boiled puppy;

powder or scrapings of unicorn and rhinoceros horns; flesh of vipers. The last three
were particularly regarded as antidotes to
poison. The viper flesh was one of the ingredients of Venice Treacle, by the 17th
century already internationally famous as
a poison antidote. The magical quality
of rhinoceros horn was recognized by the
inclusion of a rhinoceros as centre-piece of
the crest of the Society of Apothecaries.

II

Costume Accessories

According to Genesis, Chapter III, the fig tree was the first universal dress provider and it was followed by cloth made from the bast or inner bark of both fig and mulberry trees, which still apparel mankind in some parts of the globe. In more civilized lands, wicked capitalists soon put poor little silkworms to long hours of hard labour, converting mulberry leaves into fine silken threads; now, under more humane conditions, men and women and machines can do nearly as well by converting the cellulose from the tree, although initially they copied the silkworms to the extent of making the first artificial silk from actual mulberry leaves.

When it comes to dress accessories, wood has played many and varied parts: shoe heels, girdles, bracelets, buckles, combs, fans, shoe trees, etc. have all been made from wood, whilst rattan canes and osier rods have provided the structural framing for hooped skirts during several of their revivals.

In this book, *Costume Accessories* and *Toilet Accessories* are differentiated by including under the first heading only those few but interesting objects, wholly or partially of wood, which in former times were a part of costume, conveyed on the person or carried by the wearer. Objects connected with dressing, which, however, remain in the bedroom, and some account of fashion, particularly pertaining to the wearing of wigs, are described in Section XXIII, *Toilet and Bedroom Accessories*.

Buckles, Belt and Shoe

Those with frontal plates of wood must always have been rare, compared with those of metal. The finely shaped and carved, early 18th-century, boxwood shoe buckle, with steel inner frames and prongs, Plate 15, *S*, is one of a pair, both of which were formerly in the Evan-Thomas Collection; the present whereabouts of the second one is unknown.

The pair of inlaid and laminated shoe buckles, Plate 13, dating from the 1780–90 period, may well be unique. Measuring $4\frac{5}{8}$ in. long, by $2\frac{3}{4}$ in. wide, and of a type familiar in silver, these have their curves built up of four glued cross layers. The edges, painted for protection, are $\frac{5}{16}$ in. thick at centre, tapering to a knife edge at the ends. The handsome face veneering is a remarkable piece of work, for the design has to allow for curvature in section, as well as for rounded corners. The face plate is only $\frac{1}{2}$ in. wide, but in that narrow width it accommodates nine stringings and bandings. The centre is a cross band of boxwood, inlaid with alternate pin-points of mahogany and ebony. This is edged on each side with stringings of ebony and satinwood, then cross bandings of kingwood and finally, at the edges, another stringing of satinwood. Lamination, or ply construction, was used more frequently for curved work in the 18th century, than is generally realized today.

The Regency period, rosewood belt buckle, Plate 15, *T*, is mounted with chased ormolu, pierced in anthymion pattern and has frame and prongs of gilded metal.

Busks, Stay

The verb 'to busk' means to dress or attire; thus William Warner (1558–1609) 'Her face was maskt ... her body pent with busks'. A busk is a wood or whalebone stiffener for inserting in the corset or corsage. In some rural districts of England, there was formerly a custom of carving and presenting stay busks as love tokens, just as in Wales rustic lovers carved and gave love spoons and in the Dales boys carved love-token knitting sheaths for sweethearts.

These chip carved, or occasionally inlaid wood or engraved, bone busks were intended for proud display, either inserted into little pockets, top and bottom, in the fronts of bodices, or sewn on their outside through small holes, drilled at top and bottom of the busks. The majority of them are straight, a few are curved to fit the body, but all of them must have been hard, unyielding, uncomfortable love tokens; that they were used, nevertheless, is clearly shown by the considerable wear which many of them show. They range in length from 10 in. to 15 in., averaging 12 in. to 13 in.; in width, they vary from $\frac{3}{4}$ in. to 2 in. at top, tapering downwards and ending in a round or point. Some are flat; the majority are triangular in section. The facets on the faces are elaborately chip or scratch carved with love motifs. Backs are often carved additionally with intimate love messages, incised dates, and the name or initials of donor and recipient; the last may occur on backs or fronts. When two dates occur, a year or two apart, they probably denote betrothal and wedding, but when the dates are 20 or more years apart, it may mean that

the same busk was used for luck at weddings of two generations.

As on Welsh love spoons (for *Love Spoons* see Section IX), the most commonly carved motifs on the faces of stay busks are hearts, or twin hearts and roundels, the remaining space being filled with love-birds, costume figures, flower and leaf motifs, or geometric designs, varying from the coarse and simple, to finely chip carved intricacies. Whalebone or ivory busks, usually made by sailors, are generally thinner than their wooden counterparts. Additional to the usual motifs, sailor designs sometimes include ships, anchors, whales, fish and rope knots. The etched lines are sometimes filled with black or red pigment.

A stay busk in the Pinto Collection, dated 1660, is the earliest dated wooden example recorded; there is a fine specimen in the Victoria and Albert Museum dated 1675.

It is difficult to know how prevalent was this custom of carving and giving love token stay busks; certainly they are now very rare. Stay busks were only worn when fashion's vagaries decreed a wasp waist, which was invariably accentuated by a long, pointed bodice and a billowing skirt. It is interesting that this fashion recurs at approximately 100-year intervals; thus the earliest stay busks are dated between 1660 and 1700 and the vast majority were made between 1760 and 1800. One has been noted dated in the 1870s. Are we due for another revival?

The following are the details of the examples illustrated. The majority were formerly in the Evan-Thomas Collection and before that in the collection of Dr. Oxford; some formerly in the Linn Collection had also previously been in the aforementioned.

Plate 10
A. Back view of sycamore busk, 13$\frac{1}{2}$ in. by 2$\frac{1}{4}$ in.; inscribed 'When This You See. Pray Think On Me. Tho Many Miles We Distant Be. Altho We Are a Great

Way Apart. I Wish You Well With All My Heart'. The face is finely chip carved with twin hearts and roundels.

B. Plain sycamore busk, 13½ in. by 1½ in.; anatomically shaped. Possibly 19th-century.

C. Busk 14½ in. by 2¼ in., the face chip carved with a tulip in a flower pot, a leafy branch, etc. and the initials M.K.; on reverse, twin hearts and initials M.E.

D. Mulberry wood busk, 12½ in. by 1¼ in., simply carved with twin hearts, initials M.M. and I.M. and date June 15. 1785; on reverse inscribed 'This and the giver are yours forever. Thormanby. June 15'. Formerly in the Linn Collection.

E. Narrow, boxwood busk, 12¾ in. by 1⅛ in. Carved on face with a heart, initials E.S. and date 1762; on reverse, E.K. Skelton. April 10, 1762.

F. Good quality busk, 12¾ in. by 1⅜ in., carved on face with hearts, roundels, initials A.P. and date June 17. 1791. The back is inscribed 'May all this world's fair smile so gay, Shine on you both night and day. And in the next may you be blest, In Glory and Eternal Rest'.

G. Unusual busk, 12¾ in. by 1½ in., carved in low relief with the sun, a winged heart, figures in late 18th-century costume, a pair of love-birds, etc.; on reverse, the Crucifixion.

H. A heavy and finely carved busk, 13 in. by 1½ in. Initials M.I. Dated on back, 1795.

J. Outstanding busk, 11¼ in. by 1¼ in., of heavy, triangular section. The top carved with a Red Indian maid, probably Princess Pocahontas; the faces intricately carved with masonic emblems, in a fine chip carved border, and the initials T.U. and E.U. On reverse, the names are inscribed in full—Thomas Underwood and Elizabeth Underwood; the latter name is crossed through, which would seem to denote some tragedy. Probably 17th-century.

K. Small busk, 10¾ in. by 1⅛ in., chip carved with hearts and a thistle; on reverse, Priscilla Price 1790. Formerly in the Evan-Thomas and Dr. Oxford Collections.

L. Unique inlaid mahogany busk, 12⅝ in. by 1¼ in. Late 18th-century. Formerly in the Linn Collection.

M. Unusually finely chip carved busk, 13 in. by 1½ in. Twin heart motifs, etc. On reverse, initials M.S. and T.W. and date 1794. Formerly in the Linn Collection.

N. Ash busk, 13 in. by 1¾ in., neatly carved on face with hearts, roundels and initials W.A. On reverse, 'Mary I Grives 1785. Har Busk July 27'.

O. Late 18th-century busk, 13¾ in. by 2 in., chip carved with hearts, leaf motifs and initials E.M. on face; numerous initials on back. Holes for sewing to bodice. Formerly in the Evan-Thomas and Dr. Oxford Collections.

Plate 11

A. A great rarity: the earliest dated wooden busk so far recorded. 15¾ in. by 1¼ in., curved, chip carved on face with hearts and criss-cross pattern, and with sewing holes. Inscribed on back 'As a ring is round and hath no end So is my love to the(e) my fri(e)nd. Battie—Agnes 1660'. The face carved with twin hearts and chip carved diamond pattern.

B. An attractive slender stay busk of fruit-wood, 13½ in. by ¾ in., with unusually good quality relief carving. 18th-century. The back is shown here and depicts hunting and domestic scenes, carved so as to be viewed horizontally; this may be unique. The formal carving on the face is also exceptionally competent.

C. Simple busk, 14½ in. by 2⅜ in., carved with initials E.R., 1783, a heart, roundel, tulip, etc. Formerly in the Evan-Thomas and Dr. Oxford Collections.

D. Narrow and rather pointed, beechwood busk, 13 in. by 1½ in., chip carved with love-bird in a tree, and a heart. Initials G.S.M. Date 1788 and a verse on back.

E. Elaborately carved busk, 13½ in. by 1½ in. Late 18th-century. Initials M.H. on back. Formerly in the Evan-Thomas and Dr. Oxford Collections.

F. Chip carved busk, 13¾ in. by 1⅞ in. Initials M.I., dated 1785. The inset heart-shaped mirror is an unusual feature.

G. A handsome busk, 12¼ in. by 2 in., well designed and carved finely. Dated 1777 and 1781 on back. Formerly in the Evan-Thomas and Dr. Oxford Collections.

H. Unusual curved busk, 12½ in. by 1¼ in., which must have been less uncomfortable than the normal. The significance of the twins on the front is unknown. On reverse, initials E.F. and A.I. 18th-century.

J. Chip carved busk, 13¾ in. by 1¾ in. Dated 1789 on reverse. Formerly in the Linn Collection.

K. Unusually heavy busk, 14¼ in. by 1½ in., chip carved with hearts, roundels, etc. Late 18th-century. Formerly in the Linn Collection.

L. Well worn specimen, 14¾ in. by 1⅞ in. Initials S.B. and date 1782. Formerly in the Evan-Thomas and Dr. Oxford Collections.

M. Late 18th-century busk, 14¾ in. by 1⅛ in., chip carved with heart, roundel, etc. and initials I.S. Formerly in the Linn Collection.

Buttons

Among wooden buttons, only those with faces exposed and preferably decorated by carvings, painting, inlaying, transfer printing or gem studding are worthy of collector notice. A few are illustrated in Plate 15. The two carved as dog heads, J, and the two, K, carved with flowers, are walnut. The two, L and M, the so-called Irish diamond buttons, are actually made of bog oak, inset with gem cut Irish quartz. All these buttons are 19th-century.

An interesting point about buttons is that whilst all authorities agree that they originated many centuries before buttonholes, buttons as costume fasteners apparently only appeared in Europe in the 15th century. According to Harrison's *Description of England*, they were not used as costume fasteners in England until the second half of the 16th century. After describing their former use as costume ornaments among the fashionable, he goes on to say that about

1567 '. . . many young Citizens and others, began to weare Christall buttons upon their doublets, coats, and Jerkins, and then the former wearing of borders and hatbands, set with Christall buttons ceased. And within few yeeres after, began the generall wearing of buttons, of threed, silke, haire, and of gold and silver threed'. Harrison is generally most accurate and although portraits of Henry VIII and inventories of early Tudor times show that jewelled buttons were already being used by people of fashion, they appear to have been fashionable ornaments and not costume closures.

Clogs—see Section XXV, *Trade Devices: Cobblers.*

Fans

Folding fans, generally said to have been invented in Japan, were introduced to France from Italy by Catherine de Medici. Although France has remained the principal centre of fan-making ever since, a considerable manufacture developed in England after 1685, when religious persecution brought an influx of Huguenot fan-makers to London. Folding fans first attained fashion in England at the Court of Elizabeth I.

Both the guards on outer facings and the sticks were made of ivory, mother-of-pearl, bone, wood, etc. The lower parts of the thin and delicate sticks, known as the blades or brines, were ornamented by carving, inlay, fret-cutting or painting, and were secured at the loop handle end by a pivot pin. The leaves covering the upper parts of the sticks were generally formed of two layers of silk, paper, lace, parchment or 'chicken' skin (actually the skin of a newly born lamb). All these materials, except the lace, were painted with classical, biblical, pastoral or topical scenes, or with figures, flower designs, etc. Marriage fans, a popular wedding gift or memento from about 1720 onwards, might have miniatures of the bride and bridegroom, or scenes from their lives, painted on them. Additionally, black and white fans, painted with suitable subjects, were created as mourning fans.

Certain fans, mostly of eastern origin, have the upper part of their sticks widened out, ornamentally painted or fret-cut into lacy patterns and threaded with transverse silk ribbons, thus dispensing with coverings. These are known as brisé fans. Many of these are Indian or Chinese, and made from aromatic sandalwood. Seychelles fans are made of palm throughout.

All the folding fans already mentioned open out into a segment of a circle, but one group, of which open and closed examples are illustrated in Plate 14, *D*, form a complete circle, when the top tassel is pulled; when the tasselled cord is pulled downwards, the fan folds into its handle. These fans, dating from the last half of the 19th century, are Italian and have covers of olivewood. Their particular interest lies in the emphasis they give to what, in the 18th and 19th centuries, was known as 'the language of the fan', which had recognised rules. By the subtle movements of her fan, a girl could convey messages of hope, discouragement, annoyance, etc. It must have been a great help when the wielder of the fan could simultaneously study her facial expressions in the small oval mirror provided. Some fans have quizzing glasses instead of mirrors.

Rigid wooden fans, with a thin scalloped-edge board, decorated with oriental or floral scenes on a black, red, green or natural wood ground, held in a groove at the top of an ornamentally turned stick handle, gilded or of matching colour, date from the Regency or Victorian periods. They may be regarded as complementary to papier mâché.

Footwear—For clogs, patterns, sabots, wooden soles, heels, etc., see Section XXV, *Trade Devices: Cobblers*.

Girdles

Girdles, used to secure loose robes in mediaeval times, were probably always a great rarity, if made of wood. A remarkable survival is the superbly carved, French, thornwood girdle of the 14th century, Plate 12, in the Victoria and Albert Museum.

Jewellery—see Section XIII, *Nuts, Gourds, Fruit Stone, Jet and Bog Oak Jewellery*

Parasols—see *Umbrellas*

Pattens—see Section XXV, *Trade Devices: Cobblers*.

Pomanders—see Section XXIII, *Toilet and Bedroom Accessories*

Purses

Purses of wood and woody materials are quite 'finds' for the collector. Five Victorian examples are illustrated in Plate 15. The heart-shaped specimen, *F*, is of carved walnut, *E* and *G*, of coquilla. (For details of coquilla nut, see Section XIII.) The purses, *D* and *H*, are of threaded melon pips.

Scratchers, Head and Back

Personal hygiene and fashionable attire had little in common before the end of the 18th century. The only difference between rich and poor was that the former, of both sexes, perfumed their wigs, their clothing and their persons, using musk to an overpowering degree, to try and disguise the fact that only their hands and faces were not strangers to soap and water. Hence the need for the devices under this heading.

The dated 17th-century, Turkish back scratcher with silk carrying cord, Plate 14, *A*, is an exceptional example of small scale carving. Actually, the most popular back scratcher in 18th-century England was an imported Chinese ivory hand, with fingers crooked for scratching, which was mounted on a turned ebony stick. Horribly crude modern copies are on sale, but unlikely to trouble collectors. The plain lignum vitae, English head scratcher, *C*, with twist carved ivory ring for slinging from the fingers when promenading, was typical of that 18th-century elegance which accepted public poking of wigs and itching heads as normal. Men's heads probably itched chiefly through being shaved, but fashionable women had lousy heads, particularly in the 1770s, because of the hair dressing technique then in vogue (see introduction to Section XXIII, *Toilet and Bedroom Accessories*).

Toothpick Cases

Even when perfectly plain, these small boxes are invariably of the highest quality. They were made throughout the 18th and probably during the first 30 or 40 years of the 19th century and were considered as much normal social pocket equipment as a snuff box or vinaigrette. They were made of gold, silver, ivory, tortoiseshell, boxwood and ebony and when examining wood specimens, it will usually be found that the hinge and spring catch are of gold; *C*, one of the three shown in Plate 15, has its original quill-cutting knife still in the case.

The first hint of condemnation of *excessive* tooth picking in public comes in a book of etiquette published in 1834—'Do not pick your teeth *much* at table, as however satisfactory a practice to yourself, to witness it is not a pleasant thing'.

Umbrellas

The term umbrella is used here to include sunshades or parasols. As shades from the sun and emblems of rank they appear in stone reliefs of Egypt, Assyria and Persia. They were known in China B.C. In Burma, only kings and white elephants were allowed white umbrellas. The Maratha princes were 'Lords of the Umbrella' and the present King of Siam, Bhumibol, includes among his titles 'Possessor of the Four and

Twenty Golden Umbrellas'. The 12th-century Doge of Venice had a State umbrella. Women carried umbrellas in ancient Greece and Rome. In Queen Anne's reign, the folding umbrella for use against rain, came into general use in London, as a protection for women. There are, however, occasional literary references to its use by women in 17th-century England and an umbrella, probably of French manufacture, is described in a 1561 Holyrood inventory of the possessions of Mary, Queen of Scots. Daniel Defoe, in *A Tour Through the Whole Island of Great Britain*, written in 1724, refers to a terrace walk at Windsor Castle, built for Queen Elizabeth I —'As to rainy weather, it would not hinder her, but she rather loved to walk in a mild, calm rain, with an umbrella over her head . . .'. In the 17th century, a common umbrella was also kept in coffee houses for showing men to their sedan chairs, but the first man to use one regularly in London was Jonas Hanway, the noted explorer and philanthropist, in 1778. Hanway was mobbed by the sedan chair carriers, as a potential menace to their trade. (For further information on Hanway, see Section XVII, *Reading, Writing, Copying, Drawing etc.*) As late as 1787, Parson Woodforde's *Diary* records, rather apologetically, how in a blizzard at a grave side, he succumbed to having an umbrella held over him.

Early folding umbrellas were heavy and clumsy, with whalebone frames, but improvements followed in rapid succession, many of them patents, but some with only novelty value. The most important patents were that of Henry Holland of Birmingham for steel ribs, and that of Samuel Fox & Co. of Stockbridge, Sheffield, for the lighter U-section steel rib in 1852.

Regency and early Victorian ladies parasols were so small, generally about 16 in. in diameter, that now they are often thought to be children's. The slender sticks of wood or ivory, although long enough to walk with, were made to fold, Plate 17, *A*, and the bone ferrules were fitted with turned cross-bars or rings; when not in use, ladies of fashion inverted their parasols or umbrellas and suspended them from their fingers.

In the first half of the 19th century, Ashley, the noted umbrella and parasol maker of 11 Old Bond Street, Bath, enjoyed great favour with the fashionable world visiting Bath. In one of his rhyming lists of ware, published in 1811, he announced

> 'Choice Umbrellas for the Rain
> Parasols, Chinese and plain,
> Every sort made to your order
> Silk, (fast color) fringed or border
> Repaired, new covered, neatly made,
> And "Cheap" as any in the trade;'

The list of wares sold by Ashley is so exhaustive and interesting and contains so many items mentioned in this book that his 138 lines of rhyme are given in full in Appendix III.

From the mid-19th century, two London firms, William and John Sangster at 140, and Lewis and Allenby at 193–7 Regent Street, took the lead on the fashionable side of parasol design; changes in shapes from rounds to squares and in curves from near flat to deep domes, also double curves giving pagoda effects, were mostly sponsored by them, as were also lengths and styles of fringes, and the rich choice of materials and overlays of lace, embroidery, etc. After 1870, shades increased in diameter and sticks in length and strength, until they became the dignified walking stick umbrellas of the Edwardian regime, popularized of necessity by Alexandra, Princess of Wales, who walked with a slight limp, due to a rheumatic complaint. This style persisted until the 1920s, when the 'dumpy' came into fashion. Certain ladies of the old school, notably the late Queen Mary, remained faithful to their tall umbrellas until they died.

A selection of umbrella and parasol handles is shown in Plate 17. The delightful girl's bust, *B*, is boxwood, probably French, early 19th-century. The donkey head, *D*, is reputed to be one of Queen Victoria's parasol handles, portraying the head of her favourite donkey, which pulled her chair round Windsor Castle grounds; it is believed to have been commissioned in Austria by the Prince of Wales, afterwards Edward VII.

Visiting Card Cases

Visiting cards, with their elaborate etiquette, bring back to many still living, visions of Victorian and Edwardian drawing rooms, and formal 'At Home' days. Actually, the visiting card and its case date back at least to the Regency, and the 1834 *Hints on Etiquette* devotes 3½ pages to visiting cards. From it we learn

> 'If you are thrown amongst fashionable people, you must not pay a visit to a lady before two o'clock P.M., nor after four, as, if you call *before* that time, you will interrupt those avocations which more or less occupy *every lady* in the early part of the day: if *later* than four o'clock, you will prevent her driving out.
>
> On returning visits, a card left at the house is generally considered all that is necessary; but, if you are admitted, do not make a morning visit too long, lest you interfere with the engagements of the mistress of the house.
>
> Never leave your hat in the hall when you pay a morning visit, it makes you look *too much at home*; take it with you into the room.
>
> It was formerly the custom to turn down the corner of a card if your visits were intended for more than one person in a family, and it is even now occasionally done; but it is much better to leave a card for each division—that is, one for the master of the house; another for the mistress; and one for the young ladies. An old lady, desirous of complying with the fashion, of the reason of which she was ignorant, when calling on a *single lady*, turned down all the four corners!'

Visiting card cases were made of gold, silver and silver filigree, enamel, shagreen, tortoiseshell, ivory and wood. The latter might be plain, inlaid or carved. The carved case was commonly very elaborate and intricate, of aromatic sandalwood, imported, and carved in India or China. The *circa* 1855, Italian, olivewood case, inlaid with initials R.P., Plate 14, *E*, belonged to the author's paternal grandmother, Rosetta Pinto. *F* is carved sandalwood, Oriental, and *G* and *H* are inlaid, English. (For *Visiting Card Carriers*, see Section X, *Miscellany*.)

Walking Sticks and Staffs

A whole book could be written on this subject, so of necessity this entry is restricted. The sticks described here and illustrated in Plate 16, are mostly those which do or contain something. Such sticks have a long history. From the 16th century, if not earlier, up to and including the 18th century, men of fashion, when having to move among the masses, carried sticks with a pouncet box knob—that is a hollow knob, with a gold or silver outer cover and a perforated inner one, containing a sponge soaked in aromatic vinegar. It was really a stick with a built-in pomander, designed to ward off evil smells and diseases. Sometimes a second cavity, concealed below the pouncet box, was used for carrying money.

Probably the easiest of dual purpose sticks to find today are shooting sticks. Modern ones are ingenious, although hardly collector items yet, but some of their 19th-century, folding chair-stick ancestors are interesting—see Section X, *Miscellany: Seat Sticks*. Sticks containing swords are still easily obtainable; those containing umbrellas are scarce. A French, 19th-century, poacher's gun-stick, which fires through the ferrule, can occasionally be bought, but a stick with a watch in the knob handle is very rare. A late 19th-century stick containing an electric torch has been recorded.

A nice Regency malacca with silver knob, which contains a glass beaker and, below it, a long phial for brandy, is highly desirable (this feature is also recorded in a patent for parasols and umbrellas). In the late 18th and early in the 19th century, 4 ft. to 4½ ft. tall staffs for running footmen were similarly fitted; they must have been much needed. Old 'Q', the notorious 4th Duke of Queensberry, is reputed to have been the last man to keep a running footman. Other staffs, 4½ ft. or longer, were usually staffs of office and may include processional staffs and those formerly used by sextons for awakening snoring sleepers during interminable sermons. Cheaper copies of the original brandy flask sticks, grained to simulate malacca, were made in Germany between 1880 and 1900; their fittings are of thin, soft copper, silver plated. Of the same provenance and similar poor quality were ingenious sticks each containing a pen, pencil, inkpot and indiarubber.

A crude crook-handled stick of ashwood, shown in Plate 93, *C*, contains a long saw blade, held in a cut in the stem. It pivots at the ferrule end, and when unclipped at the top the springy stick can be bent until the top of the saw is clipped into the end of the curved handle; the saw then forms a V with the stick and is an efficient tool for severing small branches, or ivy from tree trunks.

The following are details of the dual purpose sticks illustrated in Plate 16:

A. contains a dog whistle in the silver mount.
B. contains a remarkably efficient woodworker's kit in the handle.
C. is a sword stick.
D. a briar pipe with a metal wind shield forms the handle.
E. is one of the French, 19th-century, poacher's gun-sticks.
F. contains a snuff receptacle.
G. when the silver handle is opened, two rectangular and one round lidded com-

partments are revealed; they may be for different varieties of snuff, or alternatively pill boxes.

H. contains a long phial for brandy in the lower part of the cane and in the upper part, alongside, a glass beaker.

J. contains an open fronted, spring metal tube, embracing 8 glass bottles, one above the other.

K. contains a cigar cutter in the handle.

L. contains a bird-watcher's spy glass. This stick could probably tell a charming story: it is inscribed on the knob 'From Lassie to Laddie, Xmas, 1885'.

The cane illustrated in Plate 291, contains a horse standard (measure) calibrated in hands. Other dual purpose sticks, not illustrated, include a telescopic fishing rod stick and another smoker's walking stick, dating from the second half of the 19th century, which is fitted full length with a hollow tube to hold cigars; surrounding the tube, in the knob, are compartments for matches.

Also for collectors of odd sticks are some of cork-oak, with part of the cork bark left on and carved to simulate a loosely furled umbrella. Sold in the Isle of Wight about 1900, they were presumably supposed to be local products, as several cork-oaks grew in the vicinity, including the one which still flourishes in the grounds of Osborne. I suspect, however, that these sticks were Portuguese imports. Made about the same period, mostly in Austria, were sticks and parasols with a delightful variety of animal heads having movable jaws, like Plate 17, *C*. Extremely well modelled, they have usually survived with their spring

lower jaws intact. Of similar provenance are rabbit heads, which move their ears. Sticks carved with 'double face', back to back heads were popular in the 18th century. Unless the subject can be identified, the significance is lost.

Many sticks have crook handles bent by steaming, but ash walking sticks with right-angle bar handles are grown by specialist foresters. Ash seedlings are transplanted after two years, shortened to a few inches and re-set at a very slight angle with the ground. The shoots then sprout and are trained nearly vertically, eventually becoming walking sticks with right angled handles running along the ground.

A French, 17th-century, boxwood walking stick, superbly carved in one piece with a grotesque head terminal to the crook handle and an intertwined foliate design with satyrs and nymphs, caryatid figures, putti, etc., is illustrated right, Plate 18. In the same picture is an English walking stick of boxwood, with a well executed terminal head of John Wesley as handle. Below the carved rope collar are six flying angels, the Crucifixion and the Road to Calvary; Adam and Eve and the serpent with the apple are represented at the base. Some details of the carvings on both these sticks are shown in Plate 19.

The 2 in. high, silver mounted, boxwood carving of a classical head, Plate 171, *A*, is probably the handle of a French cane, *circa* 1800, and the carved boxwood griffin, Plate 171, *C*, may also be off a French cane or parasol, but is difficult to date.

III

Drinking

Although, in general, treen drinking vessels were the humblest, and pewter, silver, gold, and later, glass were reserved for the ascending social scales, this is only a generality. Certain drinking vessels of wood, such as mazers and fine tankards, and drink receptacles such as wassail bowls of lignum vitae, were always expensive and highly esteemed, either because considerable skilled labour, or careful selection of rare wood, or both, were needed.

Vessels of different materials and shapes developed in various parts of the world, according to easy availability of materials and degree of skill needed to make drinking vessels from them. In tropical countries, coconut shells required little labour or skill to convert; by the sea shore, some sea shells were equally handy, and in cattle districts, horns were easily adapted. Where there was clay but little forest, the potter soon turned vessels on his wheel, and where there was more forest, the turner performed like service with his lathe, for the turner and potter are the oldest machinists in the world and their crafts are similar, in that their machines do not make, they only rotate material, which is shaped entirely by the skill of the operator.

As the continents became opened up by land and sea travel, the common nutshell of the tropics became the luxury import of Europe and because it was rare, usually

had much more labour and skill lavished on it, than it would have had in its homeland. In the 16th century, the humble coconut and African ostrich egg became the body of a rare goblet or jug, to be richly mounted in silver, with the eggshell or the nut carved by skilled artists. There can be little doubt that the egg and the nut were the basic inspiration of the man-made goblet form. Coconut drinking vessels are described in Section XII, *Nuts, Gourds, etc.* A good idea of the variety of treen and other drinking vessels in use in England early in the 17th century, is afforded by *Heywood's Philocothonista* or *The Drunkard Opened* (1635):

'Of drinking cups divers and sundry sorts we have; some of elme, some of box, some of maple, some of holly, etc.; mazers, broad-mouthed dishes, noggins, whiskins, piggins, crinzes, ale-bowls, wassell-bowls, court-dishes, tankards, kannes, from a pottle to a pint, from a pint to a gill. Other bottles we have of leather, but they are most used amongst shepheards and harvest-people of the countrey: small jacks we have in many ale-houses of the citie and suburbs, tip't with silver, besides the great black jacks and bombards at the court, which, when the Frenchmen first saw, they reported, at their returne into their countrey, that the Englishmen used to drinke out of their bootes: we have, besides, cups made of hornes of beasts, of cocker-nuts, of goords, of the eggs of ostriches; others made of the shells of divers fishes, brought from the Indies and other places, shining like mother of pearle. . . .'

The connection between wood and drinking has always been close and it seems probable that without wood many popular drinks would never had been made, distributed or served; for wood has played an essential part in wine fermenting tanks and for presses and vats and, until very recently, it was equally important in the distillery and for providing casks for brewing beer and cider. Our ancestors avoided water as a drink whenever possible and, even as late as the 19th century, gravestones in England recorded such inscriptions as this:

> 'Full many a man, both young and old,
> Has gone to his sarcophagus—
> Through pouring water icy cold
> Adown his warm oesophagus'.

In biblical days, alcoholic drinks were already well known and numerous references occur to ceremonial cups of gold and silver, but these were obviously rarities amongst drinking vessels and the majority must have been made of wood and pottery, during most of man's time on earth. In these days, it is difficult to realise that glass, although used before the Christian era, is a comparative newcomer as the universal drinking vessel and that although pewter has held a large place from the Middle Ages until the present day, it never superseded wood. Wood, until recently, remained the material not only of the common drinking vessel but also of larger-sized community vessels, which were articles of great value and probably contributors to the epidemics which periodically decimated the population.

The varieties of treen drinking vessels are more numerous and generally more valuable than any other specific group of objects in wood and, for that reason, this section of the book is lengthier than most. Drinking vessels tended to increase in variety through the centuries, rather than for new shapes to take the place of old: thus goblets and tankards, known from very early days, have never gone out of fashion; only the materials from which they are made have changed. This makes it impossible to describe drinking vessels in chronological order, although some varieties, such as horns, mazers, methers and quaichs, have reigned for a period only. Because of the wide variety of drinking vessels and ancillaries, and the fact that there are frequently definite regional differences in design, some sub-headings have been created in this section. Only items under sub-heading are arranged alphabetically.

Sub-headings
English and other drinking vessels, liquor
    containers, etc.
Scottish drinking vessels.
Irish drinking vessels.
North-west European drinking vessels.
Ancillaries of drinking.

Although certain drinking vessels, particularly some ornamentally incised ones, and certain historical vessels with silver mounts, can be dated accurately, it cannot be emphasized too strongly that the less important ones like goblets, beakers and some of the smaller bowls, can only be guessed by analogy with vessels of similar form in other materials. Admittedly, experience in judging wear, condition, etc., may help, but even these factors can be misleading and as regards design, it is not unusual to find a 19th- or 20th-century turner copying a 16th-century design because he liked it. It helps the student considerably if the copy is in a wood not introduced to Europe until recently.

ENGLISH AND OTHER DRINKING VESSELS, LIQUOR CONTAINERS, ETC.

The principal groups under this heading are beakers, goblets, mazers, wassail bowls, standing cups and tankards. Although these six groups conjure up clear mental pictures to most people, it will be found, when analysing them, that some of the divisions are by no means clear. Goblets may be described as circular, individual drinking vessels with a bowl mounted on a stem and foot. A standing cup or chalice, which is also known as a loving cup because it is passed between friends, is simply a similar, larger vessel with a bowl mounted on stem and foot. Whilst the majority of standing cups are considerably larger than goblets, there are some borderline cases. Whilst many wassail bowls are immense, some of the smaller ones are nothing more than large standing cups or loving cups; again there is no clear dividing line. To add a little more to confusion, the word hanap, used in mediaeval documents, may, on checking the description, be found to refer to any elaborate type of drinking vessel ranging from a certain type of mazer to a standing cup. Hanaper, the basket in which a hanap was stored or carried, has developed into the word hamper.

Lignum Vitae
As lignum vitae figures so largely in the history of drinking vessels from the 17th century onwards, here is a brief history of its early uses.

Lignum vitae was first imported to Europe from the West Indies and Central America about 1515, its introduction being medicinal. Its name, wood of life, was given because it was the supposed West Indian cure for venereal diseases. The first European treatise on the subject was published by Ulrich von Hutten in 1519; other treatises on the lignum vitae cure followed throughout the 16th century. The lignum sawdust, which was mixed with water and dosed to sufferers as a form of porridge, is still found sometimes among materia medica in small drawers of old apothecary cabinets. Lignum vitae shavings, also used medicinally, were sold by Eliza-

beth Barton Stent at 'The Turners Arms', Little Britain, as late as 1750.

Although John Evelyn, in the first edition of *Sylva*, 1664, and in subsequent 17th-century editions, does not refer to the special turnery quality of lignum vitae, its introduction as a turnery wood has until recently been generally accepted as being about 1660. Evelyn does refer to the oil of lignum vitae as a cure for venereal diseases, and in another part of *Sylva* he mentions it under its French name guaiacum, but he obviously must have confused it with some other species, possibly the western red cedar or *arbor vitae*, for he dismisses it as a useful timber, by saying '... fittest for the shrubby part and under-furniture of our ever green Groves, and near our Gardens of Pleasure'. Why Evelyn, who mentions the turnery qualities of so many lesser woods, fails to discuss lignum, must remain a mystery, for research into the archives of the Worshipful Company of Turners shows that we must now revise our dating and possibly some of the large wassail bowls, usually regarded as of Charles II period, may date from the reigns of James I or Charles I. When lignum vitae reached England for curative purposes is unknown, but probably its great advantages for certain specialised turnery were known by the end of the 16th century, and the turners had by then overcome the considerable difficulties of working a wood so hard and dense that it weighs some 88 lb. per cu. ft. when seasoned, and is so heavy that it sinks in water. A minute of the Turners Company, September 1, 1609, records a controversy between John Frank, an assistant, and Robert Gray, a brother of the Company. The settlement, by Company arbitration, provided that John Frank should take all the 'bark' which he had bargained for with Robert Gray, at the rate of 20s. per cwt. and should have in exchange a ton of wood, called lignum vitae, at such rate as any two men of the Company should say it is worth. A ton sounds considerable, but all that the purchaser received was approximately 25½ c. ft. of lignum vitae.

Probably the first reference to its use in turnery occurs in the Turners' records of 1605: '2 paire of black lignu vite bowlles'. In 1621, there is a reference to two pairs of lignum vite bowles given to two officials as a 'gratulation' or compliment. A later third reference occurs in Samuel Pepys' *Diary*: on November 21, 1660, he wrote 'This morning my cozen Thomas Pepys, the turner (Thomas was a Freeman of the Company), sent me a cup of lignum vitae for a token'.

The Ordinances of the Turners for 1608 show that the remarkable qualities of lignum vitae were by then already recognized for hard-wearing accessories on board ship, for it is the foremost wood recommended for sheaves and pins. Lignum vitae contains an oil which is immiscible with sea water and makes the wood impermeable; this, combined with its hard-wearing quality, still makes it the finest material in the world for bushing the bearings of ships' propellers; it was used for this purpose on the liner Queen Mary.

Although there is no record of the date, another early use of lignum vitae was, perhaps, for the 'woods' used at bowls, for which its weight, even density and ability to stand up to punishment, made and make it the ideal material.

The turner's ordinary treadle pole lathe was useless for the heavy work entailed in turning lignum vitae, so he converted it into a two- or three-man machine, by means of what was known as a 'great wheel'—a wheel of some 6 ft. to 9 ft. diameter, bolted to the floor, some distance from the lathe and driven by means of a crossed belt. The great wheel had one or sometimes two cranked iron handles, so that the turner, according to the weight of his work, could have one or two assistants providing the power. For very large and heavy work, the wheel was powered by a horse or by water.

When lignum vitae was first introduced here, it came from virgin forests and was available in sound logs of large diameter; having overcome the initial difficulties of turning this wood, so unusually suitable for hard-wearing vessels and those requiring impermeability to liquids, the turner naturally thought of making drinking vessels and pestles and mortars of it, for it provided the additional selling point that the curative qualities of the wood were supposed to pass into the drink or mixture compounded in the vessels. In consequence, lignum vitae became *the* wood for drinking bowls, goblets, loving cups, pestles, mortars, etc., in Stuart England. Prior to its introduction, the size of wassail bowls was severely limited by the diameter of European hardwoods of sound heart.

I am often asked how turned wooden cups and bowls, particularly those of woods other than the unusually tough and dense lignum vitae, stood up to the strain of hot liquids. I am also told by collectors that they have stripped the disfiguring varnish with which some later misguided 'improver' had coated their lignum vitae wassail bowls, etc. The question and the remark are closely interrelated. What does not seem to be generally known now, is that varnish is a very old protective finish. The first part of Stalker and Parker's *Treatise of Japanning, Varnishing and Guilding*, 1688, is devoted to the ingredients and manufacture of different kinds of varnish, which they state, is now so much used. Wassail bowls, posset cups, etc., when of treen, were originally coated thickly all over with varnish to protect them against hot liquids. Varnish does not, however, patinate like a waxed finish and improve with age; on the contrary, in time—and many of these vessels are now 300 or more years old—it will flake, and where the edges are fractured, damp will creep under, make the varnish opaque, and create unsightly white or grey patches. I always strip the varnish in such an instance, and I advocate doing so for appearance sake, *unless* it is intended ever again to use the vessel for its original purpose. It will sometimes be found, when removing the varnish, that colour also comes away from patches of yellow sapwood on the edge of a bowl, which have been stained in to match it up with the dark heartwood. As this stain is under the varnish, it is almost certainly original. Probably our ancestors either disliked the contrasting colours on aesthetic grounds, or else the turners coloured in the sapwood to make it appear that a bowl was 'turned' from a larger log than it really was. I always remove the stain with the varnish, because I like the contrasting colours in the natural wood. But this is a matter of opinion, which every collector must decide for him or herself.

These notes may simplify the descriptive text which now follows.

Beakers

Straight or slightly convex-sided, circular, tapering treen vessels must have been turned from very early times. Sometimes they are ornamented by horizontal bands of raised 'strapping', incised lines, beads, etc. They vary considerably in size, degree of fineness and coarseness, but being so simple and lacking in intrinsic value, it is probable that most of those existing today, were made within the last hundred years. They are found in all the native hardwoods which are free from taste or unpleasant odour, and they cannot be dated accurately. A selection of sizes and outlines are shown in the bottom row of Plate 20.

Beakers, Folding

Picnic beakers, consisting of a number of thin, concentric, tapering rings which, when pulled upwards, form a tight-fitting ringed beaker, were made to fit into a circular box, of which the bottom of the beaker formed the base, Plate 20, *h* and

j; they probably originated in silver. Between 1900 and 1910, they were made in considerable quantities in aluminium. It is probable that most of those wooden specimens, usually of ash, with crude inlay in the cover, date from the same period and were the *tour de force* of a particular turner. They cannot be considered as anything more, because the stresses set up by alternate wetting and drying of thin ash rings and the resultant swelling and shrinking must inevitably have led to warping and splitting. Although not to be considered as practical drinking vessels their making entailed considerable skill, and one made recently and presented to me is a fine example of turnery.

Bibers—see *Cups, Wine Tasting*

Bowls, Drinking

There is a small group of lignum vitae drinking bowls of which that shown in Plate 39, measuring $5\frac{1}{4}$ in. in diameter by $2\frac{1}{2}$ in. high, may be considered typical, except that it does not have a small foot rim, which occurs on the majority. There seems to be no literature regarding these individual drinking bowls, which are all of high quality and so thinly turned that they must be regarded as drinking vessels, not just liquor containers. The fact that they are often badly warped, suggests that perhaps they were used for hot posset. They appear to be a stage between the shallow mazer bowl and the drinking cup and were probably an early 17th-century essay in turning lignum.

Bowls, Mazer—see *Mazers*

Cups, Armorial Decorated, 17th-century

Considered as a group, the elaborately incised treen cups, usually known as James I armorial standing cups, are probably the rarest and most decorative English treen cups in existence. As regards their original purpose, they are also the most puzzling. I have not used the title James I armorial standing cups, because not all the cups date from the reign of James I; at least two are bowls, not cups; and at least two, which in general respects belong to the series, have no armorials on them although, like the rest of the series, they are decorated all over, and include bands of texts in their composition.

These cups are all beautifully turned and the decoration is skilfully designed. It is probably of a pyrographic nature and executed with a hot thin steel implement on a carefully prepared surface, very smooth and probably glazed first. This was difficult in the days before controlled heat was available to give a constant temperature to the steel and it is possible that patterns and inscriptions were etched or incised by fine gouging, which was then artificially darkened and the surrounding surface subsequently cleaned off. However it was done, many days of skilled labour must have gone into each cup and, as wooden objects go, they were costly.

It would be interesting to know how many of these cups were made and how many survive. I have kept a record over many years, but it has not been possible to examine all the specimens. Some of the records consulted were compiled more than 100 years ago; most of them are incomplete, vague or inaccurate regarding dimensions, dates, descriptions of crests and texts, and wood used. As the cups and bowls have changed hands, the descriptions have changed and sometimes finials, covers and even stems and feet have been lost or damaged. Out of the considerable number which I have recorded and of which I have examined a high proportion, I am satisfied that 28 are not duplicated. They consist of:

1 cup dated 1603, bearing the Royal Tudor Coat of Arms.
2 cups dated 1608, having no armorial devices.

1 cup and 1 bowl dated 1610. ⎫
2 cups dated 1611. ⎪
1 cup dated 1614. ⎪ Mostly
1 cup dated 1615. ⎪ bearing the
2 cups dated 1617. ⎬ Royal
1 cup dated 1619. ⎪ Arms of
5 cups dated 1620. ⎪ James I
1 cup dated 1621. ⎭
7 cups undated, but nearly all bearing the Royal Arms of James I.
1 cup dated 1648, with no Royal Coat of Arms.
2 cups dated 1687, bearing the Royal Arms of James II.

One of the undated specimens is more 19th- than 17th-century work, but as the modern parts are probably a replica of an original, I have counted it in the total.

According to various records, specimens are turned from pearwood, cherry, maple, sycamore and beech. Age, wear, decoration and discoloration, make positive identification of wood difficult, without damaging the specimens; but none of those which I have examined are beech, although some were alleged to be. I would not have expected any to be of beech, because it is neither a suitably stable wood for such fine turnery, nor has it the correct qualities required for fine scale and intricate decoration of this nature.

As the illustrations show, the cups vary greatly in their outline and overall dimensions, but all of those made between 1603 and 1625 have, or appear to have had, clip-over lids, with projecting rims, a stem and domed foot, and only one has no knop on the stem. The lids are of varying degrees of convexity, surmounted by knopped finials which, in the case of steeple cup types, such as Plates 55 and 56, contain spice cups in their hollow knops; the finial covers to the spice cups have a hit and miss closure. The finial and knop may, therefore, be in one or two parts, and the main cover, body of the bowl, stem and foot are separate components; fixed junctions are threaded or dowelled.

With only three exceptions, the covers,

as well as the bodies of the cups, are divided into three or four zones by formal incised borders and have the zones filled with armorials, of which one is usually the Royal Coat of Arms of the reigning monarch, normally with the initials and sometimes the date added. The other zones most commonly show two or three of the following:

Stag	(Lisle)
Wyvern	(Herbert)
Unicorn	(Ferrers)
Ostrich	(Digby)
Porcupine	(Sidney)
Elephant	(Knollys)

But not all heraldic authorities agree on the family relationship and apparently there can be more than one answer. Griffin, lion, salamander, swan, parrot, fox and flowers also occur on a few cups. The quasi-religious texts, many of the sources of which, I believe, have never been traced, are frequently very lengthy, always occur in one or two bands round the bowl and sometimes, additionally, round the finial, the cover, the foot, and even under the foot, forming concentric circles of lettering which may run to 150 or more words.

All except those made between 1603 and 1621 which I have seen, except Plate 57, appear to have been either the work of one man, or more likely, to have been made in one workshop, under the direction and supervision of one master craftsman.

The exception to all the rules, Plate 57, which is undated, must in theory have been made between 1603 and 1625, because it bears not one but two Royal Coats of Arms—one of James as James I of England, and the other as James VI of Scotland. The lettering of the texts is much more precise, better formed and in part much larger than on any of the other cups, but like all of them, is badly spaced. The style of the ornament is more sophisticated and is quite different in character, as is the shape, which is reminiscent of Common-

wealth silver. It is also one of the two tallest of these cups recorded, being 19½ in. over the finial, compared to the Elizabeth I cup, which measures 19¾ in. I would not be surprised to learn that this cup was made in Scotland; it would be interesting to learn if Scottish design was more advanced than English at this period.

Plate 58 illustrates the so-called Hickman chalice, one of the two 1608 dated cups, which have no armorials, but instead formal leaf decoration and the usual lengthy texts. The other, which has lost its lid, is very similar in design. I know of no duplication of texts or rhymes on these cups, but those on the Hickman chalice are particularly clear and typical of the general style. Under the lip-band is the inscription

> *'The Lord of Lyfe his Precious Blood hath shed from Death and Hell his chosen to redeeme such as from Sinne are risen from the dead him and his word they greatly do esteeme for that from so great Death they are set free they shune all Sinne and serve him thankfully'.*

The inscription is continued round the bottom of the bowl. Round the foot is another inscription

> *'God's word sincerely often preached and read, true Christian Soules it doth in ofte truely feed. Thereby they learn a Blessed lyfe to leade: to them Christ giveth worthy Drink indeede: his owne Deare Bloud'.*

Under the foot, in concentric circles, is the continued inscription

> *'Doth cleanse them from all Sinne. Salvation Good they so are sure to winne: Because they do feel the Power of Christes Death working in them effectually the Death of all Sinne and the power of his resurrection raising them up to newness of lyfe to serve God with a faithfull sincere loving and obedient heart so rune that you may obtain: 1608'.*

The two James II cups, dated 1687, not illustrated, have the largest bowl diameters of any, being 10⅜ in. and 10¾ in. diameter respectively. Although thin at the rims, like earlier ones, both the bowls and covers thicken up much more, and the walls of the bowls low down are approximately $\frac{1}{2}$ in. thick, at least double that of earlier specimens, which in other respects they closely resemble.

Many theories have been adduced as to the purpose for which these intriguing cups were made. The most popular is that they were fashionable Communion Cups; but treen Communion Cups had been forbidden by the Canons of Winchester as early as 1071, on the grounds that they absorbed the Host. The veto probably was not fully observed in country districts, but at the time these cups were made, Communion Cups of silver were of a form dictated by authority and a fashionable treen series would never have been made, nor would nearly all of them have borne the crests of the same noble families. It has also been suggested, by the heraldry on them, that these were the cups of royal cup bearers, but although some members of the families represented on the badges were cup bearers, it was mostly in reigns prior to James I. If replicas of these cups existed in silver, then the treen cups might possibly be try-outs or patterns for silver; but, so far as I know, there are no silver replicas. Even allowing for the Commonwealth destruction of silver, surely not all specimens would have perished, and two of the cups are, in any event, later than Commonwealth. Moreover, for try-outs, it is most unlikely that the texts would have been engraved and not surface written.

I would like to propound a new theory. It is that these cups formed part of the insignia of some exclusive 17th-century society. At Burghley House, Stamford, seat of the Marquess of Exeter, are some portraits of members of the Honourable Order of Little Bedlam, a social club founded by the 5th Earl in 1684 and reformed in 1705 by the 6th Earl. Each member had to adopt the name of a particular animal and be

referred to as that animal. As stated earlier, I have recorded 28 of these cups and there were 27 members present at the 1705 Chapter. Amongst them were

Lion (The Rt. Hon. John, Earl of Exeter, Great Master)
Stag (The Hon. Chas. Bertie)
Unicorn (Sir Godfrey Kneller)
Porcupine (Signor Antonio Verrio)
Elephant (Anthony Palmer, Esq.)

There were also present many animals not represented on the cups. The six surviving portraits of members at Burghley show, with their insignia, the 5th Earl of Exeter (lion), the 1st Duke of Devonshire (leopard), Lord Gainsborough (greyhound), Dr. Haschard, Dean of Windsor (cock), Kneller, the painter (unicorn) and Verrio's self portrait (porcupine).

Possibly an earlier society or club existed, of which the outsize Elizabethan cup of 1603 was the master cup. If such a club died out during the Civil War, the 5th Earl could well have known of its existence and if an ancestor of his were the founder, the cups might have been stored at Burghley and given him the basic idea for the Little Bedlam. Possibly some of the new members may have adopted or been given badges of members of other families who had died. Probably the six armorials which appear on nearly all cups, were those of founder members. The fact that there are two large armorial cups of the series dated 1687 could tie up with the founding of the Little Bedlam in 1684. The two cups with texts inscribed on them, but no armorials, may have been for paid officials of the club, or for guests, who would have had no badges or symbols.

Cups, Bitter—see *Cups, Goblets, Quassia*

Cups, Dipper
Dipper cups, of which a selection in lignum vitae is illustrated in Plate 21, were used in conjunction with wassail bowls and were

mostly made in the 17th century and earlier. They were filled by dipping them in the wassail bowl. They are generally of broad thimble shape, with a flat base, but a few are of ogee form. They vary from a rim diameter of 1½ in. to 3 in. and a depth of 1¼ in. to 2 in. They were most frequently made of lignum vitae, but also in maple and horn. Some are plain, some engine-turned and some silver-mounted. They were also made entirely of silver. Originally they were in sets, for use with a bowl, but the sets have usually become separated and now even single examples are rare. Some wassail bowls had lignum trays in which they stood and the trays were large enough to provide room for a row of inverted dippers, on turned finials on which the dippers, when not in use, were placed inverted.

G. Bernard Hughes has deduced that the dippers were filled by ladles, because of the risk of drips falling on clothing. It may be so, but cloths were used for wiping in eating and drinking ceremonial and certainly our ancestors would not have been squeamish about all drinking and redipping in turn. My own view is that ladles were probably not used generally until the end of the 17th or beginning of the 18th century. Some 16th- and 17th-century paintings of drinking scenes show dipper cups on tables, but no ladles; 18th-century drinking scenes sometimes depict ladling from a bowl, but I have never seen a 17th-century picture showing ladles—for details of ladles, see Section IV, *Eating* and Section VI, *Kitchen*. For further references to dipper cups, see *Wassail Bowls*.

Cups, Engine-turned Standing

The three engine-turned standing cups illustrated in Plate 26, *F*, *G* and *H*, and measuring respectively 7¾ in., 8¾ in. and 10¼ in. high, by 6 in., 7 in. and 7½ in. in diameter, could equally well be described as wassail bowls. They probably all date from the mid-17th century and are fine examples of the Stuart turner's skill in

using the eccentric lathe contrivances needed for the intricacies of rose engine turning. Although they all bear a family resemblance, I have never yet found two exactly alike. The rose or other ornament occurs not only on the bowl, stem and foot, but also under the foot of each cup. Having been told, on several occasions, by ceramic experts, that Josiah Wedgwood invented engine turning in the second half of the 18th century, I must record that at most he might have had the idea of applying it to ceramics. Joseph Moxon, in his *Mechanick Exercises*, 1696, describes both engine turning and oval turning in some detail. Charles Plumier, in *L'Art de Tourner en Perfection*, 1701, illustrates the processes and nearly all the designs found on 17th-century work, and gives copious instructions for executing the work.

Cups, Goblets, General

Goblets are individual, smaller versions of standing cups, each being a bowl on stem and foot. When devoid of ornament—and the majority are—they are usually impossible to date with any degree of accuracy. It is comparatively easy to say whether one has age or is modern, but the forms do not help, because turners modelled their treen outlines on all the glass, silver and pewter which were suitable for copying, and they were just as likely to copy a design 200 years later, as when it first appeared. A good selection of shapes and sizes is shown in Plate 20. *F* well illustrates the difficulty of dating. It follows a well-known mid-17th-century design, but in mahogany, which was not introduced to England at that period. Woods used for goblets include ash, beech, sycamore, chestnut, oak, yew, mahogany, walnut, olive and various fruitwoods. The smallest goblets were presumably made for cordials. The two well patinated goblets with Elizabethan incised ornament, Plate 26, *B* and *C*, are examples where a 16th- or 17th-century attribution can be given without hesitation. They also illustrate the lack of clear dividing line between standing or loving cups (see also *Cups, Loving*). The smaller, $5\frac{5}{8}$ in. by $3\frac{3}{8}$ in. diameter, is a normal goblet size. The larger, $7\frac{3}{4}$ in. by $4\frac{1}{8}$ in., is a borderline case.

Cups, Goblets, Historic Woods

Goblets, like snuff boxes, have often been made as mementoes from the wood of historic trees, or from wood taken from historic buildings. Thus goblets may be found made from Shakespeare's mulberry tree, or from the roof timbers of York Minster. Two examples are illustrated here. The yew wood goblet, $5\frac{1}{2}$ in. high, Plate 20, *P*, has the foot silver-rimmed and its underside covered with a silver plate, which tells that it was the gift of a Mr. Lockett of Petworth and was made in 1837 from a yew tree cut in the churchyard at Pulborough, Sussex, recorded as having been standing before the Conquest of 1066. The other cup or urn, $4\frac{1}{2}$ in. high, Plate 20, *O*, was turned from the chestnut tree at Whitelackington, Somerset, in which the Duke of Monmouth hid after the battle of Sedgemoor. The tree was blown down at the end of the 19th century; the wood was salvaged by a Mr. House and his son, and this urn was turned from it locally. In 1963, the son, Mr. H. C. House, then aged 80, presented the urn to the Pinto Collection.

Cups, Goblets, Quassia

Plate 20, *K*, is made of quassia wood. Quassia comes both from the West Indies and from Surinam. It has insecticidal, tonic and mildly aperient qualities. Quassia chips were formerly used for washing lousy heads and quassia powder went into non-poisonous fly-papers and into animal conditioning powders. Formerly, large quantities were imported for the brewing of ale and porter. Quassia goblets, with two lines of reeds, like that illustrated, were known as 'bitter cups' and imported from

Jamaica. They impart a bitter flavour to any beverage allowed to stand in them. If you have a goblet which looks like that illustrated, test it by leaving water in it and drinking it after an hour or two.

Cups, Loving

Loving cup has now come to be an alternative name for the large standing cups used for passing round and drinking healths at dinners, but formerly any drinking vessel of appropriate size, including a tankard, was used as a loving cup. Treen cups may be with or without covers, but, owing to the nature of the material and the process of turning, are almost invariably devoid of the handles which distinguish so many silver specimens. Usually they vary between 7 in. and 11 in. in height, and $4\frac{1}{2}$ in. to $6\frac{1}{2}$ in. in diameter, and may be of any suitable hardwood, lignum vitae being particularly favoured from the 17th century onwards. Examples are shown in Plate 26. The 17th-century, lignum vitae cup of chalice form, *A*, is $7\frac{5}{8}$ in. high by $5\frac{1}{4}$ in. diameter and the 17th-century, yew wood cup, *D*, is $9\frac{5}{8}$ in. high by 5 in. diameter. The larger of the two Elizabethan goblets, *B*, probably ranks as a loving cup. The $10\frac{5}{8}$ in. high cup, *E*, is said to have been used formerly as a Communion cup in a country church. The engine turned cups are described under *Cups, Engine-turned Standing*.

Cups, Milkmaid

Milkmaid cups, sometimes known as wager cups, were mostly made in silver, but a few treen examples exist. They are carved in the form of a woman in 17th-century costume, with a hollow, billowing skirt; her arms are above her head and a small milk-pail 'cup' swings between her hands. The figure was inverted and both her skirt and the swinging cup were filled with wine. On admission to the Vintners Company, each Liveryman was required to drink from a milkmaid cup. First he had to drink to the Company from the skirt, without spilling wine from either cup, and then a health to the Master from the pail—quite a difficult feat. Treen examples, usually of pearwood, generally have both cups silver mounted. Occasionally the figure is a man, and probably these rarities, dating from the 17th century, were originally made in pairs.

Cups, Nest of

A small number of covered wooden standing cups, some silver mounted, containing nests of dipper cups, were made in the 18th and possibly in the 17th centuries. They usually measure 6 in. to 7 in. in height, excluding the knop and about 4½ in. in diameter. Like treen folding beakers, they must be considered more as a *tour de force* of the turner than as vessels seriously meant for use. Apart from the fact that any assembly using them would have had cups all varying in size, possibly from pint to little more than thimble, the thinness of turning, and sometimes the choice of wood, suitable for fine turning, but not for a sequence of wetting and drying, shows that they were never intended for use. Although some of the actual standing cups are more elegant than the example illustrated, Plate 27, this one is remarkable for the number of tight-fitting cups which it contains—16 in all. Their turning individually with such accuracy required great skill. They were not, as has sometimes been stated, all cut from the same block by means of a long handled steel cutting tool, with a long curved chisel point, manipulated so that the entire centre of a bowl was removed in a single piece, and without waste. Such a tool was and is used by the turner and a highly skilled turner might be able to cut, say, every third cup of a diminishing series from the same block. If it were possible to do what has been written, then Mr. F. J. Howe of Tunbridge Wells, than whom I know of no finer turner, would be able to do it. He, however, confirms my own view that it cannot be done, and examination of the grain of nests of tight-fitting, relatively straight-sided cups,

will confirm that they have not been made in this manner.

Cups, Posset

Posset was a hot spiced drink, formerly much used as a 'night-cap' and as a cure for colds. There are many recipes, but usually the 'body' was milk, curdled with ale or wine, with lemon, sugar, cinnamon and other spices added. A posset cup was not a ceremonial vessel; it was intended for an individual or a few cronies and there is no restriction of form for it; perhaps small lidded wassail bowls were sometimes used, but more frequently the posset cup was doubtless of materials other than treen. The treen vessels described as posset cups usually have a container on the lid for spices and a separate base hollowed out for a lemon.

The best known treen vessel of this nature is that illustrated in Plate 30. It was described by the late Owen Evan-Thomas, very happily I think, as an 'Elizabethan Service of Treen', for it consists of a number of different purpose components, including a double cup of sycamore, one large and one small cup, which can be used either way up. The upper cup is surmounted by a wide projecting domed lid, which is hollow and contains a spice box. Above this lid-box is a knop which forms a handle, is also hollow and holds a nutmeg; the lower part or neck and foot of this knop forms the spice box. The cup itself stands on two hollow bases, one above the other. The upper base has a rim which holds the cup and is hollowed out to hold a lemon; inverted, it forms a stand for the pot in which the posset was heated. This upper base forms the rebated lid of the lower base which is a box, containing 10 cedar of Lebanon roundels or mats. It does appear, therefore, that this service was intended more for a loving cup ceremony with hot spiced wine, than as a posset cup. The whole 16th-century complex, when assembled, forms an imposing standing cup, 18 in. high, decorated all over with bands of typical Elizabethan ornament in sunk relief. It is probably unique today, but it is likely that there were once others, for in the Pinto Collection is a roundel box, Plate 61, of somewhat similar type and ornament, with a socket on the lid to hold a superstructure.

Much more correctly described as posset cups are the examples illustrated in Plates 21 and 53. The lignum vitae standing posset cup, Plate 21, measures 11 in. in height overall, by 5½ in. diameter. It has a covered spice cup on the lid. It stands in the rim of a heavy base, which is hollowed out for a lemon. Reversed, the base can be used as a hob, but this seems unnecessary as the foot of the cup itself is so heavy. It is 18th-century, Irish and several cups of similar form in other materials are known. The rare English, standing posset cup, with bowl of ogee outline, Plate 53, *F*, probably dates from early in the 17th century. It is a very thin and delicate piece of turnery, although almost certainly country-made, because it contains such a mixture of hardwoods. The lid and knop, the latter hollowed to hold a nutmeg, are of mulberry wood, the bowl of beech. Owing to amateurish repairs, which I have had to rectify, it has lost its patination, which gives it a falsely new appearance. I have seen two others of somewhat similar type.

Cups, Stirrup

Stirrup cups of wood are exceptionally rare. I only know of five, out of which three are in the Pinto Collection, Plate 39. None of them represents the fox mask, the most common in other materials. They all date from the 18th century; the two hound mask cups are comparatively crude. The late 18th-century, yew wood, ram's head cup is a highly skilful and sophisticated example of carving.

Cups, Travelling

Travelling cups were normally made of silver; the only wooden ones which I have found are a set of four elegant lignum vitae, ogee-shaped cups, of which two examples are shown in Plate 39. They are 3⅛ in. tall, silver lined and rimmed and complete with their two original leather cases, one of which is shown, right. Two cups nest in each case. They are not hall-marked, but probably date from about 1700.

Cups, Vendageur

Whilst I always feel that the awkwardness of these Swiss and South German vessels, such as the example left of Plate 39, makes them much more suitable as ornaments than drinking cups, they are apparently generally recognized as a group of late 16th-century drinking vessels. They follow a very close pattern, are usually carved from pear-wood, but are very rarely complete now. Both men and women figures were made, sometimes in pairs. The bearded man should be leaning on a stout knobbly staff, the knobs often of silver. The grape basket or hod on his back, which forms the cup, is usually silver mounted. The mount is missing from the example illustrated. The man's hat has a feather, his jacket is pleated, a pouch is attached to his waistband and he wears loose breeches and gartered stockings; sometimes he carries a silver-mounted water flask. He should have a seated dog, with silver collar, at his feet.

Cups, Whistling

Silver tankards with a whistle incorporated in the thumb grip of the handle are recorded, and I have found a horn spoon with a whistle in the handle, so that its user could whistle for more. Most writers claim that this custom is the origin of the phrase 'wet your whistle', but some say the phrase goes back much further and that 'whistle', in this sense, is a corruption of 'weasand', the windpipe, which in former days was sometimes spelt 'weesil' or 'wizzel'. The whistling cup illustrated, Plate 38, is, however, the only treen vessel of this nature which I have seen. It is carved from walnut, is 8 in.

long by 3 in. diameter, has a whistle in its base and is inscribed

> ' Take not from me all my store
> Except you fill me with some more
> For have to borrow and never to pay
> I call that foul play.
> —H. N. Watson, 1695 '

The cup bearing this excellent maxim, holds half a pint.

Cups, Wine Tasting, or Bibers

The curious 8½ in. high vessel, Plate 20, *D*, with small cup on a long stem, is believed to be a 17th-century wine biber, used in the cellar for tasting wine from the cask. The finely finished, 16th- or 17th-century burr maple bowl, with silver straps, mounts and handles, like a miniature mazer of 3 in. diameter, top right, Plate 39, would also have served as a taster, but for a wine steward at table.

Cups, Witch—see Section I, *Apothecary: Witch Bowls*

Decanters

The example illustrated, Plate 53, *A*, is 11½ in. high, turned from mulberry wood. It is in one piece, the bulb being hollowed out from the neck opening. It is a considerable feat of skill, but one must doubt whether it could ever have been used without splitting, although admittedly wooden bottles, well varnished, were made occasionally and appear to have had good use (see Plates 50, *O*, and 54, left).

Dipper Cups—see *Cups, Dipper*

Goblets—see *Cups, Goblets*

Horns

Though not strictly treen, mention should be made of the typical Anglo-Saxon drinking vessel, the horn. This, by reason of its awkward shape, was, it is believed, customarily drained at one draught. A complete specimen, elaborately silver mounted and dating back to the early 7th century, was found in 1883 in a grave at Taplow Court, Bucks. It is now in the British Museum. Silver mounts of others were found in the Sutton Hoo ship burial hoard in 1939 but, so far as I am aware, no other early complete horns have been found. In the Bayeux tapestry, drinking horns are shown in the scene of Harold and his Anglo-Saxons, banqueting at Bosham. At the Conquest, horns were not discarded, but they became increasingly restricted to ceremonial use and they developed one or two additional silver bands, to which silver feet were riveted, so that the horn could stand upright and need not be emptied at a single draught. Some of the silver mounting is very beautiful and the legs simulate those of an animal or bird, terminating in paws or claws. A few of them also had fine silver covers. They appear to have died out in the 15th century. In early Christianity, horn cups were used for wine at the Communion service, but in A.D. 785 the horn was forbidden. See also *North-west European Drinking Vessels*.

Jugs, Coopered

Coopered jugs were formerly made in considerable quantities, both straight-sided, tapering towards the top, and bellied; the latter required more skill, although all coopering is a skilful task, in order to create liquor-tight joints. Some of these jugs were open necked, others lidded. Apart from the fact that they are spouted, they only differ from coopered tankards in the much greater range of sizes. The woods most commonly used were oak, chestnut and pine. The bands might be of iron, copper or willow. Where carving occurs on them, they are probably Scandinavian, unlikely to be English. Owing to shrinkage of staves and eventual collapse, when not used regularly, comparatively few really old ones have survived. See also tools of the cooper, Section XXIV, *Tools, of Specialized Woodworkers*.

1 The pole lathe is the oldest type of 'turning' machine and is still used in primitive communities, particularly by chair bodgers and bowl turners, working in the woods. This photograph is of a copper engraving by the Dutch painter-engraver Jan Joris Van Vliet, born at Delft, 1610. It shows a turner working on a leg for a chair, or a part for the spinning wheel in the foreground. The pole lathe has a reciprocal action. The two puppet posts, one of which slides in the bed, the rest on which he holds his chisel, the foot treadle with cord twisted round the 'stuff', and connecting to the spring pole cradled from the ceiling, are all shown. Sometimes, in the open woodland, a bent down sapling is used as a spring. A compass and turning chisel are to be seen in the racks and on the lathe bed, and on a shelf at the back are three footwarmers, a spice(?) box, a yoke, flour barrels, etc.

2 A number of dishes of this type in silver, bronze, silver gilt and brass have survived from the 16th century, when they were used for display on buffets, at banquets. This handsome carved pearwood example, dated 1575, is a great rarity—possibly unique. It shows traces of gilding and originally may have been gilded all over, to simulate gold plate (which it would do by candle light). Alternatively, it may have been a 'try-out' by the craftsman, to show his patron, before the work in metal commenced. The dish was probably made on the Italian/German border. The scenes depict—Salome; the Prodigal Son; Christ at the Well; the Worship of the Magi; the four Evangelists. The coat of arms has not yet been traced. Through age, the dish has gone oval, now measuring 20⅞ in. across the grain and 22 in. with it (*Introduction*)

3 Mahogany, box door type, apothecary cabinet with secret compartment at back. Used or sold by Ambrose Godfrey of Southampton Street, Strand, *circa* 1750. (*Section I*)

4 Selection of 17th- and 18th-century treen apothecary jars. *B, D, G, H, J* and *K* are German. *C* and the fine yew-wood jar *F*, formerly in the Carnegie Collection, are probably English. *L* and *M* are Mallorcan-Spanish. (*Section I*)

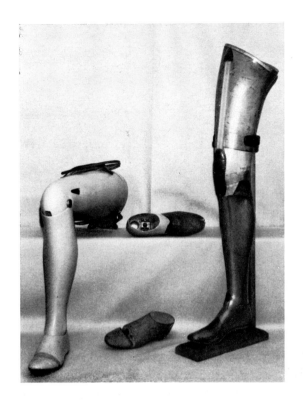

5 'Anglesey' artificial legs of willow. RIGHT: early suction type, World War I. LEFT: 1954–64 type, used with waist belt and shoulder strap. CENTRE: two willow feet in various stages of manufacture. (*Section I*)

6 *A*, Florence Nightingale bandage winder; *B*, *C* and *D*, 16th- to early 18th-century searces; *F* and *G*, two double measures; *H* and *J*, two bleeding bowls, probably 17th- or 18th-century; *E*, Anglo-French phlebotomization outfit, *circa* 1740; *K*, massage roulette; *L*, Chinese massage ball; *M*, root cutter. (*Section I*)

7 *A* to *H*, boxwood, ebony and rosewood bottle cases; *J* to *M*, various syringe cases; *N*, sprinkler cases; *O*, salve pots; *P* and *Q*, two camphor (?) containers; *R* and *S*, thermometer cases. (*Section I*)

8 *A* and *B*, dental keys, *circa* 1800; *C* and *D*, boxwood gags; *E*, 17th-century apothecary jar stopper; *F*, apothecary's scoop; *G*, witch's brew bowl; *H*, 18th-century pill silverer; *J*, nest of pill boxes used by Palmer, the poisoner; *K*, 19th-century pill making machine; *L*, pill rounder; *M*, pill box; *N*, selection of pill boxes; *O*, cachet machine. (*Section I*)

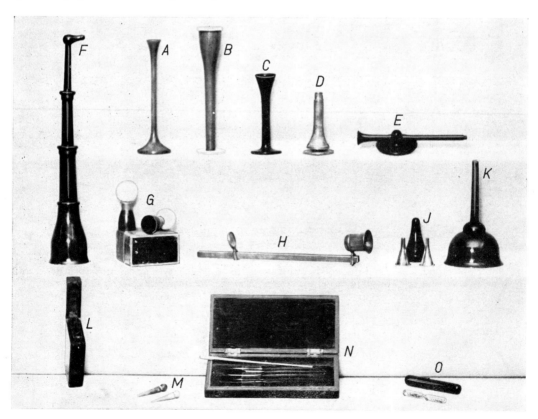

9 *A* to *E*, 19th-century stethoscopes—*D* and *E* are folding types; *F*, early 19th-century, folding ear trumpet; *G*, Dr. Ball's eye cups; *H*, 19th-century eye tester; *J*, silver funnels with lignum case; *K*, large funnel; *L*, Regency pocket instrument case; *M*, operation pegs; *N*, late 18th-century, surgeon's dissecting case; *O*, *circa* 1840, pocket thirty-second sand glass with lignum vitae case. (*Section I*)

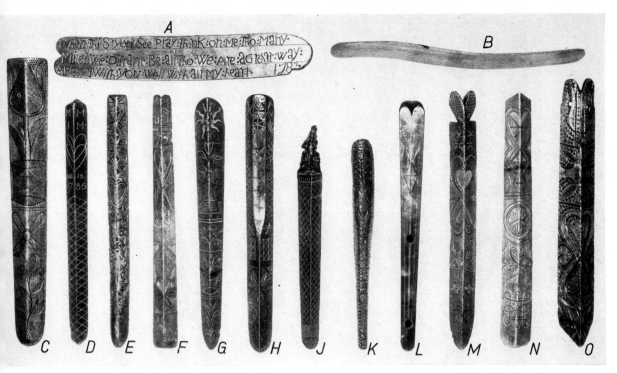

10 Stay busk love tokens. English, 18th century. For details, see text. (*Section II*)

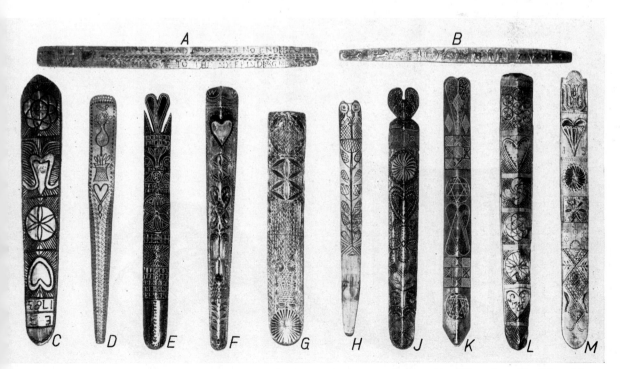

11 Stay busk love tokens. *A* is the earliest recorded dated English specimen—1660. The others, English, 18th century. For further details, see text. (*Section II*)

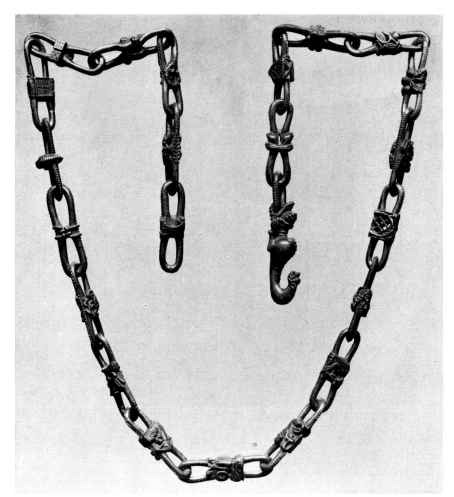

12 Superbly carved thornwood girdle. French, 14th century. *Photograph by courtesy of the Victoria and Albert Museum.* (*Section II*)

13 A pair of rare inlaid, laminated, wooden shoe buckles. English, 18th century. (*Section II*)

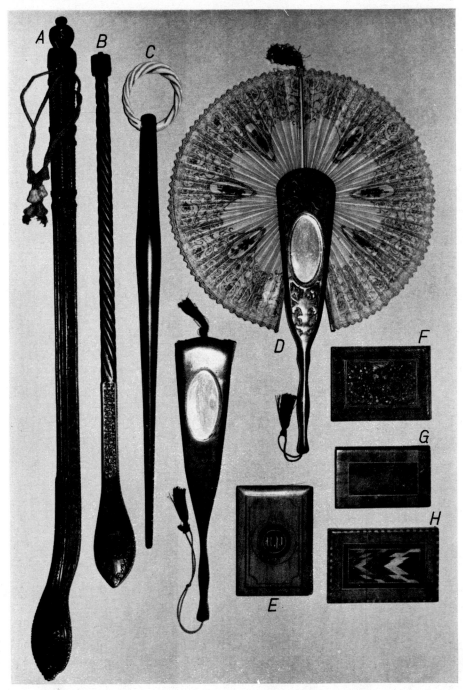

14 *A* and *B*, back scratchers; *C*, head scratcher; *D*, mirrored fans, Italian; *E*, *F*, *G* and *H*, visiting card cases.

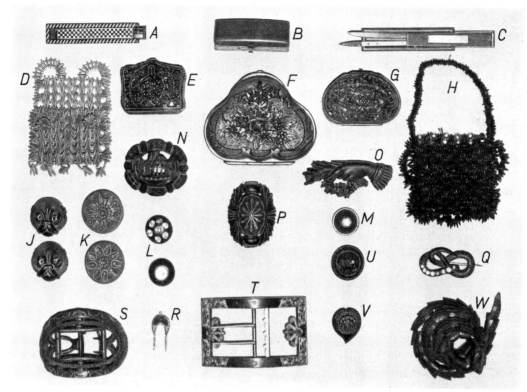

15 *A, B* and *C*, English, 18th-century, toothpick boxes. *D, E, F, G* and *H*, 19th-century purses, *E* and *G* of coquilla nutshell, *F* of carved walnut, *D* and *H* of melon pips. *J, K, L* and *M*, buttons; *J* carved as dog heads, *K* carved walnut; *L* and *M* are Irish bog oak, set with quartz. *O,* *P* and *Q* are brooches; *R*, gold mounted jet ear-ring; *S*, 18th-century, boxwood shoe buckle; *T*, Regency, rosewood belt buckle, mounted with chased ormolu; *U* and *V* are carved coconut shell costume ornaments. *W*, a carved coquilla nutshell bangle. (*Section II*)

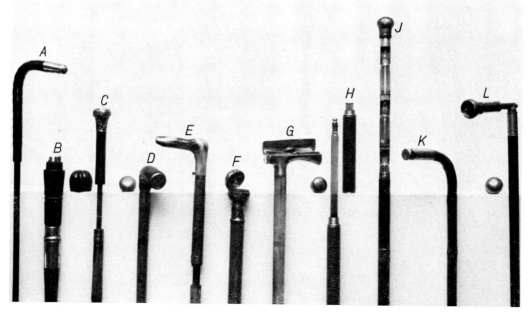

16 Walking sticks with a secondary purpose. For details, see text. (*Section II*)

17 *A*, *B* and *D*, parasol handles, and *C*, walking stick handle, described in text. *E*, 18th-century stick or parasol handle carved as a drummer boy. *F*, monkey, *G*, bulldog, and *H*, alligator, are 19th-century handles. *J* and *K*, of carved ebony, date from *circa* 1800. (*Section II*)

18 RIGHT: superbly carved, French, 17th-century, boxwood walking stick. LEFT: English, 18th-century, boxwood walking stick, carved with head of John Wesley and scenes from the scriptures. (*Section II*)

19 Details of the carvings on the two sticks shown in **18**.

20 Selection of treen drinking vessels. *D* is an early wine taster, and *E* a tumbler holder; the others lettered *A* to *V* are goblets of various shapes. In the bottom row are mainly beakers, including *h* and *j*, comparatively modern folding types. (*Section III*)

21 Irish posset cup set of lignum vitae, 18th-century; five lignum vitae dipper cups, three engine turned (*Section III*) and six 18th-century ladles, three of them English and three Scottish (*Section IV*).

22A and B Outside and inside view of the Epworth mazer of burr maple, silver mounted. 16th century. *Photograph by courtesy of the British Museum. (Section III)*

23 (BELOW) German, maple burr and silver mounted mazer of octofoil outline with handle, all in one piece. *Circa* 1500. *Photograph by courtesy of the British Museum. (Section III)*

24 (ABOVE) The Galloway standing mazer of burr maple, with engraved and repoussé silver mounts. Dated 1569. *Photograph by courtesy of Sotheby & Co. (Section III)*

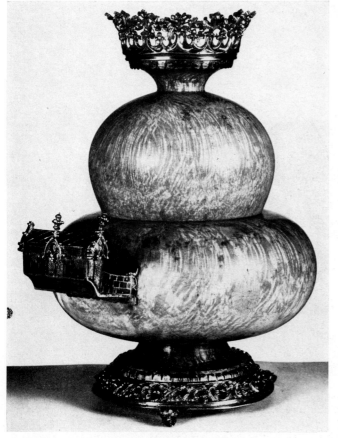

25 German double mazer of burr maple, with pierced silver gilt mounts and coat of arms in enamel. *Photograph by courtesy of the Wallace Collection. (Section III)*

26 *A, D* and *E,* 17th-century loving cups; *B* and *C,* Elizabethan loving cups; *F, G* and *H,* 17th-century, engine turned loving cups or small wassail bowls; *J,* a standing mazer, probably 16th century; *K,* small lignum vitae wassail bowl; *L,* lignum vitae tankard, 18th century; *N,* engine turned, double spice box of lignum vitae, 17th century; all the preceding are English; *M,* an unusual, 17th- or 18th-century tankard, may be German. (*Section III*)

27 Nest of 17th- or 18th-century, English dipper cups, which fit in a standing cup—a *tour de force* of the turner. *Photograph by courtesy of Gabriel Olive, of Wincanton.* (*Section III*)

Jugs, Toby

A toby jug in wood is not a very likely object for a collector to find, although I have seen several made of leather. Nevertheless, two or three wooden toby jugs do exist, all probably carved by the same man in the West of England, and so skilfully finished in a glazed polychrome in the typical Ralph Wood palette of colours, that it is necessary to handle them before being aware of the clever subterfuge. The jug illustrated, Plate 41, is 14½ in. high and, like the Ralph Wood glazed pottery examples, has prominent warts on the right cheek and left side of the nose. The tricorne hat and shoes are black, the coat and jug in his hands, brown; breeches, green; waistcoat, ochre, and stockings and shoe buckles, ivory coloured. The wood used is pine, which has been built up in glued sections. The interior is so unfinished that it could only have been intended as an ornament, or shop display. When this specimen in the Pinto Collection was illustrated in *Country Life*, 1.7.60, the owner of a similar one, except that it has a hinged lid, which the specimen pictured has never had, wrote to me saying the correspondence which came to him with his jug, suggests that these jugs were probably carved round about 1900. I would have expected the one illustrated to be about 100 years earlier. Recently, another one has come to light, this time a money box, with the slot in his tricorne hat. It is very similar in style and colouring to Plate 41, but designed as a town crier with G.R. on his bell; I am still inclined to think that some of these rare wooden 'toby' specimens were made around 1800 or earlier.

Loving Cups—see *Cups, Loving*

Mazers

In an article in *Connoisseur*, March 1949, and to a greater extent in my book *Treen* published by Batsford the same year, I established the truth about mazers, concerning which a number of misconceptions had arisen, largely as the result of the writings of W. H. St. John Hope. He had discussed mazers essentially as silver, because the largest and most important ones were mounted in, and decorated with silver. St. John Hope contended that 'The five characteristics of the mazer are: (I) the bowl; (II) the band; (III) the "print"; (IV) the foot; (V) the lid; but in most cases the last two never existed'. If they never existed how could they be characteristics? Indeed, in a later passage, St. John Hope admitted that a mazer could still be a mazer without the characteristics. Sir Charles Jackson and Evan-Thomas unfortunately accepted and confirmed or copied without question, what St. John Hope had written about the five characteristics. The latter made his arguments more involved by confusing bird's-eye maple with burr maple, and also writing that 'Of all the drinking vessels in use from the 13th to the 16th century, none were so common and highly prized as mazers'.

For students, collectors and others deeply interested, the arguments leading up to my conclusions can all be read in *Treen*, which although out of print, is obtainable from museum and some other libraries. To keep the record straight, it is only fair to add that I later discovered W. J. Cripps, another eminent writer on silver, had, by different means, reached the same conclusion that I had done, in 1878! Unfortunately his scholarly historical research was ignored by later writers; since I began writing this encyclopaedia, Cripps' valuable work has been reprinted. Below, are my conclusions.

In ancient literature, mazers are sometimes described as 'common', at other times as 'much prized'. This apparent contradiction is due to mazers being basically wooden drinking bowls. In the Middle Ages, the small, plain ones, or *murrae usuales*, were the individual drinking bowls used by monks and others; the large and elaborately silver-mounted vessels, for passing from drinker to drinker at table, were the *murrae magnae*, the valuable ceremonial vessels referred to in inventories and the most important drinking vessels used between about 1250 and 1600. As early as the reign of Henry II, who died in 1189, there are mentions in the royal household accounts of the Keeper of the Mazers. Other mediaeval references show that at Coronations certain titled families had to present to the sovereign a silver-mounted mazer or mazers, as their fee for their land. Additional to being called *myrrhine* and *de murro*, mazers are recorded in inventories as *cuppa de mazer, mazeri, maslins* and *mazerins*.

Inventories of five monastic houses recorded the following quantities at the dates quoted:

1328	Canterbury	182 mazers.
1437	Battle	32 mazers.
1446	Durham	49 mazers.
1540	Waltham	15 mazers.
1540	Westminster	40 mazers.

As these are not individually described, it can be assumed that they were all small mazers, normally used by the monks. Being of little intrinsic value, hardly any plain mazers have survived. In the few instances where they have done, they are merely old, simply turned, thin wooden bowls, which cannot be dated accurately; but a clue to their age and former purpose may sometimes be obtained by examination and identification of their wood.

Why were awkward, shallow bowls so often preferred to beakers, goblets, tankards, etc., as drinking vessels during the Middle Ages? A partial answer may be fashion, but the principal cause is the peculiar nature and form of the wood chosen, which had considerable advantages, particularly for large vessels which were to be silver mounted, but which also had serious limitations in the depths of vessels which could be obtained from it. The clue to the peculiarity of the wood is the name mazer. It appears to be derived from the old German word *masa*,

meaning a spot or speck (the origin of measles), and from *maserle*, the maple tree, sometimes referred to as the mazer tree. The connection of thought between 'spots' and maple probably arose originally because maple trees are often spotted or 'bird's-eye' marked. The cause is believed to be the action of a fungus which attacks the cambium layer, the part of the tree immediately under the bark, in which active growth takes place. Bird's-eye marking, which does not affect the strength of the tree, can occur throughout, or only in part of a tree. Bird's-eye maple was not, however, used for making mazers: the mazer wood was the much prized burr or spotted excrescence which sometimes forms on trees, most commonly just above the ground, at the junction of root and trunk, or at the forking of branches.

From denoting a certain kind of wood, the term mazer changed to meaning a drinking vessel made from maple or other burr wood. (In Devonshire, the black cherry is known as the mazer tree.) Eventually, in its broadest and later sense, mazer was used to describe a certain shape of drinking bowl, not necessarily of wood, but sometimes of silver, or silver-mounted semi-precious stone. In January 1644, John Evelyn observed, in the Farnese Palace in Rome '... mazers of beaten and solid gold set with diamonds, rubies and emeralds ...'. The simple fact is that the shape of mazers was originally governed by the common shape of burrs or burls, wart-like excrescences on tree trunks, formed by growth round a wound or dormant buds. Clusters of these small twigs or knots, grown over, gradually build up into shallow curved protuberances, which on large trees are often of considerable diameter, particularly on the butt—the junction of trunk and roots.

Alternating periods of wetness and dryness create severe stresses in wooden bowls, due to their being wet inside and dry outside when in use, with periods of alternating dryness and wetness of both sides, resulting from washing and drying after use. Moreover, they must be turned to fine limits, to serve their purpose elegantly and comfortably. No English hardwood trees which grow to large size, such as oak, elm, ash or beech, combine the qualities of freedom from warping and splits, with sound heart, toughness, denseness of grain and consequent lack of undue porosity.

When 'turned' with the grain running vertically, large vessels of these woods, however well seasoned, would leak badly from the base, and split radially. As wood has negligible longitudinal but fairly considerable width shrinkage, varying according to species and degree of seasoning before 'turning', bowls turned with grain running horizontally, gradually become oval and cannot be mounted in silver with long term satisfactory results. These short-comings were overcome by using burrs, which have irregular and contorted growth, presenting a tangled, interwoven structure, entirely different from normal long grain. Burrs, prized for veneers since early times, were, if sound and free from defects, also greatly esteemed by turners; not only were they beautiful, rare and worthy of mounting in silver, but they were also stable and capable of withstanding alternate cycles of moisture and dryness, when thinly turned into hollow circular vessels. Once it is realized that the shape and size of a burr governed the shape and size of a mazer, it is immediately obvious why such an awkward-shaped drinking bowl was adopted, as soon as it became apparent to the turners that a burr made a more stable and handsome bowl than any other part of a tree could do. Maple burrs are particularly dense and impervious to moisture, but they are usually, although not invariably small, because the maple tree itself—if you ignore the sycamore maple, which may or may not have been available here in mediaeval times—is usually a small tree in England. Shallowness and lack of diameter were overcome, in important mazers, by adding deep, outward projecting

silver rims to increase depth, size and importance. Most of the mazers still extant are these large and important ones, rimmed or banded, and mounted on foot bands of silver and silver gilt. They have a circular medallion centrally placed on the interior base. In the 14th and 15th centuries, it was known as the 'founce' or 'frounce', and since then, generally as the 'print'. Some authorities consider that it was originally inserted to conceal the lathe mark, not obviated until the chuck was invented, whilst others assert that it was derived from the umbilical boss found in Greek paterae and early Egyptian bowls. Some prints are engraved or embossed with portraits of the Virgin, others with coats of arms, stars or animals. Some surviving mazers, particularly later ones, are provided with two silver handles, affixed to straps connecting rims with bases.

The largest surviving mazer is the Great Mazer at York, $12\frac{5}{8}$ in. diameter, but only $3\frac{1}{2}$ in. deep inside the bowl. Other famous specimens include the St. Bede's Bowl at Durham and the Guy of Warwick Mazer at Harbledown; the latter dates between 1307 and 1327. There are six other mazers at Harbledown.

Sixteenth-century mazers are usually deeper, being more heavily mounted than earlier ones. Plate 22, A and B, show the exterior and also interior and print of the mazer from Epworth Church, Lincolnshire, now in the British Museum. The print, originally enamelled, is engraved with figures of St. John the Baptist and St. Andrew, the saints to whom the church is dedicated. The maple bowl, with all-over small burr marking, is $6\frac{7}{8}$ in. in diameter and $1\frac{1}{4}$ in. deep inside. The silver mount increases the diameter to $8\frac{3}{4}$ in., inside depth to $2\frac{3}{4}$ in. and outside height to 3 in. This bowl never had a foot.

In the 17th century, true English mazers died out, their place being taken by deeper bowls, usually of small diameter, some with and some without stems, and often with silver-mounted feet and rims. They were usually known as mazer cups and were made in beech, pear and maple (not burr). Simultaneously, the turners were experimenting with the newly imported lignum vitae (see *Bowls, Drinking*). An unusual English custom of the mazer period, I think chiefly confined to the West Country, may be mentioned here. It was usual to hire a 'sin-eater' at the funeral of a wealthy person. The poor sin-eater took on himself the sins of the deceased in return for a mazer bowl of maple, filled with ale, and a loaf of bread which he consumed over the corpse on its bier, as the procession to the grave commenced; he thus absolved the deceased from walking after death. He also received sixpence. He could not retain the mazer however; that was kept for the next sin-eating! The service performed by the sin-eater must, in some instances, have appeared very cheap at the price!

An unusual and beautiful German mazer, made about 1500, is shown in Plate 23. Its shape appears to have been largely dictated by the maple burr formation which is exceptionally clearly defined and beautifully marked. It is in one piece and the eight-foil edge, 8 in. in diameter, encloses a circular bowl. At one side, the burr extends outwards, forming a scallop edged handle. The foot, rim and print are silver gilt. Between the lobes of the rim are silver bosses of curly leaves, which match in character the rosette print.

In addition to mazer bowls with and without feet, some mounted on stems were made. Probably always rare, few have survived. They are known as standing mazers. It is believed that only three English specimens with feet now exist. Commander How, who added considerably to our knowledge of Scottish standing mazers*, revealed records of several Scottish examples. The two

* (See *Scottish Standing Mazers* by Commander G. E. P. How, F. S. A. Scot., *Proceedings of the Society of Antiquaries of Scotland* (vol. lxviii (vol. viii, sixth series), 1933–34, pages 394–411).

finest Scottish standing mazers are probably the Tulloch and the Galloway. The latter, now in the National Museum of Antiquities, Edinburgh, is shown in Plate 24. It is $8\frac{1}{4}$in. high, with an equal bowl diameter. The silver print in the bowl is $3\frac{5}{16}$ in. diameter, engraved

Provert 22 . Ane . good . mane . is . to . be . chosen . Aboūe . great . riches . And . louing . faūour . Is . aboue . silūer . And . Aboūe . Moste . fyne . golde . 1569

Details of the arms on the silver rim and much other interesting historical information will be found in Commander How's notes, mentioned above.

On my assumption that a mazer need have no silver mounts, then the standing cup, Plate 26, *J*, ranks as a standing mazer. Its height is 7 in., diameter of bowl 6 in. and depth 2 in. It is beautifully faded and has the bowl and foot of some burry root, closely resembling amboyna or yew. The stem is yew; the knop on the stem, reverse way up to normal, provides a very satisfying hand grip.

There is a small but important group of German double mazers which differ entirely from any of the English or other examples. Although they are found in other countries, including England, and may include in their mounts English or other continental coats of arms, it is almost certain that they all emanated from Germany. The handsome example illustrated, Plate 25, of burr maple, with silver gilt mounts, dates from the early 16th century, and measures $6\frac{7}{8}$ in. in height by $6\frac{1}{8}$ in. diameter. As will be seen, it consists of two cups one arranged inverted on the other, so as to resemble a miniature cottage loaf. It is sometimes said that the upper and smaller cup was used as a tasting vessel by the cup bearer, against the risk of poison. According to John Russell's *Boke of Nurture*, 1452, tasting, according to etiquette, was only done for those of royal blood, as a Pope, Emperor, Emperatrice, Cardinal, King, Queen, Prince, Archbishop, Duke and Earl, but no lower rank. However, lower ranks in fear of poison doubtless had their tasters. The silver gilt crown, which acts as the stand of the smaller cup when in use, contains a coat of arms in translucent enamel, set in a quatrefoil within the circle.

When I wrote *Treen*, I thought that there were between 60 and 70 English mazers in existence. Others have been made known to me since, so that counting all those belonging to churches, museums, colleges and private collectors at home and abroad, I think there must be 80 or more.

Milkmaid Cups—see *Cups, Milkmaid*

Nest of Cups—see *Cups, Nest of*

Piggins

Piggins are straight-sided, circular vessels, with an upstanding lug to act as a handle. They were used both as drinking vessels and as dippers to ladle out liquor from a large container into a smaller one. They were used as much, if not more, in the dairy, as they were in connection with alcoholic drinks. The majority are coopered vessels bound with willow or metal, and when so constructed, see Plate 50, *K*, one stave is lengthened to form the lug. A few are found turned out of the solid. See Section V, *Farm*, and also *Scottish Drinking Vessels: Luggies*.

Posset Cups—see *Cups, Posset*

Stirrup Cups—see *Cups, Stirrup*

Tankards

The vast majority of wooden tankards surviving from the past are continental (see *North-west European Drinking Vessels*). English specimens of all periods are very rare.

By A.D. 960, wooden tankards were in general household and tavern use in Britain, but whether the drinking vessels which we now know by that name were then called tankards is unlikely. The word was in common use, but it referred to an iron hooped wooden tub, used for carrying water and was employed in this sense certainly until the end of the 16th century, although a century earlier it was also applied to large beer mugs. The men who carried water from the London conduits are referred to in old records as 'tankard bearers' and the vessels they bore, as tankards. A number of references occur to tankards of this type in farming accounts and kitchen inventories of the 13th and 14th centuries.

Mediaeval drinking tankards were made of narrow staves, generally of oak or pine and usually bound by hoops of wattle. The majority were provided with wooden lids and handles and were lined inside with a coat of pitch. They were made to hold two quarts and in an endeavour to decrease drunkenness, King Edgar introduced the peg or pin tankard. He ordained that certain cups with pins or nails set in them should be made and that any person who drank past the mark or peg at one draught should forfeit a penny, of which half should be given to the accuser and half to the town in which the offence was committed. This is an early instance of encouragement to common informers. It was usual for a single tankard to be passed from hand to hand and pegs or pins divided the contents of the tankards into eight separate portions, but they do not seem to have had much deterrent effect on drinkers, for we soon find Archbishop Anselm decreeing that 'priests shall not drink to pins'. Tankards have remained in common use to the present day and the phrase 'have a peg' has passed into common usage.

Much earlier than mediaeval, is the remarkable Celtic tankard dating from between 50 B.C. and 50 A.D., now in the City of Liverpool Museum. Known as the Trawsfynnid Tankard and measuring $5\frac{9}{16}$ in. in height by $7\frac{3}{16}$ in. diameter, it is composed of strips of yew-wood arranged around a turned disc base. The exterior, which is concave, is sheathed in bronze, turned over on the inside to cover the rim. The strips are kept in position at the base by two circles of thin brass, formed into a wavy band and hammered into the end grain of the yew strips. The handle, a series of graceful scrolls, cast in trumpet pattern, is one of the outstanding examples of Celtic design.*

In *Treen*, I referred to the Glastonbury peg tankard as Saxon, and one of the earliest in existence. Unfortunately, at the time I was writing, this tankard was in a wartime hiding place and I had to rely on information that was incorrect. The tankard, a handsome specimen, richly carved with the Crucifixion on the lid and with the twelve Apostles, labelled in arches, round the body, belongs to a series of English and western European tankards carved in a somewhat similar manner about 1600.

Elaborately carved wooden tankards were very much in vogue among the wealthy in most European countries in the 17th century. Three outstandingly fine specimens, said to be much earlier, but I think of the 17th century, are in the Waterman's Hall, London. The smallest appears to be of Baltic origin; the other two probably are Swiss or Tyrolean.

A simple, 18th-century, lignum vitae tankard, which has lost its silver rim, is shown Plate 26, *L*. The body is in one piece, the handle pegged on. It measures 6 in. high by 4¼ in. diameter and next to it, is another unusual specimen, probably of birch and of baluster wine measure outline. The base is inserted, the handle, with

* *Note*: Publications on this remarkable tankard include

National Museum of Wales Guide—Plate VIII.
R. E. M. Wheeler, *Prehistoric & Roman Wales*, p. 210, fig. 85.
G. P. Ambrose, *History of Wales*.
Romilly Allen, *Celtic Art*, p. 142 and plate.
Archaeologia Cambrensis. Series 5, vol. XIII, p. 212.
E. T. Leeds, *Celtic ornament*, p. 53, fig. 20a.
Glyn Daniel, *Picture Book of Ancient British Art*.

squirrel head terminals, pegged on. On the lid is carved a dog with a bird in its mouth. It has lost its patination owing to stripping and both its date and provenance are uncertain. It may be German, 17th- or 18th-century. For other examples of tankards, see *Irish Drinking Vessels* and *North-west European Drinking Vessels*.

Toby Jugs—see *Jugs, Toby*

Vendageur Cups—see *Cups, Vendageur*

Wassail Bowls

An early instance of the term 'wassail' occurs in the account of a banquet given by Hengist, the Jutish Prince, in honour of King Vortigern. Princess Rowena, Hengist's daughter, is related to have '. . . come unto the king's presence with a cup of gold filled with wine in her hand, and making a low reverence unto the king said "WAES HAEL HLAFORD CYNING"—"Be of health Lord King"'. The response is DRINC HAEL.

'Waes-hael', 'was-haile' or 'wass-heil', the Anglo-Saxon equivalent of 'Good health' or 'Cheers', eventually passed into our language as 'wassail'. Although the term goes back to pagan times, 'wassailing' and wassail bowls have long been associated with Christmas festivities. In country districts, wassailing ceremonies survived into this century.

The word wassailing is associated primarily with festive community drinking, but in the past it also had close connections with orchards, carol singing, ceremonial processions and blessing of fruit trees. At different periods and in various places, wassailing ceremonies were held on varying and sometimes on several annual dates. These included Shrove Tuesday; Hallow E'en, October 31—still associated with bob-apples; All Saints' Day, November 1; Christmas Eve; Christmas night; New Year's Eve; and Twelfth Night, traditional ending of Christmas festivities. The last, an almost universal date, was commonly known as 'Wassil Eve'.

The blessing of the orchard connected with wassailing seems to commemorate the heathen sacrifice to Pomona. It consisted of pouring cider or ale on the roots of the trees to the accompaniment of a rhyming chant such as Herrick's

> 'Wassaile the trees that they may beare
> You many a plum and many a peare;
> For more or lesse fruits they will bring,
> And you do give them wassailing.'

The glossary to the Exmoor dialect gives 'Watsail—a drinking song on twelfth day eve, throwing (a) toast to the apple trees in order to have a fruitful year'.

In the more general wassailing ceremony, a bowl decorated with rosemary, evergreens and ribbons was carried by poor maidens from house to house, where in rhyming song the carollers invited the inmates to partake as a prelude to giving alms. 'A carroll for a wassell bowl', included in Ritson's collection of *Ancient Songs* and intended for singing to the tune of 'Gallants come away', gives a good idea of wassailing:

> 'A jolly Wassel-Bowl,
> A Wassel of good ale,
> Well fare the butler's soul,
> That setteth this to sale;
> > Our jolly Wassel.
>
> Good Dame, here at your door
> Our Wassel we begin,
> We are all maidens poor,
> We pray now let us in,
> > With our Wassel.
>
> Our Wassel we do fill
> With apples and with spice,
> Then grant us your good will
> To taste here once or twice
> > Of our good Wassel.
>
> If any maidens be
> Here dwelling in this house,
> They kindly will agree
> To take a full carouse
> > Of our Wassel.

> But here they let us stand
> All freezing in the cold;
> Good master, give command,
> To enter and be bold,
> > With our Wassel.
>
> Much joy into this hall
> With us is entered in,
> Our master first of all,
> We hope will now begin,
> > Of our Wassel.
>
> And after his good wife
> Our spiced bowl will try,
> The Lord prolong your life,
> Good fortune we espy,
> > For our Wassel.
>
> Some bounty from your hands,
> Our Wassel to maintain:
> We'll buy no house nor lands
> With that which we do gain,
> > With our Wassel.
>
> This is our merry night
> Of choosing King and Queen,
> Then be it your delight
> That something may be seen
> > In our Wassel.
>
> It is a noble part
> To bear a liberal mind,
> God bless our master's heart,
> For here we comfort find,
> > With our Wassel.
>
> And now we must be gone,
> To seek out more good cheer;
> Where bounty will be shown,
> As we have found it here,
> > With our Wassel.
>
> Much joy betide them all,
> Our prayers shall be still,
> We hope and ever shall,
> For this your great good will,
> > To our Wassel.'

Whilst recipes for the wassail ingredients varied according to local custom and the pocket, the basic items quoted in old records usually consist of good ale heated and stirred with sugar, nutmeg, ginger, cloves, cardamoms, with soft roasted small apples added, allowing at least one for each drinker. In some recipes, wines were substituted for ale. Frequently, whites of eggs were stirred in and probably the frothy appearance thus created, resulted in the drink being known as 'lambs-wool' and the bowls as lambs-wool bowls. Literary references to lambs-wool are numerous: to name but three, they occur in *Old Wives Tales* (1595), Pepys' *Diary*, Oliver Goldsmith's *Vicar of Wakefield*. A verse in Herrick's *Twelfe-Night* runs:

> 'Next crowne the bowle full
> With gentle lambs-wool;
> Adde sugar, nutmeg and ginger
> With store of ale, too;
> And thus ye must do
> To make the wassaile a swinger.'

Not all writers agree that frothiness was the reason for the name. John Brand, the antiquary, thought the softness of the composition suggested it. Vallancey traced the etymology of lambs-wool to an English corruption of La Mas Uhbal, pronounced *Lamasool* (the day of the apple tree).

Probably ordinary wooden bowls or wooden pails were used as refills for individual cups for street and orchard wassailing, but in early times in great houses and monasteries there is evidence that for the ceremonial drunk, a fine bowl of burr maple—that is, the mazer—was used. Thus an old Gloucestershire New Year's Eve drinking song runs

> 'Wassail! Wassail! o'er the town
> Our toast it is white, our ale it is brown!
> Our bowl it is made of a maplin tree,
> We be good fellows all; I drink to thee.'

In the 16th century, with the decline of the mazer, it is probable that both deeper drinking bowls and loving cups were among the treen vessels used for wassailing. The loving cups so used in the late 16th century, would most likely have been larger and more ornamental versions of the simple Elizabethan goblet, Plate 26, *B*, with the bowl considerably greater in depth than in diameter and the foot steeply sloped. These proportions, dictated largely by the comparatively small diameter in which English hardwoods of sound heart are usually found, seem to have influenced the early turners of lignum vitae wassail bowls until they found that this newly introduced dense hardwood (see introduction to this drinking section) made limits on diameter unnecessary. The late Owen Evan-Thomas, who was both antique dealer and treen collector, and who had a very high proportion of the largest and finest wassail bowls through his hands, thought that his earliest lignum vitae specimen was one of rather deep goblet proportions, with a steeply stepped base. He assessed it as *circa* 1620, which I would think about right. So far as I know, there are no lignum vitae wassail bowls inscribed with dates, and as silver mounts, in the few instances where they occur, are often of later date, it does not help even if they are hall-marked, which again is rare. In endeavouring to set up a chronology of lignum vitae wassail bowls, I suggest that those with depth of bowl 1 in. to 3 in. greater than diameter, were made during the first half of the 17th century, those with a steeply sloping foot, being the earliest. Probably few were made during the Commonwealth, but the immediate post-Restoration ones, in general design, look as though they are those examples with roughly equal bowl depth and diameter; the diameter may then have tended to increase and the depth to decrease, until by the end of the century, the lignum bowl which had come to be of punch bowl proportions, was succeeded by bowls of other materials: I have adopted this theory in ascribing dates to examples described or illustrated.

Before proceeding to further description of lignum vitae wassail bowls, I draw attention to Plate 29, an early Stuart wassail bowl, probably of sycamore, in Horsham

Museum, Sussex. If it is as early as I think, it is an exception to the general theory I have expounded, and anyway it is large for an English hardwood bowl of this type, although a few of the armorial decorated standing cups and bowls, already described, have even greater diameters. It is interesting for its form, decoration of roundels and intersecting segments and the full development of the spice cup knop on the lid, which is such a feature of some lignum wassail bowls. The diameter of the bowl is 8 in. and of the lid 10½ in.; it measures 10 in. to the top of the cup, and overall is 17 in. high.

The size and weight of large lignum wassail bowls made the ceremony of filling them at table a necessity. The number of these handsome liquor vessels which have survived, makes it apparent that, considering the small 17th-century population, the lignum vitae wassail bowl was a status symbol, and the ceremony an almost universal 17th-century fashion among those who could afford it. Lignum vitae wassail bowls were made plain, faceted, engine-turned (see Plate 26) and engine-turned and faceted, the last very rare. They were made with and without a stem and foot, and with and without a lid. Occasionally there is, inside the lid, a silver or silver and enamel 'print', decorated with a coat of arms, similar to the print in the earlier mazers. Some of those which originally had a lid have lost it. If they have a thin, plain lip, they probably originally had lids, but if they have a fairly thick and reeded or beaded rim, they are complete without lids. The lid was lifted by a centre knob, which, in a few instances, is formed as a smaller lidded cup for spices. One in Temple Newsam, *circa* 1660, on stem and foot, has a spice grater inside the lid of the spice cup, which is mounted on the main lid; it measures 21 in. overall, 13 in. to the top of the main bowl and has a diameter of 11½ in. Occasionally, there are turned finials for inverted dipper cups, mounted on the lid

surrounding the spice cup. A good example of this type, *circa* 1640, is illustrated in Plate 32; it measures 22½ in. overall, with diameter of 9½ in. One of the largest of this type still in existence, but considerably restored, was formerly in the Fripp collection. It is 30 in. high overall, 19 in. to the top of the bowl and has a diameter of 18 in.

Plate 33 is a possibly unique, early 17th-century, lignum vitae vessel—a combined pestle, mortar and wassail bowl, so that the spices could be pounded at table, in the first stage of the wassail bowl ceremony. The rim of the bowl is thin, the base heavy. The rim could not be damaged by the pestle, because it was controlled by the opening in the heavy lid; the bowl is 9½ in. high by 9 in. diameter.

A lignum wassail bowl on stem and foot may vary from about 5½ in. high, up to 19 in. (excluding superstructures), and from 4 in. to 19 in. diameter. The smallest mentioned may be described as a wassail or posset cup, although in every detail it is a miniature of the larger members of the family. The lignum cup, Plate 26, *K*, measures 5½ in. high by 5 in. diameter, compared with the wassail bowl, right of Plate 34, measuring 11⅜ in. high by 9¼ in. diameter. The most general sizes of those on stems and feet come within the range of 8 in. to 12 in high by 7 in. to 9 in. diameter; anything above this must be considered large. The most usual shape is the thimble, 1640–60, right of Plate 34, 11⅜ in. high by 9¼ in. diameter. Probably coming within the same date range, but with the bowl shallower and the stem longer, is the handsome silver mounted specimen, 9½ in. high by 8 in. diameter, Plate 31. It has three engraved silver bands and the coat of arms of the Grocers' Company and is inscribed round the rim 'Ye Gifte of Richard Rogers to Hys olde friends who meet in ye Toye roome'. The Toye, an inn much frequented by the Court, stood outside the gates of Hampton Court Palace, opposite the Mitre. It was erected either in the 16th or 17th century, demolished 1857, and a bay window of the reception desk now in the Mitre was brought from the Toye. It has not proved possible to find anything definite about Richard Rogers. Several gentlemen of that name were 17th-century Liverymen of the Grocers. A circular salt, hall-marked 1601, was given to the Goldsmiths' Company in 1632 by a Richard Rogers 'Comptroller of his Majesty's Mint'.

Central in Plate 34 is a fine and unusual, 17th-century, lignum wassail bowl, shaped like an outsize chalice, 12½ in. high by 10 in. diameter. On the left, is one of a small group of late 17th-century, lignum wassail bowls, which have never had a foot. This one measures 6½ in. high by 11 in. diameter. Another one, also in the Pinto Collection, is lidded, 10¼ in. high by 15 in. diameter and holds between 4 and 5 gallons. I have only records of four of these bowls which have no stem and foot; there is some reason to think that they may all be Scottish. There is in the Pinto Collection another 4 to 5 gallon lignum bowl unusually thickly turned, on short stem and foot, which weighs nearly ¼ cwt. when empty and measures 12 in. high by 13 in. diameter. It has a curious history engraved on a silver plate on it: it is said to have been discovered in a water course at Fahan, Co. Donegal. This may well be true, as I have never before seen a lignum bowl so scoured, pitted and, when it came to us, so hungry looking. The auctioneers' description, however, I cannot swallow, "An antique Irish 'sloake' or mazer bowl, possibly of yew wood, . . . late 14th century"! (my exclamation mark).

An unusual survival is a set of three early 17th-century matching lignum wassail bowls, 11½ in. high, which form part of the civic insignia at Hedon, Yorkshire; apart from these, I know of no others exactly alike. It is difficult to know now how often wassail bowls were originally made as parts of complete wassailing sets. Possibly matching dipper cups were fairly common and spice boxes, when not incorporated in the lid

structures of bowls, may have been made *en suite*.

Unique in its quality, beauty and completeness must be the Stuart lignum vitae and ivory wassailing suite which has been in the family of Lord Cullen of Ashbourne ever since the 17th century, Plates 35-7. This superb drinking set consists of a table, a pair of candle stands and candlesticks, a covered bowl with a spice box and dipper cup finials on the lid, and a set of silver-rimmed dipper cups. The bowl and its lid and spice box foot, the tops of the candle stands and the candlesticks, are so finely and elaborately engine turned and include such a variety of patterns that they represent almost the entire repertoire of the Carolean turner and, indeed, look like an essay founded on the plates in Plumier's *L'Art de Tourner*. The underside of the foot of the bowl is not engine-turned, as has sometimes been stated elsewhere. A feature, which at first sight appears to be at variance with the family tradition, is that the design of the table and candle stands is unmistakably Charles II, not Charles I. I feel that the answer may well lie in what is the meaning of the word 'set'. Usually a wassail bowl set consists of a wassail bowl, its dipper cups and possibly a tray. There is nothing whatever in the design of the Cullen wassail bowl and dipper cups which is inconsistent with the story that they were presented to the first Viscount Cullen by Charles I after the Battle of Naseby. I suggest that the set was already considered a priceless relic by the time of the Restoration, and that soon after that, the table, candle stands and candlesticks were created, with matching ornament, so changing a remarkable wassailing set into a unique wassailing suite.

Whistling Cups—see *Cups, Whistling*

Wine Barrels and Fountains
The dividing line between lignum vitae wassail bowls, wine barrels and fountains is thin. A few large wassail bowls, of ordinary

outline, have taps for filling their cups, but the wine barrel proper should, I think, be barrel shape, as Plate 42. I assess it as early 17th-century and have only seen four. It is made to revolve on its stem, has a bronze or copper mount and tap, and a pewter lining; its other features are clear from the illustration. It stands 17 in. high, excluding the knop and is approximately 9 in. in diameter. The lignum vitae wine fountain, Plate 40, is part of the Burrell Bequest to Glasgow Museum and Art Gallery. The photograph is unable to convey its immense size; it is probably the largest lignum vitae liquor bowl ever turned. It holds 9 gallons and measures 35 in. in height overall, with a diameter of $18\frac{1}{2}$ in. over the rim; the main bowl is $19\frac{1}{4}$ in. high. It has a syphon arrangement for drawing liquor from the lower to the upper bowl, which is sealed, except for air control, by means of the acorn finial. Below the three silver taps are drip catching bowls, each provided with a filter through which the overspill is returned to the main bowl. There are rims inside the drip bowls, which support drinking cups.

Wine Tasting Cups—see *Cups, Wine Tasting*

Witch Cups—see *Cups, Witch*

SCOTTISH DRINKING VESSELS

Scottish mazers have already been discussed under the general heading of mazer bowls and most of the other drinking vessels described under *English and Other Drinking Vessels, etc.*, were probably made and used both in Scotland and England. There are, however, two groups of vessels, mainly for drinking, which are peculiar to Scotland: these are the bicker and quaich families. Representative specimens of both are illustrated in Plate 46. The straightsided vessels of bucket form were known generally as bickers (the same root word as beaker), and the shallow curved bowls as quaichs.

Bickers

Bickers were made in a considerable range of sizes, all of which included two varieties of wood. Most commonly, the light staves are sycamore; and the alternate dark, contrasting ones of alder are steeped in peat bogs to colour them a dark red brown. Alder treated in this manner was formerly known as Scotch mahogany. Bickers are said to have been made with only a knife, but that is hard to believe; few craftsmen today could make them so well with a full tool kit. Their setting-out shows considerable geometric skill, for two of the staves, always light ones, are usually wider than the others and are extended outwards and horizontally to form concave handles. The greatest skill in the making was the 'feathering' of the staves into each other. Usually five wooden 'feathers' were cut between each stave; the cutting is so perfect that each bicker, although made 'dry', is completely water-tight. Each stave is grooved horizontally on the inside near the base, to take the bottom and the whole assembly was then tightly banded with willow. The diameter of willow strip was carefully chosen in relation to the size of bicker; so skilfully was this graduation executed, that irrespective of size of vessel, each usually has eight or nine bands round it and the careful lacing of these bands can be seen in the bicker, one from left of top row.

The uptilted bicker, one from right at top of the illustration, shows how the staves are 'feathered' into each other; the grooved-in bottom, in some fine specimens, is divided into four segments, tongued into each other. Some of these vessels have double bottoms, separated by a space enclosing a dried pea, so that you could rattle it when you wanted a refill.

The nest of bickers, centre, top row Plate 46, is a great rarity. The smallest bicker, $1\frac{1}{2}$ in. deep by $2\frac{1}{4}$ in. diameter ($3\frac{1}{2}$ in. over handles), has eight 'turns' of willow binding. The largest in the nest, $3\frac{1}{2}$ in. deep by $5\frac{1}{4}$ in. diameter ($7\frac{1}{4}$ in. over handles), has nine 'turns' of willow. This last size occurs the most frequently and the specimens showing their lacing and feathering, measure the same. Very small bickers, like quaichs, were used for spirits, mainly whisky. The medium sizes (largest of the nest) were chiefly for ale, but were also used as individual porringers. Really large bickers were known as cogs or coggies; but these vessels were made in such a large range of sizes that it seems impossible to define where bickers end and coggies begin.

Large, shallow cogs, sometimes a foot or more in diameter, were used as community porridge bowls, or as ale reservoirs for refilling individual bickers. Ale was refilled by dipping the 'luggie', the vessel shaped like a milk piggin, top left, with one stave extended upwards to form a lug or handle.

Large, oval, shallow pans, with alternate light and dark staves were largely used in the dairy for cooling, and like their English counterparts, which have all the staves the same colour, were known as keelers. Like beaker becoming bicker, it seems probable that a cooler became a keeler in Scotland, but the spelling and pronunciation were also adopted in England.

Up to 1946, we had never been able to acquire a bicker, then within 19 months we found and purchased, in different parts of England, and all apparently emanating from different sources, 14 including the nest of seven. Such an extraordinarily large haul, after years of searching, made us begin to wonder if these vessels were being planted for us. They all appeared to be genuine period specimens and their prices did not suggest that there could be any profit in faking them, but just to be sure, we sent them to the National Museum of Scotland for vetting. They were all passed as genuine, and in the last 20 years, we have only been offered three others; such are the curious things which happen to collectors. When the bicker family came into being is unknown, but their period of manufacture covers at least the 18th and a large part of

the 19th centuries. Originality and fine craftsmanship are Scottish characteristics; both are found in the light and dark staves of the bicker family and in some of the quaichs, where the simple, straight lines, and alternate coloured bands, somehow look complementary to pleated tartans and might well originate from a distant but common design source.

Quaichs

There is not only confusion between bickers and cogs, but also between bickers and quaichs, small bickers sometimes being called quaichs. The reason is doubtless that the Gaelic for both cog and quaich is *cuach*, which is also synonymous with the Welsh *cawg* and probably the Latin *caucus* and Greek *kauka*. Generally, however, 'quaich' is applied to shallow, two-handled spirit bowls. Small quaichs were made for individual use, larger ones for passing round the table as loving cups.

Early quaichs are made up of bi-coloured, feathered staves, like bickers, but even finer in their detail. The best ones have light staves of box or holly, and dark ones of laburnum or lignum vitae. The bands may be willow or silver; the handles are sometimes silver-mounted and a silver 'print' masks the centre junction of the staves in the base. Quaichs were being copied in silver before the 17th century ended. Early silver quaichs were made in simulation of coopering, even to the modelling of dummy staves and feathering. Quaichs were also hollowed from a single block of hardwood, with the spreading handles or lugs formed integrally. The usual number of handles is two, but more rarely, three or four lugs are found, see bottom left and third from right, Plate 46. Quaichs cut from the solid sometimes have silver coins embedded in the base as 'prints'. In the first decade of the 19th century, some nicely made hardwood quaichs were carved externally in a basket-weave pattern. Some of them are silver-mounted and engraved with Gaelic inscriptions; two examples are shown bottom right. All give the impression of coming from the same workshop.

The large and unusual quaich, at top of the illustration, right, is of walnut, divided into three circular troughs. The outer and middle troughs are connected by holes bored through the dividing rim, thus controlling the flow. The small centre section, never filled with liquor, has a spy glass panel in the bottom, inscribed, in faded ink, 'For its bottom is of glass, that he who quaffed might keep his eye the while upon the dirk hand of his companion'. It is another variant of the ancient custom of guarding the back of your neighbouring drinker, during the loving cup ceremony, which still survives at City Guild dinners. This specimen, although old, is only a copy of one said to have been made for Bonnie Prince Charlie, which later was in the possession of Sir Walter Scott. There is a glass-bottomed quaich at Abbotsford presented in 1745 by Prince Charles to Campbell of Kinloch. It bears the same inscription as the copy, but does not resemble it otherwise, being of conventional type.

IRISH DRINKING VESSELS

In Ireland, the use of wooden drinking vessels lingered in country districts until this century and included all the goblet and beaker types used in England. At a very early period, the Irish developed two distinctive wooden drinking vessels, the lámhóg and the mether; how far they go back in history is conjectural, for those which appear to be the earliest survivals have not been found in association with other datable objects. A number have been excavated from peat bogs.

Lámhógs

There are more survivals of lámhógs than methers; the former must have been the easier and cheaper to make and were,

therefore, made in greater quantities than methers, but both types are now considerable and prized rarities. Lámhógs—in some districts of Ireland known as piggins—are circular, downward tapering vessels, flaring out at the base, right hand half, Plate 44. They are entirely shaped and hollowed from a single block of wood. Because they were rough turned on the primitive but effective pole lathe, which had a reciprocal movement, it was possible to leave a projection at the side, which was then shaped and gouged out with hand tools, to form a comfortable handle grip. They vary in capacity and size considerably; the smallest measure about $5\frac{1}{2}$ in. in height by 4 in. in diameter and hold $\frac{3}{4}$ pint; the largest which I have seen measures $8\frac{1}{2}$ in. by 6 in., and holds 3 pints. Some are completely plain, but the majority have two horizontal bands, each consisting of two incised lines. A few, like the smallest one illustrated, have engraved on them *Céad mile fáilte*, the Gaelic for 'A hundred thousand welcomes'. Most surviving lámhógs are of willow, but they were also made in beech, elm and ash. They seem to have been the common drinking vessels of Irish taverns, at least from mediaeval times and some were exported and used in West of England and Welsh inns.

Methers

The other traditional Irish drinking vessel, the mether, is often said to derive its name from the herb drink mead, medd or meodu. No evidence has been produced in support of this theory. 'Mether', in Irish, *meadar* (f.), gen. *meidre*, means a churn or pail or a one-piece, wooden, quadrangular drinking cup. *Meadar loinithe* is a plunging or dash churn. Methers, left of Plate 44, which vary in height at least between 4 in. and 10 in., were decorative objects and probably intended much more as ceremonial drinking vessels than were lámhógs. They differ from the latter not only in shape, but also in construction, for they are made in two pieces, the bottom unit being a separate insert. The mether must have been a laborious and expensive object to make and one requiring considerable skill. It was also an awkward vessel from which to drink, for liquor had to be imbibed from one of the spouts formed by the rounded angles of the concave sides. Possibly this shape evolved because the vessel was intended as a loving cup which had the advantage of possessing four drinking places, but it is doubtful whether our ancestors were fastidious enough to consider that. The accentuation of the spout and shaping of sides varies considerably between one mether and another. All those which I have examined are of willow and they are invariably concave and rectangular on plan at the rim; occasionally this outline continues down to the base, but the majority change their form during their tapering descent and become circular at the base, which is often bound round with a willow strengthening hoop. As on lámhógs, the handles on wooden specimens are always cut from the solid block. Some methers have no handles, some have two, and some have four. Where there are four, they are usually extended downwards to form legs, lifting the body of the mether $\frac{1}{2}$ in. to $\frac{3}{4}$ in. from a table or other surface. Methers are smooth inside down to about $\frac{1}{2}$ in. from the base, where they are thickened out to form a ledge, on which the separate bottom unit is set in some kind of mastic. The bottom may be of horn or wood. I have seen one or two methers all of horn, and one of silver, dated 1706; both horn and silver specimens have applied handles. Most wooden specimens are probably considerably earlier, possibly mediaeval, but the only wooden specimen which I have seen inscribed with a date, is one in the Dublin museum inscribed 'Dermot Tully 1590'. Some of them are decorated with incised pokerwork of the emasculated interlacing lines common in the mediaeval centuries, after the flower of Irish interlacing had decayed.

Tankards

Irish wooden tankards, like English ones, have not survived in any quantities nor do they seem to differ. There is, however, a very remarkable bog oak tankard in the Pinto Collection, Plate 43. When seasoning timber by air drying, it is usual to allow one year for each inch of thickness. The wooden tankard illustrated measures $12\frac{3}{4}$ in. in height and was cut out of a log measuring nearly 8 in. square. One would, therefore, have reckoned at least eight years for the seasoning. Actually the time between the fall of the tree and the work by the turner, carver and silversmith, which converted the log into this tankard, was, according to geologists, some hundreds of millions of years, for this remarkable tankard, which weighs 10 lb. 10 oz., is made of bog oak, is completely silver lined both inside the body and in the lid, has a silver rim round the foot, and a silver handle and hinged thumb lift. The handle and combined thumb lift are designed as a gnarled and twisted branch, bearing acorns and leaves. The silver bears the Dublin hallmark for 1831, the coronation year of William IV and in that event probably lies the reason for this elaborate *tour de force*; for both its size and weight suggest that it was intended much more as a handsome commemoration piece than as an article for use. Even when empty, it is a 'two-hander'.

Bog woods vary considerably in their degrees of hardness; this specimen is one of the hardest, and the carver was wise to use the technique of a statuary and treat this as sculpture, rather than wood carving. Nor can he be faulted either in powers of observation or skill in grouping or cutting. He certainly knew his Irish types too, and has faithfully portrayed their features and has captured their lively expressions during various stages of a day or night given up to the pleasures of 'celebrating'. The lid is surmounted by a cluster of rocks, on which is seated one drinker, while his companion lolls back, draining the last drops from a flagon. The rim of the lid is carved with a band of textured laurel leaves. The same texturing, like fine toothing, forms the pleasantly contrasting background to all the highly polished, sculptured high relief figures on the body of the vessel and to the cyma curves of the lid. Below the lid is a 6 in. high frieze, consisting of 16 men, women and children—a happy rollicking band of roisterers. They form a laughing, shouting, happy crowd, singing and dancing with abandon, to the music of the fiddlers, waving hats and shillelaghs, and above all, drinking deeply from pots. One man (just in front of the handle) is screaming as a virago pulls his hair; others, worn out by their various exertions, have collapsed on the ground. Below this frieze are eight heads, marvellous portrayals of Irish types, every one completely different in features and expressions; but even today, 137 years after they were immortalised in bog oak, you could pick out all of them on the street corners of Dublin. Unfortunately, the craftsman who created this masterpiece did not carve his name on it for posterity.

NORTH-WEST EUROPEAN DRINKING VESSELS

The background to the treen drinking vessels of North-west Europe is included in the introduction to this volume, so only a description of the vessels illustrated is given here. Constructionally, they come under three headings: turnery, coopering and hollowing out of the solid. Decoratively, they may be carved, pierced and fretted, ornamentally turned or painted; sometimes several of these finishing processes may be combined.

Kasas

The huge drinking vessel, centre, Plate 47, with bowl carved from a single block, $8\frac{1}{4}$ in. high by $8\frac{3}{4}$ in. across, is a late 19th-century copy of a Swedish horned *kasa* or beaker, of a type mentioned in Olaus Magnus' work on the *Scandinavian Peoples* (1555). Commencing in the Middle Ages as beakers, from the same common stock as Scottish bickers, Plate 46, these Scandinavian versions gradually developed horns, which were eventually linked into handles by pierced and engraved scrollwork. The specimen illustrated measures $29\frac{1}{2}$ in. high overall and 22 in. across the horns. The background is painted red, except the rim of the bowl and the two horns, which expose the natural birch. It is decorated with naturalistically coloured flowers, leaves, scrolls and black incised lines. Inside the bowl, an inscription, translated, reads 'Merry Guests drink best'. Part of the Swedish Coat of Arms is painted on the exterior. At certain peasant drinking festivals, it was formerly considered quite praiseworthy to get drunk and see who could empty one of these tremendous ale buckets at the fewest draughts. The horned rims were designed to leave room for the drinker's head between the rim and the underside of the scrolled handle. When drinking, the handle passed gradually over the drinker's head, forming a wreath against the back of his neck, as he drained the last dregs.

The incised decorated *kasa*, with outward scrolling handles, terminating in crude horses' heads, is of a type which has probably been used in Scandinavia from the prehistoric age of the sacrificial horse cult. Usually hollowed out of a solid block of birch, most extant dated examples are 18th-century. The specimen illustrated is dated, under the base, 1787. A single handled kasa of crude bird outline known as an 'alegoose', is shown in Plate 48, *C*. The coopered kasa, left of Plate 47, with incised decoration, lion head handles and willow banding, is a fine specimen, probably dating from the late 17th or early 18th century; it is 5 in. deep and 8 in. in diameter.

Tankards and Miscellaneous

Wooden tankards were the commonest drinking vessels of North-west Europe over many centuries. A selection is shown in Plates 45 and 48. They are made in three parts—the turned tankard or cup, the handle pegged on, which includes half the wood hinge, and the lid, which incorporates the ornamental thumb lift and the other half of the hinge. The two elaborately scroll carved Norwegian tankards, left of Plate 45, measuring approximately 10 in. in height by 6½ in. in diameter, belong to a well known group made early in the 19th century. They are often found deliberately 'aged' by rubbing in of dark stain in the background and lightening up of the high points. The two large lion tankards, on the right, are of a type well known in the 18th century and earlier. The taller of the two, the one supported on lions couchant, is actually dated 1809. They usually have a lion or a coat of arms carved in relief on the lid, a lion rampant acting as thumb lift, and sometimes the lions couchant as feet. In the 18th century they were frequently date incised on the lid or base, usually made of birch, and early specimens may be lined with pitch and fitted with a row of pegs to show the limit to which each drinker should go. The small tankard, at the bottom of the same picture, has one of the rather typically grotesque Norwegian flat-topped carved heads on the handle, and a floral relief on the lid; it may be 17th- or 18th-century.

Also in Plate 45, the painted boat-shaped vessel, the elaborate ladle or dipper, the tumbler holder and the spoon with acanthus carving and piercings are Norwegian, probably 19th-century, although the designs were used earlier.

The 7-in. high lion tankard of baluster outline and turned from burry maple, Plate 48, *A*, like others already described, has a lion on handle/lid, and three forming feet; it is dated 1774. The Scandinavian birch tankard, *J*, of burry birch, with the natural cambium layer surface (the growth layer immediately under the bark) left on, has silver ball feet and a silver strap on the handle dated 1734. The interesting jug, *B*,

belongs to the Norwegian, 18th-century type of vessel with lion thumb lift, and lion carved on lid. Round its globular body is depicted, in virile low relief carving, a hunter shooting a boar, whilst he himself is being stalked by a bear. The overall height is 9 in., the diameter 7½ in.; the material is birch root, the handle pegged on; the spout is inserted in the body. Its use may have been for coffee or beer.

Willow-bound coopered jugs, tapering inwards to the top, with and without lids, were formerly made and used in large quantities in Scandinavia, round the shores of the Baltic and in Holland. The example illustrated, *D*, is unusual for having three spouts, to fill three drinking vessels simultaneously.

The birch burr, fluted vessels, ornamented with bone studs, *E* and *F*, are Swedish, 18th-century. Both the diagonal flutes of the double cup and the vertical ones of the tankard, occur on Swedish silver; the berry feet of the tankard also occur in silver. The tankard is engine-turned on the lid and the remarkable thinness and precision of its turning make it an example of outstanding skill, but also raise the doubt as to whether it was intended for real use, or as a pattern piece for silver.

The handsome, engine-turned, 17th-century boxwood standing cup, Plate 28, richly patinated and measuring 13½ in. over the knop, has certain design characteristics in common with the last described, but it is earlier and, although most graceful, is sturdy and doubtless was intended for use. I hesitate to define its provenance more closely than 'Baltic', for I find that connoisseurs of all the countries bordering that small sea, are happy to accept, as the work of their ancestors, this type of cup, more often found in ivory.

The fine Swedish mazer bowl of burr maple, of depressed spherical form, 7 in. in diameter by 3 in. high, Plate 48, *H*, curves inwards just where an English example is most everted. The silver rim has shell pendants and is inscribed 'Esten.Asbirosen.Anno.1625'. Ale bowls of rather similar outline, but usually somewhat larger in diameter and turned from plain wood, which was then decorated with painted floral and geometrical designs and inscriptions, were formerly used at all country festivities in Scandinavia. These bowls have come to be known in England as 'marriage bowls', although their use was general on all great occasions, including the successful ingathering of the harvest; the translation of an inscription round one reads 'When the farmer has got his grain in, then he gets a nice drink'.

A carved wooden drinking horn is rather a contradiction in terms. The Norwegian example illustrated, Plate 48, *G*, based on a mediaeval drinking horn, complete with knopped cover and eagle claw feet, must be regarded more as a *tour de force* of wood shaping and carving, than as a drinking vessel. It is 19th-century work of the same school as the two tankards, left of Plate 45. The interlaced acanthus scrolls, pearl ornament bandings, etc., are crisp and sharply defined.

DRINKING ANCILLARIES

Beer Pulls
A typical 19th-century beer pull in ebony is shown, Plate 50, *R*. Beer pulls of the same type were also commonly made in ornamental glazed earthenware, threaded with a metal rod, and also entirely of metal.

Bottle Corks
The wine bottle and cork are now so closely associated in our minds that it is difficult to appreciate that, in this country at any rate, they only came together about 400 years ago. At least another 100 years elapsed before corks became the common method of tight-stoppering wine bottles. In general, wines were drunk 'new' from the barrel until the mid-17th century, merely being brought to table in a bottle loosely stoppered with oiled hemp. Such bottles were of globular shape, blown up like a balloon, with no shoulder, the curve of the globe gradually merging into the neck. Further, having no flat base, they were either wanded—that is, encased in osier basketwork to enable them to stand upright—or alternatively they were placed at table in special stands of metal or lignum vitae.

Early corks were mostly of tapering conical form, fitting loosely in bottles, which were stood upright or stored at a slight angle in sawdust in the cellar. Some *circa* 1660 Bellarmine jugs, with their original conical corks in them, were found at the bottom of a well near St. Paul's Cathedral. Spanish corks sold at a shilling per gross in the mid-16th century and at four shillings per gross a century later. It seems likely that the rise in price continued, for they were still mentioned in inventories and wills in the 18th and early 19th centuries. Corks surmounted by carved wooden heads or figures were made in considerable quantities in Switzerland and the Tyrol during the 19th century and are still being made.

Interesting information on the dates of the introduction of various wines to England, methods of buying, storage, etc., is contained in the chapter headed 'The Wine Cellar' in *Life in a Noble Household 1641–1700*, by Gladys Scott Thomson, M.A., F.S.A., based on the household papers of the Russells, Earls and later Dukes of Bedford.

Bottle Corking and Uncorking Devices
For ease of reading, devices connected with corking, uncorking and bottle sealing are treated here as a single heading, described in chronological rather than in strictly alphabetical order. Wooden bottles are described under *Decanters*.

Corkscrews
Although early conical corks projected from the bottle necks and were withdrawn by the fingers, some early corks must have been of the tight-fitting, non-tapering variety,

because corkscrews, also known as bottle screws, screws, and steel worms, were being made in Tudor times. Their manufacture came under the auspices of the Worshipful Company of Loriners, makers of horse bits and spurs. Probably the early steel worms partook more of the nature of wine augers and broaching gimlets, both of which are mentioned in 15th-century documents, in connection with the fitting of bungs and spigots to casks. Few corkscrews survive from earlier than the 18th century and most of those of that period have a ring-turned, barrel-shaped, hardwood cross-bar handle, terminating at one end with a hog bristle bottle dusting brush, as shown in Plate 49, *F*. One with a boxwood handle, shaped like a cork, is illustrated in Plate 50, *L*. Corkscrew makers were continuously improving their bottle opening devices and perhaps one of the most effective, albeit somewhat large and elaborate, is the mahogany bottle crane illustrated, Plate 49, *K*. It probably dates from the beginning of the 19th century, exerts an enormous straight pull and removes the most obstinate cork effortlessly. Mr. A. H. Westwood, Assay Master of the Birmingham Assay Office, has drawn my attention to the fact that in 17th- and 18th-century parlance, bottle crane denoted a hollow cane, sometimes of precious metal, for piercing a cork and acting as a syphon.

Only the invention of the corkscrew made possible the insertion of tight-fitting corks, flush in the necks of bottles, the horizontal binning of wine, the maturing of wine in the bottle and the consequential development of vintage bottled wines. Bottle corking was an art and at first a difficult one.

Bottle Cork Pressers

Still to be found occasionally, are the devices used for the preliminary compressing of corks in the 18th century, so that they would swell up subsequently and fit tightly in the necks of bottles. They are hinged levers, Plate 49, *A*, usually of mahogany, and are often mistaken for nutcrackers.

Instead of the single nut cavity, however, they have two or three half-round borings of different diameters, running transversely across and opposite each other in both the levers. The cork having been compressed dry between the levers, was then quickly driven into the neck of the bottle with a mallet. The liquor in the bottle then speedily completed the swelling.

Bottle Sealers

The final operation was to seal the bottle with a signet impressed with the name of the wine. One of these 18th-century sealers, and two of its signets are shown, Plate 49, *G*; it has a hollow hardwood handle, containing several brass signets, which fit in a chuck. They are engraved port, rum, sherry, etc.

Bottle Corkers

The cork presser was finally superseded in 1860 by C. Bossalaer's patent described as 'An improved Apparatus for Corking Bottles, Jars and other Vessels', Plate 49, *E*. A modern but basically similar device, I found in common use, for corking bottles of olive oil, in the Isle of Ischia, 10 years ago. The ingenious and remarkably effective Bossalaer's invention drives a cork into a bottle neck under compression, where it swells and forms a tight fit. It is made of hardwood and in three parts—a plunger, a cover and a tube. The plunger passes through the domed cover and into a rebated, brass-lined, downward tapering tube; this is concave at the base, to fit over the neck of the bottle. In use, the plunger and cover are first removed and the cork inserted into the top of the tube. After replacement of the cover and plunger, the device is placed on top of the bottle and the plunger smartly tapped with a mallet until the cork, increasingly compressed as it is forced downwards, passes into the slightly larger neck of the bottle, where it swells out again.

Additional to the cork sealing device

already mentioned, bronze dies may still be found for impressing seals on 17th- and 18th-century glass wine bottles. They have iron tangs for fitting into wooden handles and mostly give names of purchasers of the wine, but a few are impressed with wine merchants' names and addresses. Following the prohibition of sale of wine by the bottle in 1636, wealthy families ordered wine by the barrel and had it bottled in their own bottles impressed with their names, or titles and coats of arms. Samuel Pepys recorded, October 23, 1663 ". . . to Mr. Rawlinson's and saw some of my new bottles with my crest upon it, filled with wine . . .". Some inns bearing the sign "The Boot and Flogger" are often thought to have some connection with former severe corporal punishment; this is not so. Before the days of corking machines, the 'boot' was a leather receptacle for holding a filled bottle between the knees of the operator while he drove the cork home with an instrument called a flogger.

Bottle Openers
Bottle openers, for removing the serrated metal caps from mineral water bottles, sometimes have carved wooden handles, mostly Swiss or Tyrolean, but do not rank as bygones yet. The humble hardwood, usually cocus or boxwood, device for pushing and releasing the glass marble, which sealed the fizzy lemonade bottle for 50 years from 1870, however, deserves mention. The Codd bottle, Plate 50, *Q*, was named after the inventor, Hiram Codd. His first patents for the bottle sealed by pressure of the gas against the glass ball, was in 1870. Patents for further refinements of the idea were taken out by him in 1872 and 1875. The exterior of the hardwood device for unsealing, is shown on the bottle and the interior view is on the right. It is simply a turned hollow cap, with a wooden plunger left upstanding in the middle of the circle. Fitted over the bottle and pressed downward, it dislodged the ball and re-

leased the gas and the liquid. For shop use, the device on the left was designed. It was screwed against a counter, plunger downwards, and the bottle was pressed up to it.

Carriers, Coasters, Stands (for bottles and decanters) and Pourers and Tilters

There are so many overlaps between all the above, that they are here treated under a common heading. The term coaster has come to have two separate meanings, as applied to drinking service: (1) a small tray, usually circular or piecrust edged, sometimes quite shallow rimmed, at other times with a rim up to about 2 in.; (2) a platform on wheels, essentially for passing drinks from one person to another. The overlap is understandable, for the small circular tray was also originally intended for passing drinks by sliding along the table, instead of wheeling and it should have the underside covered with baize. Sometimes the coasters were 'turned' complete with their rims, out of mahogany, lignum vitae, or other suitable hardwood, but many were made with decoratively embossed or pierced and engraved silver or Sheffield plate rims, and 'prints' in the base. Others were made of japanned iron or papier mâché. A rarity is the 6 in. diameter, fret cut, Chippendale period coaster, Plate 60, which is an example of Georgian two-ply construction. The inner veneer is vertical, to take the compression easily; the outer is horizontal. The lamination of the edge is masked by an applied moulded rim. Purpose-made plywood was used for curved work in the 18th century, much more frequently than is generally realised. It is only the mass production of plywood that is a late 19th- and 20th-century development.

A selection of treen coasters is shown in Plate 50. The 9½ in. and 9 in. diameter examples, *C* and *D*, are mahogany, mounted on castors and date from early in the 19th century. *D* was made in Kelso, Scotland.

The 2 in. thick, 10 in. diameter, burr yew-wood specimen, *A*, one of a pair, was used for the wide based Rodney decanter on board ship. The 6¾ in. diameter padauk example, *B*, with acanthus carving, also one of a pair, was probably also used on board ship. In the bottom row, the burr wood, lignum vitae and mahogany coasters, *G*, *H* and *J*, varying from 5 in. to 6 in. diameter, represent normal domestic type coasters of the second half of the 18th century. The 7½ in. diameter oak example, *E*, with egg and dart carved border, follows the fashion of 18th-century coasters with silver or Sheffield plated rims, by having a silver 'print' in the base. Whilst the majority of these coasters were simply decanter stands, made to slide easily, some were trays, large enough to hold several decanters and glasses. In the 18th century, when the ladies retired at the end of dessert, the table cloth was removed and the baize-bottomed coasters slid easily and without scratching on the polished table top. Curious ancillaries in the Common Room at All Souls, Oxford, are a long handled 'pusher' and 'puller' for bottles or small coasters. The 'pusher' has a crescent shaped terminal and the 'puller' of crook outline, forms an elongated letter J, which embraced the coaster neatly. Prince Püchler-Muskau, writing of his English tour of 1828–9, stated that the decanters were placed before the host, who pushed them on stands or in little silver wagons on wheels, to his neighbour on the left.

A very wide variety of these decorative table carriages on wheels were made in the late 18th and in the 19th centuries. Probably the earliest known silver carriage 'for sweet waters' is the silver 'wagon and tun', made in Bredau and presented to the Worshipful Company of Mercers in 1573. It moved along the table by clockwork, which is still in working order. A handsome early 19th-century wine coaster of chariot form and figure 8 plan, Plate 51, is entirely carved in walnut. It is Italian and appropriately the rims of the stands are carved

and pierced as balustrades supporting bunches of grapes. The wheels are formed of entwined serpents; three *putti* are the charioteers.

Beer coasters are larger, heavier and cruder; they are difficult to date accurately, but some are probably 17th-century. They have a very festive look particularly when brightly painted and decorated with their owners' coats of arms, as they often were. Made in many patterns and in two distinct types, they were used mostly in servants' halls, colleges, and for military reunions and other celebrations. The smaller ones were for circulating beer along the table; the larger coaster or beer wagons, which usually have a painted barrel mounted on a platform, ran along the floor. The floor type sometimes have the barrel at one end, fitted with a tap for filling tankards on the lower step at the other end. Examples are also known with a central raised platform for the barrel, which is fitted with taps on opposite sides, for filling tankards on a lower platform at each end. Table beer coasters are sometimes heavy, oblong, rimmed trays, cut from a solid block of hardwood, carved with grooves running down to a central cavity, or they are of irregular figure 8 outline, with the smaller round or oval, for the jug or blackjack, joined at the waist to a larger round or oval. for tankards or mugs. Examples of travelling beer coasters or beer wagons survive in servants' halls of several stately homes and in various museums. An unusual coaster variant is a wooden railway in the Fellows' Common Room at Magdalen College, Oxford, which carries two wheeled coasters on a cord, up and down a gentle incline, across the fireplace, from one table to another. There is a similar specimen in the Senior Common Room of New College, Oxford.

Portable wine waiters, generally made to hold six decanters, were wine carriers mounted on trolley stools, usually of mahogany, which were fitted with castors and made for circulating round the room. The tray parts, which were sometimes, but not always detachable from the stands, had upstanding rims, frequently scalloped, and matching divisions which apportioned the decanter spaces into squares. The majority, of Irish manufacture, date from the mid-18th century, have cabriole legs, and are handsomely carved pieces of furniture. Wine carriers were trays, mostly quite simple and of mahogany, rather like cutlery trays, with which they are often confused. They have semi-circular cut-outs in their deep rims, so that bottles could lie slightly tilted, with their necks projecting a little through the apertures. They have a central lifting handle, which is either a cut-out in a raised portion of the centre division or else a brass lifting handle. They were usually made to hold two, occasionally four or six bottles, and the cut-outs are at opposite ends of the trays, in order to balance the weight of the bottles. Now and again, single bottle carriers or cradles are found which usually have much deeper rims than multiple bottle carriers, so that there is sufficient height below the bottle neck aperture for a glass to stand alongside on a table, allowing the carrier to be used as a simple form of bottle pourer. Ale carriers, of any suitable hardwood, were formerly used in inns for carrying tankards. They vary in size, but are usually between 12 in. and 18 in. long, formed like a pair of book ends of inverted U outline, connected at the base by a shelf with a slight rim along each long edge and with a turned rod carrying-handle, connecting the ends near the top.

The true Georgian bottle pourer is formed as a bottle cradle, built up on a ramp, with a hinge or pivot at the top and some form of ratchet, to enable the tilt of the bottle to be adjusted as it empties. Judging by the few survivals, bottle pourers were individually designed and made in small quantities and appear always to have been of superlative quality, intended for the wealthy connoisseur. They are found both in silver and in mahogany, and usually, when holding a bottle, they appear to have been intended to simulate, in a general manner, the form of a bombard. An elaborately carved, mahogany specimen, Plate 52, is shown raised on its ratchet. Its platform, on 'bun' feet, with insert leather pads, measures 16 in. by 6 in.; it is a weighty object, being made of the so-called Spanish mahogany. The edge of the platform is carved with egg and tongue gadrooning. The cradle itself, hollowed from a solid mahogany block, is carved with grapes and vine leaf trails, with a mask of jovial horned and bearded Bacchus below the spout; the curve of the handle is both functional and graceful. It is difficult to date accurately. In its bold outline, general exuberance and the carved motifs used, it fits in equally well with 1730–40 or 1800–10. In the first period, both gadrooning and egg and tongue carving occur on a notable range of boldly carved, mahogany wine coolers on lion paw feet. The Regency period again used the aforementioned carved motifs and additionally favoured the vine pattern for wine services. Two factors support the first date. Firstly, Spanish mahogany, widely used in 1730–40, was very scarce by 1800. Secondly, the screws, which secure the platform to the ramp, are the early hand filed thread type, superseded about 1760 by the lathe cut thread.

Costrels—see *Kegs*

Decanter Stands—see *Carriers, Coasters, Stands and Pourers*

Drink Measures

Double measures of boxwood, of egg cup shape, described and illustrated in Section I, *Apothecary*, were formerly used for drinks both in the home and the bar. Tot measures of boxwood, fitted to corks, as shown in front of the mahogany lemon squeezer, Plate

49, *J*, were also used in the 19th century, if not earlier.

Flasks

A series of carefully turned boxwood and sycamore travelling flasks, which in shape exactly foreshadowed the modern vacuum flask, were made in varying sizes from 9 in. to 12 in., presumably some time during the 19th century, by the same turners who specialised in bottle cases. Two are illustrated, Plate 53, *C* and *D*. The upper portion holds a tumbler, the lower, a cork-stoppered glass bottle. Although obviously not nearly as efficient as a vacuum flask, wood is a very good insulator and they were much more effective than the metal ones which also were made. Wooden beaker cases were made in large quantities during the 19th century.

The 9½ in. high flask of disc form hollowed out of the solid, *E*, is probably Scottish, early 19th-century. The 10½ in. long, heart-shaped, carved flask, *G*, also cut from the solid, is Russian; on the back is inscribed "This bottle was taken from a Cossack who was killed by one of our men, whilst in the act of stabbing some of the British wounded after the battle of Inkerman . . . who afterwards gave it to Captn. M. D. Hammill, Commander of the Transport *Cambria*". The ingenious double beaker type flask, *H*, which screws together, is shown with some of its interior fitments adjacent; these hold liquids, dried food, salt, etc. It is obviously a very carefully thought out 'special'; not surprisingly, it is inscribed inside 'Captain Scott 1899', and it was probably used in the Antarctic. See also *Kegs*.

Ice Buckets and Wine Coolers

The earliest known English wine cooler is, I believe, the bronze specimen at Penshurst Place, made from cannons captured from the Armada and mounted on a stand of oak, made from the gun carriages. Walnut wine coolers of the 17th and early 18th century are rare. In the 18th century, the cabinet-maker was called in to assist and eventually he partially superseded the turner and cooper in making specialised metal-lined wooden equipment associated with drink. Enclosed wine coolers in a large variety of forms, usually of mahogany, but sometimes of silver, were made *en suite* with other dining room equipment. Brass-bound staved mahogany ice pails and plate carriers were also made in matching pairs.

Kegs and Other Coopered Vessels, etc.

Oak kegs have been made from the earliest times in varying sizes. The most common type are the harvest kegs, known alternatively as costrels, firkins, bever barrels or bever kegs. The willow-bound keg standing vertically in Plate 54 is of the *vivandière* type used during the Napoleonic wars and the horizontal one next to it, with glass ends, is the Swiss 'St. Bernard' pattern. Both are bound with willow. The iron-bound drum keg behind them, with two bands and a handle, is a 19th-century Welsh costrel. Flatter kegs of this type, marked W.D., were still being issued by the War Department to British troops in the last quarter of the 19th century. Farm kegs in Great Britain were more often the shape of miniature barrels and until the beginning of this century, they could often be seen at harvest time, stacked in the shade of a hedge, ready for carrying cider, beer or an oatmeal drink known as shot to the heated workers in the fields. Each keg had, fitted over the bung, an iron 'tot', which acted as a drinking vessel. Most of these kegs have leather thong handles and a vent peg, which acts as a safety valve if the keg is shaken or stood in the sun. The owner's initials usually appear on one end.

On the right, the iron-bound oak barrel on stand is a sherry barrel of a type still in use. The copper-banded oak bottle on the left is a good quality specimen and was probably made by one of the old coopers who specialised in the manufacture of oak 'jacks' (jugs).

Plate 50, *N*, the 7½ in. long keg made of cane, using the natural horizontal membranes to act as top and bottom, was an issue to Japanese soldiers in the First World War.

Ladles—see Section IV, *Eating*, and Section VI, *Kitchen*

Measures—see *Drink Measures*

Monteiths

According to Anthony à Wood, the Oxford diarist, writing in 1683 'This yeare in the summer time came up a vessel or bason notched at the brim to let drinking vessels hang there by the foot, so that the body or drinking place might hang into the water to cool them. Such a bason was called a Monteigh from a fantastical Scot called Monsieur Monteigh, who at that time or a little before wore the bottome of his cloake or coate so notched.' A monteith was, therefore, a communal cooler for drinking glasses, just as the Georgian deep glass bowls with one or two lips or notches in the rim, now usually described as finger bowls, were really individual glass coolers. Nearly all monteiths were made in silver, but my guess is that, as so often was the case, the first 'try-outs' were made of wood—lignum vitae. I have only ever seen two of these turned bowls, and the one illustrated, Plate 59, a typical late 17th-century vessel, 12 in. in diameter, is much the finer.

Spice Boxes

Nutmeg grater spice boxes, for carrying in the pocket, are described and illustrated in Section XI, *Mortars, Grinders and Graters*; most of the larger ones come into Section VII, *Kitchen*. A large 17th-century specimen, of bottle outline, turned from lignum vitae, and probably used in connection with the wassail bowl ceremony, is illustrated, Plate 53, *B*; its inside is still redolent of spices.

A smaller double spice box of lignum vitae, of the same period, handsomely engine turned is shown in Plate 26, *N*.

Spigots

Turned and tapered wooden taps for inserting in barrels are still used, but have also become collector items. One is shown in Plate 50, *P*; another, inserted in a sherry barrel, is illustrated in Plate 54. Large spigots seem to have been made in any suitable hardwood, but small ones, in the past, were usually of boxwood or mulberry. I know of no way of dating them accurately.

Step Counter for Change—see Section XXV, *Trade Devices*

Swizzling Sticks

Swizzling sticks of lignum vitae, with serrated stirring ends, are sometimes to be found, Plate 50, *M*. They do not appear to be very old.

Tankard Jacks

Tankard jacks were probably used in most taverns from early times. In England, they were usually turned from a solid block of lignum vitae, Plate 49, *C* and *D*, occasionally of boxwood, in the U.S.A. sometimes from laburnum. They were inserted into the soft pewter tankards and revolved slowly to restore the shape after rough usage. Being of ideal design for fitness of purpose, they have not changed over the centuries and cannot be dated accurately.

Tumbler Holders

Treen tumbler holders are of two types. One for protecting the fingers from a hot glass, Plate 45, is unlikely to be older than last century. The other, which may be of any goblet form, such as Plate 20, *E* and *e*, are distinguishable from other treen goblets by the fact that they taper to a point inside, to hold the early footless pointed tumblers, now usually known as toasting goblets, which really did tumble unless held.

Wine Coolers—see *Ice Buckets*

Wine Pourers—see *Carriers, Coasters, Stands (for bottles and decanters) and Pourers and Tilters*

Wine Strainer Bowls

English turned wood wine strainer bowls, fitted with a fine mesh in the base, are rare. A 7 in. diameter specimen of sycamore, probably 18th-century, is shown in Plate 50, *F*.

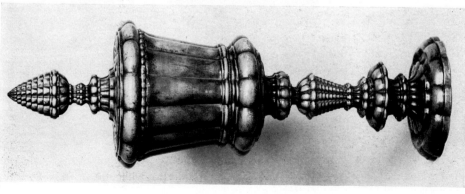

28 Engine turned, boxwood standing cup from one of the countries bordering the Baltic. 17th century. (*Section III*)

29 An unusual, early 17th-century, wassail bowl of sycamore. *In the collection of F. A. Turner, Esq.* On loan to Horsham Museum. (*Section III*)

30 An Elizabethan service of treen. The base is a box of roundels. For details of this remarkable set, see *Posset Cups. Photograph by courtesy of Glasgow Art Gallery and Museum.* (*Section III*)

31 English, 17th-century, silver mounted, lignum vitae wassail bowl. For details of the interesting inscription, see text. (*Section III*)

32 Lignum vitae, lidded wassail bowl, with spice cup and dipper cup finals. English, 17th century. (*Section III*)

33 A combined wassail bo and mortar of lignum vita English, 17th century. (*Sect III*)

34 Three 17th-century, English, lignum vitae wassail bowls; the one on the left, without stem and foot, and the one chalice form, in the centre, are rare types. (*Section III*)

35 Unique Carolean lignum vitae and ivory wassail bowl suite. *Collection of Lord Cullen of Ashbourne. (Section III)*

36 Close up view of the engine turned wassail bowl and the engine turned ivory plaques in the top of the lignum vitae table. *Collection of Lord Cullen of Ashbourne. (Section III)*

37 Detail of the engine turning on the top of one of the candle stands, which matches that on the lid of the wassail bowl, see Plates 35 and 36. *Collection of Lord Cullen of Ashbourne. (Section III)*

38 Unique whistling cup, 17th century. *Photograph by courtesy of Taunton Museum. (Section III)*

39 TOP SHELF: 18th-century carved stirrup cups and a 16th- or 17th-century burr maple wine taster. BELOW: late 16th-century *vendageur* standing cup; 17th-century, lignum vitae drinking bowl; 18th-century, silver lined, lignum vitae, travelling cups, with original leather case. *(Section III)*

40 The nine gallon capacity, English, 17th-century, lignum vitae silver mounted wine fountain with its cups, which is in the Burrell Collection, Glasgow Art Gallery and Museum. *Photograph by courtesy of the Museum.* (*Section III*)

41 A carved wood toby jug, painted in simulation of a Ralph Wood pottery jug. (*Section III*)

42 (BELOW, LEFT) Revolving wine barrel of lignum vitae. English. 17th century. (*Section III*)

43 Irish oak tankard, with carving of sculptural quality. Silver lined and with silver handle. Hall-marked 1831. (*Section III*)

44 LEFT: two Irish methers, loaned to the Pinto Collection by Belfast Museum and Art Gallery and the National Museum of Antiquities of Scotland, respectively. RIGHT: three Irish lamhogs. (*Section III*)

45 UPPER SHELF: two elaborately carved, Norwegian, 19th-century tankards and, on the right, two 18th-century 'lion' tankards. BELOW: Norwegian dipper vessels, spoon and tumbler holder, all 19th century; right, small 17th- or 18th-century tankard. (*Section III*)

46 Scottish vessels: TOP, LEFT: a luggie, a nest of bickers and two others, showing the feathers and the lacing: RIGHT: replica of the windowed quaich which belonged to Bonnie Prince Charlie, BELOW: a selection of quaichs. (*Section III*)

47 CENTRE: 19th-century copy of a 16th-century, Swedish horned kasa. LEFT: Scandinavian coopered kasa, with carved lion handles. RIGHT: a Scandinavian horse head kasa, dated 1787. (*Section III*)

48 *A*, Scandinavian, burry maple tankard, dated 1774; *B*, spouted jug, carved with a hunter, stalked by a bear, while he is shooting a boar; *C*, 'ale goose' drinking bowl; *D*, three-spouted, coopered jug; *E*, Swedish, fluted birch burr double cup, and *F*, tankard; *H*, Swedish, silver mounted mazer, dated 1625; *G*, Norwegian, 19th-century, carved drinking 'horn'; *J*, Norwegian tankard, dated 1734. (*Section III*)

49 *A*, cork presser; *B*, 'pub' step counter for change; *C* and *D*, tankard jacks; *E*, bottle corking device; *F*, combined corkscrew and bottle brush; *G*, bottle sealer; *J*, combined cork and tot measure; *K*, bottle crane. (*Section III*). *H*, lemon squeezer, (*Section VII*)

50 *A* to *J*, selection of English coasters, mostly 18th century; *K*, coopered piggin; *L*, corkscrew; *M*, swizzling stick; *N*, Japanese, cane water keg; *O*, wooden bottle; *P*, mulberry wood spigot; *Q*, Codd bottle and bottle openers; *R*, beer pull. (*Section III*)

51 Italian, walnut, chariot wine coaster, early 19th century, carved with *putti* and vines. (*Section III*)

52 Georgian cradle wine pourer, mahogany, carved with Bacchus head spout and vine trails. (*Section III*)

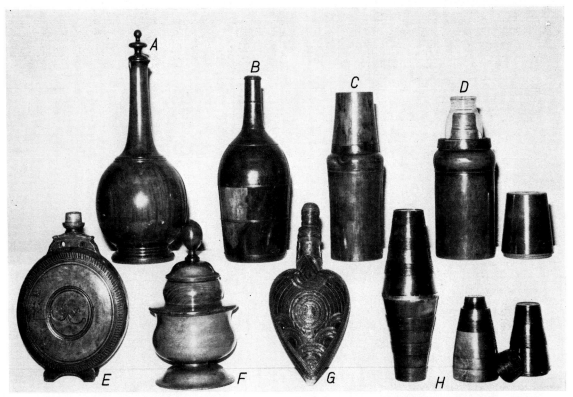

53 *A*, mulberry wood decanter; *B*, lignum vitae 'bottle' spice box, probably 17th century; *C* and *D*, 19th-century predecessors of the vacuum flask; *E*, water flask, probably Scottish; *F*, posset cup set, 17th century; *G*, Russian soldier's flask, Crimean War; *H*, Captain Scott's specially designed flask of 1899. (*Section III*)

54 Coopered bottle, kegs and barrel. (*Section III*)

55 More cups in the armorial series resemble this one in their proportions than any other. Dated 1620. It has a spice cup in the knop and is 18½ in. high by 5¼ in. diameter. *Photograph by courtesy of the Victoria and Albert Museum. (Section III)*

56 A rather more ovoid armorial cup of the series, Dated 1614. It has a spice cup in the knop and is 15½ in. high by 4¾ in. diameter. Burrell Collection. Glasgow Art Gallery and Museum. *Photograph by courtesy of the Museum. (Section III)*

Pearwood standing cup, 19½ in. high by 9¼ in. diameter, th two royal coats of arms of James as James I of England and mes VI of Scotland. This cup differs from the others described in this article, in its shape, lettering and style of decoration. *Photograph by courtesy of the British Musuem. (Section III)*

58 The 'Hickman Chalice', 13 in. high overall by 5¼ in. diameter; dated 1608, it is one of two cups with very similar formal foliage detail, instead of the more usual armorials in other cups in this series. In the Burrell Collection, Glasgow Art Gallery and Museum. *Photograph by courtesy of the Museum. (Section III)*

59 Fine late 17th-century, lignum vitae Monteith. *Collection of W. J. Shepherd, Esq. (Section III)*

60 A rare, fret cut, Chippendale period coaster—an example of Georgian two-ply construction. *(Section III)*

61 TOP ROW: lignum vitae cheese plateau; Victorian dessert knife stand; two cases for silver. MIDDLE ROW: brown oak bread bowl and Charles II lignum vitae sweetmeat bowl. BOTTOM ROW: Elizabethan roundel box; Georgian cutlery stand; burr oak fruit bowl. (*Section IV*

62 *A* to *G*, serviette rings; *H* and *J*, invalid cups; *K*, pap boat; *L*, ladle; *M*, picnic set; *N* to *P*, dish slopes; *Q* and *R*, salad servers; *S*, pastry server; *T* to *V*, sauce boat stands; *W* and *X*, treen dishes. (*Section IV*)

63 An 18th-century, mahogany, enclosed cheese cradle for a man who obviously liked cheese, but not its smell. (*Section IV*)

64 (ON RIGHT) CENTRE: knife and fork in case carved with biblical scenes and date 1611. LEFT: Italian, 17th-century, pearwood spoon. (*Section IV*). RIGHT: German, 17th-century anointing spoon, finely carved inside and outside the bowl and round the stem. (*Section X*)

65 Top and bottom views of an 18th-century, oak cheese plane, for those who had lost their teeth. (*Section IV*)

IV

Eating

During the Middle Ages, in the average household, up to the rank of at least yeoman, the sound of a table being set must have been very different from what it is to-day. There was no clatter of glass or china, nor jingle of silver; apart from a certain amount of earthenware, there was only the sound of wood to wood, as treen platters, bowls, goblets or beakers, and spoons were set on bare boards. In the squirearchy, pewter was used for salts, spoons and sometimes for tankards and goblets. Among the nobility and people of wealth—and at that time the two were probably synonymous—there were tables covered with cloths and graced with silver.

It was only during the 16th century, in Tudor England, that the national increase and better distribution of wealth, with consequent improvements in the general standard of living, commenced the downgrading and decrease in the use of treenware at table. William Harrison (1534–93), rector of Radwinter, North Essex, published his *Description of England* in 1577 and left us a wonderfully clear picture of the changes which had taken place within the memory of those still living. He refers to three things which the older men in the village particularly note. One is the increase in chimneys, the second is improvements in beds and bedding,

'The third thing they tell of is the exchange of vessel, as of treen platters into pewter, and wooden spoons into silver or tin. For so common were all sorts of treen stuff in old time that a man should hardly find four pieces of pewter (of which one was peradventure a salt) in a good farmer's house, and yet for all this frugality (if it may so be justly called) they were scarce able to live and pay their rents at their days without selling of a cow or a horse or more, although they paid but four pounds at the uttermost by the year. Such also was their poverty that, if some one odd farmer or husbandman had been at the ale-house, a thing greatly used in those days, amongst six or seven of his neighbours, and there in a bravery, to shew what store he had, did cast down his purse, and therein a noble or six shillings in silver, unto them (for few such men then cared for gold, because it was not so ready payment, and they were oft enforced to give a penny for the exchange of an angel), it was very likely that all the rest could not lay down so much against it; whereas in my time, although peradventure four pounds of old rent be improved to forty, fifty or a hundred pounds, yet will the farmer, as another palm or date tree, think his gains very small towards the end of his term if he have not six or seven years' rent lying by him, therewith to purchase a new lease, beside a fair garnish of pewter on his cupboard, with so much more in odd vessel going about the house, three or four feather beds, so many coverlets and carpets of tapestry, a silver salt, a bowl for wine (if not a whole nest), and a dozen of spoons to furnish up the suit.'

It was during the 16th century that the dining parlour came into being, but in a great house of the Middle Ages, the master and mistress and their principal guests dined with their retainers in the great hall. The standard both of table appointments and of furniture varied greatly from one end of the hall to the other. At the upper end, furthest away from the screens passage which led to the buttery, kitchens, etc., was a platform, which might be carpeted occasionally; rushes sufficed for the rest of the hall and might also act as bedding for servitors, who slept there. The table on the platform, literally the high table, commanded a view of the whole hall. Those who sat at it had their backs to the wall—much safer so; they were served from the front of the table. The master and mistress and any guests of great importance had chairs; others used stools or benches. At the long table or tables—there might be one down the centre of the hall forming a T with the top table, or a U if there were a table down each side—only forms or benches were used.

The several books of nurture or courtesy, largely books of training in manners, both for staff and children, which were written in the 15th century, give a good idea of arrangements at the high table in a royal or noble household. Table cloths must have been narrow, for one was laid down the centre of the table, a second hanging down along the outer edge, and a third likewise on the inner edge; napkins were also provided. Silver salts were placed at intervals along the high table, in front and always to the right of a place; those at the high table, therefore, all sat above the salt. To the left of the salt were placed drinking vessels and a trencher or two; to the left again, were a knife, some rolls and a spoon, all folded in a napkin and all then covered by a cloth,

until service commenced. As everyone used their fingers, to a large extent, for eating, until forks were invented, a washing table, covered by a diaper towel, was provided near the high table and thereat the diners washed both before and after their meal. On it stood a basin and ornamental ewers for hot and cold water, and plenty of towels or napkins. There was definite etiquette in eating with the fingers; Jean Sulpice, writing in 1480, says that it is wrong to grab your food with both hands, meat should be taken with three fingers. Very reasonably, he adds that people should not scratch themselves at meals and then put their fingers in food! If such advice were necessary to diners, the appalling standard of general behaviour of servitors in the 15th century, may be imagined. It is well exemplified by the admonitions contained in John Russell's *Book of Nurture*, written about 1440. Russell was Usher and Marshall to Humphrey, Duke of Gloucester, youngest son of Henry IV; his object in writing was to train worthy successors in the management and running of a great household. His instructions were not intended for the lowest classes, but for those whose education and appearance fitted them for service in a royal or noble household. Yet he thought necessary all these cautions on general behaviour in public (transposed into modern English):

(a) Don't claw your back as if after a flea; or your head, as if after a louse.
(b) Don't pick your nose, or let it drop, or blow it too loud.
(c) Don't claw your private parts.
(d) Don't pick your ears.
(e) Don't hiccup, belch, retch, or spit too far, or squirt with your mouth.
(f) Don't spit into cups or put your fingers in to remove dust, nor put your tongue in dishes for the same purpose.
(g) Don't pick your teeth or cast stinking breath on your lord.

It may be added that in the *Percy Household Book* for 1825, the instructions to footmen, although worded more politely, do not differ overmuch in their implications.

Having sketched in the background to service at the mediaeval high table, we now visit the lower tables. Here no cloths or knives were provided. Knives in sheaths were carried by all and there was self service. Treen provided the trenchers, often shared by two diners, and also the spoons, drinking vessels and salts. Roasts were served from a huge wooden dish, sometimes on legs—really a heavy topped table, with a runnel and outlet to a gravy bucket below. Stews and broths were ladled from a large wooden bowl, into smaller ones. Trenchers were scraped between courses and the same one used again; but the evidence of cuts and wear on the back of trenchers suggests that they were probably reversed between the main and final course.

Potatoes were unknown in England in the Middle Ages and bread was the most important single item of diet. For details of special trencher bread, see *Trenchers*.

Reference has been made to John Russell's advice that guests at the high table be provided with a knife each. It must be emphasized that this was something which would only pertain to people of very high rank; all ordinary people carried one or two knives in a sheath, usually of leather, hung from the girdle. The habit of carrying your own knife with you and of eating with a knife, spoon and fingers, outlasted the Middle Ages and, in general, continued throughout the 16th century. In the 17th century, with the gradual introduction of the fork, the sheath was modified to include a knife, fork and sometimes a spoon, but although, in polite society, it became more general to include cutlery in the table appointments, no traveller away from home would have been without these necessities. Samuel Pepys, at the Lord Mayor's banquet at Guildhall, October 1663, noted '. . . none in the Hall but the Mayor's and the Lords of the Privy Council that had napkins or knives, which was very

strange'. The absence of napkins was not so strange by the mid-17th century, because the general acceptance of forks meant that in polite society people no longer normally used their fingers for eating. Although Pepys does not mention the absence of forks, this can be assumed. Formerly, it took a very long time indeed for fashions at the apex of society to percolate down to the poor. As late as the 1840s, emigrants to Australia in sailing ships, had each to take one knife and fork, one large and one small spoon, one pewter or tin plate, one pint teapot and one half pint tin panakin. Doubtless, many farm lads, joining the British forces in 1914, accepted as perfectly normal, their issue of service cutlery, etc., for even at the beginning of this century, farm hands, who at harvest and certain other times were provided with their meals, had each to carry his own knife and either whittle or get one of the team boys to make his fork. Only the driver of the leading team of horses, by reason of his rank, was provided with a farm knife and fork. The disposable plastic cutlery now being supplied to aircraft passengers, is not, therefore, so new a fashion.

Although Henry VIII owned 'suckett' spoons and forks—a stem with a spoon on one end and a two prong fork on the other end for spearing ginger, plums, etc. in heavy syrup, and Queen Elizabeth I began to receive New Year gifts of rare gold, silver and crystal handled forks from 1582 onwards, their general introduction to England commenced about 1611. Thomas Coryat's *Crudities*, telling of his adventures in Italy, was published then, and in it he told at great length of Italian eating habits:

'The Italian, and also most strangers that are commorant in Italy, doe alwaies at their meales use a little forke when they cut their meate. For awhile with their knife, which they hold in one hand, they cut the meate out of the dish, they fasten their forke which they hold in their other hand upon the same dish, so that whatsoever he be that, sitting in the company of any others at meale, should unadvisedly touch the dish of meate with his fingers, from which all the table doe cut, he will give occasion of offence unto the company, as having transgressed the lawes of good manners, in so much that for his error he shall be at the least brow-beaten if not reprehended in wordes. This forme of feeding I understand is generally used in all places of Italy, their forkes being for the most part made of iron or steele, and some of silver, but those are used only by Gentlemen. The reason of this their curiosity is, because the Italian cannot by any meanes indure to have his dish touched with fingers, seeing all mens fingers are not alike cleane. . . .'

Coryat adopted the habit for eating, but not without much mockery about aping foreign ways, and for a long time, the fork in England remained primarily a server of sticky preserves, rather than an implement for eating.

Apple Scoops—see *Scoops*

Bowls, Bread, Fruit and Other Food

Bread bowls, lettered with the word BREAD, were particularly popular in the second half of the 19th century. They were an alternative to circular sycamore bread boards, similarly lettered and carved in low relief with wheat-ears round a wide rim, which is often additionally pierced in an ornamental design. The English brown (pollard) oak bread bowl, centre row, Plate 61, is a good specimen, with fanciful lettering of the 1870 period, reading 'Eat thy bread with joy and thankfulness'.

The brown burr oak fruit bowl, or compotière, one of a pair, in the bottom row, was formerly in the Dr. Carter Collection and probably dates from the 18th century; the pear, apple and banana in it are also of carved hardwoods. Standing fruit bowls or tazzas, simplified versions of Greek and Roman models, are popular examples of turnery, but the majority are comparatively modern. A few thinly turned, rather deep bowls, based on silver designs for sugar

bowls, such as the Brazil nutshell bowl, top right, Plate 199, were probably intended for sugar. The majority of turned bowls rank as general-purpose bowls, to be selected for purpose according to depth and diameter. A peculiar type of eating bowl is described under *Trenchers*.

Bread Boards—see *Bowls, Bread*

Carving Boards—see *Dishes*

Cases for Silver

A few pole-lathe turned double bowls, or bowls with covers, usually of sycamore, exist and are somewhat puzzling. As similar shaped bowls of leather, or of wood covered with shagreen, were used as cases for silver in the 16th, 17th and 18th centuries, it can be assumed that these served a similar purpose. Two examples are shown in the top row, right, of Plate 61; they measure $4\frac{1}{8}$ in. and $7\frac{1}{4}$ in. in diameter respectively.

Cheese Coasters or Cradles

In mediaeval books of household management and manners, frequent references occur to the important place of cheese in the diet. John Russell (see introduction to this section) tells how milk, junket, posset, etc. are binding and should be followed by hard cheese, to keep the bowels open. Hard cheese was also advocated after eating pears, nuts or any food that set your teeth on edge. An interesting side issue is that although casein cement, or casein glue, was only patented and manufactured commercially in Europe in 1892, Russell, writing 550 years earlier, says 'Whan stone pottes be broken, what is better to glew them againe or make them fast; nothing like the Symunt made of Cheese . . .'.

Cheese coasters or cradles are crescent shaped, usually of mahogany and provided with castors; they ran up and down the table in Georgian and Victorian times, when large families were usual. Cheese cradles generally have a thin, longitudinal division, placed off centre, so that one division would hold half a thick cheese and the other, half of a thin one; sometimes one compartment was used for cut bread instead. Eighteenth-century specimens are mostly plain and well proportioned. As the 19th century advanced, they tended to become coarser, and scrolled ends and carved embellishments were frequently added.

An 18th-century gentleman, who obviously liked cheese but not its smell, has left an interesting memento of his fastidiousness, Plate 63. It is an enclosed mahogany cheese cradle, 16½ in. wide by 11 in. high, with a hinged fall front and a rising lid, hinged at the back. A noteworthy fact about the curved part of the cradle is that it is laminated in five layers. It is widely assumed that plywood is a modern invention; it is not; only its manufacture as a sheet material on mass production lines is a comparatively modern technique. The Georgians used glue laminate construction for curved work and occasionally for large panels and, indeed, it was used long before their time, but only where essential, because made by hand, it was a slow and expensive process.

Cheese Planes

An old proverb runs 'Tis an old rat that won't eat cheese'. This has been interpreted alternatively as 'It must be a wondrously toothless man that is inaccessible to flattery' or 'He must be very old indeed who can abandon his favourite indulgence'. Whatever the interpretation may mean, it is extremely unlikely that our ancestors liked giving up the eating of hard cheese, which they esteemed both for its medicinal and its epicurean qualities. Yet with the absence of dentures, they must have found themselves in considerable difficulty when they lost their teeth at an early age, as they were wont to do, in the absence of tooth brushes and mouth hygiene. An 18th-century individual solved his or her problem by means of a special plane for slicing cheese, Plate

8—T.O.W.B.

65. This implement, now possibly unique, is made of oak, is 12 in. long and 4½ in. wide and is used upside down, the cheese being slid over it, between two guiding rims. The cutter, set at an angle of 45°, is adjustable to take off slivers of cheese of the desired thickness. On the side of the plane is inscribed:

'When with long grinding, Nature's tools are spent
To shave the cheese, Art found this Instrument'.

Without the inscription, it is doubtful if the purpose of this ingenious device would ever have been guessed.

Cheese Plateaux—see *Plateaux*

Cheese Scoops—see *Scoops*

Condiments—see *Salts*

Cutlery Boxes and Racks—see Section VII, *Kitchen*

Cutlery Cases or Stands

The 18th-century cutler frequently used 'The Case of Knives' as his shop sign, and the ornamental cabinet in which he sold a set of cutlery, which included spoons and forks, as well as knives, was known as a case of knives. In the 18th century, these cases were mostly made by specialist cabinet-makers, such as John Lane of 44 St. Martins-le-Grand, London, and John Folghan who, during the second half of the century, was in turn at Wood Street, Fetter Lane, and Fleet Street, London. Being essentially the smaller work of the furniture or cabinet-maker, knife cases are only described briefly here. The sloping hinged top knife case, with canted front corners, was known in the 17th century; early in the 18th, it developed the characteristic serpentine front with side hollows, forming a double ogee, which remained popular throughout the century, merely changing its veneers and forms of inlay, according to fashion. Knife cases were usually supplied in pairs, occasionally in threes, to stand on dining room side tables. In the last quarter of the 18th century, the sloping serpentine fronted types share popularity with Adam classical urn knife cases, which crowned the pedestal cupboards flanking the principal side table. During the Regency period, sideboards sometimes had integral knife cases, decorated with carving or ormolu mounts, in the Graeco-Egyptian taste. After the Regency, knife cases died out, because sideboards incorporated one or more baize lined, partitioned drawers for cutlery.

An 18th-century, open knife case or cutlery stand of mahogany, which is largely the work of the turner, is shown central in Plate 61. It is 9½ in. high, excluding the finial, by 8¾ in. diameter. Also in Plate 61, is illustrated a 19th-century dessert knife stand, which is rather a charming piece of Victoriana. The woodwork is finished a verdigris bronze colour; the rim of the stand is neatly decorated with fine black, white and gold beadwork, and the knives are of horn.

Dinner Mats

Wooden mats, of alternate light and dark wood, glued on to felt and made to roll up, tambour fashion, were popular in the last quarter of the 19th and first decade of this century. Like much of the 'striped' woodware, they were made in Scotland and were available in oblongs and ovals for use under dishes, and circular for under plates.

Dishes and Carving Boards

Treen serving dishes, round, oval and oblong, being plain and functional and, therefore, unchanging over many centuries, are impossible to date accurately. Being intrinsically of little value, and in the past not considered worth keeping when worn, it is doubtful if any have survived from much earlier than the 18th century, although

judged on cuts, wear and patination, some look very ancient. Experience has convinced me, however, that continual impregnation and discoloration with gravy and fat, alternated by scrubbing and surface disturbance due to cuts and abrasions, can produce a misleading appearance of age. The 20 in. diameter, sycamore dish, Plate 62, X, formerly in the Evan-Thomas Collection and the 17 in. diameter, beech dish, W, in the same picture, both show considerable wear and patination and may be 18th- or 19th-century. The rare, oval, sycamore dish, 16½ in. by 11¾ in., with runnel and gravy well, Plate 84, comes under the same date heading and so likewise, in my opinion, does the elm 13⅜ in. by 10½ in. carving board, Plate 68, D, in spite of its extensive hollowness due to wear, and its network of cut marks. Having four crude square legs, it is definitely a serving board, not a chopping board.

Dish Slopes

Some people contend that the well dish was a 19th-century invention, because mahogany dish slopes all appear to date from the 18th century. Certainly that was their heyday, but with the 19th-century large well dish, they were still needed, even though not available. Owing to distortion during firing, the china dish seldom gave a proper flow towards the well; in my childhood home, my father, after serving, always placed a knife rest under the dish, to tilt the gravy into the well. Mahogany dish slopes, as exemplified by Plate 62, N, O and P, 5½ in. to 7 in. long over handles, may be ribbed or smooth; occasionally they are decorated with carving; they were generally made in pairs, because a large dish required two at the head end.

Egg Carriers

The 12-hole, mahogany egg carrier, Plate 68, E, may be late 18th- or early 19th-century. The crude board, A, with eight cavities in the main part and one in the handle, was considered by Evan-Thomas to be a very early form of egg carrier, with salt cavity in the handle. So far as I am concerned, it is a 'dunnowhat'. Admittedly, hens' eggs were formerly smaller, but even so, these slightly ovoid holes are not the right shape for eggs lying down, nor deep enough for them to stand safely on end. Moreover, the 'handle' may not be a handle, because at the other end, holes run through the board in its thickness from end to sides, at an angle of 45°, as though some metal rod handle were inserted. It has been suggested that this was used in some ancient game. See also Section VII, for kitchen egg stands.

Egg Cups

English egg cups of different styles, in various hardwoods, are illustrated in Plate 68, B and C. When not in egg stands, I do not attempt to date them. Turners have always turned them to any shapes that take their fancy, irrespective of current fashion in silver or china. On such analogy, the yew-wood cup, extreme right, row B, is the earliest; the double ring type, in the same row, is usable either way up, with a hole going right through. In row C, the cup to the left of the one on its side, with stem alongside, together form a pair of travelling egg cups; for packing, the stems go in the cups, which fit together, forming a wooden egg.

Egg Stands

In Plate 68, F, G and H are three different styles of English egg stands. F is early 19th-century; it has the tray of mahogany, but the handle, with acorn finial, and the four cups, appear to be of some other red wood. G, with revolving tray, is an 18th-century specimen; it was formerly in the Linn Collection. Its six thin turned egg cups, which engage on pegs, and the centre pillar are of elm, and the plateau and foot of other hardwoods; this mixing of woods was very common among country turners. The early

Victorian revolving egg cup stand, with salt cavity, H, is of mahogany, with ebony egg cups, which appear much more stylish than the stand.

Feeding Cups—see *Pap Boats*

Food Bowls—see *Bowls, Bread, Fruit and other Food*

Forks—see *Knives and Forks*

Fruit Bowls—see *Bowls, Bread, Fruit and other Food*

Garnishing Skewers—see *Skewers, Garnishing*

Knives and Forks

To the treen collector, it is the beauty of a wooden handle of a knife and fork which counts. Consequently, both description and illustrations to this section concentrate on this angle. The introduction of the fork and the carrying of a personal knife in a sheath have been discussed in the introduction to this section.

In Plate 64 is illustrated a knife and fork in a finely carved wooden sheath, with silver mount engraved with flowers. The carving is dated 1611 and bears the initials W.G.W. So far, this maker, who apparently worked over a period of half a century, has not been identified, but he was probably either Flemish or German. I have recorded nine other very similar sheaths by the same man, bearing the dates 1566, 1577, 1589, 1591, 1592, 1593, 1594, 1602 and 1615. Each sheath, which is hollowed out of a solid block of heavy, dark hardwood, is divided into 24 scenes, carved with the Return of the Prodigal Son, and the Twelve Apostles, plus panels for a shield, the date and the maker's initials. There is a pierced projection on the sheath for cords, for suspending it from the girdle.

In Plate 66 is a selection of carved box-wood-handled cutlery. The well worn knife and two-pronged fork, left, have silver mounts to the handles, engraved with a coronet, with initials K and V at the sides and initial B, below. The handles are carved with figures of Faith, Hope and Charity and Justice, surmounted by six cherub heads. They are probably 17th-century, German or Dutch. The next pair, in almost mint condition, have the handles carved and pierced with open lanterns and loose rings. The subjects round the lanterns are, knife handle, David and Bathsheba, and fork handle, Joshua commanding the sun to stand still. Two tobacco stoppers, obviously from the same series and work-shop, are shown in Plate 358, Q and R. They all appear to be late 17th- or early 18th-century, probably Flemish. The handle, central in the same plate, is des-scribed under Section X, *Miscellany: Religious Carvings.*

The next knife, with handle carved with figures of the four Virtues, surmounted by a lion couchant, above two lanterns, has carved initials V.R. and date 1643; the steel blade is engraved with leaf scrolls and Antonio. The Dutch knife, with lion ram-pant holding a shield, above a wide band carved with vertical foliage and flowers, is dated 1722 on the blade, which is engraved with male and female busts in circles and an inscription which translates, 'Beauty un-accompanied by virtue is like stale wine'. This probably denotes that this knife was originally one of a pair of wedding knives. The giving to the bride of a pair of decora-tive knives, engraved with a verse extolling constancy and enclosed in a handsomely embossed leather or embroidered sheath, goes back to mediaeval times on the conti-nent, but seems to have first become com-mon practice in England at the Tudor Court. The custom continued throughout the 17th century, with the exception of the Commonwealth decade; by the end of the century, the convention was dying out in England. The handle, extreme right of Plate 66, also probably German or Dutch,

is carved with Faith, Hope and Charity and dated 1731. The salt spoon is described under *Spoons*.

At the ends of the row in Plate 67 are two outstandingly carved boxwood pen-knife sheaths, described in *Section XVII, Reading, Writing, Drawing and Painting Ac-cessories*. Next to each of the penknives is a boxwood handle, delicately carved with *putti* among foliage and a double eagle coat of arms; the two form a pair for a knife and fork and may be South German, Austrian, or North Italian. Of the other two box-wood handles in the centre, the one to the left portrays David with the head of Goliath; it is German or Flemish, late 16th or early 17th-century. To the right, mounted on a stand, is another handle, probably of the same date and provenance. It is a particularly delicate and sensitive piece of craftsmanship, depicting the Angel staying Abraham from slaying Isaac.

In Plate 81, *L* is the comparatively modern, say 19th- or early 20th-century, strictly utilitarian version of the old personal knife and fork; the rosewood handle of each implement is designed to provide a slide-in sheath for the blade of the other.

Ladles

In Plate 21 is a selection of English and Scottish 18th-century punch ladles. These may vary in length of handle from 6 in. to 12 in. Cordial ladles, which have smaller bowls, also have shorter handles, usually 3 in. to 4 in. long. English and Scottish 18th-century punch and cordial ladles differ fundamentally in construction. Scot-tish ladles, immediately left and right of centre, Plate 21, have handles threaded into bowls; of the other ladles, the English have the handle and bowl all in one piece. Admittedly, the unusual ladle, extreme left, probably the work of a sailor, has a handle junction in the knop; it also has a jug and drinking vessels carved on its bowl. Note the English ladle extreme right, shown side view on; it has a projection on the back of the handle, to prevent the ladle handle slipping into the punch bowl. This feature, quite common in the 18th century, was launched with considerable publicity, as a new invention, by makers of jam and pickle spoons some twenty years ago!

The yew-wood ladle, Plate 62, *L*, carved with a heart and roundels, was doubtless made as a love token, but it was meant for, and has had use. It may be two, three or even four hundred years old; its decoration is timeless and its shape, dictated by the twisted contours of a natural piece of yew-wood, affords no clue to age. It was doubtless used for ladling from a bowl and the naturally formed hook on the underside of the handle, as with punch ladles, prevents it slipping. The graceful side curvature and twist on the stem make it particularly easy to 'flick over' when serving, rather like the action of a Caernarvon crooked spoon (see *Spoons*). Unique it is, but so satisfying both in sculptural quality and ease of use, that if consciously designed today, it would probably win a major award.

Muffineers—see *Salts and Condiments*

Nutcrackers
Nutshells can be cracked in three ways: by striking them with a mallet or stone, by lever-applied pressure, or by building up screw pressure.

There is a paucity in early literature of references to nutcrackers. It seems reasonable, however, to assume that the 'strike' method came first and even today nut bowls with wooden mallets and anvils are sold. Whether the specially designed nut cracking device or *nucifrangibulum* to which Elyot referred in 1548 was screw or lever type is uncertain, but the earliest dated wooden specimens all seem to be lever types. Wooden screw crackers are seldom dated.

From mediaeval days, a nutcracker formed as a droll human or animal head, with articulated jaws, seems to have tickled the fancy and challenged the skill of wood

carvers. John Evelyn, in *Sylva*, mentions the ideality of boxwood for nutcrackers and the best wooden specimens were invariably made from this tough and strong wood, also so suitable for fine carving. Even so, the lower jaw, which is an integral part of the back lever, is often found chipped and sometimes both levers and lower jaws are replacements. This type of cracker is constructed with the back lever passing through a mortice in the front of the figure; the two parts are pivoted together by a boxwood or iron pin.

Accurate dating of wooden nutcrackers of 16th to 18th centuries is difficult, but careful study of those few which are carved with original dates, assists greatly. Amongst the hundred or more wooden specimens in the Pinto Collection, are examples dated 1570, 1574, 1655, 1677, 1685, 1690, 1702, 1709, 1720, 1768, 1830 and 1868. Unfortunately, some 19th-century nutcrackers reproduce earlier period designs; additionally, collectors have to beware of deliberate fakes, for early specimens are now valuable enough to attract the skill and cupidity of these deceivers.

One of the oldest surviving boxwood nutcrackers must be Plate 70, carved as an ogre. It is of fine quality, probably of French origin and would date from *circa* 1500. The nutcracker of richly patinated boxwood, shown side and front view, Plate 71, is a superb and almost anatomical carving of Hercules astride and breaking the jaws of the Nemean lion. Dated 1570, it is the earliest dated and finest wood specimen which I know. It is probably Italian and was formerly in the Carnegie Collection.

All these early examples have jaws only large enough for a cob or filbert, but often there is a secondary hollow or oval recess in the back of both levers, which will hold a walnut. Brazil nuts were not introduced to Europe until the 16th or 17th century. In Plate 71, this secondary hollow, which cannot be seen in the photograph, occurs where the dentil and guilloche ornaments meet. Whilst almonds were used considerably for flavouring, they do not appear to have been eaten as dessert in early times, so wooden nutcrackers were only called on to crack filberts or walnuts.

Most of the boxwood lever type specimens shown in Plate 69 are as early in date as the last. Possibly the oldest in this picture is *D*, depicting a French king(?), with headdress and long hose costume of the period 1480–1500. The lower jaw is broken; the right leg is a replacement. The open crown surmounting the shield is of mediaeval character, as is also the conventional lion, gripping the coat tails of the back lever (not showing in the picture). The carving bears traces of polychrome. A related type of cracker is *A*, formerly in the Evan-Thomas Collection. It appears to be 20 or 30 years later than *D*. Note the closed type of crown above the shield and the Renaissance head and foliage below it.

A rare specimen, dated 1574, possibly Florentine, is *B*, a grotesque head with the lower jaw partially broken away. Its quality is not comparable with Plate 71, but there is similar guilloche carving behind the head, as can be seen in Plate 74, *G*, where it is shown horizontally.

The 'term' figure, Plate 69, *C*, is another example of the same period. It is decorated with guilloche on all four sides and is a fine specimen and an early example of a standing figure nutcracker. Its country of origin is uncertain, but could be French, Italian or Flemish. The boxwood lever cracker with ivory teeth, *E*, is a practical and gracefully scrolled French example of the 18th century. The 17th-century merman, Plate 74, *A*, original in theme and of small size, was formerly in the Redfern and Bussel Collections; it may be English or continental. The 18th-century standing cracker, with lugubrious expression, *B*, is almost certainly English. It is a practical design, with brass lined jaws and lead weighted base to give the *coup de grace* to an obstinate nut. The fat boy, *C*, a delightful

example of Elizabethan peasant craft in walnut, *circa* 1580–90, is much the worse for wear and worm. It was formerly in the Evan-Thomas Collection.

Sophie v. la Roche noted in her diary, when crossing to Harwich from Rotterdam on September 4, 1786

'... The young Suffolk farmer (a fellow traveller) was, indeed, one of the brightest, and amused himself with his nut-crackers, which were carved and painted like mannikins with large mouths, and which he had bought for his children as portraits of young Dutchmen at Rotterdam kermis. ...'

Such a mannikin is the Punch-like figure, *D*, finished in polychrome, which depicts a nut vendor with his basket of nuts before him. It is typical of the spirited character put into late 18th-century, mid-European work, for sale at fairs in Holland, Germany, Switzerland, etc.

The crude specimen, *E*, may be 17th- or 18th-century, English. The unusually small boxwood figure, *F*, with Vandyk beard and moustache, is an English lever cracker dated 1720; it was formerly in the Redfern and Bussell Collections.

Screw-actuated wooden crackers all follow the same principle. Until the 19th century, they are mostly plain and simple; some Swiss and Tyrolean, 19th-century specimens are elaborately carved. The cavity may be round, oval, more rarely heart-shaped or square, but always with one wall of the cavity pierced with a hole threaded for a correspondingly threaded screw. Plate 72 includes a selection of charming and essentially functional screw crackers, nearly all of boxwood. The simplest and easiest to find, are the plain ring types, *M*, which were probably made over several centuries and are impossible to date accurately; usually, but not invariably, the ring is drilled right through. Next come the barrels, *F*, *O* and *P*; the last is dated 1690. Acorns, *N*, are more difficult to find. A considerable rarity is the boxwood bird on a cage, *D*. I believe that all the foregoing are English and not later than the 18th century. *H*, with body of burr maple and screw knob of boxwood, and *E*, of boxwood, carved with a double horse-head, are probably 18th-century, Scandinavian.

Ornamentally carved screw crackers, such as *G*, with heart-shaped apertures, have sometimes been described as 'English, rare, 17th-century'. I doubt this: I have seen too many similar specimens and all in good condition. They are invariably beautifully finished, but appear to have been commercially produced and a popular 18th- or possibly even early 19th-century pattern, of Scandinavian origin.

The remainder of the screw-type crackers in Plate 72 are Swiss or Tyrolean and most of them were made in the 19th century, when there were hundreds of designs from which to choose, as there still are today. Probably the earliest and most unusual, dating from around 1800, are *Q*, the yew-wood poodle, with a bone between his paws, *L*, the yew-wood cottage on a cliff, and *C*, the girl on a pedestal. The bird with a tail which unscrews, *K*, was a popular alternative to a similarly constructed crocodile, in the second half of the 19th century. From the same period also, dates *B*, the Edward Lear cross-legged figure of a man up a pole. Completing Plate 72, are two lever nutcrackers. The mannikin, *J*, polychrome finished with blue coat, red breeches and white waistcoat and hose, is one of the late 18th-century fairground figures of the same type as the nut seller, Plate 74, *D*. The seated woman, *A*, who cracks nuts in her jaws and deposits them in her basket, is a popular 19th-century alternative to a variety of gnomes, similarly posed.

In Plate 73, are some rare and interesting lever type nutcrackers, also a few which are not all they seem to be at first sight. The miserable creature, *A*, was purchased expressly for £1, to illustrate here as a warning to collectors; he is a deliberate fake, based on the valuable early king types

illustrated in Plates 69, *A* and *D*. He has several twin brothers; all are made of some comparatively soft and ill chosen wood, stained nearly black, rubbed light on the high points and with traces of polychrome carefully worked into the depressions. If you happen to meet one of the family with a broken foot, it is one that has been sent to me on three occasions in days gone by, by different dealers (probably in ignorance) and offered at prices which then varied from £5 to £15. If it is still in existence, perhaps this exposure will finally end its deceitful life! The cheerful man with ruff and beaver hat, *B*, looks at first sight to be *circa* 1620, but there is not really much age about it and I have seen two others similar. My theory is that he is a pre-Raphaelite and that he was designed by Burne-Jones for his picture 'Lorenzo and Isabella'; anyhow, he is to be seen depicted in that painting in the Tate Gallery.

The ingeniously constructed crossover, lever nutcrackers, Plate 73, *C*, *D*, *E*, *F*, *G*, *M* and *N*, differ from the lever types so far described. A carefully selected piece of hardwood, with a crooked branching grain at the head end, is used for the cross-over morticed arm; into this, the straight arm is loosely tenoned and levers against a hardwood peg in the tenon. The chip carved specimen, *C*, is probably 17th-century, Welsh. The inscription on *D*, which is of boxwood, makes it particularly interesting. It is dated May 1677, inscribed with initials A and K, and the names Ambros and King, and 'If All Bee Trew As Weemen Say Ye Night Is Sweeter Then The Day.'. It probably commemorates a marriage between a King and an Ambros. *E* and *F*, both of yew-wood, the former 5½ in. and the latter 6½ in. long, are, as usual with this type, decorated all over with incised ornament of scrimshaw type. The ornament sometimes includes English flowers and tropical palms or fish and animals. Basically, they are a 17th-century type and they are probably the work of sailors of various nationalities. I have given their dimensions to distinguish them from the larger and coarser 19th-century specimens made on the same principle, similarly decorated, and also usually of yew-wood. One is shown, *G*, which is nearly 8 in. long; another in the Pinto Collection is dated 1868. The charming little boxwood specimen, *M*, 4½ in. long, dappled all over with blobs of dark stain, in simulation of tortoiseshell and pierced with a heart-shaped opening, is engraved with the initials M.F. and date 1685. This crude simulation of tortoiseshell occurs on other 17th-century English treen. The last of this type, *N*, is English, 17th-century, probably of thorn-wood.

H, *J* and *K* are cleverly constructed one-piece nutcrackers, made from hardwoods selected for their springiness. They are not very strong and few of this type have survived; they give the impression of being more notable for ingenuity than practicability. *H*, made of ash, is decorated with acorn terminals, date 1830 and initials W.H. and M.H., which stand for William and Mary Hooke of Castle Farm, Kirby Muxloe, Leicestershire. *J* and *K* are probably 18th-century, English. The unusual boxwood lever nutcracker, *L*, with two legs but a domed top instead of a human head, is incised with flowers, a human figure, an animal and the date 1702 and is probably Danish. Made from boxwood, *O* employs a different constructional principal. It is in three parts, the strap being morticed through and the two arms tenoned and loosely pegged. It dates from the 18th or early 19th century and is probably Scandinavian. It was formerly in the Evan-Thomas and Bussell Collections. The boxwood lever crackers, *P*, is reinforced with a brass spine and has a steel pivot pin. The pattern, which is common in metal, is most unusual in wood. The jaws are studded with metal pins to grip the nut and seem to have had plenty of wear; it is probably 19th-century, English.

Highly decorative wooden lever nut-crackers were made in large quantities in the Austrian Tyrol, the Swiss and French Alps and in the Black Forest region of Germany during the 19th century, and are still being made today. Usually they are extremely competent carvings, but, being made of comparatively soft fruitwood or walnut, they will not withstand the nut cracking which confronted earlier boxwood specimens. A selection of 19th- and 20th-century, human and animal head, lever types is shown in Plate 75; those which have been used show extensive bruising of 'roofs' of mouths, and often complete slicing off of lower jaws. Late 19th-century screw types have proved little more practical, as their comparatively soft threads also give trouble. Actually, during the last century and a half, wooden nutcrackers have deteriorated into tourist souvenirs, with more ornamental appeal than practical use. This has been tacitly recognised in the last 20 years, as exemplified by Plate 75, *C* and *D*, which have the bases of the front levers widened to form standing ornaments. Celebrity subjects for the foreign market were Swiss specialities of the 19th century. Louis Philippe, *A*, and Gladstone, *B*, are typical; Bismarck was another popular subject. There is an almost unlimited range of these attractive peasant carvings, in both screw and lever type wooden nutcrackers.

Nut Picks
The two English, 18th- or early 19th-century nut picks, Plate 73, *Q*, 5¾ in. long, have handles turned from lignum vitae.

Pap Boats
When artificial feeding was resorted to for very young babies, a cow horn seems to have been the usual device used in England. For slightly older children, there were silver and pewter pap boats. Whether wooden pap boats were made and used in England, I do not know, but all the wooden pap boats and invalid feeding cups which I have

noted, are continental, mostly Swiss or Tyrolean, but some few Scandinavian. Whilst all those examined appear to be 19th-century, they are probably of a traditional form and doubtless earlier ones would have been scrapped as soon as they became worn. Basically, invalid cups and pap boats, Plate 62, are the same thing, but the larger ones such as *H*, 6 in. long and *J*, 5½ in. long, decorated with grapes and vine leaves, are for invalids, whilst *K*, 4½ in. long, with chip carved floral ornament, is a pap boat. Slightly smaller Swiss and Tyrolean scoops of similar form, but without the cover over the handle end, were used as caddy spoons. All these pap boats and scoops are decorated on the underside with formal leaf carving.

Pastry Servers
The very practically designed, French pastry server of walnut, Plate 62, *S*, is quite modern, but I believe follows a traditional silver design.

Picnic Outfits
Elaborate travelling cases fitted with cutlery, china, food containers, etc., are outside the scope of this work. There is a much smaller type of travelling canteen outfit which may, however, qualify for inclusion, by reason of late 18th-century specimens, such as Plate 62, *M*, containing a certain amount of wood. The basic idea of the design, which goes back to the 16th or 17th century was to use a beaker as a receptacle for a knife, fork, spoon, condiment and additionally, in some cases, a marrow scoop, toothpick, nutmeg grater and corkscrew; the whole outfit was then enclosed in a tight-fitting outer case, usually covered in shagreen or leather, but occasionally of silver. The most famous and elaborate repoussé silver example was that made in 1740 at Edinburgh and found in the tent of Prince Charles Stuart, after the battle of Culloden in 1746. It was sold in 1963, at Christie's, for £7,200. The example illustrated is much humbler Sheffield plate, *circa* 1790–1800, in tooled leather case. Basically, however, it is the same: the fitment, which nests in the beaker, holds a folding knife, fork and spoon with ebony faced handles and an ivory ringed, turned ebony container for salt and pepper; the marrow scoop and toothpick are missing.

Plateaux, Revolving
Revolving plateaux, to save passing condiments, etc., were used on dinner tables in 18th- and 19th-century England and also in the North American colonies. They were very much 'middle class self service' and, as such, find no reference in fashionable books of furniture design. In fact, even the contemporary name for these table centre variants of dumb waiters seems unknown. In the U.S.A., they are now known as 'Lazy Susans'. They were made in various hardwoods, mahogany being the most popular. This was not only a matter of fashion, but also because mahogany was available in greater widths than most other hardwoods, and was very free from warping, even when only supported in the centre, as these plateaux are. They vary in size from about 16 in. to 20 in. diameter, and follow wooden cruet fashion in having a spreading circular foot, with a stem rising through the plateau and terminating in a knob or ring handle; the plateau revolves between collars on the stem and is generally about 3 in. off the table. Another type of revolving plateau, essentially for cheese, is illustrated top left, in Plate 61. It is an 18th-century, English specimen, 11½ in. in diameter, with the top surface turned into concave rings, to grip the cheese or cheeses.

Platters—see *Trenchers*

Roundels and Roundel Boxes
At first thought, there may not appear much connection between a wooden trencher and a part song with a refrain. The roundel, however, is the connecting link, for thin

circular wooden trenchers, known as roundels, were decorated with 'poesies', which were recited or sung by guests, as roundelays, in the reign of Elizabeth I, James I and Charles I. Doubtless the Civil War killed both the banquets and the festive spirit of the party games in which roundels and roundelays played their part. Roundels were usually circular, made of sycamore or beech and were between 5 in. and $5\frac{1}{2}$ in. in diameter, and usually $\frac{1}{16}$ in. to $\frac{1}{8}$ in. thick.

After the more robust wooden trenchers, used for the main courses, had been cleared away, a roundel, plain side up, was placed before each diner. These roundels were used for cheese, or for the sticky marchpanes (marzipans), sugar-plums, or other confettes or 'conceits', which terminated Elizabethan or early Stuart banquets. After Grace, the roundels were reversed, exposing the ornamental side, which was painted with one or at most two verses, elaborately bordered in gilt and brightly coloured ornament, and varnished over. The verses were sung or recited by the diners in turn, probably to the accompaniment of a lute, for the entertainment of the company. Roundels were usually made in sets of 8 or 12, occasionally 24, and were kept in circular roundel boxes, which sometimes repeated on the lid, the ornamental border designs painted on the contents. Instead of the text, however, the lids are often painted centrally with the Royal Coat of Arms, flanked by the initials E.R. It is unlikely that this would have been permitted as a fashion, but even more unlikely that all these sets, painted with the Royal Arms, belonged to Queen Elizabeth, as is often claimed for a set so decorated! I suggest that the real answer is that Elizabeth I, who was thrifty, gave a box of roundels with her Arms on the cover, to members of the nobility who had given her costly New Year gifts, as was then the custom. It is probably more than coincidence that most of the roundels in boxes decorated with Queen Elizabeth's Arms, have a strong family

resemblance: they probably came from the same maker, who, as we would say now, held the Royal Warrant. Very few complete sets of roundels have survived and of those which have, the majority, in the course of time, have become separated from their original boxes.

References to roundels occur in late 16th- and early 17th-century inventories, but much more light is cast on the roundel custom by the following quotations. In *Northward Ho*, published by Webster and Dekker in 1607, a character says 'I'll have you make twelve posies for a dozen cheese trenchers'. George Puttenham, in *The Art of English Poesie*, 1589, says in a chapter headed 'Of short Epigrames called Poesies':

'There be also other like epigrames that were sent usually for New Yeares gifts or to be printed or put upon their banketting dishes of sugar plate or of March paines ... they were called "Apophoreta", and never contained above one verse or two at the most, but the shorter the better. We call them Poesies and do paint them now a dayes upon the backe sides of our fruite trenchers of wood...'

Sets of roundels could be purchased, worded to suit all tastes. Subjects included satirical verses, proverbs, Signs of the Zodiac, moralising stories, such as *Aesop's Fables*, the twelve months of the year, fruits and flowers in their seasons, and biblical quotations. Whilst the majority of roundels have their lettering central within the borders, a few are painted with central pictures and the text referring to the picture is incorporated in, or used to form the outer border. Usually the lettering is black on the natural wood, but a handsome set of early 17th-century roundels, in the Victoria and Albert Museum, is painted in gold and silver on a black ground. Eleven of another set of elaborate roundels, in the same museum, are illustrated here, Plate 77, together with the lid of the box, top centre, and the box, bottom centre, in which one of the roundels is shown. This set is of natural sycamore and each roundel, $5\frac{1}{2}$ in. in diameter, is lettered in black with red capitals and the central theme is on the subject of marriage; surrounding it are scriptural texts taken from Miles Coverdale's 1535 translation of the bible. The border consists of a black outline design on gold, and the centre has a basically red design, with touches of dark blue, olive green, pale green and yellow.

Flowers and fruit figure more commonly than any other subjects in the borders of Elizabethan roundels; usually they are stylised and incorporated in, or joined by strapwork, based on the engravings found in the popular pattern books which were imported from the Low Countries at that time. Several sets, or part sets, which have survived, much simpler than the ones illustrated and painted with verses and flowers in black, red, white and gold, are so similar to each other as to be almost certainly all from the hand of the same artist.

Although it is a contradiction in terms, a few very rare oblong roundels, about 5 in. by 4 in., have also survived. Their decoration is of the same style as on the conventional round examples. A whole set of superb quality, in absolutely mint condition, is illustrated in Plate 76. The book-shaped container measures $6\frac{1}{4}$ in. by $5\frac{1}{8}$ in., the roundels $5\frac{3}{8}$ in. by $4\frac{1}{8}$ in. by only $\frac{1}{32}$ in. thick. The box and the roundels are decorated with strapwork/Tudor rose decoration in gold, blue, green and white. The poesies are of the moralising type.

Some 17th-century sets of roundels, both round and oblong, have coloured prints stuck to the thin boards and only the texts round the border are painted direct on to the wood, the whole composition being then varnished over. Where the whole of the painting is not directly on the wood, careful examination is necessary, in order to determine not only that the whole of the composition is contemporary, but also that the picture and the board commenced life together.

As roundels are seldom found in complete sets and often without their original boxes, it follows that roundel boxes sometimes survive without their roundels. One of three in the Pinto Collection is illustrated bottom left of Plate 61. It is of sycamore, with late 16th-century incised decoration and it would have held 24 roundels of 5 in. diameter. Judging by the cavity in the lid, it formed the base of a treen cup or other object, somewhat on the lines of Plate 30.

Salad Servers

Treen salad servers, both those combining a pivot-connected spoon and fork, Plate 62, Q and R, and the separate implements, Plate 81, G and H, are seldom very old. Of those illustrated, Q may be late 19th-century and R, of pearwood, early 20th-century. Both types are still being made and the rubbing in of salad cream soon gives an impression of age.

Salts and Condiments

From earliest times, salt has been greatly venerated. 'Not worth his salt' is still a stock phrase, while among Arabs, 'There is salt between us', implies friendship. At the mediaeval top table, the salt was prepared with an ivory plane and the standing salt cellar occupied the place of honour, dividing master, mistress and honoured guests—the quality 'above the salt'—from the retainers below. Incidentally, the word 'cellar' is derived from the French *salière*, meaning salt box, and our term 'salary' has a similar derivation, the Latin *salarium* being an allowance of salt made by the Romans to their soldiers, as part payment. In the homes of the nobility, the finest salts were often masterpieces of the greatest goldsmiths and silversmiths. In more yeoman houses, treen sufficed for salts which, as the selection in Plates 78 and 79 shows, were turned in numerous varieties of shapes and sizes, mostly based on simplifications of current fashions in metal.

In the late 17th century, standing salts

tended to lose their peculiar importance and improved standards of living brought into being smaller salts, called trencher salts, often made in pairs, occasionally in sets of four and intended for individual diners. Most treen salts surviving, date from the 18th century; they are remarkable for the variety of timbers employed. Some of these woods are extremely difficult to season; consequently, the stems and feet of some salts are split widely, but never have I seen the crack extend into the bowl. This is interesting because a coating of salt is now recognized as being one of the best means of seasoning refractory timbers.

Treen salts are impossible to date accurately, both on account of time lags in country districts, and also because a turner sometimes copies a shape he likes, a hundred or more years after it was fashionable in silver or other materials. Having said that, here are some dates based largely on analogy with silver or pewter—take some of them with a grain of the contents! In Plate 78, *A, circa* 1700, is unusually elaborately turned from a handsomely marked block of laburnum wood, $5\frac{1}{4}$ in. high. *B* and *C* are 18th-century examples of mahogany, one 6 in. and the other $4\frac{1}{4}$ in. high; both originally had lids. The taller has been altered at some time and its base spoilt. Most of the salts in the bottom row are trencher types, but the majority are formed as miniature standing salts. The left-hand pair, *L*, $3\frac{1}{4}$ in. high, of mahogany, are mid-18th century design. *M*, the squat walnut example, $1\frac{1}{2}$ in. high, dates from 1760–80. *N*, of lignum vitae, is $2\frac{1}{2}$ in. high, and *O*, of fruitwood, probably plum, is $2\frac{1}{4}$ in. high; both follow silver designs of 1710–20. The boxwood salt, *P*, 3 in. high, is a good specimen of 1680–90. Right of the cruet, *Q*, a $3\frac{3}{8}$ in. high, plum or cherrywood salt of drinking cup type, demonstrates how confusing similarity of form can be. This vessel is an authentic salt, its form and exact dimensions being that of a well known pewter salt of 1740–50. *R*, a thistle-shaped,

mahogany salt, $2\frac{3}{8}$ in. high, was probably made about 1760. *S*, of teak, although only $1\frac{7}{8}$ in. high, measures 6 in. in diameter and must, therefore, have served in place of a standing salt. *T* is a 3 in. high capstan-shaped salt of *circa* 1680, made from laburnum.

U, although not a salt, resembles one outwardly and could easily be confused with one. Wooden salts, although varying considerably externally, are all characterized by shallow bowls, necessary because the impure salt became excessively damp in a deep receptacle. Salts in general only vary in depth from $\frac{3}{4}$ in. to $1\frac{1}{2}$ in., according to diameter. The vessel now described, however, is $4\frac{3}{8}$ in. high, of walnut patinated to a warm colour and has a conical bowl $2\frac{3}{8}$ in. deep, tapering to a point. It is one of the now rare stands for 17th-century glass 'tumblers', which were blown to a point.

The four receptacles with covers, *D*, *E*, *F* and *G*, are 18th-century condiment pots. *D* is finely figured laburnum and, like *E* of lignum vitae, shows contrasts between dark heart and light sapwood. *F* and *G* are country-made specimens; the latter, where split, has been repaired carefully with a gut stitch. *H* is a 19th-century pepper grinder of walnut and *J* a pleasingly shaped mid-18th-century boxwood pepper. The muffineer, *K*, is of sycamore, 7 in. high and of a form which, rare in wood, was common in silver *circa* 1700–10; it is almost paper thin and must, I consider, have been made as a pattern for silver or pewter.

The lignum vitae revolving cruet stand, with silver bottle caps, is Scottish hallmarked 1790. Wooden cruet stands are becoming scarce; the greatest rarities are those with hardwood caps to the bottles, as in Plate 79, which probably dates from *circa* 1810.

In the top row of Plate 79, *A*, $5\frac{1}{2}$ in. high, is a muffineer of *circa* 1725 and *B*, the same height, *circa* 1750. *C*, *D* and *E* are 19th century peppers. *F* is a late 19th-century pepper mill; *G* is a French, rosewood rock salt grinder of the traditional type which is still being made and *H* a 19th-century, Scottish, light and dark staved condiment pot. The imposing brown oak salt, *J*, 8½ in. high, is theoretically a 1590 Elizabethan bell salt and the oak may well be as old as that, but its outlines are too harsh and I surmise that it is one of those objects made in the 19th century from the timber of some famous building, ship or tree. *K*, a 5 in. high standing salt of beautifully patinated yew-wood and *O*, a simple but imposing 7 in. high, pearwood standing salt, are both probably authentic early 17th-century survivals. *L* and *N*, of laburnum and mahogany respectively, are probably 18th-century, but the former has had the foot cut down at some time. *M*, of lignum vitae, is a miniature of a late 17th-century wassail bowl. In the bottom row, *P*, a boat-shape, yew-wood salt, is a simplified version of late 18th-century silver; it varies from all the other treen specimens illustrated, in being the work of a carver, not a turner. *Q*, of lignum, appears to be 17th-century; *R* of walnut, and *S*, of cherrywood, I place as 18th-century. *T*, a crude, pole-lathe turned salt and *U*, an equally crude condiment pot, may be of the same period or earlier.

Sauce Bottle Stands

Sauce bottle stands are simply smaller diameter versions of the circular, rimmed coasters used for decanters. Three are illustrated in Plate 62, *T*, *U* and *V*: the first is a simple 19th-century spindle type; the others may be 18th- or early 19th-century examples.

Scoops, Apple and Cheese

There is no clear line of demarcation between apple and cheese scoops. In either, the length of the scoop portion may vary from about 1½ in. to 3 in., and the diameter from ⅜ in. to ⅝ in. Sheep shank apple scoops are found in every layer excavated in Britain from Roman times. Similar scoops, possibly used for other foods, were found by Professor Raymond Dart, of the University of Witwatersrand, while excavating the remains of Middle Stone Age man in South Africa and, therefore, one must assume that it is basically one of the oldest eating utensils in the world. With the knuckle left intact to form a handle, a shortening of the bone to 5 in. or 6 in. and a paring of the lower 1½ in. to 3 in., to leave slightly more than half the wall intact, an efficient scoop or corer was produced. Often the man who did the whittling added some scratch ornament.

Although the main purpose of an apple scoop was to enable one who had lost his or her teeth, to eat a raw apple, the longer ones were also used as efficient apple corers. Those with scoop and handle separate and threaded together, so that when reversed the scoop, which is of different diameter, is encased in the handle or vice versa, were intended for pocket use when travelling. An alternative name for a cheese scoop was a cheese spitter: in some country districts of England, apple scoops are still known as scuppits and there is a superstition that it is unlucky for anyone other than the owner to use one. It was customary, therefore, for the plain bone one, at any rate, to be thrown away on its owner's death; this may, in some measure, explain the large numbers which are excavated.

Scoops range from peasant-carved bone to the sophisticated craftsmanship of the ivory worker and silversmith. Between these two extremes, are both carved wood, and also specimens part wood and part bone, which often show considerable originality of design and skill in execution. The motifs carved on some of them indicate that they were intended as love tokens. Hand-made apple scoops were still commonly used up to the beginning of this century, particularly in apple growing districts, where they were to be found in most of the cottages. The majority of the specimens with dates carved on them are 18th-century, but they vary enormously in skill and design. Not all wood and bone or ivory specimens are carved: some are simple examples of turnery.

In Plate 80 is a good selection, as follows:

A. Natural sheep shank bone, engraved with initials S.W. and date 1747. English.

B. Boxwood scoop, carved with pierced window, heart, spade, diamond and club motifs, various initials and date 1796. English.

C. Boxwood scoop, chip carved and pierced with lanterns. English. 18th-century.

D. Fruitwood(?) scoop, carved and pierced with lanterns. English. 18th-century.

E. Boxwood scoop of unusually fine quality, carved with 8 open hearts and with lanterns and surmounted by an ape's head. On back of scoop, a carved leaf spray, and on sides, initials L.M. and date 1729. An English love token.

F. Rare boxwood scoop, carved with a crowned head and features of both sexes; probably emblematic of William and Mary. It is dated 1690 and carved with initials S.K. English or Welsh.

G. Bone scoop with hardwood handle nicely carved with squirrel and nut. 18th- or early 19th-century. Probably English.

H. Bone scoop with studded ornament, and chip carved yew-wood handle inlaid with a silver heart engraved E.W. 18th- or 19th-century. English or Welsh love token.

J. Bone scoop with boxwood handle, competently carved with crown, initials E.C. and date 1874 and inlaid with red and green composition. English.

K. Chip carved lignum vitae scoop, with lantern and loose ball. Dated 1741. English or Welsh.

L. Rare boxwood combined screw-type nutcracker and apple corer combined. English. 18th-century.

M. and N. These natural sheep shank scoops are impossible to date unless excavated from a layer containing other datable objects. N was excavated in the City of London and is more than 1,000 years old.

O., P. and Q. Turned bone scoops, probably all 18th-century, English. O and Q unscrew and reverse for travelling.

R. Unusual scoop of sycamore with 'basket' handle linked on. The rather crude ornament of flowers, heart, initials A.M.H. and date 1767, are filled with red and green sealing wax. Probably a sailor's love token. English.

S. Crudely carved hardwood scoop; probably 18th-century, sailor's or rustic work. English.

T. Simply turned boxwood scoop. English. 18th-century.

Serviette Rings

Treen serviette rings, Plate 62, A to G, are found in a considerable variety of diameters, moulded sections, and hardwoods. Swiss and Tyrolean specimens are frequently of pearwood and carved. They have also been made in boxwood, lignum vitae, walnut and olivewood; the last, often decorated with a design of circles, are usually Jerusalem souvenirs. Probably none are earlier than about 1880, when silver napkin rings are first recorded. Wooden specimens are frequently carved with numerals, for use in families, or in boarding houses. As mentioned in the introduction to *Eating*, serviettes or napkins, used in polite society during the mediaeval and Tudor periods, tended to become much less usual table appointments when forks came into general use for eating in the 17th century, and this desuetude continued in the 18th century. The French traveller, Faujas de St. Fond, noted, in 1784, that at a dinner of the Royal Society, presided over by Sir Joseph Banks, '... No napkins were laid before us; indeed there were none used; the dinner was truly in the English style.'

Silver Cases—see *Cases for Silver*

Skewers, Garnishing

Four from a set of six lignum vitae, Georgian garnishing skewers, 16 in. long, are illustrated at U in Plate 80. Each is carved with acanthus, but as is usual in the work of the turner, there is some variation in every handle, either in the positioning or number of ring turnings. This pattern was made in silver between 1750 and 1760, but a set in lignum vitae may be unique.

Spoons

Spoons appear under three headings in this volume—kitchen spoons are in Section VII, *Kitchen*, love spoons are in Section IX, *Love Spoons and Other Love Tokens*, and in the present section are eating spoons, ornamental spoons (other than love spoons) and ceremonial spoons. Ornamental and ceremonial spoons are not necessarily eating spoons in the normal sense, but they are described here as a matter of convenience and because there is often a very thin dividing line between them and true eating spoons.

Excluding Welsh love spoons, all other treen spoons formerly made for use in the British Isles, were almost invariably copies of the simplest silver and pewter, entirely devoid of carved or pierced ornament, but often of fine quality. In Plate 81, *A* and *B*, both of sycamore, are Welsh, early 18th-century in style and of the Caernarvon dolphin type, with the curious deepening of the centre part of the handle and acute upturn of the end of the handle. *C* is the finest pair of relatively plain, 18th-century spoons I have ever seen. The two spoons, of boxwood, nest into each other and when conjoined, are no thicker than an ordinary spoon. The spoon on the left, has a groove in the handle; the one on the right, has a matching tongue; both have handles which are semicircular in section. The pair, which are shown nested together in Plate 82, *L*, are inlaid with silver piqué on their handles and slightly carved on and below the knop. I do not know where they were made, but would not be surprised if the craftsman worked in the Aegean area. Alternatively, a refugee craftsman from that area could well have made them in England.

Continuing with Plate 81, *D* is one of a pair of Russian ceremonial spoons of boxwood, with handles encased in silver and translucent enamel; they are probably by Gratchov. Spoons of this type formerly played a part in the Russian and Greek marriage ceremonies. It is possible that some of the ornamentally carved spoons, which will be described in this section, were intended as christening spoons—peasant equivalents of the silver spoons which were commonly given by the wealthy as christening presents. *E* is a rather crude, 18th-century, English folding spoon, knuckle jointed in the middle of the handle. *F*, of sycamore, English, probably 18th-century, is well proportioned. *G* and *H* are described under *Salad Servers*. The Caernarvon crooked spoons, *J* and *K*, of sycamore, 18th- or 19th-century, are traditional and peculiar to Caernarvon; they are said to be particularly useful for teaching small children to eat, as the angle of the bowl, in relation to the handle, facilitates tilting into the mouth, which is true. Some of the typically Welsh porridge or broth spoons with very broad bowls are shown in Plate 147, *B*. The actual examples illustrated are very worn and appear to have some considerable age, but it must be emphasised that this centuries old type is still being made and used in country districts today, especially for eating the bacon and leek broth known as *cawl*.

The boxwood silver-mounted spoon, Plate 81, *M*, is Swedish, probably 17th-century. Lignum vitae teaspoon *N* is a nice, thin, 18th- or 19th-century, English specimen. *O* is one of a set of four sycamore, Caernarvon, dolphin-stemmed egg spoons. The simple boxwood, 18th-century spoon, *P*, is unusual in bearing the crest in silver of Lord Monson of Burton Hall, Lincolnshire; presumably it was a special spoon for some purpose for which silver was unsuitable. The yew-wood spoon, *Q*, is Welsh, 18th- or 19th-century.

In Plate 82, *A, B, G, H* and *J* are all Scandinavian; *A, B* and *H* have the typical acanthus scroll carved and pierced handles found on 18th- and 19th-century work; *H* has the best detailing and workmanship, which includes four free-standing carved twist ropes, which connect the handle to the sharply uptilted bowl; the bowls of *G* and *J* are decorated with wood engraving. Although all these spoons could be used, and *A* and *B* certainly have been, one feels that they were very much 'party pieces'. With *C*, superbly carved, pierced and inlaid with silver pinpoints, the balance goes over from practical to ornamental. St. George slaying the dragon, dolphins, snakes and vines all appear in a border of ribbon knots above a roundel; carved from pearwood and with finely formed, paper-thin, uptilted bowl, this spoon was probably made somewhere in South-east Europe, in the 18th century. It was formerly in the Evan-Thomas Collection.

D, another superbly carved pearwood spoon, with thin, finely formed uptilted bowl, has the handle centred on a sun-head, with hand bent in benediction, above an inverted thistle motif; this may well have been a christening present. It may be Scandinavian, 18th- or 19th-century. *E*, with fish handle, and *F*, carved with roundels, may be of the same provenance and date. *K*, actually a ladle, is Scandinavian and is interesting because of the ingenious selection of twisted burry grain, which has enabled the shaping of a paper-thin, but quite strong side lip. *L* has already been described in connection with Plate 81. Scandinavian spoon *M*, of burr maple, with knopped twist handle and fig-shaped bowl, may be 17th-century. The set of five Swiss Guard spoons, *N*, showing uniforms of different dates, is 19th-century work.

The name of the skilful carver of the 12 spoons in Plate 83 is, unfortunately, unknown. They are a translation into wood sculpture of the favourite subjects engraved by Jaques Callot (1592–1635), born at Nancy. Whilst still a boy, the characteristics which eventually dominated his life became apparent. In due course, they were to make him the first important artist who expressed his artistry and skill solely in engraving and never in painting. He was much attracted by the nomad life and showed masterly skill, attention to detail, and sympathy in his etchings of gypsies, cripples and beggars. He was equally successful in depicting, with satirical humour, the pomp of society of his day. His work conveys a feeling that he delved beneath the surface and studied his subjects from within. It is obvious that his sympathy always lay with the under-dogs and that his underlying aim was to help them by arousing compassion for suffering and want, whilst satirizing the follies of the wealthy. At the age of 12, Callot ran away from home and joined a band of gypsies, with whom he travelled to Florence. Later, he immortalized the features of his gypsy friends in *Les Bohémiens*, engravings published in 1622. He remained in Italy from 1604 to 1622, mostly at Florence and Rome, studying and developing his style and meticulous eye for detail. In 1622, he was invited by Charles, Duke of Lorraine, to return to Nancy and undertake various commissions, which included some of his best landscapes and crowd scenes. He remained at Nancy until 1625, when he went to the Low Countries, to make his large-scale engraving of the *Siege of Breda*. Following completion of this commission in 1628, he was called to Paris by Louis XIII, to engrave the *Siege of La Rochelle*.

About 1630, Callot returned to Lorraine, which for several years was to suffer all the agony of war and political chaos, with their aftermath of misery, maiming, poverty and begging. Callot's experience as eye-witness and artist, provided him with the material for his great dramatic masterpiece, *Les Grandes Misères de la Guerre*, and *Les Gueux* (The Beggars).

Each of the carved spoons is made from a single piece of pearwood. The short necks or stems of their fig-shaped bowls merge into moulded octagonal cappings, forming pedestals for the 12 different and life-like miniature cripples, beggars, itinerant musicians, etc. An interesting feature, adding to their naturalness, is that the statuettes are arranged at various angles in relation to the fronts of the spoon bowls. Except in the literal sense, there is nothing wooden about these sculptured figures; their creator has admirably captured Callot's poses and the facial expressions of the sorry crowd.

The man, *A*, a fruitseller, has two sticks. The woman, *B*, with a basket of circular discs—perhaps biscuits for sale—has her right leg in an iron and uses two sticks. *C* has his left leg in a sling, has lost his right hand, and uses a crutch and a stick. The flute player, *D*, with knapsack on back and dog at feet, is certainly sound in wind and shows nothing wrong with his limbs. The street musician, *E*, appears to have no disability beyond being bandy. The old crone, *F*, has deformed feet and uses a stick in her left hand, a crutch in her right. The musician, *G*, has his right leg bandaged. The sailor(?), *H*, has a badly misshapen left leg and uses crutches. The peasant woman, *J*, has two sticks. The stout elderly man, *K*, who appears to be blind, also has a bandaged left leg; he uses two sticks and has a pilgrim's badge on his cape. The elderly dame, *L*, with water flask in waistbelt, has a deformed right foot and requires two sticks. The woman, *M*, has both feet deformed and uses a stick and a crutch.

K's badge is interesting: I am told by an authority, who has studied the subject deeply, that many of those who wore beggar's garb and pilgrim's badges in the Low Countries in the late 16th century, were not really mendicants, but were members of the Beggars Party, sworn to release the Netherlands from the yoke of Philip II of Spain. They regarded themselves as pilgrims, dedicated to the journey towards freedom.

The boxwood salt spoon, bottom right, Plate 66, has a silver-gilt handle modelled as St. Simon with his saw. It is French,

16th-century. The pearwood spoon, left of Plate 64, is Italian, 17th-century.

Spoons formerly used in church ceremonies are invariably in the fine art class. The anointing spoon, right of Plate 64, is described in Section X, *Miscellany*, under the heading *Religious Objects*.

Spoon Racks—see Section VII, *Kitchen*

Sweetmeat Bowls
Judging by analogy with silver, the handsome and very thinly turned, covered bowl of lignum vitae, middle shelf, right, Plate 61, is correctly described as a Charles II sweetmeat bowl. It appears to be unique and, so far as I know, none of similar type or period exists for comparison, although one or more decoratively carved, covered bowls of boxwood or pearwood, which may have served the same purpose, survive from the Middle Ages. The lignum bowl, so highly polished that it reflects the fruit from the bowl below, is 6 in. high, excluding the knob, and 9½ in. in diameter. The copper band round the rim of the bowl appears to be a later addition, to strengthen it.

Tazzas—see *Bowls, Bread, Fruit and Other Food*

Trays—see Section XX, *Tea, Coffee and Chocolate Drinking Accessories*

Trenchers, Platters and Eating Bowls
Allusions to trenchers being thrown to the dogs, or given to the poor, occur in mediaeval documents and are puzzling unless it is realised that the Normans served their meat on a square slice of bread, known as a *tranche*. It seems probable that at the 'high table', the tranche was always placed on a rectangle of wood known as a trencher. By the 15th century, probably earlier, the squares of bread and the squares of wood, both of which were still being used, were referred to indiscriminately as trenchers.

Elaborate details have come down to us

of the way various types of bread were made, and how cut and placed at table in a noble household. Fine white bread was known as manchet and several different recipes exist for it, but none, I think, earlier than the 16th century. All agree that it was made with finely ground white flour, and it seems to have been usual to include three pints of ale and some salt, to a bushel of meal. Early 15th-century books of manners and procedure tell that 20 loaves went to a London bushel. Whilst we learn that the lord was served with new manchet for eating; his trencher bread of whole meal, which only served to mop up the gravy, had to be kept four days and it was squared up with a special trencher knife. Another special knife was provided for smoothing chipped or worn trenchers. In large households, colleges, etc., a menial was employed, known as 'scrape trencher'.

When the bread under meat custom died out, the smooth, flat, rectangular, wooden trencher, most likely of beech, which let the gravy run off, must have proved very unsatisfactory. It was probably not long before someone had the bright idea of 'turning' a circular hollow for the meat in the centre of the square and a smaller round sinking for salt in one corner. Survivals of square trenchers with one large and one small sinking are now extremely rare and valuable, although 3 dozen were valued at 9d. the lot in a 1638 inventory. Even rarer are similar trenchers with a handle extension on one edge, making them the shape of a horn-book; they may have been used by invalids or small children, taking their meal away from table. One of each type is shown, bottom right, Plate 84. The one with handle, of elm, is even more worn and scored on the back than on the face. The back has a corner salt cavity but none for meat and my theory is that this is such an early piece that what is now the back was originally used in the days of bread on wood. When it became too worn for further use, say around 1500, perhaps it was con-

sidered worth turning, because of the handle. Certain it is that the main circle was made after the board had completed its width shrinkage, for the cavity still remains near enough a true $5\frac{1}{2}$ in. circle, which is very unusual in something as old as this must be.

The other square trencher with salt cavity also shows the care with which these humble objects were sometimes treated, for where it has split, it has been held on the face with two copper rivets and plated with copper on the back. The main circular cavity of this specimen has shrunk nearly $\frac{3}{16}$ in. in its width; it is one of two in the Pinto Collection, which are part of a set which were formerly in the Evan-Thomas Collection and are identifiable as a set by reason of rather unusual grain, colouring and dimensions; the remaining 10 or more are scattered in various collections. Age, wear and discoloration make identification of the wood uncertain, but it could be a rather unusually marked sycamore. It is sometimes contended that sycamore was only introduced to England in the 16th century, because the first mention of it occurs in a herbal of that period. Others believe that it was planted here by the Romans. I find the first contention completely negative.

In the 17th century, the last change from trencher to platter took place; the square was cut away, leaving a rimmed circular sinking—the trencher had become a platter, although the two terms remained synonymous, the platter sometimes being described as a round trencher. In homes of the wealthy, the wooden platter was rapidly superseded by silver, pewter and glazed pottery, and later by china. The wooden platter, by now usually of sycamore, a good wood for scraping and scrubbing without splintering, lingered on in schools, cottages and servants' halls until the beginning of this century. Whilst, in general, patterns of wood rims changed with fashions in metal and ceramics, this is only a generalization, because country folk and turners are conservative people, who tend to disregard fashion, particularly when change brings no improvement. Certain districts and houses, too, long maintained their own special designs in wooden platters. The Fitzwilliams, Lords of Wentworth, retained their own distinctive platters or trenchers in the servants' hall of Wentworth Woodhouse. These platter-trenchers, stamped on their backs W.F. for Wentworth Fitzwilliam are ovals of sycamore, enclosing a circular sinking, top left, Plate 84. The design is good, for it leaves a wide rim at each end for condiments, whilst allowing a long edge to come close to the edge of the table, tight up to the eater. A photograph and description of one of these platters published recently, brought me an interesting letter from a lady of over 70, whose parents lived on the Fitzwilliam estate, when she was a child, the father working for the Earl and paying 2s. per week rent for his 'cottage' (her quotes) of seven rooms. On half-yearly rent days, the family were all given dinner in the servants' hall at Wentworth Woodhouse. Referring to the wooden trenchers, she writes:

'I will never forget having meat and veg on one side and turning it over for the rice pudding served on the other side. Happy days, no pep pills needed'.

The other platters in Plate 84 probably all date from the 18th century, in spite of their varieties of rims, and all are English and of sycamore, except for the second from the left, middle row, which is one of a very highly finished set of six, turned from brown burry pollard oak; these have the flat parts of their backs riveted on to a $\frac{3}{8}$ in. thick disc of ebony. They may be German, 18th-century, dessert plates.

Another wooden dinner service of yesteryear, of which two examples are shown at the bottom of Plate 84, is much more difficult to fit into chronological order. It originally consisted of 60 or more elm eating bowls, now scattered into smaller sets, but all apparently emanating originally from the same Sussex farmhouse. What is particularly unusual about them is that each 'log bowl' consists of a 3 in. thick horizontal slice of the tree, so that the eating surface is on end grain—this is a turnery technique very unusual in Europe, although common in the East and Middle East. The blocks are turned into shallow hollows, $1\frac{1}{2}$ in. to $1\frac{3}{4}$ in. at the centre and the bases are stepped in sharply, giving a silhouette similar both to wooden bowls dug up in Middle East excavations of 4,000 years ago and also some shown in Pieter Breughel the Elder's 16th-century peasant paintings. This set of bowls appears to vary considerably in age, possibly by as much as 200 years, and this suggests that when they split radially, as one would expect them to do and as many of them have done, they were replaced by others of similar type and wood, thus carrying on the tradition of this particular farmhouse. All except five of these log bowls are approximately 7 in. in diameter; the five small ones, approximately $4\frac{1}{2}$ in. in diameter, may have been used by children, or they may be salts.

V

Farm

Wooden bygones of the farm are grouped alphabetically under two main headings: (A) *Agricultural and General*; (B) *Dairy*. Although a brief general introduction is given to each section, no attempt has been made to write a technical farm history, and attention is drawn to the list of books for further reading.

(A) AGRICULTURAL AND GENERAL

The general and agricultural part of this section is necessarily limited to smaller objects of the farm, as wains, wagons and ploughs, other than breast ploughs, are outside the scope of this book. Wooden objects used in the farm brewhouse, butchery and in thatching are described in Section XXV, *Trade Devices*.

Collectors may find considerable variations between their own specimens and some illustrated, because many tools used were made either on the farm, or by a craftsman in the locality; as a result, devices differed according to terrain, type of farming practised, custom and, to some extent, even in ready availability of certain woods. Different counties also had their own local name for the same tool. Some of these different names travelled, in due course, with the colonists to North America, but in a few instances, a new name was given to an old tool in the New World.

Apple Parers

Early apple parers were of wood, except for the fork on which the apple was impaled and the special blade with which it was pared. Early in the 19th century, cast iron machines for paring apples were introduced; their use gradually spread from town to country, superseding the ingenious, individually made, wooden devices, which were essentials before the days of cold storage, when peeling and cutting of apples into rings, to dry for winter usage, was an important autumn job. I have never seen an English-made wooden apple parer, but a number of different types have survived in the U.S.A. Some were made as benches, on which the operator sat; others were clamped on tables. A particularly well made 19th-century specimen, which could be used in either manner, is shown in Plate 86, *J*. When placed with the extension board across a stool, the operator held it down by sitting on it, and the working end projected out over the apple paring bucket. The apple on the fork was revolved by one hand turning the handle of the belt drive, whilst the other pared with the razor-like blade.

Bells and Calls, Sheep, Cow, etc.

A clucket or sheep bell for the 'bell wether', with original bentwood neck hoop and leather suspension strap, is pictured in Plate 85, *D*. A shepherd's dog whistle,

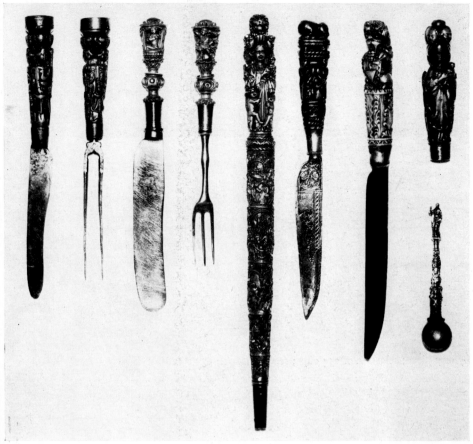

66 Selection of finely carved boxwood cutlery handles; for details, see text (*Section IV*). The centre handle is described in *Section X, Miscellany: Fine Art*.

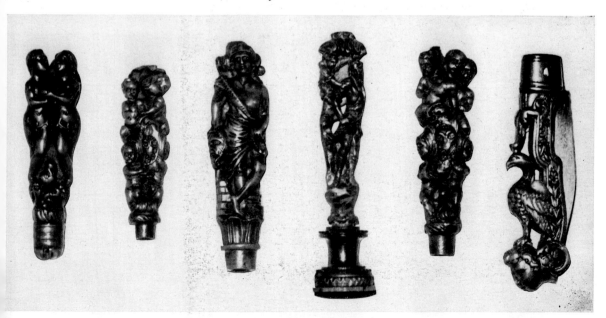

67 Four fine quality, carved boxwood cutlery handles; for details, see text (*Section IV*). Also two penknives, described in *Section XVII, Reading, Writing, etc.*

68 A mystery piece; selection of egg cups; serving board; egg stands. (*Section IV*)

69 16th-, 17th- and 18th-century, boxwood, lever nutcrackers, described in the text. (*Section IV*)

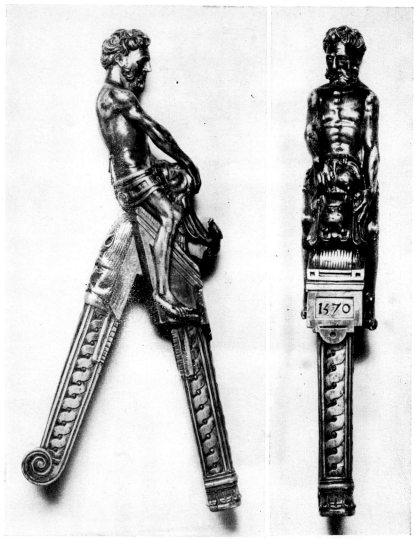

Boxwood lever nutcracker, carved
a ogre; *circa* 1500. (*Section IV*)

71 Boxwood lever nutcracker, depicting Hercules astride the Nemean lion. A
superb example dated 1570. (*Section IV*)

72 A selection of 14 screw nutcrackers and 2 lever types, all described in text. (*Section IV*)

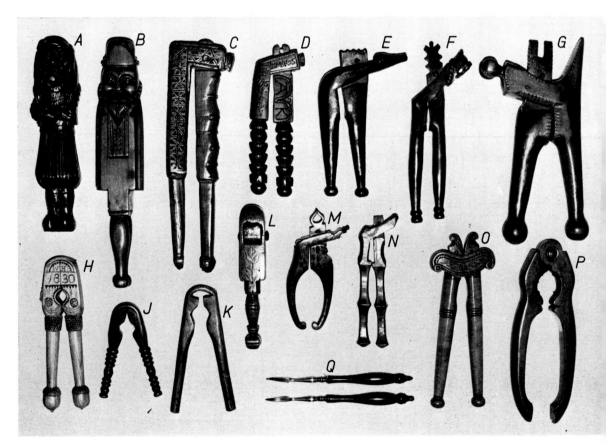

73 Lever, cross-over, and natural sprung wood types of nutcrackers and a pair of nut picks. For details, see text. (*Section IV*)

74 Six 18th-century lever nutcrackers and, at the bottom of the picture, the back of the 1574 nutcracker illustrated in Plate 69. *B.* (*Section IV*)

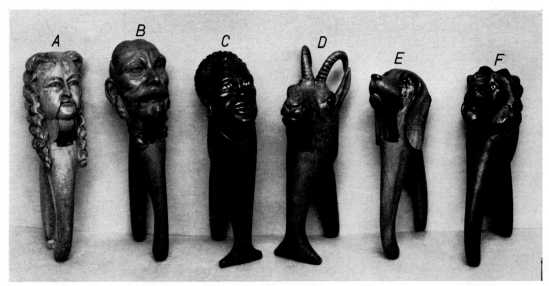

75 19th- and 20th-century, Swiss and Tyrolean ornamental lever nutcrackers. (*Section IV*)

76 A remarkable set of Elizabethan roundels of oblong shape, with their original book type container, all in mint condition. *Photograph by courtesy of the Ashmolean Museum, Oxford, where the roundels are on loan from the Bodleian. (Section IV)*

77 A fine set of Tudor roundels, with box and cover. Probably second quarter of the 16th century. *Photograph by courtesy of the Victoria and Albert Museum. (Section IV)*

78 Salts and condiments, mainly 18th century. For details, see text. (*Section IV*)

79 Salts and condiments, mainly 18th century. For details, see text. (*Section IV*)

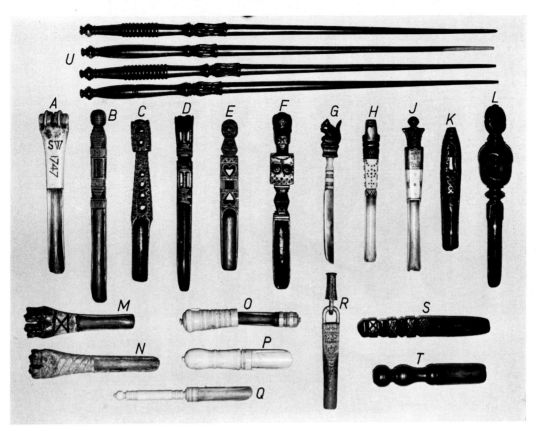

80 Four from a set of six lignum vitae garnishing skewers and a selection of apple and cheese scoops of the 18th and earlier centuries. (*Section IV*)

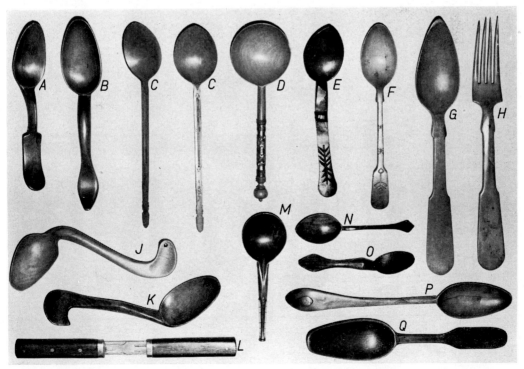

81 Selection of eating spoons, forks, etc. All except *D*, *M* and probably *C*, are English or Welsh. (*Section IV*)

82 Ornamental treen spoons from various parts of Europe. For details, see text. (*Section IV*)

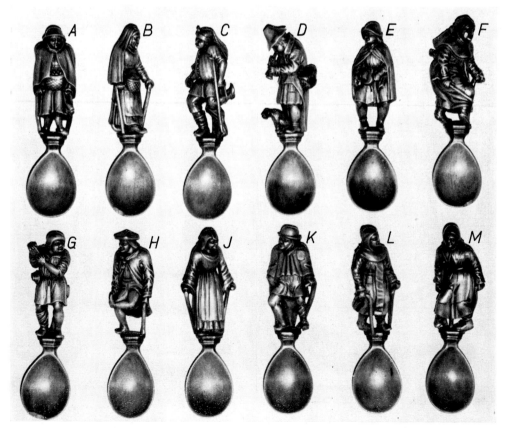

83 A rare and skilfully carved set of pearwood spoons, based on the engraving of cripples and beggars by Jacques Callot (1592–1635). (*Section IV*)

84 TOP ROW: planter from Wentworth Woodhouse and a well dish, both of sycamore. MIDDLE ROW: selection of treen platters. BOTTOM ROW: another platter, two very unusual eating bowls and two rare 16th-century trenchers with salt cavity. (*Section IV*)

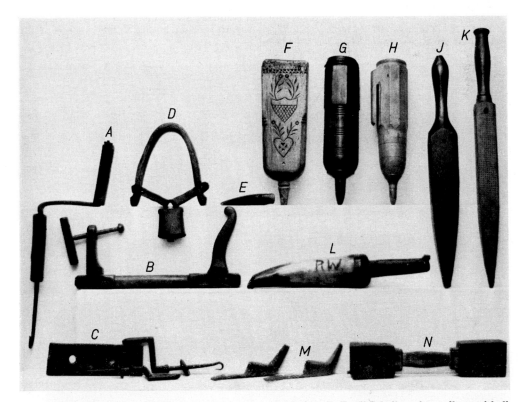

85 *A* and *B*, English wimbels; *C*, English corn stook binder; *D*, English bell wether collar and bell; *E*, English shepeherd' swhistle; *F*, *G* and *H*, Swiss hone boxes; *J* and *K* English strickles; *L*, cattle drenching horn; *M*, finger protectors, when using a sickle, Scottish; *N*, Swiss cow call. (*Section V*)

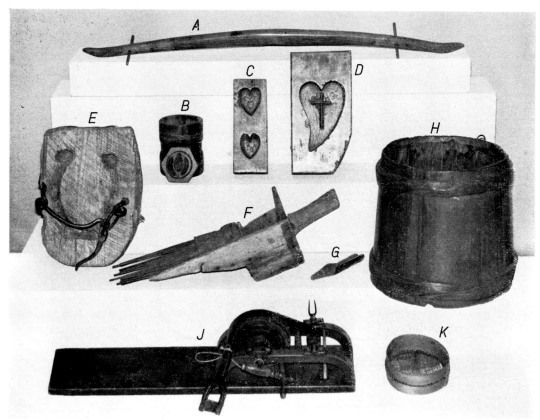

86 *Americana: A*, gambrel (*Section XXV*); *B*, unusual hexagonal butter mould from Maine; *C* and *D* Canadian maple sugar moulds; *E*, horse mud shoe used in cranberry swamps of Wisconsin; *F*, blueberry 'salt box' rake, used in the swamps in Maine; *G* and *H*, maple sap spout and bucket, Canadian; *J*, American hand-made apple parer; *K*, 'Shaker' hair sieve. (*Section V*)

87 *A*, corn shaul; *B, C, D* and *E*, selection of scoops; *F*, flail; *G*, hay fork; *H*, kneeling mat; *J*, seed lip. All English. (*Section V*)

88 and 89 Ox yokes from New Hampshire and Virginia, U.S.A. *In the Collection of Mr. and Mrs. James A. Keillor.* (*Section V*)

90 Ox yoke from Connecticut River Valley, also in the *Keillor Collection.* (*Section V*)

91 English ox yoke, from Buckfastleigh, Devon. *By courtesy of the Museum of English Rural Life, Reading.* (*Section V*)

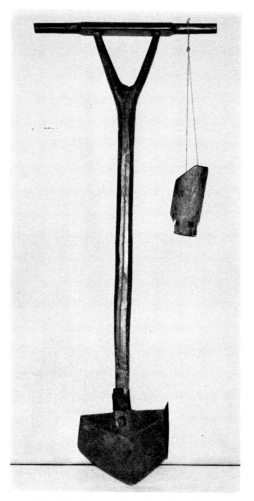

92 English breast plough. Probably 18th century. (*Section V*)

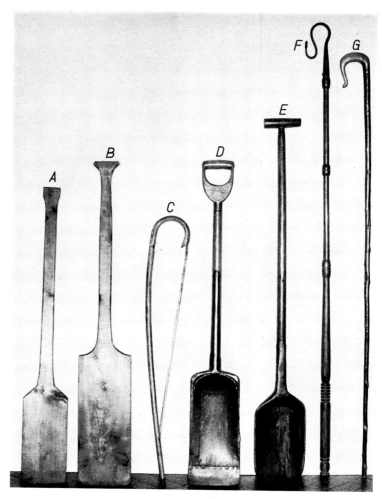

93 *A* and *B*, snow spades; *C*, ashwood saw stick; *D*, mud scuppit; *E*, grain shovel; *F*, Pyecombe, Sussex, shepherd's crook; *G*, one-piece hazel shepherd's crook. (*Section V*)

94 Oak dog tongs. Welsh. (*Section V*)

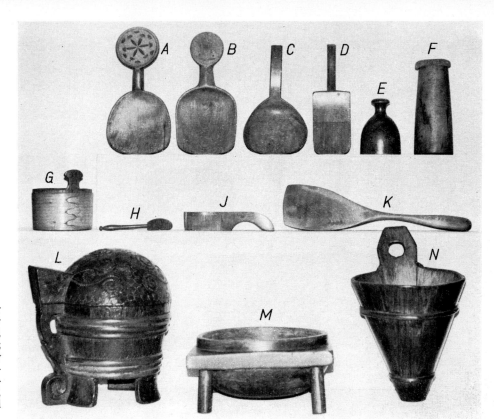

5 *A*, *B* and *C*, butter
scoops: *D*, *H* and *J*, butter
slices and curls; *E* and *F*,
butter cups; *G*, milk piggin;
I, cream stirrer; *M*, whey
bowl. All the aforementioned are English. *L*, Scandinavian butter mould, *N*,
Swiss benediction horn and
milk sieve (*Section V*)

6 *A* and *J*, butter workers; *B*, *C*, *D*, *E* and *F*,
butter hands; *G* and *H*,
milk skimmers; *K* and *L*,
dairy thermometers; *M*,
mealey begs, or butter
bowls. All from the British
Isles. (*Section V*)

97 Selection of cheese vats or chessels, and dairy bowls. English. (*Section V*)

98 Irish bog butter container and swinging churn. (*Section V*)

which may be of horn or wood, is shown at E. The cow call, N, is Tyrolean, chip carved and hollowed out of one piece. It has four wooden clappers in each 'bell' and makes a castanet-like sound when shaken.

Blueberry Rakes

The harvesting of lowbush blueberries, which begins in Maine in late July and August, is gradually being mechanized. Since about 1882, it has been carried out by hand, with special all-metal rakes of dustpan type, invented by Franklin P. Tabbut of Columbia Falls. Prior to that date, the old wooden 'salt box' rake, as Plate 86, F, was used. The closely placed steel tines or prongs (there are 18 in the specimen illustrated) project $6\frac{3}{4}$ in. beyond their iron sheath. The rake is used with an upward tilt, so that the blueberries are shaken into the pine box at the back, which has a sieve mesh bottom to let any debris fall through. The rake is $14\frac{1}{2}$ in. long, excluding the handle, and 6 in. wide; the box is 5 in. deep at the back.

Breast Ploughs

The breast plough, Plate 92, is one of the most ancient and now one of the rarest surviving agricultural tools. Its use, by gripping the handles and pressing the chest forward in a series of jerks against the 17 in. long breast bar or cross handle, constituted one of the heaviest farming tasks. Its basic form is believed to go back to Saxon times. The breast plough did not plough a furrow in the sense of a horse or mechanical plough; it did no more than pare and cleanse the top soil, which, if stony, administered severe jarring to the ploughman. Tough and sturdy though he was, he needed protection and his equipment included either a board slung round his waist, or a pair of wooden clappers, worn in front of the thighs. One of these survives and is shown in the picture; it measures $10\frac{1}{2}$ in. by $4\frac{1}{2}$ in., is hollowed out of elm and, near the bottom, has the remains of the leather strap

which buckled round the legs; near the top are two holes for the cord loop, with which the clappers were suspended from a waist belt, to avoid leg slip.

The 4 ft. 6 in. long haft of the plough is of elm, carefully selected with a balanced natural fork at the top, which tenons into the breast bar or cross bar handle. The plough blade itself is steel, with a right-angled 'counter' or sharp edged, forward projecting blade at one side. The main blade is 12 in. wide by $10\frac{1}{2}$ in. long to the point or pricket. These breast ploughs are very individual and blade dimensions vary. Total height of the plough is about 5 ft. 3 in., but it can be varied to suit the height of the ploughman, by means of iron wedges in the metal loop of the plough blade. This specimen is probably 18th-century; earlier ones tended to be 5 ft. or more in the haft.

Corn Shauls and Strikes

The 28 in. long by 10 in. wide beechwood corn shaul, Plate 87, A, is a skilful example of craftsmanship, gracefully scooped out of a 4 in. thick block and now well patinated. Corn shauls served a dual purpose: for scooping grain into a wood measure, and then for using the front straight edge as a strike for levelling off the grain. Strikes are shown in use in Egyptian stone carvings of 5,000 years ago. See also Section XIX, *Scientific: Measures of Volume*

Cow Calls—see *Bells and Calls*

Crooks, Shepherds'—see *Shepherds' Crooks*

Curry Combs

The 19th-century curry comb, Plate 105, A, consists of an ash handle fitted at a right angle to a curved iron blade, $5\frac{3}{4}$ in. long, toothed on both edges, and with a further toothed blade riveted in centrally, to form a third parallel comb, with teeth running 8 to 1 in. On a horse curry comb, the teeth are longer, run 9 to 1 in., on a flat back plate which has 4 or 6 combs on it, plus a centre spine without teeth. For horse curry combs, see Section XV, *Pastimes: Accessories of the Horse*.

Dog Tongs

In former times, farmers used to take their dogs to church; the custom seems to have pertained particularly to Wales. If the dogs commenced to fight, they were removed with a pair of dog tongs, kept handily suspended on a wall or pillar of the church. Some are still *in situ* in Welsh churches. The majority of dog tongs were iron; wooden ones are very rare. A good oak specimen is illustrated, Plate 94. It has short iron spikes in the claws, which gripped in the sheep dog's thick coat. Closed, it measures 26 in. by 7 in.; open, as illustrated, it extends to approximately 51 in. Some churches also had a dog door—an opening about 30 in. high, through which the offending animal could be ejected. One still survives at Mullion, Cornwall.

Dog Whistles—see *Bells and Calls*, also Section XV, *Pastimes: Sport;* and Section II, *Costume Accessories: Walking Sticks*

Drenchers—see *Hone Boxes, Strickles and Horns*

Farm Measures—see Section XIX, *Scientific: Reckoning, Measuring, etc.*

Finger Protectors

The finger protectors, Plate 85, *M*, each carved and gouged from a single piece of pearwood, are Scottish, probably 19th-century and were used to safeguard the fingers of the left hand, when using a sickle in the right. I have only seen three of them.

Flails

The flail has great antiquity for threshing or thrashing grain, beans, etc. It was used in the more remote parts of the British Isles until the First World War and was always individually made and of a weight to suit the user. It is still used commonly in Korea and other parts of the Far East. Alternative names for it included frail, nile, drashel, stick and a half, and 'Joseph and Mary'. A flail, see Plate 87, *F*, has three parts: the hand staff, which is held in the hand whilst swinging the shorter stick, the swingel or tail top; the two are connected together by a very strong and ingeniously constructed universal joint. The hand staff is usually of hazel or ash; the swingel is almost invariably of thorn, because the knobbly thorn knots are functional in the threshing. The joint, known as a teme, consists of the revolving, looped handstaff cap, skilfully made from steamed bent hazel, bound with tarred twine, which is connected to the leather cap of the swingel by a laced loop made of eel, snake or pig skin, or horse or cow hide. The flail had to be used with strokes spaced out, so men usually worked in pairs, delivering alternate strokes. Apart from the muscular need for the respite, the teme would have been overheated if used continuously, nonstop. It is said that this originated the saying 'Setting the temes on fire' which in due course became 'Setting the Thames on fire'.

A heavier version of a flail, with an iron swingel, connected to the hand staff by a chain, was formerly used in the building industry around Collyweston, Northamptonshire. It was known as a thrale or thrail, and was employed by the slaters to beat up their mortar which, like the slates, was made from the local limestone. The objective was to create air entrainment, or small air bubbles, which, by requiring less water in the mix, adds to the strength. The same method had been used by the Romans; now it is achieved by chemical additives to the mix.

Flour and Grain Scoops—see *Scoops*

Forks

Wooden forks can be grown, or made like the traditional English ashwood hay fork,

Plate 87, *G*, which is split, wedged and nailed through the wedge and just above it, to prevent the split travelling further. In England, a third prong was sometimes cut and wedged or inserted, instead of a wedge. Both English and continental 'grown' forks may have three, four or five tines, each being a branch carefully trained from the main stem. Those which I have seen were mostly grown in France and in the Iberian Peninsula and were made from a variety of elm. By careful training, pollarding and shaping of the growing tree, the tines are grown parallel; they are tapered almost to a point, and the outline is practically that of a conventional manure fork. The forestry fork industry, of considerable antiquity, has practically died out now, but I believe survives in the island of Majorca.

The collection of wooden forks in the the Durell Farm Museum of the Union Fork and Hoe Company, at Columbus, U.S.A., shows the versatility of the early colonists in the making and forming of forks with from four to seven tines, from ash, hickory and black walnut. In some examples, the main stem or handle is split and splayed out into four or more tines or fingers, held into a fan shape by cross dowelling and pinning. Others have the centre stem split in two and an additional tine splayed on at each side. One ingenious specimen has a malleable iron collar on the end of the handle, fitted with a cross bar, which incorporates smaller collars for four replaceable tines.

Hair Sieves—see *Sieves*

Hay Forks—see *Forks*

Hay Rakes—see *Rakes*

Hone Boxes, Strickles and Horns
A necessary accompaniment to the sickle and scythe, which needed continuous sharpening, was either a whetstone, often shortened into hone, and a hone box, or

alternatively a strickle and a grit and grease container. In the British Isles, the whetstone was either carried in a special pocket, or a leather sheath slung from the belt. In Switzerland and the Austrian Tyrol, a decorative, one-piece wooden hone box was used, Plate 85, *F*, *G* and *H*. The first may be 18th-century, the other two, 19th-century, but all are traditional in form, measure approximately 12 in. overall and each is provided with a grooved belt loop and a spike for pressing into the ground, near the place of work.

Strickles, streics, rifles, ryfles or scythe boards, Plate 85, *J* and *K*, are wooden alternatives to whetstones or hones. *J* and *K* are English and *K* is dimpled all over, to give a better holding surface for the grease and grit; it is said that the dimpled effect was usually obtained by tapping the surface repeatedly with a saw blade. *J* is $17\frac{1}{2}$ in. long, *K*, 20 in. American and French versions were flatter, did not taper and looked more like razor hones. The grease, usually bacon fat, and sand or crushed gritstone, were generally carried in a cow horn, similar to Plate 85, *L*, but with a lid instead of a handle. When closed at one end and shaped with a tapering cut at the other, like *L*, it was used as a cattle drencher, for dosing cattle.

Horse Mud Shoes
Elmwood horse mud shoes, with iron staples, as Plate 86, *E*, were used to give a horse better bearing in the cranberry swamps of Wisconsin, U.S.A. and also when cutting marsh hay. It measures $11\frac{1}{2}$ in. by 9 in. and is 1 in. thick; the impression of the horseshoe can be clearly seen. Similar devices were used in the English Fen country and were known as Fen overshoes.

Key Indicators
In days when farm labourers were illiterate, it was useless to label the keys of the pigsty, cow byre, turnip store, etc. In an Elizabethan farmhouse in Sussex, the difficulty was

overcome by having key markers, each made from an entirely different and, therefore, easily recognizable, natural honeysuckle twist, as Plate 105, *G*.

Kneeling Mats
The traditional U-shaped elm kneeling mat or 'kneeler', Plate 87, *H*, had many uses on the farm. It was also used until early in this century in the house, not least by the visiting 'step woman', who called at houses in a street and hearthstoned the front door steps.

Maple Sap Buckets and Spouts
A maple sap bucket of coopered pine, bound with hazel(?) and painted red externally, is shown, Plate 86, *H*. The wire loop, for suspending it on a nail below the sap incision in the tree, can be seen in the photograph; the bucket, 10½ in. high, is approximately 10 in. diameter at top and 11¾ in. at bottom. Plate 86, *G*, shows the 6½ in. long, ashwood spout, which was inserted in the aperture in the tree and guided the sap into the bucket. In recent years, wooden spouts and buckets have been replaced by metal. Both the bucket and spout are from Canada, but similar ones were used in the U.S.A. A tree to be tapped is usually at least 50 years old and the average yield from one tapping is 5 lb., but up to 14 lb. has been known.

Maple Sugar Moulds
Shown at Plate 86, *C* and *D*, are two early 19th-century, carved wood moulds for maple sugar, from Quebec Province, Canada. The motifs of the Sacred Heart of Jesus and the Emblems of the Passion, carved in the moulds, tie up with the Holy Week ceremonies of the Roman Catholic church, and generally coincide with 'sugaring-off time' in Quebec. For details of mould carving, see Section XII, *Moulds*.

Mud Shoes—see *Horse Mud Shoes*

Mud Shovels—see *Shovels*

Ox Muzzles
Ox muzzles of steamed and bent wood were formerly in common use in many countries. The two different patterns illustrated, Plate 108, are traditional Portuguese.

Ox Yokes
Plates 88–91 clearly exemplify some of the considerable differences there are in shapes and degree of finish of ox yokes from different countries and districts. The first three are from the U.S.A.; the last is English. Some, from parts of Europe and Asia, are different again. There are also great variations in weight. Plate 88 is a heavily ironed yoke from New Hampshire, used for pulling a stone boat. It is said that the pair of oxen weighed 5,500 lb., and they must have been very powerful, for the 5 ft. 1 in. long, elm yoke weighs 94 lb. The large ring was for the pole; the smaller one had a chain connected to the boat (sled), or a second team of oxen in front. Plate 89, cruder, with square-cut end, is from Virginia; it is 1 in. shorter and weighs 76 lb. Plate 90 is a Connecticut River Valley yoke of elm, painted blue. It is a particularly gracefully shaped type, with fine bevels. It is 5 ft. 3 in. long and weighs 57 lb. The bows of these three yokes are all of hickory, steamed and bent on a wooden form. Plate 91 is a typical English yoke from Buckfastleigh, Devon. It is made of ash, is 4 ft. 4 in. long and weighs 35 lb. This particular one has iron bows, but more often they are of steamed ash.

Peat Cutters
A peat cutter is a square-ended spade of normal length, with a right-angled, forward projecting blade at one side, like the breast plough. Thus, it is used to detach a block of peat simultaneously from the line behind and at the side of it. It looks somewhat like a smaller breast plough (see Plate 92), but

with a normal handle and without the point to the main blade.

Ploughs—see *Breast Ploughs*

Rakes

The craft of the wooden rake maker is an ancient one and, like the hay rake itself, probably remained virtually unchanged from mediaeval times until the First World War. Now, in Great Britain, it has practically died out. Tools and equipment were few and simple, but skill was needed to make the rake strong, light and suited to the terrain, for sloping fields required the head set at an angle to the stem. Details of the entirely different patterns of rakes and woods used for them, in various localities of Great Britain, will be found in *Traditional Country Crafts* and *Woodland Crafts in Britain* (see *For Further Reading*).

Root Cutting Boards

The introduction and gradual increase throughout the 18th century, in the growing of root crops for animal winter feed, led to the importance of the well worn root cutting board, such as Plate 105, *J*. It consists of a block of beech, $2\frac{1}{8}$ in. thick by 12 in. by $5\frac{3}{4}$ in., with a pivoted, slightly curved knife or splitting chopper, which falls into a parsnip shaped depression. See also Section I, *Apothecary*, and Section VII, *Kitchen*, for other cutting and chopping boards, and Section XXII, *Tobacco Accessories*, for plug cutters.

Salve Bowls—see *Sheep Salve Bowls*

Saw Sticks

The ashwood, crook-handled walking stick, Plate 93, *C*, has a groove in the stem, a pivoted metal loop in the handle and a saw blade which, at rest, nests, teeth inward, in the groove where it is held by a sliding catch at the top. The blade is fixed at the bottom on a swivelling pivot and has a cross-pin at the top; when it is tilted out and swung round, by pressing on the handle, the cross-pins on the saw engage firmly in the metal loop. It is a serviceable tool for removing small branches, or cutting ivy off trees. It is probably a 19th-century device.

Scoops, General

A selection of general-purpose wooden scoops is illustrated, Plate 87, *B*, *C*, *D* and *E*. Obviously they were not restricted to a form and might be used domestically, in a corn chandler's, a grocer's shop or many other places. Specimen *B*, of sycamore, has the remains of a patent number, indecipherable, on it. I believe it is an American patent. This type of wooden scoop was used particularly for filling bags with tea, sugar, etc. It was later superseded by the same pattern in metal. See also *Shovels*.

Scuppits—see *Shovels*

Seed Lips and Seed Cups

The traditional English seed lip or leper, for broadcasting seed, is of bent ash or oak, kidney-shaped, with an inserted, nailed pine bottom, as in Plate 87, *J*, which is 24 in. by $12\frac{1}{2}$ in. wide by $8\frac{1}{4}$ in. deep. The lip is usually bored with two holes, or fitted with two rings, on the concave side, for suspension by a cord round the neck; the concave side fits snugly across the abdomen. It was steadied with one hand holding the convex rim, or a handle on it, whilst the seed was broadcast with the other. The example illustrated has obviously had plenty of use but neither has, nor ever has had suspension hooks or holes, or a handle, so it would appear that some of these seed lips were probably suspended in some kind of sling; a few seed lips were straight sided, oblong boxes. Probably coming long before the bent wood seed lip, was one made of coiled straw ropes, but its use continued, although on a decreasing scale, throughout the 19th century.

A turned wooden seed cup, for broadcasting very small seed, is shown, Plate 105,

H; it is 2 in. high and 2 in. in diameter. Near the rim of the cup is a small hole for distributing the seed; in use, the hand covered the cup, from which the seed was shaken out through the hole.

Sheep Bells—see *Bells and Calls*

Sheep Branding Irons

Typical 19th-century sheep branding irons are illustrated, Plate 105, *D* and *E*. These are from a farm near my home. The letter and figure, which appear in reverse, have iron tags spiked into wood handles, but sometimes the handle is merely a continuation of the iron tang. Of considerable interest is the crude reverse letter P, fret cut or gouged out of wood and nailed on a 5¾ in. by 2¼ in. wood block, Plate 105, *F*. It came from a New England farm and was used with red paint for stamping an ownership initial on cattle, a very necessary precaution with common grazing or lack of fixed boundaries.

Sheep Dipping Troughs

The illustration of Cooper's all-wood sheep dip bath, Plate 109, is self-explanatory. It was made between 65 and 100 years ago, but had been repainted before photography. It stands 2 ft. 0 in. high and is 4 ft. 6 in. by 2 ft. 5 in. at the top, tapering to the base. In large measure, it superseded sheep salve dressings.

Sheep Salve Bowls

Sheep salve bowls were traditionally oval, and gouged from a single block of suitable hardwood. Of the two illustrated, Plate 105, *K* and *L*, the former is of beech, 7¼ in. by 5 in. by 2¾ in.; the latter is of walnut and measures 9½ in. by 8¼ in. by 2¾ in. Each has holes in the base for fixing it on the low trestle on which the salving operation took place. Both these specimens came from the Cumberland and Westmorland district and may be 18th- or 19th-century. Before the days of sheep dipping, sheep salving was a regular form of winter protection, particularly in the North of England; the Salvers' Meet at Wasdale Head was an annual event of great antiquity. According to an old recipe, the sheep, having been laid across a trestle on which the salver sat astride, was smeared with a mixture of butter or lard, sulphur, beeswax and tar. The purpose was both to protect against the weather and reduce the incidence of scab.

Shepherds' Crooks

Shepherds' crooks must be among the oldest implements in the world, and as they rather tend to be regarded as family heirlooms, they sometimes attain greater antiquity than do other wooden bygones of outdoor life. It is doubtful if the ancient crook ever differed much from the comparatively modern hazel example, unpeeled except at the head, Plate 93, *G*, which is 4 ft. 10 in. high. Other woods commonly used in like manner were ash and willow. Pyecombe, a small village in Sussex, has been famous for crooks with iron hooks, from the 18th century or earlier. Pyecombe crooks are known and used in every part of the world where there are sheep farms. The head was preferably made from the barrel of an old muzzle loader and so designed as to enable a sheep to be caught by the neck without injury; the blunt hook of the end of the crook has the right sized opening to catch a 'Southdown' by its hind leg. For a North of England sheep, a different sized hook is needed. The 19th-century Pyecombe crook, Plate 93, *F*, is 5 ft. 2 in. tall and has a Douglas fir turned shaft.

Shepherds' Whistle—see *Bells and Calls*

Shovels and Spades

Wooden spades and shovels were formerly made in a wide variety of designs, some general purpose, but others for specific uses. Plate 93, *A* and *B*, are two from a set of different size pinewood snow spades. Our generation, which has learnt so much, has also forgotten a lot, including, apparently, the fact that snow cakes up on an iron blade, but slides off a wooden one! Plate 93, *D*, is an iron shod and iron reinforced one-piece ashwood mud scuppit or spade from Burwash, Sussex. Scuppits are a traditional tool for ditching. Plate 93, *E*, is an ashwood grain shovel, formerly known in South-east England as a slailing shovel. For malt shovels, see Section XXV, *Trade Devices, Brew House.*

Snow Spades—see *Shovels and Spades*

Spades—see *Shovels and Spades*

Sieves
The most interesting of the steamed wood rimmed sieves used in the kitchen and on the farm are those hand woven with a mesh of hair made from horses' manes or cows' tails. They vary in size from the 4½ in. diameter specimen, Plate 86, *K*, up to 24 in. or even more. They were highly valued and carefully kept, for many hours of fine work went into each, but few have survived. There seems no difference between English, continental and American specimens. The example illustrated was made by the Shakers in New England.

Straw Twisters—see *Wimbels*

Strickles—see *Hone Boxes*

Strikes—see *Corn Shauls*

Thraa-crooks or Throw Hooks—see *Wimbels*

Wimbels
Wimbels are essentially cranked devices for twisting ropes out of straw, formerly required for binding corn stooks or shocks, making hay stacks, in some operations of thatching, and for many other country purposes. Other country names for them include wimbrels, straw twisters, thraa-crooks, throw hooks, hay-band winders, and, in Cornwall, winks. Two different English types are shown, Plate 85, *A* and *B*. The corn stook binder, Plate 85, *C*, was a follow-on device, used in the actual binding of the corn stook. It consists of a piece of board, approximately 7 in. by 2¼ in. by ½ in., with two holes bored through. A length of straw rope, previously formed in a loop at each end, was passed round the stook and through the holes in the board; two men, each using one of the iron cranked handles hooked through the looped ends of of the rope, drew them tightly together and secured them. In New England, where the term 'shock' is more usual than 'stock', the device was known as a corn shock binder.

Yokes—see *Ox Yokes;* also *Farm, (B) Dairy: Yokes*

(B) DAIRY

The prime essentials of the dairy, cleanliness and coolness, are unchanging; both have been stressed in all books of instructions from early times. Judging by some of the products and equipment which the dairymaid had to handle, her good health and physical strength were as important as her personal cleanliness. Whilst in some districts men were employed for the heaviest work, such as lifting 90 lb. cheeses and manipulating heavy presses, in other parts this work fell to the dairymaid. In any event, she had to walk considerable distances over rough ground, literally shouldering as much as 60 lb., consisting of a yoke with chains and two coopered buckets and their contents, and milking began before dawn.

The dairy itself, which in a domestic establishment might be an adjunct of the kitchen quarters, but when part of a commercial farm would be an entirely separate building, had a stone, brick, slate or tiled floor; shelves were also of slate, if possible, and the window faced North and was protected by gauze or louvres. Outside the dairy window, an elder tree was planted to keep away witches, whose malevolent activities might prevent the butter 'coming'. At least that is the usual story and undoubtedly there were superstitions, but our ancestors were pretty cute and they knew that elders repel flies, and flies in the dairy also turn milk sour and prevent the butter 'coming'. Butter never seems to have been made; it either came in response to the verse:

> 'Come butter, come,
> Come butter, come,
> Peter stands at the gate,
> Waiting for a buttered cake,
> Come butter, come'.

or it did not come. It often refused to come, particularly in thundery weather, and the process must have been especially tricky when temperatures of cream had to be tested by the fingers and when delay in 'coming' resulted in fatigue of the churn operator and lack of rhythm. When cows only calved at the natural time, not much milk was available in winter, so butter making was very much a summer occupation and butter had to be salted down for winter use.

A notice over a door or window, saying *Dairy* or *Cheese Room*, denotes that the building dates back at least to 1808, when the dim-witted politicians of that day had the bright idea of imposing a tax on domestic windows. They soon found that they had to exempt dairies, otherwise there would be no dairy produce. Ridiculous finance bills, which have to be amended out of all recognition of the original and then speedily repealed, are unfortunately not a thing of the past!

The woodware of the English dairy, excluding cheese vats, was almost invariably of sycamore, ideal for its lack of taste and smell, whiteness, ability to stand up to frequent scrubbing without roughening or splintering, and its availability in good widths, free of knots. Most of the dairy farm devices are traditional in form and impos-

sible to date accurately, but being objects of little value, they were seldom kept when worn and the majority of survivals date from the last hundred years. Some of them were being used in London less than 100 years ago, for there were dairy farms, even in such now crowded parts as Lambeth and Walworth, as late as the 1870s. In the first decade of this century, one or two cows were still kept and milked in St. James's Park and the warm milk was sold at 1d. per glass. A milkmaid, carrying her milk supply on a yoke, sold it in the Green Park, opposite Devonshire House, Piccadilly, up to about 1880 or 1890, and another milkmaid with yoke delivered in the Burlington Arcade until at least 1907.

Benediction Horn

The benediction horn/milk sieve is a Swiss dual purpose device of considerable antiquity. The example illustrated, Plate 95, *N*, is of pine, bound with willow, measuring $9\frac{1}{2}$ in. in height, excluding the lug, by $8\frac{1}{2}$ in. diameter at the top. The small lower aperture was loosely filled with a special kind of grass, when used as a milk sieve. At nightfall, the cowherdsman stood at the door or window of his hut and sang a benediction to his cattle, using the horn as an amplifier.

Bowls, Dairy

The various bowls used in the English dairy were invariably of sycamore, turned on a pole lathe and commonly measuring between 16 in. and 18 in. in diameter and 4 in. to 6 in. deep; examples are shown on the floor in Plate 97. The whey bowl, Plate 95, *M*, is turned from a $10\frac{1}{2}$ in. square of elm, not sycamore, and the bowl and block are all in one; the feet are inserted. This type, on feet, seems to be mostly restricted to the West of England. See also *Dairy Vessels*.

Buckets, Coopered

Coopered buckets formerly had many uses on the farm, and were almost entirely superseded by the lighter galvanized pails, during the last century. Very few survivals have much age, because the nature of the construction led to their falling apart when dried out. See also, *Yokes*.

Butter Bowls

The covered butter bowls, Plate 96, *M*, known in the Isle of Man as mealey begs, were pole lathe turned, in a variety of sizes and served two different purposes: (1) for taking samples of butter to market and (2) by fishermen for taking their butter rations when going out fishing, and by shepherds for taking their rations up to the higher pastures in summer, where they would bury the bowls in peat, or cover them in stones or scrub for coolness. Some of these bowls, like the Welsh one in front, which was formerly in the Linn Collection, are carved with the initials of their owners. See also, *Butter Kegs*.

Butter Churns—see *Churns*

Butter Cups

Butter cups as illustrated, Plate 95, *E* and *F*, are not butter prints; they are butter measures, which were used where an old recipe states 'take a cup of butter'. They are hollow domes, with no carving inside them and some of the cups, like *F*, are so deep that they had to be hit on the head with a mallet to dislodge the butter dome. *F* shows evidence of considerable bashing. See also butter cup prints under *Butter Prints*.

Butter Curls, Cutters and Slicers

Ribbed slicers, cutters and curlers, of sycamore, are shown in Plate 95, *D*, *H* and *J*. The last two were used more for preparing butter for the table, than in the dairy.

Butter Hands

A selection of pairs of butter hands, also described sometimes as butter patters and butter boards, is shown in Plate 96. *B* and *C*, both plain, are of yew and boxwood

respectively; *D*, unusual in having ornamental handles, and *E* are the ribbed type, of sycamore; *F* are of pine.

Butter Kegs

Butter kegs similar to the example, left, Plate 98, but not usually so complete, are occasionally excavated from Irish peat bogs. Some of them are probably hundreds of years old, preserved in the peat, and completely filled still with rancid butter, like the specimen illustrated, which came from a bog in County Antrim and is $10\frac{1}{2}$ in. high by $6\frac{1}{4}$ in. square. They are mediaeval in form, following the general outline and construction of the Irish mether (see Section III, *Drinking: Irish Drinking Vessels*), with the prominent angles and handles cut from the solid. The whole container is hollowed out of a single block, with top and bottom inserted. You can take your choice of the three theories as to how they come to be found in bogs: (1) that they were buried as a magic offering for the fairies or the gods of the harvest; (2) that the bog was used as a refrigerator and the site of the burial was lost; (3) that the Irish liked their butter rancid.

Butter Moulds

Butter moulds of tankard type, similar to Plate 95, *L*, were formerly made and used in all the Scandinavian countries and may hold 6 lb. to 8 lb. of butter. Coopered in pine and bound with willow, they are decorated externally with chip carving and punched ornament. The finest carving is reserved for the deeply cut roundel in the lid, shown in Plate 101, which makes the print on the block of butter. A Scandinavian hexagonal butter mould, which pegs together, is shown alongside. Another unusual hexagonal butter mould is illustrated, Plate 86, *B*. It is from the State of Maine, U.S.A. and is made of pine, banded with pewter; it is constructed as a through tunnel, with a removable pineapple carved print of maple, which can be slid through to any depth. The mould is $4\frac{1}{2}$ in. deep and $2\frac{7}{8}$ in. across inside. See also *Butter Prints*.

Butter Patters—see *Butter Hands*

Butter Pouncers—see *Butter Workers*

Butter Prints

Butter prints are of five distinct types and many patterns and sizes. The types are (1) flat prints; (2) ejector prints; (3) cup prints; (4) three-dimensional prints; (5) roller prints. The vast majority are of sycamore, but a few of outstanding quality are of boxwood or lime. The technicality of the carving of butter prints is described in Section XIII, *Moulds*. In the West of England and Wales, carved designs tend to be geometrical, sometimes with a strong resemblance to Scandinavian, Russian and Polish carving; some particular geometric designs may be associated with a specific town or county. In other parts of the British Isles, the prints may provide a clue as to the type of farm from which the butter came. Thus, a swan indicated river farm; a cow, mainly dairy farm; a sheep, sheep farm; flowers, a flower farm; grapes (rare), farm with a vineyard. Many are carved with the English rose, Scottish thistle, etc. Others, carved for household use, may bear the crests or initials of the family who used them.

The three canoe-shaped prints, Plate 99, *A*, are a basically Welsh type, in spite of the one on the left being carved with thistles and a rose, as well as a leek. This shape of print strays over the border and is also found in Shropshire, Cheshire and Lancashire. The specimen in the centre, carved with the heart motifs, is concave on the face and has a circular print on the handle, at the back; it appears to be older than the others, probably 18th-century.

In the next row, *B* and *C* are West of England; *D* may represent a shell or a sycamore leaf; *E* and *F* represent a crown and an anchor respectively and both have

extra sharpness, being carved from boxwood; *G* is carved with the letter P in reverse; *H* is a rare Easter butter print, carved with a cross and two eggs; *J* is a pineapple; *K* is a corn stook and *L* is a cup, carved with a rose. Cups are the most difficult to carve, as the cutting has to be done on concave surfaces, to create a butter dome; cup prints should not be confused with butter cups, which are described under a separate heading.

In the third row, *M*, *N*, *O* and *P* are West of England patterns, and *M* and *N*, which have flat, fret outlined handles, are both much earlier specimens than usual. *Q* and *R* represent Prince of Wales feathers, the latter quite a modern version; *S* is a well carved and elaborate monogram in boxwood. In the bottom row, *T* is a good quality print, well designed around a heart centre motif; *U* is from the West of England; *V*, a very rare print, commemorates Queen Victoria's golden or diamond jubilee —it has never had use and was presented to us by Miss Howard, daughter of the carver; *W* is another version of Prince of Wales feathers and *X* is an ejector type print, carved with a family crest.

In Plate 100 are more flat butter prints; *G* portrays a swan; *H*, a cow; *J*, an English wild rose; *K*, acorns; *L*, thistles; *M*, a rose; *N*, a dove(?) with olive branch; *O*, which is a cup print, a pineapple. In the same picture is a selection of three-dimensional, two-part prints or moulds, which peg together and create butter ornaments in the round. *A*, forms a beehive; *B*, a crown, formerly used at St. James's Palace; *C*, a corn stook; *D*, a swan; *E*, a boar's head; *F*, a duck.

In Plate 102 are included some of the more unusual butter prints. *A* is a ribbed butter marker, $14\frac{3}{4}$ in. long; *B*, a flower design, has a long handle, not showing in the illustration; *C* is a heavy butter print and slapper, with carved date 1885; these three are of sycamore and English. *D* and *E*, the former of boxwood and probably

18th-century, the latter of sycamore and 19th-century, are both traditional Swiss patterns, carved with edelweiss, etc. *F*, well worn, sycamore, and carved with the 'soul' motif (for soul motif, see Section IX, *Love Spoons*), may be Welsh. *G* and *H* are different sizes of a traditional Tyrolean or Swiss pattern of mould, consisting of four sycamore flaps, staple-hinged to a centre plaque, and an ash or willow band to act as a closure; one mould is shown open and one closed; they create a butter loaf with carved motifs on the top and on each of the four sides. *J* and *K* are included to show profiles of typical flat butter prints. *L* is an old 'Oxford' pattern print; it has a hole drilled right through the handle and the butter was dislodged by the dirty habit of blowing through the hole. *M* to *V* are a selection of roller butter prints, with traditional rose, acorn, thistle, leaves, geometric and lettering designs. These rollers were also used on pastry. *W* is also a roller butter print, but it has, additionally, a circular print on the handle. According to the old label which it bears, it was a wedding present in 1800.

Butter Scales

In Plate 101 are shown three types of butter weighing devices. Top left, the suspended oak beam balance, with beech saucer pans, probably has a longer history than the standing balance with turned sycamore pillar and pans, alongside. On these balances, both pans are alike, and they were used without weights; the first pound or half pound of butter was made in a mould and then placed in one pan to act as a counterbalance against subsequent ones. Survivals of both these types are rare, because they were fragile and of little intrinsic value. The wooden weighing machine shown below, although later in date, is much more unusual, because it is a wooden version of a machine designed essentially for manufacture in metal. It is stamped under the Victorian Weights and Measures Act and dates from about 1870.

For other types of weighing devices, see Section XIX, *Scientific*.

Butter Scoops

Butter scoops of sycamore, used to scoop butter out of the churn, are illustrated, Plate 95, *A*, *B* and *C*. *A* has a print carved on the face of the handle; *B* has prints on both sides; *C*, is the hook handle type. All are traditional in form. The lead-bladed, long spoon, illustrated in Plate 138, *A*, and described in Section VII, *Kitchen*, was also used for scraping butter out of a churn. See also *Scoops, General*.

Butter Slicers—see *Butter Curls, Cutters and Slicers*

Butter Workers

Sycamore butter workers, shallow, thin turned saucers, 8 in. to 9 in. in diameter, with a turned handle central in the saucer, Plate 96, *A* and *J*, were used for working the water out of butter; in the West of England, they were also known as butter pouncers.

The more sophisticated *yard of butter worker* was invented in Connecticut in 1842. Up to 1860, some twenty patents for different versions of it were taken out in the U.S.A. It is believed to have been introduced to England between 1860 and 1870. An English example is illustrated, Plate 111. All these devices consist of a trough, a yard long, and all that I have seen are 1 ft. wide. Sometimes the trough is slightly convex in length, with drainage holes at each end. The example illustrated has a fall to one corner, where there is a drain hole, stoppered when required by the ribbed head, tapered peg, which when not in use, is held in a hole in one leg, as shown. The butter worker itself is a revolving ribbed roller, which travels the length of the trough, working the moisture out of the butter. The thin yard of butter, when worked out, was rolled and carried in long, narrow, specially woven baskets. The selling of butter by the yard long antedates the invention of the American yard of butter worker.

Cheese Moulds and Stands—See *Cheese Vats*

Cheese Presses

Cheese presses work by means of a drop weight, screw pressure, or lever pressure; until the second half of the 19th-century, they were individually made, as a few of them still are. In the British Isles, they were usually plain and strictly utilitarian, but on the continent they were often decoratively carved and sometimes gaily painted, in the manner common to other peasant wood-work of the locality. A drop weight cheese press may be constructed with one heavy stone, rope or cord controlled, falling between guide posts. The stone may be seated on a wood platform, to which the cords are connected, or the stone may be fitted with an iron ring for suspension. Alternatively, the weight may consist of a number of smaller stones in a wooden box. Sometimes the press was made as a free-standing movable; at other times it was a fixture, with the posts running from floor to roof of the building in which it stood. In some instances, a beam was pivotally mounted to a tree or post, passed over the press standing nearby to form a lever, and on the far end of the beam, weights were hung at intervals, as on a steelyard. The screw-type press, Plate 107, is from Cwm Clyde Farm, Newton St. Margarets, Herefordshire. It is mainly of oak, believed to be about 120 years old and was last used 20 years ago. The stool is 54 in. wide and the height to top bar is 58 in. The illustration shows its method of operation clearly.

Cheese Prints

When pressing a cheese, a heavy board, in early times known as a sinker, was fitted in the vat on top of the cheese. The sinker is now usually called a follower. A cheese print is a carved follower for impressing a design on a cheese. Cheese prints were formerly used on special occasions and one might be specially carved with the Royal Arms to commemorate a Coronation or royal visit. Two outstanding specimens are shown in Plates 103 and 104, both bearing the Royal Coat of Arms, but some 250 to 300 years apart in age. Carved from chest-nut, Plate 103 is 19 in. in diameter and bears the late 17th-century Royal Arms. When purchased, its use seemed long for-gotten under multitudinous layers of paint, applied by successively misguided decora-tors; they had treated it as a heraldic orna-ment, ignoring the fact that the coat of arms appeared in reverse. Its stripping was a formidable task. The royal Victorian cheese print, Plate 104, *B*, probably cele-brating Queen Victoria's Coronation—the arms were altered soon after that date—is technically a much finer and deeper carving. It is 15 in. in diameter. The carved board, probably of mahogany, $1\frac{1}{4}$ in. thick, is backed with elm, making a total thickness of 3 in. The cheese prints are provided with weep holes.

In Poland, traditional heart-shaped cheese moulds, known as *Parzenica*, have attractive geometrically chip carved lids and bases, which impress the heart-moulded cheeses on both faces.

Cheese Vats and Stands

In different parts of the British Isles, cheese vats were formerly known as chessels, chesswells, chesils and chessets; in the Wensleydale district, they were known as chesfords. After the curd had been broken and settled in the tub, and had developed the necessary acidity to shrink it away from the tub sides, it was drained of whey, had salt added and was transferred to vats; a selection is shown in Plate 97. Cheese vats are turned or coopered wooden vessels, $5\frac{1}{2}$ in. to 18 in. in overall diameter and with an inside depth of $1\frac{1}{2}$ in. to 18 in., varying according to the size and variety of cheese;

those above 6 in. in depth are usually coopered. The walls of solid vats vary from ½ in. to 1½ in. thickness; sometimes they are bound with metal. In the base of most vats are weep or draining holes, placed at regular intervals and up to eight in number. Some dealers, selling these old vats as plant containers, have a nasty habit of filling the holes with plastic wood. Vats of similar size were piled one on another on a stand or shelf, left to drain and then transferred to the cheese press. Vats were made of any suitable hardwood, such as elm, beech and sycamore, elm being preferred.

Chessels or Chessets—see *Cheese Vats*

Churns
It is unfortunate that the name churn is given to a circular metal milk vessel with a tap, used for filling smaller vessels, as well as to devices used for churning cream or milk into butter. The *Oxford Dictionary* defines a churn as 'A vessel or machine for making butter in which cream or milk is shaken, beaten or broken, so as to separate the oily globules from the serous parts'. That explains why churns can be actuated in so many different ways. Having no mechanical parts, it seems safe to assume that swing churns and plunger or knocker churns came into use first. The Irish swing churn, right, Plate 98, excavated from a peat bog in County Antrim, is almost certainly mediaeval. It is oval, approximately 11 in. by 9½ in. and 12 in. high. Like many early Irish vessels, it is not turned, but gouged out of a solid block, with the bottom inserted.

The small and well worn, ring turned dash, plunger or knocker churn, Plate 110, *B*, is a type shown in 17th-century dairy illustrations and is a rare survival, which also closely resembles mortars of that period. The plunge-stick has the foot carved in corrugations. Eighteenth-century and later plunger churns mostly taper inwards towards the top and are usually coopered.

Plate 110, *D* and *E*, show two types of hand churns popular in the 19th century. *D*, an oak barrel, from Yorkshire, simple but effective, was still being made at the beginning of this century; it has three inwardly projecting dashers or ribs, each perforated with three heart-shaped cut-outs, permanently fixed lengthwise, at equal intervals, to the staves of the barrel. As the barrel revolves, the liquid swishing through the heart-shaped apertures of the dashers, forms the butter. The spring loaded pouring-in cap can be seen on top of the barrel, and the bung hole, for extracting the buttermilk, shows in front. In the Charlemont over-end barrel churn, the spindle passed through the sides and the barrel tumbles end over end. The sycamore box-churn, Plate 110, *E*, a very popular type, itself remained stationary, and the handle revolved a four-slatted paddle; the lid is loosely rebated on; the buttermilk outlet, secured by a peg, is near the bottom, on the side opposite the handle. Other types of wooden churns which may be found include eccentric or oscillating churns, with a double movement—rotary and from side to side; additionally, there are rocking or cradle churns. When churns were too large and heavy for a dairymaid to turn by hand, various devices were employed; these are described under the heading *Treadmills*.

Cream Stirrers
The yew-wood paddle, Plate 95, *K*, is a cream stirrer. These stirrers, sometimes known as mundles in the Midlands and in Cheshire and Lancashire, were individually made in a number of different patterns, usually between 10 in. and 15 in. in length. Some were fret-cut in heart designs and obviously intended as love tokens.

Dairymaid Yokes—see *Yokes*

Dairy Scales—see *Butter Scales*

Dairy Stools—see *Stools*

Dairy Thermometers

Dairy thermometers, first mentioned in 18th-century literature, came into general use during the 19th century. Two kinds are shown in Plate 96, *K* and *L*. Both have special temperature markings for dairy use, but *K* is wood framed to float on the milk, whilst *L*, shown with its sycamore case, is for dipping only. For other types of thermometers, see Section XIX, *Scientific*.

Dog Wheel Churns—see *Treadmills*

Egg Boxes

Egg boxes, divided into separate compartments for eggs, must have been made and used for centuries, but they are not the kind of thing to be kept when worn. The two shown in Plate 105, *B*, closed and *C* open, have felt-lined compartments and were a produce of the Dairy Outfit Co. Ltd., of Kings Cross, London, between 1900 and 1920.

Egg Stands—see Section VII, *Kitchen*

Followers—see *Cheese Prints*

Honeycomb Butter Rollers—see Section VII, *Kitchen: Rollers*

Mealey Begs—see *Butter Bowls*

Milk Vessels

Apart from dairy bowls, most of the other wooden vessels used in the dairy were coopered, staved vessels, bound with willow or metal bands. They varied from the shallow keeler or cooling pan to much deeper vessels, such as the $13\frac{1}{2}$ in. deep, oval milk carrying vessel shown in Plate 110, *C*; this example is Swiss. Intermediate heights and types included buckets and the various round and oval tubs illustrated and described in Section VIII, *Laundry*. The vessels made by the cooper were, in the main, very much general-purpose items, and similar ones might be found in the kitchen quarters, a laundry, dairy, brewhouse, etc.

Milking Stools

Three turned and splayed legs, driven through holes bored in a thick circular or octagonal elm seat and firmly fixed by splitting the tops of the ashwood legs and driving a wedge in each, is the traditional way of making a milking stool; it has not varied for hundreds of years. Since at least the 18th century, it has also formed the basis of the graceful but sturdy Windsor chair which, unlike all others, has a back hoop going downwards into the chair seat, entirely independently and not a continuation of the back legs, which are fitted as in a dairy stool. The three-legged stool serves several purposes: it masters uneven ground; by placing one splayed leg forward, it avoids risk of the milker tilting when leaning forward; it is lighter and easier to carry than a four-legged stool. The last point is further improved by the 19th-century example illustrated, Plate 110, *F*, which has the back of the stool cut away and comfortably shaped to accommodate a carrying handle.

Piggins

A coopered oak milk piggin, with finely 'fingered' or laced ash bands is illustrated, Plate 95, *G*. For description and various uses of piggins, see Section III, *Drinking, Piggins*.

Roller Prints—see *Butter Prints*

Scales—see *Butter Scales*

Sinkers—see *Cheese Prints*

Skimmers

Dairy skimmers are thinly turned, plain, shallow, curved saucers of sycamore. They vary in diameter from about 7 in., Plate 96, *H*, to 10 in., Plate 96, *G*. There is no way of dating them accurately.

Stools—see *Milking Stools*

Thermometers—see *Dairy Thermometers*

Treadmills

For turning large and heavy churns in the past, water wheels were occasionally used, where water power was available. But much more common was the treadmill, which might be powered either by a human or a suitable animal. Indeed, the treadmill principle was employed far beyond the dairy churn, being used for such diverse purposes as turning a circular saw or grindstone, grinding corn, pressing grapes, operating a printing press, a water pump and even a crane. At Harwich, there is still preserved a treadmill operated crane, used by the Admiralty from 1666 until the First World War. The crane was powered by 16 ft. diameter twin treadmills, each worked by a prisoner.

Treadmills for working the simple mechanism of churns were usually smaller and lighter, were of several different kinds and were placed outside the dairy and could be connected so as to operate any type of churn inside the dairy. Their heyday seems to have been about 100 years ago, but in outlying districts, both in the British Isles and abroad, they were still used between the two World Wars. The three principle varieties of treadmills were (1) the cage type, as used for the dog turned spit, see Section VII, *Kitchen*, but with a considerably larger wheel placed at ground level; (2) the upward sloping endless platform and (3) the circular platform of about 9 ft. diameter, set at an angle to the ground, as shown in Plate 106; this specimen, which came from a Welsh farm, is shown with a life-sized wooden silhouette of a dog, placed in the correct position. The *New England Farmer* of 1854, referring to one of the upward sloping, endless platforms with treadmill belt running over 12 in. diameter drums at each end, says that a gentleman extensively engaged in dairying in western New York '. . . operated it with a cosset sheep, who came at the call of a whistle and did the churning every morning. A large dog or a child will also answer the purpose well'. Correspondents in the *American Agriculturist* of 1870, illustrate the different types of churns and treadmills then in use and state that they were powered by dogs, sheep and goats. A number of other correspondents in various publications in this country, who have seen dog wheels in operation both here and on the continent, during the last half century, emphasise how eager the dogs were to work the churns and how the animals seemed to enjoy their task. In some contraptions, two dogs worked together side by side in harness. In all the wheels, moving belts, or disc platforms, the principle was the same: the dog or other 'power' was harnessed to some immovable object, so that his back peddling against the slats or, in some instances, carpeted surface, kept it moving, whilst he remained stationary. Several correspondents have referred to the commonness of the dog churns in Belgium during the 1914–18 War and at least two have recalled the drudgery when they themselves acted as churn 'powers' in their childhood. On some farms, both churns and large water raising wheels of the cage type were formerly powered by donkeys or horses. The best known donkey water raising wheel still in use in this country is that at Carisbrooke Castle, Isle of Wight, but an even finer one of oak, 15 ft. in diameter, built in 1688, was still intact on a Bedfordshire farm, up to four years ago.

Whey Bowls—see *Bowls, Dairy*

Yard of Butter Worker—see *Butter Workers*

Yokes

A traditional type of wooden yoke, with its

original chains, is shown in Plate 110, *A*. Beech, willow and elm seem to have been the woods most commonly used. Judging by old pictures, there has been no change in the pattern for hundreds of years. Although usually described as dairymaid yokes, they were, in fact, used to an even greater extent in town and country by water carriers, who normally were men. The load was a heavy one, but it was well balanced. See Introduction to this section, also *Ox Yokes*.

VI

Fire and Lighting

This section covers four subjects: (a) making and maintaining fire, (b) lighting, (c) warming and (d) fire fighting. A separate brief introduction is given to each subject.

MAKING AND MAINTAINING FIRE

Although man solved the basic problem of making fire at a comparatively early stage, all the methods employed were tedious and, under certain conditions, slow and uncertain. Fire making developed on four different lines:

   (i) A controlled version of nature's sun caused conflagrations by introduction of a burning glass.
   (ii) Striking a flint with a nodule of iron pyrites.
   (iii) Wood friction methods.
   (iv) The fire piston.

The first never developed into any modern invention. The second, when man learnt to smelt iron, became flint and steel, which was used in conjunction with the tinder box until the first half of the 19th century. In a more advanced form, it became the tinder pistol, and then the tinder lighter of the 1914–18 War period. The last, by further refinement and changing its fuel, became the petrol lighter, which has now evolved into the gas lighter.

The third method of making fire, by rubbing two sticks together, was improved by coating the end of the wood with a chemical compound, so eventually leading to the friction match.

The fourth, the fire piston, was originally limited to a small geographical area in South-east Asia, but much later the principle was rediscovered and used for a short period in the United Kingdom.

The inefficiency and inconvenience of tinder boxes were manifest; damp defeated and strong draughts delayed them; frequently they had to be operated in total darkness. Whilst under favourable circumstances a light might be obtained in three minutes, in unfavourable conditions it could take half an hour. It is not, therefore, surprising that, as late as the 1830s, it was common practice to keep at least one fire continually burning in a house, throughout the year. Hence the custom of the curfew or *couvre-feu*—a metal dome like an old-fashioned dish cover, with a piece cut out to maintain a little draught—which by law had to be placed over the smouldering embers, to lessen the risk of conflagrations at night. The curfew was not, as often stated, introduced by William the Conqueror; it was already established; he confirmed it and the curfew bell, for several centuries, was sounded at sunset in summer and at 8 p.m. in winter. Although its mandatory power has long since ceased, the formal sounding of the bell still continues, as a quaint custom, in a few districts. Thomas Gray (1716–1761) immortalized it in the lines

'The curfew tolls the knell of parting day,
The lowing herd wind slowly o'er the lea,
The ploughman homeward plods his weary
   way,
And leaves the world to darkness and to me.'

The tyranny of the tinder box was not finally broken until 1826, when John Walker, a Stockton-on-Tees chemist, invented the first friction light. There had been earlier matches, but they were not striking matches—merely sulphur-tipped, flat splinters of wood, Plate 115, *V*, strips of cardboard, paper, woven cotton or straw, mere adjuncts of the tinder box, used as secondary tinder for obtaining flame from smouldering basic tinder and conveying it to fire kindling, candle, rush or smoker's pipe. One of the racks in which these early matches were stored near the fireplace is shown in Plate 118.

There were also numerous attempts, in the late 18th and early 19th century, to devise various ingenious substitutes for the laborious tinder box; these are usually grouped together under the heading of 'Instantaneous Light Devices'. They were all rendered obsolete by John Walker's invention.

Amadou—see *Tinder*

Bellows
English bellows of all periods were usually simple, with plain leather gussets, fixed with brass headed nails through leather bindings to the face and back plates, constructed of whatever wood was in fashion for furniture. They had long, simple, brass, iron or pewter nozzles. A few Georgian mahogany specimens were inlaid and quite frequently 18th-century bellows were japanned. When overlaid with brass, stamped in repoussé designs, they are more likely to be reproduc-

tions than antiques. A few exceptionally luxurious specimens have survived from the 17th century, such as the bellows overlaid with repoussé silver sheets, front and back, at Ham House, a few pairs overlaid, somewhat unsuitably, with needlework, and one or two pairs with the wood exposed but the faces incised with ornament of heraldic beasts or coats of arms, in the style of silver of the James I period. English bellows generally average 18 in. to 24 in. in length.

In France and Italy, particularly during the Renaissance period, artistic designers and carvers lavished their skill on bellows which, mostly of walnut, were richly carved on both faces with such motifs as winged figures, scrolls, cartouches, grotesque heads, etc., in the fashion of the 16th century. Such bellows usually have long nozzles of bronze, complementing the wood carving in their elaboration, Plate 112. They may run up to 3 ft. in length.

Bellows, Blacksmiths'
These are simple versions of ordinary domestic bellows, but were made up to 8 ft. in length.

Bellows, Mechanical
Instead of leather gussets and the in and out motion imparted by closing and parting the handles, mechanical bellows have rigid wooden or metal boxings which contain a fan. This is turned by means of a cranked handle and a belt or cord drive passing over two wheels, at one side. Plain wooden specimens, Plate 113, may date from the 18th or early 19th century, but some made of or encased in brass are 19th-century. Some mechanical bellows were made to hang up, others as standing models. The latter were used for fires in basket grates and particularly for peat fires. Some 19th-century specimens were mounted on iron stands, with a pivot and ratchet at the head, allowing the nozzle to be raised or depressed, according to the height of the fire.

Bellows, Miniature—see Section XXIII, *Toilet and Bedroom Accessories: Wig Powdering Bellows*

Blow Tubes
Although now extremely rare, because their simplicity and lack of intrinsic value caused their destruction when worn or burnt, these practical but simple, straight-sided wooden pipes, usually 18 in. long and upwards and of 1½ in. to 2 in. diameter, with a crude flattened mouthpiece at one end, were probably common in olden days. They were the poor man's bellows, his lungs supplying the 'blow'. Generally being devoid of ornament, other than dates and initials, which sometimes occur, it is likely that the purpose of surviving specimens is seldom recognized. In country districts of Portugal, they have been used in this century.

Cigar Lighters
Explosive cigars did not originate as a joke. Austrian *Cigarren-Zünders* were patented by Stephen Romer of Vienna in 1834. They are tips or caps, each mounted on a small wooden stick and called a braided fusee; it was stuck into the end of a cigar and when in position, was struck against the sand-paper striker on the box. English versions were in cardboard boxes containing 20 to 40 fusees, Plate 115, *T*, but for pocket use, the tips could be transferred to a special tortoiseshell case holding six, Plate 115, *S*. *Cigarren-Zünders* were a specialized type of fusee match, which was essentially designed, not for domestic use, but for the lighting of cigars and pipes, especially out of doors. Fusee matches were patented by Samuel Jones in 1832 and were made of specially prepared and impregnated coarse, loose textured cardboard or amadou and they smouldered slowly, with a spluttering flame, which was not extinguished by wind.

Fire Pistons
These devices, Plate 116, *K*, were used at an early date by primitive people in Southeast Asia and the East Indies. They consist of a hollowed-out wood or a horn cylinder 4 in. or 5 in. long, closed at one end, and a tight-fitting removable piston. The piston is then placed in the cylinder containing tinder, struck a sharp blow and immediately withdrawn, when the air compression and engendered heat will be found to have ignited the tinder. The principle was rediscovered and patented in Great Britain in 1807, when fire pistons or syringes were made of steel and brass.

Fusee Matches—see *Cigar Lighters*

Gas Turn-keys—see *Turn-keys*

Instantaneous Light Contrivances
The numerous devices which intervened between tinder and flint methods and friction matches, were known collectively as instantaneous light contrivances. Among the earliest was the 'Phosphorous Box', invented in Italy in 1786; it contained a bottle of phosphorus and sulphur-tipped matches which, when dipped in the bottle, ignited. An improved version, introduced into England from France about 1810, had the bottle filled with sulphuric acid and the matches tipped with a hard paste, composed of potassium chlorate, sugar and gum. The majority of English instantaneous light device containers are tin; treen are rare, but a few examples, mostly stamped 'Berry's Patent', survive, Plate 114, *R* and *U*. The simple turned lignum cylinder, with projecting base and screw-on tapering dome lid, *P*, is English, 1810–25. It contains a bottle of acid in an inner ring, with matches in an outer ring; the lid also contains a projecting inner ring, which clamps tightly on the bottle of acid. *Q*, is a plain, rosewood cylinder, a French patent of approximately the same period, in which the lid, shown alongside, is secured by hit-and-miss projections. The projecting neck of the acid bottle shows in the photograph; it is spring seated, so that the top of the

bottle is always forced tightly against the inner ring in the lid. The outer ring of the box contains three separate compartments for small candles, one for matches and two others, of unknown purpose. A larger box of this type, with outer ring for matches, is shown, *T*. The more elaborate turned ebony box, *U*, with funnel-shaped top, is one of Berry's 1825 patents. It has a separate lid for the acid bottle, so that matches stored in the outer ring remained protected while a single match was dipped in the bottle. Berry's name is also found on matching lignum vitae ink bottle containers, similarly spring loaded, to avoid seepage of ink. Henry Berry was established as a merchant, at 28 Abchurch Street, London, before 1810; in 1825, he took out his patent and by 1835 he was at 466 Bernard Street, Russell Square and 14 Green Street, Theobalds Road, where he described himself as 'Merchant & Patentee for the Application of India Rubber, the only Chemical Stopper for Light, Inks, Bottles, etc.'.

Match Dispensers

Match dispensers, Plate 116, *L*, which, by means of a rise and fall action, lifted and presented a single match in a concave groove, from the bottom of a storage box or magazine, seem to have been introduced in the last quarter of the 19th century. In larger form, they were also used for presenting cigars in the same manner, and more recently they have been used for cigarettes. Match dispensers were used chiefly in public houses, tobacconists' shops, clubs, etc.

Matches, Friction

The need for tinder boxes and instantaneous light contrivances died soon after 1826, when John Walker invented and sold his first 'friction' lights at 1*s*. per box of 100, including a piece of sandpaper, between the folds of which the match head was inserted and pulled sharply, causing it to ignite—provided the head remained attached. This wonderful labour-saving invention initially achieved little popularity and Walker only sold 250 boxes in the first two and a half years. Little over a century later, no fewer than 8,640,000,000 were sold in Great Britain within a similar period. Walker, indentured to become a doctor, abandoned medicine for chemistry and during his fire-making experiments, a stick, which had been dipped in a composition of potassium chlorate and antimony sulphide, ignited when rubbed accidentally and gave birth to his invention. Walker's matches contained no phosphorus. Because he was not commercially minded, Walker never advertised and made no attempt to sell outside his district; nor did he take out a patent. About 1829, Samuel Jones, a London chemist, of "The Light House", Strand, marketed 'The Lucifer', a copy of Walker's friction light, and made a fortune —the first of many made from Walker's invention. 'Lucifer' passed into history as an alternative name for match.

It is interesting that if matches were made of a quick firing wood, they would be consumed too rapidly, so they are made chiefly from aspen or white Canadian pine, which ignites so slowly that they must be coated with paraffin wax at the head end, in order to create an inflammable vapour. Watch the wax ooze out on the next one you light.

Matches, Friction, Protective Boxes for

Phosphorus matches were introduced to England, by German and Austrian chemists, about 1830 and their greater ease in striking gained them quick popularity. Their liability to spontaneous combustion from a knock, or through exposure to warmth, was so great, however, that it strictly limited them to home use and urgently necessitated provision of special containers, known as 'Protective Match Boxes'. These, like instantaneous light contrivances, were mostly metal. Tinned iron were commonest, but brass, copper, white metal, marble, bone and ivory were all made. Treen specimens, which are rather difficult to find, are invariably carefully turned from selected hardwoods, of which lignum vitae and ebony were the most popular. An early lignum vitae protective match box, made specially for the first friction matches, is illustrated, Plate 114, *V*. The two lignum buttons at the top are lined with glass-paper and the match was pulled through them to strike. Some protective match boxes are combined with candle holders, Plate 114, *M1* and *M2*.

Berry was not very lucky with his 1825 patent, so far as instantaneous lighting devices were concerned, for Walker's 1826 invention, especially when it was commercialized by Samuel Jones, rendered the acid bottle obsolete; so Berry, caught with a stock of his two-ring lignum containers, converted some of them into protective boxes, by fitting circular strikers into the centre compartments, formerly housing the bottles of sulphuric acid; consequently, instantaneous light contrivances and protective match boxes are sometimes found with similar exteriors. Apart from these converted examples, protective match boxes usually have sinkings under their bases for circular strikers of glass-paper. Other exceptions are the rather rare Irish bog oak 'castles', Plate 114, *E1* and *E2*, which have circular rings to simulate stonework; these rings act as strikers. Most protective boxes have a small brass or bone boss inserted— see numerous examples Plate 114—either at the top or near the edge of the top, for holding a single wax match—'the good night match'. This was used while getting in or out of bed, after extinguishing, or before lighting the gas; it was also used for sealing letters.

Protective boxes, Plate 114, *A*, *B*, *C*, *E2*, *G*, *H*, *K*, *L*, *N*, *R*, *S*, *W* and *X*, were probably made between 1830 and 1860. The brass-banded examples, *D1*, *D2*, *D3*, *D4*, *J*, and the novelty 'top', *O*, were products of the 1870s, as was also Plate 115, *H*. With the invention of safety matches and improve-ment in the manufacture of non-safety types, it was no longer necessary to have protective match boxes for table use and they were soon superseded by open containers. At first, these were turned like their predecessors, but in the last quarter of the 19th century, they were carved into a number of novel and amusing forms, Plate 115, *A* to *G*, and *P*, and Plate 114, *E1*.

Matches, Pocket Boxes

Gold, silver and plated match boxes for pocket or watch chain were popular from the mid-19th century up to the First World War. Some of the cheaper alternatives were of wood. The majority, of the rather few which have survived, are continental. A selection is shown, Plate 115. *J*, simulating a book, is English; the ribbed 'leaf' edges is the striker and, in most instances, only the presence of strikers makes it possible to identify these small boxes as definitely for matches. *L* is Irish, of bog oak, carved in relief with ruins. *M* is Russian; *N*, of thuya, is probably English and *O*, Finnish. *Q*, with a double pivoted lid, is Swiss, and *R*, of pearwood, with a tambour action, could well be German, Austrian or Swiss.

Spills

Candle lighting and open fires made the use of spills sensible and economical in the past. Apart from paper, spills were made either of flat slivers of wood, or rolls of curled shavings. The flat slivers or 'spelk' were cut on a spelk plane, the same tool which was used for spelk basket making. The tubular shaving spills were tightly and automatically curled as they passed through the special plane, shown Plate 116, *G*. In the U.S.A., it was known as the H. W. Yates Improved Cigar Lighter Plane. Shavings from the plane, Plate 116, *G*, are shown in the spill vases, *A* to *F*.

Spill Vases

No Georgian nor Victorian sitting room was complete without one or a pair of spill vases. Sometimes, spill vases were included in a smoker's compendium, or were adjuncts of a churchwarden pipe stand. Some vases of goblet form, now often described as drinking vessels, but with rims much too thick for drinking, are really spill vases. The selection shown in Plate 116, *A* to *F*, contains spills from the spill plane, *G*.

Taper Boxes

Taper boxes were nearly always of metal or cardboard. The candle-shaped specimen illustrated, Plate 117, of rosewood, is the only wooden example identified by the author. It is 13 in. long.

Tinder

The usual tinder in domestic tinder boxes was charred linen rags, but dry grass, powdered leaves, rotten wood, down from birds, and amadou were all used. Amadou, or German tinder, is a fungus which grows on dead trees and, when prepared, looks like brown washleather.

Tinder Boxes

Any strong box of wood or iron, if of suitable size, served as tinder box. Leather tinder pouches were also made for travellers. A considerable number of iron and a few wooden candlesticks had circular tinder boxes in their bases; an example is shown, top left, Plate 125. Candle boxes quite often included, at one end, a tinder and flint compartment with an inner lid, under the main sliding lid. A much worn and charred, ancient tinder box, formerly in the Owen Evan-Thomas Collection and quite impossible to date accurately, is illustrated, bottom left, Plate 117; the smaller compartment has an inner lid, to keep the tinder dry. A Dutch, 18th-century, pocket tinder tube of coquilla nut and ivory, silver mounted, is shown, Plate 115, *K*.

Tinder Pistols

These were used in western Europe, in houses of the wealthy, during the 17th and 18th centuries. They seem to have been produced in England from early in the 18th century. The well made English example, with ashwood butt, Plate 116, *J*, was made by J. Savige of Wolverhampton. It is fired by the trigger, which releases the flint against the steel and simultaneously opens the tinder box, ejecting the spark into contact with the tinder. A candle socket is provided alongside. A much smaller and neater tinder pistol, contained in a metal case, the size and shape of a walnut shell, was made in Japan in the 17th and 18th centuries.

Turn-keys

Long, wood-handled turn-keys, with a metal end grooved to fit over a gas tap, essentials for turning on and off gas jets above arm reach, were used in conjunction with telescopic metal taper holders, at least until the first decade of this century. Now, the turn-keys have nearly all disappeared. The brass terminal of the $28\frac{1}{2}$ in. long, beech example illustrated, Plate 118, is formed as a hand grasping a book. On the other end of the $\frac{5}{8}$ in. diameter rod is a brass ring for hanging the turn-key on the wall, usually at the side of the fireplace. It was a registered design of October 6, 1844.

LIGHTING

From fire making, we pass to light. Cave dwellers used firebrands; most ancient civilisations used oil lamps; some Pacific islanders used candle-nuts. In Roman times, candles were made with a sliver of papyrus reed, impregnated with sulphur as a wick, and dipped in tallow. John Evelyn wrote, in 1670, that splints of woods of the hornbeam, piceaster (pine) and pitch-pine were all formerly used as candles in Europe. In remote districts in Europe and Asia, they have continued in use in this century. The Middle Ages used oil lamps, as well as rush-lights and soft tallow dips, which gradually developed into the hard candles used today. In general, the principle of artificial illumination remained the same from the dawn of history until the end of the 18th century; it was by means of burning a wick of some kind, either in animal or vegetable oil, or fat to form a lamp, or a candle.

The 19th century saw a race between improved oil lamps, gas and electricity. Colza oil lamps, introduced about 1836, were the early Victorian 'party' lights, until they were superseded, in 1853, by lamps burning paraffin or kerosene. Gas was discovered as an illuminant, in 1795, by William Murdock, who lit his own house with it, but popular prejudice slowed its general adoption. Boulton and Paul gave the new medium a fillip by lighting their works with it, at the end of the 18th century, and gas street lighting, commencing in Pall Mall in 1809, soon spread to many important London streets, superseding oil lamps on standards, a few of which had been installed as early as 1684. The 19th century was half way through, however, before even better class London homes had gas services extending higher than the reception rooms and in many houses, owing more to fear than cost, gas never reached the bedrooms, candles continuing as the only illuminant until electricity cheapened. It must be remembered also that early gas was not such a great improvement on candles: at first it was smelly, noisy, fed by fluctuating pressure and merely a raw, flickering flame, emerging from a hole at the end of a pipe. 'Batswing' and 'fishtail' burners followed, but not until Welsbach, in 1885, invented the incandescent mantle, did gas become a steady, white light.

Candelabra and Wall Sconces—see *Chandeliers*

Candles

A chandler's apparatus has been excavated from Herculaneum. A fragment of a candle, believed to be of the 1st century B.C. is in the British Museum. First written references to candles occur at the end of the 2nd century A.D. Fine wax candles were in royal and ecclesiastical use from early days in England; Alfred the Great (871–99) used wax candles, calibrated into twelves to tell the hours of the day. This was actually an ecclesiastical use, as the divisions were for prayer times.

The first advance on rush-light, in the ordinary home, was the soft tallow 'dip', which was merely a thicker rush-light or wick, repeatedly dipped in tallow, or other suitable fat, until it had attained the required diameter. The poorer people made their own candles, but in the 15th century, if not earlier, in important towns, travelling candlemakers visited the larger houses at regular intervals and made candles for the servants from the kitchen waste fat, accumulated in barrels. Such candles gave a poor, flickering light and needed frequent snuffing or trimming of their crude, loosely twisted, round wicks, which burned slower than the fat and tended to fall into it. One may gather this from the irascible Swift's ironic instructions to a butler and footman:

'Let your sockets be full of grease to the brim, with the old snuff at the top, and then stick on fresh candles. It is true, this may endanger their falling, but the candles will appear so much the longer and handsomer before company. When your candle is too big for the socket, melt it to a right size in the fire, and to hide the smoke, wrap in a paper half-way up. Sconces are great wasters of candles, therefore your business must be to press the candle with both your hands into the socket, so as to make it lean in such a manner that the grease may drop all upon the floor, if some lady's head-dress or gentleman's periwig be not ready to intercept it; you may likewise stick the candle so loose that it will fall upon the glass of the sconce and break into shatters; this will save yourself much labour, for the sconces spoiled cannot be used. Snuff the candles with your fingers then throw the snuff on the floor, then tread it out to prevent stinking: this method will very much prevent the snuffers from wearing out; you ought also to snuff them close to the tallow, which will make them run and so increase the perquisite of the cook's kitchen stuff, for she is the person you ought in prudence to be well with. And snuff the candles at supper as they stand on the table, which is much the surest way, because, if the burning snuff happens to fall out of the snuffers, you have a chance that it may fall into a dish of soup, sack posset, rice milk or the like when it will be immediately extinguished with very little stink'.

This reference to the butler's and footman's perquisite of candle ends is authentic 18th-century custom. It is related that the original Messrs. Fortnum and Mason, two footmen at the Court of Queen Anne, obtained their capital, to set up in business, from the legitimate sale of candle ends from St. James's Palace. Truly they waxed fat! Susanna Whatman, in her 18th-century housekeeping book, gave her advice more politely than Swift: 'The first thing a Housekeeper should teach a new servant is to carry her candle upright.'

Wax candles came into use, in the homes of the wealthy, in the 16th century, but were very expensive and very much 'party' lights elsewhere, until the end of the 18th century. They cost as much as 30s. per lb., not only because of their costly ingredients and their tendency to shrink while cooling, but also because their sticky nature precluded moulding them and they had to be rolled. As late as 1794, we find Parson Woodforde recording in his diary '... Dined at Mr. Mellish yesterday. Mr. Mellish treated very handsomely indeed. Wax candles in the evening ...'. In 1795, he records '... To Yollop, Haberdasher, for half a dozen pound of Kensington or London Mould candles, 4 to the lb. paid him 5/-....' These would have been tallow candles, which then cost 5s. to 7s. 6d. per 6 lbs.—much less than wax, but in 1654, moulded tallow candles had cost 5s. for 12 lbs., so inflation is nothing new.

With the opening up of the whaling industry in the 18th century, the excellent but expensive spermaceti candles came into use. Spermaceti vaporizes easily, burns cleanly and these candles provided an improved and steadier standard of lighting. They were formerly used for measuring candle power. Sir John Filmer, in his journal, recorded, April 14, 1758 'Paid John Lorum in Naked Boy Court in the Strand, for 1 dozen of spermaceti candles, no 3 to the pound, £1.7.0'.

Moulded candles had been introduced in the 15th century or earlier, but were always much dearer than dips. Metal moulds were usually employed, but the earliest were of wood (see *Candle Making*). The hard composite candles of today are a 19th-century invention, as was also the flat plaited wick, designed to bend downwards into the flame and be totally consumed. Until these came, footmen had to remain in attendance, to snuff candles dripping from chandeliers and to trim wicks. This was no mean task: at the coronation banquet of George II, Westminster Hall was lighted by 1,800 hanging candles, additional to those on the tables. At a function which I attended at Goldsmiths' Hall, between the two wars, the fine old hall, some 80 ft. by 40 ft., was lit by 250 candles and the light, though beautifully soft, was very subdued. With our bright and evenly lit rooms of today, it is easy to forget the dim light in the rooms of even 100 years ago, with their pools of wavering light from scattered candles.

Candle, Auctions by

'Auction by the candle' or 'Auction by inch of Candle' often appears in 17th- and 18th-century sale bills; it included not only small merchandise, but also houses and ships. The purchaser was the last bidder before

99 TOP ROW: Welsh canoe-shaped butter prints; BELOW: English butter prints. For details, see text. (*Section V*)

100 Two upper rows, mainly three dimensional butter prints; below, and at sides of centre row, circular butter prints. All English. (*Section V*)

101 English butter weighing devices, the interior print of the Scandinavian butter mould shown closed in Plate 95 *L*, and a Scandinavian hexagonal butter mould. (*Section V*)

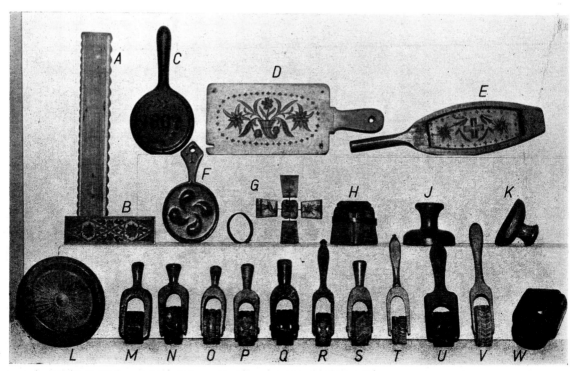

102 *A, B, C, F, J, K,* and *L* English butter prints; *D, E, G* and *H*, Swiss butter prints; *M* to *W*, English butter or pastry roller prints. (*Section V*)

103 Royal Stuart cheese print.
(*Section V*)

104 Royal Victorian cheese
print. (*Section V*)

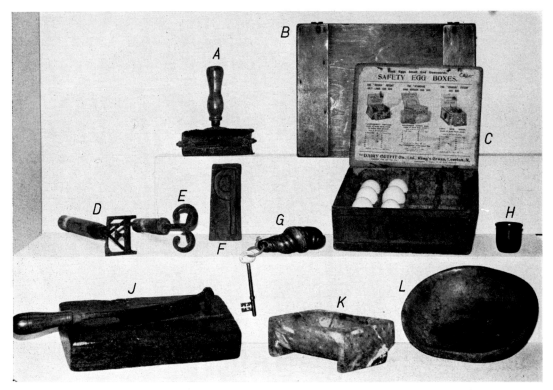

105 *A*, cow curry comb; *B* and *C*, egg boxes; *D* and *E*, sheep branding irons; *G*, key indicator; *H*, seed broadcasting cup; *J*, root chopper for cattle feed; *K* and *L*, sheep salve bowls. All the foregoing are English. *F*, New England wooden stamp for ownership initial on cattle. (*Section V*)

106 Dog disc wheel, for turning the box churn on the right. Welsh. (*Section*) *V*

107 Screw type cheese press from Herefordshire; *circa* 1845. *By courtesy of the Museum of English Rural Life, Reading.* (*Section V*)

108 Two types of ox muzzles; both Portuguese. (*Section V*)

109 Cooper's sheep dip. English. (*Section V*)

110 *A,* milk or water carrier's yoke; *B,* early type of plunger churn; *D,* barrel churn; *E,* box churn; *F,* milking stool with handle. All the foregoing are English. *C,* Swiss coopered milk vessel. (*Section V*)

111 Yard of butter worker. English. (*Section V*)

112 Two fine specimens of carved walnut bellows, with bronze nozzles. Italian, 16th century. Formerly in the Ledger Collection. (*Section VI*)

113 Standing bellows, mechanical, for peat fire or basket grate. English or Irish, 18th or early 19th century. (*Section VI*)

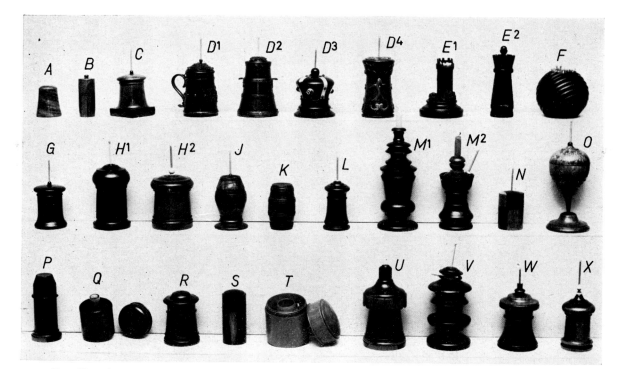

114 *P* to *U* are instantaneous light devices, *circa* 1810–25. The remainder, except *F*, are all protective match boxes made between 1826 and 1870; *D*1 to *D*4, *J* and *O*, are the latest and *V* probably the earliest. *M*1 and *M*2 combine candle holders. For further details, see text. (*Section VI*)

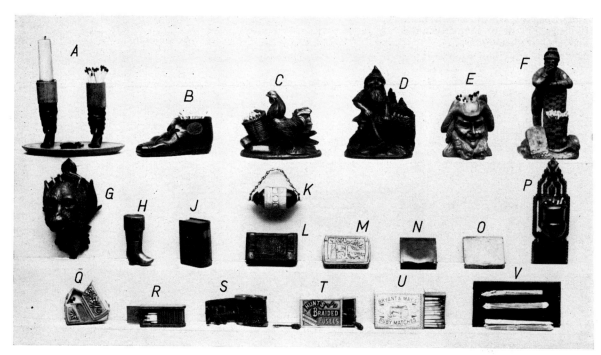

115 *A* to *F*, open match containers, *circa* 1875–1900; *A* and *B*, boots and shoe, probably English; the others, Swiss or Tyrolean. *G*, a monkey head, and *P*, a 'Gothic' fret cut design, Swiss or Tyrolean wall-type match holders, *circa* 1875–1900; *J*, *L*, *M*, *N*, *O*, *Q*, and *R*, pocket match containers of the same period; *K*, pocket tinder tube, Dutch, *circa* 1780. *S*, tortoiseshell case of *Cigarren-Zünders*, *circa* 1834; *T*, Hunt's Braided Fuses, *circa* 1850; *U*, Ruby Matches *circa* 1926; *V*, early secondary tinder 'matches'. (*Section VI*)

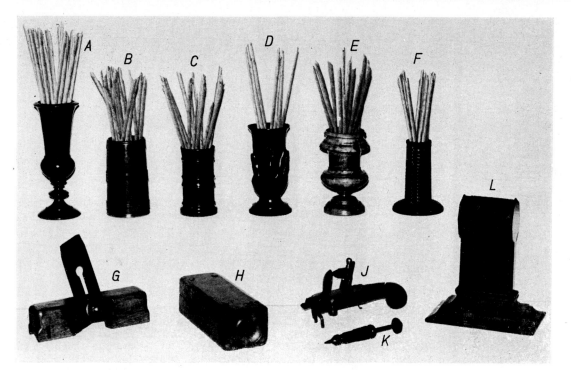

116 *A* to *F*, spill holders, all English except the carved hand specimen, 18th and 19th century; the curled shaving spills were made on the spill plane, *G*. *H*, exterior of Tudor candle mould (shown open in Plate 120, *J*). *J*, tinder pistol, English, 18th century. *K*, early fire piston, *L*, mahogany match dispenser, English, late 19th century. (*Section VI*)

117 TOP ROW: oak candle box, oak rush light box, rosewood taper holder, mahogany candle shield, all English, 18th-century. MIDDLE ROW: oak candle box, English, 18th century; oak nightlight holder, Welsh, 19th century. BOTTOM: at ends of row, old tinder box and 18th-century mahogany candle shield, both English; in between, a Dutch and a Norwegian food warmer, both 18th century. (*Section VI*)

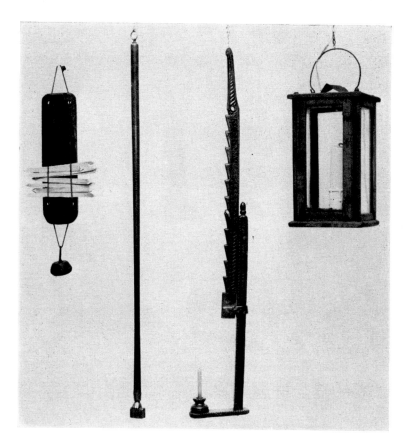

118 Early, English, oak rack for storing matches (non-strike); the cord is kept taut by the lead weight; English gas turn-key, the actual key of brass, formed as a hand grasping a book, at the end of a long wood handle; rare English or Welsh ratchet hanging candle holder, dated 1669; wood lantern, Alsatian, 18th century. (*Section VI*)

119 Unusual type of English adjustable candle stand, 18th century or earlier; candle mould stool for 24 candles, 18th or early 19th century. (*Section VI*)

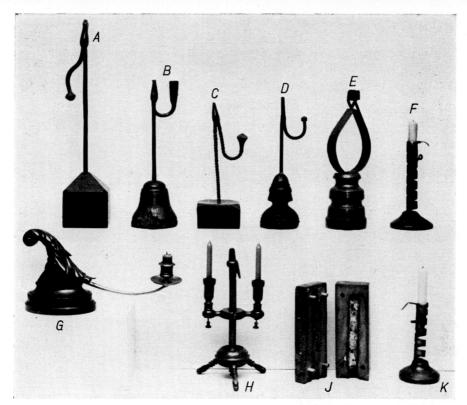

120 *A* to *D*, rush-light nips, English, probably 18th century; *E*, a Scottish puirman, probably 18th century; *F* and *K*, coil steel spiral adjustable candle holders on wood bases, English, probably 18th century; *G*, Regency, mahogany and brass candle arm; *H*, rush-nip and adjustable twin candle holder of boxwood, 18th century; *J*, very rare, 16th century, beechwood candle mould (shown closed in Plate 116, *H*), containing original 'fat' candle. (*Section VI*).

121 Selection of English, 18th- and 19th-century candlesticks; English, 18th century, candle stands and food warmer, and a French or Belgian, 18th-century, carved candle box. For details, see text. (*Section VI*)

122 Finely carved pearwood candlesticks and travelling folding lantern, French, late 17th century; burr wood saucer candlestick, 18th century; olivewood snuffer tray, a rarity in wood; wooden candle extinguisher. (*Section VI*)

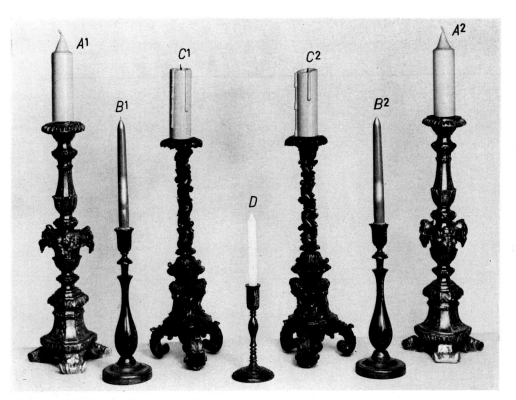

123 Fine candlesticks of the 16th, 17th and 18th centuries. For details, see text. (*Section VI*)

124 English candlesticks—*A* 18th century, adjustable, mahogany; *B*, 19th-century, carved walnut candelabrum; *C*, early 18th century, mahogany; *D* and *E*, 18th century, mahogany; *F*, walnut, 17th century. *G*, Scottish, 18th century; *H, J, L* and *M*, all English, 18th century; *K*, the triple twist, is probably 19th century, Spanish. (*Section VI*)

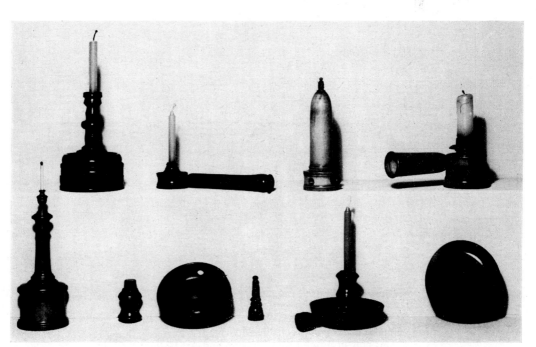

125 Travelling candle holders; English, 18th and 19th century. For details, see text. (*Section VI*)

126 Foot warmers of the 17th, 18th and 19th centuries. For details, see text. (*Section VI*)

127 English bed wagon, probably 18th century. Formerly in the Rev. C. J. Sharp Collection; now in Birmingham Museum and Art Gallery.

28 Scottish kelchin for drying pinewood splints, for use in a puirman. *Photograph by courtesy of University of Aberdeen.* (*Section VI*)

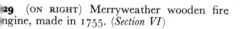

29 (ON RIGHT) Merryweather wooden fire engine, made in 1755. (*Section VI*)

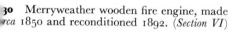

30 Merryweather wooden fire engine, made circa 1850 and reconditioned 1892. (*Section VI*)

131 Bacon rack from Somerset. The frame is carved and moulded round the side rails. Probably 17th century. (*Section VII*)

133 (ON RIGHT) Top and underside views of a unique Welsh basting stick inscribed: This.Bastin.Stick.I.Give.My.Host.To. Bast.His.Wife.For.Not.Bastin.His.Rost.By.Me.Edward. Webster.1646. (*Section VII*)

132 (BELOW) Oak bread oven door and 'print' combined, from Chard, Somerset, carved as a mermaid with mirror and comb; it may date from the 17th century. (Section VII)

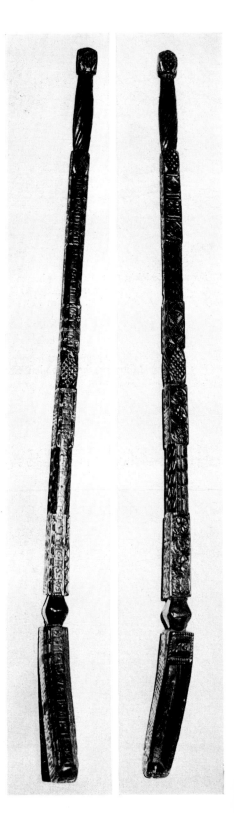

the candle expired. Samuel Pepys attended many Admiralty auctions by the candle and in 1662 recorded

> '... observed one man cunninger than the rest that was sure to bid the last man, and to carry it; and inquiring the reason, he told me that just as the flame goes out the smoke descends, which is a thing I never observed before, and by that he do know the instant when to bid last, which is very pretty.'

Candle-Beams

References to candle-beams occur in English literature, from the Middle Ages onwards. Originally, they appear to have been structural beams in open roof halls and churches, which had on them a row of candles, mounted in fixed iron sockets. In the 15th century, the term was sometimes applied to chain-suspended chandeliers—cross-bars of wood, similarly fitted with metal candle holders or spikes and forming an X on plan. If the wood framing was in the form of a circle or wheel, it was more frequently described as a corona.

Candle Boxes

English candle boxes, long, plain and rectangular, were usually made of oak, mahogany or elm. The sliding covers are generally bevelled, to slide in the end and side grooves. The cover may act as a top or a front: the boxes, being made to lie flat or hang on the wall, have a hole in the back extension, for a hook or nail to pass through, top left, Plate 117. The hexagonal box, illustrated immediately below, is very uncommon in wood, although this shape is sometimes found in metal; this oak example was formerly in the Gordon Roe Collection. Continental candle boxes are sometimes carved, Plate 121, A.

Some candle boxes have, at one end, a small compartment with inner pivoted lid, to hold tinder, flint and steel. Double candle boxes, with two narrow sliding lids and two parallel compartments, one subdivided into two smaller sections, were also combined candle and tinder boxes, one of the small sections being for tinder and the other for steel and flint. Single boxes of candle box form, but divided across into two sections, as described, are treen tinder boxes, bottom left Plate 117.

The use of candle boxes is already so far forgotten that they are often described as knife boxes. It is noteworthy that the first recorded use of mahogany in England was for a candle box, made by a cabinet-maker named Wollaston of Long Acre, at the end of the 17th century.

The general place for candle boxes was the foot of the staircase leading to the bedrooms, where candlesticks were grouped on a table or ledge, ready to light you to bed. In old houses, a recess or niche in the wall at the bottom of the stairs, now occupied by ornaments, was designed for candlesticks.

Candle Extinguishers

These are small 'dunces' caps', Plate 122, sometimes described erroneously as candle snuffers. Wooden ones are rare.

Candle Holders, Ratchet

Most of these useful devices for adjusting height of light source and keeping the height of the burning candle constant, were of iron. The majority were floor standing models. Hanging examples, on the lines of that illustrated, Plate 118, and dated 1669, are extremely rare. On this specimen, which is probably Welsh, the actual candle socket is a replacement.

Candle Holders, Travelling

Package candle holders, designed essentially for travelling, only seem to have come into vogue about 1800. As a generality, those made until about 1830 hold candles of only $\frac{3}{8}$ in. to $\frac{1}{2}$ in. diameter and, of necessity, include no provision for matches. Later specimens usually hold modern type candles up to $\frac{7}{8}$ in. diameter. A selection is shown, Plate 125. Top left is an 18th-century candle holder with tinder box in base; this type is common in metal, but rare in wood; the stem unscrews from the box. The next specimen, made of rosewood, is the first of the true travelling models, the obelisk; it dates from the Regency period, does not incorporate a tinder box, but no longer necessitates packing the candle separately. The handle, which is pictured screwed into the side of the base, is a hollow tube, threaded externally at the tapering end and internally at the wide end. When not used as a handle, it screws on top of the base and protects the candle. Its general appearance, when closed, can be visualised from the next example, of boxwood, which holds the larger diameter 1830 candle and has a thread-stoppered cavity in the base to hold three or four precious matches; the other hole takes the threaded end of the cover, when in use as a handle. Extreme right, is a slightly later and clumsier, boxwood model, with a box in the base to hold a quantity of matches. Both these last described examples have recessed glass-paper strikers under their bases.

The boxwood specimen, left of the bottom row, is an oddity difficult to fit into period sequence. Its resemblance in outline, however, to Victorian glove powdering flasks of 1860–70, suggests that date. The guiding factor in its design may well have been its maker's desire to create the outline of a classical urn surmounted column, on a plinth. This has resulted in a tube which holds only a $\frac{3}{8}$ in. candle and the utility of having the tube also serve as a handle has been lost. The match box in the base, however, is larger than in any previously described examples and the urn forms a socket for the 'good night match'.

The last examples shown in Plate 125 are chamber candlesticks, ingeniously made in pairs which screw together for travelling. In England, they are usually known as 'Brighton Buns'. They probably originated in Italy and are said to have been known in

the 17th and 18th centuries. English ones only seem to date from the 19th century. They vary considerably in quality and in size, ranging from $3\frac{1}{2}$ in. to 6 in. in diameter. Italian examples are usually of olivewood, like the specimen here shown open. The closed 'bun', English, is yew-wood, but English ones were made of any suitable turnery wood. Their working principle is that each half 'bun', or saucer, has a small central upstand. One upstand has an internal, and the other an external thread, so that they will screw together. The candle holders or sockets likewise have alternate threads, so that they will screw into or on to the respective upstands. The two candle extinguishers also have threaded extensions on their closed ends, which screw into holes in the sides of the saucers and act as handles. Sometimes there are no holes in the sides of the saucers and then there were probably no extinguishers included in the outfit. When screwed into a complete 'bun' for travelling, there is space inside for the two candle holders and two extinguishers. Apart from 'Brighton Buns', wooden chamber candlesticks of saucer type, with side handles, are rare but not unknown.

Candle Making and Candle Moulds

Countrymen probably discovered, at an early period of civilization, that an effective candle mould could be made from a length of dried cow-parsley stalk, cut between the knuckles; this method continued among the poor to within living memory. The first man-made moulds were single ones, gouged out of wood and made in two halves, to peg together. Possibly the oldest now in existence, and maybe unique, is that illustrated, open, Plate 120, *J* and closed, Plate 116, *H*. It measures 8 in. by 3 in. by $2\frac{1}{2}$ in. and its survival and finding are interesting, for Mrs. Pinto discovered it amongst ancient lumber in the cellar of a farmhouse, the *new* part of which dated from the reign of Elizabeth I. It still had its original kitchen waste fat candle in it, as shown. Beech is not usually a long-lasting wood and this artefact has undoubtedly survived only because the cellar of damp limestone has petrified the outside, whilst the inside is so saturated with fat that the normal weight of the wood is greatly increased. According to old records, wooden candle moulds were also made in batteries, like the later metal ones. Generally, moulds of iron, tin, pewter and pottery appear to have superseded wooden ones during the second half of the 16th century. Although single metal ones were made, the majority of domestic moulds were in batteries, which made up to 1 or 2 pounds of candles, of varying sizes, at a time. Commercial batteries might make 200 or more at a time. Candles were formerly sold according to the number which went to the pound. Thus, you might buy a pound of long nines, twelves, or short sixteens.

Most of the battery moulds were all metal, including their stands, but some were metal moulds, inserted in wood stools or stands, Plate 119. The actual moulds, usually but not invariably tapering, were inverted, pointed ends downwards. The candle making process was the same for moulds of all materials. Wires were laid horizontally along the bed over each line of moulds. The wires were held in position by passing through holes in the upstands, each end of the stool. The stands were then inverted, and wicks were threaded through the pointed end of each mould, leaving a short length projecting at the lighting end. The long lengths passed through the moulds and were then knotted on to the wires. The candle stool, which had been on its side during the knotting operation, was then stood upright and the wicks had to be arranged carefully to ensure that they passed centrally through each mould. After this, pouring could commence. With all these slow and fiddly operations, it will be readily appreciated why dipped candles were so much cheaper than moulded ones. Some of the cheapest dipped candles were made like rush-lights, with rush wicks, but moulded candles had woven wicks. The various improvements in wick processing are outside the scope of this book, but in some 18th- and 19th-century households, candle wicks were finely knitted and dipped in boracic, to give clean, bright burning.

The old candle mould stool of pine, Plate 119, 18½ in. high by 19¼ in. wide by 6¾ in. deep, with 24 inverted iron moulds arranged in three rows, presumably made 2 lbs. It is probably 18th-century, although there is no way of dating such an object accurately. It was, however, a common object in the kitchen quarters of 18th- and 19th-century homes and might be used by household staff or itinerant candle-makers, usually women.

Candle Moulds—see *Candle Making*

Candle Screens or Shields

These must have been essentials in draughty rooms, to stop candles guttering. The majority of screens were made of brass, silver or japanned iron. Probably few were ever made of wood, because the greater difficulty of bending would have made them expensive, compared with metal. The few extant are all 18th-century, mahogany examples, Plate 117. So far is their use already forgotten, that a pair in the U.S.A. were recently advertised as 'unusual decanter stands'.

Candle-Stands

These are often confused with wig stands of the same period, but the latter are, in fact, mushroom topped—see Section XXIII, *Toilet and Bedroom Accessories*. Most surviving candle-stands are of the 18th or early 19th centuries and they were originally made and sold in pairs, Plate 121, *G, H* and *J* (only one of each pair is illustrated). Although varying in their turning, English examples follow a basically similar design. A hollow stem of baluster or vase outline is threaded into a circular foot, which is sometimes lead weighted. A circular tray, with slightly upturned rim, is fitted with a solid rod stem, which slides up and down in the lower hollow stem, and is adjustable at varying heights, by means of a wooden set-screw. Manual height adjustment kept the source of light reasonably constant, as the candle burnt down. A few candlesticks were made with height adjustment, obviating the use of a candle-stand, Plate 120, *F*, *H* and *K*, and 124, *A*, all described under *Candlesticks*.

Floor standing candle-stands, pedestals or torchères, are outside the scope of this work, except for those which incorporate a candle holder, and the majority of those are of iron. There were, however, three types made in wood, particularly in the 18th century. One had a threaded wood stem or pillar, on which were mounted one or two threaded candle brackets, adjustable in height by turning them on the stem. The second had a ratchet adjustment and the third, illustrated, Plate 119, which probably dates from the 18th century and is of oak and elm, has a friction rise and fall action.

Candle-stands, Lace-makers'

If the rays of light from a candle are passed through a water-filled glass globe, they are refracted and emerge as a concentrated beam. In England, the globe or flask is known as a flash, but the American terminology of water lens or refractor is more logical, because that is precisely its function. That this principle has been employed at least from the 17th century and by lace-makers is undoubted, but it was also used by cobblers, glove-makers, limners, jewellers, watchmakers, wood engravers and probably in many other close work trades, where a comparatively small circle of bright, unwavering light was all that was needed. At least one well-known engraver today, still uses a candle lit water lens for her fine work, claiming that it is much kinder on the eyes than any modern illuminant.

A lace-maker's candle-stand, with most usually four flashes in wooden holders ranged round a single candle, provided a bright circle of light on four lace pillows grouped round it and enabled four of the poorly paid workers to work by the light of one comparatively expensive candle. Nearly all English lace-maker's candle-stands are crude, three-legged stools of milk stool variety, with five holes in the top, of which four, spaced round the perimeter, are for the flash holders, and one centrally placed for the spring controlled rise and fall candle holder: the flame had to be kept at a reasonably constant height, to concentrate the light on the pillows. The early or mid 18th-century, oak pillar and tripod lace-maker's candle-stand—see Section XXI, *Textile Workers' Devices*, Plate 333—must be considered as an exceptional quality piece, more likely to have been used in an English manor house, than in a cottage. The glass flashes are modern.

For lone lace-makers and others engaged on close work, single flashes on stands, or in hollow holders of candlestick form, were available. Some flash holders, like the flashes, were of glass. On the continent and in the U.S.A., oil lamps often provided the illuminant for the flashes in the 18th cenbury, but oil does not seem to have been used in England, for this purpose, before the 19th century and even then candles remained more common.

Candlesticks

Candlestick is so ancient and well established a word that it is useless now to try and restrict its usage to the pricket type, which was the ultimate development of the pointed stick or spike on which a candle was originally impaled. Properly speaking, the socket type is a candle holder. Safety-wise, wood was never a suitable material for making candlesticks, unless their sockets were lined with metal; otherwise, if somebody were not handy when the candle reached its end, the candlestick became a well fatted torch, which set the room and ultimately the house on fire. Nevertheless, in all probability, more candlesticks made of wood than any other material were formerly found in humble homes, because wooden candlesticks of simple design were the cheapest and easiest to make; moreover, our ancestors seem to have been fatalistic about fire and remarkably careless, considering open fires, naked lights and that so many lived in closely packed wooden houses, with thatched roofs. In spite of frequent occurrences of devastating conflagrations and terrible loss of life, in the 16th century they used curtained oak bedsteads, which often had candle ledges just above the pillow line of the bedhead.

For the reasons already stated, really early wooden candlesticks are about the rarest form of treen. There are probably now extant, none of *simple form* of earlier date than the 16th or 17th century; even if any of those periods are now found, they will probably be singles and not the pairs, in which they were originally made. A damaged wooden candlestick had no value and became firewood unless elaborate and valued as a work of art. Another reason for the survival of palatial and ecclesiastical carved wooden examples is because they are mostly pricket types and their tops were always protected from burning by a metal grease pan. An exception in early socket types, is the well-known 15th-century Beaufort pair at Winchester.

It is dangerous to be dogmatic about dates of antique candlesticks, even when their design features are outstandingly obvious. The same designs continued century after century and no man, on appearance of the wood, can tell whether a wooden piece is 300 or 400 years old. Moreover, burning of sockets, and scraping off, and polishing in of grease runs, create a quick patination and gives an entirely false impression of age to candlesticks.

Whilst in England, very early treen domestic candlesticks were probably simple,

humble pieces, this was not necessarily the case on the continent; but in England, wood came into fashion for domestic candlesticks in the 18th century, and as these specimens usually had metal or metal-lined sockets, a fair number of pairs have survived and some representative specimens are illustrated, Plates 121, 122, 123 and 124. Because of the conservatism of the turner (and sometimes his client), it is emphasised that dates given must be regarded as very approximate and have been assessed by analogy with designs in silver, brass, pewter, copper, ceramics, etc.

Two fine pairs of candlesticks, of which one pair is probably 16th-century, Italian, are illustrated, Plate 123. The pair, *A1* and *A2*, 21 in. high, of gilt pine, consists of hexagonal columns formed with three large and three small sides, decorated with classical carved mouldings and cherub heads, whose respective outstretched wings meet. They stand on three rather flat scrolled feet and are typical of designs in wood and bronze of their period. Their condition is good, considering their probable age. The much more unusual pair, *C1* and *C2*, $19\frac{3}{4}$ in. high, of pearwood, are patinated to the colour and lustre of bronze. They are late 17th-century design and have twisted pillars with intertwined flowers, and knops which act as canopies for three beautifully executed cherub heads, with wings folded in the manner beloved of Grinling Gibbons. Their acanthus scroll carved feet curve gracefully inwards. Their prickets, which appear to be original, are also wooden, so it may assumed that they were never intended for use, but were wood patterns made as a 'try-out', probably for bronze— for wood 'try-outs', see *Introduction*, page 6.

Two French candlesticks of pearwood, in the fine art class, are illustrated in Plate 122. Such candlesticks were included in pairs in dressing table sets of the late 17th century. The designs with fine low relief carvings of flowers and scrolled foliage are usually described as by Cesar Bagard of Nancy. For further details of Cesar Bagard, see Section XXIII, *Toilet and Bedroom Accessories*. Similar designs occur in silver of the period.

Little seems known of simple treen candlesticks until the end of the 17th century; one earlier, a German specimen of pricket type, dating from *circa* 1500, is in the Victoria and Albert Museum.

Analogy with metal gives a good idea of 15th-, 16th- and 17th-century wood forms and it is a popular fallacy that although the socket candle holder was introduced in the 14th century, it was uncommon for domestic use until at least 200 years later. This is incorrect: the Romans used socket candlesticks, which may have been lost again in the Dark Ages and not re-introduced until the 14th century, but paintings of domestic interiors, from the mid-15th century onwards, almost invariably show socket types. The pricket, especially for candles of larger diameter, has continued in churches to the present day.

The 12½ in. high, baluster turned, walnut candlesticks, Plate 123, *B1* and *B2*, are a genuine old pair, which approximate to the silver design of 1794. The slender baluster and ring turned mahogany candlestick, *D*, is 7⅞ in. high and inlaid with flowers. It is Dutch, *circa* 1740–50. The two therm-shaped, mahogany candlesticks on square base, Plate 121, *D1* and *D2*, have brass necks and drip pans and are typical Regency pieces of *circa* 1810–20. The two small ebony candlesticks, *E1* and *E2*, copy a late 18th-century design.

Somewhat of a speciality of the· turner were 'twists'; there are solid twist, both of rope or 'Dutch' type, as well as English double rope or 'barley sugar', also the more airy 'open double twists', like Plate 121, *F1* and *F2*, and 'open triple twists', as Plate 121, *C1* and *C2*. They have all enjoyed popularity ever since the 17th century and as open twists are regarded by turners as exhibition pieces, they will

probably continue in similar form for many years yet. The dates of individual specimens are problematical. They are delicate and, even if treated carefully, break easily, so it is likely that most existing specimens were made during the last century. The 'triples', Plate 121, *C1* and *C2*, are oak, probably about 100 years old; the 'doubles', *F1* and *F2*, of good quality, are walnut and probably date from 1800–10. In all modern specimens so far examined, the turners have removed the centre cores from inside the twists with a drill, then pelleted the holes at the end. The older ones, such as those illustrated, are scooped from the sides, and without holes at top or bottom.

Many people exaggerate the importance of the shape of candle sockets and contend, because of the prevalence of 17th-century 'cotton reel' and straight cups in metal, that urns, vases or inverted bell shaped cups were all 18th-century innovations; all these shapes occur in earlier work, particularly Italian Renaissance. The 18th century, apart from certain ornamental detail, was mainly a classical revival. In candlestick bases, there are two distinct styles: flat bases, which seem to have originated in western Europe, and cylindrical, deep bases, sometimes slightly conical, which came from the East. They chased each other in and out of fashion, the 15th- and early 16th-century popular 'flat' largely giving way to the 'deep' cylindrical in the late 16th and early 17th, after which the pendulum swung again. During most of this period, however, the top of the base was the drip pan and not until the mid-17th century did the drip pan separate from the base and start climbing upwards, staying half-way for some time, but reaching the underside of the cup generally between 1675 and 1700. By 1800, the pan had tended to become a separate metal or glass disc on top of the cup, relieving the candlestick itself of all drips.

The only candlesticks entirely of wood, which provided height adjustment to compensate for the burning of the candle, were probably the ratchet candle holders already described, see *Candle Holders, Ratchet*. A few partially wooden candlesticks with metal adjustments were, however, made. In England, the commonest in the 17th and 18th centuries were probably the coil steel spirals, on wood bases, Plate 120, *F* and *K*. In North America, the wire or 'bird-cage' was more favoured, for raising the candle 'lift' on two or more vertical wires. A much more sophisticated device than either is the English, 18th-century candlestick with square brass collar, controlled by set-screw, which operates two candle arms on a mahogany obelisk, Plate 124, *A*. Other interesting candlesticks in Plate 124 include *C*, an 18th-century, English specimen in mahogany, and *D* and *E*, also early 18th-century. *G* is mahogany with brass cup, Scottish, last quarter of the 18th century. The imposing Charles II, walnut specimen, *F*, one of a pair, looks younger than its age, because some misguided person had stained and polished it a plum red, and it has had to be stripped. *H* and *L*, each one of a pair, are lignum vitae, English, 18th-century. *J*, one of a mahogany pair, with 'cotton-reel' candle sockets and delicately turned stems, is English, 18th-century. *K*, one of a pair of elaborate, carved, double twist candlesticks, turned from walnut and other hardwoods, is probably Spanish, 19th-century. *M*, one of a pair of unusual English candlesticks, may well be 17th-century.

Horizontal metal and wooden candle arms, to clamp on the edge of a table or shelf, were made throughout the 19th century. In wood, they were usually of rod section, provided with a number of elbow pivot joints, which gave them a considerable range of action; they were a speciality of the Tunbridge turners. An interesting and attractive variant, although providing much less range, is the heavily weighted, acanthus scrolled, oval, mahogany block, with brass side arm, Plate 120, *G*. It is English, *circa* 1820–30.

Chamber Candlesticks—see *Candle Holders, Travelling*

Chandeliers

The words chandelier and candelabra both have great antiquity and have long been interchangeable English terms for multibranch candle holders. In old inventories, they are sometimes referred to as hanging candlesticks. Since the 17th and 18th centuries, the great age of elaborately carved candelabra, the term chandelier has been reserved for the hanging variety; candelabrum, plural candelabra, is now more usually reserved for the standing multibranched candlesticks. The terms are so used here.

On account of both reduction in weight and cost, many of the multi-tiered, many branched, gilt chandeliers which still grace 17th- and 18th-century halls and apartments, are of gilded wood and not metal, as they first appear to be. All the great 18th-century cabinet designers and makers, and mirror frame carvers, including Thomas Chippendale, illustrated carved chandeliers and girandoles or wall sconces in their range of products. On the continent, particularly in South Germany, Switzerland, Austria and Portugal—the deer hunting countries—great chandeliers of antlers were made, from the 14th century onwards. Some of these antler chandeliers had their points mounted with polychrome finished, carved wooden figures or busts, which formed the candle sockets.

The design of the candelabrum did not lend itself to manufacture in wood. One of a pair, dating from about 1870, made of walnut, ingenious but hideous examples of misplaced Victorian ingenuity, is illustrated Plate 124, *B*.

Coronas—see *Candle Beams*

Girandoles—see *Chandeliers*

Kelchins

Kelchins were crude wooden cradles, with

frames of hurdle construction and an ash, or other suitable springy wood, loop handle, like Plate 128, which is a rare survival. From early times, they were suspended from the ceiling, near the fireplace, in Scottish cottages and farmhouses, and were devices for drying the splints of resinous pine or 'fir candles', which were often used there for lighting, instead of rushes as in England. See also *Puirman*.

Lanterns or Lanthorns

Although horn for lantern sides diminished in use at the end of the 16th century, being largely superseded by glass, all the great 18th-century designers still used the term lanthorn, instead of lantern. Lanterns fall under two headings—small portable, single candle lanterns, for carrying in the hand or fitting to vehicles, and large, multi-candle lanterns, for use in halls or on staircases, where draughts would have made open chandeliers a menace. In England, portable lanterns almost invariably had metal frames. On the continent, wood framed, portable lanterns seem to have been used considerably. The traditional 18th-century example, Plate 118, came from Alsace.

Eleven elaborate rococo designs of carved wood and brass hall lanterns are illustrated in the 1762 edition of Chippendale's *Director*; more appear in Ince and Mayhew's publication of the same year. There are also frequent references to them in the accounts of both Georgian cabinet-makers and specialist manufacturers of brass lanterns. Some of these hanging lanterns were vast, up to 8 ft. in height and holding up to 18 candles. Some were open at the top; others were provided with hinged, framed glass doors. In some instances, these lanterns were serviced from the staircase; in others, they were provided with pulleys, for letting down.

Some of the 18th-century wall lanterns are wood framed and some metal. Generally, they have mirror or burnished metal backs to increase light reflection, and they must have needed daily polishing. Like the hanging varities, some are open at the top, others provided with doors.

Night-light Holders and Food Warmers

Not surprisingly, straightforward night-light holders of wood are rare. The charmingly naïve, but quite undatable oak chapel, with stained glass windows, Plate 117, is Welsh. It has a very charred candle ledge behind it. The proud woodworker father, who probably designed and made it, obviously created a grave fire risk, although no doubt the illuminated windows delighted and comforted his small child.

The majority of wooden night-light holders are combined with pap warmers. Mostly they were made in ceramics, both pottery and porcelain, and they are usually described by the French term *veilleuses*. Wooden specimens are described later under *Warming: Food and Foot Warmers*.

Night-light Lanterns, Collapsible

Survivals are extremely rare, understandably as they must have constituted an exceptional fire risk. They were made to pack flat for travelling. The framing was usually of metal, but one in tortoiseshell has recently appeared in auction. Whether they were ever made in England is unknown. The wooden specimen, Plate 122, is an example of the fine carving of the school of Cesar Bagard of Nancy and dates from the second half of the 16th century. For further details of Cesar Bagard, see Section XXIII, *Toilet and Bedroom Accessories*. The base on which the night-light sat, doubtless on a metal plate, the top rim and the hinged cover are, as is usual with this work, of pearwood. The 'lantern' is of paper; the paper is not original.

Pickwicks—see Section XXII, *Tobacco Accessories: Tobacco Stoppers*

Puirman

The puirman, or poor man's splint holder, was the Scottish equivalent of the English rush-light holder. The spring iron or steel tongs, mounted on an iron or wood base, Plate 120, *E*, gripped the long resinous splint, which was burnt at an angle of about 30° out of horizontal.

Rush-lights

Rushes were prepared as rush-lights by cutting them in late summer or autumn, soaking them in water, drying them in the sun and then peeling them, but leaving one strip of peel to strengthen the pith, which acted as the wick. The rushes were then coated with kitchen fat, by passing them through a boat-shaped pan of melted bacon or mutton fat. If dipped several times, a rush candle resulted. The best description is given in Gilbert White's *Natural History of Selborne*. White states that a good rush, 2 ft. 4 in. long, will burn for 57 minutes, and that rushes costing 3*s*. per lb., went 1,600 to the 1 lb.

Rush-lights were used by the Romans and Greeks and described by Homer, 12th century B.C., and they were still used in country cottages 100 years ago.

Rush-light Boxes

These containers, Plate 117, usually of oak or mahogany and mostly dating from the 18th century, are rare and seldom identified correctly. They are made to stand or hang and generally measure about 13 in. in height, plus the extension for wall hanging. They are 3 in. to 4 in. wide and 2 in. to 3 in. deep, open at the top, and usually have a viewing 'window', low down in front.

Rush-light Nips

Rush-lights were too long, slender and fragile to be held upright, when lit; they had special iron holders of weighted pincer form, which gripped them firmly, allowed for adjustment of angle and easy moving along of the rapid burning rush. Rush-light nips generally have iron stems and nips and wooden bases, sometimes roughly squared, at other times simply turned. Some are floor standing models, with adjustable ratchets to raise or lower the light. Crudity of base shows cheapness more certainly than antiquity. Generally, bases of 18th-century specimens, when turned, are steeper in profile than 19th-century ones. The examples illustrated, Plate 120, *A* to *D*, are probably all 18th-century. The side cup, which is a part of one 'leg' of some hinged rush nips, such as *B*, acted as a candle holder for special occasions, or as a douser for the rush; on early specimens, the cup is smaller than on 19th-century examples.

Some rush nips were intended as wall brackets. When so designed, the iron stem is bent in L-shape and the return piece is roughly pointed, for driving into an upright timber post.

A rare boxwood combined rush nip and adjustable twin candle holder tripod is shown, Plate 120, *H*. When the knobs under the candle sockets are pressed upwards, the candle ends are ejected; the candle sockets are brass lined.

Save-alls

Save-alls are small, usually square sheets of iron, fitted with an upturned iron spike, to allow candle stumps to be used to the end. Occasionally, a square of thick wood, with a nail driven in and the head filed off, served the same purpose.

Scioptric Balls—see Section XIX, *Scientific: Optics*

Snuffer Trays

The only wooden specimen so far noted, is the olivewood example, Plate 122, which follows a well known English, 18th-century silver design.

Wall Sconces—see *Chandeliers*

WARMING

Portable warmers for hands, feet, beds and food have doubtless existed ever since man has colonized cold parts of the world. The majority of the devices, such as heated bricks, and metal, stoneware or rubber bottles for beds, hot water containers of different shapes, for use in muffs, and as pre-heaters for boots, or even curved to strap over the stomach, are outside the scope of this book.

Bed Warmers and Wagons

Warming pans of silver, copper or brass are simply circular containers, with hinged lids, for charcoal or embers; they have been used for many centuries and were slid up and down the bed by means of a long handle. The container usually has a diameter of approximately 13 in. to 16 in. and the overall length is about 42 in. In some examples, the lid is pierced in an ornamental pattern.

Bed wagons were more often bed airers than bed warmers, to be placed on the bed, under the covers, in a little used bed-chamber.

The 18th-century bed wagon, as illustrated in Plate 127, is a cage, sometimes of iron, but more often of wood, usually with steamed and bent ashwood hoops and spars, enclosing a pan of charcoal in an iron brazier; iron plates fitted above and below, protected the bed clothes from burning. Bed wagons are said to have been in use in England in the 16th century. As most of the existing specimens originally came from Sussex, it is possible that their manufacture was a branch of Sussex trug making.

A bed wagon, priced at one guinea, appears in an account from George Seddon to Joseph Robinson Pease, which is preserved in the Victoria and Albert Museum. Seddon, who had a very large showroom and cabinet factory in Aldersgate Street, well described in the diary of Sophie v. la Roche (*Sophie in London*, 1786), would probably have 'bought in' such an item.

Bed wagons of split cane, with a can of hot ashes, hung from a hook from the top spar, are still used as ordinary bed warmers in remote parts of the mountain districts of North Italy.

Food Warmers and Foot Warmers

The grouping together of old-time food warmers and foot warmers may, at first sight, seem curious. In their simplest form, they were, however, basically similar, made in different sizes and sometimes of different materials.

Food Warmers

The food warmers, which also doubled up as night-light holders—see *Lighting, Night-Light Holders*—were usually made in ceramics, both pottery and porcelain and the majority which have survived are comparatively simple circular pedestals, with an opening at the bottom in front, for inserting the heating unit, and a circle cut out of the top, to form a seating for a teapot, chocolate-pot, warming bowl or posset cup, which in most instances were probably made *en suite*, although few complete units have survived. The heating/lighting unit, usually a pottery container, was filled with oil and fitted with a wick, or a night-light was used; sometimes, when no light was required, charcoal was used, in a metal pan.

In France, these food and drink warmers were known as *veilleuses*, and the name was adopted in other countries, including England. *Veilleuses* are found in many countries, including England, France, Switzerland, Germany, Italy, Russia, Spain, Portugal and the Far East.

The oddest material for making *veilleuses* was probably wood and the fact that so few have survived is doubtless due, not to their having been uncommon, but because of their inflammability. Most of the wooden examples appear to have come from the Baltic countries, particularly from Friesland

and Scandinavia—countries in which wood is the most common material and where a virile peasant tradition of woodware and wood carving has existed for many centuries. Plate 117 illustrates two food warmers, a small one, probably Dutch, and a larger, carved oak Norwegian specimen, 6 in. wide and 5 in. high, dated 1761. Both are charred under the top, as one might expect. Plate 121, *K*, is a 4 in. high, English, 18th-century, oval food warmer of reeded mahogany, lined with brass. In a painting of a lady drinking chocolate, by Jean-Etienne Liotard (1702–89), a mahogany *veilleuse*, of very similar design, is shown on the floor alongside the lady.

Foot Warmers

Most 17th- and early 18th-century wooden foot warmers still extant are Dutch or Scandinavian rectangular boxes, on the lines of the good Scandinavian example, left, middle shelf, Plate 126. The door is fitted with a turn-button, and the elaborately pierced panels in the door, sides and top disseminate the warmth. Foot warmers of this type usually measure about 9 in., by 8 in., by 8 in. in height, have brass carrying handles and are chip carved all over, generally in geometric designs of centre roundels and corner lunettes, with the piercings forming part of the design. Occasionally, naturalistic flower, leaf and animal designs are employed. Additional to being useful necessities in cold climates, with draughty houses having brick or stone floors, they also served as household ornaments, when not in use; they were then hung from a ceiling beam, which explains why carving under the base is as elaborate as that which covers the other surfaces. A painting by Cornelius Bisschop (1630–74) shows a girl using a Dutch carved foot warmer, of the general variety described.

More scientific and efficient types of foot warmer were made both in England and Holland in the 18th century, and are shown centre and bottom, Plate 126. They consist of a flat board of wood, from 14 in. to 17 in. wide, covered in copper, on which was mounted centrally a 5 in. to 7 in. wide oak box container, sometimes with metal liner, and vents in the lid. The perforated box sent the heat up under the user's skirt and also carried it along the copper covered convector foot plates each side. In certain variants, such as that central in the same plate, there is a slat-topped heater box in the centre, with perforation at the base of the sides, carrying the heat through to lower boxes each side, on which the feet rested.

During the 18th century, both in England and in Holland, round and oval wooden foot warmers came into vogue; both are illustrated in Plate 126. Like the earlier ones, they contained charcoal pans, and had brass carrying handles. Some had marble tops. All these portables were used not only in the house, but also in vehicles and were carried to the cold stone-paved churches; in some churches, foot warmers could be hired for the equivalent of 1*d*. a service.

Also during the 18th century, circular wooden foot warmers with brass hot water containers in them and brass carrying handles, were introduced, centre, top shelf, Plate 126. They were usually about 10 in. in diameter and 5 in. to 6 in. high. They continued in use in England and Holland, well into the 19th century.

For horse carriages in England, a considerable number of footstool warmers were used, top right, Plate 126. This is a rectangular, polished rosewood veneered frame, 10 in. square, by approximately 3½ in. in height, and contains a flat metal hot water tank. The hinged lid or cover is an open frame with fleece lined turkey wool-work stretched and nailed over the framing. Some of us are old enough to remember the successors of carriage foot warmers— copper hot water 'bolsters', which occupied the centre of the floor in long distance, separate compartment trains.

FIRE FIGHTING

Fire Fighting Equipment

Although English history lays much stress on the Great Fire of London of 1666, which destroyed 13,200 buildings in four days, few seem to realise the appalling frequency of other fires, formerly involving whole streets or districts in London and other cities of Britain. Bearing in mind the closely packed timber-framed buildings with thatched roofs in early times, the paucity of fire-fighting equipment and the absence of fire-fighting organization, the extent and frequency of the conflagrations is not remarkable, particularly as the citizens seem to have adopted a fatalistic outlook and showed complete disregard, not only of care and commonsense, but also of the laws enacted for the protection of their lives and property.

Although most writers have copied each other in stating that chimneys were almost unknown in England until the 15th century, this statement is completely incorrect. It seems to be based on the fact that large halls, up to and including the 15th century, often had centrally placed hearths, with the smoke ascending to a louvred cupola in the roof above; a few single storey and possibly single roomed primitive dwellings followed the same pattern, but although our ancestors were certainly tough, it is a great mistake to think that the majority of them endured this kippered existence. Norman castles had their wall fireplaces, with short stone flues, some of which still survive, and quite obviously mediaeval houses of two or more storeys, with several rooms on each floor, neither could nor did adopt the open hearth plan. It can be safely assumed that in the 13th century, domestic chimneys were common but a grave fire risk, for from sloth, stupidity and probably, in many instances, poverty, people built their domestic chimneys, whenever possible, of wood! As early as the reign of Edward II (1307–1327), a law was enacted in London '. . . that no chimney be henceforth made, except of stone, tiles, or plaster, and not of timber, under pain of being pulled down'. Only rigorous enforcement of this law eventually brought the dangerous practice to an end. Abuses were still being punished 150 years later.

Other laws of Edward II, appertaining to London, made provision for stone party walls to be continued above the roofs, to form fire barriers, for houses henceforth to be roofed with lead, tile or stone and not with straw or stubble. Citizens were also required to '. . . have a ladder, or two, ready and prepared to succour their neighbours in case misadventure shall happen by fire'. They also had to have '. . . before their doors a barrel full of water for quenching such fire . . .' and, probably most important of all, it was laid down that in every ward, there should be provided '. . . a strong crook of iron with a wooden handle, together with two chains and two strong cords . . .'—namely, a fire crook or thatch hook—see *Thatch Hooks*.

Fire Buckets

Early fire buckets were of coopered wood, or copper riveted leather. In the 19th century, the much lighter canvas buckets came into general use. It is doubtful if any early coopered wooden fire buckets survive. There would be no way of distinguishing a fireman's wood bucket from one used by a water-carrier or a milkmaid.

Fire Engines

The Dutch engineer, Jan van de Heyden, 1637–1712, known in England as Jan van der Heide, made the first manual fire engine in 1672. It was a tank and pump on wheels, with flexible leather hose. Richard Newsham, a London engineer, between 1721 and 1725, added the air chamber to fire engines, an important development, which converted the former series of water spurts into a continuous stream. Several of Newsham's manual engines survive.

These early blacksmith/carpenter-made

wooden engines were only 5 ft. to 6 ft. long and had quite small tanks, without inlets, and had to be filled continuously from a bucket chain. They had approximately 2 ft. diameter iron-rimmed solid wood wheels and were difficult to turn, as there was no swivel on the front axle. A Merryweather wooden engine, dating from 1755, is illustrated, Plate 129.

Engines gradually grew larger during the 18th century and in the early 19th century, a number were made which could be pulled manually or by horse power. The wooden fire engine in the Pinto Collection, Plate 130, made about 1850 and formerly owned by the Earls of Darnley and used at Cobham Hall, Kent, has large open wheels, swivel axle and a good-sized tank with side lever pumps, and an inlet with strainer. It seats five men a side, and may be drawn by two or three horses. It has leather and canvas hose and is in working order. The date 1892, painted on its sides, denotes when it was reconditioned.

About the mid-19th century, steam power was first used for operating fire pumps, and before the end of the century Merryweathers of London were building engines motivated by steam. The wheeled fire escape, as opposed to ladders carried on engines, was invented by Abraham Wivell, in 1837.

Early fire hoses of copper-riveted leather were immensely heavy and difficult to roll and unroll. They were not generally superseded by canvas until the second half of the 19th century.

Thatch Hooks
Some thatch hooks for dragging thatch from burning cottages and houses still survive. In spite of the law, party walls were not always of stone or brick before 1666, even in London. In many country places, the walls seldom continued above the roof, until recent times. The only way, therefore, of creating a fire-break, in a terrace of thatched buildings, was to tear down the thatch and isolate the doomed building or buildings from others which had not yet caught alight. The chain-hung hooks were mounted on 16 ft. to 20 ft. long poles and were wielded by several men, or harnessed to horses, as necessary.

Fire Services

Fire brigades existed in ancient Rome, but not until 1698 do we hear of firemen in England, when the Hand-in-Hand, a London insurance office, appointed 'firemen' from among the Thames watermen. Early in the 18th century, individual insurance companies commenced forming their own brigades, with their own engines and other equipment. They marked the building which they insured, with their fire marks or fire plates—now collector items— and at first only fought their own fires. In 1832, the London Fire-Engines Establishment was formed, by an amalgamation of the fire-fighting organizations of 30 insurance companies. James Braidwood, chief of this first 'Establishment', had managed the Edinburgh brigade from 1824, three weeks before the great Edinburgh fire of that year. His experience in that fire, led to his making the Edinburgh service the finest in the United Kingdom, before he transferred to London, where he reorganized the service.

The 1861 Tooley Street Fire, in which brave James Braidwood lost his life, destroyed two million pounds worth of property and led to the passing of the Metropolitan Fire Brigade Act, 1865, the merging of the London Fire-Engines Establishment, and the Royal Society for the Protection of Life from Fire, and the establishment of the London Salvage Corps. In 1866, the Metropolitan Fire Brigade was established and standardization of equipment followed. In 1888, the brigade, came under the L.C.C. and in 1904, it became the London Fire Brigade. Quite appallingly, the provision of fire-fighting services in the provinces remained permissive and not obligatory, until the coming Second World War cast its shadows in 1938.

As a temporary war measure, the regular fire brigades and the war-time Auxiliary Fire Services were amalgamated into a National Fire Service in August 1941, with a total strength of 213,000 whole and part-time men and women serving, and more than 20,000 appliances.

VII

Kitchen

The early mediaeval kitchen seems to have been a timber structure with a central hearth, the smoke escaping through louvres above. It was built away from the main building, to lessen the danger from fire. Before the end of the mediaeval period, kitchens in large establishments had changed to stone or brick structures, with one or more open fireplaces with wide arches and flues in the thickness of the walls. Thereafter, until the end of the 18th or early in the 19th century, the development of the kitchen was slow, consisting largely of gradual improvements in cooking equipment. In the planning of many great houses until well into the 18th century, the kitchen remained well away from the house, not because of the risk of fire, but to avoid the smell of cooking. To ensure as far as possible against tepid food, passages for trolleys with huge covered dishes, and even kitchen railways were built, as at Shobdon Court.

The 19th century and this one, have been the real revolutionary period in kitchens; basically, there was no great difference between the *circa* 1340 kitchen illustrated in the Luttrell Psalter, the 16th-century kitchen at Hampton Court and the Regency kitchen at the Brighton Pavilion, because the method of cooking was the same. During a period of at least 500 years, roasting was by means of a turn-spit in front of an open fire; boiling and stewing

were carried out in pots, some of huge size, suspended over an open fire, or in pots on legs, stood in the fire; bread and pies were baked in brick ovens, built into the walls. Such changes as occurred were mostly due to fashions in food, gradually increasing availability of coal, improvements in and increase of varieties of implements, and in the changing emphasis of use of various devices, due to the modifications aforementioned.

During the mediaeval period, equipment was sparse, and boiling, stewing and making of hotch-pots more common than roasting; this was partially due to the absence of fresh meat in winter, but probably even more to the lack of forks and the consequent reliance on spoons for everything not eaten in the fingers. Log fires for cooking resulted in the use of skillets and other pots with legs, including kettles, which could stand in the hot ashes, or legless pots for suspension from hooks and chimney cranes. With increased use of coal during the 17th century, fire baskets and grates came into use, and pots and pans lost their legs.

A surprising development of 17th-century cooking by coal heat was Monsieur Papin's Digestor, a pressure cooker invented 250 years ahead of its time. John Evelyn recorded, April 12, 1682,

'I went this afternoone with severall of ye Royal Society to a supper wch was all dress'd, both fish and flesh, in Monsʳ Papin's digestors, by which the hardest bones of beefe itselfe, and mutton, were made as soft as cheese, without water or other liquor, and with less than 8 ounces of coales, producing an incredible quantity of gravy; and for close of all a jelly made of yᵉ bones of beefe, the best for clearness and good relish, and the most delicious that I had ever seene or tasted. We eat pike and other fish bones, and all without impediment; but nothing exceeded the pigeons, which tasted just as if bak'd in a pie, all these being stew'd in their own juice, without any addition of water save what swam about the digestor, as *in balneo*; the natural juice of all these provisions acting on the grosser substances, reduc'd the hardest bones to tendernesse; but it is best descanted with more particulars for extracting tinctures, preserving and stewing fruite, and saving fuel, in Dr. Papin's booke, publish'd and dedicated to our Society, of which he is a member'.

Thanks to coal, the heating of spits became easier to control, roasting became more popular and the importance of the flesh hook—a wooden-handled iron pitchfork with upward curved prongs, set at right angles to the handle—waned because it was no longer required for pulling out large joints of meat from vast cauldrons. The long-handled colander type of spoon shown in the Luttrell Psalter still continued in use, and mortars figure largely in kitchen illustrations from the 14th to the 19th century.

In theory, roasting and baking both denote the same thing—cooking by radiation. In practice, there is considerable difference in the flavour of meat and poultry that has been cooked on a spit, as opposed to the same foods baked or roasted in an oven. Few will deny that the flavour induced by the free evaporation of the spit roast is superior to that of the vapour enveloped meat cooked in an oven, even although oven design has recently improved greatly and is very different from that of the Victorian kitchen range or kitchener, which was more or less standard-ized about 1851 by Evans, Son & Co. of 33–4 King William Street, London. The kitchener was the last stage of development of the improved kitchen range invented by Thomas Robinson in 1780, but only adopted very slowly in British homes.

Nevertheless, that range, with its central fire-box, side ovens, hobs, dampers and back boiler, need for frequent stoking and adjustment, not to mention emery paper and blacklead, all of which would speedily drive a modern cook out of the kitchen, was revolutionary and in its day a compendium of baking, boiling and water heating, which represented a substantial saving of labour, as opposed to the various separate components which previously served the same purpose. These, in brief, were the bread and other brick-built baking ovens; the open fires, with a multiplicity of hooks, swinging cranes and ratchet adjustable hangers for suspending pots above the fire; and the revolving spits across the front of the fire for roasting meats, game and poultry. In a large kitchen, this sometimes entailed having as many as four open fireplaces. A fire-dog each side of the fire had a series of hooks projecting in front. These acted as supports and bearings at each end, for the 6 ft. to 8 ft. long steel spits revolving in front of the fire at an appropriate height, with a long pan for the dripping, below. When not in use, the gleaming spits were kept horizontally, one above the other, in a notched rack over the mantelshelf.

By the beginning of the 17th century, spits were turned by at least five different methods: manually, by man or boy, as in the Middle Ages; by a dog; by means of a chain running over a cogged pulley, to which was attached a weight, wound up by a winch; by clock-work; or by a smoke jack. The first needs no explanation; it was lowly, hard and hot drudgery; to call a man a turnspit or skip-jack was a term of contempt in the 17th century. When a turnspit-dog was employed, the poor animal was incarcerated in a treadmill or wheel, usually located high up on the wall beside the fire-place. The action of the dog 'back-peddling', was transmitted to the pulley wheel on the spit, by means of cords and intermediate wheels. The smoke jack was a vane in the chimney, turned by the up-ward current of hot air. It was the kindliest and most labour saving motive power for the spit, but being expensive to install was usually only found in large and wealthy households. A smoke jack and spit remain *in situ* in the late 16th-century kitchen of Burghley House, Stamford, and another in the kitchen of the Brighton Pavilion. In 1660, Samuel Pepys was intrigued by the ingenuity of Mr. Spong, the instrument maker '. . . especially his wooden jack in his chimney, which goes with the smoke, which indeed is very pretty'. A wooden smoke jack sounds rather a bad fire risk!

The term kitchener was originally applied to one employed in a monastic kitchen. Not the least of the advantages of its Victorian successor was the provision of some hot water by taps to sinks, basins and baths, instead of the interminable trek with kettles and cans. By the end of the 19th century, the cook and the household generally, were being assisted by auxiliary gas cookers and hot water circulators and the half century reign of the kitchener was nearly over. Early in this century, gas, and a little later, electric cookers superseded solid fuel cookers, at least in towns. With the advent of refrigerated ships, cold storage and more latterly deep freezes, it has be-come normal to convey meat and other perishables across the world, keep them for long periods and have them available for the table all the year round.

Contemporary with these changes, there has been a complete revolution in the appearance, size and amount of labour in-volved in a kitchen. Even since my child-hood, it has changed from a large, cream painted, albeit somewhat gloomy chamber, with floor to ceiling cupboards and a huge dresser, accommodating china on its upper shelves, and on its counter covered in American cloth, a row of deep drawers below and, lower still, an open compart-ment with black painted pot-board for pre-serving pans, fish kettles, etc. Additional familiar kitchen features were the narrow shelf for trays and the wall hooks for gradu-ating sizes of dish covers. Gone are its ancillaries of scullery and pantry, the former with copper, and stoneware sink, the latter with teak or lead-lined sink. Gone, in favour of plastics, are also many of the wooden gadgets formerly considered kitchen essentials, although some of the treen items are staging a come-back. Now we have a small, bright and colourful, clinical, labour saving room, fitted with purpose-made, plastic-surfaced ranges of fitments, which include stainless steel or enamelled iron sinks, garbage disposal units, refrigerators, so good that they have almost superseded larders, and eye-level cookers, some with revolving spits, which once again roast meat properly.

As with the spit, so the wheel has gone full circle in another way. In the small home of today, it has become quite com-mon for part of the kitchen to be set aside for meals, just as it was in the farmhouse or cottage kitchen, before the days of the kitchener. Then, even a small kitchen-living-room had a huge fireplace with bread oven at the side and usually another brick oven for baking pies or heating plates, a brick or stone hearth, fire dogs, chimney crane, pot hangers, inglenook seats, and often also with small windows inside the arch. Larger houses had a separate bake-house. Space was also found on a fireplace ledge or wall for the salt box, which had to be kept dry. On the main ceiling was the bacon rack, well out of reach of marauding rodents.

What is not generally realized today is that food has become less highly seasoned as it has become more freshly available. In the Middle Ages as, indeed, long after, while transport remained bad, and before root crops were introduced, there was lack of winter pasture and cattle were slaughtered in the late autumn, except those kept for breeding, and those so kept only bred at the natural times. In consequence, most of the winter meat and fish available was salted, for fish brought inland was likely to be stale; winter fruits were mostly dried.

The absence of fresh meat in winter was the reason for the multitude of large and handsome pigeon cotes and pigeon lofts, which were built during the Middle Ages and in the 16th and 17th centuries. In early times, only the lords of the manor and clergy were allowed to build cotes and this was a great hardship to the farmers and cottagers, whose grain was raided. But laws were harsh and a thief who stole pigeons could be hanged; F. G. Emmison, in *Tudor Food and Pastimes*, records that between Easter and Michaelmas 1551, 1,080 pigeons were taken from the pigeon cote at Ingatestone Hall, Essex. Pigeons made a valuable addition to the menu of any manor house and pigeon cotes with 365 holes, one for each day of the year, were fairly common; some cotes contained 1,000 or more holes, all accessible from potences.

The need for highly spiced foods may be appreciated by reference to some of the most common penalties of 'punishment by pillory' recorded in *Liber Albus of the City of London*, in the reign of Edward I, between 1275 and 1296. 'For selling putrid meat' is the most frequent charge, but it is run close by selling 'stinking pigs, putrid pigeons, stinking capons, rotten fish and stinking eels'. It is no wonder that vast quantities of spices and herbs were used in cooking, by those who could afford them, and it is enlightening to read old recipes and other documents and see how many flavourings were available in quite early times. Rosemary, sage and thyme are native herbs, and saffron was grown in England (Saffron Walden) from the 14th century. It was valued medicinally and for dyes and was much used in sauces, together with ginger, cinnamon, cloves and onions, all of which were also valued medicinally. A Guild of Pepperers existed in London as early as 1180. Nutmegs, dill, cummin and aromatic seeds such as fennel, coriander, caraway and mustard have been used since biblical times. Honey and almonds were both used in England in mediaeval cooking and, in fact, of the flavourings now used, only vanilla appears missing from the English kitchen until the 18th century. All the imported spices and other flavourings were subject to customs duties at an early date. Among those listed, with the dues payable, in the 13th-century section of the *Liber Albus of the City of London*, are pepper, sugar, cummin, almonds, ginger, small spices (such as cloves, mace, cubebs and nutmegs), cinnamon and anise. Other foods then being imported included figs, raisins, rice, dates, chestnuts and 'confectures of spicery'.

Bacon Racks

Bacon racks or cratches, formerly a normal feature in kitchens of homes not large enough to have a bacon or ham-curing loft, were designed on two different principles. One was a slatted rack, fixed to the rafters, with a fall flap or hinged doors at one or both ends; steps were needed to reach it. The other was a rack raised or lowered by means of cord and pulleys. The majority of the rise and fall type were of hurdle construction, but in the West of England, a more decorative style was sometimes used, rather like a latticed bed tester. A Somerset pattern is illustrated in Plate 131. The pine frame, which is both carved and moulded on the outer faces of the rails, is tenoned and pegged into the oak corner stumps, which have turned knobs. The slats are halved over each other. This style is traditional, the example illustrated measuring 52 in. by 49 in., and probably 17th-century; it will be noted that some of the diagonal slats are missing. The cratch served the dual purpose of seasoning the bacon in the smoke from the fire, and keeping it clear of rats and mice.

Basting Sticks

With spit cooking, basting had to be done frequently and by hand. The fat floating on the liquid in the dripping pan was used, not the gravy itself. The frequency and manner in which the operation was executed were just as important as stopping the revolution of the spit at the right moment, to ensure the roast being 'done to a turn'. The implement used for basting in the 17th and 18th centuries was known as a basting stick. It was basically a long handle, curved downwards and scooped out at the far end to form a trough for the fat. Affixed to it and extending out beyond the trough was an iron or pottery ladle or spoon, which was fed with fat through a hole in the end of the trough. Being generally of no intrinsic value, few such early implements have survived, but one, a Charles I example, Plate 133, almost certainly Welsh, still exists, doubtless only because its ornamental shaping, the quality and intricacy of its fine carving and the nature of its inscription, have made it unique.

It is cut from a single piece of yew-wood, 36 in. long and is patinated to a rich bronze colour. Although the numerous changes in its section, throughout its length, give the impression of turnery, it is actually all whittled by a knife or chisel. All surfaces except those reserved for the inscription are neatly and intricately chip carved with roundels, diamonds, ropes and other geometric designs of the type found on Welsh love spoons and knitting sheaths, but it is no love token. The incised inscription on it reads as follows:

THIS.BASTIN.STICK.I.GIVE.MY.
HOST.TO.BAST.HIS.WIFE.FOR.
NOT.BASTIN.HIS.ROST.   BY.ME.
EDWARD.WEBSTER.1646.

It is also carved with the initials M.G.

How it came into the Pinto Collection is of interest to collectors. When I first saw it, it had its original iron spoon projecting through the end of the trough and it was in a West End saleroom, in a lot with a French casket. I only wanted the stick, but I left a bid which I thought would secure it. I was the underbidder and it went to a West End dealer friend. Owing to being ill at the time, I did not visit him for several weeks. He had only been interested in the casket and said that he would gladly have given me the stick, which he considered valueless, but he had sold it in a lot to a Dutch dealer, the previous week. He wrote to the Dutch dealer, who had by then sold it at the Utrecht Antique Dealers' Fair. Two years later, it turned up at the Grosvenor House Antique Dealers' Fair. By now, due to lack of understanding of its correct use, it had lost its iron spoon, and the slot through which it passed had been carefully filled in. It was also priced at five times the original amount which it and the casket together had fetched. I refused to buy at the price asked and as it was not sold at the Fair, I eventually secured it at a more reasonable figure.

Biscuit Prickers—see *Muffin Prickers*

Boards, Chopping and Pastry

Pastry and chopping boards are usually quite plain and not very old, being thrown away when worn.

Bowls

Bowl turning is described in Section XXIV, *Tools of Specialised Woodworkers*. Often there is no distinction between a wooden bowl used for eating, in the kitchen, dairy, laundry, or for other purposes. They simply varied according to diameter and depth. Large ones are usually of sycamore, small ones of beech. A 17½ in. diameter bowl is shown in Plate 135, *A*. In Plate 136 are five beech bowls. *K* was excavated from a 16th-century layer in Old Street, London. It is pole lathe turned, like the small bowls *P, Q* and *R* which, in the absence of such evidence, are impossible to date. The 8 in. diameter bowl, *O*, with lug and spout cut out of one piece, is very unusual, being the result of painstaking gouging, not turnery.

Bowl Stirrers and Scrapers—see *Spatulas and Spurtles*

Boxes, Food—see *Dry Store Jars, Bentwood Boxes and Flour Barrels*

Bread-crumb Graters—see Section XI, *Mortars, Grinders and Graters*

Bread Oven Doors

In town kitchens, the brick-arched, half-moon-shaped, bread oven opening was usually closed by a loose iron door, secured by a button. In country districts, it was not unusual to use a piece of hardwood, which dropped into a groove in the brick cill of the oven floor and was secured at the top by a turn-button. The wooden panel, usually perforated with a few vent holes, became charred on the back in time, but probably lasted indefinitely. The ancient oak bread oven door, Plate 132, from Chard, Somerset, is carved in intaglio on the face of the board, so that it also acted as an ornamental print or stamp, $15\frac{1}{4}$ in. wide by $11\frac{1}{2}$ in. high. It may date from the 17th century. When used as an oven door, the charred mermaid of Chard had to stand on her head to perform her toilet with a comb and mirror.

Bread Slicers

Commercially produced bread slicers were a feature of design and patents in a number of countries during the second half of the 19th century. The American slicer, Plate 134, *A*, was patented by the Arcadia Manufacturing Co. of Newark, New York, under various patent numbers, between 1885 and 1891. It has $\frac{1}{16}$ in. slice thickness adjustments, up to 1 in. It is 21 in. long and mainly of elm, with cast iron fittings,

other than the steel knife. Behind the sliding panel, with its diagonally set, adjustable knife, is a folding wooden bed and an upright end fence. The loaf is placed on the bed, tight up against the fence, and pushed against the sliding knife panel as it passes backwards and forwards.

Much simpler is the English device, *E*. It consists of a pivoted cutter with beech handle, guided between two bent beech hoops, fixed to a beech bed, with a spring-loaded adjustable fence, which determines the thickness of the slices. It is undated, but was probably made about 1900. See also *Vegetable Slicer*.

Cabbage Pressers

Cabbage pressers, for squeezing out water, are larger versions of 'mushroom' darners, usually with the button end about 5 in. in diameter. One is shown in Plate 135, *H*. They are normally turned from beech and are traditional in form.

Caramel Rollers—see *Rollers*

Choppers

Kitchen choppers are usually short spades with a turned crossbar handle. The blade may be straight on the cutting edge, or convex for use in a chopping bowl. Twin-bladed, double-handled choppers like *D*, Plate 134, are uncommon; it appears to be a 19th-century specimen.

Cratches—see *Bacon Racks*

Cucumber Slicers—see *Vegetable Slicers*

Cutlery Boxes—see *Spoon Racks*

Dog Driven Spit

The different methods of turning a spit are described in the introduction to this section. The only one which comes under the heading of wooden bygone is the dog wheel or cage, Plate 146, and survivals are very rare. Some were built into the wall, as shown in the reconstruction of an old kitchen; others, probably the majority, were boxed out on the face of the wall. The small dog was placed in the treadmill of the cage and as it walked forward, the wheel reversed and turned the spit. The connection is by means of the leather driving thong, looped round the variable speed, grooved driving wheel of the shaft, which transmits dog power, via a loop on the fireplace beam, to the wheel of the spit. The wheel illustrated is in original condition, probably dates from the early or mid-18th century and measures 36 in. in diameter and 9 in. in width. For details of other animal driven devices, see Section V, *Farm: Treadmills*.

Dry Store Jars, Bentwood Boxes and Flour Barrels

All wooden jars with stoppers or close fitting lids are, in effect, dry store jars and in the absence of labels or other evidence, it is impossible to be certain which were used solely in the kitchen. Possibly a few of those illustrated in Section I, *Apothecary*, were used in the kitchen. A very distinctive type, which seems to be peculiar to Sussex, but the exact purpose of which, unfortunately, appears to be lost, is represented by Plate 135, *D*. This example is 16½ in. high and I have found another the same size, and three lesser, of which the smallest is 7 in. high. It seems likely that they are combined jars and measures. In Plate 137 are three other different types. *A* is very much a translation into wood turnery, of a pottery design. *C* is somewhat puzzling. It is coopered in mahogany, with three brass bands; it tapers towards the top and has a tight fitting lid, with knob; the inset base, shown towards the camera, is chip carved to form a print or stamp. I know neither its nationality nor purpose, but it looks to be 19th-century. Both the appearance and design of *R* suggest that it is not later than 18th-century.

In the same way that you formerly went to a bowl turner and selected a bowl to suit your particular purpose, so you went to a bentwood box-maker, or 'band box' maker, selected a box of the size you wanted and used it to house anything from dried herbs to butter, cheese, bread or cakes, or from hats to any other articles of clothing, and in smaller sizes, from pills to boot buttons. Bentwood boxes, therefore, are only described in this section because some of them were used for dry stores, but they could be and were used for many other purposes. They may consist of either three or four principal components—the top, the bottom, the box rim and, in English and American examples, the lid rims. The top and the bottom are pine, for the easy nailing or pegging on of the rims. The wood used for the rims varies according to when and where the box was made. The design limits the shapes to rounds and ovals. Bentwood boxes have been made for hundreds of years, and so well made that they last hundreds of years. It seems probable that the cradle of bentwood boxes was Scandinavia, although they have been made in almost every other country where suitable wood is available for cutting thinly, and steaming and bending the rims.

Examples of bentwood boxes are shown in Plate 138, of which *F, G, J, K, L* and *M* are Scandinavian. All these are of pine throughout, with square or fingered lap joints, laced with willow, and every component joined with wood pegs—no metal anywhere—making the boxes ideal for any food purpose. *F* and *G*, which are 18th-century specimens, are decorated with chip carved and gouged ornament; *J, K* and *L*, the last 21 in. long, are probably second half of the 19th century and are ornamented by steel punches and simple gouging. These later boxes continue to be well made, even though the ornament is dull. Note also that they have willow loop handles on the lids, which do not occur on earlier specimens. Basically, the method of opening and closure remains the same, irrespective of age. The upstanding pegs or horns, which are such a typical feature, are shouldered to engage slots which are cut out of the ends of the lids. By springing the horn towards the end of the box, the lid is released, and lifts off; it goes on easily by pressing it downwards, along the curved edge of the horn. On the 18th-century boxes, release of one end of the lid is by the same method, then it can be tilted up above the peg head, when it is swivelled round, not lifted off. At first sight, this procedure looks impossible with round box *F*, because it has four pegs, but the answer is that only two are fixed to the box rim, the other two being merely ornaments on the lid.

The attractively decorated, 11 in. diameter, convex-lidded cake box, chip carved in a floral pattern, signed, and dated 3 April 1822, was probably made as a love token; the willow lacing of the lap joints is particularly good. It follows the English and American style of tight fitting rimmed lid. In England, bentwood, 'chip', or band boxes were made for storing documents as early as the 15th century and are listed in early 17th-century inventories—see also Section XIV, *Parcelling, Postage, Sealing etc.: Skippets*. They were given the name band box because they were used to store the fashionable bands or ruffs; the larger ones always seem to have been used much more for costume and its accessories than for food. By the commencement of the 19th century, the term 'band box' and bonnet or hat box were practically synonymous. English band boxes are quite plain, usually with a square lap joint and both this and the junctions of rims with tops and bottoms are nailed. The bent rims are made from steamed beech, oak, ash, hazel or pine.

American bentwood boxes, sometimes called spit boxes, divide into three types—Colonial, Shaker and factory made. There must have been many of them among the luggage of the early colonists from Europe. Early Colonist boxes usually have lap joints of rims fastened with nails, but the rims themselves fixed to lids and bottoms with wooden pegs. As in Europe, various woods were used for rims of the multi-purpose lap-jointed boxes.

Shaker boxes were uniformly well designed and executed. The tops and bottoms are always of pine, the rims of maple, on medium size boxes, only $\frac{1}{16}$ in. thick; lap joints are neatly fingered and all junctions are secured by copper nails. The Shakers, an American celibate religious community, active for 150 years from the mid-18th century, made some of the most practical, simple and aesthetically satisfying objects of home and farm in the New World. The Shaker oval box *H*, 8¼ in. long, is inscribed, in the lid, that it was made in 1856 by the Rev. Joseph Johnson of the Ministry Enfield, near Hartford, Connecticut. Compare the fingering of the joints on this box with those on Scandinavian boxes *J* and *K*, made about the same time.

English and American bentwood boxes were factory made in the 19th century and have machine-made nail fixings. They were sometimes supplied in 'nests' of up to a dozen sizes.

Some English flour barrels, like Plate 144, *J*, come into the bentwood construction technique; they have sliding gate action bolts and are impossible to date accurately. So also are the traditional willow bound, coopered pine flour barrels, like Plate 144, *G*, which were used over a long period both in England and America, and also served basically as butter and sugar tubs. The square flour box, tapering slightly towards the top and fitted with a sliding handle, secured by a peg, Plate 144, *H*, was an awkward type of container, made in England in the 1870s. Like so many household objects of that period, even including iron hot water cans and hip baths, it was usually grained externally in imitation of a particularly sickly fumed oak. See also *Salt Boxes*.

Egg Stands
Double-decker egg stands, with neatly turned corner posts, Plate 136, *N*, made to

hold 12, 24 or 48 eggs, were to be found in all Victorian and Edwardian larders and also in dairies.

Egg Timers

Egg timers, Plate 136, *H* and *J*, have been kitchen essentials for hundreds of years. They were merely small and short term members of the sand glass family, and their larger brothers were also to be found, at one time, on every kitchen mantelshelf, for timing cooking operations. *H* is an 18th-century, standing specimen; *J*, made about 1860–70, is pivotally mounted on a wooden plaque, which screws on a wall. For dating of sand glasses, see Section XIX, *Scientific*.

Flour Barrels—see *Dry Store Jars, Bentwood Boxes and Flour Barrels*

Food Boxes—see *Dry Store Jars, Bentwood Boxes and Flour Barrels*

Fruit Pulpers

The long-handled wood implement, Plate 138, *E*, with the faceted head, rather like an enlarged lemon scoop, is alleged to be a fruit pulper, possibly for pumpkins, but no corroboration has been obtained.

Funnels

Wooden funnels, of which a good selection is shown in Plate 136, *E* and *F*, were formerly to be found in the kitchen, chemist's dispensary, wine shop, etc. Funnels show all the individuality of the turner, and his ability to make useful objects attractive, without ornamentation; no two are exactly alike. The last four unscrew at the bulb, which contains, or should contain, a wire strainer. The general outlines are traditional and appear both in 17th- and 18th-century engravings, and also in silver and pewter examples.

Garnishing Moulds

Wood-handled, steel garnishing moulds of similar type to Plate 142, *M*, were made in a variety of designs for food decoration. *M* has a rosewood handle.

Ginger Sifters—see *Sifters*

Griddle Boards—see *Riddleboards*

Haver Boards—see *Riddleboards*

Hobs

Although wooden hobs may not seem very practical for hot pots, they were, in fact frequently used, not only in the kitchen, but also in the workshop for glue pots; if made of certain hardwoods, they soon cover themselves with a protective coat of char. They do, however, become unsightly and, therefore, are usually thrown away when worn. The Elizabethan tilting hob, Plate 135, *E*, is believed to be a unique survival. It consists of a triangulated openwork grid, with extension arms tenoned and pegged 'dry' into an upright post, toothed to form a ratchet and grooved to take a movable bracket. When a pot is stood on the hob, with its handle resting on the bracket, it may be tilted by simply raising the bracket on the ratchet, thus making easy the ladling out of the last of the liquid contents. The hob, which· is made of various English woods, is extensively charred, but the thin cross-slats are easily replaced by sliding in new ones.

Icing Guns

The icing gun, Plate 139, *C*, consists of a tinned iron cylinder with a solid sycamore plunger. The lower part of the cylinder, which terminates in a narrow rim, is detachable by means of a bayonet fastener. Seated on the rim is a loose metal disc, with a central star-shaped aperture. Presumably there would originally have been a set of such discs, with apertures shaped for different icing sugar ornaments. It probably dates from the 19th century.

Iron Holders—see *Kettle Holders*

Jelly Mould Stands

Hardwood stands for copper jelly moulds, consisting of eight solid wood blocks and a centre handle, similar to Plate 139, *F*, are to be seen in the Regency kitchen at the Brighton Pavilion.

Jugs

Wooden jugs in general are described in Section III, *Drinking*. A small and very crude jug is illustrated in Plate 136, *G*. It is interesting both because the jug, its handle and its spout are all cut out of the same block, and because the relationship of spout to handle show that it was intended for left-hand pouring.

Kettle and Iron Holders

The insulating qualities of wood made it an ideal material for holders for lifting metal devices being heated over an open fire. The kettle or iron holder of mulberry wood, Plate 141, *K*, consists of two segmental leaves with brass hinges; it was formerly in the Evan-Thomas Collection and probably dates from the 18th century. In 1953, in Belfast, I found sycamore holders on sale as the latest thing. The modern ones only differed from the old design in having a length of spring steel pinned round the leaves, so that they sprang open, when the hand pressure was released.

Knife Boxes—see *Spoon Racks and Cutlery Boxes*

Ladles (Kitchen)—see *Spoons*, also *Muffin Ladles*

Lard Squeezers

The lard squeezers, Plate 137, *D* and *E*, are from the U.S.A. They consist of two boards, roughly shaped and hinged with leather. They were obviously made by the handyman, as required. Doubtless similar crude but effective devices were used in England, before the all-metal, 19th-century lard press was produced commercially.

Lemon Squeezers

When lemons were first introduced into England is unknown, but an early mention occurs in a rare 16th-century sheet of woodcuts of *London Cries*, now in the British Museum. No. 3, '*The Orange Woman*', runs

> 'Fine Savil oranges, fine lemmons, fine;
> Round, sound, and tender, inside and rine,
> One pin's prick their vertue show:
> They've liquor by their weight, you may know.'

Probably lemons were still a rarity in the 16th-century England, as I know of no recipes of that century which mention them; but certain sauces which, at that time, used fennel, verjuice or vinegar, were made in the 17th century with lemon juice.

In Sir Hugh Plat's *Delightes for Ladies*, published in 1602, recipes are given for 'Lemmons in Marmelade', 'Lemmon moulded and cast' and 'Lemmon Juice kept all the yeere'. Instructions for the marmelade read

> 'Take ten Lemmons or orenges & boile them with halfe a dozen pippins, and so drawe them through a strainer, then take so much sugar as the pulp doth weigh, and boile it as you do Marmelade of Quinces, and then box it up.'

Moulding and casting the lemon was a complex recipe for making an edible sugar ornament, coloured with saffron and cast in alabaster moulded round a lemon. Plat's instructions for preserving lemon juice are too long and involved to quote.

Early lemon squeezers were always made of close-grained hardwood. The three basic principles which were employed are still used for their successors in glass, china, metal and plastics. Plate 140 shows them all—lever, screw and scoop. On the top shelf are three hinged lever type squeezers. Left, rather a rare type, dating from the 17th century, is made of lignum vitae. It has a slight hollow carved out of the inside face of each lever, so that it will readily grip a half lemon. It has to be held vertically

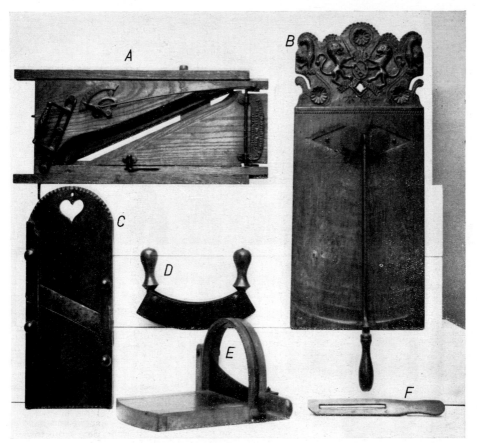

134 *A* and *E*, American and English bread slicers respectively, late 19th century; *B*, Dutch *saladier*, early 18th century; *C*, English vegetable slicer, and *F* cucumber slicer, both late 19th century; *D*, twin-bladed chopper, 19th century. (*Section VII*)

135 *A*, sycamore kitchen or dairy bowl; *B*, strainer spoon; *C*, short-handled bowl; *D*, Sussex dry store jar; *E*, unique Elizabethan tilting hob; *F* and *G*, boxwood potato masher and rolling pin, made *en suite*; *H*, cabbage presser. (*Section VII*)

136 *A* and *B*, steak beaters
shortbread mould; *D*, moulds
removing dents from pewter sp
E and *F*, assortment of funnel
jug cut from the solid and des
for left-handed pouring; *H* and *J*
timing sand glasses; *K*, 16th-ce
beech bowl; *L* pork pie mould
podger; *N*, egg rack; *O*, bowl
spout and handle; *P*, *Q* and *R*,
pole lathe turned bowls. (*Section*

137 *A*, *C* and *R*, dry store jars;
H and *M*, various handled stra
D and *E*, American lard pre
F and *G*, kitchen spoons; *J*, *O*, *P*
Q, handled bowls or ladles
scoop; *N*, piecrust roller. (*Section*

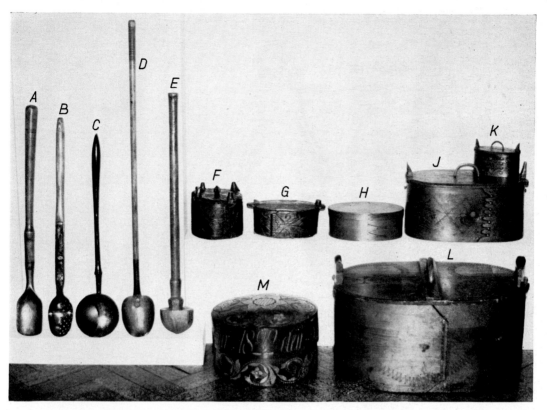

138 Various long-handled, English and Scottish, kitchen implements and bentwood boxes of Scandinavian and American origin, all described in the text. (*Section VII*)

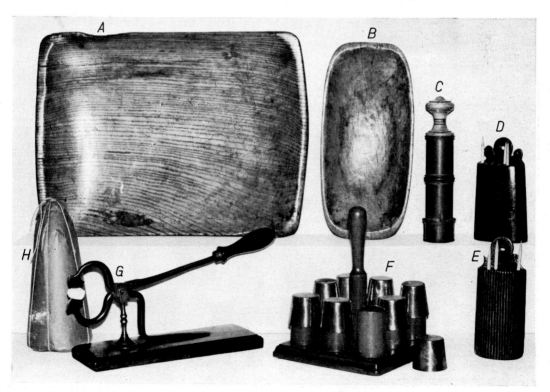

139 *A* and *B*, salting or pickling dishes: *C*, icing gun; *D* and *E*, Welsh skewer holders; *F*, jelly mould stand; *G* and *H*, sugar nippers and sugar loaf. (*Section VII*)

140 Lemon squeezers, 17th to 19th century. For details, see text. (*Section VII*)

141 *A, B, C, D. E, F, G, H* and *J*, spice containers; *K*, kettle holder; *L*, biscuit pricker; *M*, potato masher; *N* and *O*, muffin pricker and measuring ladle; *P*, sifter or dredger. (*Section VII*)

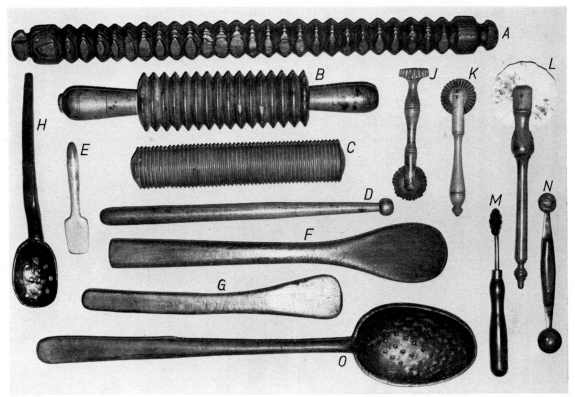

142 *A* and *B*, oatmeal rollers; *C*, caramel ribber; *D*, spurtle; *E*, *F* and *G*, spatulas; *H* and *O*, strainer spoons; *J*, *K* and *L*, pastry markers or jiggers; *M*, garnishing mould; *N*, potato ball maker. (*Section VII*)

143 Selection of kitchen salt boxes. For details, see text. (*Section VII*)

144 *A*, salamander; *B* and *C*, oven peels; *D* riddleboard; *E* and *F*, pie peels or boards; *G*, *H* and *J*, flour barrels. (*Section VII*)

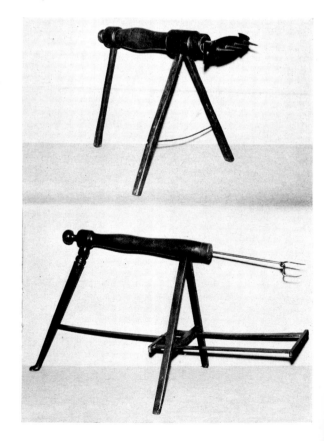

145 At top, a toasting dog. Below, an object of uncertain use. For theories, see text. (*Sect. VII*)

146 18th-century dog wheel, showing drive transmission to the spit. In the collection of *John H. Fardon, Esq. (Section VII)*

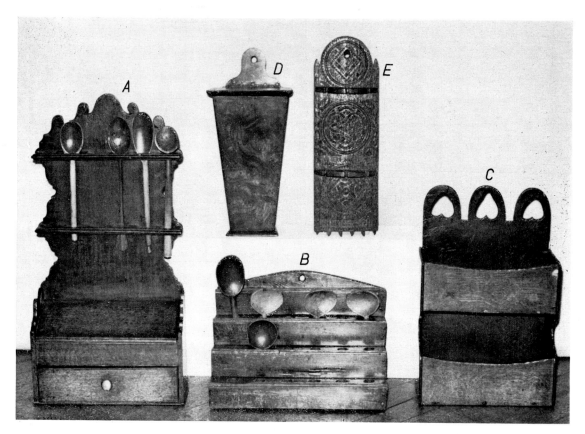

147 *A*, English combined spoon rack and cutlery holder; *B*, Welsh step spoon rack; *C*, English two-decker cutlery holder; *D*, English cutlery box; all 18th century. *E*, Friesland spoon rack, dated 1632, converted from a mangling board. (*Section VII*)

148 English linen press, oak, early 19th century. (*Section VIII*)

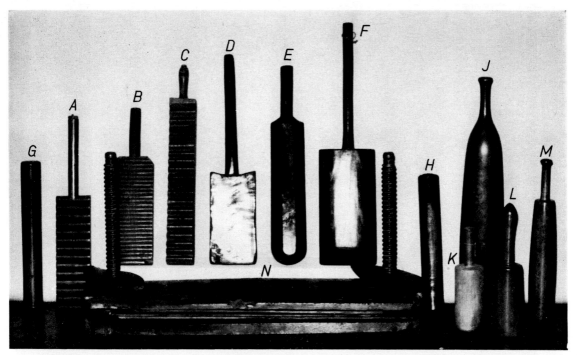

149 *A* to *F*, washing bats; *G* and *H*, rollers, English, 18th and 19th century; *J* to *M*, washing beetles; *N*, rare, Welsh stocking press, probably 17th or 18th century. For further details, see text. (*Section VIII*)

150 Continental washing bats or batlets, 18th or 19th century. For details, see text. *Photograph by courtesy of Haslemere Museum.* (*Section VIII*)

151 *A*, two tennis ball brushes; *B*, *C* and *D*, gauntlet and glove hands; *E*, German dust bellows; *F*, breeches board; *J*, tub for washing glass, etc.; *K*, 19th-century knife cleaning machine; *L*, early 20th-century suction cleaner; *G*, carved button stick and *H*, one of ordinary Services issue type. For further details, see text. (*Section VIII*)

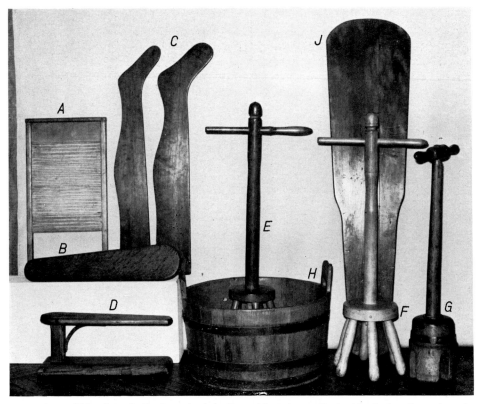

152 *A*, scrubbing board; *B*, sleeve board; *C*, stocking airers; *D*, double-decker sleeve board: *E*, *F* and *G*, various types of dollies; *H*, wash tub; *J*, skirt board. For further details, see text. (*Section VIII*)

153 *A* and *B*, two Friesland mangling boards, 18th Century; *C*, Scandinavian mangling board, 17th or 18th century; *D*, French or Flemish mangling board, dated 1649; *E* and *F*, two Norwegian mangling boards, early 19th century; *G* and *H*, two rollers. For further details, see text. (*Section VIII*)

154 English box mangle, *circa* 1810. For further details, see text. (*Section VIII*)

155 English rocker washing machine, *circa* 1862. In the Parker Collection. (*Sect. VIII*)

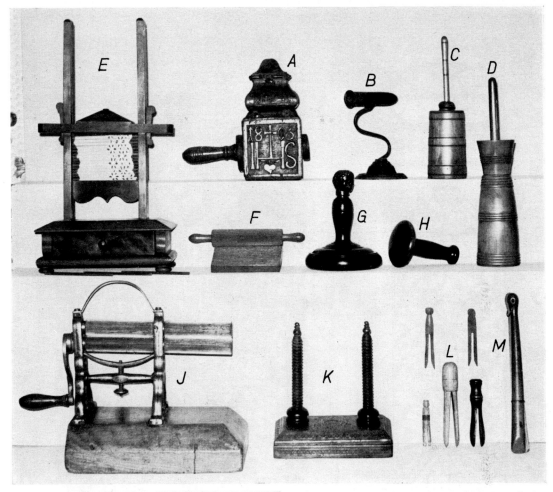

156 *A*, carved winder, dated 1805; *B*, goffering iron stand; *C* and *D*, lace dollies, both English, 19th century; *E*, goffering stack, early 19th century; *F*, crimping board, 17th or 18th century; *G* and *H*, two lignum vitae slickenstones, English, 17th or 18th century, the one carved with a blackamoor's head; *J*, goffering machine, English, 18th or early 19th century; *K*, Italian lace press, 17th century; *L*, at bottom, two blanket pegs and, to the left, clothes peg carved as a miniature man, two ordinary 19th-century pegs above; *M*, lace tongs. For further details, see text. (*Section VIII*)

157 Thomas Bradford's rotary washing machine with wringer, *circa* 1857. *Photograph by courtesy of Hoover's.* (*Section VIII*)

158 Two large and elaborate 19th-century Welsh love spoons. For details, see text. (*Section IX*)

159 Selection of Welsh love spoons. For details, see text (*Section IX*)

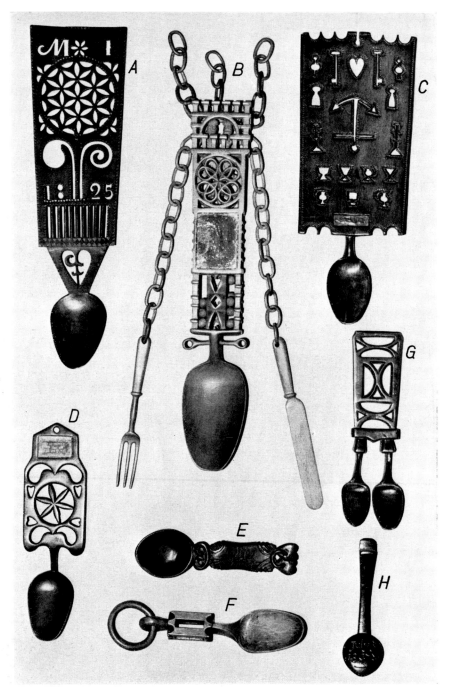

160 Selection of Welsh love spoons. *H* is dated 1720. For other details, see text. (*Section IX*)

above a bowl. On the right is its direct descendant; it has deeper hollows in the levers and is the most commonly used 18th- and early 19th-century lever type. In between is an 18th-century, mahogany lever squeezer, shown open in Plate 49, *H*, which employs a slightly more scientific approach; it is used horizontally, with one lever held above the other; the lever held uppermost is provided with a projecting button, carved with radiating grooves, against which the half lemon is pressed; the lower lever is scooped out to form a 'cup', into which the juice flows from the inverted half lemon.

The lemon squeezer on the right of the middle shelf, also probably of the 18th century, is a further stage in the evolution of the same idea. In this example, there is only one 'leg' which, like the last, is provided with a raised button; this single leg is hinged to a frame containing an insert wooden hollow, pierced to form a strainer. When the frame is placed across a bowl and the lever is pressed down against the inverted half lemon, the juice flows into the bowl. This is a typically country-made piece; the handle is oak, the frame mahogany and the button of boxwood. Like the other lever types so far described, it is English. Later versions of this have an inserted china strainer.

At the bottom of the picture, the large and imposing lever squeezer, mounted on a stand, is French; it is attractively carved in walnut and dates from the 18th century. It is an important looking object, one imagines too decorative to have been intended for kitchen use, so perhaps it figured in some table ceremonial, such as adding fruit juice to a communal punch bowl. The design is extremely practical, as the slope of the upper platform, on its long and short fluted columns, impels the juice down the carved runnel and spout, into the bowl placed on the base platform.

The urn-type lemon pressers, on the right at the bottom of the photograph, were popular in the late 18th and early 19th centuries. They are invariably of boxwood and they take apart and fit together at the horizontal line, either by screwing, or by means of a 'hit and miss' action catch. The cross-bar handle actuates a long wood screw, which passes through into the interior of the urn and terminates in a large, flat button end. The lemon is first decapitated or cut in halves and then placed in the urn; the downward thrust of the screw forces the button on to the lemon and ejects its juice through the spout. The complete urn shape, with the spout at the bottom, is the usual type; the example with flat base and side spout is unusual.

Both lever and screw lemon squeezers remove juice by external pressure on the rind, but the lemon scoops, shown at left, with flanged domed heads, operate by inserting and turning them in half lemons, so as to scoop out the insides. Both the specimens shown probably date from the 18th century. The boxwood example on the centre shelf is Irish; it has many more fins or flanges than the English specimens, of which one in mahogany is shown below. An almost identical model to this, but made of plastic, was on sale after the last war.

Marmalade Feeders—see *Podgers*

Mincers
English mincers with only the mechanism of steel, but the whole of the box casing of wood, are very rare but do exist. I have only seen one, which must have been 18th or early 19th century.

Mortars—see Section XI, *Mortars, Grinders and Graters*

Moulds
A sycamore Scottish shortbread mould, of traditional type, is shown in Plate 136, *C*. Sometimes the carving includes a thistle in the centre. For other ornamental moulds, see Section XII, *Moulds*.

Muffin Ladles

The pearwood muffin ladle, Plate 141, *O*, holds exactly the correct amount of batter for one muffin.

Muffin and Biscuit Prickers

A muffin pricker, with hardwood handle and iron pins, is shown in Plate 141, *N*. Biscuit prickers, following the same principle, were also made in various shapes and sizes; one is shown, *L*. There were always an even number of pins; an odd number of pricks was considered unlucky, as was baking an odd number of loaves. For *Biscuit Prickers*, see also Section XII, *Moulds*.

Oatbread or Oatcake Slices—see *Riddleboards*

Oat Crushers—see *Rollers*

Oven Peels

Oven peels were wooden spades, long-handled—4 ft. to 6 ft. long—for loaves of bread, Plate 144, *B* and *C*; short-handled for pies, *E* and *F*. The peels for loaves have blades 8 in. to 10 in. wide and those for pies 6 in. to 8 in. They were used for thrusting loaves and pies into the brick oven, and for withdrawing them. They are usually of sycamore, beech, ash or chestnut, are traditional in form and impossible to date accurately. Pie peels were always made in one piece, but some oven peels have the handle spliced into the blade, as *C*; some have rectangular iron blades. The latter were used for removing the ashes of the wood fire, which was kindled in the oven, to heat the bricks before the loaves went in. In the English home, Friday was always the day reserved for baking and great care was taken to see that the fire of dry faggots, brushwood or furze, brought the oven to just the right temperature.

Oyster Measurers and Oyster Openers

A simple but effective oyster opener, in Colchester Museum, is a wooden block, hollowed out to take a large oyster; it has a lid cut from a smaller block, which is leather hinged and swings over half the hollow, clamping down the oyster while it is opened with a knife. On the outside of the lid is a brass plate, bearing the name J. Barlow and the Hanoverian Royal Arms.

An oyster measurer is a small frame with a handle and an oyster-shaped aperture, like a hand mirror without its glass. Any oysters which passed through the opening were thrown back.

Pastry Markers

Pastry markers are also known as jiggers and, in the U.S.A. particularly, as pie crimpers. The most common is represented by Plate 142, *K*, which is of boxwood. In the 1860s, James Howard of Chesham, Bucks., invented a machine for cutting the profile of the teeth on the wheel. His prototype, or master pattern from the machine, was presented to the Pinto Collection by his daughter. Apart from accelerating the making, the machine-cut wheels are regularly toothed and sharper than the earlier ones, cut with a V tool, sometimes assisted by a triangular file. The Howard family still make pastry markers at Chesham.

In Plate 142, *J* is an earlier hand-made specimen, with a 'new moon' toothed crimper on the opposite end to the wheel. It is also of boxwood, but many of the hand-made ones are sycamore, which is easier to cut, but does not retain its sharp teeth as well. *L* is late Victorian, with a $2\frac{3}{4}$ in. flower decorated china wheel; crimpers with similarly outsize wooden wheels were made in the 1870s. Walrus ivory crimpers, sometimes decorated with scrimshaw work, were made by sailors of many nationalities, as gifts to their sweethearts.

Peels—see *Oven Peels*

Pickling Dishes—see *Salting Dishes*

Pie Moulds

The pie mould or pork pie rammer, Plate 136, *L*, was the 'inside former' used for 'evening out' the walls before filling the pie-crust. It is simply a solid block, usually of beech or sycamore with a handle, all turned out of one piece; it was available in a range of sizes.

Pie Peels—see *Oven Peels*

Podgers

The 19th-century beechwood block, Plate 136, *M*, with vertical grooves on opposite sides, and an undulating base, of what nowadays is described as parabolic form, is a podger. The podger is a feed stick for feeding meat for sausage making, or peel for marmalade making, into a mincer.

Pork Pie Rammer—see *Pie Mould*

Potato Ball Makers

The hardwood handle with, at each end, a steel bowl with a hole in the base, Plate 142, *N*, is a potato ball maker, probably 18th-century. Identically the same design is made today, the bowls plated and the handle plastic coated.

Potato Mashers

Potato mashers were always turned from a single block, usually of beech or sycamore, but the best quality specimens, like Plate 135, *F*, were of boxwood. Like this one, they were often made *en suite* with a rolling pin, *G*, because in olden times, the pair was considered a lucky wedding gift. The octagonal 'club', Plate 141, *M*, is presumably a potato masher of unusual form.

Riddleboards

Riddleboards, as example illustrated in Plate 144, *D*, usually range between 16 in. and 20 in. in width and may be square, or longer than wide by an inch or two, plus the short handle. For the following information on their use and alternative names, I am indebted to Mr. Frank Atkinson, Director of the Bowes Museum, Barnard Castle, who published the result of his scholarly research in *Gwerin*, Vol. III, No. 2, 1960, under the title of *Oatbread of Northern England*.

Riddleboards were formerly used in the North of England and Scotland for making oatcake or oatbread and the boards scored diagonally to form 1 in. or slightly larger squares were also known as bakbrades in Cumberland, backboards in the Bolton Abbey area, riddlingboards around Ingleton, Wharfedale and Lancaster, ruddling boards in Skipton, and reeing boards in Lancashire generally. The mixture of oatmeal and milk or water was poured on the riddleboard, which had been previously sprinkled with dry oatmeal. It was

> '. . . then transferred by a sliding motion on to a piece of dry flannel. Beneath the flannel lay the *spittle*: a handled board, and by means of this the flannel was flung across a hot stone—the bakestone. Thus the oatmeal batter was spread on the bakestone and the flannel fell away, ready to be replaced for the next oatbread.'

The spittle closely resembled a wooden pie peel (see *Oven Peels*), with a blade $9\frac{1}{2}$ in. or 10 in. wide by 11 in. or 12 in. in length.

In Scotland and North-east England, oatbread was often known as haver or riddle cake and in North-west England as haverbread or riddlebread. There were also regional differences in the making, as described by Mr. Atkinson.

Rollers and Rolling Pins

As stated under the heading of *Potato Mashers*, these and rolling pins were often made to match, as a wedding gift. The pastry roller, Plate 135, *G*, is an example of the old custom. Convex rolling pins of the type Plate 137, *N*, of various hardwoods, were used for making curved pie crusts thin in the middle, thicker round the edges. Ribbed rollers were used for numerous purposes, probably many more than their common names suggest. In Plate 142, *A* is a traditional Welsh oatmeal crusher, *B* is the Scottish or North of England equivalent and *C* is a caramel ribber. A roller about 9 in. long by 3 in. diameter, known as a honeycomb roller, was used for imparting a honeycomb pattern, for display purposes, on the top surface of Irish butter, imported in boxes.

Saladiers—see *Vegetable Slicers*

Salamanders

Salamanders, Plate 144, *A*, have a wood handle fitting into an iron socket, riveted on to a flat, circular blade or plate. The blade was poked into the fire until red hot and then held over pastry or pie crusts, to brown them.

Salt Boxes

Supply of salt has never presented any difficulty in the British Isles, with no town more than 100 miles from the sea. But even without salt panning, there are abundant deposits in Cheshire and elsewhere. Although salt refining has improved greatly in this century, the hygroscopic nature of the mineral makes it necessary to keep it as dry as possible. In damp climates, the natural place for a kitchen salt box has, therefore, always been in the fireplace opening, or on the kitchen mantelpiece. In consequence, British salt boxes usually have provision for hanging or standing. A selection of traditional types from various countries is shown in Plate 143; accurate dating is almost impossible. *A* is of oak and may be Dutch or Danish. All parts are pegged together, no metal being used; it may be 17th- or 18th-century. *B* is Scottish; this design in pewter was known in the 17th century. The light and dark staved example illustrated is a particularly good one, probably late 18th- or early 19th-century; the majority of this pattern which are still extant, are likely to be about 100 years later.

C, from Hinderloopen, Holland, is 18th- or 19th-century, decorated with a black painted fern design, on a red background. *D*, a particularly nice English box, veneered with bird's-eye maple, rosewood, etc., probably at Tunbridge Wells, dates from about 1790. *E*, a larger and heavier English 'farmhouse' version of the same sloping top design in oak, is 18th-century. *F*, a traditional Spanish, country-made, two compartment type, for rock and granulated salt, is hollowed out of a block of oak, has a lid which pivots on the osier handle, and is believed to date from the 18th century. *G*, formerly in the Evan-Thomas Collection, is hollowed out of a solid block of hardwood, attractively carved and probably 17th-century. *H*, a rare salt or dry store box, probably Dutch, shaped to an octagon and hollowed out of a block of elm, is chip carved with roundels, lunettes and tulips, and dated 1611. With a box gouged out in this manner, it is almost impossible to ensure accuracy for the lid to fit properly in more than one position. To overcome this difficulty, the maker carved X-crossed boxes each side of the tulip shown in the picture; a similar crossed box, at one spot on the lid, ensures that the lid engages correctly. For details of customs pertaining to salt, see *Salts*, Section V, *Eating*.

Salting Dishes

The salting or pickling dish, Plate 139, *A*, is of elm and measures $19\frac{1}{2}$ in. by $14\frac{3}{8}$ in. *B* is of beech, $13\frac{3}{4}$ in. by $6\frac{1}{2}$ in. These shallow dishes for salting or powdering of meat, were made in a considerable number of different but entirely unstandardized sizes. They are not to be confused with salting or powdering tubs or troughs, in which the salted down carcases of the 'autumn kill' were preserved for winter eating. These troughs were not necessarily of wood; in stone counties, they were of the local material and resembled large stone coffins. Those in the cellars of Dunsland House, Devon, are of granite.

Scoops

Scoops are mostly described in Section V, *Farm*, but the hook-handled scoop illustrated, Plate 137, *K*, is a type which was particularly used in the kitchen for flour, oatmeal, etc.

Shortbread Blocks or Moulds—see *Moulds*

Sieves—see Section V, *Farm*

Sifters

Sifters, dredgers, casters, are alternative names for sprinkler topped, cylindric containers of the type illustrated, Plate 141, *P*. In pewter or tinned iron, such a container would have had a loop side handle, but in wood such a feature adds too much to cost. The sycamore example shown has been used for ginger. These simple treen specimens are impossible to date accurately on design, as this was unchanged over several centuries.

Skewer Holders

Steel skewers with loop handles were suspended from a special skewer hook in English kitchens, but I have never been able to identify any special English holder or receptacle for the formerly much more common beechwood skewer. There is, however, a very pleasant looking and practical wooden skewer holder entirely peculiar to Wales; two examples are shown in Plate 139, *D* and *E*. Both are D-shaped in plan; the plain one is cut from a solid block of walnut; the other, reeded, is of sycamore; both are made to hang or stand, and each is drilled for eight skewers.

Slicers, Bread—see *Bread Slicers*

Slicers, Vegetable—see *Vegetable Slicers*

Spatulas and Spurtles

Even north of the border in Scotland, whence come spatulas and spurtles, there is some confusion of terminology. Generally, however, the drum-stick-like porridge stirrer, Plate 142, *D*, is described as a spurtle, but in some districts, it is known as a thieval. The various shaped flat-bladed stirrers and bowl or pan scrapers, *E*, *F* and *G*, are spatulas. Both types of implements have a long history, but are seldom old, being discarded when worn. They are traditionally made of sycamore or beech, but some modern spatulas are of boxwood.

Spice Boxes

Of the spice boxes illustrated in Plate 141, the two small, turned, barrel-shaped, Elizabethan specimens, *H* and *J*, are the earliest; *H*, $3\frac{1}{2}$ in. high, probably dates from before 1600, and *J*, just after. *H* is made as a double cup, the lid being an inverted cup of larger diameter than the box. *J* is $2\frac{1}{2}$ in. high and has a hit-and-miss action lid. Both are decorated with scratch ornament, *H* of the Tudor and *J* of the James I period; they may be English or Welsh. *G*, $6\frac{1}{2}$ in. diameter, of walnut, an early example of the radiating divisioned boxes which are still found convenient for spice today, dates from the 17th century and, in the manner of that period, has a rimmed lid with a central threaded aperture, which screws down tightly on a correspondingly threaded column, making it air tight. Even today it is redolent of the valuable spices which its four compartments once held. It may have been made in England, Switzerland, Germany or France, and was formerly in the Evan-Thomas Collection. The Regency example, *F*, of sycamore, decorated with red and black lines and a centre inlaid circle of figured walnut, was probably made at Tunbridge. It has six labelled radiating compartments and a removable, central grater; it is the direct ancestor of the iron spice box of similar form, japanned in various colours and used in most Victorian kitchens.

Sussex spice boxes of sycamore, formed as a column of boxes which screw into each other, *C*, were actually made over the border at Tunbridge, Kent. They were made in the late 18th and throughout the 19th century. Each compartment is labelled and the clue to dating is in the labelling and finishing. Early ones have script lettering on scrolled labels; Regency examples, such as *C*, are printed on scrolled labels; Victorian specimens have printing on straight labels. Early ones have a well rubbed down, hard varnished finish, later ones a poor varnish, which scratches easily and shows white abrasion marks, but some of these have been stripped and refinished. The number of boxes in a tier varies from two (possibly incomplete) up to 10. *D*, of yew-wood, and *E*, of oak, not labelled, are probably from other English counties. *B*, of masur birch, with four boxes, which when inverted nest ingeniously into each other, is probably Finnish export. *A* is a German, 19th-century spice cabinet of drawers, to hang or stand.

Spoons, Handled Strainers, Ladles, etc.

Examples of the traditional English beech kitchen spoons are shown in Plate 137, *F* and *G*, and in the spoon rack, Plate 147, *A*, and one is among the Welsh spoons in Plate 147, *B*. Apart from the spoon bowls gradually becoming more elongated ovals, they have not changed from illustrations of the Middle Ages. The same remark applies to the various long-handled wooden strainers of spoon, slice and ladle types, illustrated in Plate 135, *B*, Plate 137, *H* and *M*, and Plate 142, *H* and *O*. Of the short, hook-handled strainers, Plate 137, *L*, of sycamore, is an earlier type than Plate 137, *B*, but the latter, with a convex handle and concave bowl of planewood, forming a continuous sinuous curve, is particularly pleasing, both to eye and to hand grip. The 15 in. long, hook-handled ladle, Plate 137, *J*, served many purposes, as did also the short handled ladles, scoops or bowls, *O*, *P* and *Q*. *O*, a 19th-century type has the handle threaded into the bowl; *P* and *Q* are

made in one piece. *Q*, a particularly large and attractive, one-piece object of honey coloured maple, cleverly cut so that the 6½ in. diameter bowl is of burr, whilst the handle is long grain, is probably American Colonial, although bought in England. The implements, Plate 138, *A* to *D*, are wood handled, but metal ended. *A*, 24 in. long, which has a lead end, was used for scraping butter out of a wooden vessel. *B*, 23 in. long, has a perforated copper spoon, and *C*, 21½ in. long, with a tinned iron perforated spoon fitted with a crescent-shaped, perforated cover, seems to be a speciality strainer. *D*, 33 in. long, is called a spathe in Scotland and is used for transferring oatcakes from board to griddle. Nearly all these implements came from the kitchens of Ashburnham, Sussex. For details of other spoons, see Section IV, *Eating*.

Spoon Moulds

Both wood and iron moulds were used for making pewter spoons, but the 18th-century, mahogany spoon moulds, Plate 136, *D*, were not made for this purpose and do not fit together, as do the moulds used in making. One block is carved with the convex impression of the back of a spoon and the other with the concave of the inside, and they were used for hammering the dents out and restoring the shape of the soft metal.

Spoon Racks and Cutlery Boxes

Spoon racks and cutlery boxes of the types illustrated in Plate 147 are essentially farmhouse kitchen and cottage pieces, individually designed and made. Sometimes the spoon rack, cutlery box and a drawer were combined in one piece, like the 18th-century, English, oak rack, Plate 147, *A*, which is 25 in. high; this example is interesting for having incorporated into it, an ingenious secret compartment for money, with access from a sliding panel at the back. More often the old spoon racks are like the upper part of this one, with the cutlery box separate, as in *C* or *D*. The former is a nice 'double deck' oak crudity, the back of which its maker pierced with hearts, as a love token. *D* is a familiar 18th-century shape, but is unusual in being made of burry elm. Sometimes boxes of this type, in mahogany and oak, are inlaid on the front with a crossed knife and fork. For the more sophisticated dining room knife cases, see Section IV, *Eating*.

The Friesland spoon rack of oak, Plate 147, *E*, is dated 1632 and neatly carved with roundels, etc. Quite apart from the inscription on it, the way the spoon ledges cut across the design and the way the hole for suspension cuts into a diamond, show that this is the lower part of a mangling board. I would guess that the conversion was made soon after the board was carved.

Spoon racks of most European countries consist of backboards and ledges with holes or notched out openings to grip the spoon handles. But even in spoon racks, the Welsh were individualists and step-type racks, like Plate 147, *B*, were peculiar to Wales. Usually they are quite plain, but occasionally the pediment, pierced for suspension, is fret cut in the manner of Welsh love spoons.

Spurtles—see *Spatulas*

Steak Beaters
Steak beaters and butter mauls are the same implements—mallets with diamond-toothed heads; they have remained virtually unchanged for centuries. A large and a small one are shown in Plate 136, *A* and *B*, both of beech. A steak beater with Dresden china head is illustrated in Plate 312, *J*.

Strainers
Wooden strainers, usually of sycamore, of the same type as tea strainers, but with long handles to seat over bowls, were formerly made. Very few have survived.

Sugar Nippers
After first breaking up the sugar loaf with a sugar axe or hammer, sugar nippers of steel, some with turned wood handles, were used for breaking it further, for use at table. Nippers of various sizes were used, some two-handled implements, others mounted on wooden stands, like Plate 139, *G*, which is shown with an original 1½ kilo., blue paper wrapped sugar loaf, *H*, alongside. Sugar loaves were made in various sizes and weights, ranging up to 55 lb.; below 12 lb., the rounded-top loaves were called loaves, but above that weight they were usually pointed and known as cones. The Sugar Loaf was a popular 18th-century grocer's sign.

Thieval—see *Spatulas and Spurtles*

Tilting Hob—see *Hobs*

Toasting Dogs
Toasting dogs, or toasting stools, made from a variety of English hardwoods, seem to have been more common in the North of England than in the South, and they were used for toasting kippers and other delicacies; sometimes they have an iron plate below the fork, which slides forward to catch the drips.

The example at the top of Plate 145 has a fish-shaped iron plate to its fork. The name 'dog' is much more apt in some country-made survivals, because sometimes a right-angled bend, with a smaller branch jutting at the angle, has been used to form the body, tail and back leg, and the two front legs are made from a natural fork, dowelled into the body.

Stools of the type shown below, Plate 145, have caused much controversy. The majority of writers and museum authorites contend that they are a more sophisticated form of toasting dog, with a sliding rack for a dripping or fat tray. Another school of thought, to which I belong, believes that the resemblance of these more elegant objects to toasting dogs is fortuitous and that possibly they are connected with wool carding. So far, we cannot prove our point, but these factors favour it: (*a*) nearly all these stools come from Yorkshire and other wool districts; (*b*) the sliding tray, to hold the alleged drip pan, would not only have blazed merrily in the fire, while the kipper toasted, but (*c*) anything put on it or on the fork (which I do not believe is original to the stool) would overturn this delicately balanced stool unless the knob end were weighted; (*d*) real toasting dogs show sign of burning, the others do not; (*e*) most old hearths are brick or stone and the legs of real toasting dogs show considerable wear; (*f*) a turned leg, with graceful taper and pad foot, as pictured, could never have survived hearth use.

Vegetable Slicers
The early 18th-century, pearwood *saladier*, Plate 134, *B*, with carved cresting, is probably Dutch. These highly decorative root cutting boards were used in all western European countries. Some of the most attractive come from Alsace. They were used in apothecaries shops for cutting roots into manageable size for grinding, in the kitchen for preparing salads, and in France, and probably also in other countries, for cutting the long bread rolls at table.

The English vegetable slicer Plate 115, *C*, with adjustable diagonally set knife, is probably of about the same date, but very sober by comparison, its only ornament being a chip carved edging to the head and a heart-shaped opening. Its smaller brother, the cucumber slicer in mahogany handle, *F*, is stamped Gidney, Dereham; the Gidney family were ironmongers in Dereham, Norfolk, between 1845 and 1890. For other root cutters, see also Section I, *Apothecary* and Section V, *Farm*, and for plug cutters, see Section XXII, *Tobacco Accessories*.

VIII

Laundry and Cleaning Devices

The principles of fabric washing doubtless go back for as long as men and women have worn clothes and had bed clothes. According to a lecture given by F. Courtney Harwood, starch was used by the Egyptians 3500 B.C. and by 2500 B.C. the Pharaohs had Royal Chief Washers and Royal Chief Bleachers. In the tomb pictures at Beni Hasan are representations of washing being carried out under the supervision of the chief washer. Among Greek and Roman writers, Homer and Pliny both give accounts of washing. Basically, the process sequence was always the same—washing in a river, tank or tub, treading, pounding with a stone or wooden bat, rinsing, followed by a crude form of mangling, and laying out to dry; but the fabrics varied according to climate and indigenous materials most readily available. Thus, Egyptians used flax linen, Indians used cotton, Chinese largely used silk, and western Europe, including Britain, used more wool than cotton, linen or other fabrics, until the end of the Middle Ages.

No accounts of old-time laundering are complete without the words buck, lye and whitster. Whitster is the old English word for launderer and laundress. The buck or bucking usually refers to the periodic 'great wash' carried out by the whitsters. Both 'buck' and 'whitster' occur in Shakespeare's works. Buck was sometimes used to denote the staved, coopered washing tub in which the clothes were steeped in lye. A smaller coopered vessel, with sloping sides, was naturally a bucket. A buck basket was a wash basket, and the verb 'to buck' could mean to wash, boil, bleach and dress. It is easy to see how, in the 18th and early 19th centuries, a clean and well dressed young man became known as a buck.

Lye is the alkalized water used for the washing. It was made basically from oak or beech ashes, mixed in boiling water with slaked quicklime. The process was quite complicated; there were many boilings and strainings, and various additives, which often included human and/or animal urine. Soap remained expensive until early in the 19th century and it was only made and used for washing clothes in well-to-do households; others used a soap substitute composed of balls of hog's dung in lye made with wood ashes and chamber-pot water. The beastliness of the practice was commented on by several 16th- and 17th-century writers. Harrison, in *A Description of England*, 1577, after describing duties of a hogsherd, goes on to say (modern spelling)

'In some places also women do scour and wet their clothes with their dung, as others do with hemlocks and nettles: but such is the savour of the clothes touched withall, that I cannot abide to wear them on my body, (any) more than such as are scoured

147

with the refuse soap (chamber-pot lye), than the which, in mine opinion, there is none more unkindly savour.'

It is questionable whether the infrequently changed clothes smelt worse before or after bucking and one can well understand that the final touches by the lavenderer—later corrupted to launderer—were essential.

In a great household, at least from the 16th to the 19th century, there was a fully equipped laundry and the whitsters, or laundry maids, were sometimes part of the permanent staff, employed on other duties between times. In a medium sized house, there would be a laundry room and the washerwomen were called in periodically, arriving at dawn and working all day in the wet and steamy atmosphere, skirts tucked up and barefooted, for treading the buck, and at other times with pattens or clogs on their feet—for pattens and clogs, see Section XXV, *Trade and Craft Devices: Cobblers.* In a small house, the procedure was the same, but the kitchen or scullery served for the buck and the mangling might be taken home by one of the washerwomen, who had a box mangle and did mangling at 1*d.* per dozen small articles, 2*d.* per dozen large, for those in her vicinity. In the 19th century, it became increasingly common for the washerwoman to call for dirty clothes and bring them back clean. The practice gradually developed into the modern laundry.

In different household accounts, the 'cycle' of the buck varies enormously. In a few 17th-century households, clothes were washed once per fortnight, but once per month, or once per quarter was more common, and half yearly and annual bucks are also recorded; perhaps, and let us hope that, these were more in the nature of spring cleaning of household effects. Sometimes the buck coincided with the departure of a family from town house to country seat, or vice versa. Thus, Gladys Scott Thomson, in *Life in a Noble Household* (the Bedford family) records that in July, 1675, at Woburn, after the Duke's family departed for London

	£	s.	d.
'For washing sheets and napkins before the great wash when the two masters was in town		2	0
For four pounds of soap		1	0
For six pounds of candles		2	6
For three women one day to wash		4	6
A woman two days to help to dry up the linen		3	0
For oil, ashes and sand to scour		1	8
A woman to scour two days		3	0
For washing of twelve pairs of sheets at 4d. per pair		4	0'

At Bedford House, London, similar preparations took place

	£	s.	d.
'For soap for the great wash when the family left for London		4	6
For two women to wash after his lordship's being in town		3	0'

Although their work was so hard, washerwomen or laundresses were notoriously ill paid. Margaret Wade Labarge, in *A Baronial Household of the Thirteenth Century* (the household of Simon de Montfort and Eleanor, Countess of Leicester), remarks that the average rate then was only 1*d.* per day. Petronilla, the Countess of Leicester's laundress, did also receive '. . . her shoes for the Easter term (worth 12*d.*) as well as an additional payment of 15*d.* on May 31st for the laundry at Christmas.'

It is clear, from old records, that the poor were always filthy and lousy, both in their persons and their ragged clothing, but there is reason to think that the wealthy, who could afford better clothing and had reasonable facilities for washing, were not as unpleasant in mediaeval times, when they wore loose garments, secured by pins and girdles, as they were later, when bewigged, and when underclothing became tighter and more voluminous and over-garments were numerous, elaborate, gorgeously bedecked with ribbons and lace and, in many instances, tightly secured by buttons, stay laces and buckles. Moreover, in the 17th and 18th centuries, rooms were better heated than in mediaeval times, and at receptions grossly overheated by the addition of myriads of candles, which likewise had been sparsely used earlier. Whilst there were always some people who washed themselves and changed their linen frequently, they made news until the end of the 18th century, and it is these exceptions who naturally have left the fullest accounts of the stench of society of their day. An interesting early account of a lord who used his laundress to wash his head weekly, occurs in the 13th-century Giuseppi M.S. of *The Wardrobe and Household Accounts of Bogo de Clare*, 1284–6 (*Archaeologia LXX*, 1920, London).

In this section, most of the devices mentioned are of the laundry, but a few other specialised wooden cleaning devices are described. The commonest of all, brooms and brushes, are almost entirely omitted, because they are seldom collector items.

Airers

Being crude arrangements of cords and wooden slats, and posts or pulleys, the general airers, shown in old prints, have hardly ever survived. A few 19th- and possibly 18th-century clothes horses, with webbing hinges, may still exist, but are no different from those made a few years ago. The various types with collapsible arms, radiating out from a centre, all seem to date from near the end of the last century, or later.

Airers, Stocking

Wooden boards, shaped like a leg, Plate 152, *C*, which came from Ashburnham, Sussex, were made from any suitable hardwood, or of pine, were smooth and rounded on all edges and provided with a hole near the top, for suspension from a line or hook. Although probably used quite early, survivals are unlikely to be earlier than 18th

or 19th century. Parson Woodforde, in his *Diary* for March, 1801, relates 'A pair of Stockings that happened to be out just by the back Door upon some Wooden Legs to dry were attempted to be taken off by some Person or another, but being wet they cd. not pull them off.'

Bats or Beaters

Bats or beaters were originally adjuncts of performing the washing in streams, when the clothes were placed on stones or rocks and beaten with wooden bats; the practice still pertains in more primitive communities. Bats are made in one piece, from various hardwood; there are two forms— (1) plain on both faces, sometimes with bevels on the back edges of the blade and (2) cross-ribbed on one face, so that they could also act as rubbing boards. When used in conjunction with rollers, they also served as mangling boards (see *Mangling Boards and Rollers*).

Most of the bats illustrated, Plate 149, *A* to *F*, came from the North of England, where they were used more commonly than in the South. They vary in length from 19 in., *B*, to 29 in., *F*, in width from 3¼ in. to 7½ in., and in thickness from 1½ in. to 2½ in. They probably all date from the 18th or 19th century, but being of traditional form, their appearance changed infrequently. A woman hitting a man with a washing bat is carved on an oak misericord of 1401, in Carlisle Cathedral; like an illustration of 1582, *Harleian M.S.*, it shows that early washing bats were more shovel-shaped, with wider, shorter blades.

On the continent, North-west Europe particularly, washing bats or batlets were most decorative. In Plate 150 are five examples, of which four are chip carved, probably all late 18th- or early 19th-century; they vary in length from 13 in. to 21 in. *A*, *B* and *C*, are Norwegian, two of them carved with hearts, denoting love tokens. *D*, is Russian and *E*, Dutch. All except the last are painted in bright colours.

Beetles

The washing beetle, a large and heavy club, was an alternative to the bat and, to some extent to the dolly, for pounding the dirt out of clothes, etc. It is still used in primitive communities. The 29 in. long, elm beetle, Plate 149, *J*, is probably 18th-century, the 12 in., 15½ in. and 19½ in. specimens, *K*, *L* and *M*, 19th-century.

Bellows, Dust—see *Dust Bellows*

Breeches Boards

The shaped board for use in whitening coachmen's buckskin breeches, Plate 151, *F*, is English, 19th-century.

Button Sticks

Button sticks, Plate 151, *G* and *H*, were used for cleaning uniform buttons. The button was put through the circular hole in the stick and slid along the slot, the wood protecting the uniform from the polish. The unique carved boxwood example was probably inspired by an armoury, in which some wood craftsman soldier was stationed.

Cap Crown Smoothers

In height and outline, cap crown smoothers resemble 18th- and early 19th-century, baluster turned wig stands (see Section XXIII, *Toilet and Bedroom Accessories: Wig Stands*), but only the base of a cap smoother is of wood; the stem and knob are of iron or steel and a brass mushroom cover fits over the knob. The iron knob was heated in a fire, the brass cover replaced and the damp cap smoothed over it.

Clogs—see Section XXV, *Trade and Craft Devices: Cobblers*

Crimping or Gathering Boards and Rollers

Crimping boards and their correspondingly grooved or serated rollers, Plate 156, *F*, were used for forming the minute crimpings, gatherings or ruckings, on 17th- and early 18th-century fabrics. The fabric was first starched, then damped, placed on the board and rolled, until the desired strip of small pleats was formed; when used for gathering or rucking, the pleats were subsequently stitched at the top. The board, about 5 in. square, and roller are usually of boxwood; they are frequently wrongly described as dairy butter implements.

Dollies, Washing

Washing dollies, in different parts of the British Isles, also known as dolly pins, poss sticks and peggy sticks, Plate 152, *E*, *F* and *G*, are plunging, stirring and pounding devices, for working detergent fluid through and dirt out of clothes, etc., in a wooden wash tub. They are a logical development of the beetle and bat and are still used in country districts.

Basically, 19th-century and later specimens consist of an upright turned pole of ash or elm, through which passes a turned cross-bar handle, 13 in. to 15 in. long, at a height of 32 in.; at its lower end, the pole fits into either a circular beech 'stool', about 9 in. high, on 4, 5 or 6 turned elm or ash legs, such as *E* and *F*, or an elm dome, about 7 in. high, with 4½ in. high arches cut through from each side, like *G*, or a metal cone with louvres in the sides. Earlier dollies, probably used up to about 1800 or 1810, were cut out of one piece, except for the cross-bar handle, had the upright left square, but stepped out about 1 in. on each face at the usual step level, to give a larger plunging area, and with arches cut right through from each face. In William Tucker's *The Family Dyer and Scourer*, published in 1817, it is stated that the only apparatus required is a dolly and a tub.

Dust Bellows

Doubtless, ordinary fire bellows were also used for blowing dust out of awkward corners, before the days of suction cleaners; there were, however, also special dust bellows. A German, all-wood specimen, 21 in. long, made about 1900, is shown, Plate 151, *E*. It is believed to have been used particularly for pianos.

Gathering Boards—see *Crimping Boards*

Glove Hands or Trees

Glove hands on stands, Plate 151, *B* and *D*, were used in laundries for drying gloves, in shops for display, and in workshops during making. Most surviving examples are of beech and date from the 19th century. Those for ladies are 8 in. to 9 in. high plus a 2½ in. turned stand, and for gentlemen, 10 in. high plus the 2½ in. stand. Gauntlet hands, *B*, 18 in. high plus a 2½ in. stand, were for whitening the coachman's buckskin gauntlets. All are made in three sections, which join together with sliding dovetail slots—thumb and index finger in one piece, middle finger separate, and third and fourth fingers joined. The flat hands, like *C*, with all the fingers cut from one piece and the thumb pivoted in front, were used by glove makers.

Goffering Stacks and Machines—see *Poking Sticks*

Ironing and Pressing Boards

Ironing boards, simple, smooth, round-edged boards, usually of sycamore, but also of oak, elm and pine, are found in a variety of shapes and sizes, for skirts, Plate 152, *J*, trousers, *B* and sleeves, *D*. The last two are sometimes made as "double deckers", like *D*.

Keelers—see *Tubs*

Knife Cleaning Machines and Knife Boards

Knife cleaning machines, circular wooden drums, usually about 16 in. in diameter, on cast iron feet, first appeared about 1850. They have a cranked handle, central on one side, which revolves a drum, or grooved wheel, fitted with diagonal leather leaves,

16—T.O.W.B.

Plate 151, *K*; three knives can be inserted at one time in brush lined brass apertures in the perimeter and a fourth hole allowed for funnelling in the emery knife powder. The knife blades fit into the groove of the wheel and, as it revolves, they are stropped and cleaned by the leather leaves, and dusted free of knife powder by the brushes, as they are removed from the apertures. Leading London manufacturers included George Kent of High Holborn; Samuel Nye of Oxford Street; Alfred Peirce of Oxford Street; Worth & Co. of Harrow Road, and J. T. Wedderburn of Hammersmith.

Although, judging by survivals, rotary knife cleaning machines must have sold in many thousands, they never superseded the traditional stropping and cleaning knife boards, faced with leather, or, from the 1840s onwards, with kamptulicon. Kamptulicon was a mixture of india rubber, gutta-percha and cork, mounted on canvas. The boards were used in conjunction with emery powder. In 1866, there were 11 manufacturers of knife cleaning machines in the London trades directory. In 1928, the number had dropped to six. Soon after, the entry ceased: stainless steel had ended the drudgery.

Lace Dollies

Lace washing dollies are turned vessels, almost invariably of sycamore, shaped like miniature milk churns, Plate 156, *C* and *D*. They are made in three parts—the main vessel, 5 in. to 6½ in. high, with a 3 in. to 3¼ in. diameter base, a lid, which sometimes incorporates a collar and may add 2½ in. to the height, and a plunger. The plunger stick passes through a circular aperture in the centre of the lid or collar and has a circular wooden disc base, which is perforated with ¼ in. diameter holes, arranged in a circle, ¼ in. to ½ in. in from the edge. The holes may vary in number from three to seven. As befits their purpose, lace washing dollies are smooth and well finished inside and out. All that I have seen, appear to date from the 19th century.

Lace Presses—see *Presses*

Lace Tongs

Lace tongs of sycamore, Plate 156, *M*, were used for removing lace from washing dollies. They usually have a copper loop at the pin junction of the blades, for hanging up, and another loop, which slides up and down the blades, for gripping and releasing the lace.

Laundry Tallies—see Section XIX, *Scientific: Tallies*

Line Winders—see *Winders, Line*

Linen Presses—see *Presses*

Linen Smoothers—see *Slickenstones*

Mangles

Box mangles are said to have been invented in the 17th century, but most of those surviving date from the 19th. In Thomas Chippendale's accounts for Nostell Priory, January 20, 1768, is the entry:

'To a large strong wainscot mangle
to go by a Wheel and Pinion complete
£14 . 0 . 0.'

It sounds a high price for a box mangle, in terms of 18th-century money, so probably it was a fine one, made by Chippendale, although he, like the other large furnishers of his day, factored to some extent, when executing complete furnishing contracts.

One of the earliest patents for improvements in box mangles is that taken out, in 1791, by Thomas Hughes, a turner and press manufacturer. Hughes first appears in a London Directory for 1817, as one of 13 London manufacturers of mangles. The three earliest entries under this trade heading are in the 1790 Directory—Baker & Son of Fore Street, Joseph Hampson of 52 Long Lane, Smithfield, and J. T.

Oxenham of 402 Oxford Street. As the London entries only fluctuate between 11 and 14 manufacturers from 1817 to 1866, whilst the number of provincial makers (North of England especially) rises steadily during the same period, it appears that the ponderous box mangle was mainly manufactured on a commercial scale for roughly the first 60 years of the 19th century. By about 1860, the intolerable heavy drudgery of this machine was being rapidly superseded, in progressive establishments, by the much smaller and easier to use, spring-loaded roller wringing and mangling machines (see also *Washing Machines*), but in backward districts, box mangles were still being used up to the 1914–18 War.

The box mangle illustrated, Plate 154, is 7 ft. 0 in. long, 3 ft. 1 in. wide, and 3 ft. 0 in. high, excluding the iron superstructure. It is of oak, and with the box filled with stones, the total weight is nearly a ton. It was made by the aforementioned Baker & Son, probably between 1805 and 1810; now, 160 years later, Baker's are still leaders in laundry equipment. The weighted box runs backwards and forwards over the loose rollers, around which the clothes are wound. When it reaches the end of its travel in each direction, it automatically tips, so that the rollers can be removed, for taking away mangled clothes and replacing them by others. The box is guided by boxwood wheels, set in the sides of the top rails. Although some of these box mangles are rope or leather strap driven, the majority like this one, have chains. The big wheel at the back acts as a flywheel and the smaller one, with peg teeth, provides the automatic reversing device, so that the handle is always turned in one direction. The folding pawls on the centre frame engage with the brackets at each end of the box and tilt it at the end of its travel.

Another firm with a long history of leadership in laundry equipment are Thomas Bradford & Co. of Salford. They were one of the last to effect improvements in box mangles—a patent of 1857—and they continued to make and sell them at least up to 1878, although by then, judging by their advertisements, wringers and washing machines were a much more important part of their trade.

A little jingle that was still being sung 80 years ago, ran:

'Cheer boys, cheer!
My mother's bought a mangle.
Cheer boys, cheer!
She's filled it full of stones.
Cheer boys, cheer!
She makes me turn the handle,
Cheer boys, cheer!
It nearly breaks your bones.'

A miniature box mangle of pine, 16½ in. long by 7½ in. wide may be a child's toy, or a real device for 'smalls'.

Mangling Boards and Rollers

Mangling boards, Plate 153, *A* to *F*, were formerly used in many parts of Europe, but more particularly in Scandinavia and Friesland. The board, which may vary in length from about 27 in. to 38 in. and in width from 3 in. to 6½ in., was used in conjunction with a roller, Plate 153, *G* and *H*, 1½ in. to 2½ in. in diameter and 17 in. to 18 in. in length. The practice was to wind the wet articles round the roller, which was then run backwards and forwards on a flat surface, by firm downward pressure, applied to the mangling board, held at right angles above the roller. The action was, therefore, a hand version of the wheel and chain operated box mangle, trundling its load of stones over the washing-wound rollers.

Scandinavian and Friesland mangling boards are usually handsomely carved, and the former often brightly painted on the face, for they had the secondary purpose of being ornaments in the home and a reminder of the man's prowess in carving. Making an attractive mangling board was part of the winter's *husflid* (for *husflid*, see *Introduction, Background to Folk Art*), and when not

in use, it either hung on a wall of the living room, or outside the entrance door to proclaim that washing was taken in. Some of the boards have carved inscriptions on them, declaring that X washes white, mangles, glazes, etc.

Friesland, having much less forest than Norway and Sweden and that being largely oak, the mangling boards are mostly of this material, only ½ in. to ⅝ in. thick, slightly convex on the geometrically carved face, about 4½ in. wide and parallel in width. They are not usually painted, have no handles, but are normally pierced near the top, for hanging up; the two shown, Plate 153, *A* and *B*, are 17th- or early 18th-century. *D*, also of oak and without handle, is French or Flemish, carved with fleur-de-lis and date 1649.

Scandinavian mangling boards, *C*, *E* and *F*, are thicker, 1½ in. to 2½ in., heavier, often tapering in width, and made of birch or pine; occasionally, they are carved with geometric designs, but more often with naturalistic scenes in relief, or with a mixture of both, and enlivened with bright paint, green and red being particularly popular. They generally have handles, which are commonly shaped as a horse or lion; *C* is late 17th- or 18th-century, *E* and *F*, 19th-century.

Napkin Presses—see *Presses, Linen, Napkin*

Pegs

A well made wooden peg gripped much firmer and could take more punishment than its weakly, spring controlled, plastic successor. Pegs dating back 100 years or more are now very scarce, those carved in the form of a man, considerable rarities. Blanket pegs are larger, heavier versions of clothes pegs, like the two large ones, Plate 156, *L*; the small one on the left is one of the rarities carved as a miniature man. Cheap pegs, of almost any available wood of suitable texture were whittled by gypsies, but the best were turned by coopers and turners, from carefully selected hazel, willow, ash, hickory or beech, and only from a branch cut at the right spot, to ensure a non-splitting, springy peg; this was just below a Y-shaped fork. The round head of the peg was shaped out of the wood just below the fork, as this contained tough twisted grain wood, which would ensure that the opening in the peg would not spread up into a split.

Peggy Sticks—see *Dollies, Washing*

Poking Sticks and Goffering Stacks and Machines

Poking sticks were the forerunners of goffering irons, stacks and machines, and were as essential tools for ruffles as was the starch itself. First references to starch appear in English 14th-century documents, but its introduction to the fashionable English scene dates from the mid-16th-century era of ruffs. John Stow, in his *Annales of England*, 1594, says that Mistress Dinghem van der Plassen of Flanders introduced the art of starching here in 1554. Mistress Dinghem and some of her compatriots set up a school for teaching ladies and laundresses the arts of folding, pleating, starching and the making of starch. It was not possible to employ heat for the setting of the pleats of ruffs and bands in early Elizabethan times, because it was done by moistening them with a starch solution and folding them, while wet, over a wooden or bone poking stick of the desired dimension. Harrison (*Description of England*) states that steel poking sticks were introduced in 1573–74, and thereafter heat could be used and the process was made much simpler. It is doubtful whether anything so simple and commercially valueless as a 16th-century poking stick has survived. How would one recognise it anyhow?

Goffering irons, stacks and machines, Plate 156, were all used in the 17th, 18th and 19th centuries. The stack illustrated, *E*, mainly of elm, dates from around 1800. It carries on the Elizabethan tradition of cold crimping, by weaving the damp, starched cambric in and out of the wooden 'quills', which are held under pressure of the vertically sliding top bar, secured by wedges. Spare quills are stored in the drawer. Three of them are shown in front of the stack.

The goffering or gophering machine, *J*, dates from before 1800 and is finely made of steel and brass, mounted on a 3½ in. thick oak base. The ribbed brass rollers are hollow and hot circular irons are inserted before use. The fabric is fed between the rollers, which are revolved by means of cogs, actuated by the cranked handle. Spring tension is upwards, thrusting the lower roller against the upper.

Poss Sticks—see *Dollies, Washing*

Presses, Linen, Napkin and Lace

Pressing was a linen room operation, the last stage before the clothes and linen were put away with lavender and rosemary. Woollens did not receive such sweet smelling treatments; they were stored with ground-up old clay pipes in little bags, to keep away moth. Presses were made in various sizes, of which linen were the largest, napkins the medium, and lace the smallest size. The first two follow a common form of construction. The lower leaf or base of the press has upright posts secured centrally at each end; the posts are connected together at the top by a head rail. The wooden screw which applies the central pressure, is provided with a cross-bar handle and is threaded through the head rail, and connected at the bottom direct to the cross batten strengthened upper leaf of the press, which it can raise or lower. The upper leaf has slots cut out at each end; these notch round the uprights, which serve as guides. Linen and napkin presses were both made in considerable numbers in the 17th, 18th and 19th centuries. They can only be dated accurately by comparison with constructional details and period features of furniture. Country-made examples are found in almost any English hardwood; town-made are usually of oak or mahogany and may be plain, carved, or inlaid. They may be found on plain bases, on bases incorporating a drawer, such as Plate 148, which is of oak, on open stands, or on chests of drawers. Sizes vary considerably. Linen presses may measure anything from 18 in. by 24 in. to 24 in. by 36 in. on plan; napkin presses usually measure 12 in. to 15 in. by 8 in. to 10 in.

Lace presses are much rarer, quite small and of entirely different construction. The work put into their finish and decoration suggests that they were generally used by the lady of the house, as they are found occasionally handsomely carved, or with 'windows' cut in the top surface of the upper leaf, enclosing *petit point* or beadwork panels. They generally measure 8 in. to 10 in. long by 4 in. to 5 in. wide. They have two threaded hardwood uprights, secured to the bases; these 'screws' pass loosely through holes in the upper leaf; pressure is applied by means of hardwood nuts. The example illustrated, Plate 156, *K*, is Italian, 17th-century, probably of cypress wood, with boxwood screws and lignum vitae nuts. It is decorated with low relief carving, similar to embossing on leatherwork of the period. The top is decorated with lions rampant, supporting an eight-point star, in a surround of foliage. The bevels and sides have linked diamond ornament. There is simulated tooling under the base. Lace presses were made in the 17th and 18th centuries, but few survive. I have never seen a 19th-century specimen. They are sometimes confused with playing card presses. For differences, see Section XV, *Pastimes*.

Presses, Stocking

Stocking presses are so rare that the example illustrated, Plate 149, *N*, is the only one which I have seen. It came from the private laundry of a remote house in Wales. It is all of elm and measures 41 in. by 9½ in.,

with a base 2⅛ in. thick and top leaf 1⅜ in. thick. Although crude and heavy, it follows the principle of a lace press, with the two screws passing through the upper leaf, and pressure applied by means of boat-shaped elm nuts. Stockings were apparently pressed between intermediate boards and the press contains three, ½ in. thick, with U-shaped slots at each end, so that they are kept in line by the screws. The whole artefact is very wormy and decayed and probably dates from the 17th or 18th century.

Pressing Boards—see *Ironing Boards*

Rucking Boards—see *Crimping Boards*

Scrubbing Boards

It is believed that ribbed wooden scrubbing boards of the type illustrated, Plate 152, *A*, originated in Scandinavia and the manufacture spread to other countries during the 19th century. During recent years, the ribbing has been made of glass and other materials, but the pattern is now practically obsolete.

Slickenstones

Slickenstones, also known as linen smoothers, are mushroom-shaped objects, used 'cap' downwards, in a circular sweeping movement, for smoothing and, to some extent, glazing damp linen. The average diameter of the cap is 5 in. to 6 in., but they occur from about 3½ in. They were usually made of glass or marble, but very occasionally of lignum vitae. Two 17th- or 18th-century specimens, in this material, are shown, Plate 156, *G* and *H*; their base diameters are 3½ in. and 5½. respectively. *H*, which stands 7¼ in. high, is competently carved with the head of a blackamoor, wearing ear-rings; it is probably unique.

Stocking Airers—see *Airers, Stocking*

Stocking Presses—see *Presses, Stocking* .

Suction Cleaners

The vacuum cleaner comes into the age of electricity, metal and now plastics, but the idea was developed earlier, using wood and leather bellows, to suck the dust into a bag. 'The Pom' suction cleaner, Plate 151, *L*, registered in 1913, had already developed the mouth, shaped as on a modern vacuum cleaner. The dust bag is removable by releasing two butterfly nuts at the base.

Tennis Ball Brushes

The hardwood brushes, Plate 151, *A*, with their bristles facing inwards into a half dome, are effective, and although manufactured until recently, seem to puzzle many people.

Tubs and Keelers

The cooper, with his carefully built up staved and hooped watertight vessels, was, to some extent, a competitor of the turner, who turned the mainly smaller wooden vessels out of the solid. But for vessels too large to be made from one piece, the cooper reigned supreme until enamelled and galvanized iron and, more latterly, copper, aluminium, stainless steel, certain special ceramics and plastics gradually displaced him from his traditional markets.

Coopered tubs of various diameters and depths were general-purpose vessels, used largely in the laundry, the brewery, for the occasional bath in the bedroom, etc., from early times. William Tucker (see *Dollies*) stated that a tub, for use with a dolly, should be 2 ft. 6 in. deep, by 2 ft. 0 in. diameter at the top and 14 in. at the base. The round tub illustrated, Plate 152, *H*, measures 11 in. in depth by 21½ in. at the rim, and is of the type used on a bench or stool. In houses which did not possess a teak or sycamore sink, the oval tub, Plate 151, *J*, 7 in. deep and 16 in. by 12 in. in diameter, was an essential, for glass, china and silver, which could not be washed in stone or stoneware sinks.

Keelers are shallow tubs, 3 in. to 6 in. deep, used for 'smalls' in the laundry, and for cooling liquids in the dairy, kitchen, brewery, etc. See Section V, *Farm: Keelers*.

Troughs

Troughs, usually of sycamore, some fitted on stands, were made commercially for the laundry in the late 18th and throughout the 19th century. Most 18th-century and earlier engravings show only tubs and keelers in use. Baker of Fore Street, London, and Thomas Bradford of Salford (both mentioned under *Mangles*) were among the well-known makers of troughs. Straight-sided troughs, approximately 5 ft. 6 in. long by 2 ft. 11 in. wide and 2 ft. 7 in. deep, with a central division across, were for rinsing and blueing. Shallower tapering troughs, approximately 5 ft. 6 in. long by 1 ft. 10 in. wide at top, 1 ft. 6 in. wide at base and 1 ft. 4 in. deep, on a 1 ft. 10½ in. high stand, were for washing; they usually have a small triangular soap shelf in the angle formed by the division with one end. Late 19th-century specimens were sometimes made of teak. Both types of troughs have waste holes and were stood over open gullies. They had to be filled laboriously from cauldrons.

Washing Machines and Wringers

The modern rotary washing machine, a circular drum rotating in an octagonal trough, and actuated by a geared handle, turned by hand, was invented by Henry Sidgier, Upholder, of London, in 1782, patent No. 1331. In 1790, at the Hanbury Hall sale of the effects of Henry Cecil, later Lord of Burghley, a washing machine was purchased by Dr. Treadwell Nash for £1 12s. 6d. It may well have been a Sidgier washing machine. Why this eminently practical and advanced looking machine disappeared, it is hard to imagine, for the next one of which I have a record, made about 1900, was a very retrograde affair and was simply a poss stick, worked by a geared handle, set upright in a lidded trough.

The rocker wooden washing machine, Plate 155, was one of the novelties of the 1862 International Exhibition. Thomas Bradford's rotary washing machine of 1857 (virtually Sidgier's with a mangling or wringing attachment), Plate 157, was the prototype of a large range of machines which appeared in the 1860s and 1870s. Wringers were also made as separate machines contemporary with box mangles, before the latter died out. In the 1860–70 period, Bradford's produced a shuttle washer which was geared to tilt backwards and forwards and was a cross between the rocker and the rotary.

Winder, Line

Wash line winders are usually strictly utilitarian objects, without any collector interest. The winder illustrated, Plate 156, *A*, is one of those curious objects which occasionally turn up to intrigue and delight the antiquarian. It is carved and hollowed out of a solid block of willow(?) and measures 9 in. in height by 4½ in. wide by 3½ in. deep. The winder spindle is much worn; it is very fragile, in an advanced stage of decay and badly worm eaten. At first sight, it appears to be early 17th century, but it is clearly carved with the date 1805, sacred initials above a heart and other initials in the three sides of the solid worked moulding. One can only assume that either (*a*) it was made by a woodworker of 1805, as a replacement of an earlier one, or (*b*) that he made it to harmonize with a 17th-century lead rainwater head on the building or (*c*) that he was inspired by a Jacobean newel post.

IX

Love Spoons and Other Love Tokens

The custom of making useful objects and carving love emblems, initials or names, and dates on them, was formerly widespread among rustic and maritime communities in many countries. Furniture was sometimes so treated, but more often the practice applied to smaller domestic objects. Where these objects served a useful purpose, additional to being tokens of love, they are described and mostly illustrated in other sections of this volume. Useful wooden articles, which sometimes served a dual purpose, include Valentine gift boxes, and mirror cases and H combs, Section XXIII, *Toilet and Bedroom Accessories*; stay busks, Section II, *Costume Accessories*; lace bobbins, knitting sheaths and continental flax swingles and scutching knives, Section XXI, *Textile Workers' Devices*; continental washing bats and mangling boards, Section VIII, *Laundry and Cleaning Devices*; snuff spoons, Section XXII, *Tobacco Accessories*; money boxes and continental feather-bed smoothers, Section X, *Miscellany*; ell rules, Section XIX, *Scientific*; marriage bowls, Section III, *Drinking*.

Many love tokens were made of material other than wood, some by the donors, others produced commercially; although it is not always possible to say whether they were intended as proposal, betrothal, marriage, birth or anniversary gifts, it may be of interest to list a selection. Jewellery included posy rings—rings engraved with a line of poesy or poetry—some of which go back to mediaeval times. Also under this heading are inscribed heart-shaped lockets for suspension, or as features of brooches or rings and sometimes forming frames for miniatures. Hand-worked costume connected with betrothal, marriage and birth has frequently included complete and elaborate outfits or specific garments, ranging from embroidered head-dress, kerchiefs and aprons, to gloves, garters and slippers. In the Iberian Peninsula, artificial flowers, delicately carved from the pith of the elder tree, were formerly used as love tokens. Sailors of many nationalities, in the days of sail, conveyed their love messages by means of verses and scrimshaw pictures scratched on whalebone and tusk ivory. Ashore, they bought Bristol glass rolling pins, decorated with verses and girl's names and sometimes used them to bring in contraband liquor. At home, not so handy lovers could buy their love messages ready inscribed on Sunderland lustre, or Newcastle or Stafford pottery. Heart-shaped pincushions, worked in beads, or with names or messages spelt out in pin heads, were popular love gifts in 19th-century England, and heart-shaped tablets of soap, impressed with a cradle and separate soap baby, were Victorian natal gifts.

In the British Isles, the pre-eminent love

token which served no secondary purpose, was the Welsh love spoon. It was essentially a message from a rustic or sailor, who might be illiterate or tongue tied and found it easier to convey his feelings in traditional symbolism, carved in wood. To a lesser extent, the same token was used in the West of England, in Scandinavia, Switzerland and neighbouring districts, as well as other continents. Occasional variants were a wooden knife, fork, sugar tongs or carved handle terminating in a marriage shoe, or two chained miniature shoes. These often intricately pierced spoons and related objects were never equivalents of engagement rings; they were preludes to courtship—questions in wood, made and offered by the man, to signify a desire 'to spoon', a term which came into use in Victorian times. The village belle, if a coquette, might have several love spoons hanging in her cottage. The symbolism of the spoon, as applied to courting, probably originated in spoons of similar size fitting closely. In Trotter's *Distressed Seamen*, 1789, occurs the sentence 'They are stowed sponways, and so closely locked in one another's arms that it is difficult to move'.

The Welsh love spoon custom goes back at least to the 17th century; the National Museum of Wales possesses a fine specimen dated 1667. The majority, however, of these valued and carefully preserved bygones date from the second half of the 18th and the 19th centuries. If no date is carved on them, they are difficult to judge, because in the country, fashion passed them by, and a young man might take a much earlier spoon as his model. It has been said that handles with four-sided pierced lanterns which often have loose balls running up and down in them, and that glass 'windows' with names behind them, only date from the 19th century. These statements are incorrect. The 'lantern' occurs on the 1667 spoon and was common in the 18th century; so also were glass 'windows', but the majority of 'windows' are 19th-century and some late

ones were probably commercially made. Other erroneous beliefs are that swivel links in wooden chains were only made after 1870 and that all painted or varnished love spoons are continental.

Spoons were usually made from readily available local hardwoods, the clean, easily carved sycamore being favourite. Sometimes a spoon is made of a foreign wood, but even without this clue, its carved motifs, such as a chain, anchor, ship, dolphin, camel, etc., will pronounce this the work of a sailor, whiling away tedious hours on board a sailing ship. Some sailor-carved specimens have incised lines filled with red or black wax.

The most common carved motifs are hearts or twin hearts; sometimes the spoon bowl is shaped as a heart with a rib down the middle, denoting 'We two are one'. Nearly as popular as hearts, on 19th-century spoons, were 'soul' motifs—pierced outlines of 'comma' shape, usually, but not invariably, inverted and arranged in pairs. How this particular motif came to be included in Welsh symbolism is a mystery, for these are ancient Egyptian symbols for the soul, representing the nostrils, through which the soul was believed to escape at death. Some writers have claimed that this 'comma' is really the Indian pine motif, so popular on 19th-century Paisley shawls from about 1816 onwards. On grounds of date, I do not think there is anything against this theory, but it does not fit in with the symbolism of the other motifs, and I think it more likely that some paper on the Egyptian soul motif, printed in English, was disseminated in the 19th century.

Other carved or pierced designs which occur, include a small house, or a keyhole, meaning 'My house is yours'; a spade, also denoted by carving the spoon bowl in that shape, signified 'I will dig for you'. Some people aver that the wheel motif also betokens 'I will work for you'. Twin bowls, sprouting side by side from the base of one handle, represent an alternative way of saying 'We two are one'. One or more small spoons or spoon bowls, each side of one or two large ones, are said to indicate the desire for a family, and the number; I feel, however, that there may be occasional exceptions to this theory, and not only because the little ones are sometimes carved as knives and forks!

As a generalization, and it is nothing more, love spoons with very large, flat and intricately pierced handles are more often 19th-century, than earlier. But locality also counts; Pembrokeshire spoons with large, thick, coarsely carved panel handles are sometimes earlier.

Two unusually large and elaborate sycamore love spoons are illustrated, Plate 158. That on the left, cut from a thin board, 29 in. by 5¼ in., can be dated between 1820 and 1830. At the top is a simplified version of the 1820 hobby-horse cycle. Below is silhouetted Telford's Menai suspension bridge, with four arches one side and three the other, built between 1819 and 1826. A three masted sailing ship of the same period, wheel, keyholes, hearts, souls and five spoon bowls all appear in the lacy tracery of this skilfully composed wooden love letter; according to tradition, it says 'I am yours heart and soul, my house is yours, I will work for you and when we marry, may we have four children'.

The other specimen came from Penrhyn Castle, North Wales, and is cut from a board 24 in. by 11 in., with the hook-on spoons all separate. It forms a multi-pierced wooden Valentine, surmounted by a simplified coat of arms, with numerous cut-out hearts, crowns, love-birds, vases, wheels and rabbits. It is not clear whether there is connection between the rabbits and the 31 small spoons, nor is it known whether the girl heeded the warning and the carver died a disappointed bachelor!

Study of the various photographs in this section will show the prevalence of wooden chains connected to love tokens. The wooden chain, in fact, has been used to symbolize both the links of marriage and of prison, and sometimes merely to show the skill of the carver. In Plate 159, A, the pair of spectacles, linked by chain to the swivel-mounted pair of spoons with lantern and ball handles, carved from a 24 in. long block of pearwood, is said to have been made by a French prisoner in Lewes gaol in 1850; assuming this is true, the chain could have had dual meaning. The remainder of the specimens in Plate 159 are all Welsh. B, of sycamore, is 19th-century; several variations of this design exist. The wide panel spoons from North Wales, always make the spoon bowl look disproportionately small; the example C, which is also sycamore and 19th-century, is fret cut with keyholes, roundels, heart and soul motifs and has an integral chain of seven links, connecting the 'horns'; it has initials J.J. cut in, and a chip carved design filled with red sealing wax, which suggests the work of a sailor. D, probably from North Wales, is an early type, with curved thumb lift and lantern and balls, and could be 17th- or early 18th-century. E, sycamore, with spade-shaped bowl, and lantern and keyhole in the handle, may be 18th- or early 19th-century. F, an unusually narrow, fret cut, boxwood spoon, may be 18th-century. G, an uncommon design of interlaced scrolls in fruitwood, may also be 18th-century. H, is a good quality maplewood spoon, the graceful curves of which do not show in the front view; with its integral chain of eleven links, it measures 15½ in.; it may be 18th- or early 19th-century. Of the same period is the neat little spoon, J, pierced with three hearts. K, is a 19th-century, dolphin stemmed, sycamore spoon, with heart pierced handle. The 11 in. long, sycamore spoon, L, with integral ring, chip carved lantern with four balls and twin stem below, connecting to a well shaped bowl, has a special place in my heart, because it is one of the first two pieces of treen which I acquired. Possibly because of this favourable prejudice, I regard it as one of the most crisp and satisfying carved love spoons which I have ever seen. I bought it for 8*s*. 6*d*. in the Caledonian market when I was a boy, 50 years ago.

All the spoons in Plate 160 are Welsh. *A*, probably from North Wales and neatly chip carved round all the fretted openings, tells its story with initials, date and love motifs. *B*, is a terrific example of Welsh patience combined with considerable technical skill and ingenuity; the naïvety of design, however, results in a rather overwhelming impression of 19th-century busyness. The whole intricate composition, including the five chains, but with the exception of the cross link through the stem above the bowl, is or was cut from a single block of pearwood. Actually, the knife is a replacement, carried out in planewood. The main handle is pierced and carved from all four faces; in side section, it shows a centre division vertically, so that there are four lanterns, each with three balls, in the lower compartment, two separate pierced roundels lie behind the mirror panel, and above the mirror there are three separate windows, behind each other. Looking out through the arch above are a little man and woman, presumably representing donor and recipient, carved in the round. The piece of mirror inserted in front, was probably to avert the evil eye; there was often a considerable amount of superstition mixed up with love tokens, and pieces of mirror, too small to be useful, were included in other varieties of love tokens. *C*, a 19th-century, broad panel type, is pierced with keys, keyholes, heart and anchor and, more originally than most, with candlesticks, jugs, and goblets; a sinking just above the spoon bowl, would originally have held a name. *D*, pierced with heart and soul motifs, grouped round a roundel, has the name Catherine Davies and a Welsh inscription in its glazed window; it could be late 18th- or early 19th-century. *E*, with handle terminal of twin hearts, all carved from yew-wood and inscribed Two Fayth-

ful Hartes United, is, I think, a 19th-century commercial product. *F*, is probably 19th-century, neat and unpretentious, but cleanly carved from pearwood. *G*, another neatly fretted spoon with twin bowls, proclaiming 'We two are one', is probably late 18th- or early 19th-century. *H*, plain and simple, is the earliest dated specimen in the Pinto Collection—July Ye 18.1720.

All the spoons and forks in Plate 161 are Welsh also. The clumsy but unusual pair of leaf-carved spoons, suspended from a framed mirror, *A*, total length 15 in., probably came from Pembrokeshire and might be dated between 1870 and 1900. The mirror, sight size $3\frac{1}{2}$ in. by $2\frac{1}{4}$ in., is just large enough for use, or may be another example of the evil eye superstition. The $13\frac{3}{4}$ in. long pearwood spoon, with heart-shaped bowl, *B*, is a well designed and competently executed example of the lantern and ball type; it may be 18th- or 19th-century. The same general remarks apply to the six-prong and four-prong forks, *C* and *D*, each of which has four lanterns, with balls in the lowest part of the stem, another behind the X, and a swivelling ball in the heart-shaped opening, forming a junction with the chain. Forks are much rarer than spoons and seldom of such good quality as these two, which show a common design ancestry. The total length of forks and chains are 16 in. and 15 in. respectively. *E*, a simple sycamore spoon and impossible to date, has the letter A carved on the handle and a double bowl, divided by a centre rib, denoting 'We two are one'. *F*, is an early 19th-century, beechwood, panel-handled spoon, carved with heart and soul motifs and diamond fretting against an all-over chip carved background. *G*, an ingenious and original piece of work, comprising three keys and a whistle linked to a ring, all carved from a single block of mahogany, brings us back to a question: are these the keys to the girl's heart and the whistle to call the carver, or are they the work of some wretched prisoner, whiling away the interminable hours by making a facsimile of his gaoler's keys and whistle?

The earliest date-carved Welsh love spoon recorded, is one of 1667, with curved thumb lift handle and two lanterns with balls, inscribed with the initials L.P.; it is in the National Museum of Wales. Plate 161, *H*, is an exact replica, except that the initials are E.W., which, according to a faint written inscription in the bowl, stands for Elizabeth Williams. I think that this replica is unlikely to be earlier than 1800. *J*, is another spoon of this same type, but I believe that this example also was made in the 19th century.

Like the two preceding plates, all the objects in Plate 163 are Welsh. The bunches of spoons on a ring, *A* and *D*, may not appear as spectacular at first, as some of the more elaborate examples already illustrated and described. But just think of the sheer technical skill in *A*, and the amount of labour involved in the setting out and cutting of the six graceful, perfect matching 'children' spoons, with fig-shaped bowls, the 'mother' spoon and the ring, which are carved, not turned, all out of a single block of sycamore. The block, I estimate, must have been at least 16 in. long, 8 in. or more wide and 4 in. thick. The ornamentally incised bands are as simple, neat and masterly as the rest of this remarkable nest of spoons from Cardiganshire, which I take to be 19th-century. *D*, also from Cardiganshire, is probably earlier, much cruder and has only four spoons of similar size, arranged in pairs; the symbolism, if any, is not apparent to me. *B*, is another of those deceptively plain and simple compositions which involved considerable skill and labour. The chain links are very thin, well matched and precisely cut; so are the lanterns and balls. The total length is nearly 29 in.—everything cut from the one sycamore plank. I would think that it dates from 1800–10. The 19 in. long chain, *C*, with two lanterns and balls, a swivel link and a benediction hand, is said to have been

carved by a Napoleonic prisoner in Cardiff Gaol; how long a period did each link represent?

In Plate 162 are a number of love spoons, not Welsh, and some unusual love tokens, mostly from Wales. First the spoons; *B* and *G*, are probably sailors' love spoons. The former is carved with a rope twist stem, and a star surmounted by a kneeling camel. The latter has a cleverly carved looped handle, decorated with incised wavy lines, stars and zig-zags, with a rope knop terminal. *C*, shown inverted, is crude and appears to be a very early specimen. The inside of the bowl has a centre ridge of the 'We two are one' pattern, like Plate 161, *E*. The whole is painted in polychrome, and the back, shown in the picture, represents the Tree of Life or Knowledge, with the trunk entwined by the serpent. Well carved, probably 18th-century, and almost certainly Scandinavian, *D* has some symbolism on which I have been unable to obtain any information. At the top is a mermaid with her hands resting on a shield. Below the rope-edged platform, a well delineated hand grasps a pair of legs with hoofs at the upper and boots at the lower end. *E*, is a love spoon of excellent quality and unknown provenance. The open crown at the top has hearts carved on each side of the inner cushion; below, is another piercing, heart-shaped back and front, with twin heart piercings each side. On the back of the spoon bowl are intertwined initials; it probably dates from the 18th century. *F* is also of very good quality, with an unusually thin handle and bowl, the latter exceptionally tilted, necessitating cutting out of at least a 2 in. thick block. The unusual feature is that in the handle, there is a loose revolving wheel, cut out of the solid. The handle and ring are chip carved in diamonds and circles; the provenance and date are unknown. *A*, cut from a single block of mahogany, is a rather mysterious object, possibly a sailor's love token; it is 10½ in. long by 1 in. square. It contains two

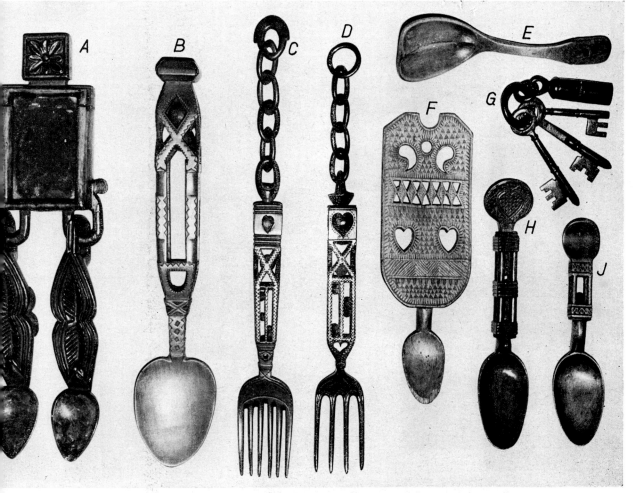

161   Selection of Welsh love spoons and a ring with keys and whistle. For other details, see text. (*Section IX*)

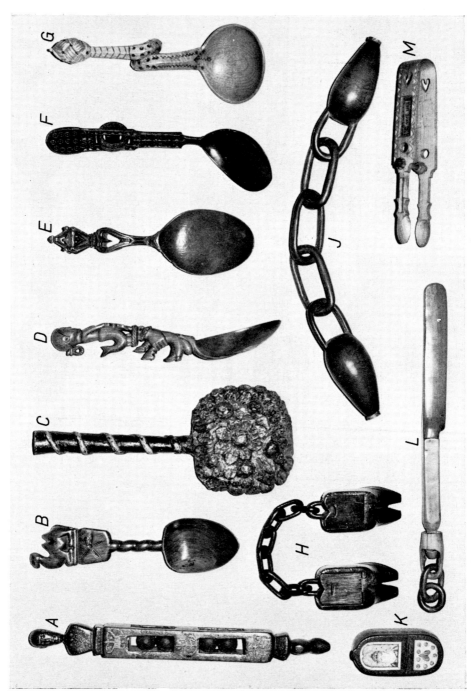

162 Love spoons and other love tokens from various parts of the world. For details, see text. (*Section IX*)

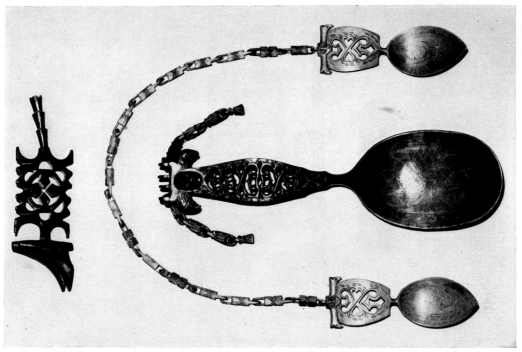

164 Norwegian love spoons and one of a pair of Welsh (?) carved and fretted stands of unknown purpose. For details, see text. (*Section IX*)

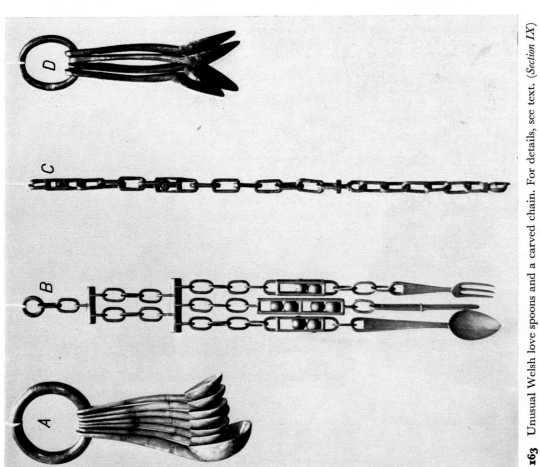

163 Unusual Welsh love spoons and a carved chain. For details, see text. (*Section IX*)

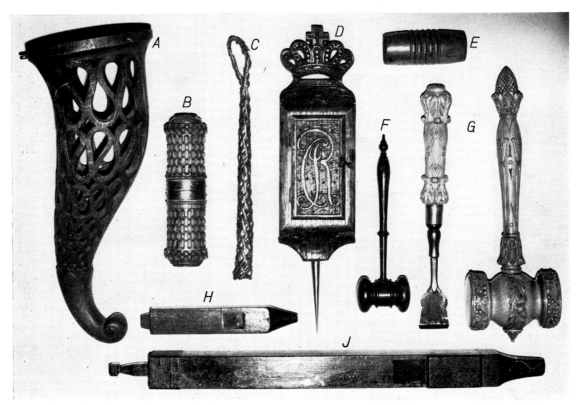

165 *A*, a remarkable wooden cornucopia; *B*, 19th-century apprentice's indenture box; *C*, woven split-cane wife lead; *D*, Scandinavian Fiery Cross box; *E*, bicycle handle-bar grip; *F*, chairman's gavel; *G*, ceremonial chisel and mallet; *H* and *J*, pitch pipes. (*Section X*)

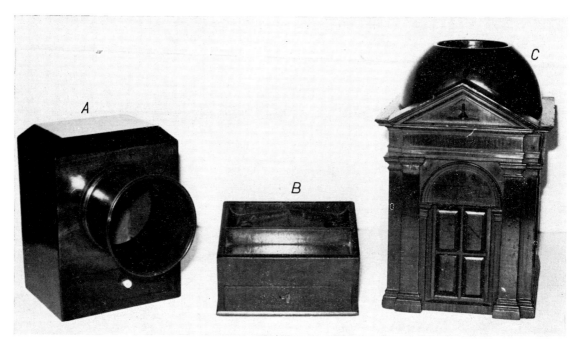

166 18th-century, mahogany ballot boxes. *C*, is a Masonic box, designed as a temple (*Section X*)

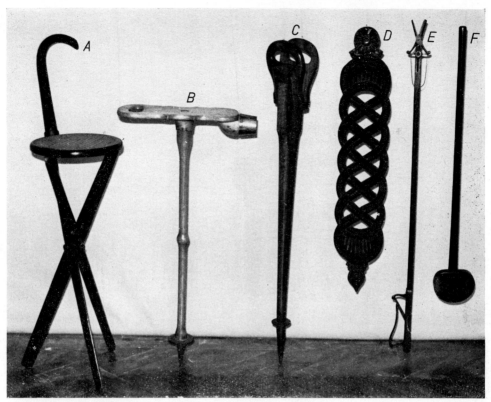

167 *A, B* and *C*, 19th-century, folding seat sticks; *D*, carved oak bell pull (?); *E*, Victorian flower picker; *F*, feather bed smoother. (*Section X*)

168 Selection of collecting and money boxes. For details, see text. (*Section X*)

169 Swiss, carved standing cups. 19th century. (*Section X*)

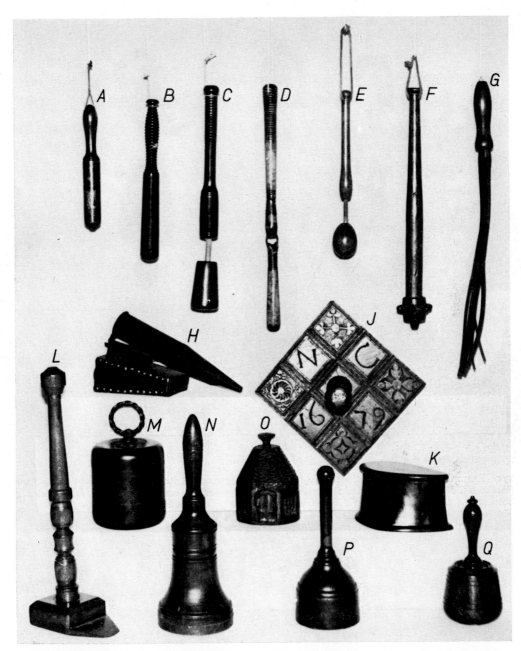

170 *A* and *B*, truncheons; *C* to *E*, life preservers; *F*, club or bludgeon; *G*, cat-o'-six-tails; *H*, bee keeper's bellows; *J*, church hat peg, dated 1679; *K*, World War I propellor box; *L* to P, selection of wooden door porters; *Q*, ceremonial stone laying mallet. (*Section X*)

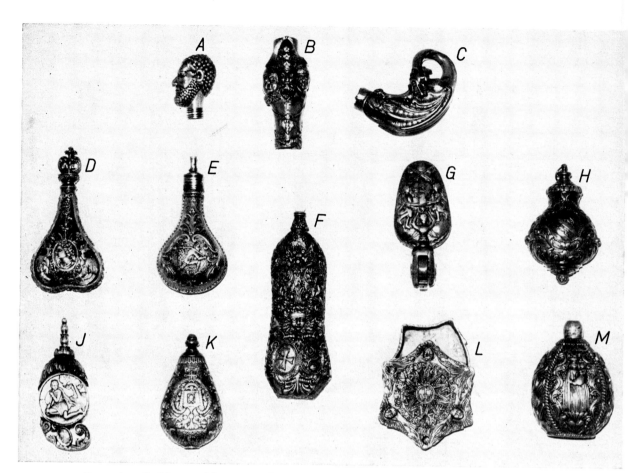

171 Examples of 16th- to 18th-century fine art in boxwood. *A* and *C*, handles of sticks or umbrellas (*Section II*). *D*, *E* and *J*, scent flasks (*Section XXIII*). *B*, probably a cardinal's staff; *F*, *H*, *K* and *M*, chrism bottles; *G*, folding chrism spoon; *L*, probably a wafer box. (*Section X*)

172 Carved and hand painted angels from a presepio set by Georg Anderl of Munich. (*Section X*)

173 An Arab stallion from the same set as Plate 172. (*Section X*)

174 A rare, 19th-century, American Aeolian harp, shown open and closed. (*Section X*)

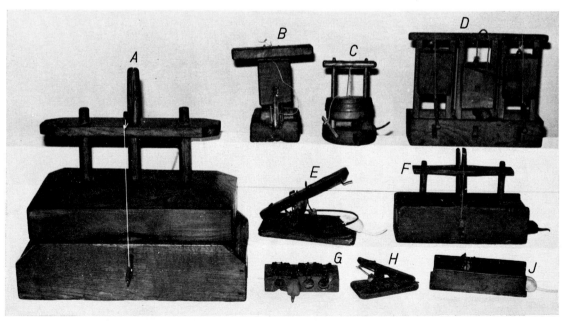

175 Selection of rat and mouse-traps. For details, see text. (*Section X*)

176 A wooden *velocipéde, circa* 1866. (*Section X*)

177 TOP LEFT: cylindric walnut mortar and pestle, and the bowl mortar below, are typical shapes for large mortars. TOP CENTRE: 18th- or early 19th-century coffee mill, of a type used in coffee houses and large households. TOP RIGHT: D-shaped kitchen grater on oak plaque, 18th or early 19th century. BELOW: the large breadcrumb grater, from Ashburnham, Sussex, has the practical feature of a drawer to receive the crumbs. (*Section XI*)

178 *A* to *E*, *G* and *H*, selection of mortar-graters; for details, see text. *J* to *V*, apothecary mortars, 17th to 19th century, mostly of lignum vitae and varying in height from 2¾ in. to 6¼ in. The trumpet shaped specimen, *P*, is of laburnum wood. (*Section XI*)

179 Selection of mortars. *B* is dated A.D. 1659 on base and is the earliest dated wood specimen known. The octagonal salt mortar, *F*, is so impregnated that the salt oozes out in damp weather. For further details, see text. (*Section XI*)

180   Coffee mills dating from 1660/80 to 1851. For details, see text. (*Section XI*)

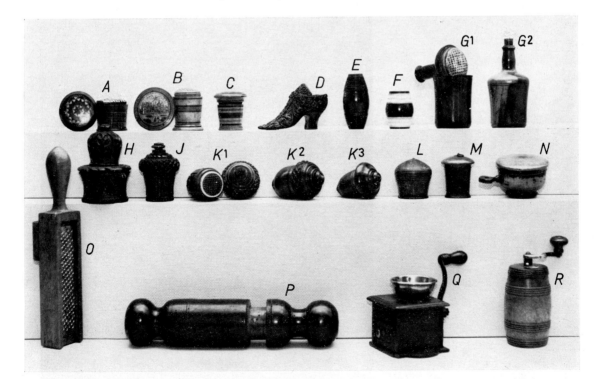

181   TOP AND MIDDLE ROW: section of pocket spice graters, with kitchen grater at each end of middle row. For details, see text. The shoe, *D*, is a finely carved specimen dated 1707.   *O*, a kitchen specimen with travelling compartment at back; *P*, an 18th-century grinder-roller; *Q*, a mill for grinding pepper for filling casters; *R*, a pepper mill for grinding at table. (*Section XI*)

182 The skilled carver selects a tool. (*Section XII*)

183 The outline of a cow takes shape under the carver's swift, firm strokes. (*Section XII*)

184 ABOVE: one side of the fine, boxwood, Nürnberg cake mould, dated 1567, with casts from both sides. BELOW: hexagonal marchpane mould, dated 1779, shown in sections, together with cast. (*Section XII*)

185 A crude elm mould carved with a dolphin and heart, and name S. Plum. (*Section XII*)

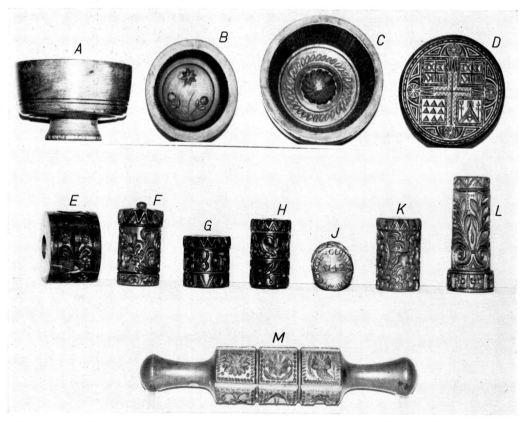

186 TOP ROW: flummery moulds and a coptic bread stamp. MIDDLE ROW: French, 18th-century, box-wood roller prints. AT BOTTOM: fondant roller, English, probably 18th century. (*Section XII*)

lanterns, each with two balls, is surmounted by a male bust, and its base terminal is a man's boot. The decoration, which is all over and entirely in brass pin heads, includes, on the man's chest, a heart. Below the bust are crowns on the front and sides and initials G.T. and M.R. at the back. Between the lanterns are, in front, a crown and on the other sides, a tankard, goblet and bottle. Below the lanterns, the decorations are a spade, heart, diamond and club; on the boot is another heart. I would think that it is 19th-century, Welsh.

The antiquity of the symbolism of the shoe or boot in connection with luck and marriage, dates back to the bible, when the plucking off of a shoe denoted the confirmation of a contract for redemption or change of ownership, which could include marriage. Thus, in the *Book of Ruth*, we read

'Now this was the manner in former times in Israel concerning redeeming and concerning changing, for to confirm all things; a man plucked off his shoe, and gave it to his neighbour: and this was a testimony in Israel. Therefore the kinsman said unto Boaz, Buy it for thee. So he drew off his shoe. And Boaz said unto the elders, and unto all the people, Ye are witnesses this day, that I have bought all that was Elimelech's, and all that was Chilion's and Mahlon's, of the hand of Naomi. Moreover, Ruth the Moabitess, the wife of Mahlon, have I purchased to be my wife. . . .'

The connection between footwear, luck and marriage still persists with the miniature silver shoe on the wedding cake and the tying of a boot or shoe to the back of the vehicle in which the newly-weds commence their honeymoon. Even in childhood's fairyland, Cinderella's crystal slipper is the symbol of her luck and her royal marriage.

The Welsh marriage shoes, Plate 162, *H*, each pair connected by a chain, all cut from the solid, and the shoes hollowed out to form boxes with sliding lids, are believed to have a long country history. It was formerly a charming marriage custom to

carve and give them to the bride and groom, with a knob of coal in one pair of shoes and sugar in the other, to ensure that the couple never lacked warmth and sweetness or sustenance. The twin solid boots with fret cut panels behind and handles extending backwards and slightly upwards, shown at the top of Plate 164, are one of a pair and look late 19th-century and Welsh. They are presumably love tokens, but whether they had a secondary purpose, I have been unable to ascertain.

Returning to Plate 162, the late 19th-century snuff box, *K*, with bone insert frame enclosing a picture of girl, and bone insert below, fret-cut with a heart, is perhaps more a love keepsake and memento than token, in the sense of the spoons. *L*, the wooden knife with chain and swivels, is just a variant of love spoons. *M*, a pair of chip carved, bentwood sugar tongs 'for the sweetie' is a commercial production of the late 19th century, when the custom of making and carving love spoons was falling into decay. These tongs, which really rank as wooden Valentines, were sold with a glass window in one or both sides, behind which the donor could insert his message. The example illustrated has 'Mrs. Evans' in one window and 'March 1892' in the other.

The chained pear shaped flasks, *J*, which are 3 in. long, and others like them but smaller, mostly only 1½ in. to 2 in. long, puzzled me for many years. They appeared on the market from time to time, always with the consistent story that they were Welsh pledging cups, used in some betrothal ceremony. So far as these flasks are concerned, the story is fabricated, and the 'Welsh pledging cups' are African snuff flasks, which someone has been carefully re-finishing and selling very profitably. I never believed the story, because the woods were African species and the 2 in. to 2½ in. long chain links were too coarse for Welsh work. I had long suspected that these chained flasks, like some chained spoons, were made by certain African natives; I once measured a pair of African spoons with chain, coarsely but quite skilfully cut from a single piece of wood, which was 6 ft. 4 in. long. The final link in the wooden chain came when I acquired a pair of carved wooden African head rests, chained together with a wooden chain and having 'Welsh pledging cups' suspended from their outer edges. An illustrated letter to *Country Life* (February 4, 1965), showing the African flasks, Plate 162, *J*, and the head rest with its flasks, included for comparison, produced considerable and interesting correspondence from Britons living in, or who had lived in various parts of Africa, and also from ethnographical museums in different parts of the world. What is now established is that the flasks, Plate 162, *J*, and the head rest which I illustrated, are of Zulu origin, although both types of objects and the chained spoons were made and used by other tribes. The chained head rests are much more common than the flasks. There is some doubt whether either were ever made as love tokens for traditional use, or whether they represent a kind of fantastication of African custom developed for the European curio hunter. They mostly seem to have been made between 1902 and 1920. One of my correspondents in Natal, South Africa, has been told by his Zulu servants that the snuff flasks are shaped to represent the padlocks on leg chains; he makes the additional interesting point that all the tribes who formerly made these objects are from areas where the Government Services were previously largely recruited in Britain and contained a fair proportion of Welshmen in the police and prison services. He adds further, that the best collections of chain work are owned by persons who had connections with one of these services, and surmises that possibly it was taught unofficially in the prisons, by Welshmen. So once more we have some tenuous connection between love, Welsh love tokens, chains and prison.

The pair of Norwegian chained love spoons, with engraved bowls, Plate 164, are cut from a block of sycamore 36 in. long by 2¼ in. wide by 1½ in. thick. I judge this pair to be about 60 or 70 years old, but they appear to have a long tradition, although rather more crude specimens are still being made as tourist attractions. Chained spoons carved on the same principle, but in different patterns, were also made in the Alpine districts of central Europe. The large sycamore spoon, 14 in. overall, central in Plate 164, with carved and pierced handles, human head and eagle head terminals, and chain pendants, is also Norwegian, and probably early 19th-century.

X

Miscellany

In this section are illustrated and described various entirely unrelated wooden objects which do not come under any of the other section headings. They are arranged alphabetically.

Aeolian Harps

Musical instruments played by man are excluded from this encyclopaedia, not only because of the considerable scope of the subject, but also because the 'woods' are an incomplete study without the metal 'winds'. The Aeolian harp is the one exception, being a wooden instrument played not by man, but by the winds, and named after Aeolus, Roman God of the Winds. The rare example, shown open, Plate 174, *A*, and closed, Plate 174, *B*, was made in 1862 by Jno. Simpson, a retired American sea captain. It is constructed mainly of Virginia walnut, inlaid with brass discs and diamonds of mahogany, plane and other light woods. It has two sounding boxes with pine tops and is 32 in. long, $5\frac{3}{4}$ in. wide and $6\frac{1}{4}$ in. high, when closed. The upper and lower sections are hinged together at the back. There are two strings, one above the other, at the back, and four on the lower sound box. The aperture, which is $2\frac{1}{4}$ in. high in front, tapers to $\frac{3}{4}$ in. at the back.

The instrument is played on a windy day, by laying it flat and closed, in the bottom of a sash window, which is shut down on it, with the narrow side of the harp aperture facing outwards. Its eerie sounds, much more resembling certain notes of an organ, than those of a harp, are heightened if any gaps in the window opening at the ends of the harp, are masked out.

Anointing Spoons—see *Religious Objects*

Apprentices' Indenture Boxes

Cylindric boxes, usually between 4 in. and 6 in. long, of the type used for knitting and netting needles, and also for pens and pencils, are sometimes found with rather more decoration than normal and also with initials or names and dates on them. It is always possible that such examples were originally intended for apprentices' indenture rolls. A 19th-century turner apprentice's ornamentally turned, oak indenture box is illustrated, Plate 165, *B*.

Ballot Boxes

There is a close connection between the words ballot and bullet, the word ballot being derived from *ballota*, a round bullet. Correctly speaking, ballot is simply the ball used in the procedure of secret voting, or voting by ballot, and the ballot box is the receptacle in which the ball is placed; but the term is now taken to cover votes cast into a box by means of marked but unsigned cards or papers. Voting by ballot goes back to ancient Greece and Rome and has spread from those centres to all parts of the world where constitutional governing methods prevail. English reformers demanded the use of the ballot box for elections at the beginning of the 19th century, but not until the passing of Forster's Ballot Act of 1827 did secret voting become obligatory in all our parliamentary and municipal elections, except parliamentary elections for universities. Elections by ballot for Guilds, Livery Companies, Chartered Companies and clubs, however, go back considerably further in Great Britain and although by no means common, were used in the 17th century.

There are at least two distinct ways of balloting for election, each requiring a different type of box. In one method, white and black balls were used and the ballot box had a single compartment into which the hand was thrust through a circular wooden sleeve, shaped like an old-fashioned telephone mouthpiece. The balls fell into a drawer below the opening; when the drawer was opened, if it contained all white balls, the candidate was elected; if there were one or more black balls in the drawer, he was 'black-balled'. Plate 166, A, shows a single drawer, Georgian mahogany box, 9½ in. high, 7 in. wide and 6 in. deep; the 'sleeve' is 5 in. in diameter. A variant of this type of box, Plate 166, B, has inclines running downwards from the centre of an open-topped box. The inclines are marked 'For' and 'Against', or 'B' and 'W'. At the bottom of each slope is a hole, through which the black and white balls drop into a single drawer below; such boxes were used behind a screen.

In the other method of balloting, the balls need only be of one colour, because the box itself is divided into two compartments, for the 'Ayes' and 'Noes' respectively. The single entry box is still used, but when the hand is inserted in the circular opening, it is found that inside there is a division, and the ball can be dropped to left

or right, into either of two drawers. Such boxes were made either with the 'telephone' sleeve in front, or with an apertured dome on top. An ingenious architectural version of the domed box is shown, Plate 166, C, an 18th-century, English, Masonic ballot box. It is designed as a classical Masonic temple and is a fine example of cabinet making, executed in Spanish fiddleback mahogany. The dome, open in the centre 'to the sky', in the manner of the Pantheon in Rome, has a division, shaped like a steeply pitched roof, a few inches down inside. The slopes divert the balls to left or to right, into the drawers, inlaid on their faces with the letters A (Aye) and N (Noe). The pediment is inlaid with a Masonic compass, square and plumb. The sides and back of this handsome box are each divided vertically into two panels, with solid moulded framing. The dimensions are 13½ in. high, by 9 in., by 9 in.

The largest, most elaborate and probably the earliest surviving ballot box in this country, is the one which has been used since 1676 by the Worshipful Company of Saddlers, for the annual election of its Master and Wardens. The box, however, goes back to 1619, when it was commissioned by Sir John Holloway, a member of the committee of the East India or 'John' Company, as it was often called. Sir John realised the dangers inherent in voting for membership of the committee by show of hands. He accordingly had the box made, produced it at a meeting in 1619 and suggested that voting by ballot should be adopted. He was, however, like so many inventors, in advance of his times. Doubtless with a view to winning the King's approval, Sir John had the King's initials and Royal Coat of Arms painted in full colours on a panel of the box, to the left of the central 'sleeve' opening, with the arms of the East India Company in a balancing panel on the right; it was all of no avail however, for James I is said to have declared that 'he would have no Italian tricks browght into his kingdom'. Eventually this magnificent box, rejected by the East India Company, passed to the Saddlers. Magnificent is the right word too, for this solid oak box, 18 in. high, $17\frac{3}{4}$ in. wide and 13 in. deep, is designed as a fanciful triple-domed pagoda, partially inlaid and partially painted. It is also an important example of fine craftsmanship of the period and one of the earliest examples of English *chinoiserie*, ante-dating, by about half a century, the general use in England of lacquer in imitation of the Oriental work imported by the East India Company. The name of the artist employed by Sir John is unknown, but undoubtedly the same man was responsible for the ornamental work on two small cabinets and a set of roundels in the Victoria and Albert Museum.

Bath Chairs—see *Vehicles*

Bed Beaters—see *Feather Bed Beaters*

Bee Keepers' Bellows
The bee keeper's bellows, Plate 170, *H*, was used for subduing bees by means of smoke. The iron nozzle is detachable, for allowing burning rag or paper to be inserted in the combustion chamber, which is connected by an aperture to the bellows; actuation of the bellows causes the emission of a cloud of smoke. The example illustrated is English, 18th- or 19th-century.

Bell Pulls
Various carved and pierced wooden strips, sometimes gilded, were mounted on strips of needlework or other fabrics and used as the handles of bell pulls in past times. The rope twist carved, oak specimen, Plate 167, *D*, which measures 25 in. by 5 in. by $\frac{7}{8}$ in., is said to be off an 18th-century bell pull, but I am not convinced that this was the original purpose of this one, nor another also in the Pinto Collection.

Bicycles—see *Vehicles*

18—T.O.W.B.

Bicycle Handle-bar Grips
The bicycle handle-bar grip of beechwood, Plate 165, *E*, was a wartime substitute during the shortage of rubber, in the Second World War.

Card Carriers—see *Visiting Card Carriers*

Cat-o'nine-tails—see *Life Preservers*

Ceremonial Tools
Ceremonial tools of considerable elaboration were made for presentation to the notabilities invited to lay foundation stones of buildings, or to launch ships. Such tools as squares, mallets, chisels, etc., often bear silver plates commemorating the ceremony and for ship launchings are sometimes found in a fitted case, with a picture of the ship in the lid. A ceremonial boxwood mallet and chisel, Plate 165, *G*, are believed to have been used in a 19th-century ship launching. A ceremonial stone laying mallet is pictured, Plate 170, *Q*.

Chrism Bottles—see *Religious Objects*

Chrism Spoons—see *Religious Objects*

Collecting and Money Boxes
Offertory, collecting and money boxes are indivisible subjects. Those which interest collectors are mostly of wood, iron and pottery in considerable variety. A selection of wooden examples is illustrated, Plate 168. The ancient specimen, *A*, painted on a black ground with a skull and crossbones on the raised backboard, and with crossbones on both sides and front of the tray rim, was for collections for grave-diggers. One of a pair of walnut box stirrups, banded with steel, *O*, is alleged to have been an offertory box, at one time, in Pewsey Church, Wiltshire; they are suspended by steel loops, and probably were hung on long poles or rods and passed down the pews by a collector from each end, as were those 18th-century carved pine cherubs,

holding wooden rings, now mostly used as light pendants, although originally each had a bag suspended from the ring. Eighteenth-century church offertory boxes, such as *K*, *L* and *M*, are mostly circular, with a handle attached. The Scottish type, *M*, may have a safety lip covering nearly half the top, or be formed like a spittoon, *K*.

The earliest surviving wooden money boxes are iron bound 'trunks'—hollowed tree trunk chests, each with three different locks, sometimes seen in parish churches. Henry II, in 1166, ordered that trunks should be placed in all parish churches to receive offerings of the faithful for the relief of the Holy Land. It was ordained that each trunk be secured by three keys, one to be held by the priest, the other two by reliable parishioners.

Although alms boxes now invite contributions for many purposes, the most universal appeal in days gone by was 'God's penny' for the poor. Samuel Pepys' *Diary* mentions the Dutch and French customs of hanging in places of entertainment, a poor-man's box and Pepys recalls being told '. . . that it is their custom to confirm all bargains by putting something into the poor people's box, and that that binds as fast as any thing'. 'Poor's' boxes are often fascinating examples of wood carving. A delightful specimen at Halifax (Yorkshire) Parish Church is the life-sized carved figure of 'Old Tristram', who in his lifetime collected alms for the poor so assiduously that after death the old man, with flowing locks and full beard, was fittingly commemorated grasping his alms box with gnarled fingers. In early Christian times, general charity boxes in churches were opened on Christmas Day and the contents, known as the 'dole of the Christmas box', were distributed by the priests on Boxing Day. By Tudor times, the Christmas box had come to mean a collecting box for gratuities, carried round by apprentices to their masters' customers. Now, the term Christmas box is applied to the gift itself.

Some of the most interesting poor's boxes belong to the ancient City Livery Companies; some of their contents are 'fines' for minor misdemeanours, such as failing to appear at a Court meeting without adequate excuse, or appearing improperly dressed—that is, without a Court badge. A rare and handsome poor's box owned by the Worshipful Company of Glass-Sellers, was presented to the Company by John Green Senr. in 1690. It is in mint condition and is veneered with fine floral marquetry of the period and also the Royal Coat of Arms, the Arms of the Company, and of the City of London.

Money boxes exist in great variety, some highly ornamental. Wooden Bibles, like *B*, with money slots in the 'leaves' were popular as Bible Society, 19th-century collecting boxes. Also in the 19th century, tartan and transfer ware money boxes and turned beehives, like *N*, and barrels had a vogue. A possibly unique carved money box, designed as a George III toby jug and finished in polychrome, was sold at Sotheby's recently.

Some children's money boxes are described in Section XV, *Pastimes*, and a unique specimen is illustrated, Plate 225. Simple examples in Plate 168, are *H*, a miniature drop leaf table and *J*, a chest of drawers, both 19th-century.

Of the boxes in Plate 168, not already described, *C*, is a trick opening, clip together, six-piece money box, made about 1850–60. *D*, shaped like a sauce boat and made in one piece from some unidentified hardwood, has a silver plate on it engraved 'Madras'. The box made from various hardwoods, *E*, has two mouths, one for large and one for small coins, within twin heart-shaped bands of bird's-eye maple; similar bands occur on all four sides, the front one enclosing initials E.A.P. The box, probably Welsh, 18th-century, opens by unscrewing the base. The interesting 17th-century, 'sick' offertory box, *F*, is of fruitwood, with iron mouth plate and lock plate.

It is protected from withdrawal of money by a chain link curtain, hanging inside. On the front is a Spanish silver plate, embossed with a monstrance and cherub heads. It was formerly in the F.A. Crisp and Bussell Collections.

The inlaid 'book', *G*, is not a money collecting box but a money safe, for concealing among books in a bookcase. Many variants of this type of concealment are known.

Cornucopia

The classical horn of plenty is by no means an unusual symbol to find carved in wood, both in the round and in relief, but it is usually a solid block of wood, and merely part of an ornamental grouping. I have only ever seen two hollow wooden cornucopia—the pair, of which one is shown, Plate 165, *A*. Whether you admire such things is a matter of taste, but there is no doubt that these two cornucopia, 12½ in. long, made of oak (not laminated), are a remarkable technical achievement. They are each constructed in two halves, with straight, longitudinal glued joints, back and front, and they have not warped nor split since they were made, presumably some 200 years ago. They are not bentwood, but have been laboriously carved, hollowed, and pierced with a tear drop shaped lattice, from hard oak and with such accuracy of shaping that the joints have to be searched out. They look newer than they are because, when purchased, they had been stained and varnished a bright plum red, and they have had to be stripped.

Crutches

Crutches are not usually of interest to those collectors who are able bodied. But a pair of 'wine crutches', illustrated in *Country Life*, May 12, 1955, would undoubtedly be an attraction. They are single columns of mahogany, ornamentally turned and fluted and fitted at the bottom with heavily weighted, half round bases, which appear to be about 8 in. in diameter, and they have well padded arm rests at the top. They appear, from the photograph, to be only about 35 in. high, so that they would fit comfortably under the arm-pits of a Georgian tippler and prevent him falling out of his chair.

Cups, Ornamental, Swiss and Tyrolean

Swiss and Tyrolean standing cups, originally largely cottage products of the long snow-bound winters, have probably been made over a long period, but most of those which I have examined, appear to date, at the earliest, from the 18th century, whilst the majority are 19th-century. They rank essentially as ornaments and are usually turned and carved from pearwood or sycamore. They are built up from a number of parts, dowelled and glued together. Considerable skill is shown in the carving, which is sometimes heightened by staining. The designs frequently suffer from an *embarras de richesse*. Three examples are shown, Plate 169. The cup *A*, 10½ in. high by 4 in. diameter, is an ambitious but rather naïve example of rustic-romantic. The stem is a gnarled tree, below which are seated two men and a dog. Rustic scenes run round the bowl of the cup, which is shadowed by the twig pierced overhang of the lid. The lid, in turn, is surmounted by a mountain with sheep, and a cow being milked. The large pearwood cup, *B*, 17 in. high by 5½ in. diameter, is technically fine, but the design is over-ornate, mixed in its motifs, and typical of the 1851 Exhibition period. The Pope's Swiss Guards act as supporters for the cup, which has a frieze of historic figures round the body, between horizontal bands of roses and acorns. The gracefully curved lid, carved with stylized acanthus, is surmounted by Canova's wrestlers.

The dragon surmounted cup, *C*, is another skilful example, part stained; the handles are carved out of the solid, and some of the floral motifs are free standing.

Curtain Rings

Curtain rings, usually of mahogany, were turned by the million, in various diameters to suit curtain poles, throughout the 19th century. Each is fitted with a screw eye, to take the drapery hook. The mahogany poles have usually been re-used for other purposes, but the heavily turned finials have often survived and have sometimes been adapted for feet of 'made-up' pieces of furniture.

Door Porters

Door porters have largely been superseded, in recent years, by spring-loaded fittings which screw on to doors and exert friction pressure on the floor. The majority of door porters were always of metal and some of the traditional cast ornamental specimens are being reproduced. The commonest wooden ones were boxes enclosing a brick, but being further covered by carpet, felt, or thinner fabrics, they have not much appeal for wood collectors. However, patient search will bring to light much more interesting examples, and a selection, probably all 19th-century, English, but some could be earlier, is shown, Plate 170, L to P. The 19 in. high, combined door porter and door wedge, L, is of turned beech. The example of elm and beech, shaped to represent a weight with iron lifting ring, M, was a popular design. The 15½ in. high, bell-shaped specimen, N, and the oak specimen, carved as a thatched cottage, O, are both lead weighted. P, one of a pair, is turned from oak.

Feather Bed Smoothers

English feather bed smoothers, such as Plate 167, F, 26 in. long, were plain and strictly utilitarian objects, usually made of lignum vitae since the 17th century; they are impossible to date accurately. The continental *bâton de lit*, destined for smoothing the marriage bed, was often, like the Welsh love spoon, a hand-carved gift from the man to his sweetheart. The custom of carv-

ing and giving feather bed smoothers was particularly prevalent in rustic areas of the Vendée.

Fiery Cross Boxes

The Fiery Cross, now associated in most people's minds with that unpleasant organization the Klu-Klux-Klan, is one of the Klan's borrowings from the remote past. In bygone days, the fiery cross, fire cross, convocation stick, or message arrow, was a specialized branch of the beacon or fire signal system—not a general warning, like the chain of beacons used to signal the advent of the Spanish Armada, but more of a telegram delivery service for conveying specific and urgent messages and summonses to remote parts of a kingdom or territory. Olaus Magnus describes the custom as having been used by the Goths, but does not say that they originated it. In the Scottish Highlands, Scandinavia and the Faroe Islands, it was known from very early times and lingered until well on into the 18th century. The fiery cross, not necessarily cruciform, sometimes an arrow, was scorched or burnt to denote urgency, and might be used to call for the rapid assembly of the clan to a religious or political convocation, or to seek assistance in finding a murderer, etc. If the call were a summons to war, a scorched arrow was dipped in the blood of a slaughtered animal. When the chief dispatched the cross, stick or arrow by messenger, it was relayed by a rota of further messengers to the limits of the territory and there were heavy fines for not passing on the message. If the messenger found no one at home, he transfixed the message to the door post, with the arrow or a spike.

Collectors may be puzzled as to the purpose, if they find a small cupboard, with hinged door, enclosing a shallow cavity, gouged out of the solid wood; these cupboards are generally about 10 in. long and bear a family resemblance to the one illustrated, Plate 165, D, which measures 9½ in., plus the steel spike, is 3½ in. wide and ⅞ in. deep. I have now seen three of these small cupboards, two of oak and one of elm, all differing slightly in size and carved detail, but all including in their motifs a cross, a crown and the cipher C.R.; one, additionally, is plated with brass at all angles. These are Norwegian or Danish church convocation arrows; the box or cupboard contained the official message, and if no one were at home, the messenger, often a farmer, spiked the message arrow '*bud stikke*' to or beside his neighbour's door. Only those boxes used for church messages are surmounted by the cross, and the cipher and form of the crown may differ according to the name and date of the monarch. C.R. is the most likely to be found, because there were no less than 10 Norwegian and Danish kings named Christian, 15 Scandinavian kings named Charles and also Queen Christina of Sweden. The example illustrated, and believed to be 18th-century, probably bears the cipher of Christian VI or VII.

Flower Pickers
The Victorian, trigger operated flower picker, Plate 167, *E*, is 32 in. long and is marked Thornby of London. His name does not seem to appear in any directories. I assume the device to be late 19th-century.

Gavels
The popular 18th-century shape for a gavel, Plate 165, *F*, is still being made today and although old and new are readily distinguishable, it is not always possible to tell an 18th-century from a 19th-century one. The old example illustrated is rosewood; other popular materials were lignum vitae, boxwood and ivory.

Hackney Chairs—see *Vehicles*

Handles—see *Religious Carvings*

Hat Pegs
Hat pegs are not generally of much interest, but one from Loxton Church, Somerset, merits an entry. The peg and its carved backboard, Plate 170, *J*, are of elm and the board is decorated as shown, including initials N.C. and date 1679. The initials do not agree with those of the incumbent of the period, although this interesting relic has long been known as parson's hat peg. The peg itself continues through a hole in the board and would have been embedded 5½ in. into the masonry.

Ice Picks
Ice picks are plain, stiletto type, steel spikes with wooden handles, which usually bear the marks of blows from a mallet. They do not seem to differ from other large stiletto-like tools used in various trades.

Life Preservers
Under this heading will be found grouped, a selection of weapons, some of which were probably just as much offensive as defensive. They are illustrated, Plate 170, *A* to *G*. The Victorian beechwood truncheon, *A*, 9½ in. long, is painted V.R. on a blue background. The 19th-century, lignum vitae truncheon, *B*, is 12 in. long; it was probably a private citizen's. *C*, *D* and *E*, are variants of the type of weapon most generally known as a life preserver; all are English and may date from the 18th or early 19th century. *C*, 17 in. long, is of mulberry wood, with a leather cord connection between handle and striker. *D*, 18½ in. long, is of ash, with a metal link, and *E*, is boxwood, with leather-covered cord connection between handle and egg. *F*, is an ashwood, knob-kerry type of club, with iron-studded ring at the striking end. *G*, is a cat-o-'six-tails, with beech handle. The 'cat' was a whip, originally with three leather tails, but in the reign of James II, the number of tails was increased to six, and later to nine. The brutal severity of the punishment was greatly increased by the number of knots in the tails.

Mole Traps—see *Rodent Traps*

Money Boxes—see *Collecting Boxes*

Mouse Traps—see *Rodent Traps*

Nativity Figures—see *Religious Objects*

Pitch Pipes

The mahogany pitch pipes, Plate 165, *H* and *J*, adjustable by means of a sliding stop, are 7 in. and 18 in. long respectively and were formerly used in churches which had no organ, to give the keynote before singing commenced. They are English, probably 18th-century.

Presepio Figures—see *Religious Objects*

Propeller Boxes

The curious shaped box, Plate 170, *K*, was made from the damaged propeller of a First World War aircraft. There are many of these boxes in existence, made of laminated mahogany and American walnut and varying in their size and curvature of outline, according to how far from the hub, the section was cut. The making of souvenir trinket boxes from damaged blades was a favourite occupation of Royal Naval Air Service and Royal Flying Corps mechanics. The actual hub was sometimes converted into a clock or barometer case.

Rat Traps—see *Rodent Traps*

Religious Objects

Large statuary, and religious carvings which are fixtures of the Church, are outside the scope of this work. Certain secular objects sometimes carved with religious motifs, such as planes, snuff rasps, tobacco stoppers, knife and fork handles, walking sticks, etc., are described under their appropriate headings. This leaves anointing and chrism spoons, chrism bottles, wafer boxes, etc. and Nativity figures, which are described and illustrated here and, as would be expected, include some exquisite examples of fine-scale carving.

Anointing and Chrism Spoons, Chrism Bottles and Wafer Boxes

The anointing spoon, right of Plate 64, is of pearwood, finely carved round the border with inscriptions. Outside the bowl is a depiction of the Annunciation, and inside, the Adoration. On the stem, are the Virgin and Child on one side and a Saint on the reverse; it is German, 17th-century. The fine, rare, boxwood folding chrism spoon, Plate 171, *G*, is carved externally with the Papal Coat of Arms, and inside with the Annunciation; it is 16th-century, probably French, and was formerly in the Evan-Thomas Collection. In the same illustration, are four fine quality chrism bottles, all hollowed out of solid blocks of boxwood. *F* is a rare and unusual, flattened bottle of snuff rasp shape, 6 in. long and probably intended for carrying in the pocket. It is finely carved with a cherub head, mitre, cross, orb, etc., set in foliage. It is probably Italian, of the 17th or 18th century. Of more conventional shape, *H* is an attractive, French, 17th-century flask, with a monogram and coat of arms set in classical acanthus scrolls. *K*, $3\frac{3}{4}$ in. high, is carved with a monstrance on one side and a coat of arms on the reverse and the date 1723; it is probably Italian and was formerly in the Evan-Thomas Collection. *M* is carved with the Virgin and Child on the exposed face, and the Crucifixion on the reverse. It has the Tree of Life on the ends, and is French, 17th-century.

L is a rare and unusual star-shaped boxwood box, hollowed out of the solid and pivoted in a case also cut from the solid. The style of the work suggests a 17th-century, English origin, and the motifs and inscriptions that it was intended for Eucharistic wafers; it measures 3 in. by $\frac{7}{8}$ in. Another box intended for wafers, is shown among the coquilla nut objects, Plate 192, *D*. A very few exquisitely carved boxwood censers of French or Italian provenance were made in the 16th century and in their outline, they resemble larger versions of Plate 171, *H*.

Handles

A remarkable boxwood handle, centre of Plate 66, probably intended for a flabellum or censer, is 11¼ in. long and is minutely carved in zones with the stories of Joseph and his Brethren, and the Judgment of Solomon. It is surmounted by a lion couchant above cherub heads, and the Virtues It is 17th-century and may be North German or Dutch. Plate 171, *B*, a carved boxwood handle, 3⅝ in. high, is carved with the head of a Pope and three other heads, back to back, all linked by a Cardinal's hat. One of the heads has an order round his neck, the ribbon inscribed Sens Komi (or Korri) Order; there seems to be some allusion here, perhaps political, which is not clear. Possibly the head of a 17th-century Cardinal's staff, this carving was formerly in the Trapnell Collection.

Walking stick or parasol handles, Plate 171, *A* and *C*, are described in Section II, *Costume Accessories*, and scent flasks, Plate 171, *D*, *E* and *J*, in Section XXIII, *Toilet Accessories*.

Presepio Figures

The arrangement of miniature scena depicting the birth of Christ is a Christmas custom going back at least to the Middle Ages, when groups of wandering students, appropriately garbed, performed Nativity plays in churches and other public buildings in different parts of Europe. The next stage seems to have been the carving of life-sized wood figures as permanent decorative features in mediaeval churches. Such figures included not only the Holy Family, but also adoring shepherds, angels and wise men. The size of figures must have imposed a limitation on what could be done in the way of stage backgrounds and doubtless because of this, there gradually evolved

the miniature Nativity tableaux, to be brought out each Christmas and arranged as ingeniously contrived three dimensional stage sets. To allow for perspective, angels, humans and animals, in one set, are usually made to different scales. A part set in the Pinto Collection has some sheep and goats, intended for the foreground, larger than the cow and bull.

Presepio or Nativity figure tableaux have been and still are used in most parts of Christendom, but the most famous carvers and modellers of this miniature artistry between the 15th and 19th centuries, were Italians, Germans, Tyroleans and Swiss. Italian presepio makers tended to model visible parts of dressed figures in terracotta, with cork and wire bodies, rather than carve them from wood; but they used a large variety of materials, including wood, wax, cork, metal and clay, in order to obtain their verisimilitude. The largest school of Italian presepio modellers worked in Naples in the 18th century, when the fashion for presepio arrangements, or Christmas crèche scenes, reached not only the apex of its popularity, but also the height of extravagance, both in quality of workmanship and elaborateness of settings. Nor were presepio tableaux confined to churches: they were also a domestic custom and although princes vied with each other in magnificence of costume, jewels and number of figures in new and ever more ornate settings, the humblest citizens also had simple crèche scenes set out in a room, or on their house tops. Some of the greatest sculptors did not disdain to work on presepio. One of the most gifted was Giuseppe Sammartino, born 1720, whose life-size recumbent figure of the veiled Christ, in the chapel of San Severo at Naples, is recognized as one of the sculptural masterpieces of the world. Sammartino's presepio figures, of which some are preserved in the wonderful collection in the museum at Naples, are noted for their vigorous modelling, perfect colouring and their remarkable range of facial expressions. In his lifetime, Sammartino did not enjoy such fame as the less gifted Francesco Celebrano, who was employed to make presepio for the Bourbon king, Charles III. Another famous Neapolitan presepio worker was Sammartino's pupil, Guiseppe Gori, who was unusual in that he seems to have made his living entirely by creating presepio figures. He sometimes worked on miniature scena in collaboration with Sammartino. Like certain painters, he included figures of his patrons and their friends in the 'crowd' scenes.

Neapolitan 18th-century Nativity scena stray a long way from the simple setting of the Nativity story and become a centrepiece to the gay pageantry, colour and elaboration which Neapolitans adore. The costume and accessories of the figures are essentially 18th-century and backgrounds almost invariably represent Naples and environs, not Bethlehem. Vesuvius is sometimes seen smoking in the background and Roman or Grecian ruins appear frequently in the tableaux. These include street scenes, with shops displaying merchandise and drinking, dancing and merry-making crowds, with musicians playing various instruments, ragged beggars, and street vendors figuring prominently. The animal kingdom, too, in the joyous and theatrical Neapolitan scena, is extended to include considerable variety of animals and farmyard birds. The processions of the Three Kings gave the Neapolitans wonderful opportunities for using their riotous imagination to introduce snake charmers, elephants and camels, as well as gorgeously jewelled silk and brocade costumes and a galaxy of gifts.

The German and northern Swiss carvers kept more to the spirit of the Gospels, although, as with the Italians, their presepio were very much 'Hamlet in modern dress' and against a northern background. In one 18th-century German scene, one of the Kings, a negro, has a gold watch dangling from his belt. Nevertheless, in their Nativity representations, they rarely introduced incongruous figures, and the backgrounds are usually simple and appropriate, with miniature fir trees and log cabins figuring prominently. Their work is essentially traditional wood carving and, at its best, the expressions on the faces of figures convey great beauty, piety, adoration, joy, etc. The Swiss carvers generally used a more glyptic and virile approach to their work, deliberately showing the gouge marks on their carvings. The German presepio carvers, mostly Bavarians, followed the Neapolitan technique, and the painted wooden figures closely resemble those of terracotta. In the Bavarian National Museum at Munich is the finest presepio collection in the world—some 8,000 figures, collected and presented by the 19th-century Munich banker, Max Schmederer.

It is unexpected to find the most famous exponent of traditionally carved miniature Nativity figures coming on the scene so late as the latter part of the 19th century. However, the outstanding and most highly esteemed master in this Bavarian branch of wood sculpture was undoubtedly Georg Anderl of Munich, who was born at Altenerding, near Erding (Oberbaycrn) in 1868 and died in 1928. His parents were smallholders and quite poor. In his young days, he earned his living as a drayman at a Munich brewery. He married in 1897 and turned to carving Nativity figures in his spare time. Although untaught, his genius was such that, within a year, he was able to give up driving and, thereafter, support himself entirely by the wonderful skill of his hands. Anderl's friend Körner, who coloured the figures, equalled Anderl's skill in the carving. Anderl's wife helped him by dressing those figures intended to be clothed. Whilst Italian presepio figures usually have terracotta heads and crystal eyes and, if clothed, have cork bodies and wire joints, German figures, such as Anderl's, have carved and painted eyes and, if intended for clothing, have wooden bodies with wire joints, which allow them to be arranged standing, astride a horse, sitting, or kneeling. In the Pinto Collection are 32 of Anderl's masterpieces, all carved from pearwood. They belong to his post-1910 period, when he was at the height of his powers; Plate 172 shows a group of Anderl's angels and Plate 173, an Arab stallion from the same set.

Rodent Traps
Rat and mouse traps, apart from some Victorian labyrinthine, all-metal patented devices, come under three principal headings—drop weight, spring break-back, and cage type. The first did not vary in any way between the Middle Ages and the late 19th century; this is the only excuse for most of the 18th- and 19th-century examples still extant, being commonly described as mediaeval. In the Merode altarpiece of the Annunciation, painted in 1425 (Metropolitan Museum of Art, New York), the right-hand panel shows St. Joseph making drop weight mouse traps, which, it is quite clear, are basically the same and work on the same principle as Plate 175, *A, B, C, D* and *F*. Of these, *A* is actually a double-ended drop weight rat trap, mainly of elm, 19 in. long and with an elm weight which, when released by the bait nibbler, could be guaranteed heavy enough to flatten any rat; I doubt whether it is earlier than 19th-century. *B*, a crude, 5 in. square, oak mouse trap, working on the same principle is considerably older. *C* is the traditional Selsey, Sussex, circular mouse trap, made of beech and 5 in. in diameter; it may be 18th- or 19th-century. *D* is a triple, drop weight mouse trap of oak and ash, 12½ in. long, which works on the same principle as the others; it may be 18th- or 19th-century. *F*, of pine, with oak drop weight, 11 in. long, is the mouse size version of oak trap, *A*.

E is a spring, break-back rat trap, presumably 19th-century; *H* is the smaller edition for a mouse. *G* is a four hole, spring mouse trap, made of walnut, which catches mice by their heads when the baited springs are sprung; traps of this type were made in the 19th century, with varying numbers of holes. *J* is a 19th-century double-ended spring cage type mouse trap, 8 in. long, made of beech; it has a division across the centre and catches two mice alive. For another ingenious type of mouse and rat trap, see *Wife Leads*.

Mole traps were usually all iron and of the downward thrusting fork type, but a variety with a wooden 'tunnel', for sinking in the mole run, is illustrated diagrammatically, on the next page. When the mole touches the toggle or wedge in the centre of the tunnel, it releases the holding string of the spring and is caught in the noose, irrespective of whichever end of the tunnel it approaches. Although said to be ancient, I think it doubtful if this trap principle was applied before the 19th century; a similar device, all metal, is still being made.

Seat Sticks
Seat sticks are usually described as shooting sticks, although they serve a much wider purpose. No one has yet designed the perfect one, either in wood or metal; most of them are either unsafe, uncomfortable, too heavy, or have all three disadvantages. Three of the woodworker's attempts to provide the solution are illustrated, Plate 167. The best is probably *A*, which is made of bentwood, with a cane seat. It was either made by Michael Thonet of Vienna, or was based on his technique; it probably dates from 1850–60, is strong, light, folds flat, and is less uncomfortable than most others; a variant of the design, with the same folding action, has a webbing seat. *B* has a threaded socket underneath the centre, and another at one end; when not used as a seat, the horizontal member is unscrewed and screwed on vertically, forming a rather clumsy handle. The all-wood ancestor of the modern shooting stick is represented by *C*.

Sedan Chairs—see *Vehicles*

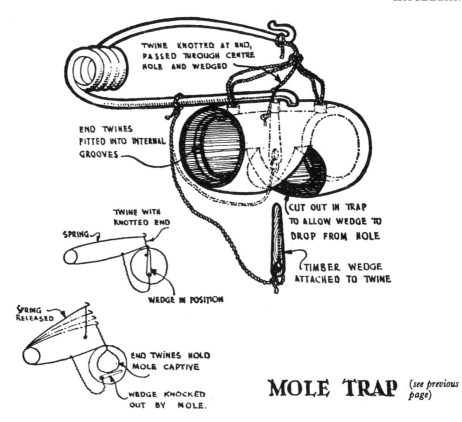

TWINE KNOTTED AT END,
PASSED THROUGH CENTRE
HOLE AND WEDGED

END TWINES
FITTED INTO INTERNAL
GROOVES

CUT OUT IN TRAP
TO ALLOW WEDGE TO
DROP FROM HOLE

TIMBER WEDGE
ATTACHED TO TWINE

TWINE WITH
KNOTTED END

SPRING

WEDGE IN POSITION

SPRING
RELEASED

END TWINES HOLD
MOLE CAPTIVE

WEDGE KNOCKED
OUT BY MOLE.

MOLE TRAP *(see previous page)*

Sledges—see *Vehicles*

Swiss Standing Cups—see *Cups, Ornamental, Swiss and Tyrolean*

Vehicles—Small
Large vehicles are outside the scope of this encyclopaedia. Some of the smaller fire engines are described in Section VI, *Fire and Lighting,* and the specialized hand propelled vehicles of itinerant traders receive mention in Section XXV, *Trade and Craft Devices.*

Bath Chairs
There appears to be no evidence that the wheeled invalid chair, or Bath chair, originated at Bath, although in the 18th, 19th and early years of this century, it was much in use there, as indeed it was at Harrogate and other spas. A good, early 19th-century specimen was formerly kept at a public house near my home, but whether it was used for a resident invalid, or wheeling home drunks, is unknown. Some Bath chairs, including the aforementioned, were designed for pushing or pulling by an attendant, or for drawing by a donkey or pony. See also *Sedan Chairs.*

Bicycles—see *Velocipedes*

Hackney Chairs—see *Sedan Chairs*

Sedan Chairs
Although they represented two distinct classes of the same vehicle, hackney hire chairs and privately owned Sedan chairs are both usually described now as Sedans. The Sedan took its name from the town of Sedan, where it is said to have been invented; it was introduced to the Court of James I by the Duke of Buckingham and very soon its use spread from being

essentially a privately owned vehicle for people of means, to a licensed and numbered hackney, to be hired from stands in the streets, or from public houses and inns, which found it advisable to keep one or more on the premises, long before anyone thought of breathalysers. The first London licences were granted to Sir Sanders Duncombe in 1634. Like the mini-car, the Sedan was popular because it was not only cheap, but also eased congestion by carriages in the streets.

Sedan chairs were enclosed armchairs, carried by two chairmen or bearers, by means of long, removable poles, passed through two rings fixed to each side of the vehicle. The Sedan continued in use up to about 1825 and some late examples have a wheel at each side, and two fixed poles, requiring only one chairman. The popularity of the Sedan began to decline in the second half of the 18th century, as the folding umbrella became less clumsy and more acceptable.

Survivals of the plain, essentially utilitarian, black leather covered hackney hire chairs are rare, but the elaborate private sedans, with hand-painted panels displaying their owners' crests, are well represented in museums. Some of the best examples have lift-up tops, so that passengers could enter and leave without disarranging their elaborate coiffures.

Sledges

Winters in the past, in Great Britain, were sometimes more severe than they are now, and travelling conditions were much worse, by reason of bad roads and lack of municipal snow clearance and de-icing services. In many parts of the country, horse and pony drawn sledges were commonly used, up to the end of last century. Two good, 19th-century specimens, a horse drawn four-seater, used by the Earls of Darnley at Cobham Hall, Kent, and a pony drawn two-seater, driven by a doctor at Guildford, Surrey, are in the Pinto Collection.

Velocipedes

Velocipedes, or boneshakers, being bicycles mainly of wood, merit inclusion here, but for the evolution of bicycles in general, see *Further Reading*.

The Draisienne of Charles, Baron von Drais de Sauerbrun, first exhibited in Paris in 1818, may be considered as the father of two wheeled cycles, although it had no pedals and the rider had to thrust at the ground with his feet. In 1819, the Rev. Edmund Cartwright built a four wheeled cycle, or quadricycle, propelled by pedals, but the pedal idea applied to two wheeled cycles, or bicycles, does not seem to have become really popular until the 1860s, when the Pierre Michaux *vélocipède* appeared in France and its equivalent, the boneshaker, in England. A Michaux *vélocipède* of 1865–7, Plate 176, has wheels entirely of ashwood, with iron tyres and an iron-shod ash backbone, or curved connecting bar between back and front wheels. As the pedals were connected direct to the front wheel and their speed of rotation would have broken the legs of a rider going downhill, iron leg rests were provided on a front extension of the backbone; going downhill, the rider travelled with his legs horizontally in front of him on the rests, and steered as best he could by means of the cord attached to the handlebars.

It is interesting to consider the changes in transport which took place in a lifetime. My father, born in 1863, who died at the comparatively early age of 67 in 1930, saw the boneshaker in use in his boyhood, rode a 'penny-farthing' and lived into the age of common travel by air.

Visiting Card Carriers

During the days when the ceremony of leaving (visiting) cards was in vogue, a receptacle for cards always stood in the entrance hall. It might be any ornamental platter or 'waiter' of silver, papier mâché, china, wood, etc., but sometimes it was a specially designed, carved pedestal or wall bracket, known as a card carrier. Popular forms for pedestals in the round and brackets in relief, were figures of negroes, jesters and monkeys, supporting platters. Occasionally, a pair of hall figures may be found with one designed to hold a card platter, and the other a flambeau.

Wafer Boxes—see *Religious Objects*

Wife Leads
The woven split cane wife lead, Plate 165, C, has long been made and used by the Caribs of the West Indies; now, it has become a tourist souvenir. Slipped on to the wife's finger at the open end and held on the man's finger by the loop at the opposite end, the diamond mesh loop elongated and gripped the finger tighter, the more she tugged. In larger diameter, baited and anchored to the floor, the same device has been used as a mouse and rat trap. It has also been adapted and used for drawing the ends of cables through ducts.

XI

Mortars, Grinders, and Graters

Mortars, mills, querns, grinders, graters—
although these terms cover a large range of
sizes and devices, which may be very
different from each other, there are, in certain instances, very thin dividing lines between one type and another. All are intended to reduce comparatively large
material to smaller particles, or powder,
by means of pulverization.

The origin of the process is lost in antiquity. Proverbs, 27, 22, tells us 'Though
thou shouldest bray a fool in a mortar
among wheat with a pestle, yet will not his
foolishness depart from him'. In Isaiah
occurs the passage 'What mean ye that ye
beat my people to pieces and grind the
faces of the poor?' Excavations in Palestine
and other ancient civilizations have disclosed vast quantities of querns, mortars and
varied pulverizing devices which basically
have not changed during the last 2,000 years.

Probably the sequence of pulverizers was
(1) the hollow mortar with pestle or
pounder, both of which can be found provided by nature, (2) the grinder or simple
quern, consisting of two specially shaped
stones, (3) the grater, formed by a perforated metal plate, (4) the mechanical
toothed mill, operated manually or by
various forms of power.

Graters

Graters are basically perforated metal
sheets, usually with all the holes punched
through from the backs, and the burred
edges of the punctured pimples forming the
grating surface. Where it is desired that the
whole grating operation shall take place on
the surface, the design is effective, but if the
residue is required to pass through the
grater, then such a device is inefficient.
The French, Germans and Italians realized
this at least as early as the 17th century, and
they designed their snuff graters (see snuff
rasps, Section XXII, *Tobacco Accessories*)
scientifically, so that the dust really did pass
through into the receptacle. The lines of
holes in these graters are usually arranged
diagonally, sometimes with two diverging
lines of diagonals meeting at the centre, to
form chevrons. The ingenuity, however,
lies in the direction of the punch holes: one
line is punched from the front of the plate,
the next one from the back, and so on. This
creates alternate diagonal lines of mountains and valleys. The tobacco is grated on
the sharply burred mountain range and the
snuff falls through the face stamped holes
in the valleys. English and Dutch, 17th-
and 18th-century rasps do not show this
refinement and, indeed, the principle never
seems to have been adopted in England,
even when the grater was intended also to
act as a sieve.

The general-purpose kitchen grater, D-
shaped on plan and now entirely made of

tinned iron or plastic, was, until nearly the mid-19th century, a blacksmith-made sheet of punched blued iron, secured to a wooden backplate. A typical 18th- or early 19th-century specimen, on oak plaque, Plate 177, measures 13 in. by 8 in. Less than half the substance grated on it passes through. The same applies with the giant 18 in. by 13 in. pine-framed bread grater with drawer, from Ashburnham, Sussex.

In Plate 181 is a selection of spice or nutmeg graters, most of which were for carrying in the pocket, in the 18th and early 19th centuries, when spiced mulled wines were in favour. Although silver pocket graters were probably made in the greatest quantity, there was a good quality range of English turned graters available in hardwoods and coquilla nutshell (see Section XIII, *Nuts, Gourds, etc.*) The most popular shapes were acorns, *K1*, *K2* and *K3*, barrels, *E* and *F*, buckets *A*, *B*, *C* and *M*, and wine bottles, *G1* and *G2*. The acorns, *K1*, *K2* and *K3*, are made of coquilla, as are also some barrels, but some are of mulberry wood. The bottles, *G1* and *G2*, are of mulberry, as is the 18th-century bucket, *M*, but the Regency buckets, *B* and *C*, are of sycamore, decorated with red and black lines and with hand-painted or paper applied pictures on the lids, depicting views of Brighton Pavilion, *B*, or Tunbridge Wells Pantiles, etc.; these were probably all made at Tunbridge Wells, like the mosaic-lidded rosewood grater, Plate 181, *A*. Whether mulberry wood is particularly suited to retaining the flavour of nutmeg, I do not know; possibly a specialist turner had a stock of that wood. There seems to be no record of nutmeg graters made from Shakespeare's famous mulberry tree (see Section XX, *Tea, Coffee and Chocolate Drinking Accessories*).

The boxwood shoe nutmeg grater, Plate 181, *D*, finely carved with cupids and foliage and dated 1707, has the grater in the sole and is a rare and outstanding specimen. The shoe neatly holds a nutmeg.

H and *N* are kitchen graters; *H* is late 19th-century and *N* is Regency period. The ingenious, tall specimen, *O*, is late 19th-century; it holds a nutmeg in a spring-loaded travelling compartment pressed against the back of the grater; when this is slid backwards and forwards, the nutmeg is automatically grated.

Grinders

Grinders are divided into two varieties—mechanical grinding mills, and mortars with tight fitting abrasive tipped pestles. Mills for coffee, paint, pepper and other spices, etc. (for further information on spices see Section VII, *Kitchen*) all follow the same principle, varying only in their sizes and outlines. The majority of surviving wooden mills were intended for coffee.

The background to coffee drinking will be found in Section XX, *Tea, Coffee and Chocolate Drinking Accessories*. On coffee's introduction into England, the beans are said to have been brayed by a pestle in a mortar. Naturally this laborious method of pulverizing, quickly created demand for a more mechanical contrivance. Between 1657 and 1659, Thomas Garraway of tea and coffee house fame, announced 'That Nicholas Brook, living at the sign of the "Frying-pan", in St. Tulie's Street (Tooley Street) against the Church, is the only known man for making of Mills for grinding of Coffee powder, which Mills are by him sold from 40 to 45 shillings the Mill'. This was very expensive, considering the different purchasing power of money, then and now, but the mills were fine examples of craftsmanship, turned from heavy, costly lignum vitae (for details of lignum vitae, see Section III, *Drinking*), with grinding cogs of hand-forged steel. The few survivors are now collectors' pieces; when the mechanism is intact, it is usually virtually unworn. Until recently, 18th-century specimens were not too hard to find; then, unfortunately, the mechanism was removed from many good specimens, to convert them into table lamps.

Plate 180 shows the evolution of coffee mills; they may be dated as follows: *A*, 1660/80; *B*, 1700; *C*, 1706; *D*, 1700/10; *E*, 1750; *F*, 1760/70; *G*, 1790; *H*, 1800 onwards; *J*, 1851. *A*, *B*, *E*, *F* and *G* are turned from lignum vitae; all these follow the same basic layout. At the top, they have a feed-in for beans, which pass into the grinding chamber and thence into the coffee powder compartment below. The wood parts are threaded together; the handles fold and fit in the lower compartment. All except the more practical one, *G*, have screw-on lids; these enclose the spindle and add considerably to the aesthetic charm. The classical urn type, *E*, of 1750, is particularly elegant; *F* and *G*, were probably more popular, as they are frequently illustrated on 1760–90 period grocers' trade cards, and 'At the Sign of the Coffee Mill' grocers' sign boards.

All the mills so far described are English, but *C* and *D*, with drawers in the base, are probably Dutch and Italian respectively. If, as seems probable, the pull-out drawer type originated on the Continent about this time, it took nearly a century before adoption in England. The imposing Dutch, font-like mill, *C*, is notable in two respects; its date, 1706, is engraved on it, and it is hollowed from a maplewood burr, with all mouldings worked on the solid, not applied. It has a burnished steel base tray and feet and steel band round the top. The smaller, Italian, walnut mill is inlaid with brass piqué; the circular upper part is brass. *H*, *circa* 1800, of mahogany with pewter funnel, is the prototype for nearly all grinders made since. *J*, reverting to the earlier construction, is made to simulate a corked bottle, and was possibly an 1851 Exhibition novelty.

Eighteenth- and early 19th-century inventories sometimes refer to 'a coffee mill fixed and a pepper mill ditto'. The coffee mills would have been for use in a coffee house, coffee shop, or large household and of the type illustrated in Plate 177, which is boxed in oak, and was also used for grinding many materials other than coffee. The pepper mill would be a smaller version, as Plate 181, *Q*, for filling pepper casters, as opposed to the pepper mill, *R*, shown alongside, for grinding at table. Before the pepper mill was invented, pepper was ground or broken by shaking it in a perforated, screw-together, two-piece hollow sphere or quern, containing a marble.

Mortars, Grater Type

Mortars are of two kinds, mortar-graters and open mortars. A selection of mortar-graters is illustrated, Plate 178, *A* to *E*, *G* and *H*. They were used by apothecaries, tobacconists for snuff, and in various other trades. Those illustrated vary in height from 4 in. to 6 in., excluding their pestles. *A* and *B*, are of walnut, Italian, 17th-century. *C* is a rare Elizabethan carved oak specimen, *circa* 1600; it is the earliest wooden specimen I have seen. It was formerly in the Fripp Collection. All these have, or have had, perforated iron plates nailed on the bottoms of their pestles. *D*, English, probably 18th-century, has toothed blades, crossing each other, inserted in the end of the pestle. The crude specimen *E*, formerly in the Evan-Thomas Collection, appears to be early, but cannot be dated accurately. The bun-turned snuff or spice box, *F*, and its companion, *G*, a two-section grater, English, probably 17th-century, have hit and miss action connections, the former between lid and box, the latter between the grating and the lower storage chamber. The pestle, in this example, grinds the tobacco leaves, or spice, through a perforated plate, into the lower compartment. *H* is a lignum vitae, 18th-century mortar-grater, one of a pair, from Ashburnham, Sussex.

The 18th-century spice grinder-roller, Plate 181, *P*, is hollow, has a metal-studded pestle and is a dual purpose variant of the grater type mortars already described.

Mortars, Open Type

Mortars vary in size from large font-shape floor-standing types, about 33 in. high, utilized in large scale business and in great households, down to 3 in. or 4 in. high specimens, used by apothecaries for individual prescriptions, and domestically. Floor-standing types were turned from any suitable large tree, elm, oak and pine probably being the most common; usually, a marble or stone bowl mortar was inserted in a hollowed out aperture at the top. Sometimes the pestle for such a mortar will be found with a ring screwed in, or a hole bored through the handle, because the pestle was often suspended by a cord from a ceiling pulley and counterbalanced by a lead weight. An 18th-century specimen with this feature was, until recently, still *in situ* in a Grosvenor Square, London, house.

Small and medium sized wooden mortars and their pestles were usually made of lignum vitae, on account not only of its hardness, sound heart and impermeability to liquids, but also because its imaginary medicinal qualities were supposed to benefit the mixture being compounded.

Two of the most typical shapes for large mortars are illustrated in Plate 177; the bowl mortar measures 13½ in. in diameter and the cylindric walnut specimen is 13½ in. high by 7½ in. in diameter. Medium-sized mortars are shown in Plate 179. They vary in height from 6 in. to 8½ in. *A*, the plain cylindric example, is decorated with black and red painted bands; *B* is the earliest English dated wood specimen known; it is hexagonal, 7½ in. high, of lignum vitae, and is inscribed on the base A.D. 1659. It was formerly in the Carnegie Collection. *C*, the only certain non-English specimen pictured here, is of unknown provenance; it appears to have considerable age and is decorated with an incised pattern of noughts and crosses. The lignum vitae mortar, *D*, formerly in the Evan-Thomas Collection, is typical of mid-18th-century turnery.

E is a simple, 18th-century, lignum vitae mortar; wooden mortars of this type are still being made in Spain and Portugal. *F*, a crude octagonal salt mortar of beech, is quite a rarity; it is so impregnated, that the salt oozes out in damp weather. *G*, a bell-shaped mortar of walnut, which may be English or French, has the unusual feature of a side handle. *H*, the 18th-century, quadruple lugged and spouted elm basin mortar, 8¾ in. in diameter, is a very rare shape in wood, although common in marble and Wedgwood ware.

The small apothecary mortars, Plate 178, *J* to *V*, vary in height from 2¾ in. to 6¼ in.; most of them are turned from lignum vitae and are of traditional shapes, which were used at least from the 17th to the 19th century. This remark applies particularly to the four beaker mortars, *K*, *Q*, *R* and *S*. The 6¼ in. high, trumpet mortar, *P*, is of laburnum wood; *U* is a common shape in bronze, but unusual in wood.

XII

Moulds

The art of intaglio or reverse carving, to produce a matrix which can be reproduced indefinitely, is highly skilled and very ancient. The Egyptians employed intaglio extensively on hardstone signets; other ancient civilizations also used carved moulds for mechanical reproduction of lettering and ornament, or the making of useful objects. A finely carved heraldic die or shallow mould of boxwood, which is probably connected with Napoleon's invasion of Egypt, is illustrated in Plate 261, *L*. On one of the orders is the date 1801.

Additional to wax seals, numerous other objects have been made or ornamentally shaped in moulds; these include clay pipes, and lead tobacco jars (see Section XXII, *Tobacco Accessories*), toys (see Section XV, *Pastimes*), lead horn-books (see Section XVII, *Reading, Writing, Copying, Drawing, etc.*), compo or plaster ornament for walls, ceilings, mouldings, picture and mirror frames, glassware, bronze wool weights, and every kind of edible confection which can be moulded (see also Section V, *Farm: Dairy* and Section VII, *Kitchen*).

The materials which have been used for different kind of moulds include silver, iron, various kinds of stone, notably alabaster, terra-cotta and above all, wood. For finely detailed, sharply defined ornament, close grained boxwood has been first choice for all types of moulds where it was desired to take many impressions, without blurring of outline. Some of the original box and cherrywood moulds made for Robert Adam's compo ornament are still in use after 200 years. Boxwood, being so slow growing, has always been expensive, and is also hard to carve, so other hardwoods were chosen for work where the detailing was not so fine, or the number of impressions required was unlikely to be numerous. The prime qualities required of wood for most moulds are that it should be close grained, well seasoned, free from knots, not liable to warping, splitting or undue shrinkage, under variable temperatures and during alternate cycles of wetting and drying and be unlikely to roughen, chip or splinter when scrubbed. Additional to these exacting requirements, there are two more essentials for food moulds—freedom from taste or unpleasant smell. Woods which meet all these tests and are found in all varieties of moulds, include pear, cherry, apple (the traditional choice of the Bohemian glass workers), plum, sweet chestnut, sycamore and lime. The last is rather soft, but being a very quick cutting wood, is sometimes preferred to the more usual sycamore for butter prints and pastrycook moulds. Beech and elm were sometimes used for the coarser gingerbread and other food moulds.

Although so many carved wooden moulds are now bygones, the carving of butter prints still continues with its traditional skills unimpaired. Plates 182 and 183 were photographed at the Chesham workshops of Howard Brothers, who number notabilities in most parts of the world among their customers. In Plate 182, the expert carver is seen at his bench, about to choose a gouge from the large selection before him. In his left hand he holds down a blank butter print in a specially shaped rest. In Plate 183, the outline of a cow is taking shape under his swift, firm strokes. To the onlooker, it is remarkable that a man can carve so accurately 'free hand' in reverse, particularly those three dimensional moulds, Plate 100, *A* to *F*, which fit together accurately and cast the model in the round. For butter prints, drawings are only used for 'specials' and, contrary to general belief, the expert intaglio carver only uses a mirror for crests or lettering. For his normal work, he keeps a tray of damp silver-sand beside him, and with it takes progress impressions of his work and also checks that the final impression is to his satisfaction. This brief description may be taken as typical for all ornamental intaglio carving, but where 'one offs' were required, a drawing was pasted or traced on the wood, and where a mould was required for making rather than ornamenting an object, such as a clay pipe, the sections and dimensions of the mould would be checked to fine limits.

Wood moulds may be considered under two main headings—for edible and non-edible objects. The majority are easily distinguishable by the nature of ornament, or the shape of objects, but instances occur where one cannot be sure. These are mostly moulds for narrow ornamental borders, largely traditional designs, such as acanthus, egg and tongue, reel and bead, etc., which were used both around cakes and also for wall, ceiling and mirror surrounds. The same woods, largely boxwood, were used for both purposes; but decorators' moulds rather tend to be thicker than those of pastrycooks', and if they have screw or

nail holes in the backs, showing that a backing or thicknessing piece was originally fixed, you can be sure that the mould was for compo or plaster. As a generality, but it is no more, decorators' moulds are 1 in. to 2½ in. thick, plus a fixed backing-piece, usually of another hardwood, which may be as thick or thicker; they are also often numbered with black paint on white painted end grain. The paint afforded protection against splitting and made selection easy from racks in the moulder's workshops. The pastrycooks' moulds usually vary between ½ in. and 1¼ in., but these are not the limits: I have found 1½ in., 2 in. and even a couple of church festival outsize moulds 2½ in. thick. Kitchen moulds are never painted on the end grain, although they may have written or stamped markings referring to designs, or giving carvers' names. Nor are they ever backed by another board, and often they are carved on both faces, occasionally on the long edges as well. Unless made of boxwood, culinary moulds, being unbacked, tend to be worn and rounded on both back and front edges.

I have given these details at some length because prices of culinary moulds are now high and ornamental mould collectors have to beware of two kinds of fakers. For the existence of the first, they have only themselves to blame. The criteria for value should be (1) the quality of the carving and of the wood used—they go together; (2) the rarity of the subject or the interest of the design; (3) the age, particularly if datable reasonably accurately. Indiscriminate collectors have, however, elevated another worthless consideration above these: 'Is it for food, or not?' If it is, they are prepared to pay three or four times as much as they would for a handsomely carved decorator's mould of considerable interest. The consequence is that some of the most interesting decorators' moulds have had their backing boards removed and the screw holes filled, or they are reduced in thickness to eliminate the holes, the paint is removed from the ends and the backs and ends are rounded and aged artificially; unfortunately, the difference in price obtained justifies the labour.

The second kind of fake is made possible by the mistaken belief that all crudely carved food moulds must be very old. A few crude ones are ancient, but very few; nearly all modern ones, however, are crude, lacking in detail and produced as cheaply as possible. They are still being made, in Holland and Belgium especially; they are usually for 'cookies' in the form of dogs, cats and other undatable subjects. After some use, they are sold and eventually bought for much more than their intrinsic value by bargain hunters, mainly in markets. To simulate age more convincingly, some of these moulds are deliberately burnt. This, in fact, establishes them at once as fakes, because no genuine old food moulds ever went near an oven, or other source of heat (bread oven door moulds excepted). Even gingerbread was not baked in wood moulds, as so many people believe. Mrs. Pinto has carried out considerable research on this subject and has found that none of the old gingerbread recipes included any *eggs*, *fat* or *flour*: the main ingredient was breadcrumbs and the mixture was never baked; it was pre-cooked by boiling. Using old recipes, Mrs. Pinto obtained excellent impressions from wooden moulds. The gingerbread made by this method, and in accordance with a recipe of 1609, is a very dark brown, of rather a rubbery consistency, highly spiced with ginger, liquorice, aniseed and cinnamon, with a background flavour provided by claret. To our taste, it compared unfavourably with modern gingerbread. A recipe of 1656 produced a much more palatable gingerbread.

As previously mentioned, decorators' moulds, when in use, were always backed, but food moulds, never. The reason was that the multiplicity of fancy food moulds in a pastrycook's or large family kitchen created a serious space problem: to prevent the "wooden library" becoming too cumbersome, a number of individual gingerbread, cake, biscuit or sugar icing designs were often cut into both sides of a board, known as a "card". The juxtaposition of carvings on a "card" is often incongruous, to say the least of it. For example, the Crucifixion may be found next to Puss-in-Boots on one card, and on another, Moses and Aaron are alongside the Duke of Wellington; yet another depicts St. Catherine with her wheel, Queen Elizabeth I, and a wedding coach!

Theoretically, one would think it more natural to wish to bite effigies of those we loathe, rather than those we admire, but obviously such moulds formed reminders of personages or dates, and delicacies of former days were often shaped as saints, royalty, and popular heroes. It must, however, have seemed somewhat sacrilegious to eat St. Catherine, lese-majesty to nibble at Queen Elizabeth I, and a dangerous risk to bite off the Duke of Wellington's head! The nearest to a criminal in a carved mould is probably "Punch", who was a gingerbread favourite at fairs during many centuries. The gingerbread stall, with gilded gingerbreads or 'fairings', was, according to old records, the children's prime favourite from mediaeval times. It is related that when St. Bartholomew's Fair, held annually at Smithfield from 1123 onwards, finally closed in 1850, the gingerbread stall was the last survivor. The most famous gingerbread seller of fiction, was Ben Johnson's 'Joan Trash' in *Bartholomew Fair*, produced at Bankside in 1614. The most noted in real life was a very foppishly dressed, 18th-century, London man, known as Tiddy-Doll who is shown selling his gingerbread in Hogarth's picture of the hanging of the 'Idle Prentice' at Tyburn.

The ease with which gilding peeled off gingerbread gave us one of our popular sayings and we can imagine children licking gingerbread 'horn-books', with which they were enticed to learn the alphabet.

Horn-books are described in Section XXVII, *Tuition*; the gingerbread horn-book custom is commemorated in two rhymes. The first, written by J. Crane in 1835, runs:

'The bakers to increase their trade
Made alphabets of gingerbread
That folks might swallow what they read
All the letters were digested
Hateful ignorance detested'.

The second, from Matthew Prior's *Alma*, runs:

'To Master John the English Maid
A Horn-book gives of Ginger-bread
And that the Child may learn the better,
As he can name, he eats the Letter'.

No records exist of when the idea originated of heightening gastronomic anticipation by staging a magnificent display, but we can be sure that the art of making food attractive by moulding it in decorative form has a long history, because enjoyment of food, and skill in carving, all go back a long way. Accounts of great mediaeval banquets and books of etiquette, and Tudor and later household recipes, show that it has long been usual to adorn the festive board with elaborately moulded confections, which included enormous pies, brawns, jellies, cold meats, cakes, marchpanes (marzipan cakes) and various sugar confections simulating real or legendary birds and beasts, or fantastic and monumental edifices embellished with royal statuary, crowns, coronets, coats of arms, fountains, sporting scenes, cannons, hearts, bells, saints and ecclesiastical insignia, babes in cots, lover's knots, or other motifs appropriate to the personage or occasion which it was desired to honour.

In former times, a hostess could order, from a specialist mould-maker, a relief portrait of her principal guest, or one carved specially to commemorate his or her memorable feats or red letter days. Several carvers in the 19th century, who specialized in pastry and biscuit mould

carving, stamped their moulds. The name of William Henry Mathews of 22 Lant Street, Borough, appears on good quality moulds made between 1839 and 1851. Alfred Mathews seems to have succeeded soon after that date and continued at least until 1878. William Hawkins, of 4 Vigo Street, Piccadilly, made high grade special moulds at least between 1838 and 1851. Carvers' stamps of earlier than 19th-century date are rare.

Casts from confectionery moulds provide some of the finest relief records of costume, both of important personages and of the more ordinary citizens of the 16th to 19th centuries. For the collector, casts placed alongside their moulds add enormously to interest. They can also be used as most appropriate decoration on dining room walls. A curious sidelight on the former importance of the decoratively moulded pie is the effect which the flour tax had during the Napoleonic wars. Temporarily, it almost banished the elaborately enclosed pastry pie, but in so doing, it created a new industry. The enterprising Josiah Wedgwood produced 'pie pots' in a non-porous stoneware, officially known as cane-ware. His 'pies', more often described as 'crock pies', were pots to hold hot stews, and they reproduced perfectly, the colour of a pastry pie, done to a turn; they were available in the decorated moulded shapes fashionable in the last decade of the 18th century. A number of other potters followed Wedgwood's lead in the early years of the 19th century.

CULINARY MOULDS

Commencing with culinary moulds, here are descriptions of the selection illustrated.

The finely carved Nürnberg, boxwood, cake mould, Plate 184, measuring 11½ in. in diameter, is the earliest dated specimen I have seen. On one side is a stag amongst foliage and on the reverse, the double-headed, crowned eagle and date 1567.

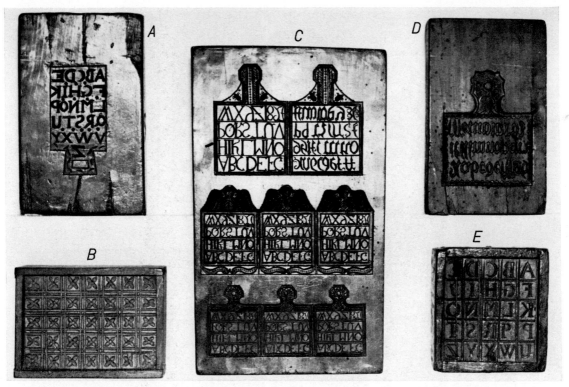

187 Mostly single and multiple gingerbread horn-book moulds. (*Section XII*)

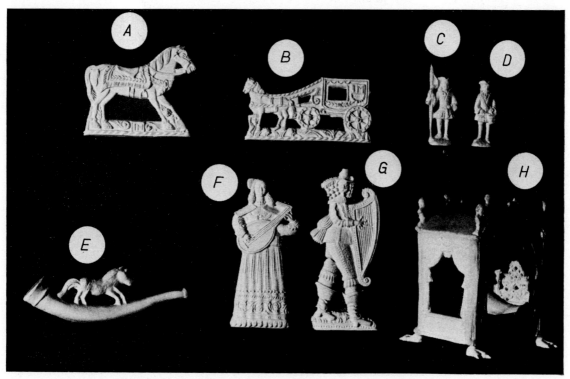

188 Sugar casts from some of the moulds shown in Plates 191, 192 and 193. (*Section XII*)

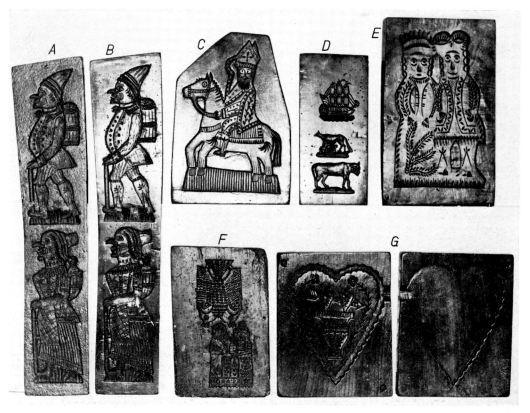

189 *A*, cast-iron mould of Punch and Judy, obviously made from *B*, the carved mould; *C*, a Russian St. Nicholas mould; *D*, *E* and *F*, country-made gingerbread moulds; *G*, back and front of a Valentine cake mould. (*Section XII*)

190 English or German, 18th-century equestrian mould and mould of a fashionable young lady of the eighteen-eighties. (*Section XII*)

191   *D* shows one side of the unique mould for the 18th-century four-poster bed, Plate 188, *H*. *A* is a fine Regency mould; *B*, *C* and *G* are 17th century, and *E*, 18th century. The casts from *F* are shown in Plate 188, *A* and *B*. (*Section XII*)

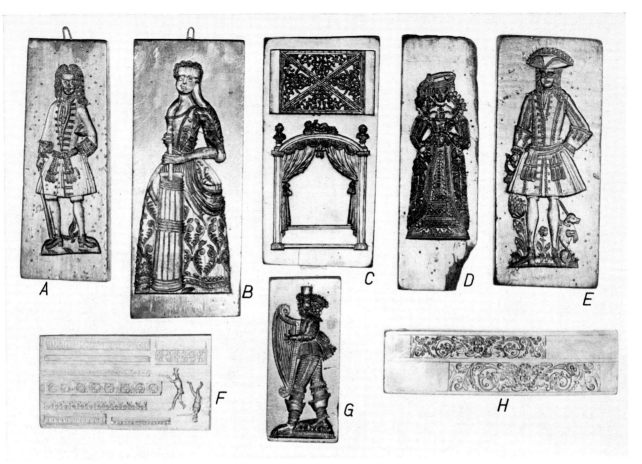

192 *C* shows the mould for the tester and bed side part of the four-poster, Plate 188, *H*; *G*, the mould for the 17th-century gallant, Plate 188, *G*; *F* is a Regency mould; the remainder are 18th century. (*Section XII*)

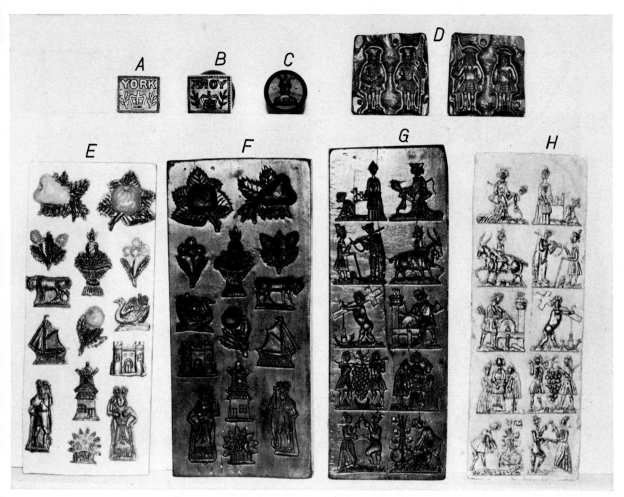

193 *A* and *B*, case and boxwood mould for a York wine biscuit; *C*, finely carved mould and biscuit pricker; *D*, two sides of the mould for the 18th-century sugar soldiers, Plate 188, *C* and *D*; *F* and *G*, 'card' moulds for biscuits, with their casts, *E* and *H*. (*Section XII*)

194 Ornamental sugar moulds, including, *A*, two sides of the mould for the 'clay' pipe, Plate 188, *E*; *B* and D, moulds for birds, *C*, baskets, *E* 'tick-tocks', *K*, mottoes, *G*, alphabet letters, and *L*, christening cake. (*Section XII*)

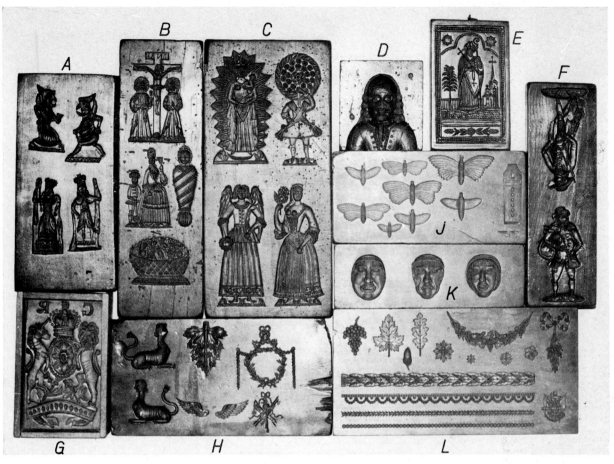

195 *A, B, C* and *F*, 'card' moulds for gingerbread; *D* 18th-century mould, probably for gingerbread; *E*, a Greek church mould, carved on both sides. The remainder of moulds in this plate are 18th- and 19th-century, for sugar ornaments. (*Section XII*)

196 Boxwood moulds for compo ornament—*A*, masonic; *B*, fox mask and brushes; *E*, centrepiece for portrait frame of champion jockey; *F*, 'Revelations'. For details of other moulds, see text. (*Section XII*)

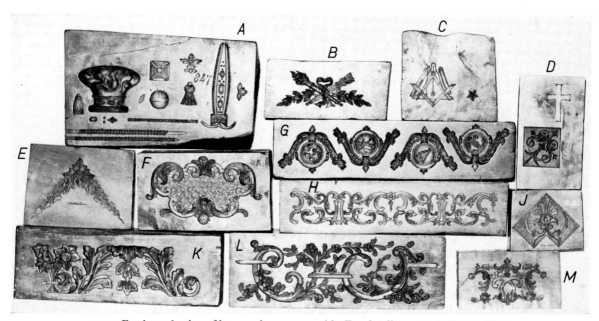

197 Further selection of boxwood compo moulds. For details, see text. (*Section XII*)

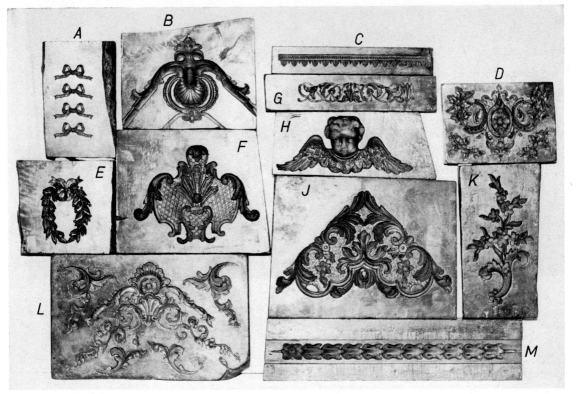

198 Further selection of boxwood compo moulds. *A*, the ribbon bows, is an Adam mould. Most of the others are also 18th century. (*Section XII*)

199 TOP ROW: Napoleonic Corsican gourd bottle; South American gourd bowl, shown inverted; outer Brazil nutshell; compotiere turned from Brazil nutshell. BOTTOM ROW: Chinese moulded cricket cage gourd; two finely engraved Chinese gourds; outer Brazil nutshell, partially stripped, showing the nuts peeping through; bowl turned from Brazil nutshell. (*Section XIII*)

200 Two Chinese floral brooches and a braclet 'stone' carved from peach stones. (*Section XIII*)

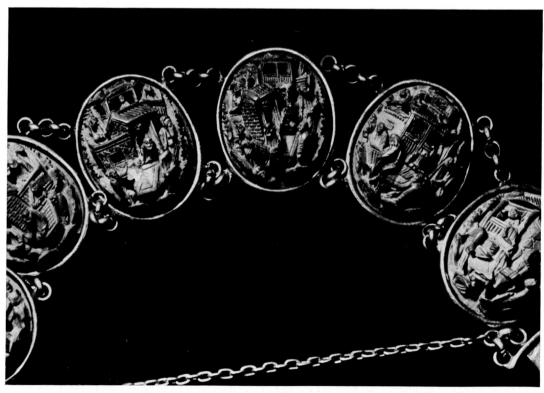

201 Enlarged details of Chinese bracelet peach stones. (*Section XIII*)

203 Bugbear view of two French and one Mexican coconut flasks. (*Section XIII*)

204 Details of some of the finely carved panels of the three coconuts shown in Plate 203. (*Section XIII*)

202 Charles II, silver mounted coconut cup, dated 1669. For further details, see text. *Photograph by courtesy of Glasgow Museums and Art Galleries.* (*Section XIII*)

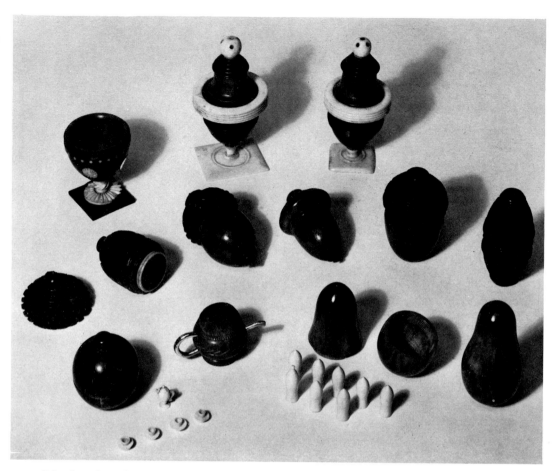

205 Selection of mostly plain coquilla nutshell objects. English, 18th or early 19th century. (*Section XIII*)

206 Carved coquilla nutshell snuff boxes, flask, and *étui*. Continental, 18th and 19th century. For details, see text. (*Section XIII*)

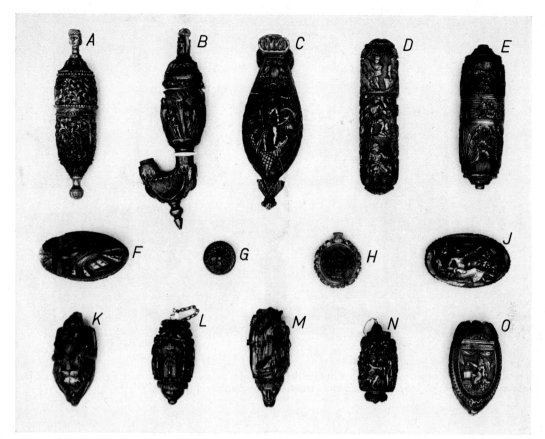

207 Finely carved coquilla nutshell snuff boxes, flasks, etc. Continental. Mostly 18th century. For details, see text. (*Section XIII*)

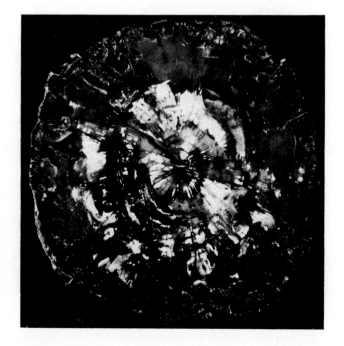

208 Slice of petrified wood from the Petrified Forest of Arizona. (*Sect. XIII*)

209 *A*, mediaeval-type skippet; *B* and *C*, sealing outfits; *D*, lawyer's deed rack; *E*, wafer signet and water box; *F*, 1840 stamp perforator; *G*, John Gamgee's 1870 patent stamp dispenser. (*Section XIV*)

210 English domestic posting boxes, *circa* 1872 and 1900 (?). (*Section XIV*)

211   Selection of string boxes; *B* and *C*, early 20th century, the remainder 19th century. All English except *B*.
For details, see text. (*Section XIV*)

212   Selection of English, 19th-century string boxes. For details, see text. (*Section XIV*)

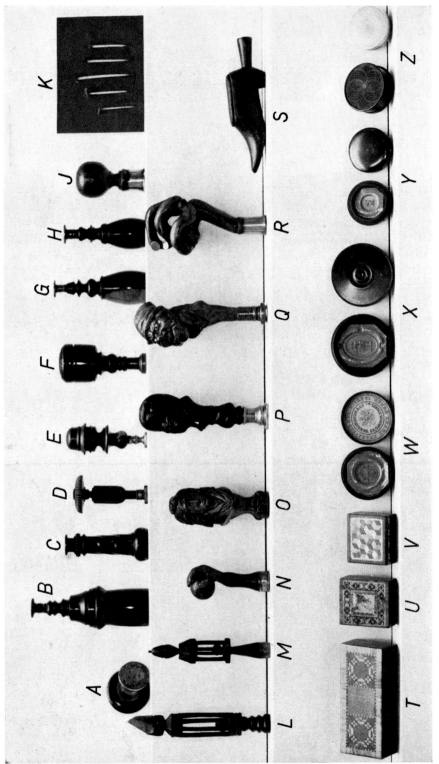

213 *A* to *J* and *L* to *S*, selection of signets; *K*, Babal Indian thorn pins; *T*, *U* and *V*, stamp boxes; *W*, *X*, *Y*. *Z* and *Z1*, seal boxes. (*Section XIV*)

Casts from the two sides are shown alongside. It was formerly in the Bussell, Sir William Lawrence, and Rosenheim Collections. Below, is another rare specimen, dated 1779. It pegs together and forms the ornamental hexagonal marchpane (marzipan) cake shown alongside. It was formerly in the same collections as the Nürnberg mould. The particular delicacy which was cast in the crude mould Plate 185 is uncertain. It is of elm, has inside dimensions $11\frac{1}{2}$ in. by $9\frac{3}{4}$ in. by $2\frac{1}{2}$ in. and turns out a rectangle, face moulded with the name S. PLUM, two rosettes, a dolphin and a heart; it has the weep holes usually found on cheese moulds.

In Plate 187 are mostly gingerbread horn-book moulds, the custom for which is described in the introduction to this section. *A*, may be 18th- or early 19th-century; on the back of it is carved a windmill for a gingerbread fairing. *B* is a repetitive florette design, and *C*, a multiple mould for three different patterns of horn-books, dated 1827. *D* is an earlier Gothic lettered horn-book; *E* is a 17th-century alphabet mould, with the old type of Q and the V omitted.

In Plate 186, *A*, *B* and *C*, are three from a set of 18th-century flummery moulds, which came from Essex. They are of sycamore and vary in inside diameter from $3\frac{1}{4}$ in. to 5 in. and in depth from $1\frac{1}{8}$ in. to $1\frac{5}{8}$ in. Flummery was a popular 18th-century dish. *The Experienced English Housewife* by Elizabeth Raffald, 1769, gives this recipe:

Put one ounce of bitter, and one of sweet Almonds into a Bason, pour over them some boiling Water, to make the skins come off which is called Blanching, strip off the skins, and throw the kernels into cold Water, then take them out and beat them in a Marble Mortar, with a little Rose Water to keep them from Oiling, when they are beat, put them into a Pint of Calf's Foot Stock, set it over the Fire, and sweeten to your Taste with Loaf Sugar, as soon as it boils strain it thro' a Piece of Muslin or Gawz, when a little cold put it into a Pint of thick cream

and keep stirring it often, till it grows thick and cold, wet your Moulds in cold water and pour in the Flummery, lit it stand five or six hours at least before you turn them out; if you make Flummery stiff and wet the Moulds, it will turn out without putting it in warm Water, for Water takes off the Figures of the Mould and makes the Flummery look dull.

N.B. Be careful you keep stirring it till cold or it will run in Lumps when you turn out of the mould.

Mrs. Pinto tried the recipe, which turns out quite easily from the moulds.

D is a 5 in. diameter coptic bread stamp; another print is carved on the handle at the back. The same design is said to have been used for more than 1,500 years, and these stamps are still being carved in various diameters. *E* to *L* are finely carved, French, 18th-century, boxwood roller prints. Nearly all have the fleur-de-lis included in their designs and some, which include the Cross and Emblems of the Passion, were doubtless used for Easter cakes. The majority have carved motifs on the ends, additional to the patterns on the perimeter. One is stamped Guillaume A. Gorge. 1747, and another Josephe Mignon, 20 Janvier 1748. The fondant roller, *M*, probably also 18th-century, is English and carved with roses, acorn, thistle, corn stook, strawberry, heart, shell, etc.

One of the rarest moulds in the Pinto Collection is of boxwood, carved on both sides with the components of an early 18th-century bridal bed, for topping a wedding cake with a miniature sugar 'four poster'. This probably unique mould also requires considerable skill from the ornamental sugar worker, particularly in curving the tester without damaging the intricate carving on the underside, which unfortunately cannot be shown in the picture of the casting, Plate 188, *H*. In Plate 191, *D* is the side of the mould with the carving for the head, the foot, the two pillows and the claw feet. Plate 192, *C*, the reverse side, shows the underside of the tester and the side of the bed. This mould may be English or Dutch; the sugar model is 4¾ in. high, 3½ in. long and 2¾ in. wide.

Continuing Plate 191, *A*, of pearwood, shows finely cut ornament for a Regency Graeco-Egyptian decorated cake, *circa* 1810. *B*, showing a youth in the fashionable costume of 1660, is probably a contemporary carving. *C*, a particularly sharply detailed boxwood carving of a Court lady playing a mandolin, *circa* 1630, has her harp-playing gallant on the back, shown in Plate 192, *G*; the sugar casts from this mould are in Plate 188, *F* and *G*. Two well carved trumpet playing cherubs, *circa* 1700, are depicted, Plate 191, *E*; on the back of the mould is a three-dimensional bust, which confirms this dating. *F* shows a gaily caparisoned horse and a wedding coach, the sugar casts from which are shown Plate 188, *A* and *B*. *G*, fragile and wormy, shows a grand lady of 1630, with her spinning wheel and distaff. Of those not already described in Plate 192, *A* is a Hanoverian gallant, *circa* 1755; *B*, a fashionable lady playing dairy-maid *à la* Marie Antoinette, *circa* 1765; *D*, a belle, about 1635, and *E*, also carved on the back, *circa* 1755. *F*, carved with figures and borders on both sides, is a fine quality, Regency, boxwood example for ornamental sugar moulding. *H*, another very good quality boxwood border mould, carved on both sides, is 18th-century work.

Plate 189, *A* and *B*, Punch and Judy, have unusual interest. The subjects have been popular gingerbread fairings for several hundred years and moulds depicting them are not particularly rare. The extraordinary coincidence in this case, is that having bought the carved wooden mould, *B*, (probably early 18th-century) in 1946, we then found the cast iron replica, *A*, of the identical mould, 10 years later and many miles distant from the first purchase. One can assume that the subject was so popular, that in order to avoid the cost of new carvings at frequent intervals, iron cast moulds

were made, but this is the only instance of a wood original and iron replica which I have ever seen; the figures from it are 9¾ in. high. *C* is a Russian St. Nicholas (Santa Claus), probably 19th-century. *D*, English, 19th-century, is a 'card', with three separate subjects on the face shown, and four on the reverse. *E*, another crude 'card', may be a 19th-century depiction of 18th-century gingerbread costume figures, 10 in. high. On the back is a 10 in. high cock-a-doodle-do. *F* is an even cruder card: on the face pictured, is a bird (upside down), and Moses and Aaron; on the reverse side, are the cat and fiddle, and Cinderella's slipper; congruity of subjects is not a feature of these country-made specimens. *G*, a two-piece elm mould, turns out a delicious looking iced Valentine cake, shaped as a heart, 7½ in. high.

It is difficult to imagine how some of the large moulded ornaments were used. The fashionable horseman, left, Plate 190, second half of the 18th century, stands 13½ in. high, perhaps not too tall for a gilded gingerbread fairing and quite in the design tradition: alternatively, it might have been for a German moulded metal ornament. Flat-backed, moulded, tin ornaments and toys, including some tin soldiers, were being made at Nürnberg in the 1770s, but whether any of the figures were as large as this, seems doubtful. The 16½ in. high moulded figure, right, Plate 190, is even more of a puzzle. This charming young lady, dressed in the height of fashion of the 1880s, would have been a real sweetie, cast in coloured sugar; but a single tier cake more than 16½ in. high seems formidable, whilst if laid horizontal on the cake, it would have appeared more like a tomb effigy. However, some of the apparent cake moulds—those for Church festivals especially—are even larger. One of a Russian patriarch in full regalia is 3 ft. high; an early Italian mould with a monstrance on one side and a Roman warrior on the reverse, is carved from a block of walnut 26 in. by 17 in., by 3 in. in thickness.

Plate 193, 194 and 195 are cake ornament, biscuit and gingerbread moulds of normal size; many of them are of the 'card' type, carved on both sides with a variety of unrelated motifs, arranged indiscriminately, but primarily to fit the maximum number into the board. Plate 193, *A* and *B*, are the cast and the boxwood mould for a York wine biscuit. *C* is a very finely carved boxwood combined biscuit stamp and pricker; the design is the head of a mediaeval king. *D*, of boxwood, are the back and front of the 18th-century, three dimensional mould for the delightful $2\frac{3}{8}$ in. high sugar soldiers, casts of which are pictured, Plate 188, *C* and *D*. *F* and *G* are 'cards', with their casts alongside. Being largely fruit, flower, animal, nursery rhyme and religious motifs, they are not easy to date, but I think *F* could be as late as 19th-century, but *G* not later than 18th. Among the eight 'biscuits' on the back of *G* is a neat miniature hornbook; both cards are carved on both sides.

The sugar clay pipe with a horse on it, Plate 188, *E*, was cast in the three-dimensional mould, Plate 194, *A*; it doubtless brought as much pleasure to 19th-century children as the sugar 'tick-tocks', *E*; the mould has larger watches on the back. The sugar mottoes, *K*, are, or certainly were favourites 60 years ago: the six mottoes, three each side, spell out 'Do you love me', 'Will you marry me', 'Forget me not', 'I will', 'I will not', 'I love you'. *B* and *D* show an unusual subject, birds, and like one for butterflies, Plate 195, *J*, they require considerable skill by the sugar worker, who has to bend the wings of each bird or insect, to give it verisimilitude. Plate 194, *C*, could be 18th- or 19th-century; the King and Queen, and Punch and Judy, who are on the reverse side, are shown in Plate 195, *A*. Plate 194, *F*, is exceptionally deeply cut with a crisp border design of grapes and vine leaves; on the reverse side are numerous well carved motifs, including two sizes of coats of arms of the Prince of Wales. *G* is

a 19th-century sugar alphabet biscuit mould, with letters on both sides; the carver, in his zeal to save space, has carved some of the letters back to front, the L and P on the side illustrated, and the S and R on the reverse. Moulds *H* and *J*, carved on both faces, are good quality, sharp impressions of iced cake ornaments and borders; *H*, is probably 18th-century and *J*, stamped W. ROFF, BEDFORD, 19th-century. *L* is a traditional Italian christening cake mould of a babe in swaddling clothes.

Plate 195, *A* and *J*, have already been mentioned. *B* and *C* are interesting and fairly competently carved 'cards'. The strange juxtaposition of religion and fashion on *B* is clearly shown. The idea of treating the Crucifixion as an edible decoration seems most distasteful; on the same card, note the 18th-century lady with her black page boy and infant in swaddling clothes. *C*, also 18th-century, has a paschal lamb, elaborate five-point star, fish and infant in swaddling clothes on the reverse side. *D* is a good 18th-century bust, probably for gingerbread and *E*, a Greek(?) church mould, carved with archbishops on each side. *F*, an 18th-century fairground gingerbread mould, has Punch and a jovial monk on the back. *G*, of pearwood, makes a confection with a rather fanciful rendering of the Hanoverian Royal Coat of Arms on it. *H* is a very fine quality, carved boxwood mould in the Greek taste of the early 19th century; the back is carved all over with the diamond pattern often used on the iced walls of cakes; one edge of the $1\frac{1}{8}$ in. thick mould is carved with oval link chain pattern. *K*, another good quality carving, makes three, three-dimensional heads; the backs of the heads are cut into the reverse of the mould. *L* is equally well cut with cake icing decorative motifs and borders and on the back, with diamond pattern. *H*, *J*, *K* and *L* all came from the same pastrycook source and may be the work of the same carver, a man with considerable skill in intaglio carving.

COMPO MOULDS

Some idea of the interesting subjects and fine quality and detailing which exists in moulds for compo, mostly carved in boxwood, can be seen in Plates 196, 197 and 198. These all appear to be 18th- or 19th-century.

In Plate 196, *A* consists of masonic emblems. *B* shows a fox mask and brushes. *C*, detailed with leaves and fruits, is carved on the back with the carver's or owner's mark, (H?) Owlett. *D* is deeply cut with flying cherubs, urn, flower motifs, etc. *E* was doubtless the centrepiece of a frame for a portrait of a champion jockey; it is signed by the first-rate 19th-century mould carver either John Peter Wall of 188 Strand, London, or James Charles Wall, of 31 Paternoster Square. The first was working in the mid-19th century, and the latter in the last quarter.

F produces a plaque of REVELATIONS CHAP. XX & XXI, in a sunburst above clouds. *G* is carved with a formal border, coronet, garter, etc. *H* has, on the left, a very finely carved order of the King of Prussia. *J* is probably a detail for a corner of a picture or wall panel frame.

Plate 197, *A*, is a $2\frac{1}{4}$ in. thick block of boxwood, unbacked: the reason for this considerable thickness is to get the depth for the crown which is carved more than $1\frac{1}{2}$ in. deep, quite a feat in boxwood. *C* is masonic and *G* depicts heraldic badges. The others, all well carved, are, I think, self explanatory; *J* is carved by Wall.

A further fine selection of wall panel moulding and picture frame motifs is shown in Plate 198. *A*, the bows of ribbon, is marked (Robert) 'Adam Ribbon'. *C* is stamped Ashmead, 10 Duke St., Grosvenor Square. Ashmead was originally a brush manufacturer, first appearing in the Directories at the above address in 1825. From 1827 until 1851, he described himself as Brush-Maker, Ivory-Turner, Military and Naval Cockade-Maker, and Naturalist or bird stuffer; if he also added in mould carving, he was extremely versatile. *G* bears Howlett's stamp. *J* is unusual in having the stippled effect produced by silver headed pins or studs, a technique most unusual in carved moulds, although found fairly often in textile printing blocks.

Additional to the names of carvers of compo moulds already mentioned are the following, who sometimes stamped their work:

Lucien Mound, 1 Hanway St., Oxford St., London and 1 Sutton St., Soho Square; *circa* 1860.

Jonathan Taylor, 84A Margaret St., Cavendish Sq., London; *circa* 1860.

Charles Foster, 2 Francis St., Lower Marsh, London, S.E.; *circa* 1875.

A. Mound, 37 Francis St., Tottenham Ct. Road, London; *circa* 1875.

Richard Mound, 18 Windmill St., Tottenham Ct. Rd., London; *circa* 1890.

XIII

Nuts – Gourds – Fruit Stone, Jet and Bog Oak Jewellery – Petrified Wood

Gourds

Gourds are the fruits of a group of climbing or trailing plants of the *Cucurbitaceae*, which are closely related to melons and cucumbers. They are native to warm, temperate and tropical parts of the globe, require plenty of moisture, and are all rapid growing annuals. Some are cultivated for food value, others for ornament and for their woody rinds which, when dry, harden and make useful and attractive receptacles. The fibrous interior skeleton of one of these gourds, the *Luffa cylindrica*, is the bath-tub loofah. They grow naturally in various flask shapes, such as pear, fig, truncheon, egg, etc., and can be partially bandaged or corsetted while growing, in order to develop unusual outlines. In China, they are, by an ingenious method, sometimes encased in intaglio carved moulds whilst growing, so that when they mature and fill out the interstices of the moulds, they appear to be carved or moulded. A Chinese gourd cricket cage (wire mesh not original), which has been enclosed in a hexagonal mould whilst young and supple, is bottom left, Plate 199; it tells the story of fertility. Cricket cages of this nature are traditional love tokens in China. For further information on moulded gourd cricket cages, see article entitled *Chinese Impressed Gourds*

Reconsidered by Professor Schuyler Cammann, *Oriental Art Magazine*, Vol. X, 1964.

In their various countries of origin, scooped-out gourds are used as flasks, or cut segmentally to form natural spoons. For export particularly, they are decorated by etching or engraving the surface and either pigmenting the etched lines, or the surrounding surface. Corsican gourds treated in this manner usually portray Napoleon, as one might expect, and some of them are extremely well executed. A small Napoleonic gourd scent flask is shown right of Plate 388. A large flask, top left, Plate 199, skilfully portrays Napoleon with three of his officers on board the Bellerophon; the scene is framed in a formal laurel wreath and scrolled ribbons; on the reverse side, an eagle, carrying a sword, flies below a sun rayed crown.

Two small Chinese gourds from the province of Kansu, North-west China, bottom row, Plate 199, are engraved with figures and Chinese characters; the work is of a very high order. A late 19th-century, $8\frac{1}{4}$ in. diameter bowl gourd, shown inverted in the same picture, has been ebonised and then etched with the arms of the South American Republics and dates of their independence.

Jewellery

For many centuries, the Chinese and Japanese have been famous for the fineness and intricacy of their carvings. Little larger than some precious stones and, in fact, valued similarly and often mounted in gold or silver to serve as necklaces, bracelets, brooches and ear-rings, some of the carved peach stones and canarium nuts are gems of art. They vary considerably in quality of workmanship, but the best are undercut and pierced through and through, until they attain a lace-like quality. It is difficult to imagine how they are ever created, because the average European needs a strong magnifying glass merely to study the detail. The colour of the fruit stones and nut shells varies from buff to bronze; the subjects may be humorous gnomes or animals, paper-like flowers, or a complete street scene with figures and buildings, which have open and closing shutters, all portrayed in the compass of half a peach stone. In Plate 200, much enlarged, are two Chinese floral brooches, and a bracelet 'stone' of a scene with trees and a house in the background, and a merchant in the foreground, displaying a jar and casket to three others seated at a carved table. Plate 201 shows enlarged details of some of the peach stones in a bracelet. They portray an amazing amount of perspective in a thickness of $\frac{1}{4}$ in.; with a good glass, it is possible to examine the expressions of the four to seven animated figures in each scene and every brick in the background buildings is clear. P. de Rossi, a lady artist of Bologna, working in the 15th and 16th centuries, carved some minute work on peach stones.

Purses made of melon pips sewn together, Plate 15, *G* and *H*, and some intricately carved cherry stone bangles and necklaces were made both in Europe and South Africa during Victorian times. During this period also, a considerable amount of jewellery and other small objects was made from dense, dark brown or black peat impregnated woods, known collectively as bog oak, although often they are other species. In general, such work, both English and Irish, has little artistic merit.

Wood can become mineralised in several different ways; coal is the best known. In the artistic sphere, the related jet—lignite rendered black by fossilization and impregnation with bituminous matters—has been prized for jewellery since early times, enjoying recurrent periods of popularity, particularly for memorial jewellery. According to Pliny, the name jet is derived from Gagas or Gages, a town and river in Lycia, Asia Minor, from which the material was first obtained. In England, the main source of supply is Whitby, Yorkshire, where the jet was formerly extracted in large quantities from a bed of shale, 25 ft. to 30 ft. thick, belonging to the Upper Lias. The best jet is a dense black and possesses a resinous lustre. It is sometimes known as black amber, because it becomes electrified when subjected to friction.

In Britain, jet beads have been found in early Bronze Age deposits. Gaius Julius Solinus, in the third century A.D., mentions the abundance of jet in Britain. Whitby jet ornaments reached the apex of their popularity in the 19th century. Jet was worn as mourning for William IV. For some years after the death of Albert, the Prince Consort, ladies presented at Court were requested to wear no other jewellery. Jet enjoyed a renewed vogue for sentimental jewellery of remembrance, during and immediately after the Crimean War and the Indian Mutiny.

The first of the 19th-century jet workshops in Whitby commenced operations between 1808 and 1810; by 1850 there were 50, with an annual output of £20,000. The peak came between 1870 and 1880, when some 200 workshops had an annual output of between £80,000 and £90,000; thereafter, the trade in jet ornaments declined rapidly. Spain is now the main source of supply of jet, but Spanish jet is softer than that from Whitby and when ground to a fine edge, will not retain it like the Whitby material. In the 19th century, the cheaper Spanish jet was used mainly for beads, lockets and crosses, but that from Yorkshire was preferred for cameos, crisply carved combs, bandeaux, ear-rings, brooches, aigrettes, dagger or arrow pins for the hair, hatpins and other ornaments. A selection of jet and bog oak jewellery and buttons is shown in Plate 15.

Nuts, Brazil

Each hard-shelled segmental Brazil nut, which we eat or press for oil, is one of 12 to 22 which, when growing, is contained in another hard outer shell, nearly spherical, about 6 in. in diameter. An outer shell is shown, top row, Plate 199, with below it a partially stripped shell with the nuts peeping through. On the right, top row, is a cup made from an outer shell; below it, is a bowl of the same substance. Brazil nut treen often puzzles collectors because it has no grain in the normal sense—merely a mass of short, hard, yellowish fibres. When turned and polished, it is often taken to be a modern moulded particle or chipboard product.

Nuts, Coconuts

Coconut palms are among man's best friends. Every part of the tropical tree has economic value. The fleshy kernel, esteemed when fresh, is valuable copra when dried, being about 70 per cent fat and a basic ingredient of margarine, detergents and oil-cake. In the tropics, the trunk is used in housebuilding and bridging, and in England it is used for walking sticks, etc., under the name of palmyra; the leaf-stalks and midribs have such diverse uses as canes, brooms, needles and pins. The husk, which thickly surrounds the outer shell, is used for matting, ropes, etc., and the leaves for thatching, basket-work, curtains and hats. Finally, the shell has, for many centuries, been the raw material of all kinds of nut treen, including flasks, bowls, spoons, etc.

In their native lands, being a never-ending crop and, therefore, the commonest form of eating and drinking vessels, little labour is usually expended on ornamenting them. As early imports to Europe, however, they, like ostrich eggs, were great rarities—costly objects to be carved by skilled craftsmen and converted into silver-mounted goblets, or to form bodies of jugs. It seems probable that nature's ovoids, nuts and eggs, have had considerable influence on the shape of drinking vessels.

When coconuts were first introduced to Europe is unknown, but in 1259 a Bishop of Durham was able to bequeath his '*cyphum de nuce Indye cum pede et apparatu argenti*'. In the 14th century, a few more mentions occur, and in the 15th and 16th centuries, references to coconut standing cups and jugs occur fairly frequently in inventories of the plate of the nobility. Tudor examples usually have pierced and fret outlined silver straps connecting the rim mount with the stem of the cup or foot of the jug. The practice continued during the 17th century, but the straps became plainer.

The Charles II, silver-mounted coconut goblet, Plate 202, is divided by narrow silver bands into three panels, illustrating incidents in the flight of Charles after the Battle of Worcester. In one panel, the King's head and that of Col. Carles peer from the foliage of the Boscobel oak, while two Cromwellian troopers ride below. A ribbon stretches across the tree trunk, bearing the picture of the three Crowns and the inscription '1000 PVND-FDK'. The second panel depicts the King, dressed as a servant, riding into a pond near a castellated house, while a man whips on the horse. The third panel, which can be seen in the illustration, shows the King on horseback with Mrs. Jane Lane, who assisted his escape, seated behind him. The silver rim is dated 1669. Coconuts continued to be used as bowls of goblets in the 18th and 19th centuries but, in general, and there are exceptions, the nuts were left plain and polished and the ornament was confined to the silver.

Coconuts have also been used in their entirety as flasks, with carving used to accentuate the 'bugbear' marking. They vary enormously in quality of work; some of the crudest are souvenirs carved by sailors visiting the tropics, but often they are valuable as historic documentaries of costume and episodes. Three of the finest quality carvings are shown in Plates 203 and 204. Plate 203 depicts the accentuation of the natural bugbear eyes into grotesque faces and Plate 204, with the nuts arranged in the same order, shows more the quality of the work. The variations in natural ovoids make them difficult to 'set out' in formal designs. The three illustrated, each have four panels on the 'sides', with the spaces between the borders filled by finely carved scrolls and foliage. The largest nut is fitted with glass eyes, a silver spout and ivory studs for suspension as a flask. Its panels are of mythological subjects, beautifully executed in Empire style. This nut and the centre one, which has its panels carved with trophies, are reputed to be work of French prisoners of the Napoleonic Wars; both show great skill and certainly give the impression that time was no object. The small nut on the right is, in some ways, the finest work of all. It was carved in Mexico and in addition to the intricate panels depicting Mexican legends, it is inlaid with silver sprays of leaves, forming borders. The eyes are mother-of-pearl and in the carved eyebrows, the artist has microscopically carved his name, Pedro Peralta.

Nuts, Coquilla

All the objects illustrated in Plates 205, 206, 207 and 368, *C* to *K*, are made from coquilla nutshell. Until Mrs. Pinto and I carried out our research in the 1940s, the possibility of these objects being nutshells was generally ignored or ridiculed. Except for the 'eggs', they were invariably described by dealers as burr or root wood, or as figured walnut. The full story of our findings, which were greatly helped by Dr. F. N. Howes of the Royal Botanic Gardens, Kew, was set out in articles in *Apollo*, February and April, 1950, which resulted in the word coquilla coming back into general use among collectors and dealers.

Coquillas are the nuts of the *attalea funifera* or, as the Brazilians call the palm, the *Piassaba*, which has an extensive distribution on the eastern side of South America, where it grows in swampy ground or partially flooded land on the banks of rivers. The same palm is one of the sources of piassava fibre, which has been used in bass brooms for many centuries.

The first clue to coquillas came when one of these extremely brittle objects broke; I found a complete absence of long grain in any direction, and difficulty in gluing, owing to the oily nature of the material. I suspected then that these objects were nutshells; my suspicions deepened when I found that, owing to an obvious limitation of size, components were frequently built up into larger objects by threading together 'rings', or by threaded dowelling of one part to another; this again pointed to difficulty in using an adhesive. Proof came when I eventually found, inside one specimen, the three eyes or 'bugbear' markings, which are characteristic of many nuts.

Coquilla's characteristics are—shape and size of a hen's egg; generally a rich brown colour, with a handsome tortoiseshell-like mottle; very hard and takes a high polish; brittle and of an oily nature. Incidentally, if broken, the edges to be joined should first be treated with a strong solution of washing soda, when they can be glued satisfactorily.

Coquillas were introduced to western Europe in the mid-16th century and enjoyed popularity for small turnery and carved objects, at least until the end of the 19th century. The illustrated catalogue of the International Exhibition of 1862 states that 'It is from the shell then, and not from the kernel, as in the case of the vegetable ivory, that the turner makes from coquilla nuts the numerous pretty objects now commonly seen in the shops. It is especially adapted for ornamental handles of cabinet drawers, and other similar small articles . . .' In the past, they have also been extensively used for walking stick and umbrella handles, bell pulls, pomanders, scent flasks, purses, buttons, pincushions, rosaries and rosary cases, *étuis*, pipe bowls, receptacles for miniature toys, dice cups, spinning tops, small ornamental cups, urns and boxes, muffineers, pocket spice boxes and, above all, for snuff boxes. The oily nature of the material makes it ideal for keeping snuff in condition, without drying out.

I have been unable to establish names of manufacturers, or actual centres of working and much more research is needed, but the character of the objects, particularly when carved, shows that they were produced in England, Germany, Holland, France, Italy and probably other European countries bordering the Mediterranean. The products vary considerably in age, selection of material, quality of carving and finish. The best, usually 18th-century, are beautifully designed, crisply carved and hand polished; they rank as fine art. The worst, made on the Continent, from immature yellow nuts, lacking mottle, are varnished, often a sickly orange colour, and their decoration consists of a monotonous pattern of 'blind' drilled, or through pierced, circular holes. These mostly date from the second half of the 19th century.

Coquilla 'eggs', which are the natural nut shape and, therefore, the commonest, originally often contained rosaries, with beads also of coquilla, and were sold, in the 1870s, outside the Madeleine in Paris, the Pantheon in Rome, etc. Some eggs, pierced all over, were used as sachets. Dice cups, bottles, flat circular boxes, barrels, fret edged baskets and egg cups were other items in this range. Some objects of the type described, have a small knop at the top, pro-

vided with an 'eye' or window, containing souvenir views.

Much more attractive are the plain turned objects, Plate 205. These are all cleanly polished, selected mottled shells, probably fashioned in England in the late 18th and early 19th century. The items in this group (only some of which are illustrated), include acorn shaped, pocket nutmeg graters for mulled wines (see Section III, *Drinking*), ivory ringed muffineers, walking stick knobs, serviette rings, silk or cotton barrels, pincushions, spinning tops, match containers, apple and pear shaped boxes containing miniature 'ivory' toys, such as dominoes, draughts, skittles, and tiny tea and coffee sets. The ivory used for the toys is vegetable ivory, actually the inside nut of the corozo or ivory palm from tropical South America; this is, or formerly was, largely used for making buttons.

In the 18th and early 19th centuries, a range of quaint and amusing human figure snuff boxes were fashioned from coquilla nutshells, in Germany and Holland; mostly they represent town or village characters, rather than famous personages. Many are deliberately grotesque; a few have animal or frog bodies and human faces. Very occasionally, one finds a mythological or religious subject. Plate 368, *C* to *K*, shows a selection. The 'body' uses a whole nut; the head and the feet, of coquilla, bone or ivory, are pegged on. Lids are hinged at the back and the human figure boxes are opened by lifting the coat tails. An example, face down, is shown with lid open, Plate 206, *C*. Hinges are formed out of the coquilla shell and this is a weakness; they are often broken. Buttons and other clothing accessories, also eyes, are often of carved bone, occasionally, mother-of-pearl.

Also in Plate 206, are some different types of coquilla snuff boxes. *A* and *E* are French and, despite the mediaeval roundel heads which occur on both sides of the boxes, are 19th-century productions. The first two snuff boxes of this type, carved with

'Romayne heads', which I found some 40 years ago, were very worn and I thought that they were genuinely mid or late 16th-century; their crude construction, with the end pieces pegged to the thick walls of the central nut, which forms the snuff cavity, and their rather clumsy brass hinges, all lent support to the theory. I am sometimes asked why this type of box often has an oval cavity inside the lid: the answer is that the 'wall' of the shell has been left thick for strength, and the cavity formed by the nut has not been completely planed out. Over a period of time, I have found a dozen or more, some as sharp as the day they left the carver's shop. When they are found in this fresh condition, the fruit and flower wreaths, which band the end pieces, can be seen to be basically 'Biedermeier' rather than Tudor period; moreover, I have since found other coquilla objects, such as the needlecase shown open, Plate 206, F, which are decorated in like manner, but certainly made in the last century. The flask, D, which has a ferocious bugbear face, with silver mouth and silver-mounted glass eyes, is a much higher grade object. It comes under 'Mediterranean' heading and certain features suggest Sicily. The carving is fine in scale, deeply undercut and much of it free standing. Like a number of objects of related type, it depicts mythological subjects connected with the chase; they all include, in their compositions, very human looking angels or winged mortals, hunting dogs, dead game, trophies, birds, climbing vines, flowers and pomegranates. The oval snuff box, B, which has these same features on the reverse side to that illustrated, has silver hinges.

Plate 207 shows a few of the infinite variety of objects and styles found in the upper range of carved coquillas. The flask, A, is probably Sicilian and 18th-century; it is a good example of the winged figures set amongst fine and intricate leaf carving and piercing; the figures, which are on the back, unfortunately do not show in the picture. B is a lidded pipe bowl, French or Flemish. The ship snuff box, C, with Neptune standing on a crocodile, belongs to a rather rare series of ship snuff boxes, varying considerably in size and quality; the silver hinged lids are on the 'deck'. Some models, such as this, are about 6 in. long and are made up of three nutshells pegged together; others are much smaller and made from one nut, plus a small section to form the carved figurehead. Generally, subjects are French men-of-war of the Napoleonic period; the ships usually have their names carved on the sterns, and below decks are apparently depicted with accurate number of decks, guns, gun-ports, etc.

D is an 18th-century wafer box, probably Flemish, vigorously carved with episodes from the life of Jesus; I have never seen another resembling it (for wafer boxes, see Section X, *Miscellany: Religious Objects*). E is an early 19th-century, French, floral carved, cylindrical box. F and J are 18th-century, silver-hinged snuff boxes, both probably French. F is carved with musical trophies; J depicts Daniel in the lion's den. G is a 19th-century sachet and H, a perfume flask. In the bottom row are mostly 18th-century flasks. K, country of origin unknown, depicts a bearded Chinaman. The natural tuft on the end of the nutshell has been left to form the hair. L is a chrism bottle from Mount Athos and M and N, also chrism bottles, depicting scenes from the scriptures, are probably Italian and Greek respectively (for other chrism bottles, see Section X, *Miscellany: Religious Objects*). O, the silver-hinged snuff box, is French, carved in a pseudo-Oriental style.

A 'snake' bangle of coquilla nutshell is illustrated in Plate 15, W; bangles of similar design in ebony, with quartz eyes, were also made in India during the last century. Two coquilla nutshell purses, E and G, are shown in the same plate.

Petrified Wood

The most interesting and highly prized

results of wood transformed into rock, are examples from the several petrified forests which exist in various parts of the world, where the wood-rock has assumed a palette of gorgeous colouring. Two of the most famous of the petrified forests are situated in the U.S.A.—one at the Yellowstone National Park in Wyoming, Idaho and Montana, the other in Chalcedony Park, Arizona. The remains of both forests lie at 8,000 to 9,000 ft. above sea level.

Scientists differ in their opinions, both as to date and manner in which the transformation occurred. The most generally accepted view is that these mineralized logs were transformed from living trees of a tropical forest, about a hundred million years ago. The transformation is conjectured to have taken place in two stages: first a volcanic upheaval overthrew the trees and then, when they were prostrate, hot geysers emerged, bearing silicon in solution, which submerged them. It is believed that the rich oxides of Arizona then intermixed with the silicon and the cell tissues of the trees were filled by the silicious solution, which solidified. There is no conjecture about the results: these trees have become rock, composed of a most wonderful mixture of interblended agate, jasper, jade, calcite, amethyst, etc., etc., reinforced with wood fibres and only three degrees less hard than a diamond.

The polished slice, shown in Plate 208, is one of two outstanding specimens from the Arizona Forest, which were displayed in the Paris Exhibition of 1900. They are each 1 in. thick and one measures 11 in. across, the other 16 in. It is unfortunate that the vivid reds, yellows and greens and flashing white cannot be shown in the picture. But what can be seen clearly is the wood structure, with its bark, annual rings and heart shakes. All the specimens examined show that the wood was undergoing decay before being filled and preserved by the various media which subsequently solidified. On some specimens, traces of fungi (*mycelium*), causing decay, are plainly visible. Microscopic examinations have revealed that some of the wood is of the genus Araucaria, or Norfolk Island pine of the southern Pacific, familiarly known in Great Britain as the monkey puzzle tree.

The trees are mostly found projecting from volcanic ash and lava, which is covered with sandstone to a depth of 20 ft. or more. They also lie exposed in gulches and basins, where water has worn away the sandstone. Some of the logs are enormous, with butts up to 7 ft. in diameter, but they are usually broken across the grain in many places, in true rock fashion. Whilst the quantity of material is great, sound sections are rare. Quite rightly, the forest is now strictly protected against exploitation.

XIV

Parcelling, Postage, Sealing and Document Storage

As stringing of packages, sealing and postage are frequently subsequent operations to reading, writing, drawing, etc. it is advisable to read this section in conjunction with Section XVII, *Reading, Writing, Copying, Drawing etc.*

The evolution of postal services in Great Britain was very gradual. First mention of a postmaster in England occurs in 1533. The society of foreign merchants in London organized a service for the dispatch of foreign letters, to and from England, early in Elizabeth's reign; in 1568, the government established a State post office for foreign letters. Private, as opposed to official letters depended on private carriers until between 1632 and 1635, when internal postal services were instituted between the principal towns in the United Kingdom and fixed rates were decreed from a minimum of 2*d.* for up to 80 miles, 4*d.* to 140 miles, etc. During the 17th and much of the 18th century, the post office, although a state institution, farmed out or leased the postal service to a postmaster, in return for an annual rental payment. Between 1653 and 1677, rentals increased from £10,000 to £43,000 per annum. In 1680, Robert Murray and William Dockwra set up a 1*d.* post in the London area. Ralph Allen of Bath is the great name in the 18th-century

history of lessee postmasters. He invented, organized and put into operation the cross roads or cross post horse system in 1720, which greatly speeded up the post and increased post office revenue. His personal profits are said to have averaged £12,000 per annum, for 46 years, and he did much good with his wealth. In 1783, to try and cut down on mail robberies, John Palmer suggested to William Pitt changing the postal service from horsemen to mail coaches. Despite great opposition, the experiment was tried the following year and increased the average mail speed from 3 to 10 miles per hour, whilst decreasing robberies. By 1802, there were six daily postal deliveries in the London area, and from most parts of the country letters were dispatched to London twice daily. The London area rate had increased to 2*d.* and letters to the extremities of England and Wales cost up to 10*d.*, whilst remote parts of Scotland and the Orkneys were as much as 1*s.* 4*d.*, and to some parts of Ireland a letter could cost as much as 1*s.* 6*d.* The next development in carrying was the steam train, which speeded the post again, although postal rates were not reduced.

The really great name in the postal service, Rowland Hill, proposed reforms in 1837 which, after the usual opposition, were brought into effect in 1840. These included issue of the first postage stamps in the world and a universal penny post for letters up to ½ oz. to anywhere in the United Kingdom. A new Sir Rowland Hill is much overdue, to decrease mail robberies, to speed up and increase the number of deliveries and to lower postal rates.

Babla Pins—see *Pins*

Deed Racks

The solicitor's adjustable deed rack, Plate 209, *D*, probably remained in common use until the mid-19th century. Yet its purpose is now so entirely forgotten, that it is usually thought to be a textile winding device. The mahogany example illustrated, is English, early 19th-century; length is 11 in., width between uprights 4 in., height 11 in. and peg centres are at 1 in. intervals. Originally there would have been a number of pegs to separate the folded documents of one subject, or one client, from another.

Domestic Posting Boxes—see *Posting Boxes*

Pins

The earliest pins were probably thorn, sharpened wood and fish bones, but bronze pins have also been found during excavations of early dwellings in Egypt and neighbouring countries, and in Swiss lake dwellings. In India, Babla pins, Plate 213, *K*, made from natural thorns, and as sharp as any steel pin, are still gathered and used. Opinions differ on when metal pins were first imported to England from France and when they were first manufactured here, but all the experts agree that initially they were expensive and that 'pin money' was no mean allowance. It seems probable that pins were being imported into England, for the wealthy, as early as the 14th century. William Harrison, the Elizabethan chronicler, who is usually reliable in writing about his own times, said in 1587, that in

about 1572 '... Englishmen began to make all sorts of Pinnes, and at this day, they excell all nations'. This probably refers to brass pins, which held sway until well into the 19th century. Iron pins were made in England in the 15th century and Acts of 1483 and 1543 banned imports to encourage the home trade. Royal ladies, however, seem to have been above the law, and both Catherine of Aragon and Catherine Howard favoured French pins. Pins were a luxury in the 16th century and a particular New Year's gift. In Paris, no master pinmaker was allowed to open more than one shop for the sale of pins except on New Year's Eve and New Year's Day, when the husbands bought their wives pin allowances for the New Year. For further information on pins, see Section XXI, *Textile Workers' Devices*.

Posting Boxes

After 1840, when Sir Rowland Hill's post office reforms had established a cheap, regular and reliable service, letter writing increased rapidly. In 1840, 76 million letters went through the post; 1841, 169 million; 1850, 360 million; 1898, 2,186 million. In country houses remote from a post office, it became customary to have a posting box in the hall, which was emptied at intervals by a manservant, who rode to the nearest post office with the letters. These domestic letter boxes varied considerably in design and quality, but nearly all are alike in having a window in which were inserted times of collection and rates. Two neat and particularly high grade examples are illustrated, Plate 210; both are 16½ in. high. The delightful miniature of a street pillar box was registered as a design, by John Batson of Brewer Street, Golden Square, London, in 1872. It is of masur birch and has the posting compartment leather lined.

The box from Trowell Rectory, Nottinghamshire, is veneered with macassar ebony, lined with satinwood, has silver-plated fittings and was registered by Chapman,

Son & Co., of Aldersgate Street, in 1877. The clock was made by Charles Frodsham, 115 New Bond Street. This very restrained design does not look in the least like the fashion of 1877 and bearing in mind that Frodsham's did not move from 84 Strand to New Bond Street until the beginning of this century, I suggest that this posting box was really made between 1900 and 1910 and that Chapman continued to use his original registered design number to try and keep competitors from copying.

Scales

Domestic letter scales of brass, in Victorian times, were frequently made with postal rates engraved on them. There were two types—the pivoted balance used with a series of weights, stored in circular slots in a wooden base, and a moving beam type, also mounted on a wooden base.

Seal Boxes

Turned seal boxes, Plate 213, *W*, *X*, *Y* and *Z*, the last engine-turned, were usually of lignum vitae, but occasionally of boxwood, as *Z1*. They were presented by signet engravers to their customers and each box contained a specimen seal from the die ordered. The label most frequently found in the lid is that of Warrington & Co., of 23 Garrick Street, London, engravers to Queen Victoria.

Sealing Wax Outfits

Prior to 1840, gummed flap envelopes were unknown. Their acceptance was slow and for some years after, many people continued to fold and seal their writing paper with sealing wax or wafers (see *Signets* and *Wafer Signets*). Octagonally faceted, circular sealing wax outfits, decorated with Tunbridge wood mosaic, in 'Berlin wool' patterns, on rosewood ground, were popular in the 1840–50 period. Most of the Tunbridge makers sold them in a wide variety of mosaic patterns, and varying considerably in quality, and in diameter; heights range

between 3 in. and 4½ in., excluding the candle holder on the lid; Plate 209, *C*, may be considered typical. Inside the larger ones is a central circular compartment for the signet, with four radiating compartments for sealing wax and candles. The spirit lamp sealing outfit, Plate 209, *B*, has an 1833 hall-mark on the silver mount of the glass bottle. It is mounted on a boxwood pedestal, joined by the platform to a holder for the sealing wax. Two fluted rulers, illustrated Plate 267, *K* and *L*, have each a wafer signet at one end, and at the other end a candle holder which unscrews, forming a cap to a cavity for a candle.

Signets

The use of intaglio carved gems and other hardstones as signets was current in Babylon, Egypt, Assyria, Rome, etc., long before the Christian era. Signet rings have been fashionable ever since, and fob signets for men enjoyed a vogue in the 18th and 19th centuries. A signet may be required for two different purposes: (1) to act as a closure to a folded paper; (2) to authenticate or give legal force to a document. Personal domestic signets were essentials for the first purpose until the introduction of gummed envelopes, but they might also serve the second purpose. Signets were made of gold, silver, hardstone, etc., or with handles of wood, bone, ivory, etc., and the actual intaglio crest, monogram, initials, or name, usually engraved into hardstone, silver, brass, or steel. A selection is shown in Plate 213.

Usually, but not invariably, signets engraved in the manner described above, were for use in conjunction with sealing wax, but signets with a criss-cross pattern on the stamping end, which may be of silver or brass, or carved direct on wood end-grain, were for wafers. Wafers (see *Wafers and Water Boxes*) were small discs of flour, mixed with gum or gelatine which, when moistened, were used cold for sealing letters, attaching papers, or receiving the impression of a seal. Plate 213, *D*, *F*, *G*, *L* and *S* are all wafer signets; *F* is engraved with a monogram; the others have the more usual criss-cross pattern. *F*, *G* and *S* have cavities to hold a supply of wafers. The following are alphabetical descriptions of the wood-handled English signets, Plate 213. *A*, turned lignum vitae, 18th-century, was formerly in the Evan-Thomas Collection; *B*, ebony, mid-19th-century, has a centre compartment in the handle for sealing wax, with an outer ring for matches and a striker on the base; *C*, ornamentally turned lignum vitae, is mid-19th-century; *D*, an ornamentally turned boxwood and cut steel wafer signet, is also mid-19th-century; *E*, according to an old label on it, belonged to Lord Brougham and is silver-mounted and made from oak of York Minster. Many souvenirs were made from the oak of York Minster roof, following severe fires in 1829 and 1840. This seal was probably made following the 1829 fire, because Lord Brougham was living abroad most of the time after 1834. Another connection between Lord Brougham and seals is mentioned later in this heading. *F*, lignum vitae, 18th-century, has a cavity box for signets in the handle; it was formerly in the Evan-Thomas Collection. *G*, of lignum vitae, is also probably 18th-century and is similarly fitted; *H* and *J*, lignum vitae, silver-mounted, and boxwood respectively, are 18th-century; *L* and *M*, lantern and ball types, are probably both 18th-century; the former, with shoe handle, formerly in the Evan-Thomas Collection, may be Welsh. *N*, a silver-mounted hand grasping a ball, is probably 18th-century. The disagreeable looking man, *O*, is a good carving in boxwood, dated 1819, and is unusual in being unmounted and having the monogram of the signet engraved direct into the boxwood end grain. *P* is a fine, but not photogenic, 18th-century carving in ebony, silver-mounted; the subject is a wild cat pouncing on a bird. *Q*, dated 1791, has considerable character; the material is exceptionally

hard and heavy, but has grain and may be petrified wood or bone. *R*, 18th-century, is a silver-mounted natural root twist. *S* is a wafer seal with wafer box in the shoe.

It is not always possible to differentiate between a signet and a tobacco stopper (see Section XXII, *Tobacco Accessories*), although the former is usually a larger object with a larger base, and the initials, monogram or crest on a signet appear in reverse. But some signets and tobacco stoppers are approximately the same size and have no engraving on their bases, so they may have been used for either, or both purposes. I have also found wooden wafer signets with charred criss-cross pattern end, which have obviously been used as tobacco stoppers.

Important Corporation seals are usually matrices or hinged metal moulds, into which wax is poured. The mould of the Great Seal of England is freshly designed and made in silver at the beginning of each reign, when the old one is defaced. The present Great Seal is a direct descendant of the one made for Edward the Confessor more than 900 years ago. From 1761, when the office of Lord Keeper of the Great Seal was abolished, the Lord Chancellor has been the custodian. When Lord Brougham was Lord Chancellor, from 1830 to 1834, he was concerned in two curious episodes concerning The Great Seal. Lord Lyndhurst had been Lord Chancellor at the time of George IV's death, but had resigned with the rest of the Government. Lord Brougham became the new Lord Chancellor. It was customary for the old matrix to be given to the Lord Chancellor and both noble lords claimed it. The new King solved the problem by having the old matrix broken on the hinge line and one face presented to each claimant, set in a silver salver. In 1834, Lord Brougham visited Scotland during a parliamentary vacation; as was customary, he took the Great Seal with him. During a somewhat lively house party, Brougham, not so customarily, permitted the ladies to make pancakes in the matrix of the Great

Seal of England; William IV, when he learnt of it, was not amused!

Skippets

One of the earliest prizes in treen connected with writing, likely to come the way of a collector, is a skippet—usually a basin-shaped wooden box, turned and hollowed from a single block, and which was used for storing sealed and folded parchment documents throughout the Middle Ages and spasmodically until the 17th century. A very well preserved specimen, dating probably from the 16th or 17th century, is shown, Plate 209, A. This skippet measures $6\frac{3}{8}$ in. in diameter and $3\frac{1}{4}$ in. in height, but wooden examples exist from 2 in. in diameter up to approximately 10 in., and in *cuir bouilli* they were made considerably larger. The lids are secured by leather thongs, passing through holes in the lid and corresponding holes in the rim of the bowl. With the primitive woodworking tools of the mediaeval period, a well fitting, rectangular, plank box involved considerable labour (see Section XXIV, *Tools of Specialized Woodworkers*), and a large number of deed boxes must have been needed. This appears to be the only reason for producing skippets by the quick and inexpensive turnery method, for otherwise it does not seem logical to form comparatively deep circular bowls as storage receptacles for folded documents, particularly as the bases of turned skippets are always domed, making it almost impossible to stack one on another. Two small turned skippets in the Public Records Office, one $3\frac{1}{2}$ in. and the other $3\frac{3}{4}$ in. in diameter, dating respectively from the 14th and 13th century, have downward pointing nipples turned under the centres of their bases, making stacked storage even more difficult. I cannot imagine the reason for this deliberate feature, unless the boxes were centred and stood on woven rush rings, similar to those used for protecting the seals. Skippets are turned with the grain running vertical, which has ensured that they have remained round, but usually they have, in course of time, developed shakes round the perimeter. Another type of mediaeval, round or oval wood skippet, which had a flat base, was a bentwood box made from thin slivers of wood, bent round and riveted and with lid and base similarly thin. There were also two other alternative mediaeval containers for sealed documents, circular woven hampers of 'twyggys' (wicker hampers), and pouches or bags of canvas or leather, drawn tight with a cord or ribbon at the neck. Parchment records which had no seals attached were rolled up, and 'Keeper of the Rolls' is a very ancient office.

Stamp Boxes

Stamp boxes date from the 1840 period onwards. The Tunbridge wood mosaic makers, always quick to seize the opportunity of a new line, were rapidly off the mark and made some neat specimens, Plate 213, T, U and V. Sometimes, they have an actual 1d. stamp glued on as a centrepiece, like U, but the most interesting to the treen collector is one with the stamp, natural size, made in mosaic and containing no less than 1,000 tesserae in the Queen's head alone!

Stamp Dispensers

The need for an automatic stamp dispenser must have been felt soon after postage stamps were introduced by Sir Rowland Hill in 1840; a number of patents were taken out in the second half of the 19th century, for automatic vending machines for stamps and other small objects. The oak cabinet, $9\frac{1}{2}$ in. by $8\frac{1}{4}$ in., by $3\frac{3}{4}$ in., Plate 209, G, is one of the variants of John Gamgee's English Patent 2828, for an 'Automatic Vending Machine', Oct. 27, 1870. It was '. . . designed for the purpose of effecting the automatic sale in railway stations, exhibitions, bazaars, shops, or other public buildings or places, of small or essential objects'. Each compartment under the plate glass panel holds six pennyworth of stamps. When sixpence is inserted in the slot in the glass and the knob in front is pulled, the stamp-holding disc revolves and brings a loaded compartment round to the front opening in the glass. The dispenser is in full working order.

Stamp Perforators

The first 1840 postage stamps were not perforated; the wood-handled device, Plate 209, F, with sharp toothed revolving steel wheels, a stamp width apart, overcame the difficulty.

String Boxes

Until the end of the 18th century, cotton and silk were sold in skeins; it seems probable that the balling of string and the introduction of string boxes were only slightly earlier than the first commercial cotton reels of 1820. Plate 211 and 212 show a good selection of treen string boxes, mostly of the 19th century and all English except Plate 211, B. Plate 211, A, the primrose and gold painted lady, could well be the earliest specimen, circa 1800. Her companion, B, the Italian gentleman with string emerging from his cigar, is one of the latest, circa 1910. The apples, D and J, are somewhat uncommon as string boxes, and the sycamore egg in a lignum vitae cup, E, is very unusual. String 'barrels', F, G, H, K and L, were particularly popular in the 19th century; usually they have cutters on their taps. K is of boxwood, the others of lignum vitae. G with its ivory strip ornament dates from 1860–70, the other barrels, somewhat earlier. Small barrel string boxes and designs like O, were often made en suite with matching match boxes (see Section XI, Fire and Lighting). Both O and the sphere N, are of lignum vitae, probably mid-19th-century. In Plate 212, B, of lignum vitae, 7 in. high, is the most typical shop counter string box of the 1870–1900 period; it has a cutter blade on the knop. A, C, E, F and K are also lignum vitae, and good examples of mid-19th-century ornamental turnery. The helmet, D, spinning top, G, and acorn, J, are turned from masur birch. D pairs up with a helmet ink pot (see Section XVII, Reading, Writing, Copying, Drawing etc.), and G, bearing the label of Mascart of Baker St., and circa 1900, pairs with a match stand (see Section VI, Fire and Lighting). H, an unusual 19th-century, satin-wood box, is turned to represent a weight, with brass ring lift and insert cutter. L, burnt in simulation of tortoiseshell, probably dates from 1810–20. M, the beehive, and N, the 1887 Jubilee crown, are turned boxwood.

Wafer Signets and Water Seal Boxes
(see also Signets)

The wafer signet and water seal box, Plate 209, E, formerly in the Evan-Thomas Collection, probably dates from the 17th century and may be unique in wood. The water box and the metal-tipped signet are both of boxwood, the former inlaid flush with a continuous trellis binding of pewter.

XV

Pastimes

☆   ☆   ☆

Pastimes is probably a better heading than amusement, for a section hard to define and extremely broad in its scope. If anything, 'pastime' may be too wide a term, as according to the *Oxford Dictionary*, it covers 'That which serves to pass the time agreeably'. Certain other subjects in this book, such as stitchcraft and cookery, could, therefore, qualify as pastimes to some, but being laborious to others, are described under other headings.

To divide this section conveniently, I considered such sub-headings as Amusement — Adult; Amusement — Children; Board Games; Card Games; Toys; Sports, etc. Further reflection showed that no such divisions exist, and finally I decided on:

Indoor Pastimes

(1) Toys, Models, Miniature Objects and Miscellaneous Amusements.
(2) Games and Puzzles.

Outdoor Pastimes

(1) Ball Games and Miscellaneous Amusements.
(2) Archery, Hunting, Riding, Shooting, Skating, Luring, Decoying and Bird Scaring.

Even so, there are still not entirely clear lines of demarcation between indoor and outdoor amusements: merels, *bilboquet*, tops, etc., can all be played indoors or out.

Descriptions of such pursuits will be found under whichever heading appears to have been the most common usage in the past.

With a subject large enough for several books, it has been necessary to be extremely selective in this section; in general, more space has been given to pastimes which were popular in the past, but are now little known, than to those which are popular today and have changed little from the past.

As wood was the most common material for toys, and entered largely into the equipment of nearly all games and sports from the beginning of civilization until less than 100 years ago, only objects of stamped iron, moulded lead and plastic are outside the scope. Most of the latter are old objects in new dress; pastimes seem to be unchanging, although some of them only appear in fashionable cycles. Toys of fashion, either transient or recurrent, require distinguishing from basics, which are either unaffected or affected only in their trappings, from antiquity to the present day. Basics include balls, bats (in their widest sense), tops, hoops, skipping ropes, boats, spades, buckets, stilts, dolls, soldiers, animals, whistles, drums, etc.

Whilst no one can quarrel with pastimes which teach good manners or advance useful knowledge, one of the most bestial of man's outbreaks, from time to time, has been the use of toys for inculcating cruelty into children. I do not refer to soldiers, guns, etc., but to such calculated viciousness as the Nazi practice of giving to children, miniature knouts, whips and instruments of torture, to encourage race hatred in the young, and to the late 18th-century French Revolution miniature guillotines for beheading doll aristocrats.

In differentiating between toys and miniature objects, as distinct from games and puzzles, I have considered an object as a toy if you make up your own game with it. With games, there are rules, a programme and, with most, a spirit of individual or team rivalry and a desire to win. With a puzzle, there is a problem, and an urge to succeed in solving it.

INDOOR PASTIMES

Toys, Models, Miniature Objects and Miscellaneous Amusements

Many, probably the majority of toys, are miniature editions of human beings, the animal kingdom, and objects used by adults. Wooden toys have doubtless been made from early times, everywhere where there are trees. The Germans were the first in Europe to develop a woodland craft into a large export industry. They were also pioneers in cheap stamped metal toys, descendants of the moulded, flat-back, tin figures made by the Hilpert family of Nürnberg from 1775 onwards. From the 1840s, they were challenged increasingly by U.S.A. manufacturers. Until the end of the 19th century, British manufacturers were only dominant in the most expensive part of the wood and mechanical metal toy market. Now, in many branches, plastics particularly, they are second to none.

Henry Ford once declared that all history is bunk. So far as establishing where most *basic* toys originated, he was right. Who can say, with certainty, in what country children first played with tops, dolls, toy soldiers, etc.? The most one can ever determine is where a major advance occurred in the improvement of design, technique of manufacture, or conversion of a woodland or cottage craft into an industry. Toys are the permanent inhabitants of the kingdom of make-believe, in which children dwell for a brief spell, and to

which adults return from time to time, if they remain young in heart.

Animals
Miniature animals, whittled from wood, are among the earliest and generally the most unchanging toys in every civilized country. Periodically, stylized animals, such as Louis Wain's amusing 'Mew-Si-Cal Cats', *circa* 1910, which have a squeaker bellows behind each painted wooden figure, enjoy a short vogue, but after a time, children return to the traditional types. The ingenious method of making Noah's Ark animals is described under *Noah's Arks*; some details of Crandall type figures will be found under *Crandall's Patents*, and of Shoenhut circus animals under *Shoenhut Patents*. It seems probable that boxed sets of zoological animals, complete with cages, and sets of farm animals with hedges, fences, sheds and farm equipment, were both late 19th-century developments.

Automata—see *Moving Part and Mechanical Toys*

Baby Cages—see Section XXVII, *Tuition: Baby Cages*

Baby Houses—see *Dolls' Houses*

Balancing Toys

The simplest forms of balancing toys, based on a low centre of gravity, are figures with lead-weighted, half-ball bases, which always return to the upright after being knocked over. Some of the most ingenious are the many variants of the equilibrist on a high stool, right of Plate 217. By movement of the arms holding the weighted curved rod, the figure will lean forwards or backwards, pirouetting round on the stool, or it will hang by its toes. This type of ingenious toy probably developed in India, China and Burma; rather crude modern examples are being made in the West Indies. See also *Crandall's Patents* and *Schoenhut Patents*.

Crandall's Patents and Other Articulated Toys

Benjamin Potter Crandall, who manufactured baby carriages and toy prams from 1830 onwards, is best known for 'combed' interlocking letter blocks, known as 'Crandall's A.B.C. Building Slabs', patented 1867, and for various flat silhouetted, painted, articulated wooden figures, with riveted joints, made to stay in any desired position, and usually known nowadays as Crandall *type* figures. When Crandall's patents ran out, they were widely copied; except for certain known figures, such as the George Washington memorial figure of 1875, shown bottom right, Plate 214, John Gilpin and his horse and Crandall's acrobats of the same date (not illustrated), which balance on each other's heads and hands, it is difficult to know whether they are genuine Crandall's or not. There was, of course, no patent in riveted or pinned joints; it lay in the method of tonguing the figures into grooved stands and connecting them by means of tongues and grooves with each other, and also various objects, such as hats, stools, desks, etc. The figures in the top row, Plate 214, are from a set entitled 'The Village School', sold under the August 1877 registered trade mark of H. Jewitt & Co., of 27 Red Lion Square,

London, who were importers of fancy goods in the 1870s; they employ the Crandall principle.

Central in the middle and bottom rows, is a selection of Peter Pan articulated character figures, *circa* 1904. These do not have the Crandall grooved stands, nor do the dog, cat and rabbit (not a part of the set), bottom left. The large, comical and multi-jointed dog, is the ultimate development of the idea, with jointed and pivoted head and even jointed toes; it was probably made about 1910.

Dolls

Dolls are, perhaps, among the earliest playthings, but not all early miniature figures were dolls in the modern sense of the word. The Chinese tomb figures of the Han Dynasty and the Ushabti or miniature slave figures, to serve their masters in the hereafter, found in Egyptian tombs, are cases in point; so also are African fetish and fertility symbol dolls and witch dolls formerly used in many parts of the world. Dolls of Catholic countries are often really religious figures from nativity scenes—see Section X, *Miscellany*, *Presepio Figures*. Greek and Roman children had jointed wooden, baked clay and rag dolls. Wood seems to have been the principal material for dolls at least until the 19th century, although challenged in the upper price range by wax, papier mâché and china for heads.

Leslie Daiken considered that Dutch dolls, known in 17th- and 18th-century England as 'Flanders babies', and in America as 'peg dolls', really originated in the Thuringian Forest in Germany, like so many other wooden toys; *Deutsch* corrupted into Dutch, does sound the obvious answer. According to Lady Antonia Fraser's *A History of Toys*, the Nürnberg wooden doll makers were noted for jointed dolls early in the 15th century, and *Dockenmachers*, doll-makers, are mentioned in Nürnberg records of 1413. *Tocke*, which became *Docke*, originally meant a block of wood, so it is clear that the *Dockenmachers* were wooden doll makers. In that part of the world, *Docke* rather than *Puppe,* is still the more usual term for doll. The crude, rough, modern Dutch doll, with no joints at elbows or knees, is a very poor descendant of its long line of carefully modelled ancestors. However, it is cheap and, like the doll made from a clothes-peg, rags, wishbone and sealing wax, it is often preferred by rich as well as poor children, to the most expensively produced Pandora or fashionably dressed doll.

The doll stall keeper in the Victorian stall, Plate 215, is a Dutch doll, and some of her smaller sisters are shown on her counter; one, under 1 in. high and fully jointed, is so small that it does not show. I designed the stall and had it made as an appropriate background for displaying a number of miniature objects. Pedlar dolls, with baskets, trays or booths, began to appear in England about 1800 and were popular ornaments under glass shades, throughout the 19th century. They were rarely bought complete, but, like the example illustrated, were gradually assembled, sometimes to include miniature objects made by the owners.

Among the miniature objects in the top row, Plate 216, next to the 3*d.* piece, *D,* put in for scale, is a wonderful little American costume doll, *C,* the face and head made from a wheat-ear. *B* is a Swiss 19th-century, miniature carved pearwood peasant girl, with all her worldly possessions on her head.

In Plate 220 is an unusual example of a crying baby doll in swaddling clothes; the head is wax, the body of papier mâché. The wood bellows under the mattress, when pressed, actuates the mouth and produces the sound. I have no information on date or provenance, but assume it to be French or German, 19th-century. A clockwork swimming doll, with wood and metal limbs and cork-filled body and head, was made in Germany by Simon and Haltrig, about 1905. The cleverly designed Schoenhut

doll, Plate 217, is described under *Schoenhut Patents.* See also *Puppets,* and *Moving-part Toys.*

Dolls' Furniture—see *Models and Miniature Objects*

Dolls' Houses, Model Kitchens and Model Shops

Dolls' houses, until about 1850, were known as baby houses. They are believed to have originated in Germany and the Low Countries in the 16th century. A 17th-century dolls' house is preserved in the Historisches Museum, Basle, and among the unrivalled collection in the Bethnal Green Museum is a Nürnberg baby house dated 1673. Among many other outstanding specimens in the same museum, are the Tate baby house, *circa* 1760, another *circa* 1740, and the Dingley Hall house, *circa* 1874. Included in some wonderful examples in the London Museum, are the Blackett baby house, *circa* 1740, and the Lansdowne baby house, *circa* 1860; Queen Victoria's and Princess May of Teck's unpretentious dolls' houses, meant as playthings, are also there. Most of the other really outstanding examples still extant, also date from the 18th century or later, and generally those which come under the 'outstanding' heading, never were playthings: they were designed as scale models of houses or palaces, to be kept in cabinets or displayed in the drawing room. They were backgrounds for miniature works of art, attractions for guests and meant to be gazed on by children but, with few exceptions, not handled by them. They are now of tremendous historical value, not only architecturally, but because they faithfully mirror a forgotten background of living and, in certain instances, among the miniature objects are some of which no full-size prototypes are known to exist.

An outstanding 18th-century baby house, which was meant as a child's plaything, is the well-known Westbrook baby house, all of oak, including its arched stand, typical of the Queen Anne period. It was made in 1705 and presented to little Miss Westbrook of the Isle of Dogs; it is now owned by Mrs. Cyril Holland-Martin, one of her descendants. Other superb 18th-century baby houses in private collections, are the Uppark, Queen Anne period house and the slightly later Nostell Priory house; both are furnished with delightful scale models of their respective periods and there is a tradition that the young Chippendale, when a Yorkshire apprentice, made some of the miniature furniture at Nostell.

Twentieth-century miniature wonders include Titania's Palace, invented, designed and decorated by Sir Nevile Wilkinson, and the magnificent Batty dolls' house, made by T. Batty Esq., of Drighlington, near Bradford, between 1908 and 1930; it is at present on view on Brighton West Pier and is considered by many to rival Queen Mary's dolls' house, displayed at Windsor Castle. It is impossible, in a few words, to describe this latter masterpiece and if a visit is impossible, then resource should be had to the illustrated *Souvenir Book* and other literature mentioned therein. Suffice it to say, it is not a toy—it is a 1 in. scale model of an idealized royal palace of the 1920s, designed by Sir Edwin Lutyens and richly furnished and decorated, and with miniature pictures painted by some of the greatest artists of the day. It is perfect in detail down to the postage stamp size books in the library, toys in the nursery and the period royal cars in the garage.

Up to the end of the reign of George III, dolls' houses were exclusively the toys of wealthy homes, but during the 19th century, commercial production brought them into a much wider income group, and the dolls' houses, both made in England and imported from Germany, were designed as suitable backgrounds for dolls of working class, middle class and aristocrats. The dolls' houses, whether four-room or twelve-room, accurately reflected the low standards in architecture, decoration and furniture, but also mirrored improvements in comfort, such as the change over from hip baths, to baths with taps and plumbing.

Miniature furnished rooms, as opposed to complete houses, have as long, possibly a longer history than dolls' houses. The so-called Nürnberg kitchen, which was an educational plaything, to teach the child the elements of housewifery, was imported to England from both Germany and the Low Countries, from the 17th century onwards.

Miniature shops, like baby houses and miniature rooms, came under two headings —scale models, glass enclosed to be gazed at with admiration, or toys to be played with. Most of the latter, such as the grocer's, post office, sweet shop, pastrycook's, etc., are 19th-century or later commercial products; but the models, although probably produced earlier, have continued to be made to the present day, because model making is a fascinating pursuit—see also *Models*. I have no doubt that the miniature butcher's shop, Plate 219, made about 1920, gave as much pleasure to its creator as it does to viewers of all ages. The appropriately dressed butcher is entirely of carved and realistically painted wood, like everything else in the shop, except the miniature carving knife, steel, saw and hooks. The extreme accuracy of the equipment, and of the joints, pigs, rabbits, ducks, sausages, etc., suggests that this was made by a butcher, turned model maker, using odds and ends of wood and few tools. The case is 16 in. wide, 11 in. high and 9 in. deep.

Engines—see *Vehicles*

Equilibrists—see *Balancing Toys*

Forts

Children's forts presumably have as long a history as toy soldiers and men's fortresses and castles, but most of those surviving are 19th-century products, designed so that the base forms a box to hold turrets, curtain walls, ramps, draw-bridges, portcullis, etc. As one would expect of warlike toys, they are mostly of German manufacture.

Hoops and Minders

Hoops have probably been played with by children ever since the wheel was invented. Hoops are depicted on early Greek vases and in mediaeval European illustrations. In England, the traditional hoop is of steamed beech, and in my childhood, about 60 years ago, cost from 3*d*. to 6*d*., according to size. I think this included the wooden stick, or minder. Noisy iron hoops were controlled by a hook and handle apparatus, known as a skimmer. 'Hoop play' was a Victorian gymnastic exercise, part of training in deportment.

Jack-in-the-Boxes

Jack - in - the - Boxes, spring-compressed snakes, etc., in their present form, go back no more than 150 years, but an earlier form of the Jack, worked by cogs and a handle, probably originated in the Orient.

Jesters' Baubles

Jesters' baubles go back at least to the Middle Ages and must be considered more as an adult's than a child's toy. A good specimen, carved walnut, dating probably from the early 17th century, is shown, Plate 218, *A*. A jester was maintained at Glamis until near the end of the 18th century.

Jumping Jacks—see *Moving-part Toys*

Kites

Kite flying is a very ancient amusement and is believed to have originated in China, about the 3rd century B.C. Its fragile nature and low intrinsic value make the kite unlikely ever to become a collector's item.

Magic Lanterns—see Section XIX, *Scientific, Magic Lanterns*

Marionettes—see *Puppets*

Minders—see *Hoops*

Miniature Furniture—see *Models and Miniature Objects*

Model Kitchens—see *Dolls' Houses*

Model Shops—see *Dolls' Houses*

Models and Miniature Objects

Nearly all toys are miniatures of objects used by adults, but some are so small that they are miniatures of toys. Miniature objects, perhaps furniture more than most, exert fascination for children and adults alike. Dolls' houses, model kitchens and shops are discussed earlier under that heading. Some of the furnishings of a doll's house and the wares of a miniature shop are shown on the pedlar doll's stall, Plate 215. These include a miniature gramophone, dolls, tea sets, woodworkers' and painters' tools, shoes, soldiers, a tiny merry-go-round, etc., all of wood.

In general, model furniture tends to be larger than dolls' house furniture, but the scale alone does not settle the purpose for which the furniture was made, and although quality, or lack of it, often makes the intention clear, there are instances where it is a matter of opinion. Boxed suites of low grade, 19th-century and later, dolls' house furniture, make no pretensions of being scale models, but some better pieces, as shown bottom row of Plate 221, could be models or 'dolls' house'. The 3*d*. piece on the chest shows their scale. The beautiful little 18th-century mahogany piecrust table on pillar and four claws, is too delicate to be meant as a plaything. The miniature lyre-end work-table, fully fitted inside with mirror in lid, the three-drawer chest with marble top and the round dining table, which opens out concertina-wise, are all fragile and well made German models, yet they are known to have been the dolls' house playthings of Sara Rothschild, born 1840, at Frankfurt. The towel rail and high chair also, although not mass produced, are, I think, 19th-century dolls' furniture.

What of the larger pieces, top row, Plate 221? Many people would say models, not toys; but the oak chair-table and the continental wardrobe, although a cut above the general run of dolls' furniture and not too bad either as scale or period models, were mass produced not very long ago. The 18th-century, mahogany, scale model of a three-tier dumb waiter is in a different class. It is true to scale, beautifully made, and probably ranks as a toy of contemplation in an 18th-century baby house.

With Plate 222, the Victorian, walnut dressing table, $15\frac{1}{2}$ in. high and 12 in. wide, *circa* 1860, a splendid model of a hideous piece, we come to a rather specialized type of miniature furniture, which includes a lot of well made and finished, circular tip-up tables and other Victorian specialities. Here, there are four schools of opinion: (1) apprentices' passing-out pieces; (2) travellers' samples and shop window display objects; (3) toys; (4) models. In the furniture and joinery trades, it is most unlikely that the apprentice's passing-out piece ever existed. Actually, I believe this story is a hoary myth, so far as most trades are concerned. An apprentice became a journeyman by serving his time and thoroughly learning every branch of his trade; not only was there no need for a 'passing-out piece', but the employer would never have tolerated such waste of time during employment, and there were few hours of daylight which did not come into the employer's time. Most of the so-called apprentice pieces were made during the last 100 years. I have never heard of an apprentice's passing-out piece and when I first worked at the bench in the cabinet and joinery trades nearly 50 years ago, I worked alongside old men who had already been in the trade 50 years or more. None of them had ever made a passing-out piece, nor heard of the custom,

and as the further you go back in history, the harder was the manual worker's lot, you can be pretty sure that the woodworker's 'passing-out piece' is just romance. Some superb pieces of miniature furniture and joinery, particularly model staircases, were made at the bench by learners, but they were made by the boss's son or other relatives, as a pleasant training exercise, not by apprentices working hard in order to live. So we are left with travellers' samples and window displays, toys and models and, from experience, I would say that any of these three solutions may be correct of almost any piece. In my boyhood, I knew a retired Victorian furniture traveller who had a number of these models in his home, which he had carried in his travelling days; he also knew that they had been used for display in the days of small shop windows. I have met and, indeed, employed woodworkers who made model furniture, much too good really for playthings but, nevertheless, intended for their children's dolls. Finally, I have known several men, usually elderly and semi-retired, whose hobby it was to make models. One of the best modellers I ever met was a semi-retired solicitor, in whose workshop I spent many happy childhood hours watching as the most exquisite Queen Anne and Georgian bureau bookcases took shape under his skilled hands; he tooled the leather for the fall flaps, turned all the miniature draw knobs himself and did his own polishing. He also taught me that there is no such thing as an accurate $\frac{1}{8}$ scale model of a piece of antique furniture with small drawers. In a full size Queen Anne bureau of fine quality, stationery divisions may be only $\frac{1}{8}$ in. thick and the sides of the small drawers $\frac{1}{4}$ in. thick. To make the dovetailed drawer sides $\frac{1}{32}$ in. thick and the divisions $\frac{1}{64}$ in. thick in the model was obviously impractical.

Of the all-wood objects shown, Plate 216, *A*, is a traditional Salzburg peasant tree, whittled from a single piece of wood. *B* and

214 Crandall patent articulated wooden figures of the 1860–70 period and later figures based on the same principles—for details, see text. (*Section XV*)

215 Pedlar doll's stall. Most of the miniature objects are Victorian; the assembly is modern. (*Section XV*)

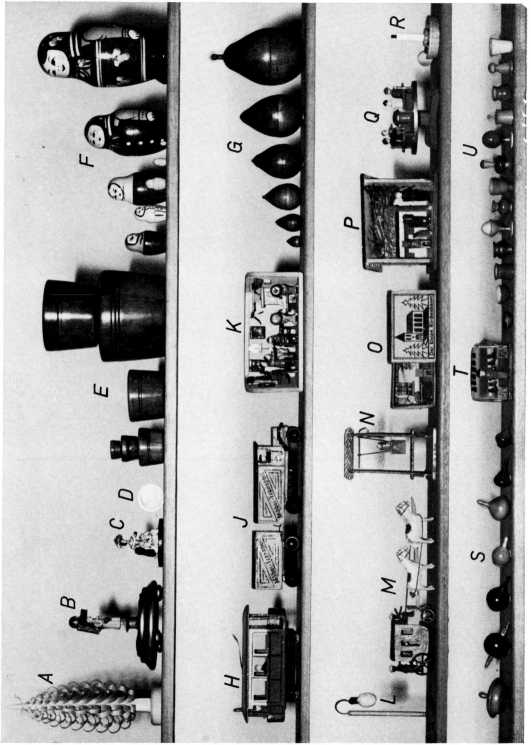

216 Models, miniature toys, tops, nests of toys, etc; 19th and early 20th century. The threepenny piece, *D*, gives the scale. (*Section XV*)

217 LEFT: Schoenhut's patent doll and circus animals, which stay in any position. RIGHT: the equilibrist was originally developed in the East. (*Section XV*)

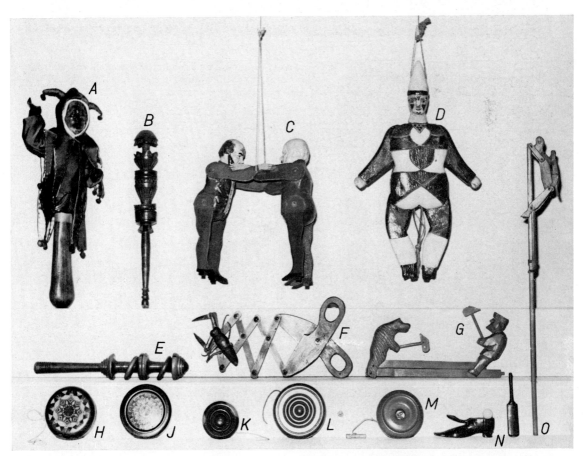

218 *A*, jester's bauble; *B* and *E*, rattles; *C*, political wrestlers; *D*, Jumping Jack; *F*, *G* and *O*, Victorian penny toys; *H*, *J*, *K* and *L*, yo-yos; *M*, warbler disc; *N*, miniature shoe trap and bat. (*Section XV*)

219 Victorian model butcher's shop, all carved from wood, except the knife, steel, saw, etc. (*Section XV*)

220 Crying baby doll, actuated by a bellows under the cushion. 19th century. (*Section XV*)

221   18th- and 19th-century model and doll's house furniture. (*Section XV*)

222   Model of a Victorian walnut dressing table, *circa* 1860. (*Section XV*)

223 Individually made, English 19th-century, oak weather cottage. (*Section XV*)

224 Victorian model fairground swing-boats, 'Ann' and 'John'. (*Section XV*)

225 Victorian child's fort money box; a coin placed on the soldier's head swings through the slot in the wall and rings a bell. (*Section XV*)

226 Noah's ark, Saxony made, *circa* 1840, with nearly 300 inmates. (*Section XV*)

227 Lathe profiled wooden rings, which show how the basic outlines of Noah's ark animals, etc., were cut from segments. *Photograph by courtesy of the Royal Botanic Gardens, Kew. (Section XV)*

228 Interior of a superb, 17th-century, inlaid games board from Eger, the backgammon side. (*Section XV*)

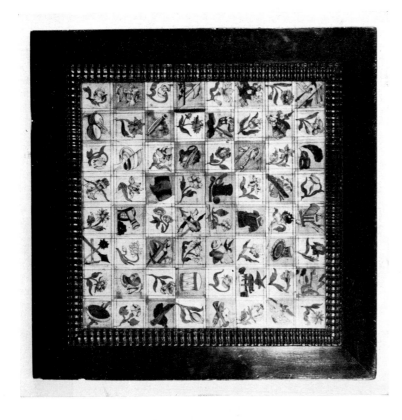

229 The inlaid draughts or chess side of the same board. (*Section XV*)

230 The relief carved inlay face of the same board. (*Section XV*)

231 On the left, 17th-century, die-stamped wooden draughts; right, the relief-carved light and dark draughts for the backgammon board, Plate 229. A, (*Section XV*)

232 Table croquet set; quoits; a variant of bagatelle; billiard cue collett; shove ha'penny board. (*Section XV*)

233 *A*, mentor's cards; *B* to *E*, dice cups; *F* and *G*, games markers; *H* and *K*, 19th-century and 17th-century card presses; *J* and *L*, chip carved domino and card boxes; *M*, *R* and *S*, cribbage boards; *N*, inlaid draughts; *O*, Pope Joan board; *P*, tee-totum ball; *Q*, box for 'chips'. (*Section XV*)

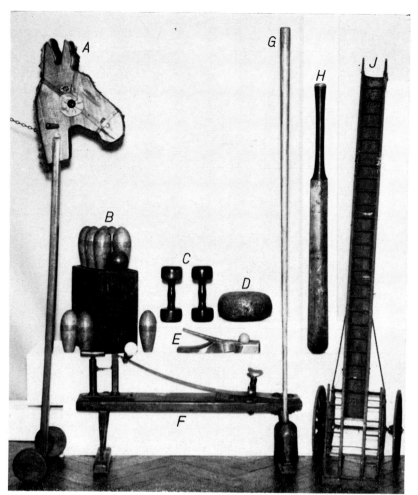

234 *A*, hobby-horse; *B*, skittles, dated 1796; *C*, lignum vitae dumb-bells; *D*, lignum vitae 'cheese'; *E*, shoe trap and ball; *F* and *G*, knur and spell; *H*, historic practice cricket bat from Cobham Hall; *J*, model fire escape and safety chute. (*Section XV*)

235 A giant English chess set, early 17th century. The kings are 12 in. high the pawns 7½ in. (*Section XV*)

236 *Principal Events in the History of England to the Reign of George III*—jig-saw puzzle published in 1815. (*Section XV*)

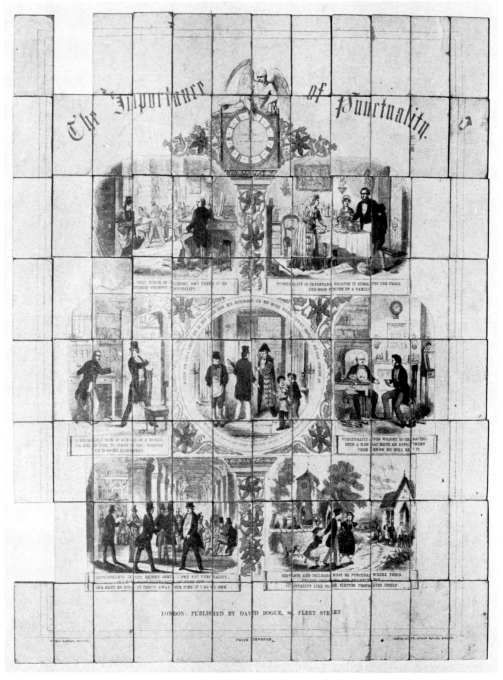

237 *The Importance of Punctuality*, a moralizing Victorian jig-saw puzzle. (*Section XV*)

238 and 239 An elegant French dicing machine, made by Charles Gallonde about 1739. *Photograph by courtesy of Sotheby & Co. (Section XV)*

240 Various games boards—for details, see text. (*Section XV*)

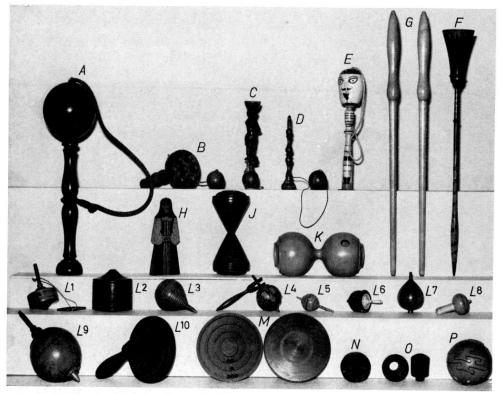

241 *A* to *E* and *F*, *bilboquets*; *G*, diavolo sticks and *J* and *K*, diavolos; *H*, Russian costume figure skittle; *L.1* to *L.10*, tops; *M*, 'Pigs in Clover' game; *N* and *O*, puzzle boxes; *P*, Chinese jigsaw puzzle ball. (*Section XV*)

C are described under *Dolls*. *D* is a 3*d.* piece to show the scale. *E*, *F* and *G* are nesting toys, traditional work of wood turners in many lands. *E*, the nest of six boxes, is Italian; *F*, the eight nesting dolls, are modern Russian versions of the traditional *Matreshka*; the pears, *G*, are Hungarian. The tram, *H*, lorry and trailer, *J*, room, *K*, lamp, *L*, coach, *M*, well, *N*, matchbox schoolroom, *O*, stable, *P*, roundabout, *Q*, and cobbler's shop, *T*, are German, *circa* 1930. Incidentally, a large range of German 'matchbox' wooden toys was made at that time. The chamber candlestick, *R*, is a modern English version of traditional dolls' house furnishing. The miniature tops, *S*, are described under *Tops*, and the brightly enamelled miniature turnery, *U*, some of paper thinness, is Indian made, late 19th century.

Models need not necessarily be highly finished to be charming. I think the gaily painted fairground swing boats 'John and Ann', Plate 224, prove this; they are suitably crude, but proper working models —a real joy to any child.

The 48 in. high fire escape and safety chute, Plate 234, *J*, is such a carefully made model that, although a delightful toy, it could well have been made for demonstration purposes.

Money Boxes, Children's
Money boxes in general are described in Section X, *Miscellany: Money Boxes*. Children's money boxes only differ in making the box itself attractive to the eyes of a child, or in introducing an element of fun into the placing of money into the slot. Under the first heading come boxes shaped as pigs and other animals, human faces, miniature furniture, etc. The second includes a wide range of brightly coloured, American made, 19th-century, mass produced iron boxes, formed as busts, each of which is provided with a moving hand, in which a coin is inserted; by pressure on a lever, the hand tilts the coin into the mouth of the figure.

An English variant is the individually made, 18th- or 19th-century, wooden toy, which has a pivoted balancing part on which a coin is placed. When the balance is swung, the coin passes into a slot, which may be the open mouth of an animal, or an aperture in a building, etc. An amusing 19th-century example is shown, Plate 225. The coin is placed on the flat head of the pivoting soldier; when he is set in motion, the coin jumps through the opening in the tower, simultaneously ringing a bell. Coins are removed by raising the flag, which elevates a door at the back of the castle.

Moving-part and Mechanical Toys
Moving-part toys originated in Europe as woodland crafts, but in Egypt, wooden crocodiles with moving jaws, and other toys on wheels have been found in tombs of 500 to 1100 B.C. They have, therefore, not only considerable antiquity, but also many of the forms are traditional and as popular today as they ever were. They first came to Great Britain from central and eastern Europe, but whether the familiar European types originated in Russia, Poland, Germany or other adjacent countries, is unknown. One of the oldest is the pecking chicks, in which the birds are arranged round a circular board, heads pointing inwards. In the centre of the board is a hole through which are passed guide strings from the chicks to a wooden ball suspended pendulum-wise; when a rotary movement is imparted to the ball, the chicks raise and lower their heads in realistic manner. Other popular variants are the Admiral, who climbs up a mast, the monkey on a stick, and the woodman and bear. The monkey, with a young one on its back, is shown, Plate 218, *O*; in my boyhood, I can remember being given one, cost 1*d.*, sold by one of the pavement sellers outside William Whiteley's in Westbourne Grove. The woodman and the bear, Plate 218, *G*, raise and lower their sledge hammers by pressure on the end of the baulk. The lobster, *F*,

opens and closes its claws by movement of the scissors handle of the lazy tongs.

The wooden Jumping Jack, Plate 218, *D*, actuated by pulling a cord and usually painted as a harlequin, goes back at least to the 18th century. The example illustrated has rather a poignant story. Some 90 years ago, an old, maimed sailor sat each day on the sands at Broadstairs, Kent, making Jumping Jacks, with the aid of a knife, some wood and tins of paint. It must have been a poor living, for it took him a day to make and paint each one in four colours, and with a face on each side. In 1880, a bride on her honeymoon was given this actual toy by her husband, and kept it over the years. Her son and grandson played with it, and when they went to live abroad, she still kept the toy of happy memories. In 1940, a bomb wrecked her London home. The old lady, then 80 years of age, told this tale to the warden who salvaged what was left of her possessions, including the Jumping Jack, which she insisted he should have. The warden's children played with it, and after they grew up, he offered it to us in 1960. In 1962, we were given another almost identical one, also with the tradition of the maimed sailor maker. Now two still strong and agile Jacks, children of the old sailor's skill, are able to jump together in unison again.

The wrestlers, Plate 218, *C*, depicting Mr. Gladstone and Lord Derby, brought politics into the English nursery in the 1860s. I suspect, however, that these were German toys, because there were variants of the personalities suitable for different countries and one pair with international appeal, entitled 'The Two Strongest Men in the World', was sold by Albert Mayer, importer of continental novelties, 63 St. Paul's Churchyard, London, E.C.

Mechanical toys, as opposed to moving-part toys, have a very long history, going back to Hero of Alexandria, who invented and produced mechanical toys worked by heat, water and mercury; in some of his devices, he employed pneumatic and hydraulic action.

In the 18th century, the French held supremacy in elaborate and expensive automata, usually dressed wooden figures, worked by clockwork. In the 19th century, the Germans, Americans and Japanese entered the market and soon produced much more popularly priced mechanical toys. From the 1870s, vulcanised rubber springs were combined with wheels and escapements to give more natural movements to automata.

Musical Boxes
Small, wood encased musical boxes, brightly painted or decorated with coloured pictures, and actuated by a cranked handle, date from the 19th century onwards. They were mostly made in Switzerland and Germany.

Nesting Toys—see *Models and Miniature Objects*

Noah's Arks
The Noah's Ark occupied a privileged place in the Victorian home. It was the one toy which was not kept in the nursery. For six days of the week, it usually reposed in a cupboard in one of the 'grown-up' rooms. On Sunday, the seventh day, it emerged to tell its enthralling bible story to generation after generation. It is true that, as the years passed, the dove with olive branch, painted on the roof, gradually became shabby; Noah, Shem, Ham and their wives and all the beasts, birds and insects inside the ark, gradually declined in number; some lost limbs and other members, and usually they acquired tooth marks on their 'suculent' paint. Being a 'once-a-week' toy, an ark may survive the hands of three or four generations and still be complete enough to delight yet more. A few years ago, Mrs. Pinto and I were given the ark, Plate 226, which had been in one family for at least three generations and was probably made

about 1840. It is still wonderfully complete and it seems remarkable that nearly 300 creatures can pack into such a small space; but they do, although when arranged in their pairs, with a small space between each couple, they stretch in a line for 30 ft. from the ark. The carved wooden figures in this particular ark cover a wider range than in most, for in addition to the usual quadrupeds, ranging from giraffes and elephants down to dogs and badgers, there is also a wide selection of monkeys and birds and, from the insect world, beetles, spiders, grasshoppers and ladybirds; only the reptiles are unrepresented. As is usual, there is a glorious disregard of scale, which becomes particularly apparent when a ladybird is placed alongside an elephant.

These wooden playthings of yesterday, which are said to have originated at Oberammergau in the 16th century, were mostly made in Saxony, throughout the 19th and early 20th centuries. The method of forming the animals was most ingenious and by no means as lengthy nor as arduous as might at first be thought, for the animal outlines, as shown, Plate 227, were 'turned' on a lathe. A circular ring, cut to the basic profile of each animal, was turned from softwood. The head end was always at the inner edge of the circle, because the head end is always narrower than the tail end, so when the animals were rough sawn out of the segments, they automatically appeared the correct shape. This method eliminated a lot of the rough work, but left legs still had to be separated from rights and various sharpening up of features had to be carved; tails, ears and horns also had to be carved, inserted and glued into holes and finally the clever and intricate painting had to be done. So eventually, in spite of the degree of mechanization imparted by the lathe, the amount of handwork, at increasing rates of pay, made the production uneconomic and the old industry virtually died out and gave way to the moulded toy. During the Napoleonic wars, some attractive straw-work arks, with hand-carved animals, were made for sale by French prisoners-of-war at Norman Cross and other English prisons.

Optic Devices—see Section XIX, *Scientific: Optics*

Perambulators—see *Vehicles*

Puppets

Puppets are figures, until recently largely or wholly of wood, and actuated in one manner or another by human agency. They may conveniently be divided into four types, all of which were probably known in the early Mediterranean civilizations. Hand or glove puppets are the simplest type and, for the travelling showman, have the great advantage of taking up little space. For slapstick comedy, such as Punch and Judy, they need and have solid wooden heads, but for more delicate artistry, the heads may be papier mâché. A loose garment is attached to the head and the manipulator inserts his arm into this, in such a manner that the forefinger goes into a hole in the base of the head and his thumb and second finger each control one of the wooden hands. Punch, a descendant of the 16th-century Italian *Pulcinella*, on coming to England in the 17th century, became blended with *Vice* of the morality plays and the mediaeval *Fool*; eventually he became completely anglicised by marriage with Judy, association with the dog Toby, the policeman and Jack Ketch, the hangman; he still remained, however, a popular and unrepentant old blackguard.

Rod puppets are basically the same, but larger and with the head mounted on a rod, smaller rods going to the arms, thus allowing the operator to control his puppets without raising his arms above stage level.

Marionettes are multi-jointed puppets, controlled by strings, held by the operator above the proscenium opening. A well constructed marionette, with its nine or more strings attached to the 'crutch' held by a skilled operator, can be made to imitate, in miniature, all the antics of man or animal. In the 18th century, special marionette theatres were built in great houses and the palaces of the nobility in several European countries and there were several marionette theatres in the west end of London. In the Middle Ages, marionettes were used in church morality plays, but even then, there was a long tradition behind them, dating back to pagan times.

Shadow puppets are flat cut-out figures, usually but not necessarily Oriental in style. They are made on the same principle as Crandall figures (see *Crandall's Patents*), but loosely jointed and string controlled. They are manipulated between a translucent screen and a strong light, in such manner that only their shadows are visible to the audience. Their origin and their cult is mostly confined to the East and Middle East, where they are said to have great antiquity. They probably originated in Indonesia.

Rattles

In countries where they thrive, gourds were possibly the first baby rattles. Because a rattle so often finds its way into a baby's mouth and acts as a tooth cutter, wood was not a favoured material, but two wooden baby rattles, turned with loose rings, are illustrated, Plate 218, *B* and *E*. The first is Swiss or Tyrolean and the second, English; both are probably 19th-century.

Rocking Horses

It appears from old engravings, that the rocking horse developed early in the 17th century and that at first, it was a boxed, flat topped, wooden rocker, with a seat at the rear and a horsehead mounted in front. Before the century ended, the rich child's nursery toy was a realistic steed, mounted on a rocking sledge, but cruder types were still made throughout the 18th century. The 19th century saw the development of the modern type on stand, which 'gallops' on two parallel iron pivots.

Schoenhut Patents

Albert Schoenhut, a descendant of a family of German doll makers, made a great name in the U.S.A., from the 1870s onwards, with his balancing toys. His first major success was with ball-jointed animals, tensioned by elastic, Plate 217. These he developed into his popular 'Humpty-Dumpty Circus', which enabled a child to arrange any number of wooden circus figures, animals and equipment, in any pose or act which they had seen performed at a real circus. His final triumph was the Schoenhut carved wooden doll, Plate 217, with spring-loaded universal joints, U.S.A. Patent, January 17, 1911.

Soldiers

Until the coming of the stamped tin and moulded lead soldier, now largely superseded by plastics, wooden soldiers reigned supreme. They were largely made in the Thuringian forest belts and other well wooded areas of central and eastern Europe, by the makers of Noah's Ark figures and animals. In spite of mass production competition from other materials, turned wooden soldiers are still being made.

Theatres

The familiar terms 'Penny Plain, Tuppence Coloured' originated in Regency England as a description of cards depicting actors and actresses, famous at the time. In fact, they were early 'pin-ups', often decorated with tinsel, silk, satin, velvet, etc. Later, the description was applied to the toy cardboard and wooden theatres and their characters, covered in printed coloured paper, but except for very small ones, these cost shillings, not pence. They reached zeniths of popularity in the 1830s, 1870s and around 1900. Toy theatres might be models of a particular London theatre with all the cast of a popular production, movable from above on hooked wires. In my childhood nursery, a model of the old Savoy Theatre, probably made between 1885 and 1900, by the noted Pollock family, with the cast of 'The Mikado', still delighted my sisters and me in the first decade of this century.

Tops

Tops rank among the eternal unchanging toys. Children have probably played with them ever since pines grew cones and cone-shaped stones have existed. The most satisfying are those turned from box, lignum vitae or other suitable hardwoods. As bas-reliefs and yields from excavations have shown, tops have been spun in every civilization, and all the recognized types were defined at early dates. Plate 216, *S*, shows a selection of small examples in ebony, boxwood and lignum vitae. Larger ones, of similar types, are illustrated, Plate 241, *L*. *L1*, *4*, *5*, *6* and *9* are humming tops, probably all dating from the first half of the 19th century; *L1* and *9* are boxwood; *L4* is Tunbridge stickware mosaic, rather too delicate a construction for the hard life of a top, and few of this manufacture survive. *L5*, also made at Tunbridge, has early 19th-century painted decoration. *L10*, of mahogany, winds with a winder, like a humming top, but is a solid disc-top and probably 18th-century. *L2* is a Regency, rosewood, whipping top, inlaid with mother-of-pearl. *L3* and *L7* are the unchanging type of peg top; the first has an inlaid mother-of-pearl disc, similar to *L2* and may be the work of the same turner.

Toy Shops

Until the mid-19th century, rich markets for French and German miniature dolls and furnishings for dolls' houses were the stalls of Lowther Arcade, stretching from west Strand to Adelaide Street (later Gatti's Restaurant), Soho Bazaar, Cremer's Toy Warehouses in New Bond Street and Regent Street, and Hamley's of High Hol-

born, who moved to Regent Street in 1892.

Trains

Model wooden trains were on sale in England in the 1840s. Except for large engines and tenders, which a child could pull along outdoors, or pedal himself in, the wooden toy train was soon superseded by metal. It is open to question anyway, whether a train ranks as a boy's toy, or his father's!

Tumbler Toys—see *Balancing Toys*

Vehicles

Wooden toys on wheels were known in Egypt more than 1,000 years B.C. Since then, miniature vehicles of every kind and period and some of no period—just boxes on wheels—have delighted children of succeeding generations. Many of the most attractive miniature wheeled vehicles are models of regional types, such as the gaily painted Sicilian carts with plumed horses, Oriental rickshaws and various Indian toy conveyances. One of the most popular vehicles of all, which may count as an indoor or outdoor toy, the doll's pram, does not appear to have been produced, other than as an extreme luxury, before the 1830s. Not until the 1850s did the name perambulator, hitherto an alternative name for the waywiser (see Section XIX, *Scientific: Dial Registers*), become the common name for a baby carriage.

Weather Cottages

The more or less standardised Swiss or Tyrolean weather cottage, with its little man with umbrella and his wife in summer attire, are too well known to need description. The device is really a hygrometer, with two figures, serving as pointers, actuated by an arrangement of a bunch of hairs, which lengthen or shorten due to changing atmospheric humidity. An English, 19th-century, hand-made version is illustrated, Plate 223.

Indoor Games and Puzzles

The majority of indoor table games, in which wood is the predominant material, are board games. As the term implies, the board is or was originally of wood, and the words board and table were, to some extent interchangeable in mediaeval times, when table meant the top only, as distinct from the separate trestles which supported it.

In mediaeval documents, the term 'tables' at first meant the game of backgammon; soon it applied to chess also and before 1500, it had become the generic term for both. In 17th-century documents, 'playing at tables' may mean almost any game played on a board or table. The divisions, colourings, or markings on one board may serve several games—chess, draughts, etc. The pieces or 'men' likewise, may be used for several games—draughts, backgammon, etc. For this reason, boards and the pieces or 'men' are described separately.

Methods of 'dressing' boards, rules, scores and procedure in play of board games, are outside the scope of this work.

Backgammon

Backgammon, which has a history of more than 1,200 years, was known throughout Asia as *Nard* in early mediaeval times and was introduced to Europe by the Arabs, via Spain, in the 13th century. At first it was called Tables in England (*Tric-Trac* in France); it acquired its present name in the 17th or early 18th century. It is a game for two players, using draughts on a board consisting of two parts or tables, each inlaid or otherwise marked out with twelve points. The moves are made by the two players, one using light and the other dark draughts, and each alternately throwing two dice. As a raised bar between the two tables is a feature of the game, it is usual for the backgammon board to consist of two hinged 'wells' which, when closed, hold the draughts, cups and dice, and when open

have the backgammon board inside and a draught/chess board on the outside. In the 18th century, and still more during the Regency period, games tables were made with draught board tops and a well below for backgammon. In the 19th century, there was a vogue for leather-covered boards, designed to simulate two large books when closed.

A superb 17th-century Eger inlaid backgammon board is illustrated, Plate 228. For further details of this fine example, see *Eger Work*.

Bagatelle

Bagatelle is played on an oblong baize-covered table, varying from 6 ft. to 10 ft. in length and 1½ ft. to 3 ft. in width. At the semicircular upper end are nine numbered cups or holes, into which it is the objective of the player, using a cue, to drive eight white and one red ball. There are many variants of bagatelle with additional hazards; in Cockamaroo or Russian bagatelle, the ball is driven through an arrangement of pins, holes, arches and bells. One of the variants, probably intended as a children's game in the first half of the 19th century, is illustrated, centre of Plate 232. The pine board is attractively covered with marbled paper on the outside, and inside with coloured prints in mock Japanese style. See also *Billiard Accessories*.

Billiard Accessories

Billiards is believed originally to have been an outdoor game, played on a lawn. When it came indoors, not later than 1429 in France, it retained its grass green as a cloth covering for the table. Elizabethan inventories show that various noblemen in England possessed billiard tables in the 1580s. After the Restoration, billiards became a popular game and references to playing the game occur several times in Pepys' *Diary*, whilst Celia Fiennes and Daniel Defoe note various billiard tables in the course of their tours. At least two 17th-century, English billiard tables have survived. A description of how to make a billiard table is included in Robert Howlett's *The School of Recreation,* published in 1684. Actual 18th-century examples are not much more numerous than 17th-century; the Parham billiard table, made about 1750 and now at Temple Newsam, is probably the finest English, 18th-century example extant. Of particular interest are the two maces or cues, one stamped Metcalf, which appear to be contemporary with the table. They are approximately 4 ft. 6 in. long and terminate in wide, paddle shaped shoes, curved in section; one is of lignum vitae, the other lignum vitae laminated on to box. They are almost identical to the mace which is with the 1690 billiard table at Knole, and have a close family resemblance to those shown in the well-known 1694 engraving of Louis XIV playing billiards. Evidently the change to the straight, tapering cue did not occur until after the mid-18th century.

Nineteenth-century wooden bygones of billiards include not only cues, but also boxes for cue tips, sometimes bearing makers' names, and boxwood colletts for holding billiard cues with captive chained file, for working through slots to roughen the end of the cue—see Plate 232, right of the miniature pin-table. Quite common are score boards to screw on the wall, and billiard cue racks, sometimes combined with a boat or shell shaped stand, to hold chalk.

Boat Game—see *Boat Puzzle,* under *Puzzles, Miscellaneous*

Cards and Card Accessories—see *Playing Cards*

Carpet Bowls—see *Bowls,* under *Outdoor Pastimes*

Chess and Draught Boards
Square boards, inlaid or otherwise marked out with 64 alternate light and dark squares, are used for chess and draughts and for other games, including fox and geese. They were sometimes known as chequer boards and have great antiquity, but when and where they originated is unknown. The name 'Chequers' for inns denotes that the game was formerly available there for patrons. During the 17th and 18th centuries particularly, some very fine inlaid boards were made, embellished with low relief carving on the borders. Many of the boards, from the 17th century onwards, are hinged to form a double box, or two wells; draughts or chess are played on the flush side and the wells are marked out for backgammon (see *Backgammon*). A very fine 17th-century board of this type is illustrated, Plates 228–230. For details, see *Eger Work*. An outsize, crude, but interesting board is illustrated, Plate 235, and described under *Chessmen*.

Chessmen
In chess, the board, with 64 alternating light and dark squares, is arranged so that a light square is on the right of each of the players, sitting opposite each other. Chess is believed to have originated in India in the 6th century A.D. and to have been introduced to southern Europe by the Moroccan Arabs, in the 8th or 9th century. It is claimed that the Normans introduced it to the British Isles in the second half of the 11th century. The date may well be about right, but bearing in mind the sophistication of the hoard of 12th-century, walrus ivory chessmen found in 1831 in the Isle of Lewis, it seems just as likely that chess came to Britain from Scandinavia. The Lewis chessmen are now divided between the British Museum and the National Museum of Antiquities of Scotland, Edinburgh.

Chess has long been played in every civilized country and chessmen have been carved in many varieties of hardwood, common and semi-precious stone, ivory, bone and amber, and made from silver, bronze, pewter, brass, enamel on copper, porcelain, pottery and glass. The dividing of the opposing sets into armies seems to have occurred at an early date, with both foot soldiers and cavalry and the royalty of the countries concerned sometimes realistically depicted. But not all sets have a military bias; some depict immortals, others the king and queen and their court, or characters from plays, or animals; bears are particularly popular in eastern Europe.

Some sets rank as major works of art, whilst at the other end of the scale are the gigantic chessmen and table, Plate 235, very satisfying in their bold but simple turning. Their scale is such that they might have served the inhabitants of Brobdingnag. This rare set is English and dates from early in the 17th century. Probably they were used in some 'great hall', where they would have looked appropriate. The size of the 'men' has to be seen to be believed; the dimensions are as follows:

Kings	12 in. high by $3\frac{1}{4}$ in. diameter.
Queens	$10\frac{1}{4}$ in. high by 3 in. diameter.
Bishops	$9\frac{1}{4}$ in. high by $2\frac{5}{8}$ in. diameter.
Castles	9 in. high by 3 in. diameter.
Knights	8 in. high by $2\frac{3}{4}$ in. diameter.
Pawns	$7\frac{1}{2}$ in. high by $2\frac{3}{4}$ in. diameter.

The set is complete and in a remarkably fine state of preservation. It has suffered from worm at some time, some pieces have split as the result of unequal shrinkage and there are a few replacements, but substantially it is as made, some 350 years ago. All the 'white' and most of the 'black' men are beech, but some of the latter are ash. Time has faded the 'blacks' and darkened the 'whites' until now it is difficult to distinguish some of the one from the other.

The table is most interesting; it measures 3 ft. 5 in. square, with each of its squares $4\frac{1}{2}$ in. across. The board is of adze-finished pine, the underframing of oak. There is no doubt of the age of either, but I am sure that they did not start life together, al-

though the board is screwed to the framing by old, hand-made screws. I think that the underframing was cut down to support the top, which originally was a loose board. The underside of the pine board is inlaid with an inner and outer square of banding, typical of the borders of Nonsuch chests, made between 1580 and 1640. It may denote that someone of that period had an inlaid table top or board and found it convenient to make a chess board on the reverse side, for all the squares are applied and are about $\frac{3}{16}$ in. thick, or it may have been made originally as a reversible board and ornamental table top, or as the lid of a box for the chessmen. It is also possible that the inner and outer squares of inlay are not mere ornament, but were used in some now forgotten game.

Cockamaroo—see *Bagatelle*

Counters and Counter Boxes
Until recently, when plastics have largely taken over, counters and 'fish' have usually been made of bone, ivory, mother-of-pearl, and metal, rather than of wood. Some of the wooden cases or caskets for counters are, however, worth collecting. A good 19th-century, cushion-topped, heart-shaped casket of pearwood is shown, Plate 233, Q; the cavities for eight oblong and eight circular engraved ivory counters are hollowed out of the solid.

Cribbage
Cribbage, an essentially English game, is said to have been invented by Sir John Suckling, the poet (1609–42); it is really an improved version of an older game called noddy and is a card game for two to five persons. The interest for the treen collector is in the cribbage boards or markers, which are extremely diverse and attractive. The boards may be oblong, oval, square, triangular or round, and are provided with holes in which the bone or ivory score pegs are inserted. Three examples are illustrated,

Plate 233, *M*, *R* and *S*. The first is a 19th-century, Tunbridge mosaic example, inlaid with various colours; it is 12¾ in. long, with peg cavity in one end. *R*, probably 18th-century, mahogany, has a peg receptacle below the bowl. *S*, *circa* 1780, is a very good quality, Tunbridge inlaid (not mosaic) specimen, formerly in the Evan-Thomas Collection. It is 7¼ in. long, with small peg drawer in the base. Cribbage and other games boxes and markers were a Tunbridge speciality. Some Tunbridge mosaic boxes for card games in general, have inlaid cribbage marker boards forming the lids. See also *Games Markers*.

Dice and Dice Cups

Dice cubes, marked in dots 1 to 6, have been used for gambling from the earliest times. Dice of baked clay, stone and ivory have been found in early Egyptian tombs. Herodotus mentions dice among the games played by the Lydians and dice have been excavated from numerous sites of early civilizations. In one of the *Bokes of Curtasye*, written about 1430, advice is given to avoid dice-playing and warnings were plentiful throughout the Middle Ages. Boxwood and blackwood dice are not uncommon, but seldom appear to have much age, early ones being mostly of the other materials already mentioned.

Many cylindric vessels described as dice cups, are not really so. A true dice cup has a multiplicity of grooved rings inside, no particular number; these rings catch the angles of the cubes when shaken and cause them to turn. A selection of 18th- and 19th-century dice cups of lignum vitae, boxwood and ebony, is illustrated, Plate 233, *B* to *E*. A screw-lidded dice barrel, for travelling or pocket use, is shown at *T*.

Dice are now used almost entirely for deciding moves in the play of a game, but formerly hazard, which is purely dicing, was a popular and sometimes expensive gambling game of chance. Many people have lost fortunes at it, and not only

through loaded dice. Although there are 36 possible combinations in the fall of two dice, the chances of each of them turning up are not equal: 2 and 12 can be obtained by only one combination; 3 and 11 by two combinations; 4 and 10 by three combinations, and 7 by six combinations, so it is as well to realize this before betting on dice! See also *Teetotums*.

A most elegant dicing machine, French, mid-18th century, really a forerunner of the one-armed bandit, recently came to light; it is illustrated, Plates 238 and 239. The curvaceous casket is veneered with kingwood and ormolu mounted; the beautifully finished interior mechanism is probably by Charles Gallonde, clockmaker and designer of scientific instruments, who worked between 1737 and 1775. A similar device by him, signed and dated 1739, has been recorded. When either of two cords, at the side of the casket, are pulled, three dice cylinders revolve, and on coming to rest, show their faces in three openings.

Dominoes

The origin of dominoes is unknown, but all authorities are agreed that they were used in Italy at the beginning of the 18th century and found their way thence to other countries. A complete set consists of 28 oblong 'stones', each divided into squares and marked from double blank to double six. The numbers are formed in black dots engraved on to ivory or bone, which is backed by ebony or blackwood. Some of the boxes are attractive, such as the chip carved, Welsh box with sliding lid, probably 18th-century, Plate 233, *J*; it is gouged out of a solid block, divided into two unequal compartments for dominoes and dice, each enclosed by a separate sliding lid.

Draughts

Draughts is a very ancient game, for which the present rules and the 64 squares board (see *Chess and Draughts Boards*), are believed to have become standardized in the 11th century. Homer, in the first book of *Odyssey*, describes something which sounds uncommonly like draughts, as the game which the suitors of Penelope played. Rameses III, in a relief in Thebes, is depicted playing draughts with a lady. The opponents in the game use 12 'black' and 12 'white' draughts respectively, but the draughts being usually of wood, are more correctly described as dark and light, and in some ancient specimens, there is now not much difference of colour between the opposing 'men'.

Unlike the simply moulded boxwood and ebony draughts generally in use from the 19th century onwards, earlier draughts are individually designed and ornamented by die stamping, carving or, even more rarely, by inlaying. The two lines of draughts, five light and five dark, left of Plate 231, are $2\frac{1}{4}$ in. in diameter, date from the late 16th and early 17th centuries, and were pressed from medal dies, each commemorating a different event. They are mainly German and most of them bear dates between 1590 and 1700, and inscriptions in German, Latin and French. Draughts of this period were often turned and pressed or carved from a single block, but these particular specimens, and the others comprising the set, consist of two separate plaques, held apart by a centre tongue which is a part of the turned rim. The complete set of 2 in. diameter, finely carved, 17th-century draughts, right of Plate 231, belongs to the backgammon board, Plate 228, and is described under *Eger Work*.

The inlaid draughts, Plate 233, *N*, are most unusual and must have been the work of a patient and skilful inlayer and turner. He managed to work out 30 different combinations of circles and segments in woods of various colours, sometimes combined with ivory or mother-of-pearl. Each draught has a central hole at the back, and fits on to a peg on the mahogany stand. The set may be 18th- or 19th-century. Early sets of draughts sometimes have the 'whites' of

bone or ivory and the 'blacks' of wood or jet; pottery and coloured glass sets have also been made.

Écarté Boxes

Écarté, a card game traceable back to early in the 16th century in France, only became popular in England during the Regency. Shallow, cushion-topped, oblong boxes, with lids curved down to the four corners and made to hold 32 cards (the 2, 3, 4, 5 and 6 of each suit are removed), 16 each side of a centre division, were imported from France. These boxes, extremely well made, are usually veneered with burr maple or satinwood, with one or two lines of glittering faceted marquisite studs forming a border to the lid and, in the centre, the word écarté, also in marquisite.

Eger Work

During the 17th century, the small city of Eger, in the western corner of Bohemia, was the centre for a highly skilled group of specialist craftsmen in relief marquetry. Whilst marquetry or intarsia is normally flat, the Eger craftsmen built up their pictures from a carefully selected palette of hardwoods of different colours and markings, about $\frac{1}{4}$ in. thick, which they glued on to a suitable background, and then carved and contoured their pictures, creating a rich combination of relief and marquetry. Sometimes in a scene, the foreground figures only are emphasized by relief carving and the more distant background is left in conventional flat intarsia. The technique enabled the depiction of human figures and costume to be much more realistic than with flat intarsia. In consequence, the Eger workshops rather specialized in crowd scene panels. In a mythological, court, or biblical scene, the ladies sometimes have necklaces, ear-rings and hair ornaments inlaid in silver; in an animated battle scene, set against a landscape with distant castles, the warriors will have their shields inlaid with silver. These rich and elaborate relief panels were mainly used for altar fronts, doors and drawer fronts of cabinets and caskets, and the exteriors of draughts, chess and backgammon boards. The panels were usually framed in pearwood, stained black, and finished with the characteristic wavy mouldings then in vogue. The work of the Eger craftsmen was largely used for princely gifts, and consequently, even in the 17th and 18th centuries, it was found at courts all over Europe. In recent years, it has been common to attribute it all to Adam Eck (1604–64) of Eger; but, even if this were not absurd on grounds of it being the output of only one man or one workshop, modern research has established that a considerable number of workers and workshops were engaged in the craft, some rather mediocre but several of them of the same outstanding technical and artistic brilliance as Eck.

As hardly any of them signed their work and several were members of large families, it is impossible to assign Eger work to any one man, in the absence of documentary evidence. The Eck family, through at least four generations, were among the masters, and Adam was the most famous. Equal in importance was Hans Georg Fischer (1578–1669), who signed his work, or included his initials H.G.F., and the Haberstumpf family, who were related to the Ecks. Johann Karl Haberstumpf (1656–1742), Adam Eck and Hans Georg Fischer are generally reckoned as the three greatest of the Eger relief intarsia workers, and it is reasonable to attribute the unsigned but oustanding games board, Plates 228–30, and the draughts, right of Plate 231, to one of the first two.

This games board, which is described in *Egerer Reliefintarsien* by Heribert Sturm (published 1961), is in the Pinto Collection; it is framed in black stained pearwood, with the usual wavy mouldings. The face of the box-board, Plate 230, shows a typical battle scene, converted from an engraving into relief intarsia. The back of the box,

Plate 229, is flat inlaid for draughts, with the squares alternately decorated with martial and floral motifs. The inside, Plate 228, inlaid elaborately for backgammon, uses floral and martial trophies for the 'points'. The 28 draughts, right of Plate 231, probably belong to the backgammon board and are in their original tooled leather cases. The 'white' draughts, of boxwood, have Eger relief intarsia plaques of European kings on their face sides and carved cartouches, giving names of the kings on the backs. The black, ebony draughts have Roman emperors, crowned with green laurel wreaths, on the face and named cartouches on the backs. There must originally have been chessmen and smaller draughts for use on the draughts board, which has squares too small for the 2 in. diameter draughts illustrated.

Fox and Geese

A yew-wood board for a game similar to Fox and Geese, dating from the 10th century A.D., is in Dublin Museum. Records of the game occur in 1300 A.D. Icelandic sagas and, under various names, it seems to have been played in Britain for many centuries. There are several versions, but in all, the object is for a fox to break through a line of geese; the geese may vary in number, from four upwards, according to the type of board used. The fox and the geese are distinguished by two colours of draughts, marbles, or pegs, and the game may be played on an ordinary draughts board, or a specially marked solitaire board. The ancient oak board, repaired with copper, Plate 240, *B*, which it is impossible to date, is said to have been used for one of the Fox and Geese variants.

Games Markers

Games markers of the type shown, Plate 233, *F*, are used for a number of card games. They are usually made in pairs and basically consist of rectangles of polished hardwood, with two lines of numbers and peg holes;

at one end is a cavity to store pegs, enclosed by a turn button. There seems no reason why such markers should not have a history as long as the games for which they were used, but I have never seen any which appear to have been made before 1820. If inlaid, they are always french polished, and the alternatives are usually Tunbridge wood mosaic, transfer ware, or tartan ware, all of which suggest a 19th-century fashion. Another type of marker, apparently of the same period, with flick-over ivory strips, mostly used for whist, is shown, Plate 233, *G*. Billiards and cribbage markers are mentioned under those headings.

Gaming Laws—see *Archery*, p. 235

Halma
Halma or hoppity was introduced about 1890; its treen, consisting of 52 small, knop surmounted, conical 'men', dyed in four colours (13 men in each colour) was mass produced and without interest.

Hazard—see *Dice*

Hoppity—see *Halma*

Jack Straws—see *Spellicans*

Jig-saws—see *Puzzles*

Lotto or Loto
Lotto, the direct ancestor of housey-housey and bingo, was a popular Georgian and Victorian table game, played with numbered, turned counters or discs, on cards. The Victorian set, in original box, Plate 240, *F*, has raised red lettering on sycamore counters and was probably made by Jaques —for Jaques, see *Puzzles, Miscellaneous*.

Mentor's Cards—see *Playing Cards*

Merels
Merels, one of the oldest and most universally popular games in all parts of Great Britain in the past, is said by different authorities to have been introduced by Romans, Danes and Normans. Of the three, the Romans must win, on the evidence of a Roman tile, depicting a merels board, excavated at Silchester, but a marked stone of the Stone or Bronze Age, found in a burial site in County Wicklow, Ireland, suggests that the game was played in the British Isles even before the coming of the Romans. There is also evidence of the antiquity of merels in China, India, Ceylon, Russia, Greece, Scandinavia, West Africa and the Amazon Valley. It was played indoors, with pegs as 'men', on a grooved and drilled board, like the 18th-century, Spanish mahogany example, Plate 240, *D*, or scratched on a table in an inn, or chalked on a barn floor, and using coins, counters or marbles as 'men'. Outdoors, there were specially marked turf greens, where children were used as the pieces, or the markings were cut into clay or sand, and sticks, stones, beans, cones or conkers were used as 'men'. But whatever the scale and nature of the board, merels is essentially a game for two players, and is marked out like the board illustrated. The aim, as in the basically similar noughts and crosses, is to get three men in a row, without intervention of an opponent's piece. The opponents move in turn, each commencing with nine men. Alternative names for merels in England are legion. They include marells and morrels; miracles in Oxfordshire and Cheshire; tick-tack-toe in Northamptonshire; peg-meryll and marriage in Derbyshire; ninepenny marl and madells in Wiltshire; fivepenny-morris in various other parts of England, and most generally, nine-men's-morris or nine-men's marriage.

In *A Midsummer Night's Dream*, Titania says:

'The nine-men's-morris is fill'd up with mud;
And the quaint mazes in the wanton green
For lack of tread, are undistinguishable'.

As late as 1897, to celebrate Queen Victoria's Diamond Jubilee, a game, using boys and girls as pieces, was played at Saffron Walden. Merels was played by old and young alike, and by clergy as well as laity. Witnesses to the universality of the game, are merels 'boards', scratched by monks on the stone seats of early cloisters in Westminster and other abbeys, and Salisbury and other cathedrals; by children on flat tomb stones in churchyards and, presumably by choir boys, on wooden choir stalls for use during long and tedious services.

In 1842–3, a 'new' game was registered, 'The Royal Game of Nine Holes', the circular mahogany board for which, is shown, Plate 240, *E*. The game was played by two persons, each having three marbles of different colour; the object of the game is to get three balls of a colour in a straight line, along any of the lines that are marked on the board.

Nine-men's-Morris—see *Merels*

Nine Pins—see *Outdoor Games, Skittles*

Noddy—see *Cribbage*

Pin Table—see *Bagatelle*

Playing Cards
No one knows for certain where or when playing cards originated. They were well known in China before A.D. 1000; mention of them commences in European literature in the 14th century. By the mid-15th century, the manufacture of playing cards was sufficiently well established in England, for a ban to be placed on imports; it was not effective, however, and further complaints were recorded in the 16th and 17th centuries. Charles I granted a Charter to the Worshipful Company of Makers of Playing Cards in 1628. A square walnut card table, *circa* 1580, inlaid with playing cards, survives at Hardwick Hall. The earliest European playing cards were known as *tarots* and there were 78 cards in a pack. Playing cards, during their long history,

have varied considerably in markings, size and number in a pack. Apart from four-suit packs, most of the specialized educational and fancy card games, usually for children—such as *Pit*, *Happy Families*, and various question and answer games—usually have a comparatively short history, going back no further than the last century. A Regency interrogatory card game, entitled 'Mentor's Cards', with its original box, is illustrated, Plate 233, *A*; it was published by Edward Wallis, of 42 Skinner Street, London, and consists of 50 general knowledge question cards and two answers cards—see also Section XXVII, *Tuition: Wallis' Revolving Alphabet*. For playing card printing blocks, see Section XVI, *Printing and Woodcut and Engraving Blocks*.

Playing Card Boxes
The majority of ornamental boxes for playing cards and games markers now extant, date from the 19th century. Some of the most attractive fitted boxes were made in Tunbridge wood mosaic. An 18th-or early 19th-century, Scandinavian, chip carved, sycamore, two-pack box, is pictured, Plate 233, *L*.

Playing Card Presses
Old playing cards were limp, hand-coloured and valuable. They were placed in presses, to flatten and preserve them. A rare, French, 17th-century carved walnut press is shown, Plate 233, *K*. It measures $13\frac{1}{2}$ in. long by $4\frac{3}{4}$ in. wide. Such presses are often confused with lace presses, which have end, not centre screws—see Section VIII, *Laundry*, Plate 156. A mahogany playing card press for a number of packs is illustrated, Plate 233, *H*; it was probably used in a 19th-century club.

Playing Card Stands
Playing card stands are simple rebated strips, usually of mahogany, each with 13 diagonal cuts, so that a 'hand' of cards may be stood in the rack, with the major

part of each card visible to the player only. They are used in double dummy bridge, and by one-handed players. They are still made.

Pope Joan

A Regency Pope Joan board, with its labels of applied and varnished paper and the decoration between, painted on natural sycamore, is illustrated, Plate 233, *O*. It measures 10 in. in diameter. Victorian examples are usually 11½ in. in diameter, have backgrounds painted green, red, black or yellow, and the decoration applied by transfers. These boards were probably made at Tunbridge. Pope Joan, named after a legendary mediaeval Pope, is a gambling card game for a number of people. I have not traced any records of it before the beginning of the 19th century.

Puzzles

Dissected and Jigsaw Puzzles

The largest and best known group of wooden puzzles are jigsaws, which became popular in England during the 18th century, as a supplement to formal teaching. Who originated the idea, we shall probably never know for certain. Early pictorial puzzles were essentially educational, and the first recorded were for teaching geography and history; these were soon followed by biblical story and historical event puzzles and subjects such as processes of manufacture, general knowledge and, in Victorian times, very uplifting and moralizing themes.

Early jigsaw puzzles, known as 'Dissections' or 'Dissected Puzzles', were issued and sold by print and map makers. Change of nomenclature from dissected puzzles to jigsaws only took place in the 19th century. It would not be surprising to learn that John Newbery, the publisher and bookseller of St. Paul's Churchyard, a man who really understood children, was the originator of jigsaws, but there is no proof that he was. However, after his death in 1767,

his family successors teamed up with John Wallis, a cartographer, who later claimed to be the inventor of jigsaws. Newbery was a great character and an extraordinary mixture. From about 1744, he built up a prosperous business in books and newspapers, concocted and sold pills, powders and other weird cures, and was also a printer and publisher, who achieved considerable fame in his day as a pioneer writer of children's books. His books were not only a novelty at that time, in being entertaining as well as educational, but they also anticipated the modern trend for free gift schemes. With his *Little Pretty Pocket Book*, which he published in 1744, and probably wrote, he gave away for 'Little Master Tommy' and 'Pretty Miss Polly', a letter from Jack-the-Giant-Killer, a ball for Tommy and a pincushion for Polly, so undoubtedly he had the right sort of imagination and sensitive understanding to devise jigsaws for children. He was also a great philanthropist and a good friend and benefactor of such famous authors as Dr. Johnson and Oliver Goldsmith. An eccentric, hustling, bustling man, he was always in a hurry and always late for appointments, which brings us back to jigsaws, for there is little doubt that the designer of *The Importance of Punctuality*, Plate 237, published by David Bogue, of 86 Fleet Street, about 1851, must have known about Newbery, who died in 1767.

Despite its sententiousness, this puzzle appears to have drawn its inspiration from the life of the Georgian children's friend and particularly what Dr. Johnson said about him. Newbery was always looking at his watch and muttering 'Late again, late again', and Dr. Johnson humorously immortalized him as Jack Whirler, in *The Idler*, saying 'His business keeps him in perpetual motion and his motion always eludes his business. . . . He cannot stand still because he is wanted in another place, and he is wanted in many places because he stays at none. When he enters a house, his first declaration is that he cannot sit down; and so short are his visits, he seldom appears to have come for any other reason but to say that he must go.' The pompously moralising captions under the seven tableaux in *The Importance of Punctuality*, read:

'Punctuality is the very hinge of business; and there is no successful(?) method without punctuality'.

'Punctuality is important because it subserves the peace and good temper of a family'.

'A disorderly man is always in a hurry; he has no time to speak to you, because he is going elsewhere'.

'When he gets there he is too late for his business or he must hurry away before he can finish it. What we call time enough, always proves little enough as poor Richard says'.

'Punctuality gives weight to character, such a man has made an appointment, then I know he will keep it'.

'Appointments indeed become debts; I owe you punctuality. If I have made an engagement with you and have no right to throw away your time if I do my own'.

'Servants and children must be punctual where their leader sets them the example. For punctuality like other virtues, propagates itself'.

The third and fourth captions seem too close to Dr. Johnson's writings about Newbery, for the wording to be merely coincidental.

In addition to John Newbery's successor, Elizabeth, some of the best known early names associated with dissected puzzles were John Wallis, Edward Wallis, William and Samuel Darton, Thomas Kitchin, Carrington Bowles and the Cremer family. Thomas Bowles, print seller, was established at St. Paul's Churchyard in the first half of the 18th century; whether he made dissected puzzles, I have been unable to trace. Carrington Bowles, of the same address, first appears in the *London Directory*

in 1768. A puzzle of the Kings and Queens of England, printed by him, is dated July 1787. John Wallis, map, book print seller, according to Miss Rachel Young, M.A., of Norwich Museum, commenced making dissected maps about 1760. He first appears in the *London Directory*, at 16 Ludgate Street, in 1777. Edward Wallis, who took over about 1820, soon moved to Islington, where he remained until 1840; he first used the term 'dissected map manufacturer' in his 1826 advertisement. Thomas Kitchin, map and print seller, engraver and royal hydrographer, was at 59 Holborn from 1763 until 1777, when he disappears from the London directories, although later dated puzzles by him exist.

A puzzle entitled *The World Dissected on the Best Principles for Teaching Geography*, is arranged as two 14 in. circles enclosing the eastern and western hemispheres respectively, with borders of countries hand coloured. Judging by dates of 'recent discoveries', printed on the map, all in the 1770s, it was published in the last quarter of the 18th century. It bears no name, but a similarly produced and labelled 'Europe Dissected' was sold by Elizabeth Newbery of St. Paul's Churchyard in 1793-4. The dissected map has never lost popularity. Crutchley's *Map of England*, one of 'Cremer's Popular Dissections' from W. H. Cremer Jun., the 'European Toy House', 210 Regent Street, was particularly popular about 1870, and others still appear under the jigsaw label.

The fascinating and ambitious production, Plate 236, is entitled:

Engravings of the Principal Events in the History of England to the Reign of George III. Dissected for Children. Price Ten Shillings in a Box.

The sheet may be had, for the use of schools, price Three Shillings.

In its forty-eight 3 in.-square tableaux, it covers events from the ancient Britons to the death of Nelson. At the bottom of the picture is printed 'The characters in each event are represented in the appropriate Costume of the different periods'. It was published, December 1815, by William Darton, Josh Harvey and Samuel Darton.

The Progress of Cheese, a puzzle arranged in 12 sequences, in rococo gold frames, appears to be a Regency pastiche, probably by John Wallis, who also published *Progress of Coffee, Progress of China Making*, etc.

A Victorian puzzle, *The Royal Nursery*, has a crude, hand-coloured, varnished picture on the lid, and another inside, additional to that on the cedar puzzle; all three are coloured differently. It was published by Dean & Co. of Threadneedle Street, and judging by the ages of Victoria and Albert's four children, depicted with them and the nurse, must date from about 1847.

Soon after the mid-19th century, some puzzles were made more difficult and interesting by introducing pictures on both sides. An early example is one which has 'The World Dissected' on one side and 'Robinson Crusoe' on the reverse.

Dissected picture puzzles, at least until the mid-19th century, are usually on $\frac{1}{4}$ in. thick mahogany or cedar and enclosed in mahogany boxes with sliding lids, labelled with the maker's name and sometimes a title for the puzzle. From about 1850, varnished-over pictures are sometimes pasted on lids, and boxes are of pine or mahogany, with the puzzles pasted on mahogany or whitewood, with a plain backing paper to equalise the pull.

Until about 1840–50, puzzle pictures, apart from maps, usually consisted of a number of small scenes, to be arranged in sequence. Generally these scenes are divided by wavy line cuts, with no cuts across the tableaux; dovetail heads, to hold the whole puzzles together, are used sparingly, if at all, and then only round the perimeter. It has sometimes been stated that this is because fret saws were not yet invented, but

this is untrue: the equivalent of modern fret saws were made and used for marquetry from the 16th century onwards, but they were hand made and consequently expensive and variable in quality. Individual pieces of early puzzles are usually large, 2 in. to $4\frac{1}{2}$ in. being common, but some are larger.

Miscellaneous Puzzles

Under the heading of miscellaneous puzzles are included such diverse ones as the Boat Puzzle, Pigs-in-Clover, the Chinese Puzzle Globe, various puzzle opening boxes and the geometric puzzles sold at Tunbridge in the 19th century, in small, square, mosaic decorated boxes. The boat puzzle, Plate 240, *J*, consists of a mahogany board, with black inlaid lines representing the two banks of a river; a carved ivory or bone boat travels in a groove from bank to bank. There are six peg holes along each bank and two in the boat, and three white and three black pegs. The white pegs represent gentlemen, the black their slaves; the pegs with dots above their heads, are the only ones who can row. They have to cross the river in such manner that the whites are never outnumbered by the blacks on either river bank, or in the boat. In a variant of the game, there are three jealous husbands and their wives to cross the river, and they have to do it so that none of the women are left with any of the other men, unless the respective husbands are also present. The puzzle was registered in 1842–3 by Jaques and Son, of 102 Hatton Garden, ivory and hardwood turners and manufacturers of chessmen, billiard and bagatelle balls. Jaques was a well-known manufacturer of games involving turnery, including not only the above, but also ringolette (see *Quoits*), squails and lotto.

Pigs-in-Clover, a game with small marbles or metal balls which, by careful tilting, are guided into the clover or centre of a maze, is usually an all-metal game. The only wooden example I have seen is the turned elm, one-piece board, Plate 241, *M*, shown with its lid alongside; with its paper-thin partitions, it is a fine example of turnery. It was made about 1840, by the great-uncle of the man who presented it to the Pinto Collection. The 3 in. diameter Chinese globe puzzle, Plate 241, *P*, is a jigsaw formed as a wooden ball; it must be as difficult to make as it is to assemble. A faceted hardwood ball, Plate 241, *N*, turned with a design of concentric circles on each facet, is really a sovereign or shilling box. It is opened by pressing on one of the concentric circles and pushing a rebated cylindric box through the 'ring' of the ball, as depicted, Plate 241, *O*. Whilst most of these boxes, which are made of padauk or rosewood, only have the circle decoration, *N* has Tunbridge mosaic centres to each circle, and it is possible that all the puzzle boxes of this type were Tunbridge novelties.

Quoits

The origin of the quoit is the Greek and Roman discus, a flat, solid disc of stone or metal, thrown as a trial of strength or skill. In modern parlance, a quoit is a ring of wood, metal or ivory, thrown to encircle a pin or number. It may be played indoors or out, with the pin mounted in a board or stand, or driven into the ground, or embedded in a box of clay. A simple, single peg, Victorian quoit for a child is shown left of Plate 232.

A complete and very well made *Ringolette or Parlour Quoits* in the Pinto Collection, Plate 251, made by Jaques (see *Puzzles, Miscellaneous*) about 1840, is described as 'A new and amusing game played on a 6 ft. telescopic mahogany board with Rings, Standards, etc., adapted for any number of players.' It has numbered ivory rings and ivory pegs and cost originally £5 5s. 0d.; with wooden rings and pegs, it cost £3 13s. 6d. This particular set came from the Earl of Darnley's servants' hall at Cobham Hall, Kent.

Race Horse Game

The Race Horse Game was, I understand, played in public bars in the 18th and early 19th centuries. Survivals of horses and jockeys are now very rare. Seven of a set of 10, which came from an East Anglian 'pub', are illustrated, Plate 242. The horses are placed with hind legs on a table, as shown, or along the front of a bar; they are balanced by a weighted, slightly curved spring-steel strip, attached to each horse. When set rocking, the jockeys realistically move backwards and forwards, and the horse heads, with reins attached, move in unison. Each horse was set in motion at the word 'go' and the player whose horse rocked the longest, scooped the pool; the one whose horse became motionless first, stood the next round. There were numerous variations of the rules.

Ringolette—see *Quoits*

Roulette

Roulette is played with the aid of a wheel, usually of mahogany, and a green baize covered, marked table, extending lengthwise in front of the wheel. The wheel, which has to be made and balanced very precisely on a pivot, is cylindrical and has the upper surface divided into 37 or 38 compartments, each of which is numbered correspondingly to a marking on the cloth. The croupier spins the wheel, and by a hand throw, sends a small ivory ball round the upper part of the basin. After describing an irregular course determined by the studs, it eventually comes to rest in one of the compartments, numbered 1 to 36, or in one of the two zeros. There are eight methods of staking. I have never seen a wheel which appears to be earlier than 18th century, but roulette is said to be a development of an earlier game.

Royal Game of Nine Holes—see *Merels*

Score Boards—see *Games Markers*

Shove Ha'penny

Shove ha'penny or shovel-board, in mediaeval times known as shove grout, is mentioned in Shakespeare's *Merry Wives of Windsor*. Henry VIII played for high stakes and 16th- and 17th-century tables, marked out for shovel-board, have survived. From the 18th century onwards, portable marked boards, like the one right of Plate 232, have generally been used. The old game remains popular in public houses and country inns.

Solitaire

Solitaire, a game for one, as its name implies, reached Great Britain from the Continent in the 18th century. It is played on a circular board, with pegs or marbles, and all the holes except the centre one are filled at the outset. The moves are made by 'jumping', the marble or peg which is 'jumped over' being removed. The object is to leave the last one in the centre. Boards which can be used for solitaire, vary in the number of pegs or marbles, Plate 240, *A*, *C* and *G*, and other games can be played on some of these boards. *G*, which has an upright, hollow, carved figure of mediaeval appearance, which acts as a tube down which the marbles may be dropped to dress the board, gives an impression of great antiquity, but I believe this is largely spurious. As a generality, 19th-century mahogany boards are french polished and have a runnel round them for discarded marbles; 18th-century boards are waxed and have no runnel.

Spellicans

Spellicans, also spelt spillikins and spillicans, and alternatively named Jack Straws, is a game for an unlimited number of players. Like so many other games, it is said to have originated in China, at a remote period. It has been played in England since early in the 18th century. The number of pieces in a set, usually of bone, ivory, or a wood veneer, vary from 24 to 100. There are also differences in scoring, some sets having numbered spellicans, the values of which, added together, determine the winner, whilst other sets are unnumbered, the winner being the player who hooks the largest quantity. The object of the game is simply to withdraw them, one by one, with the hook, without disturbing the remainder of the heap, which has been thrown in disorder on the table; when any are disturbed, the turn passes to the next player.

Both wood and bone sets are often decorated in colours, but are usually fret cut into various outlines from thin, flat slivers. Occasionally, flat spellicans are mounted into turned heads, but the exceptionally fine set, Plate 244, is the only one I have seen where each piece is individually carved. Another interesting feature is that this set is housed not in a box but is fitted in its original 19th-century, turned boxwood 'bottle case', which contains the original directions and list of 24 spellicans and two hooks, all of which are named and all but one intact. The detailed directions announce:

'Spellicans, a game for promoting steadiness of hand. The Sandalwood of which they are made came from the site of Tippoo's Palace, Seringapatam' (captured 1799).

The spellicans and the points they score are described:

Top left Bow, 5. Spear, 1. Latch key, 10.
Bottom left Spoon (the only one broken), 5. Axe, 5. Pipe, 15.
Second row Ladder, 15. Tongs, 20. Button hook, 20. Sabre, 5. Saw, 10. Rifle, 10. Stilt, 5. Boat hook, 1. Bear pole, 25.
Third row Garden fork, 15. Shovel, 10. Flag, 5. Mallet, 10. Poker, 1. Hoe, 10. Paddle, 5. Twig, 5. Snake, 15.

Squails

Squails, Plate 240, *H*, was described by Jaques (see *Puzzles*) about 1840 as 'A new round game of skill. Played on an ordinary table by any even number of players not exceeding 8, affording capital fun and amusement. Price 8/6, Superior 10/6'. The set illustrated is 'superior', with eight each turned ebony, boxwood and rosewood squails, further differentiated by different colour leather centres. A special medallion, supplied in the box, was placed centrally on the table, with the squails in a circle round it. The players took it in turn to project their squails from their position round the perimeter. The winner was the one who finished with the greatest number of squails near the medal. The calibrated 'swoggle' was used to settle differences. Basically, the game is a combination of shove ha'penny and bowls. Under the name of 'Skayles' or 'Keels', it goes back to the 16th century and is mentioned in Sir Philip Sidney's *Arcadia*.

Table Croquet—see *Outdoor Games, Croquet*

Tables—see introduction to this section

Teetotums
A teetotum, or totum, a many-faceted spinning top, with each side numbered, serves, in many respects, the same purpose as thrown dice, but if made 'true', there is an equal chance of any number turning up, which is not the case with dice. Probably for this reason, the Victorians considered it less vicious, and preferred it particularly for children's games, where a move depended on the turn up of a number. The gambling game, of staking on a teetotum, is recorded in 1753. A variant of the teetotum top, is the mahogany teetotum ball, Plate 233, *P*.

Toad-in-the-hole
Toad-in-the-hole, Plate 243, probably originated in England in Tudor times. Since then, it has been played in many parts of the world, including Argentina, where it is known as *Sapo*. It was formerly a popular game in the servants' halls of great houses, such as Cobham Hall, Kent, and Ashburnham, Sussex. The oak board illustrated, probably dating from the 18th century, would originally have had a metal toad, with gaping mouth, where the replacement letterbox-like opening is now. The game is a forerunner of the pin-table and is played by throwing lead discs, about the size of a George III 'cartwheel' twopenny piece. The aim is to throw the discs through holes in the board, which are guarded by various hazards. The discs fall down the chutes to the numbered front barrier, which shows the scores. The 'toad', guarded by a paddle wheel hazard, is top score, 2,000. The hazards to the lesser scoring holes are trap doors, shields and hoops.

Whist Markers—see *Games Scorers*

OUTDOOR PASTIMES
Outdoor Ball Games and Miscellaneous Amusements

This section is mainly devoted to ball games, but also includes dumb-bells, clubs, diavolo, hobby-horses, jumping sticks, spades and yo-yos.

Bandalores—see *Yo-yos*

Bilboquet
The game of *bilboquet*, in England known as cup and ball, was popularized in late 16th-century France by Henri III, and from a children's game, became the craze of the court and nobility, thence passing to all strata of the populace. Engravings of the period show that it was played *en masse* in parks, gardens and streets. At the Stuart court, it was also the vogue, and although its popularity has waxed and waned, it has

since encircled the world and still has its devotees in various countries. It is probable that the game has an earlier and more primitive origin than the above suggests, for the Eskimos are said to have played it in the spring from time immemorial, as a rite to hasten the return of the sun. The real game is played with a captive ball, about 1 in. in diameter, attached by string to a stick, surmounted by a cup, but there are variations. The aim in nearly all versions of the game, however, is so to manoeuvre the stick and ball, as to toss the ball into the cup. The ball and cup are usually of lignum vitae, boxwood or ivory, and a selection is shown, Plate 241, A to E; it will be seen from A, that when not in use, the drilled-out ball may be secured on the opposite end of the stick to the cup. The lignum vitae example, D, is typical of the 18th century. A, an outsize, lignum vitae specimen, $13\frac{1}{2}$ in. long, was probably intended for shop display. The ball weighs $1\frac{1}{2}$ lb.; if dropped on one's hand, it would probably break a bone. C is an interesting specimen, with stick carved in the form of a lad in early 19th-century costume. B is a Victorian variant, of boxwood, with seven numbered depressions in the end plate, each scoring a different figure. E is a modern Mexican variant; the drilled-out wooden head has to be caught on the spike. F is one of a pair of paint decorated Regency cup sticks, used for catching a non-captive, light-weight ball; it was a game for two. In a Victorian version, the cup was spring-loaded on the stick.

Bowls

Allusions to bowls go back to the 12th century in England, but as the references are to citizens taking their pleasure *in jactu lapidum*, the bowls were stone. The Southampton town bowling club was founded in 1299 and by this time hardwood bowls were probably used. From the 17th century onwards, 'woods' were always of lignum vitae; the bias was introduced in

the reign of Elizabeth I. During the mediaeval and Tudor periods, several parliamentary edicts imposed penalties for playing bowls, because the game competed with archery.

Some very large, lignum vitae bowls and cheeses of various diameters appear in antique shops from time to time and the bowls are a puzzle to collectors. Two of the bowls in the Pinto Collection are $7\frac{1}{2}$ in. and $8\frac{1}{2}$ in. in diameter respectively. They were purchased in Southsea and were said to have come from a naval bowling alley at Portsmouth, where bowls of different sizes were used. This naval connection seems correct, for lignum vitae bowls of varying sizes, from 3 in. to 15 in. diameter, are used for bowling down the wooden runway of the skittle alley at the Royal Naval College, Greenwich, and I am told that there are or were similar alleys at Malta and Singapore Naval Establishments. A giant bowl, reported to have been 18 in. in diameter, and known as 'Hairy Mary', disappeared from Greenwich during the war. See also *Skittles*.

A considerable number of carpet bowls of pottery, decorated with tartan, were made in Scotland during Regency and Victorian times. Sets of lignum vitae carpet bowls, with boxwood jacks, are more rare. A set in the Pinto Collection has bowls of $3\frac{1}{4}$ in. diameter, and a smaller set, $1\frac{3}{4}$ in. diameter, is for table use. Both are perfect miniatures in lignum vitae, complete with bias.

Clubs—see *Indian Clubs*

Cricket

The cricket bat, Plate 234, H, has considerable historic interest. It is a Crawford Exceller No. 5 boy's size, sold by Wisden's in the 1870s, and it has been cut down carefully to 2 in. width, probably for precision in practice. It came from Cobham Hall, Kent, seat of the Earls of Darnley. It was used by one of the famous 'cricketting Blighs', probably the Hon. Ivo Bligh, afterwards

8th Earl of Darnley, who captained the team which brought back the Ashes from Australia, in the winter of 1882–3.

Cricket appears to have evolved from mediaeval stool ball, in which a three-legged stool (still known in the antique furniture trade as a cricketting table) took the place of the stumps and bail. The first known reference to scholars playing at 'crekett' occurs in 1550 in the Guildford (Surrey) Corporation Court Books. A curved bat, more like a hockey stick, was used in the 18th century, together with two stumps and a bail laid across the top. This persisted until 1775, then the third stump was added. Light weight and resilience make the fast-growing willow the ideal wood for cricket bats, and the preferred variety, the close bark willow, *Salix Coerulea*, grown mainly in East Anglia. The tree is normally cut at 15 years. After splitting into clefts, seasoning takes place for about two years. The handle, made from some 16 strips of Sarawak cane, laminated with thin strips of rubber, is shaped to fit into a V, cut into the head of the blade, and glued.

Croquet

The ancestor of croquet was pele-mele, pell-mell or pall-mall, but the rules were not the same, and the mallet with a shaft some 3½ ft. long, had an oval head slightly curved and the ends hooped with iron. The ball, of approximately 2½ in. diameter, was boxwood. The game was a cross between golf and croquet. The player could tee his ball up on sand for the first shot, and the ground surface was a mixture of sand and earth, covered with powdered cockle shells; Charles II had an official cockle strewer, and a 'Master of the Mall' at that part of St. James's Park which later became the street now known as Pall Mall. The game was introduced to Scotland from France, and brought south by James I. Samuel Pepys, on April 2, 1661, recorded 'So I into St. James's Park, where I saw

the Duke of York playing at Pelemele, the first time that ever I saw the sport'. The name is derived from the Italian *palla*, a ball, and *maglia*, a mallet, via the French *paille* and *maille*.

Croquet in its present form was introduced to England about 1850 and the rules and equipment have been modified from time to time. The balls, originally of hardwood, are now composition. Table croquet became popular in the second half of the 19th century and sets in boxes, complete with green cloth, cost from 14s. to 42s. for a 'superior set' by Jaques (for *Jaques*, see *Puzzles*). A superior set is illustrated, left of Plate 232.

Cup and Ball Game—see *Bilboquet*

Darts

Darts, the public house descendant of archery, has an ancient but apparently unrecorded history. The circular board or target is usually of elm, or any other suitable wood, faced with pig bristle or cork. Darts are of many kinds, but the most common are weighted, feathered and about 6 in. long.

Diavolo

Diavolo or diabolo, which was a craze in England between 1910 and 1914, was even then a revival of a very popular French game of 100 years earlier, well commemorated in coloured engravings. The aim was to juggle or balance the wooden diavolo on a thin string held between two long, wooden sticks or handles, Plate 241, *G*, and throw it in the air as many times as possible, catching it each time without allowing it to fall to the ground. Two wooden diavolos are illustrated, Plate 241, *J* and *K*. The first, of cocos wood, is probably of the 1810 period; the second, which is a singing diavolo, is beautifully turned and hollowed out of boxwood, and appears to be identical with one illustrated in an early 19th-century, French, coloured engraving, entitled *Le Bon*

Genre, No. 5, Leçon de Diable. At the outbreak of the First World War, some of the diavolos of the singing type were being made of metal with rubber tyres.

Dumb-bells

Dumb-bells have been used in England for muscular exercise since the 18th century. The majority have always been of iron, both for weight and cheapness. The type with steel compression springs in the hand grip was invented by Eugene Sandow. People in what is now described as the upper group income had dumb-bells turned from lignum vitae, which gave the necessary weight, with warmth to the touch. A very large, heavy and unusual pair in the Pinto Collection have ball ends. A conventional pair is shown, Plate 234, *C*. It is impossible to say whether either pair are 18th- or 19th-century.

Golf

Scotland can claim to have given golf to the world, but it is extremely doubtful if the Scots invented the game. The Romans played a game called *paganica*, with a crooked stick and a leather ball stuffed with feathers. In England, during the reign of Edward III (1327–77), a similar game flourished under the name of cambuca or bandy-bull. A bandy is an old term for a curved stick or club, hence 'bandy legs'. The earliest depiction of a golf player is, I believe, of 14th-century stained glass in a small panel of the great east window of Gloucester Cathedral. The player's head is missing and his club, as in Dutch 16th- and 17th-century pictures, looks more like a hockey stick. It has long been known that golf (Dutch, *Kolf*) was an early game in Holland, but whether earlier than in Scotland is unproved. In Scotland, it had become so much a national sport by the mid-15th century, that Acts of Parliament were passed in 1457, 1471 and 1491, forbidding it, as a menace to archery. The feather-stuffed golf ball continued in use

until superseded by gutta-percha in 1848. Meanwhile, the crooked stick had gradually evolved into a club with a hickory shaft and heads first of apple and pearwood, and later of beech and persimmon. These, in their turn, like the solid gutta-percha ball, have been superseded. Clubs can best be dated by comparison with examples in museums, or diagrams in encyclopaedias.

Hobby-horses

There are two types of hobby-horses— the mummer's or morris dancer's, and the child's; both have great antiquity, but which appeared first, is a matter of conjecture. The mummer's hobby-horse is a wicker cage draped with fabric, and with a hole in it near the front end, large enough to take the body of a man. The cage is fastened round the mummer's waist and the rear end, fitted with a tail, sticks out behind like a bustle. The man wears a horse head mask, and his gambolling animates the whole contraption. The other hobby-horse, one of the earliest and most eternal of children's playthings, is, in its simplest form, merely a stick with a horse-head, which the child 'rides' astride, with the head up in front and the stick bumping behind. In a slightly more sophisticated version, Plate 234, *A*, probably 19th-century, the stick at the rear is fitted with a T cross-bar and wooden wheels. According to Antonia Fraser, the hobby-horse was known to the Greeks. Certainly it shares the honour with hoops, tops, marbles, balls, rattles and toy windmills, of being one of the few toys which frequently appear in English, French and other western European mediaeval illustrations.

Hockey

Hockey or bandy, shinty in Scotland, is one of the crooked or curved stick and ball games which has gradually evolved over the centuries. The *Oxford Dictionary* notes it back to 1527. Originally, the curved stick was the hockey, shinty or bandy, and the ball was the hockey, shinty or bandy snug. It has been suggested that the frequent cry of 'shinty hock' on the field, used to mean mind your shins or hocks and it may be the origin of at least two of the alternative names. The game was not properly organized nor the modern rules formulated until 1883, when the 23 oz. ash blade, with curved handle, became standardised.

Indian Clubs

Indian clubs attained their highest degree of popularity in Victorian and Edwardian England. They are of various hardwoods and are presumably direct descendants of the clubs used by jugglers. Some outsize pairs of clubs—pairs of clubs of normal shape, but much too large or heavy to swing—are found from time to time. There is a pair, made of lignum vitae, in the Pinto Collection and I know of several similar plain pairs, all between 20 in. and 24 in. high. A pair of oak clubs, decorated with carving and 32 in. high, was illustrated in *Country Life* in 1957, but the ensuing correspondence produced no answer as to the purpose of these giant clubs.

Jumping Sticks

Jumping sticks, uprights with holes at intervals for pegs to support a loose bar, and firm bases, are too familiar on the sports field to need any description. An unusually well finished, rosewood pair of the early 19th century, probably used in a private indoor gymnasium, are shown used as the supports for suspended ell rules, etc. See Section XIX, *Scientific*, Plate 298.

Knur and Spell

Knur and spell, or northern spell, is a variant of trap-ball (see also *Trap-Ball*). It is and always was almost entirely confined to the northern counties of England. Its origin probably goes back to mediaeval times and the equipment gradually improved, whilst several methods of scoring developed. The rather elaborate apparatus

used in the second half of the 19th century is illustrated, Plate 234, *F* and *G*. The spell, *F*, 26 in. long by 5 in. wide, is made of heavy hardwood with metal fittings. The knur is the ball, formerly of ivory, lignum vitae, or boxwood. *G* is the pummel, kibble, or striking stick, 50 in. long, with shaft of hickory and head of maple or hornbeam. Towards the end of the 19th century, the balls were made of pot—'potties'—which drove further, and the shafts of the striking sticks were changed from hickory to ash. The game is for two players, each usually having 20 'rises' or 'knocks' and the winner was he who drove the knur the greatest distance. An alternative game was scoring by skill in driving the knur into variously numbered areas of ground and adding the totals. In the apparatus illustrated, which closely resembles Captain Bogardus Patent Ball (shooting) Trap, an adjustable length of spring steel is bolted at one end to the upper surface of the spell; the far end, lightly held by a trigger mechanism, is provided with a shallow brass cup, which holds the knur. When the T handle of the catch is struck by the player, the spring is released, the ball rises in the air and the player strikes with his striking stick. The game was played mostly by adults and sometimes for heavy stakes.

Merels—see *Indoor Pastimes, Games and Puzzles: Merels*

Nine-pins—see *Skittles*

Pell-mell—see *Croquet*

Quoits—see *Indoor Pastimes, Games and Puzzles: Quoits*

Shoe-trap—see *Trap Ball*

Skittles

The game now known as skittles or nine-pins was, in the 14th century, called kayles in England and kyles in Scotland; it is said to have been introduced from the shores of the Baltic. The close association of the bowling alley with the inn is ancient and still extant in London and other parts of England; the phrase about life not being 'all beer and skittles' has long been common parlance. In the Pinto Collection are two sets of skittles, one large set of painted 'pub skittles', probably early 19th-century, and a rare set of 5 in. high, lignum vitae skittles and 2¼ in. diameter, lignum vitae ball; this set, Plate 234, *B*, is particularly interesting, because it is complete with its original sliding lid, oak box, dated 1796. In some parts of the country the ball as shown in the set is used, whilst in other parts a flat, lignum vitae 'cheese', like the 7 in. diameter, ancient specimen, Plate 234, *D*, is hurled or bowled along the rock-maple floored alley. The modern ten-pin bowling is an elaborate version of a very ancient game. Enfield skittles is a parlour game played on a framed table, with skittles and an ivory or boxwood ball, driven by a billiard cue. A 5½ in. high, light-weight, Russian wooden skittle, silhouetted as a human figure and polychrome finished, a survivor from a table set, is shown, Plate 241, *H*.

Three-pins is an ancient East Anglian field game; the heavy turned wooden pins, of vase shape, are set up in a triangle at the end of a 32 in. long plank, in a field, and bowling is with an iron shod cheese. The object, as with nine-pins, is to knock over all the pins with one shot.

Spades

The child's one-piece sand spade of beech, made in a wide range of sizes during the 19th and early 20th century, is rapidly becoming a wooden bygone, superseded by the metal blade, collared on to a wooden stem. See also Section V, *Farm: Shovels and Spades*.

Three-pins—see *Skittles*

Tip-Cat—see *Trap Ball*

Trap Ball

Trap ball is an ancient member of the same family as knur and spell, and has many names in different parts of England, such as trap and ball, bat and trap, trippit, etc. When the trap is shaped like a shoe, the game is sometimes known as shoe-trap. All versions call for the same components—a wooden trap and bat, and a soft ball. The trap is a solid block of wood, morticed out to take a pivoted trigger, the lower end of which rests in a hollow under the ball. When the upper end is struck downwards by the player's bat, the ball rises and is hit with the wooden bat. The trap may be a plain oblong, or shaped like a 17th-century shoe, Plate 234, *E*, carved from beech, with the ball resting in a hollow in the heel. This shape of shoe is a convention and does not necessarily denote age; the same pattern, I believe, has been made in this century. In a Bartolozzi engraving of 1788, in the Pinto Collection, boys are shown playing shoe-trap, using an upward curved, one-piece bat of elongated pear shape. Nowadays, the one-piece wood bat is flat and much more of an elongated and narrow tennis racquet shape. A delightful and well made miniature shoe and trap, with bat of cricket bat type, is illustrated, Plate 218, *N*; it is presumably a 19th-century model. Trap ball is played by two teams, not two individuals as with knur and spell. The scoring, too, is quite different; only distance counts in the hitting, runs being scored, as in cricket. In tip-cat, which is essentially a children's game, there are only two components—the striking piece and the small wooden piece or 'cat' which is struck. Both are such home-made, expendable crudities that they never attain antiquity or merit a collector's attention.

Warbler Discs

The boxwood warbler disc, Plate 218, *M*, which looks like a yo-yo with an aperture

242 The race-horse game. For
details, see text. (*Section XV*)

243 Toad-in-the-hole. For details, see text. (*Section XV*)

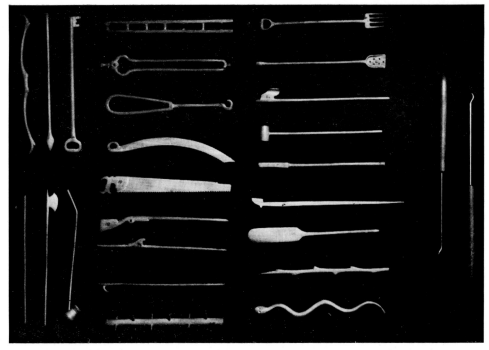

244 Set of individually carved spellicans, made from the cedar of Tippoo's Palace, Seringapatam. (*Section XV*)

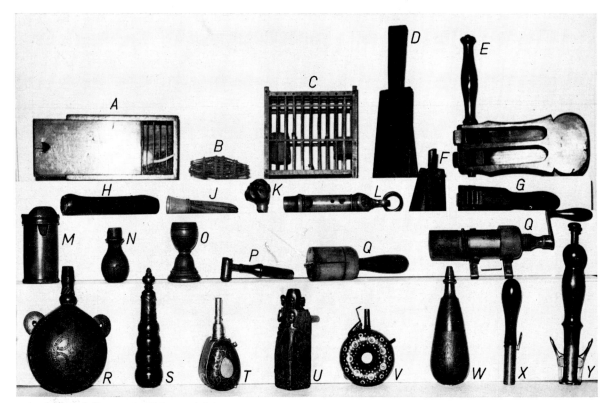

245 *A, B* and *C*, mouse, cricket and linnet cages; *D, E, F* and *G*, bird scarers; *K*, dog whistle; *H, J, L, M* and *N*, bird calls; *O*, gun periscope; *P*, shot pourer; *Q.1* and *Q.2*, cartridge 'turning down' machines; *R* to *W*, powder flasks; *X*, device for making cartridge containers; *Y*, cartridge extractor. (*Section XV*)

246 *A* and *B*, 19th- and 18th-century game carriers; *C*, pigeon ringing device; *D* and *E*, bird scarers; *F* to *J* and *N*, riding boot jacks; *K*, riding boot lifts; *L* and *M*, whip holders. (*Section XV*)

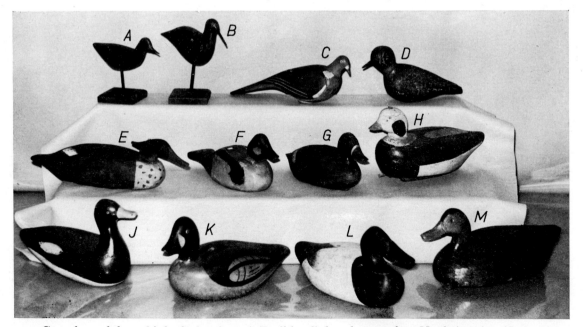

247 Carved wood decoy birds. *C*, the pigeon is English; all the others are from North America. (*Section XV*)

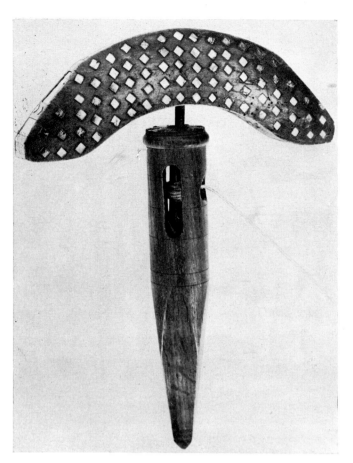

248 Cord operated lark lure; Italian, 17th century. (*Section XV*)

249 Clockwise lark lure; French, 18th century. (*Section XV*)

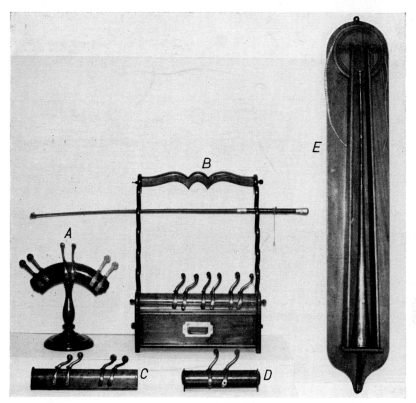

250 *A*, rare 18th-century spurs stand; *B*, combined spurs and whip stand; *C* and *D*, spurs stands; *E*, combined coaching horn and whip stand. (*Section XV*)

251 Ringolette, or parlour quoits board, made by Jaques of Hatton Garden, about 1840. (*Section XV*)

252 TOP LEFT: English 19th-century, calico printing block; CENTRE: mid-18th century 'Chinoiserie' block, probably French; BELOW: English, 19th-century block for printing details on hessian bales for export; RIGHT, English, 17th-century, floral textile printing block. (*Section XVI*)

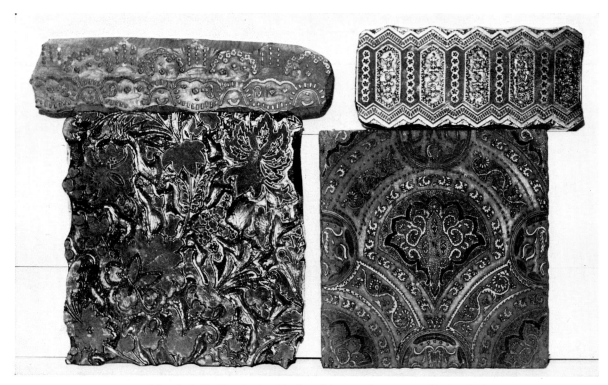

253 Macclesfield silk printing blocks, 18th or 19th century. (*Section XVI*)

254 Macclesfield silk printing blocks, 18th or 19th century. (*Section XVI*)

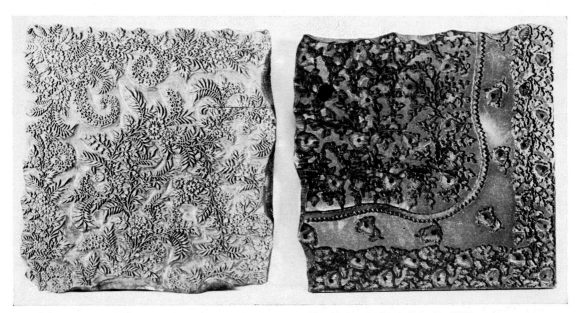

255 Macclesfield silk printing blocks, 18th or 19th century. (*Section XVI*)

256 A Macclesfield silk printing block, 18th or 19th century. (*Section XVI*)

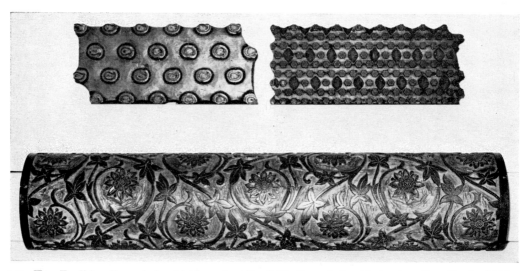

257 Two English calico printing blocks and an English roller printing block, *circa* 1800. (*Section XVI*)

258 17th-century woodcut block, with St. Roche and St. Sebastian in one half and the Virgin crowned in the other half. Probably Spanish. (*Section XVI*)

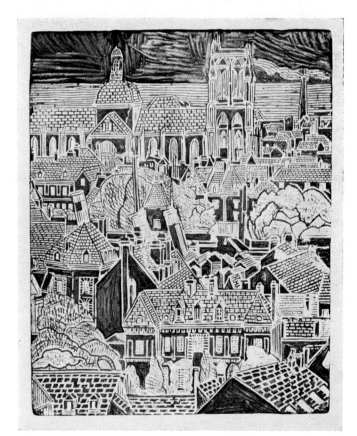

259 Woodcut block of 'Roofscape with church at Dieppe'; design by Charles Ginner, execution by T. Lawrence. First quarter of the 20th century. (*Section XVI*)

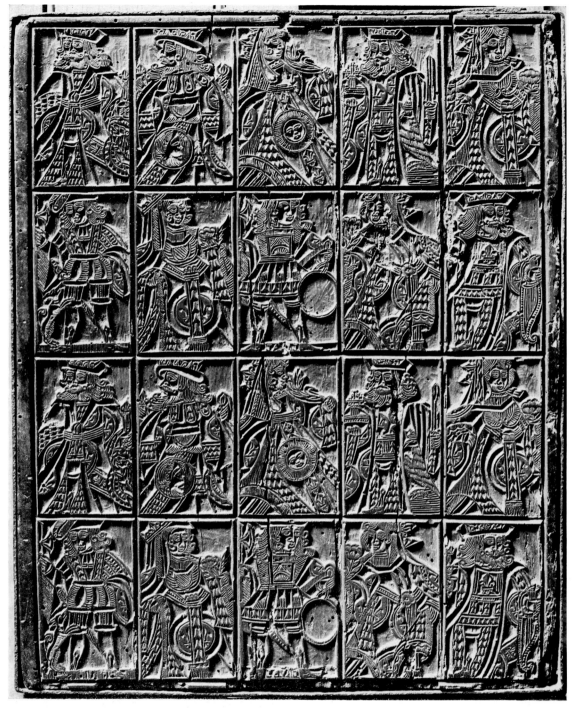

260 French, multiple playing card woodcut block, printing ten court cards in duplicate. First half of the 18th century. *By courtesy of the Wallace Collection.* (*Section XVI*)

261 Selection of fine wood engraving blocks, *A* to *K*. The pulls from them are shown in Plate 262. (*Section XVI*). The boxwood die or mould, *L*, is described in the introduction to *Section XII, Moulds*.

262 Pulls from the wood engraving blocks, *A* to *K*, illustrated in Plate 261. (*Section XVI*)

263 *A*, early 19th-century hectograph; *B* to *M* and *U*, ink containers; *N* to *Q* and *V*, pen wipers; *R* and *S*, inkstands; *T*, pen stand. (*Section XVII*)

264 *A*, *B*, *C* and *M*, writing compendia; *D*, *E*, *G*, *H*, *J* and *K*, travelling inkpots; *F*, combined pen and inkpot; *L*, ceremonial writing outfit; *N*, *Q* and *R*, ink containers; *P* and *V*, rare inkstands; *O*, *S*, *T* and *U*, pounce pots. (*Section XVII*)

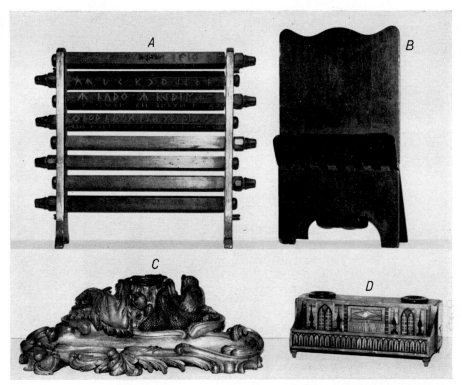

265 *A*, Welsh peithynen; *B*, ingeniously constructed book rest, half opened (shown fully open, Plate 282, *B*); *C*, 1851 inkstand; *D*, Regency inlaid inkstand. (*Section XVII*)

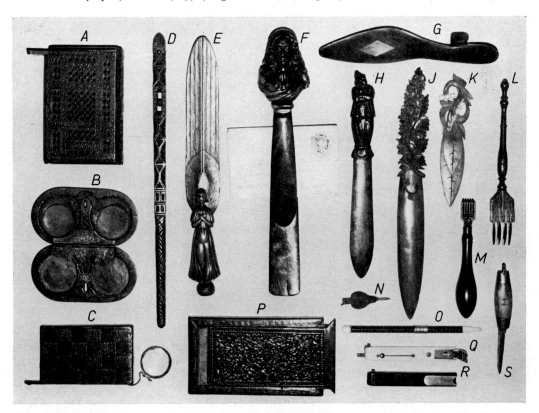

266 *A*, fine case for prayer book, *circa* 1500; *B* and *C*, rare 18th-century spectacle cases; *E to K*, paper knives. *F*, representing John Milton; *L* and *M*, music liners; *N* and *O*, revolving pencils; *P*, Persian wax tablet case; *Q* and *R*, quill pen cutters; *S*, Scandinavian folding knife (*Section XVII*); *D*, fescue. (*Section XXVII*)

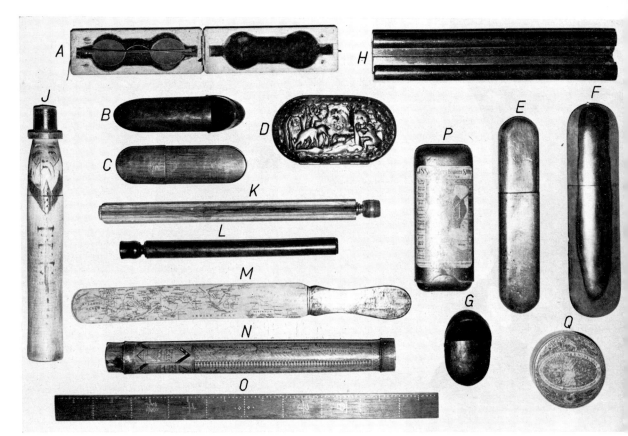

267 *A, B, C, E, F* and *G*, 19th-century spectacle cases; *D*, outside of case, Plate 266, *B*; *H*, book rest, Plate 281, left, when folded; *K* and *L*, combined ruler and sealing outfits; *M*, Victoria Jubilee paper knife; *O*, Chinese ruler; *P*, German crayon outfit; *Q*, nib box (*Section XVII*); *J* and *N*, pencil boxes. (*Section XXVII*)

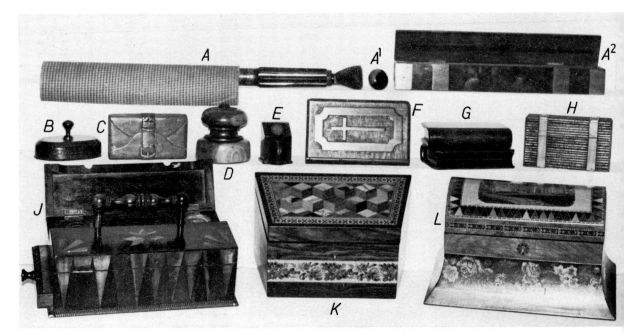

268 *A, A1* and *A2*, the components of hectograph, Plate 263, *A*; *B* to *G*, paper weights; *H*, postcard box; *J, K* and *L*, Tunbridge mosaic inkstand and two stationery caskets. (*Section XVII*)

269 *A, B, C* and *D*, scriveners' knives. The other items all in Tunbridge wood mosaic: *E, F* and *G*, paper weights; *H* and *J*, spectacle cases; *K*, paper knife; *L* and *M*, pen trays; *N* to *Q*, rulers. (*Section XVII*)

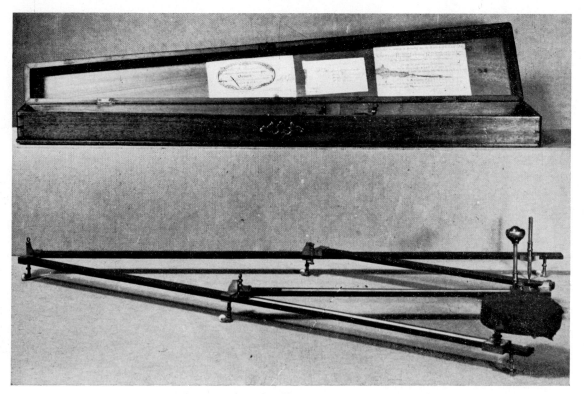

270 Pantographer of 1766–7, with its case. (*Section XVII*)

272 and 273 Mahogany travelling bookcase. English. Mid-18th century. (*Section XVII*)

271 Folding library pole ladder. English. 18th century. (*Section XVII*)

in the centre, was a Victorian child's amusement, but probably has a considerably older origin. When the string is oscillated, the disc emits a warbling note.

Yo-yos

The name yo-yo was so well popularized, some 50 to 60 years ago, that most of us who were young then, delighted in the grooved wooden disc, which could be made to run up and down a piece of string; we had, however, no idea that our latest plaything was only a revival of one which, under other names, had enthralled earlier generations of adults and children. It was known in the Far East in quite ancient times and suddenly swept France and England in the 1790s. In France, it was called the *emigrette* and in England, the bandalore. It either continued in vogue in England or had another revival in the 1820–40 period, when it was sometimes made, somewhat unsuitably, in the fragile Tunbridge wood mosaic, Plate 218, *H* and *J*; such specimens, if in good condition, are rare and prized. More ordinary and robust specimens in yew and boxwood are shown, Plate 218, *K* and *L*. The 1910–20 yo-yo craze swept America as well as Europe and travelled back again to the East, whence it had originally come. Post Second World War, the yo-yo reappeared, this time in plastic.

Archery, Hunting, Riding, Shooting, Skating, Luring, Decoying and Bird Scaring

This section is devoted mainly to outdoor sports and the sportsman's equipment, rather than to games and games accessories. Items concerned with horse welfare will be found in Section XXV, *Trade and Craft Devices: Farrier*. Although a certain number of weapon ancillaries, such as powder horns, cartridge moulds and extractors, shot pourers, etc., are included among the wooden bygones in this section, it is felt that weapons, in general, are outside the scope of this volume. The chief exceptions are those which are primarily defensive or for keeping order. Offensive weapons are, in the main, of metal; the subject is too large and specialized for inclusion here, and, moreover, weapons of war are incomplete as a subject without armour. As H. E. Palmer wrote in *The Woodworkers' Ballad*

'All that is moulded of iron
  Has lent to destruction and blood,
  But the things that are honoured of Zion
  Are most of them moulded of wood'.

That is very true, so although archery is now a peaceful pursuit, it only ranks for a heading here by reason of the far reaching effects which it has had on our gaming laws.

Archery

A witness before the Royal Commission on Gaming in 1958, described our gaming laws as 'bow and arrow legislation' and he was speaking the literal truth. In 1388, Richard II commanded servants and labourers to cease from games including dice, and directed them to practise archery. This was an early act made in the interests of national defence, and further acts with the same purpose in mind, were made in 1409, 1477 and 1541. In the last, dice, cards and backgammon were among the games specifically prohibited. Until the 17th century, no distinction was made between games played for amusement and exercise, such as bowls or tennis, and games of chance played for money. Not until 1845 was the act of 1541 repealed, so far as it affected games played for exercise.

Bird Calls—see *Calls*

Bird Cages—see *Cages*

Bird Decoys—see *Decoy Birds*

Bird Scarers

I have come to regard the cost of bird scarers as merely a surcharge on the cost of growing greenstuff and fruit for birds. But hope springs eternal in the human breast and I still go on experimenting with the modern versions of the various devices which our ancestors used—excluding the boy at 2*d.* per day! He was probably the most effective of all for, additional to his clappers, rattle or swinging tin containing pebbles, he also threw stones at the marauders and sang one of the old bird scaring rhymes. In Hertfordshire, a favourite was

> 'Shoo birds aw-a-ay,
> For tuppence a da-a-ay,
> Through hedges and ditches,
> You little black witches,
> Sha-lo, Sha-lo, Sha-lo'.

Bird clappers, made of three layers of hardwood, loosely hinged with leather and the centre leaf extended up to form a handle, are illustrated, Plate 245, *D* and *F*; they are impossible to date. One of the commonest varieties of scarer rattles is shown, Plate 245, *E*. This pattern, both with single and double ratchets, has had many uses besides bird scaring. It became the early 19th-century police rattle and householder's anti-burglar alarm; in the last war, it was issued to air raid wardens, to sound in the event of a gas attack, and the large number made for this purpose accounts for the presence of many which show no signs of age nor wear. A pivoted type, which operated by shaking it, probably originated earlier. As a generality, but no more, 19th-century rattles are made of beech, earlier ones of oak. The two carved wood bird scarers, Plate 246, *D* and *E*, with flailing arms, are 19th-century variants of the ancient windmill; *D* may be American. The blackbirds in the grounds of our house,

competed to use *E* as a perch on hot days; his flailing arms kept them cool—so much for bird scarers!

Boot Jacks and Boot Lifts

Boot jacks, contrivances for aid in removing riding boots, have been made in two basic types—permanent standing jacks, as exemplified by Plate 246, *N*, and various folding patterns, such as Plate 246, *F*, *G*, *H* and *J*. The principle is the same with all of them: the horseman stands with one foot on the jack and eases off the heel of the boot in the slot provided. *N*, English, 18th-century, made of mahogany, was the most elegant and efficient, where space and purse allowed. It has steadying hand grips and is made for a spurred boot; the pivoted gate swings forward to hold the toe down. The folding types, *F*, *G*, *H* and *J*, are all basically the same, but *G*, of rosewood, is a lady's jack, made in the form of a lady's leg, and contains one of its original lifts; *H*, of walnut, when closed, simulates a pistol; *F*, and *J*, are mahogany. All are English, probably 18th- or early 19th-century. *K* is a pair of riding boot lifts with horn hook and yew-wood handles; they are probably 18th-century and less common than lifts with steel hooks.

Cages—Bird, Cricket, Mouse, etc.

Cages all follow the same principles—enclosures with bars close enough to prevent the occupant escaping, but far enough apart to allow air, light and view. Until well into the 17th century, bird cages were in two classes: cages for fattening birds in the kitchen, and cages in other rooms, where the bright plumage and song or speech of the prisoners entertained their gaolers. Basketmakers were probably the earliest makers of simple woven, domed cages in all sizes, but wickerwork being a perishable material, no early examples have survived, nor were such cages of sufficient value to be mentioned in inventories. Iron, brass and copper wire cages were also used in mediaeval times and a 15th-century iron cage, discovered near Avignon, is now in the Metropolitan Museum, New York. The captive bird in a gilded cage, whose misery was vividly described by Chaucer, is no figure of fiction: a French inventory of the possessions of Charles V in 1380, lists cages of gold, garnished with pearls, emeralds, sapphires and other precious stones. Other cages, at various periods, have been made of silver, Sheffield plate, glass rods, hand-painted metal and hardwoods, sometimes decorated with ormolu and studded with precious stones, porcelain plaques or crystal drops; cages of varied architectural forms or furniture styles, in a blend of fashionable hardwoods and wirework, were long the height of fashion. In the 18th century, when cabinet furniture was largely controlled by the proportions of classical buildings, many bird cages became architectural microcosms; they simulated not only town houses and country villas, in mahogany and other hardwoods, but also portrayed, in their façades, all the current fashions and conceits of Palladian mansions, Gothic churches, Indian pavilions, Chinese pagodas and French chateaux. In fact, from the front, they resembled some of the most palatial dolls' houses of the period (at least one has been converted into a doll's house), with wire grille windows, but the tops and backs were generally entirely of wire. These mansion cages, some of which were made at Tunbridge and decorated with wood mosaic, were made to stand on special tables. G. Bernard Hughes has recorded that, in the 1860s, James Quin of Kidderminster was making reproductions of 18th-century Gothic cages in mahogany; another century having now passed, these can deceive the collector of today. A simple cage for a linnet, one of the birds which suffers worst in captivity, is shown, Plate 245, *C*.

Crickets are greatly esteemed in China for their song. A traditional Chinese cricket cage made of split cane, as are so many Chinese bird cages, is illustrated, Plate 245, *B*. A moulded gourd cricket cage is described and illustrated in Section XIII, *Nuts, Gourds, etc*. A Georgian child's mahogany mouse cage, with back and front sliding panels, is shown, Plate 245, *A*.

Calls

Calls, mostly of whistle type, are shown, Plate 245, *H* to *N*. The carved bulldog head, *K*, is a high-pitched dog whistle. The others are all audible lures, carefully designed to imitate realistically, the calls of various wild birds; most of them, additional to blowing, require some skilful manipulation with the finger over a hole or holes. *M*, of mahogany, simulates the cooing of a pigeon. A few wooden calls are friction, not blowing devices. *G*, which is often confused with bird scarers, is a corncrake call, which imitates the well-known rasping sound in short bursts, by turning the ratchet twixt finger and thumb. See also *Lark Lures*, and *Decoy Birds*.

Cartridge Devices

The device for making containers for cartridges for 12-bore guns, Plate 245, *X*, consists of an ebonised handle with a brass barrel. Pressure on the lever at the side of the barrel, ejects a 'flick' knife, which cuts off the cardboard tube to correct length; it was made by George Hawksley, of 74 Strand, London, *circa* 1830–40. See also *Shot Pourers*.

The extractor for 12-bore spent cartridges, Plate 245, *Y*, has a fruitwood handle and bronze(?) fittings; the side lever grips are spring actuated, and the handle is spring loaded, for ejecting the cases. There is no maker's name, but it gives the impression of a date around 1800.

Plate 245, *Q* and *Q1*, are two slightly different English patterns of 'turning down' machines, used in hand filling 12-bore cartridges. *Q* is operated with both hands, whilst *Q1*, shown open, with a cartridge in it, screws on to a bench. Both are of box-wood with brass fittings and date from *circa* 1870.

Cricket Cages—see *Cages*

Decoy Birds

Probably the oldest man-made decoy birds extant, are some specimens of North American Indian work, in the Museum of the American Indian in New York City. They are made of reeds, bound with flat rushes, pigmented and augmented by real feathers. They are believed to have been made about 1,000 years ago and were discovered in the Lovelock Cave in Nevada, in 1924. Carved wooden decoy birds have doubtless been made from very early times, but there is an almost complete dearth of history until late in the 19th century.

The word decoy, contracted from the Dutch words *Ende-Kooy*, formerly indicated the duck trap or cage, into which wild fowl were decoyed, through a netted 'pipe' or tunnel, either by using semi-domesticated birds or painted wooden ones, as the lure. John Evelyn, in his *Diary* for March 29, 1665, describes a decoy laid down in St. James's Park by Charles II. Nowadays, the decoy bird itself is usually described as a decoy and it is curious how old wooden ones seem to have disappeared in the British Isles, since being superseded by rubber and papier mâché. The decorative carved wooden specimens cannot all have been destroyed, yet all I have been able to purchase here are pigeons, one of which is shown, Plate 247, *C*, and I have had a gift of mallard ducks and drakes from a friend in Scotland. Apart from these, all those in the Pinto Collection have come from the U.S.A., where old wooden decoys attract great interest and thousands are still extant; the Shelburne Museum, Vermont, has more than 1,000 specimens, and a lavishly illustrated descriptive catalogue, which no decoy collector should be without. There is also a *Decoy Collector's Guide*, published bi-monthly in the States, where decoys are now 'big business'.

So far as I can judge from the very limited number of British specimens which I have examined, they tend to be more carefully finished than American specimens of similar age, but the modern North American decoys, carved from balsa wood, are most realistically shaped and painted.

The nature of the work for which decoys are intended, water birds particularly, their low intrinsic value, and their need of paint maintenance and repair, all mitigate against their having a long life. In consequence, most of those in museums and private collections have been made during the last 100 years, probably the majority in this century. Generally, the older decoys are cruder, but even when basically inaccurate, they are frequently designed very carefully indeed to throw the right shadows and even the crudest have considerable character and naïve charm. Some of the U.S.A. decoy carvers have been identified, by idiosyncrasies in their work—name stamps under the birds, regional characteristics, and the choice of woods, which are varied, although pine is the most common for the bodies and a selected hardwood for the heads of the water birds, which are a separate insert into the bodies; so also are long beaks, and legs of shore birds, but the bodies and heads of the shore birds are usually carved out of a single block. Water birds generally have a lead weight inserted or applied to the underside of their bodies, to make them float realistically. Some late 19th-century American water bird decoys are hollow, made like a soup tureen and lid. The neck is fixed from inside the 'lid' part of the body, and the lead weight screwed inside the base. The two halves were then dowelled together, the joint sealed and the whole carved. Great care was taken with the painting, to ensure a surface which did not glisten after rain. A decoy duck and drake, on a small island in our pond, not only attracted a live pair, but they nested alongside them, a few years ago.

Of the selection in Plate 247, *A* is presumably a plover; *B* is a New Jersey dowitcher snipe; *C*, the only English decoy shown, is a pigeon; *D* is a black-breast; *E* is an American merganser; *F* is a duck; *G* is a male scaup; *H* is a cock old squaw, stamped T.W.D.; *J* is a grey coot; *K* is a Burrow's golden eye duck; *L* is an American canvasback; *M*, a black duck. See also *Lark Lures*.

Fishermen's Accessories—See Section XVIII, *Sailors', Sailmakers' and Fishermen's Devices*

Fleams and Mallets—See Section XXV, *Trade and Craft Devices: Farrier*

Game Carriers
The English, 19th-century, machine-made, oak, portable game carrier, Plate 246, *A*, with pivoted brass gates at the opposite ends of two parallel grooves, is a direct descendant of the 17th- or 18th-century, hand-made oak carrier, Plate 246, *B*, with two central hinged oak gates. The necks of the shot birds are passed through the gates into the grooves and the birds are suspended by their heads. The carriers are both 19 in. long.

Gun Periscopes
The hour-glass shaped, $3\frac{1}{2}$ in. high, turned sycamore cup, Plate 245, *O*, painted black inside, with the aperture going right through the neck, is said to be a periscope for checking that insides of barrels of fire-arms were clear. The barrel is viewed through an aperture in the side of the lower cup, which is fitted with a tilted base mirror. It seems quite practical and appears to have considerable age, probably 17th- or 18th-century, English.

Horns—see *Powder Horns*

Horse Curry Combs—see Section V, *Farm*

Horse Hoof Parers—see Section XXV, *Trade and Craft Devices: Farrier*

Horse Tail Dockers—see Section XXV, *Trade and Craft Devices: Farrier*

Horse Tooth Rasps—see Section XXV, *Trade and Craft Devices: Farrier*

Horse Twitches—see Section XXV, *Trade and Craft Devices: Farrier*

Horse Standards—see Section XIX, *Scientific: Measuring Sticks*

Lark Lures
Decoys and lures for trapping or shooting birds can be grouped under three main headings: visual deception, vocal imposture and curiosity appeal. The lark lure comes under the last heading. The insatiable curiosity of larks and their attraction to anything glittering, makes it easy to bring them within shooting range. Although the lark lure was formerly used in England as well as on the continent, the specimen shown, Plate 248, was probably made and used in 17th-century Italy, where it was known as a *specchietto*. The crescent-shaped head, 10 in. across, is of walnut, studded with inlaid rectangles of mirror. It is fitted on an iron pin, which pivots in a pointed wooden stake, driven into the ground. The so-called sportsman hid himself nearby, pulled a cord attached to the spindle, which revolves at great speed, scintillating light in all directions and attracting the lark overhead. The cord, when dropped, rewinds itself on the spindle. Plate 249 shows a labour-saving French version, made in the last quarter of the 18th century by Alexandre Cochet of Morbier. It is powered by clockwork, has two 9 in. blades which revolve in opposite directions and runs for 45 minutes.

The eating of song birds in England goes back at least to the 15th century; John Russell, in his *Boke of Nurture*, advises that larks, thrushes, etc., should be flavoured with salt and cinnamon and that the master should be served with the legs, but if still hungry, should be given the wings. Sir Hugh Plat, in *Delightes for Ladies* (1609), says that sparrows and larks should be boiled in mutton broth with mace, sweet butter and parsley, seasoned with sugar, verjuice and a little pepper. Gervase Markham, in *The English Hous-Wife* (1656), gives a recipe for roasting a shin of beef, loin of mutton, lark and capon together. This mixing of lark and meats, seems to be the ancestor of the steak, kidney and lark pudding or pie, still offered in English restaurants between the two wars; I hope it is no longer available.

In *Systema Agriculturae or the mystery of Husbandry Discovered*, by John Worlidge, 2nd edition 1675, advice is given on snaring larks:

'... place in the middle of the verge of your Net an Instrument made to move nimbly, by plucking it with a small line or packthread to and fro; on which should be fixed some pieces of Looking-glass, that by the continual whirring motion of it, the glittering of the Looking-glass by the reflection of the Sun in the eye of the *Lark*, allureth her down to the Net, especially if there be a *Stale* (decoy).

When one or two are in the compass of your Net, let them alone until they attract more Company to them: Preserve some of them alive, that you do take for *Stales*.

But if you cannot conveniently get a live *Stale* shoot a *Lark* and draw out his Intrails, and dry him in an Oven in his Feathers, with a stick thrust through him to preserve in a posture convenient: This *Stale* may serve near as well as a living one ...'.

Tired larks and other song birds, on their way home from Africa to northern Europe, have regular stopping places. Readers of Dr. Axel Munthe's wonderful *Story of San Michele* will remember the chapter entitled 'The Bird Sanctuary'. The author describes the fate of the poor birds visiting Capri, until eventually he was able to buy the mountain of Barbarossa and make it a bird sanctuary, thereby saving, he estimated, at least 15,000 birds a year. I quote two passages from his book:

'They came just before sunrise. All they asked for was to rest for a while after their long flight across the Mediterranean, the goal of the journey was so far away, the land where they were born and where they were to raise their young. They came in thousands: wood-pigeons, thrushes, turtle-doves, waders, quails, golden orioles, sky-larks, nightingales, wagtails, chaffinches, swallows, warblers, redbreasts and many other tiny artists on their way to give spring concerts to the silent forests and fields in the North. A couple of hours later they fluttered helplessly in the nets the cunning of man had stretched all over the island from the cliffs by the sea high up to the slopes of Monte Solaro and Monte Barbarossa. In the evening they were packed by hundreds in small wooden boxes without food and water and despatched by steamers to Marseilles to be eaten with delight in the smart restaurants of Paris'.

and

'Do you know how they are caught in the nets? Hidden under the thickets, between the poles, are caged decoy birds who repeat incessantly, automatically their monotonous call. They cannot stop, they go on calling out night and day till they die. Long before science knew anything about the localization of the various nerve-centres in the human brain, the devil had revealed to his disciple man his ghastly discovery that by stinging out the eyes of a bird with a red-hot needle the bird would sing automatically.'

Mole Traps—see Section X, *Miscellany: Rodent Traps*

Mouse Cages—see *Cages*

Mouse Traps—see Section X, *Miscellany: Rodent Traps*

Periscopes—see *Gun Periscopes*

Pigeon Ringing Devices
The ingenious pigeon ringing device, Plate 246, *C*, puzzles many people. When it was invented, I do not know, but this particular specimen, made of a mixture of hardwoods, is undoubtedly 19th-century work. The right-hand end of the base block screws down on to a bench, leaving the lever end projecting outwards. By depressing the lever, the four wires pull on the four rods and open the four curved claws outwards, stretching the rubber band, which encircles their upper ends, and makes it easy to insert the pigeon's foot into the band.

Powder Horns or Flasks
Although the majority of old powder flasks are horn, they sometimes belie their name by being hollowed out of wood. A high proportion of the wooden specimens are Scandinavian, and among these is a well-known group which follow the general outline of Scandinavian water flasks and snuff flasks, but comes between these two groups in size. Plate 245, *R*, is a representative, early 19th-century example, with integral lugs for hanging by a cord; it measures 5 in. across. The simple specimens, *S* and *W*, are probably both English and date from the 18th or early 19th century. *T* is a handsome, French or English, silver-mounted and silver inlaid burr maple and horn flask; its decoration is similar to that on pistols of the 1740–50 period. *U* is Scandinavian, carved with typical heads and low relief hunting scenes, 18th- or early 19th-century. Formerly in the Evan-Thomas Collection, *V* is inlaid with bone and metal certosina work; it is Italian, either 16th- or 17th-century.

Rat Traps—see Section X, *Miscellany: Rodent Traps*

Shooting Sticks—see Section X, *Miscellany: Seat Sticks*

Shot Pourers
The shot pourer, Plate 245, *P*, has depth adjustments in the brass cup for 1, 1⅜ and 1¼ oz. shot; the handle is lignum vitae. It was made by G. and J. W. Hawksley of 74 Strand, London. See also *Cartridge Devices*.

Skates
The earliest ice skates were made of bones of deer and many museums in northern latitudes have on display ancient excavated specimens which have been well ground down by friction with ice. Some of them appear to have been sledge runners, and others were tied to the feet. When wooden skates with iron blades were first introduced is unknown, but they are clearly shown in Dutch and other 16th-century paintings. The Edinburgh Skating Club was founded in 1642.

The skate, Plate 429, *A*, is one of a pair, with sycamore stocks and leather harness, as used in the Lincolnshire Fens about 1890. *B*, with elm stocks, is the traditional Dutch and Flemish pattern.

Spurs Stands
Spurs stands generally consist of a length of polished hardwood, profiled to fit the inside of a spur, provided with holes at intervals and suitably capped off at each end. Plate 250, *C* and *D*, which may be 18th- or early 19th-century, are typical. I have only seen two like the rare, crescent-shaped, standing type, Plate 250, *A*, which is of well patinated mahogany and dates from the 18th century. The first, I saw over 20 years ago and was asked 25 guineas for it in the West End of London; I did not buy it. The second, the one illustrated, I saw six weeks later, on the pavement, outside a junk shop in Bideford, price 7s. 6d.! I have never seen another. Spurs stands are sometimes combined with whip racks, as in the early

19th- century example, Plate 250, *B*. For further details, see *Whip Holders*. All the specimens illustrated are English.

Stable Logs—see Section XXV, *Trade and Craft Devices: Farrier*

Stirrups
Steel stirrups are outside the scope of this volume; but one of a pair of carved wood foot muffs with iron strap, which also acted as a stirrup, and being of wood gave considerable protection against freezing, is shown, Plate 428, *E*. This type, which has many centuries of tradition behind it, and is found with a wide range of decorative motifs, mostly carved on birch, was formerly normal horseman's equipment in northeast Asiatic Russia, Mongolia, Scandinavia, etc.

Toxophily—see *Archery*

Turning Down Machines—see *Cartridge Devices*

Whip Holders
Excluding the metal cup in which the stock of a whip was held upright beside the seat of the driver, there are two main ways of storing whips not in use. One is by winding the thong round a grooved segmental holder such as Plate 246, *L*, or a completely grooved wheel, as *M*; the other method is to use a horizontal notched rack, like the combined whip holder and spurs stand, Plate 250, *B*. The oak holder, Plate 246, *L*, is sharply V-grooved to grip the thong, holds seven whips and includes a harness peg; it is English, 18th-century. *M*, of mahogany, 18th- or early 19th-century, is Irish and holds two whips; the same turned wheel pattern was used in England. The centre-threaded button unscrews, to expose the screw hole for screwing the disc to the wall. Plate 250, *B*, a neat design in mahogany, probably dates from the Regency period, although the same layout has been used up to recent times. This particular example is made to take apart by undoing six brass set screws, and was particularly useful for export, and also for cavalrymen and riders generally, when travelling abroad. Plate 250, *E*, of mahogany and late 18th- or early 19th-century, is a considerable rarity, a combined coaching horn rack and whip holder.

Whistles—see *Calls*

XVI

Printing (Textile and Wallpaper) and Woodcut and Engraving Blocks

Wooden printing blocks may be considered under three main headings: (1) blocks for printing textiles or wallpapers, in which, with few exceptions, each block consists of a motif or a part of a pattern which is only completed by joining up to other different blocks, or by adjacent repeats of the same one; (2) woodcut blocks; (3) wood engraving blocks. Although (2) and (3) are entirely different, they will both serve the purpose of providing the whole block for a complete illustration, but with a woodcut, a single block may only represent one stage in the final picture.

When collecting either wood engraving blocks or textile printing blocks, or both, a unique original is acquired and the blocks themselves are highly decorative. With textile printing blocks, the size varies downwards from about 20 in. by 20 in., to about 9 in. by 9 in., whilst wood engraving blocks may be as small as 1 in. or 2 in. square, but neither type is necessarily a square. Moreover, the subjects in both types of blocks are unlimited, so that pulls or prints taken from them can be used to produce black and white coloured pictures suitable for decorating a wide range of objects, including room backgrounds, furniture, and smaller objects. An added thrill of collecting wood engraving blocks is that additional

to each one being an original, you may acquire one by a real master and be able to relate it to the book or other illustration for which it was created. In the past, I was fortunate enough to acquire a Thomas Bewick, a Lucien Pissarro, a Branston (pupil of Bewick) and, thanks to her own generosity, some blocks by Joan Hassall, one of the greatest living exponents of wood engraving. I have still to obtain a Birkett Foster, or any blocks made from the elfin-like child drawings of Kate Greenaway, or works of Walter Crane.

WALLPAPER AND TEXTILE PRINTING BLOCKS

It is probable that hand block printing originated in China, India or Egypt. Certainly there is evidence that it was practised in the East and Middle East at an early date. In Europe, it developed in the Middle Ages, but whether paper or textile printing came first is unknown. Limitation of the size of paper, however, restricted early block printed paper to sheets used primarily for decorative box, trunk and cupboard linings. Wallpapers came later and until the late 17th century, consisted of quite short lengths joined together. Hand block printing, although now the mark of quality,

243

was originally an attempt to bring a decorative background within the reach of a higher proportion of the population. The printed textile was a less expensive substitute for brocades and needlework used in costume and soft furnishings, and the hand blocked wallpaper had the same relationship to the patterned fabric wall hanging.

Blocks used for hand block printing of textiles are usually built up to a thickness of about 2½ in., consisting of four or five plies of pearwood, sycamore or plane, arranged with the grain of alternate layers at right angles, to avoid shrinkage or warping; two oval holes, carved out of the back, form finger grips. The face pattern of old wood blocks is carved so that the pattern, often both delicate and intricate, stands out in relief. Modern blocks usually have a metal face. Some fascinating old wood blocks occasionally come to light, with designs formed by as many as 50,000 brass pins hammered into, and projecting ¼ in. above the face. The labour was enormous—the effect, the delightful *pointillé* or half-tone. Some large textile printing blocks involving bold splashes of colour, have the raised portions consisting of wood rims, which are hollowed out and filled flush with felt.

The use of wood blocks for textile and wallpaper printing is well described in these extracts from *Campbell's London Tradesman*, 1747:

'The Calico-Printer is employed in printing or staining Cotton and Linen Cloath. We had the first Hint of this Branch of Business from the *Indies*, where those beautiful Cloths called *Chints* are made to the greatest Perfection. We have gathered of late some of the Principles of this Art; but fall short of the *Indians* in striking their Colours: Ours come short of theirs both in their Beauty, Life and Durableness: They exceed in all Dies, but especially Reds, Greens, and Blues.

The *Indians* paint all their Callicos with the Pencil; which they do very expeditiously, and at a prodigious low Price, as may be computed from the first Price of this Commodity: But their Patterns are wild, and all their Figures, except Flowers and Plants, are monstrous. The honourable *East-India* Company have been at a vast Expence to find out the Secret of their Die, especially of Red, but to no purpose; all Trials that have been made have fallen short of the true *Indian* Chint.'

We perform our Printing in a different Manner: It is properly Printing. We took the Hint from the *Hamburghers*, who first fell into that Method. It is performed in this Manner: The Pattern is first drawn upon Paper, the whole Breadth of the Cloth intended to be printed; the Workman then divides the whole Pattern into several Parts according to its Largeness, each Part being about eight Inches broad and twelve Inches long; each distinct Part of the Pattern thus divided is cut out upon wooden Types; the Cloth to be printed is extended upon a Table, and the Types, being covered with the proper Colours, are laid on, and the Impression is left upon the Cloth. They begin to lay on the Types at one End of the Piece, and to continue to the other, and no Interstice or Vacancy is to be seen between. When the whole Piece is thus printed, the Cloth is washed and bleached, to take off any accidental Stains it may have received in the Operation: It is then dried, calendared, and laid up in Folds fit for the Shop. This is the Manner in which Cloths of several Colours are printed or stained. There is another Method used with such as are designed only of one Colour, *viz.* Blues; that is Blue and White. The Part of the Cloth which is designed to be White is waxed on both Sides with Bees-Wax, and then the Piece is put into a Vat of prepared Blue Die: The Part unwaxed receives the Blue Tincture, and the Wax keeps the other Part White. The Wax is then taken off, and the Cloth made up as the other.'

He continues that calico printers

'. . . employ three sorts of Hands: The Pattern-Drawer, the Cutters of the Types, who are likewise the Operators in Printing, and Labourers to assist in the Washing, etc. The Pattern-Drawer is paid according to the

Variety and Value of his Designs; and the Printer who cuts nicely may earn while employed Half a Guinea a Day during the Printing Season, which lasts from *April* till *September*, after which they are but little employed.

A Youth designed to be bound to this Art ought to have a Genius for Drawing, a good Eye, and a delicate Hand, for the Figures they cut in Wood are frequently very minute: He requires no Education but Reading, Writing, and to be early taught the Principles of Drawing.... Paper-Hangings are printed after the same Manner, and may properly enough be called a Branch of this Trade. Flock Paper-Hangings are performed in this Manner: They take Flock, which are the Cuttings of Cloth, taken off with Sheers by the Cloth-Dressers. This they chuse of the Colour the Paper is designed to be, and cut it with an Engine, as small as possible, till it becomes as small as fine Powder. The Figure which is designed to be represented on the Paper is drawn with Gum-Water, or drying Oils, and while it is yet wet the Flock-Powder is sifted upon it through a fine Sieve: That Part of the Powder which falls upon the oiled Part, sticks and represents the Figure designed, and the rest that falls upon the dry Paper is shaken off. If the Paper is to be of more Colours than one, suppose Red, Green, and Blue, that Part of the Pattern which is designed to be Red is first drawn in Oil and the Powder sifted over the whole Paper, which is allowed to dry thoroughly; then the Green is drawn and sifted upon in the same Manner: When that is dry, the Blue is ordered as the two other Colours. In this Manner Paper of this Kind may receive as many Colours as you please....'

One of the most unusual decorative uses for old wallpaper printing blocks is to be seen at a farm at Harpsden, near Henley-on-Thames, Oxfordshire. A large quantity of blocks of the 1795–1830 period was rescued from an old paper mill at the Oxford end of the weir across the Thames at Marsh Mills; after creosoting, they were then fixed to the exteriors of the walls of three barns, giving a most unusual textured effect.

In Plate 252, the block top left is unusual, because the leaf and stem pattern is cut back and is the part left unprinted. It was used by Sir Elkanah Armitage of Manchester in the 19th century, for printing on calico. Next to it is a mid-18th-century *Chinoiserie* block for printing linen or cotton, probably French. Below, is a block for printing the yardage, bale number and trade mark of Williamson's of Cleckheaton on hessian bales for export; it is early 19th-century. On the right, the floral textile printing block is English, of the 17th century.

The blocks illustrated in Plates 253 to 256 are all for printing Macclesfield silk; some were used in the 18th and others in the 19th century. The block, bottom left, Plate 253, has felt inserts in the large leaf masses. The finely cut block, bottom right, has felt in the darkest portions, and *pointillé* in the centre of the motifs. The equally fine example, top right, has felt inserts between the alternate vertical motifs.

In Plate 254, the block on the left consists of rather crude outlines of birds and foliage. On the right, the corner portion of a striking design of horse heads, has felt inserts in the heads and in the scrolls of the border.

In Plate 255, the left-hand block is an unusually fine and intricate fern and floral carving, all wood. The right-hand block, showing a textile corner with border, has felt inserts between the carved motifs. Plate 256, entirely carved wood, is large for a one-piece wood block; it measures 21 in. by 16 in. In Plate 257 are two more of Sir Elkanah Armitage's 19th-century calico printing blocks, and below, an English, carved hardwood roller printing block, used about 1800, for 27 in. wide cotton or linen. Roller printing was not established until 1790 and by 1802 wooden rollers, on account of their tendency to warp, were almost entirely superseded by metal.

WOODCUT AND ENGRAVING BLOCKS

Woodcutting goes back to A.D. 175, when the text of the Chinese classics was knife cut from wood blocks and impressions were taken from them. Printing from wood blocks is believed to go back to the 6th century in China and the 8th century in Japan, but these early wood blocks were generally letterpress, not pictorial. Whether wood-cutting was introduced to Europe from the East or was discovered independently is unknown, but ornamental woodcut blocks for textiles and vellum were used in Rhenish monasteries in the 12th century. Early in the 15th century, when paper making had become an established industry, wood block printing was used extensively in Germany, Holland and Flanders. The earliest wood-cuts known in a book printed in English, occur in *The Mirrour of the World*, issued in 1480. The original use of wood blocks in Europe, as in Asia, was for letterpress work and it was only with the advent of Albrecht Dürer (1471–1528), probably the greatest creative artist in wood block cutting of all time, that the full pictorial possibilities were explored and realized. Some of the most attractive 16th-century woodcut blocks are for initial letters with pictorial backgrounds.

In the mid-15th century, a Frenchman, Bernard Milnet, invented a method of drilling holes in a block to give a white on black stippled effect, which was known as *criblé* (drilled). The process soon fell into disuse, its place being taken by the cross hatching method of shading, the earliest example of which occurs in a book, *Voyage to the Holy Land*, printed by Brey-denack in 1486. No great technical development then occurred until the latter half of the 18th century, when Thomas Bewick (1753–1828) revolutionized the industry by creating end-grain wood engraved blocks of boxwood. Until his time, wood-cutters used comparatively soft hardwoods, such as pear, and cut their pictures with a knife, rather like a joiner's marking knife, or removed the wood with a gouge along the grain of the wood. The life of such blocks was limited and there was a tendency to show grain on the reproduction. Bewick, searching for a method which would give clear cut impressions indefinitely, experimented with the already known idea of engraving on the end grain of a hard, dense wood, such as box or holly and it was Bewick who developed the technique to perfection. In wood engraving, various types of gravers, Plate 419, *K*, take the place of the knife as principal tool. Because its steel is wedge-shaped in section, the width of a graver cut varies with depth. This highlights the other great difference between wood cutting and wood engraving. In the older method, the woodcutter made his drawings with black lines on the white-wood block and then laboriously cut away all the wood from between the black lines. Bewick's method created a picture comprising single stroke white lines engraved on a black background, the width of line being varied simply by depth of cut. In this process, skill in lining largely takes the place of cross hatching and becomes the obvious method of obtaining graduation of shade, with more delicate detail than is possible with woodcuts.

Owing to the limitation of size of box-wood, large blocks are built up out of sections approximately $3\frac{1}{2}$ in. by 2 in. by $\frac{7}{8}$ in., or 4 in. by $2\frac{1}{2}$ in. by $\frac{7}{8}$ in. and the craftsmanship of jointing has to be very fine and true. The edges of sections are plough grooved and fitted with loose tongues, and slots are made in backs of sections for the nuts of coach screws, which are used to draw the pieces tightly together. The whole block so formed is then planed and scraped smooth. Maple, which is obtainable in larger size blocks than box, is also used. Some engravers next apply a paint wash and draw direct on it; others make their drawing on paper and paste it on the block.

Wood engraving imposes considerable eye strain and until recent improvements in artificial lighting, it was normal practice to use a water flash to concentrate light rays—for a description of use of a flash, see Section VI, *Fire and Lighting: Candle Stands, Lace-Makers'*.

A good 17th-century pearwood woodcut double block, portraying St. Roche and St. Sebastian in one half and in the other half, the Virgin Mary crowned in glory, is shown Plate 258; it is probably Spanish. A remarkable French, 18th-century, multiple, playing card woodcut block, Plate 260, prints 10 court cards in duplicate. In the upper half, left to right, are King of Clubs, King of Diamonds, Queen of Spades, King of Hearts and Queen of Clubs; 2nd row, Knave of Spades, Queen of Hearts, Knave of Clubs, Queen of Diamonds and King of Spades. The sequence is repeated in the lower half of the block which measures $14\frac{1}{2}$ in. by 12 in. printing cards $3\frac{5}{16}$ in. by $2\frac{1}{8}$ in. The block was probably owned by Nicholas Barat of Laval; the name Laval is printed below the Knaves of Clubs, who have had their medallions erased. This was probably done when the privilege of printing cards at Laval was abolished in 1751; cards were only printed between 1720 and 1751.

The interesting woodcut block (which has been chalked to make it stand out) 'Roofscape with church at Dieppe', Plate 259, was designed by Charles Ginner (1878–1952) and cut by T. Lawrence. Ginner was one of a group of painters which included Sickert, and Gilman, popular in the first quarter of this century. This woodcut is illustrated in Herbert Furst's *The Modern Woodcut*, John Lane, 1924.

A selection of fine boxwood engraving blocks are shown, Plate 261, 'A to J, with chalked outlines. The pulls from them are illustrated, Plate 262. A is an 18th-century picture of Temple Church, Bristol, with its leaning tower; B is a mid-18th-century 'chapbook' block; C is by Thomas Bewick (1753–1828); it was probably executed during the last quarter of the 18th century and was used by Rusher of Banbury to illustrate *The History of Goody Two Shoes*. D is a finely detailed block, commemorating the London International Exhibition of 1874; E is a very original idea for a change of address card, superbly executed by Miss Joan Hassall; the style of F suggests that it is by one of Bewick's pupils, possibly Jackson. G was engraved by Branston Jun., another pupil of Bewick; it has his mark on one edge. The block was used for Pennant's *Antiquities of Scotland*, published in 1841. H, by an unknown engraver, is from a design by Mulready for a mid-19th-century edition of *The Vicar of Wakefield*. J is a vigorous engraving of rowdies in a carriage, engraver unknown, *circa* 1845. K is a Regency woodcut block for a leatherworker's billhead; the bathchair of the period is interesting. For details of L, see Section XII, *Moulds*.

XVII

Reading, Writing, Copying, Drawing, Painting and Modelling Ancillaries

As reading and writing are often preliminaries to sealing and postage, some of the devices mentioned or described here, are also referred to in Section XIV, *Parcelling, Postage, Sealing, etc.* The ancillaries of reading, writing, copying, drawing and painting are, in this section, treated as one subject, arranged in alphabetical order and not subdivided. There are several reasons for this: (1) background materials used for some of the pursuits are often alike; (2) the implements or devices used are also, in some instances, alike; (3) there is confusion of terminology in old descriptions of these implements; (4) there is sometimes no clear line of demarcation between the occupations. For instance, the earliest writings, some of which were with the brush, consisted of stringing together meaningful pictorial symbols, which in time developed into the letters of the various alphabets. Conversely, some of the latest paintings and drawings consist of linking together meaningless doodles!

In different civilizations, wood, baked clay, stone, papyrus and parchment have all served as background materials for painting, drawing and writing; additionally, both wax, engraved with a stylus, and slate have a long history of usage for temporary jottings; some of the cases for wax writing have survived. Pictures and writings on all the other materials mentioned have come down to us from the older civilizations, including wooden account books, and writing boards of the Graeco-Roman period, 2nd century A.D. The last two were lime-washed and then scrubbed for re-use. By reason of bulk and weight, baked clay, stone and wood all imposed limitations additional to the amount of surface preparation needed before the writer or artist could commence his labours. But even parchment or vellum, after the lengthy preliminary operations, still had to be pounced (see *Blotter Cases* and *Pounce Boxes*), before it could be used for writing. So for that matter did the ultimate—paper, until comparatively modern times.

The name paper is derived from papyrus, the Egyptian reed which preceded it as a writing material. The Chinese are said to have invented writing paper about the end of the 1st century A.D. It took 1,000 years to reach Europe, being brought to Spain by the Moors in the 11th century. In the 12th century, paper mills were established in France and 100 years later, the manufacture spread to Italy, thence to Germany, the Low Countries and England. The first recorded mill for paper of writing quality, was John Tate's Sele Mill near

Stevenage, set up about 1490. His watermark was an eight-point star in a double circle. Watermarks date back to the 13th century in Italy, and different marks were used for different sizes of paper. At an early date, the *fogliocapo*, folio sized sheet, became anglicised as foolscap. John Spillman, a German, who set up a mill at Dartford, Kent, in 1588, used a fool's head with cap and bells as his watermark. Harrison records Spillman's as the first writing paper mill in England, but this in incorrect: there were several before his, but probably not so large. The earliest paper mill still working in England, is Turkey Court, Kent, established about 1690. In the 18th century, James Whatman, father and son, took over the mill and made it famous for the fine paper which still bears their name.

In the 15th century, it was the invention of printing which gave the fillip to the development of paper. As few could write, the supply of vellum sufficed, and was doubtless and rightly considered more permanent for important written matters. Paper really only superseded it for writing, other than legal, in the 16th century. If paper for writing took so long to become usual, it was nothing to the time which elapsed before blotting paper came into general use; this is more fully discussed under *Pounce Boxes*.

It was the second quarter of the 19th century, around 1840, that was the writer's, particularly the letterwriter's, time of emancipation from the worst drudgery. Then, for the first time, matches were available to light the candle; gummed envelopes obviated the labour of sealing the missive itself; postage stamps and a penny post arrived; blotting paper at last banished pounce; and there was no longer need to cut and sharpen quills (see *Pen Cutters*)—steel pens to suit all tastes were on sale.

The confusion of terminology of implements used for writing, painting and drawing, to which reference was made earlier, is well exemplified by 17th- and 18th-

century descriptions of so-called penwork decoration on wood. The term itself is misleading to modern ears. The words pencil and pen were both used loosely and confusingly by 17th- and 18th-century authors; directions for penwork make it clear, as do the examples themselves, that brushes of varying fineness were used much more than pens. Although pen, in the sense then used, always means a quill, reference is sometimes to it being cut sharp or blunt, to form a nib, whilst at others allusion is to quality or pointedness of hairs, showing that a quill was to be used as a brush holder, as it still is today. When reference is made to pencil, unless blacklead pencil is stated, a small brush or pencil brush is meant. Pencil brushes most favoured for penwork were of camel hair, sable, swansdown and squirrel, held in duck, goose or swan quill, according to size.

Learning in England commenced in the monasteries. The monks not only read books, they made them. Until the introduction of printing, the great majority of the beautifully illuminated manuscripts and sumptuously bound books were the work of monks. By the 12th century, if not earlier, all great monasteries had their scriptoria for writing and painting, and cloisters for reading. On one wall of the cloister stood the 'almeries' or cupboards for books, whilst opposite, each monk had his separate 'carrell' or pew, fitted with a seat and sloping reading desk. Monasteries and colleges of the 15th century had libraries fitted in the modern manner with desks like church lecterns, to which the volumes in use were chained; bibles in churches were secured in similar manner. With the more general distribution of learning, which followed the introduction of printing in the 15th century and the dissolution of the monasteries in the 16th, libraries became less a special appurtenance of the church, but it was not until the 17th century that reading had become general enough to cause the creation of any special-purpose domestic furniture. It was the 18th century which saw the heyday of ingenious folding pole ladders for libraries, and steps which turned into chairs or folded into cabinets, library tables with special reading attachments, reading tables with rise, fall and tilting actions, adjustable book rests and swing reading brackets.

Artists' Dark Mirrors—see *Claude Lorraine Glasses*

Blotter Cases

Blotter cases, with polished wood or leather covers, were on sale from about 1840. Some of the most attractive were decorated by the enterprising wood mosaic workers of Tunbridge. The classic story is that blotting paper was discovered accidentally at Hagbourne Mill, Berkshire, where Mr. John Slade made paper by hand early in the 19th century. About the year 1840, some workmen omitted the essential ingredients of size from the manufacture and the result was the output of a quantity of what appeared to be waste. Luckily, someone used a piece of the 'waste' to write a note and the outcome was 'Slade's Original Hand Made Blotting', which soon had the seal of approval placed on it by being used regularly by Queen Victoria. Eventually the business of Slade's passed by marriage to Mr. Thomas B. Ford, with the consequence that all the world now knows 'Ford's Blotting'. Basically, this is probably true so far as commercial production of superior blotting paper is concerned, but it was a rediscovery, for blotting paper, according to *Chambers's Encyclopaedia*, was known as early as 1465 and sheets of absorbent unsized paper have been found in several 18th-century account books, with proof on its surface that it was used for blotting the entries. In 1823 Matthew Boulton recorded buying 4 quires of blotting paper, but the fact remains that the long reign of pounce did not end until about 1840.

Books and Book Covers

To Germany, the world owes both printing and the word book. The original book was a tablet of beech wood. Early printed books consisted of leaves fastened together and protected by beech wood covers. The connection between beech and book is exemplified by the German *Buche*, beech, and *Buch*, book. Wooden covers of ancient books, even when finished in the most opulent manner, such as the priceless 10th-century *Golden Codex*, faced with gold and carved ivory, have the ornament applied as a covering to the beech wood; all wooden book covers carved in relief, are rare, early ones especially. A Swiss or Tyrolean, 19th-century, relief carved pearwood album cover is illustrated, Plate 284.

Bookcases, Travelling

Bookcases, generally, are outside the scope of this volume, but two rare and unusual cases for books qualify for inclusion. The pearwood prayer-book case, Plate 266, *A*, measuring $4\frac{3}{4}$ in. by $3\frac{1}{4}$ in. by $1\frac{3}{8}$ in., is carved and finely pierced in a Gothic design and has a pierced sliding shutter at one end. It dates from the end of the mediaeval period, *circa* 1600, and may be German or Italian; a very similar example is in the Wallace Collection. The decoration may be compared with the mediaeval H combs, Plate 382.

Not until well on in the 19th century, did the lending library become general. Until then, the traveller who wanted interesting reading matter at journey's end, had to take it with him. Travelling chests of drawers, desks, and even knock down chairs, tables and beds were well known examples of speciality cabinetmaking in the 18th century; a much more unusual example of the cabinet-maker's craft of that time was the travelling library, which was used by the student going to college, or by the traveller on land or sea. A good example, *circa* 1760, in mahogany, with wired doors in the Gothic taste, is shown in Plates 272 and 273. Closed, it forms a cube 18 in. by 18 in. by 18 in. The corners and angles are protected with flush inset brass angles. The back and front, which are each framed up to form four sunk panels, are provided with heavy brass carrying handles. Probably, it originally had additional loose solid panels, made to fit inside the rather delicate traceried inner doors, to protect them from the bumping of the books in transit.

Book Markers

Book markers of veneer, sometimes with scenes etched or painted on them, are mostly modern; the same remark applies to thin, twin-bladed paper-knife book markers (see *Paper-knives*). Early in the 19th century, some attractive coloured silk book markers, terminating with Tunbridge geometric wood mosaic buttons, were included in the large range of Tunbridge products.

Book Rests

Adjustable and folding book missal and newspaper rests to stand on a table, have a long history, but the majority extant, date from the 18th century or later. Nearly all fold flat and rise by means of a ratchet, but some specimens are ingeniously designed and constructed, so that the whole contraption condenses into a small space for travelling.

A good, early 17th-century example of a French, turner-made missal stand in walnut, 15 in. by 15 in., is shown open, right of Plate 281. The gate, turned with rings similar to those on the horizontal pivot bar, engages on a central ratchet bar correspondingly ringed, which runs from back to front of the base frame. Apart from the iron hinges, the whole specimen consists of wood turnery. On the left, is an ingeniously thought out, adjustable and collapsible stand for books, newspapers, music, etc. Fully extended as shown, it is 17 in. high and 18 in. wide, but the two upper extension rods can be swung in an

arc and used as diagonals for a 9 in. high bookstand. Closed, as shown Plate 267, *H*, it forms a block only 9 in. by 1¾ in. by 1¼ in. It is made of cedar and is presumably 19th-century, English.

The handsome Tunbridge wood mosaic book rest, Plate 282, *A*, dates from about 1840. The background veneer is bird's-eye maple, coloured grey by immersion in the local chalybeate water. The roundels are in various coloured woods and the border in Berlin 'woolwork' pattern. It is backed with rosewood, measures 14 in. by 11 in. and is one of the best quality Tunbridge products. *B* is one of those ingenious one-piece folding book rests which were the speciality of a Mr. Gates of Brighton, some time in the 19th century. Despite the fact that the maker's label on the earlier examples gives Gates' address as 42 Church Street, Brighton, and on later ones, as 7 Crown Street, Brighton, I have been unable to trace the date when he operated. I have seen several of these book rests with integral solid hinges operating without a pin, and the whole device is made from one piece of wood, which is cranked at the hinge line and divided in its thickness so as to form two ¼ in. thick fold-flat flaps. Various explanations have been offered of how these rests were made, including a very full exposition, in the *Woodworker*, December 1964, but none of the explanations which I have heard or read, are or could be correct, so far as these particular examples are concerned; I confess to being mystified. The specimen illustrated measures 16 in. by 8 in., plus the pivoted extensions; others which I have seen, are wider. Neat and practical, *C*, which is of mahogany, measuring 8¾ in. by 6¾ in. when closed, is identical with one of the four illustrations of book rests in Plate XXVI of Ince and Mayhew's *Universal System of Household Furniture*, published in 1762.

Claude Lorraine Glasses

Small, circular, convex, dark glass mirrors,

4 in. to 6 in. in diameter, usually in ebonised wood frames, were used up to the end of the 19th century by artists, to concentrate the features of a landscape in subdued tones. The actual glass may vary from black to grey or blue. The term Claude Lorraine glass was used both for a dark coloured mirror in which an artist painted the reduced and subdued version of the chosen landscape, whilst turning his back on the original, and also for an unsilvered dark glass through which an artist could view the scene. This second version was particularly useful to etchers and engravers who worked in monochrome. Some artists considered the Claude Lorraine glass an important and admirable adjunct. Ruskin considered it 'one of the most pestilential inventions for falsifying nature and degrading art, which ever was put into an artist's hand'.

Cone or Conic Section

The boxwood cone or conic section, Plate 294, *E*, probably dates from the 18th century, but similar conic sections were used by the Greeks. They have been used ever since in working out mathematical curves, such as ellipses, parabolas, etc.

Copying Machines—see *Hectographs*

Crayons

Crayon pencils in general have little interest for collectors. A case of German crayons made by J. S. Staedtler for military map making, at the time of the First World War is shown, Plate 267, *P*. The crayons are keyed by numbers to colours for topographical and other landscape features charted on one side of the case. On the reverse side are symbols for infantry, cavalry and artillery formations, etc.

Desks, Portable

Portable wooden desks have a long history, but the majority which survive, date from the 19th century. There are two distinct types. The first, which have sloping tops and were intended for use in different places in the home, were made in many patterns; the second type are rectangular fitted boxes, usually flush brass bound, made to fold over, and unfold to form a continuous slope and designed essentially for travelling. Originally they had leather outer cases, now usually lost. During the second half of the 19th century, the travelling desk boxes were gradually superseded by leather attaché cases fitted for stationery and writing requisites.

In 1930, I invented and patented a cabinet tray with a thin flexible plywood cover. When the tray was pulled forwards, the cover was automatically drawn backwards in the side grooves of the cabinet. By pushing the tray back, the cover was replaced. In 1947, I purchased the portable desk box, Plate 277; it employs identically the same principle, but more ingeniously, and was probably made between 1775 and 1790! In this delightful little mahogany desk, 14 in. wide, 10 in. deep and 7½ in. high, the drawer actuates a reeded tambour, backed with canvas. The movements are cleverly timed, so that when the drawer is fully extended, it supports the sloping, leather-lined, open flap; when closed and locked, it locks the whole desk, the flap when closed, being securely held down by the tambour. Under the tambour are ink and pounce pots and pen tray, and under the back flap, a well and two small drawers.

The best of the travelling desk box type, *circa* 1810, is well exemplified by that in Plates 274 and 275; this is rather a large specimen, 20 in. by 10 in. by 7 in. high, with flush inlaid brass corners and lifting handles. When open, it provides a 20 in. by 8 in. baize-lined writing surface. Additional to the two wells, one of which still contains quill pens, there are ink and pounce pots and a pen tray, below which is a compartment still containing cuttlefish (see *Pounce Boxes*). Emerging from the right side, below the upper well, Plate 274, is a 20 in.

long, elaborately fitted toilet drawer, containing two lead-lined boxes and two similarly lined, lidded compartments, as well as several other open compartments, subdivided by $\frac{1}{8}$ in. thick mahogany partitions. Originally, these open compartments would have been enclosed by an easel type mirror, now missing. Additional to serving as writing desks and toilet or dressing cases, these large compendia were also intended to be used as reading or drawing desks. A fillet with two pins in it, which, when not needed, rests in the lower well, will fit into two brass-lined holes in the lid, which may be raised on a strut and ratchet to the desired angle, Plate 275. Two first-class makers of these speciality fitted boxes, during the Regency period, were Thomas Lund of 57 Cornhill, London and W. Gaimes who was next door at 56—see also *Stationery Cabinets*.

Hectographs

James Watt, of steam engine fame, was the inventor, in 1780, of a copying machine or hectograph. When Watt's patent expired in 1794, numerous hectographs based on his invention, were produced. Two views of one, made *circa* 1800, are shown Plate 263, *A* and 268, *A*. The brass-bound mahogany case, which holds the roller, is an integral part of the process, and the grooved handle of the roller projects through a slot in the end of the box. To operate, the waterproof sheet attached to the roller, Plate 268, *A*, is unwound and laid on a flat surface, and the document to be copied is placed face upwards on it. A sheet of tissue paper is then damped with water, by brushing with the badger brush, Plate 263, *A1*, which is stored in the hollow lignum vitae handle of the roller. In Plate 268, *A*, it is shown emerging from the handle, the screw cap of which is alongside, *A1*. The document is then covered with the damp tissue and the waterproof sheet, and the three layers are tightly rolled round the roller, which is placed in the box, Plate 268, *A2*. Its lid is now shut and the roller rotated round and

round, whilst pressure from the lid is exerted on the roller. If the original is written in copying ink, on paper that is not highly sized, a perfect copy is obtained. The copy is in reverse, but the tissue paper is so thin that it can be read right way round on the reverse side. Addition of vinegar to the water used for damping, increases the intensity of the copy, as stated in Watt's patent.

Inkpots and Inkstands

Inkpots or wells of glass or china were formerly enclosed in a wide variety of treen containers. Some 19th-century specimens have more novelty value than artistic merit, but earlier ones usually have considerable interest. An inkpot, although complete in itself, is only one component of an inkstand, called a standish—stand and dish—until the end of the 18th century.

In general, writing table accessories were made in three grades—for the wealthy, silver, porcelain, enamel or various materials, ormolu mounted; pewter for the slightly less wealthy; treen or woodware came mainly at the lower end of the social scale. The treen of writing, having little intrinsic value, consequently survived in the smallest quantities.

The best quality standishes or inkstands usually included one or more inkpots, a pounce pot and a pen tray or holder. Some 18th-century specimens also incorporated one or two candle holders, a bell to summon a servant, and also made provision for sealing-wax and other small objects.

Inkpots

The earliest inkpot illustrated is Plate 263, *K*, which was probably used by a professional scribe in late mediaeval times, who had it slung by a cord from the neck or girdle. The cord passed through holes in the projecting ears of the cover and bottle. The cover could be raised on the cords, when desired. This rare survival, decorated externally with scratch lines, follows the general outline of ink-horns. It is made of some dense hardwood and has no liner; the lower part forms the bottle and has a long shouldered spout, which fits snugly into the cover. Also in Plate 263 are a number of 19th-century novelty inkpots. *B* is turned to represent a hand bell; *C*, a good quality ebony helmet, forms a pair with the string box helmet, Plate 212, *D*; *D* is a simple turned pot with a pivoted throw-back lid; *F*, Swiss or Tyrolean, and probably intended for a child, is a carved cat's head enclosing an ink-well. *G* is one of the Oriental snake infested skulls, intended for the European market; it is a smaller version of the skull tobacco jar, Plate 363, *L*; *H* is an ornamentally turned basket-weave pot, a type popular in 19th-century offices; *J* is a well-head novelty, the bucket enclosing an inkpot; *L* is a Ransome patent travelling inkpot, *circa* 1900; *M*, a Swiss ragged boot; similar 19th-century boot carvings are also found holding matches or an ash-tray; *U*, of oak, was possibly hung on the wall of a 19th-century church vestry and used for signing the register.

In Plate 264, *A*, *B* and *C*, all Regency period writing compendia, and some used for travelling, unscrew in sections and hold an ink bottle and pounce and wafer compartments. *F* is a combined pen and inkpot, *circa* 1840; the pen reverses into the neck, so that when closed, the whole forms a vase with finial. *L*, the leaning tower, 12½ in. high, turned from ebony and handsomely carved in horizontal rings, gives the impression that it was a memento, probably created specially for some important 18th-century signing ceremony. It unscrews in several places and contains a scroll cavity, ink-well and pounce box. *D*, *E*, *G*, *H*, *J* and *K* are 19th-century travelling inkpots. Most of them are spring loaded, so that the neck of the bottle presses tightly against a rubber cushion in the lid—for details of this arrangement, which was originally Berry's patent, see Section VI, *Fire and Lighting: Instantaneous Light Devices*.

M, a 19th-century bottle novelty, turned from ebony, contains compartments for ink, wafers and sealing-wax; *N*, a capstan ink-well, is turned from wood of H.M.S. Britannia. *P*, the fine quality, 18th-century, lignum vitae, engine turned inkstand, forms an imposing standing cup, with holes round the perimeter for 54 quill pens; it was formerly in the Dr. Carter Collection. A faded parchment in it proclaims that it belonged to that remarkable man, Jonas Hanway (1712–86). Hanway, noted traveller and philanthropist, spent much time crusading for child chimney-sweeps and poor children generally. He was a governor of the Foundling Hospital, an advocate of Sunday schools and co-founder of the Marine Society. He was jeered by the mob and reviled by sedan chair carriers as a menace to their trade, being the first man who regularly carried an umbrella in London. He was a bitter opponent of the 'vice' of tea drinking and waged a wordy war about it with Dr. Johnson and Oliver Goldsmith. He was an inveterate writer of tracts, pamphlets and letters and, in his excited moods, probably broke many quills. *Q*, 19th-century, is a pleasant design of an ink-well ball with hinged lid, mounted on three smaller balls.

Inkstands or Standishes

The earliest treen standish which I have seen is Plate 264, *V*. By comparison with stands depicted in 16th- and 17th-century paintings, by analogy with pewter, and by resemblance of outlines of the components with other treen objects of known date, and also taking into account condition, this is of 16th- or at latest, early 17th-century date. It consists of a 9 in. diameter, 1⅛ in. thick, solid sycamore platform, on which is mounted centrally a scroll or quill-pen box; surrounding it are three fixed ebonised pen holders, and between them, loosely pegged in, are an ink-well, a pounce pot and an open holder, presumably for sealing-wax. *R*, a 19th-century office stand, is hollowed out of a 6 in. diameter block of rosewood, 4 in. thick and contains three ink bottles.

Plate 265, *D*, an unusual inkstand, neatly inlaid with various woods in the Regency Gothic style, *circa* 1810, gives the impression of being the product of a man who was an expert in straw marquetry. Pressure on a piece of the inlay to the left of the pounce box releases a secret drawer in the right-hand end. Of about the same date, or perhaps 10 years later, Plate 268, *J*, is a high-class example of early Tunbridge wood mosaic, intended for the centre of a part-ner's desk. The background is rosewood, the top decorated with stars and lunettes, and the sides with vandyke pattern. Lids open from both sides and it contains ink and pounce pots, seal compartment, pen tray and a drawer.

At first sight, Plate 265, *C*, carved in limewood, appears to be an example of 1760 rococo. Careful examination of the rather exaggerated scale of the scrollwork and trophies of the chase, and comparison with a carved clock case in the *Art Journal Illustrated Catalogue*, makes it almost certain that this was the work of W. G. Rogers, who won prizes in the 1851 Exhibition for his fine carving.

Plate 263, *R* and *S*, are two Victorian novelty piano inkstands, probably made about 1870. The upright piano, *R*, veneered with burr walnut, has the inkstand under the keyboard cover; the 'body' is occupied by a five compartment stationery rack. The miniature walnut grand piano, *S*, con-tains two inkpots, a pen wiper and two stamp compartments.

Lay Figures

Jointed wooden figures representing ideal proportions of the human body, have been used by artists for several, perhaps many centuries. They probably originated in Italy or Greece and have been used not only by artists and sculptors for posing of the bare limbs in various postures, but also for the arrangement of draperies, and a refined version was used for costume display and for tableaux. They are found in all sizes from a few inches high up to full size. Speci-mens of both types, at least from the 17th century, have pivoted ball joints at neck, shoulders, elbows, wrists, thighs, knees and ankles, so arranged as to allow for natural bending and turning at all these junctions; a few of the artist's larger lay figures have finger joints, but faces are expressionless and hands and feet are always crude. The majority are carved from pine, a few from mahogany. An 18th- or 19th-century artist's male figure, 22 in. high, and a late 19th-century female, 19 in. high, both of pine, are illustrated, Plate 283. Character figures, such as the 18th-century Neapolitan ex-ample of an old man, shown on the model-ling stand, have finely modelled features and beautifully detailed hands and feet. One of their uses was by tailors for showing the latest fashions. Although entirely secu-lar, they were made by the carvers of presepio figures—see Section X, *Miscel-lany: Presepio Figures*.

Library Steps and Ladders

Georgian libraries were usually lofty and their owners men of elegance, who disliked having ugly folding steps on view. But steps were needed to get at the upper shelves, and some of the most attractive and ingenious dual-purpose furniture ever designed were the various types of 18th-century library steps which converted into tables, chairs and stools. An alternative was the library ladder, which telescoped into an inconspicuous pole, Plate 271. Some formed a square section, and others, like this one, had *D* section uprights and became round poles when closed. Each upright is grooved centrally, the rungs are inserted in the grooves and either hinged or pivoted at each end so that they may be concer-tinaed by pressing one upright (in this example, the right hand one) upwards and inward towards the other. When brought together, the two halves lock into a pole.

As an instance of how the same device may be invented twice, the late Sir Edwin Lutyens, who knew nothing of the 18th-century specimens, starting afresh on the library ladder problem, arrived at exactly the same solution for a client in 1928.

Limner's Easel

The limner's, or miniature painter's easel, Plate 282, *D*, is of yew-wood. Some parts are missing, notably the 'table' on which the painting was placed, which pivoted between the uprights of the U, and the magnifying glass which fitted in the rebated opening of the horizontal frame. This latter is adjustable in height by means of a set screw, but the purpose of the peg alongside, I have been unable to ascertain. This rarity is unlikely to be later than 18th-century, but may be considerably earlier. The limner was one of the workers, who at night always used a candle stand or flash stand as described in Section VI, *Fire and Lighting: Candle Stands*.

Missal Stands—see *Book Rests*

Modelling Stands or Stools

Turned wood modelling stands, constructed like adjustable piano stools with hard tops, are usually mounted on three splayed legs, with a rise and fall, threaded, centre pillar passing through two rings which anchor the supporting legs, see Plate 283. The modelling stool may be a miniature like this one, meant for arranging a lay figure, or it may be large enough to form a seat for a human being, or a stand for an object or group of objects being copied by a circle of students. This 19th-century example has height adjustments between $6\frac{3}{4}$ in. and $8\frac{1}{4}$ in. and, like full-size specimens, has a removable foot rest.

Music Liners

The music liner was an intermediate stage between the individual ruling of lines for music and the ready ruled sheet. Two English examples are illustrated, Plate 266, *L* and *M*. Formerly in the Evan-Thomas Collection, *L*, has a turned walnut handle into which are inserted four separate, divided brass liners or nibs, which were dipped in the ink to rule simultaneously the four lines for ecclesiastical chants; it is $6\frac{7}{8}$ in. long and may be 17th- or 18th-century. *M*, 18th-century, has a lignum vitae handle, is 5 in. long, and works on a more advanced principle. The five-toothed brass terminal is all in one piece, and ink is inserted into a circular cavity which provides a reservoir, flowing direct to the five points.

Newspaper Rests—see *Book Rests*

Paint Boxes

The late Percy Macquoid, on page 54 of *The Age of Mahogany*, when referring to an artist's cabinet, said

> 'Paint-boxes and tubes of colours were unknown during the 18th century; the colours were kept in powder or bladders and in the drawers of tables or cabinets . . .'.

Percy Macquoid was correct about oil colours being kept in bladders: tubes for oil paints did not come in until 1845, but colour cakes were invented about 1770. Macquoid's statement is often incorrectly quoted in support of cake colours being a 19th-century invention.

Reeves & Son, founded in 1766, have in their museum, a wooden paint-box manufactured in 1769 and used by Rear Admiral Isaac Smith (then a midshipman) on Captain Cook's second voyage of discovery, 1772 to 1775. Reeves & Son invented cake colours and in 1781 the Society of Arts (now the Royal Society of Arts) awarded them the 'Greater Silver Pallette' for their invention. The Greater Silver Pallette is still in their possession and in the brush tray of the 18th-century mahogany paint box, Plate 278, is a facsimile of the letter of presentation, reading

'Gentlemen. Society for Encouragement of Arts, Manufactures & Commerce.
Adelphi May 17 1781

I am desired by the Society to return you their thanks for the Obliging Present you have been pleased to make them, of a Box of Colours prepared by You for the Use of Painters in Water Colours. An Art so well adapted to the purpose of Forwarding that Elegant Branch of polite Arts, could not fail of being acceptable to the Society. I am Gentlemen, Your most obed humble servant

Saml. More
Secretary.

Messrs. Reeves { Colour manufacturers to
No. 80 { Her Majesty & His Royal
Holborn { Highness the Prince of
Bridge { Wales.'

Plate 280, shows another and more elaborately fitted Reeves paint-box, *circa* 1780, of mahogany; it is complete with its finely engraved trade label and original, mostly unused, cake colours, embossed with coats of arms and colour designations, with a drawer below for mixing bowls.

A Regency period mahogany paint box, Plate 279, bears the *circa* 1815 period label of R. Ackermann's Repository of the Arts, 101 Strand, London; it is virtually the same as Reeves' box of 35 years earlier.

Palettes

At Burlington House are three 18th-century artist's pearwood palettes. One, which belonged to Sir Joshua Reynolds, is of the conventional shape made in china. The other two, one of which belonged to Hogarth, are shaped like thin versions of oat-cake slices.

Pantographers

That ingenious device the pantograph, mechanically tracing a figure similar to a given figure, but enlarged or reduced in a definite ratio, has never changed or been improved since 1668, the date about when it was probably either invented or first brought into use in England. At first it was known as a parallelogram and then, in the 18th century, as a pantographer. The fine example illustrated, Plate 270, is of ebony and brass, complete, and in full working order and with its original mahogany case behind it. The trade label of Benjamin Cole at the Orrery in Fleet Street, London, in the lid of the case, establishes the date of this particular instrument as 1766–7, when Fleet Street was first numbered, because on the label is added in ink, No. 136. Readers of Samuel Pepys' *Diary* will recall the numerous references to his friend Mr. Spong, the ingenious instrument maker from whom he purchased most of his mathematical instruments, from 1660 onwards. On October 27, 1668, Spong first told Pepys about the parallelogram. On December 7, Spong demonstrated it and Pepys ordered one to be made for him; it was delivered January 16, 1669.

Paper Knives

The paper knife is usually regarded now as an adjunct of the writing desk or table, used for slitting open envelopes, prior to reading correspondence. Paper knives, however, were used long before gummed envelopes were invented, around 1840. In fact, paper knives have been used as long as books have been made, and the more important use for cutting book pages has only died out slowly and very recently. Even now, a paper knife is still required as a preliminary to reading the more precious books, printed on hand-made paper and plain paper knives were used by 'hand folders' of book leaves. Without doubt, gummed envelopes gave a great fillip to demand for paper knives of brass, ivory, bone, wood, etc.; most of the wooden ones which are now collected, including those decorated with Tunbridge wood mosaic, like Plate 269, *K*, also those of tartan and transfer ware, date from 1840 onwards. In the last quarter of the 19th century there was a fashion for paper knives of exaggerated size, 12 in. to 16 in. long. Some of these outsize specimens are elaborately carved cane or wood imported from the Orient and sometimes confused with staybusks (see Section II, *Costume Accessories*); others are Swiss or Tyrolean tourist souvenirs, with carved gnomes or animal heads on the handles. During the same period, extra large *de luxe* paper knives were made with ivory blades and repoussé silver handles.

The more normal range of paper knives vary between 5 in. and 12 in. in length and some of the short ones, such as the Swiss, mid-19th-century example, 5½ in. long, carved with lilies of the valley, Plate 266, *K*, have thin twin blades so that they could act as combined book markers and page cutters. Dating from about the same period or perhaps a little later, are *E*, an original design, 10½ in. long, in boxwood, with the folded wings of the angel forming the blade, *G*, Italian, olivewood, carved as a mule, *H*, a statuette, and *J*, which is of pearwood, finely carved and undercut with roses and forget-me-nots. *F* is in a different class and considerably earlier. It is of mulberry wood, 11 in. long and very skilfully carved with a bust of John Milton; it may be 17th- or 18th-century; it has twin blades, so cut that they act as a combined paper clip and paper cutter. Plate 267, *M*, 13 in. long is a transferware Queen Victoria Golden Jubilee souvenir, given away by the Eastern Telegraph Company. On the face shown is a map of the world giving the Company's cable routes; on the reverse, is a calendar for 1887. Another popular Victorian type, not illustrated, was a paper knife shaped as a bricklayer's trowel. Plate 269, *K*, is a Tunbridge mosaic example.

Paper Weights

The majority of paper weights are of metal, but some have been made from dense, heavy hardwoods, such as lignum vitae or boxwood; others are hollowed out and laminated so as to encase a lead weight. One of the most charming is the miniature, 18th-century, inlaid mahogany cutlery case, Plate 268, *E*, 2¼ in. high, which is lead weighted. *B* is Indian made, 19th-century, finely inlaid with a Takashi brass design. *C*, lead weighted, and 19th-century, is carved to represent a miniature strapped concertina file. *D*, also lead weighted, is turned from laburnum and is impossible to date accurately. *F* is formed as a carved boxwood prayer book; *G* shows two plain carved walnut book paper weights; the last three are 19th-century. The Lucerne lion, carved from a block of walnut, has been a popular subject for a paper weight for more than a century. Tunbridge wood mosaic paperweights, in geometric designs of the 1820 period, are represented by Plate 269, *E*, *F* and *G*, which are lead weighted. Paperweights in Tunbridge wood mosaic are uncommon.

Peithynen

The Welsh can claim to have invented a 'book of treen'; it is known as a peithynen or LLYFR PREN—wooden book. An example is shown Plate 265, *A*, and it consists of a frame containing a number of revolving three, four or six sided sticks, on which are inscribed, with a knife, numerals, the alphabet, the Lord's Prayer or bardic verses. Characters which normally are curved, appear angular on a peithynen, so that they can be easily notched out with a knife. Although interesting to the collector, the peithynen's claim to great antiquity is not borne out by investigation and it appears to have been largely a hoax, perpetrated by Iolo Morgannwg and his associates in the 18th century. Sir John Morris Jones, writing about it (*A Welsh Grammar*, 1913) says:

'Among the "traditions" invented by the Glamorgan bards in support of their claim to be the successors of the druids was the "wooden book"; although all the accounts of it are in Iolo Morgannwg's handwriting,

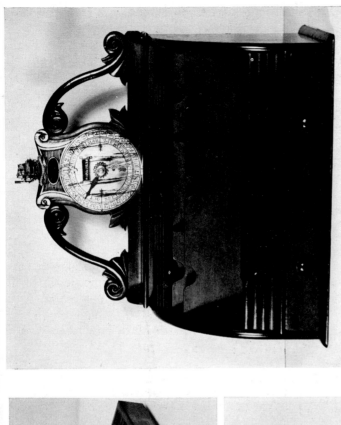

274 and 275 Two views of mahogany, travelling desk box, fitted for reading, writing and toilet, *circa* 1810. English. (*Section XVII*)

276 (TOP RIGHT) The Stockton-on-Tees stationmaster's tambour fronted, mahogany stationery cabinet, commemorating No. 1 Locomotion of 1825. (*Section XVII*)

277 (BOTTOM RIGHT) Ingeniously designed portable desk in mahogany, *circa* 1780. English. (*Section XVII*)

278

279

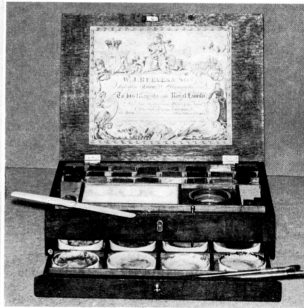

278, 279 and 280 Paint boxes—278 and 280, by W. & J. Reeves, *circa* 1780–1; 279 by R. Acker-mann, *circa* 1815 (*Section XVII*)

281 19th-century, mahogany, adjustable folding book rest (shown closed in Plate 267, *H*), and 17th-century, adjustable missal stand. (*Section XVII*)

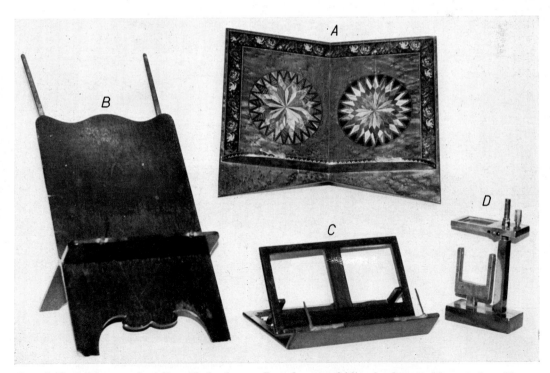

282 *A*, Tunbridge mosaic, adjustable book rest; *B*, mahogany, folding book rest with extensions (shown half closed, Plate 265, *B*); *C*, 18th-century, adjustable folding book rest, designed by Ince and Mayhew; *D*, limner's easel, 18th(?) century. (*Section XVII*)

284 Swiss or Tyrolean album, with carved pearwood covers. 19th century. (*Section XVII*)

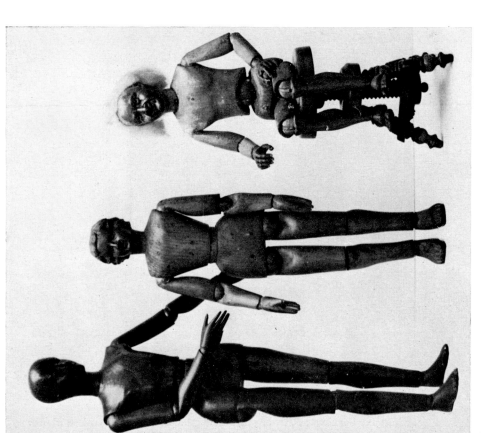

283 English, 19th-century lay figures and modelling stand, and an 18th-century Neapolitan character figure. (*Section XVII*)

285 Assortment of wooden devices; *A* and *B*, hanks; *C*, reeving block; *D* to *H*, fids; *J*, dinghy plugs; *K*, belaying pin; *L, P* and *Q*, pulley blocks; *M*, fender; *N*, mast head truck; *O*, dead-eyes. (*Section XVIII*)

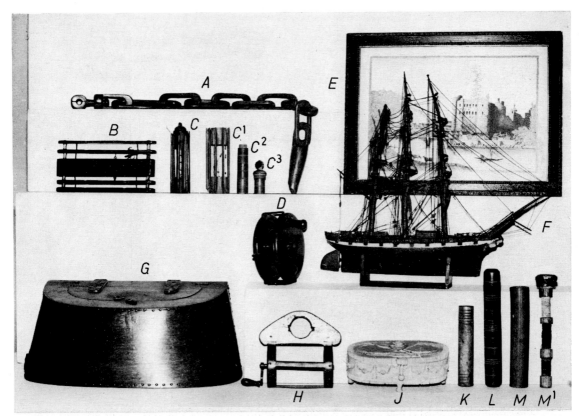

286 *A*, sailor made wooden chain; *B* and *C*, fishermen's companions; *D* and *H*, fishing reels; *F*, ship model for sailing; *G*, bentwood creel; *E* and *J*, examples of cork work; *K* and *L*, sailmaker's needle cases; *M* and *M1*, spool holder and spool. (*Section XVII*)

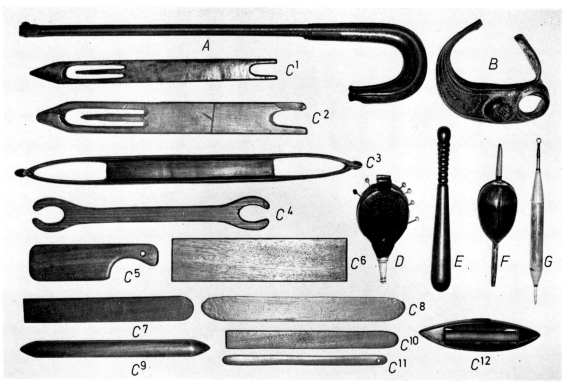

287 *A*, poacher's folding pocket gaff; *B*, sailmaker's palm, *C*, *1* to *12*, netting tools; *D*, oak bellows memento pin-cushion; *E*, priest; *F* and *G*, floats. (*Section XVIII*)

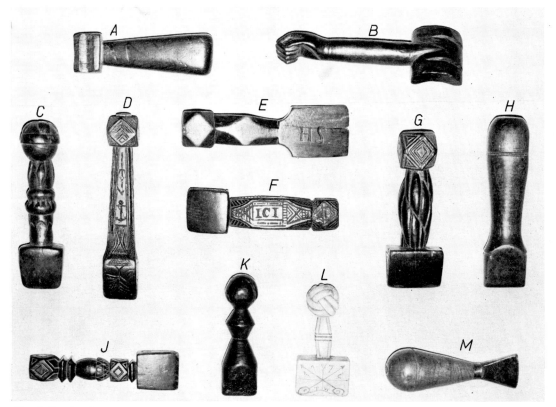

288 Sailmakers' tools: *A* and *B*, serving mallets; *C* to *M*, sailmakers' liners. *A* and *M* are 19th century, the others 18th century or earlier. (*Section XVIII*)

289 TOP: freedom scroll container, in the form of a wooden cannon; LEFT: 18th-century sextant; RIGHT: early traverse board. (*Section XVIII*)

290 Mahogany waywiser by R. Banks, Strand. London, *circa* 1790–1800. (*Section XIX*)

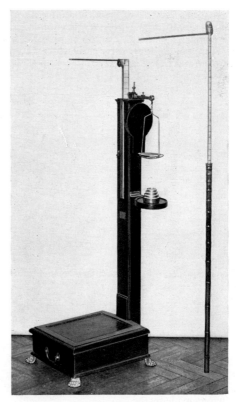

291 Georgian, mahogany cased, personal weighing machine, 18th century; walking-stick horse standard, 1872–3. (*Section XIX*)

292 *A*, watch repairer's 'parts' boxes, which nest together, as shown, *B*; *C*, watchmakers' and jewellers' eye glass, with case; *D*, wooden forceps used for jewels; *E*, glass-topped jewel boxes; *F*, jeweller's vice; *G*, prism viewers; *H*, Chinese wind and water compass; *J* and *K*, English compasses; *L*, exterior of the Italian, walnut case of the balance shown, Plate 302, *H*; *M*, micrograph; *N*, rare, early 17th-century set of Napier's bones, with original case below; *O*, ring measuring stick (*Section XIX*); *P* and *Q*, 18th-century, copying lathe turned boxwood reliefs. (*Section XXIV*)

293 Russian watch of boxwood, pearwood and maple, made by the celebrated Bronikov brothers; early 19th century. (*Section XIX*)

294 *A,* McFarlane's calculating cylinder; *B,* 18th-century, boxwood, pocket sundial; *C,* sundial by Kleininger, 18th century; *D,* 18th-century pocket sundial; *F,* Connecticut wooden clock movement; *G,* exterior of the carved walnut case of the diamond merchant's balance, Plate 311; *H,* Charles II sundial casket, with its floating compass and dial tray, *J. (Section XIX); E,* conic section (see *Section XVII*)

295 Mail and passenger coaching dials, 18th century. *(Section XIX)*

296 *A*, zograscope, and *B*, its special viewing print; *C*, Russian abacus; *D*, Oriental abacus; *E*, chuck-rum counting board; *F*, the Duboscq stereoscope; *G*, stereoscope based on a design by Oliver Wendell Holmes; *H*, lignum vitae scioptric ball, 18th century. (*Section XIX*)

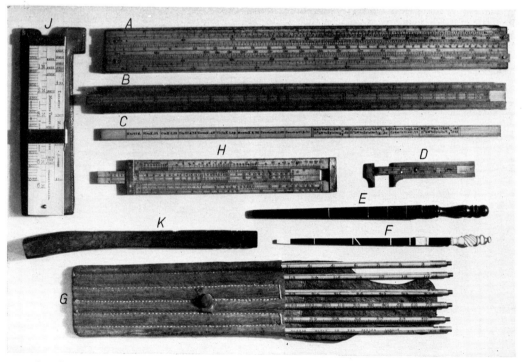

297 *A* and *B*, boxwood slide rules, *circa* 1800 and 1775 respectively; *C*, a slide from the 1775 rule; *D*, engineer's boxwood gauge; *E* and *F*, quarter ell rules for the pocket, 18th century; *G*, set of exciseman's boxwood measuring rods, in original case; *H*, Farmar's publican's stocktaking rule, 19th century; *J*, officer's calculator, World War I; *K*, tally stick, dated 1795. (*Section XIX*)

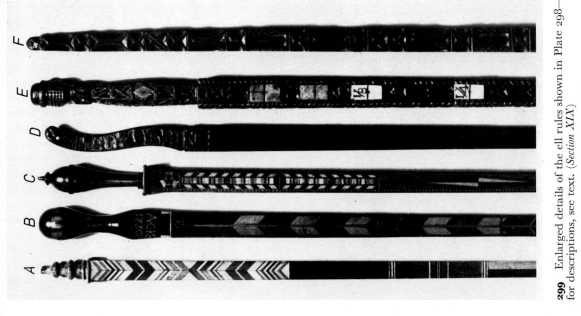

299 Enlarged details of the ell rules shown in Plate 298—for descriptions, see text. (*Section XIX*)

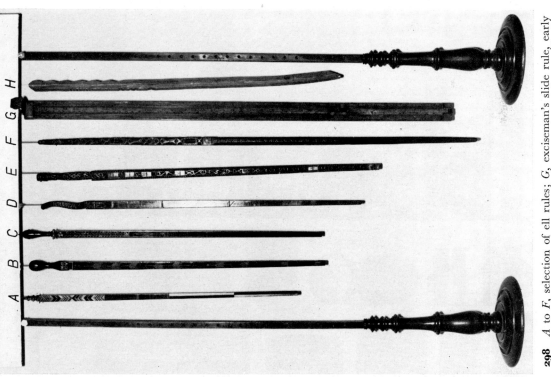
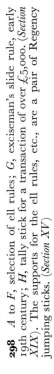

298 *A* to *F*, selection of ell rules; *G*, exciseman's slide rule, early 19th century; *H*, tally stick for a transaction of over £5,000. (*Section XIX*). The supports for the ell rules, etc., are a pair of Regency jumping sticks. (*Section XV*)

300 *A,* 17th-century sand glass; *B,* Maelzel's metronome of 1816; *C,* reversible, wall-type sand glass; *D,* 18th-century hydrometer bulbs; *E,* Nurnberg microscope, *circa* 1780; *G,* 18th-century, Culpeper microscope, with its specimen slides, *F,* and oak case, *H.* (*Section XIX*)

301 Measures of volume, both turned and of steamed bentwood—for details, see text. (*Section XIX*)

302 *A*, Hinderloopen, Dutch, 18th-century, perpetual calendar; *B*, *C* and *G*, open and closed views of 18th-century, pocket coin balances; *D*, Chinese 'banjo' bismar; *E*, Turkish, pocket coin balance; *F*, 16th or 17th-century steelyard; *H*, 17th-century, Italian coin balance in walnut case, the exterior of case shown in Plate 292, *L*; *J*, 18th century coin balance in case, with interesting label—see text. (*Section XIX*)

303 Rare, 18th-century, perpetual calendar. (*Section XIX*)

304 Magic lantern, mainly of mahogany, *circa* 1830. (*Sect. XIX*)

305 Unique wooden working model, which demonstrates Bremme's engine patents of 1879 and 1886. (*Section XIX*)

306 The *Achromatic* Stereoscope, with original mahogany cabinet and slides, *circa* 1850. (*Section XIX*)

307 (TOP LEFT) Scandinavian, carved oak tally board, dated 1772. In the Collection of Mr. and Mrs. Christopher Sykes. (*Section XIX*)

308 (LOWER LEFT) A Yorkshire miner's tally board of the 17th or 18th century, probably unique. In the Collection of T. R. Nevin, Esq., T.D., LL.B., J.P. *Photograph by courtesy of G. Bernard Wood, Esq. F.R.S.A.* (*Section XIX*)

309 (TOP RIGHT) Rare leather covered oak, laundry tally board, second half of the 17th century. Collection of A. Golding Barrett, Esq. (*Section XIX*)

310 Rare, oak framed, brass disc laundry tally, second half of the 17th century. Formerly in the Collection of the Rev. C. J. Sharp, now in the Collection of W. J. Shepherd, Esq. *Photograph by courtesy of Sotheby & Co.* (*Sect. XIX*)

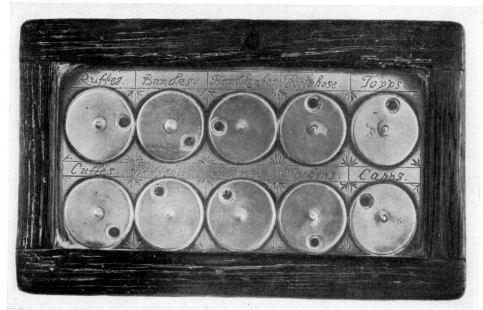

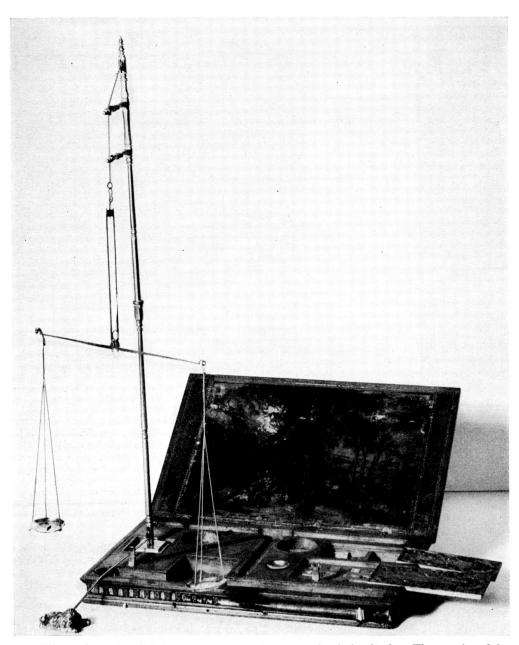

311 Diamond merchant's balance, in carved walnut case, simulating leather. The exterior of the case is illustrated, Plate 294, *G*. An exceptionally fine quality outfit, dating from *circa* 1650. (*Section XIX*)

contemporary evidence of its existence in the early 17th century is afforded by Rhys Cain's satirical englyn . . . but it cannot be traced further back. The "bardic alphabet" called *coelbren y beirdd* was a conventional simplification of ordinary characters adapted for cutting on wood; its letters are derived from the handwriting of the period, as

$\downharpoonleft\, b;\ \rangle\, d,\ \downarrow\ \vee\, (e),\ \wedge\, h,\ \vee\, n,\ \vee\, r,$

except where it was easier to adapt the Latin capitals, as

$\wedge\ A,\quad \zeta\ G.$

With one or two exceptions, such as $\sqcup$ Ll, the "derived characters" denoting consonant mutations, so far from proving the coelbren's antiquity, are its very latest development, Pughe acknowledging himself to be the author of five of them. . . . No manuscript is written in it, for the simple reason that it was easier to write ordinary characters than the coelbren caricature of them. . . . The wooden book consists of squared inscribed sticks in a frame; it was called *peithynen* from its resemblance to a weaver's reed. . . . The absurdity of the supposition that such a device ever served any serious purpose of literature is manifest when one considers what a cartload of wooden books would be required to carry the contents of a small manuscript volume.'

Pencil Boxes—See Section XXVIII, *Tuition*

Pencils

Wood cased black-lead pencils have been made in England since the 16th century, but probably none earlier than 19th-century are likely to be found now. The revolving or propelling pencil was probably a 19th-century invention and is usually all metal. Two examples, mainly of wood, are illustrated, Plate 266, *N* and *O*. The first is designed to represent a 2 in. long bellows. *O*, with ivory terminals, has an external silver collar which moves up and down a spiral cut on the wood; it is stamped Lund Patent London.

Pens, Pen Cutters and Pen Knives

The pens used by most of our ancestors between Roman times and the 19th century, were the quill and the reed or cane. Both were sharpened into a nib shape, carefully split and dipped in ink. The word pen is still synonymous for the wing feather or quill of a goose or swan, or a writing implement. Quill pens and ink were formerly peddled from door to door. In a 16th-century series of woodcuts of *Criers* in the British Museum, No. 11 shows the 'Pen and Ink Man' with the ink bottle slung behind him on his pedlar's stick and a bunch of quills in his hand, while he cries

'Buy pens, pens, pens of the best,
Excellent pens and seconds the least;
Come buy good ink as black as jet,
A varnish like gloss on writing 'twill set.'

The Romans had a metal pen; examples have been found at Pompeii and Herculaneum, but between these ancient ones and the birth of the steel pen in the 19th century, the natural materials held sway. There were experiments with metal in the 18th century and also with tipping quills with various hardening agents to avoid the skilled and laborious shaping at frequent intervals. Until the end of the 18th century, pens were shaped manually either by the scrivener's open knives, with varied ornamental carved handles, such as Plate 269, *A*, *B*, *C* and *D*, all of which date from the 18th century or earlier, or by the folding pocket knife, known as a pen knife. The handles of early penknives were sometimes considerably greater works of skill than was the cutting of a good quill or cane nib. In Plate 67, on the extreme left, is a superb quality Italian, 16th-century specimen, with the silver-mounted boxwood handle carved to represent Adam and Eve, with the serpent holding the apple; the tree behind them forms a sheath for the knife. Last right, is another beautiful specimen, French, 16th- or 17th-century, portraying an eagle perched on a cherub head. The Scandinavian, strictly utilitarian, all-purpose pocket knife, which folds into a barrel-shaped, maple sheath, Plate 266, *S*, has a long tradition behind it, but is still made in several sizes.

Early in the 19th century, the pen knife began to shed its original function, when Joseph Bramah and James Watt, two all-round inventive genii, both designed little devices such as Plate 266, *Q* and *R*, which first cut a perfect profile for the nib, by pressing down a lever on the quill, and then slit it with the little knife which slides out of the end. *Q* has an ivory, and *R* an ebony handle, otherwise they are similar.

The development of steel pens was slow. Samuel Harrison of Birmingham was making steel pens in 1780 and Jacob Wise, of Newington Crescent, London, commenced manufacturing his 'elastic steel writing pens' in 1803; about 1830 James Perry, Joseph Gillott and Sir Josiah Mason, all of Birmingham, followed with improvements in manufacture by machine. Thomas J. Palmer, supplier to the Royal family, owned the Royal Quill Pen Manufactory at East Grinstead, Sussex, where he also sold steel pens about 1840; whether he manufactured them is not known. I have his comprehensive price list. His attractively labelled box, Plate 267, *Q*, containing 50 steel pens (nibs), sold at 2*s*., 3*s*. or 3*s*. 6*d*. according to type; he was still listing quills also at this time. References to fountain pens occur in 18th-century literature. Richard Boult, a Cheapside jeweller, 1744–1753, stated on his trade card that he sold them. Fanny Burney in her *Diary*, 1789, recorded 'Then I took a fountain pen, and wrote my rough journal'. Perhaps the jeweller sold some kind of tube with a feed to a nib, on the lines of Scheffer's patent Penograph, which was advertised by J. H. Farthing, The Improved copying and writing machine and polygraph manufactory, 42 Cornhill, London, in *Robson's Directory*, 1826–7. Scheffer, the patentee, was Jno. Scheffer, 'Inventor of the life

preserver in case of shipwreck', of 6 Bedford Place, New Kent Road. The Penograph, according to the advertisement, patronised by George IV, was made in gold and silver, with metal or quill nib, the size of a pencil case, and holding enough ink for 10 to 12 hours' writing. From the illustration and description, it appears to have been a fairly advanced device, but the possibilities could not have escaped the notice of earlier writers with an inventive turn of mind, that both quills and canes, the former tapering at the upper end to a point and the latter with natural cross membranes at intervals, are natural reservoirs. It only remains to fit a tapering wooden plug, slightly nicked on the side, which presses against the nib and you have a fountain pen of sorts, which writes reasonably on the back of the nib. To test my theory, I made one, and it works, but it has to be stored upside down and cannot be carried in the pocket, which is probably why the world had to wait for precision made instruments, before an efficient fountain pen could be produced.

Pen Knives—see *Pens, Pen Cutters and Pen Knives*

Pen Stands and Trays
Horizontal tiered pen stands, as opposed to vertical pen holders, only became practical when the straight steel-nibbed pen replaced the curved feathered quill. In consequence, pen stands, usually with space for an ink pot, nearly all date from the second half of the 19th century and are of metal. Plate 263, *T*, is an amusing example of wood borrowing from a metal design and executed in fretwork. The woodworker's more usual contribution to pen storage was the pen tray, normally scooped out of the solid and measuring 9 in. to 10 in., by 2½ in. to 3 in. The Tunbridge wood mosaic manufacturers also made pen trays but their technique necessitated their framing the trays up out of five or nine

components, as illustrated, Plate 269, *L* and *M*, both probably made about 1840—see also *Ink Pots and Stands*.

Pen Wipers

There is little doubt that the steel pen gave birth to the penwiper. Ink does not cake on a quill pen, as it does on a steel one, and it is significant that the Oxford Dictionary gives 1848 as the date for the word penwiper. The spring-loaded, rosewood, vase-shaped penwiper Plate 263, *V*, cleans a nib between two velour pads, when the top button is pressed down. It is stamped patent, but without name or date. The boot pen-wiper Plate 263, *O*, contains a brush. *P* is designed as a miniature boot brush and mud scraper, the scraper part forming two wells for nibs or stamps. *Q*, another type of miniature shoe brush, is veneered in quartered kingwood and may be French. *N*, a miniature olivewood fan, enclosing four different coloured felt leaves, is Italian. All these examples were novelties of the second half of the 19th century.

Pole Ladders—see *Library Steps and Ladders*

Pounce Boxes

The pounce box was used from mediaeval times until the mid-19th century, but although keeping its name, it changed both its purpose and the constituents of the pounce at different times. Pounce boxes, pots or sand dredgers, have been made of wood, porcelain, enamel, glass, pewter, silver and other metals. When incorporated in inkstands—mostly in the 18th century and made to match the inkpot—they proved a considerable nuisance to writers, who sometimes found themselves throwing ink instead of pounce on their paper.

The original use of pounce was to scour, or smooth and degrease skins—that is, vellum and parchment—to form a suitable surface for writing; even then it was necessary to use an iron gall ink, which was mixed with gum in order to get adherence.

Early pounce was composed of powdered cuttle-fish or pumice, mixed with sand-arach resin, reduced to a fine powder and rubbed into the surface. An ivory pounce box of a type used for scouring is illustrated, Plate 264, *T*; I cannot date it. When paper generally superseded parchment, a different kind of pounce was required: scouring was not needed, as early writing paper was virtually unglazed and deficient in size, but preparation was needed to prevent the writing being blurred. It was then that the cylindric pounce box, with perforated saucer-shaped top, came into use, so that the paper could be cupped and the valuable pounce tipped back into the box. This second edition of pounce was powdered sandarach, which is why the pots or boxes are sometimes known as sand dredgers. The powdered sandarach was sprinkled on the paper and the resin was rubbed in with the fingers, or a pad, to prevent the ink spreading. Early books had this same disadvantage for scholars who were in the habit of making their notes in the wide margins. Sir Hugh Plat, in his *Jewel House of Art and Nature*, gives advice on pouncing margins with sandarach, tied up in lawn or cambric, before writing. At the end of the 18th century, when writing paper had been so improved that no pouncing was needed, it seemed as though the reign of the pounce pot was over. However, it had a new, although short lease of life, because the ink stayed wet on glazed paper, and blotting paper not having yet come into fashion, pounce was needed as a drying agent. This new pounce was usually powdered chalk, but biotite was also used. Biotite, powdered magnesia mica, adhered to the ink and gave it a sparkling frosted effect. The three pounce pots, Plate 264, *O*, *S* and *U*, the first two of lignum vitae, and the last of boxwood, are 18th-century specimens—see also *Blotter Cases*.

Quill Pen Cutters—see *Pens, Pen Cutters and Pen Knives*

Rulers

Old cylindric, ebony, lignum, and rose-wood rulers have survived in large quantities, but flat ones, unless ornamental, seldom reach antique status. Some attractive Tunbridge wood mosaic examples, all 9 in. long and calibrated in inches, are illustrated, Plate 269, *N*, *O*, *P*, and *Q*. The first two in Berlin 'woolwork' designs, date from about 1845. *P* and *Q* are 10–20 years earlier. The rosewood ruler, Plate 267, *O*, is Chinese, inlaid with brass points which calibrate (inaccurately) in Chinese inches, each representing 1½ English inches. The inlaid symbols mean 'Wishing you a hundred children and a thousand grand-children'. For rulers combined with signets, see Section XIV, *Parcelling, Postage, Sealing*.

Scriveners Knives—see *Pens, Pen Cutters and Pen Knives*

Slates

Although wood-framed slates, such as Plate 450, *B*, are now generally regarded as bygones of child education, they served a much wider purpose in previous centuries. They were often used as household reminder shopping and laundry lists, for sums, and they also served for all kinds of temporary notices and announcements in shops and workshops. In the absence of makers' names on the frames, there is usually no means of dating them accurately.

Spectacle Cases

Although spectacles properly belong to Section XIX, *Scientific*, they are so often a necessary adjunct of reading and writing, that their cases are illustrated and described here. Some early spectacle cases are said to have had wooden frames, but I have never seen any. As with so many early discoveries, the Chinese are sometimes credited with the invention of spectacles. The earliest European mention seems to be that of an 11th-century Arab writer.

Roger Bacon explained the principles of glasses in 1266 and the monks of Pisa and Florence were using spectacles in the 13th century. Amongst the earliest depictions, the following are cited. A fresco in the church at Treviso, painted in 1352, shows Cardinal Ugone wearing spectacles. Van Eyck's painting of the Madonna, 1436, in the museum at Bruges, shows the donor, Canon Van Der Paele, kneeling at the side and holding spectacles above an open book. A painting of St. Matthew on the *circa* 1460 screen at Cawston Church, Norfolk, shows the short-sighted Saint wearing spectacles. A sculptured figure of a prophet, *circa* 1480, in Munich museum is depicted wearing spectacles. A 15th-century stone corbel head at St. Martin's Church, Salisbury, is similarly depicted. The best known English representations of early pince-nez spectacles are on two statues of St. Matthew in Henry VII's Chapel, 1502–12. One shows the Saint with spectacles half-way down his nose, peering at an open book, whilst a boy angel below, obligingly holds up an inkpot. A pair of spectacles are carved on the 1537 tomb of a priest in the old church at Whichford, near Stratford-on-Avon.

By 1629 spectacle making in England was an important enough craft for Charles I to grant a charter to the Worshipful Company of Spectacle Makers '... for better order, rule and government of spectacle makers ... touching and concerning the art or mistery in the making of spectacles'. In the mid-17th century, green tinted spectacles were the latest thing for those suffering with bad sight. Oliver Cromwell and Samuel Pepys both took to them.

A rare and early spectacle case, well worn and of walnut, carved on one side with a hunting scene, and on the reverse with a landscape, is illustrated, Plate 267, *D*. It is handsomely mounted and hinged with engraved brass which is dated 1726, and is probably Dutch. The interior view, Plate 266, *B*, shows the date engraving and the original round lens pince-nez spectacles. Also containing original spectacles of similar type is Plate 266, *C*, an English, carved beechwood case of card case type, with sliding shutter. It is carved with initials R.H. and date 1775 and was formerly in the Lewis Clapperton Collection. A clumsy but unusual end-hinged case of cylindric type is pictured, Plate 267, *A*. I do not think that the spectacles belong, although both they and the case are 19th-century. *B* and *G* are the more common tilt-end spectacle and eye-glass cases of the 19th century, and *C*, *E* and *F* are representative of 19th-century slide-on wood cases. *C* was made in 1857 from the 12th-century wood of old London Bridge. Both the slide-on and tilt-end types of case were made in the 19th century in transfer and tartan ware, and in Tunbridge wood mosaic; mid-19th-century Tunbridge examples are illustrated, Plate 269, *H*, hinged, and *J*, tilt-end. For eye testing devices, see Section I, *Apothecary*.

Standishes—see *Ink Stands*

Stationery Cabinets
Although many 18th-century sloping top, serpentine-fronted knife or cutlery cases are now fitted for stationery, these are later conversions; I have seen no portable stationery cabinets of earlier than 19th-century date. In the 18th century, stationery was normally kept in the special compartments of desks and bureaux, or in the drawers of writing tables, leaving the writing surface as free as possible. It was left to the 19th century, to clutter increasingly all horizontal surfaces, even those meant primarily for work. Two of the most popular mid-19th-century shapes, for domestic stationery cabinets, are the slope top, Plate 268, *K*, 9 in. wide, and the dome top, *L*, 10 in. wide. These two particular examples are decorated with Tunbridge wood mosaic, but the same outlines were used for plain and figured veneered and leather-covered caskets. A small casket

of the same period, carved to represent a strapped, reeded trunk, with two compartments for postcards, is shown, Plate 268, *H*. Considerably larger cabinets, divided in their depth, with some of the stationery compartments fitted inside the backs of a pair of locking doors, were used sometimes on tables in offices, writing rooms of hotels, etc.

An imposing mahogany stationery cabinet with a leather-backed tambour shutter enclosing stationery compartments and accommodation for pens, ink and pounce, and with two drawers below, is illustrated, Plate 276. It measures 16½ in. wide by 10 in. high, plus the 7½ in. high, scrolled pediment and is an object of considerable historic interest in its own right, being an early 19th-century stationery cabinet, which once graced the office of the stationmaster at Stockton-on-Tees. Its particular interest lies in the heavily engraved brass plate, which forms the centrepiece of the carved pediment, and was probably made in the engine workshops. The dial is a perpetual calendar with two hands: the long hand points to the date and the short one to the months on the inner ring. The days of the week are engraved on a brass roller, in a 'window' above centre. In the ribbing in the scroll is an oval 'window', presumably for the stationmaster's name. Surmounting this is the outline of a four-wheeled engine with a tall stack, the whole engraved in considerable detail. On a scroll below the engine is inscribed 'No. 1 Locomotion 1825'. This is the engine which preceded the 'Rocket' by four or five years. See also *Desks, Portable*.

Travelling Bookcases—see *Bookcases, Travelling*

Travelling Writing Outfits—see *Ink Pots and Stands*

Wax Tablet Cases
Both wooden and ivory cases, gouged out to

form shallow trays, and fitted with protective sliding shutters were formerly used to hold a layer of wax, on which to write with a stylus. The recess for the wax is only about ⅛ in. deep and a normal overall measurement for the case is 6 in. or 7 in. by 3 in. or 4 in. To erase the writing, the tray was left in the sun, with its shutter removed. The geographical area of usage of wax tablets was wide, embracing at least the Mediterranean basin and the Middle East. Some of the most beautiful specimens, both pictorially painted and relief carved, were Persian. A handsome Persian specimen, carved with flowers and foliage on both faces, and ornamentally stamped with stars on the edges and inside the lid, is shown, Plate 266, *P*. It dates from the 17th century.

XVIII

Sailors', Sailmakers' and Fishermen's Devices

☆　　　☆　　　☆

As there is often no clear-cut division between tools and devices used by sailors, sailmakers and fishermen, there are no sub-divisions to this section.

The superseding of sail by steam, and wood by metal in ship-building, converted many everyday tools into wooden bygones during the 19th century. The various devices used in rope making are described in Section XXV, *Trade Devices*. Ship's figureheads are discussed in Section XXVI, *Trade Signs, and Ships' Figureheads, etc.*; the connection between the two is well brought out in Charles Dickens's *Dombey and Son*, where Sol Gills, the ship's instrument maker, is so proud of his little wooden midshipman effigy in obsolete naval uniform

> '... which thrust itself out above the pavement, right leg foremost, with a suavity the least endurable, and had the shoe buckles and flapped waistcoat the least reconcilable to human reason, and bore at its right eye the most offensively disproportionate piece of machinery (a sextant) ....'

'A callous, obdurate, conceited midshipman, intent on his own discoveries', as Dickens also described him, is believed to have been 'The Little Wooden Midshipman' sign outside the premises of William Heather, Norie and Wilson, in Leadenhall Street, and later in the Minories; the mid-

shipman stood outside the door from 1795 until 1917, and is still cherished inside the premises of Imray, Laurie, Norie and Wilson, publishers of charts and nautical works at St. Ives, Hunts.

Some love tokens made by sailors, will be found in Section IX, *Love Spoons and Other Love Tokens*, as well as under *Mementoes* in the present section.

Back Boards, Skiff—see *Skiff Back Boards*

Belaying Pins
The mahogany belaying pin, Plate 285, *K*, is 16½ in. long, the handle accounting for 7 in. In nautical parlance, to belay is to coil a running rope, such as a brace or bowline, round a belaying pin, cleat or kevel, so as to secure it. Belaying pins were stored in holes, bored in line, in long narrow boards known as fife rails, which were securely fixed inside the gunwales of sailing ships, opposite each mast. Each pin was always used for its own particular rope. In a 'rough house', a belaying pin was a useful weapon!

Chains, Wooden—see *Mementoes*

Cork Objects
Sailors and fishermen of many nations

formerly used vast quantities of cork for lifebuoys, life jackets and floats. Having plenty of offcuts, and leisure often unwanted and unpaid, they earned spare-time money by their skill and ingenuity in making relief pictures, models and other decorative objects from the easily worked material. The 19th-century cork picture of Haverfordwest, Plate 286, *E*, is signed P. V. Santille. It utilises slab cork for buildings, figures, boat, cows, etc., and granulated cork for tree foliage, shore, etc.

The finely carved cork casket, Plate 286, *J*, is also 19th-century work, probably English. The lid has a naturalistic rose for handle and the lid rim and sides are carved with fluting, festoons and swags. The interior is lined with blue silk; inside the lid is a cut-out cork picture of an Oriental landscape and seascape.

Cork is the outer part of the bark of the cork oak tree, which grows to perfection in Portugal, whence it is exported to all parts of the world. This outer bark is a recurrent crop, which is carefully stripped from the trees every 10–12 years.

Creels

Fishermen's creels have been made of wicker or osier work from time immemorial, occasionally of leather. The word creel, in this sense, can only be traced back to the 19th century. Izaak Walton and his contemporaries, also 18th-century writers, refer to fish panniers. A wooden creel such as Plate 286, *G*, must be a rarity. It is quite light, made of thin steamed mahogany, bent and brass nailed round a mahogany top frame and pine bottom; it has leather hinges and remains of leather shoulder straps. It is almost certainly English and may be 18th- or 19th-century; its greatest dimensions are: length 14½ in., width 6 in., height 6 in.

Dead Eyes

Dead eyes, Plate 285, *O*, are round, laterally flattened blocks, each pierced with three holes, through each of which a lanyard is reeved; the illustration shows the method of passing the lanyards through the holes. Dead eyes were used for extending the shrouds; they acted in effect as adjustable rope fixtures, like sliding buckles on a cord. The pear-shaped, elm object, Plate 285, *C*, is a reeving block.

Dinghy Plugs

The nest of three ribbed, beechwood cones, which fit into each other, Plate 285, *J*, were used for stopping leaks in life-saving dinghies in the Second World War; earlier, they were used for light craft of canvas, etc.

Fenders

Fenders are used for fending off—nautically, that is for preventing damage by a boat bumping against a ship, or against a wharf or quay. Traditionally, a sailing ship's fenders were lengths of old cable, rope balls, or rope or cork bolsters, sewn up in canvas by a sailmaker. Nowadays, old tyres often serve the purpose. The springy, woven rattan ball fender, approximately 6 in. in diameter, Plate 285, *M*, is the Oriental version of the rope ball and probably comes from Malaya or Dutch East Indics.

Fids

Fids, Plate 285, *D* to *H*, are conical hardwood 'carrots' tapering to a point at one end, and in general varying from about 9 in. to 18 in. in length, but both longer and shorter ones are known. The largest which I have recorded, is in Worthing Museum and measures 52 in. in length by 11 in. diameter at base. Like those illustrated here, it is of lignum vitae, which has been favoured for the purpose since the beginning of the 17th century, although some fids were also made of boxwood and of whalebone. Diameters at base vary considerably and it is not unusual to find fids, say 14 in. long, with any base diameters from 1½ in. to 3 in. Fids were and are used to open the strands of a rope in splicing, particularly for insertion of the 'thimble'. Small fids were mostly used for the bolt ropes of sails, larger ones for splicing cables. Fids were also used for making the grummets which are fitted over bases of shells, to protect the copper driving bands. Iron versions of fids are known as marling-spikes, marlin-spikes, or stabbers.

Figureheads—see Section XXVI, *Trade Signs, Ships' Figureheads, etc.*

Fishermen's Companions

The fisherman's companion, Plate 286, *C*, is of boxwood, 5¾ in. high; each of the 10 winders on the outer circle, which is in one piece, holds a separate line and hook. The four weight boxes, which screw into each other, when combined form the centre cylinder, and are detached *en bloc*, by unscrewing the key; this neat English device, which is illustrated on an 18th-century trade card, was formerly in the Evan-Thomas Collection. A slightly larger one, taken apart, is shown alongside, with the winders, *C1*, three of the weight boxes, *C2*, and the top weight box and key, *C3*. An English combination sportsman's companion, of mahogany, is shown at *B*. It consists of a shot and cap box with sliding lid, placed centrally, with two winders at each side; this specimen is probably 19th-century, but the same type is still being made today.

Fishing Rods

It is doubtful whether the basic principles of fishing rods have changed since the dawn of civilization. Rods themselves have gradually become more civilized, advancing from the natural branch, via natural cane and the laminated split cane, to the subtle, flexible strength of the Guiana greenheart. These, in their turn, are now being superseded by fibre-glass and steel. Ordinary fishing rods do not normally become by-gones, but the poacher's rod occasionally

survives. A Chinese specimen in the Pinto Collection, is housed in a quite ordinary looking, stout walking cane, 34 in. long, carved with an ape and a coiled snake; when the ferrule of the stick is removed, three telescopic lengths of graduated cane extend the rod to 9 ft.

Floats

Two fishermen's floats are shown in Plate 287, *F* and *G*. *F* is a cane and quill slider float; *G*, a cork egg and quill float. Both types are still in use, the latter usually painted red above, and black or green below the water line.

Freedom Scrolls

An unusual freedom scroll container, in the form of a cannon, made of Virginia walnut, is shown in Plate 289. It is probably English, 18th- or early 19th-century. Appropriate caskets were used ceremonially, when a ship was presented with the freedom of a port or city.

Gaffs

The usual poacher's gaff, being essentially a steel implement, is outside the scope of this book. The folding pocket gaff, Plate 287, *A*, dating from about 1900, may qualify for inclusion because the hook folds into an oak handle, carved as a sea-horse. Closed, it measures 17 in., open, 33 in.

Hanks

Two steamed oak hanks, of different size, are shown in Plate 285, *A* and *B*. They were formerly used on staysail hoists on sailing ships, instead of rope grummets. They were introduced about 1860 and were first made of wood, later of iron.

Liners—see *Sailmakers' Liners*

Markers—see *Sailmakers' Liners*

Mast Head Truck—see *Truck*

Mementoes

Sailors were great makers of mementoes (see also *Cork Objects*, *Scrimshaw Work*, and *Ship Models*). The wooden chain, Plate 286, *A*, with swivel hook and whistle, all carved out of the solid, was a popular type of carving. Some of the saddest mementoes are those made from the timber of famous wrecks, like 'Lusitania', 'Tuscania', 'Royal George', etc. A bellows pincushion made from the black oak of 'Royal George', with an inscription dated 1782, picked out in brass pins, is illustrated, Plate 287, *D*.

Model Ships—see *Ship Models*

Needle Cases

Two sailmakers' needle cases, containing their original triangular section, curved, sailmakers' needles, are shown, Plate 286, *K* and *L*. They measure 5 in. and 7½ in. in length respectively. They are simple, ring turned, cylindric boxes, of the same type that were also used for knitting needles, pencils, etc. They are probably 19th-century, but there is no way of dating such objects accurately.

Netting Tools

A selection of traditional netting tools, mostly of mahogany, is shown, Plate 287, *C1* to *C12*; some are round in section, others flat; they vary from 5 in. to 10 in. in length. *C4* and *C5* are different types of netting gauges; *C12* is a boxwood shuttle.

Nocturnals

The nocturnal or night dial, for finding the time at night by the stars, appears to have been invented early in the 16th century, and to have continued in general use up to the end of the 18th. The earliest examples known are Italian and German. The night dial was complementary to the sundial by day, but neither superseded the sand glass, which, despite the introduction of mechanical clocks, remained the standard time-keeper at sea, until well into the 19th century. Nocturnals were made both of boxwood and of brass, and they are beautifully designed and sometimes handsomely engraved with ornament. The instrument takes the form of a date disc, with a projecting handle or index arm; the outer edge of the disc is graduated in days and months. A smaller revolving concentric disc is provided, with a serrated outer edge graduated in minutes and hours; this can be set on the outer scale, according to date. The movable index arm, concentric with both discs, is provided with a straight edge, which passes through the centre of both discs. Some nocturnals have a lunar dial and tide calendar engraved on the back.

Otters

An otter is a now illegal poacher's fishing device. It is not illustrated, because a picture will not help, as basically it is merely a board bevelled to a point at each end and with a heavy lead keel on one edge. The specimen in the Pinto Collection, which is Scottish, is 15 in. long, 6¾ in. deep and ⅝ in. thick. It has cords and a line attached to it and is sailed out, upright, into the current, the lead keel keeping most of it submerged. Numerous 'droppers' of gut, with trout flies on them are attached to the line and set in quick motion by the first 'bite'. A full description of the otter and its working will be found in *The New Poacher's Handbook* by Ian Niall (Heinemann, 1960).

Palms

A sailmaker's palm of leather, Plate 287, *B*, was an essential of the craft. It was worn on the right hand, with thumb through the hole and the head of the needle resting in the metal thimble, inserted in the leather. The 19th-century specimen illustrated, was made by W. Smith and Son, the needlemakers of Redditch.

Plugs—see *Dinghy Plugs*

Presses—see *Sailmakers' Liners*

Priests
The miniature lignum vitae truncheon, Plate 287, *E*, 6½ in. long, was called a priest because it was used to administer the *coup de grâce*, or last rites, by knocking a salmon or trout over the head.

Pulley Blocks
Pulley blocks of three sizes, 4½ in., 8 in. and 10 in., are illustrated, Plate 285, *L*, *P* and *Q*. Elm is the traditional wood employed for the blocks, with the grooved pulley wheels or sheaves of lignum vitae; as early as 1608, the turners were recommending lignum vitae for sheaves and pins—see references to lignum vitae in Section III, *Drinking*. Pulley blocks used on land for lifting tackle, do not usually have reeving grooves for ropes in the blocks.

Reels
A 'Nottingham' fisherman's reel of mahogany, *circa* 1900, is illustrated, Plate 286, *D*. The centre pin reel of elm, Plate 286, *H*, is a traditional type and may be late 18th- or 19th-century.

Reeving Blocks—see *Dead Eyes*

Rope Making Equipment—see Section XXV, *Trade and Craft Devices*

Rubbers—see *Sailmakers' Liners*

Sailmakers' Liners
Liners, markers, presses, rubbers and smoothers are all alternative names for the same sailmaker's tool. A fine selection is illustrated in Plate 288, *C* to *M*. Liners were used for smoothing seams in canvas. This was achieved by pressing and rubbing the heart-shaped ends of the liners away from the user and flattening the double line of waxed twin stitches into the canvas, so deliberately making 'dead men'. Sailors, as one might expect, formerly made their own tools, and took pride in designing and finishing them well, and making them decorative, without allowing ornament to mar fitness for purpose. Liners made in one piece were usually of either a dense hardwood, such as lignum vitae, or walrus ivory. Liners in Plate 288, *C* to *L*, with the possible exception of *H*, are at least as old as the 18th century. *M* is late 19th-century, commercially made and has a thick steel blade. Here are points of interest of some of the specimens. *D* includes in its decoration, on the sides not visible, a heart, diamond, harpoon and flower pot, an axe and hatchet and the name Will Clark; *F*, a heart, diamond and anchor; *L*, of walrus ivory, with bucket-knot or Turk's head terminal, has the points of the compass and initials T.W. on one face and a crowned heart, containing a crucifix, on the reverse.

Sailors' Mementoes—see *Mementoes*

Scrimshaw Work
Scrimshaw work is the name given to surface scratched pictures and decorative motifs executed by sailors on walrus ivory, whalebone, seashells and hardwoods. Whalers of all nationalities seem to have indulged in the pastime, judging by the numerous depictions of whales, seals, walruses and penguins. Sometimes designs show implements like harpoons or anchors and some of the designs are geometric. Certain decorative motifs show that objects were intended as love tokens; bone stay busks and wooden love spoons, knitting sheaths, nutcrackers and coconuts, as an instance, are sometimes found embellished with scrimshaw love devices.

Serving Mallets
Like sailmakers' liners, serving mallets, or serving boards, Plate 288, *A* and *B*, were devices used in sailmaking. *A* was in use at the beginning of this century; the more decorative specimen, *B*, 6 in. long, with

handle formed as a clenched fist, is 18th-century. The concave, crescent-shaped blade, fitted over the rope which it was desired to serve, or sew to the canvas. The tool was used for straining or drawing tight the spun yarn, sailmaker's twine or sisal hemp. The two parallel grooves, which run down and score 'V's in the edge of the blade, are for straining on the yarn. The sailmaker's rhyming formula for using this tool, ran as follows:

'Worm and parcel with the lay,
Turn and serve the other way.'

According to the *Manual of Seamanship* (1937), to worm, parcel and service a rope, is to preserve it from wet or chafe. Worming is done to fill up the space between the strands of the rope with spunyard or small rope, to render the surface smooth and round for parcelling and serving. Parcelling a rope is laying round it, with the lay of the rope, strips of old canvas, tarred, from 2 in. to 3 in. wide, according to the size of the rope, before serving it. Serving a rope has already been described. 'Service at the end of a rope' is the old nautical term for a whipping.

Sextants
A sextant is an instrument of navigation for measuring the angular distances of objects, by means of reflection. It resembles the octant and quadrant and may be traced directly back to the cross-staff and Davis' back-staff. The English, 18th-century example illustrated, Plate 289, is of ebony, ivory and brass, the case of mahogany.

Ship Mementoes—see *Mementoes*

Ship Models
Ship models are a fascinating subject, and one for a book, not a paragraph. Professionals and amateurs have vied with each other in producing scale models, correct down to the smallest detail. Some of the finest models of the Napoleonic period were made by prisoners-of-war, from bones of the animals used for their rations. A sailor-made ship model of 'Sardinia' of 949 tons, built at Nova Scotia in 1856, is illustrated, Plate 286, *F*. From the viewpoint of accuracy, this is a poor model: masts are too close, bowsprit at wrong angle, and rudder about three times the size it should be. This last, particularly suggests that the model was built primarily for sailing.

Ships in bottles reflect too much from the glass to photograph in detail. Bottled ships are still made and very often the models used are of a bygone age, but in general, it is not too difficult to distinguish old from new, chiefly by the much finer detail of the old work. The glass may help, but ships, like wine, are sometimes new even when in old bottles. Ships which have modelled landscape or seascape backgrounds in the bottle, are not usually made by British sailors; some of the best of them are the work of South American sailors.

Skiff Back Boards
Skiff back boards are horizontal boards, fret outlined along the upper edge and painted with the skiff's or owner's names, addresses, dates, scenes, etc. They are often highly decorative. A selection is displayed at Watermen's Hall, 18 St. Mary-at-Hill, London.

Smoothers—see *Sailmakers' Liners*

Spools
A sailmaker's spool, wound with three different colours of yarn, is shown alongside the wooden cylinder in which it fits, Plate 286, *M* and *M1*; the cylinder is decorated with scrimshaw work.

Traverse Boards
The ingeniously designed traverse board, for recording the course sailed, appears

first to have been recorded in 1627; it was still used in some sailing ships in the 19th century. The example illustrated in Plate 289, is a rare and fine specimen of early date; it could be late 17th- or early 18th-century. The circular part of a traverse board was marked with a series of 32 radial lines, one for each compass point; along each line, eight peg holes were bored, one for each half-hour of a watch. Several pegs were provided, so that the quartermaster could record the course sailed during each half hour of the watch, and these pegs were tethered by a thin cord to a pin fixed in the central hole. The horizontal part varies from one specimen to another, although all appear to have four rows of peg holes; the number of holes along each row is not, however, the same in all ex-amples (in the instrument illustrated, there are 10 holes, representing the integers 1 to 10 and 3 representing the fractions $\frac{1}{4}$, $\frac{1}{2}$ and $\frac{3}{4}$ respectively). These peg holes are said to have been used for recording the speed of the ship for each hour of the watch. In this way, the navigator had a detailed record, at the end of the watch, of the course of the ship during the watch. The circle of the $\frac{3}{4}$ in. thick board measures $9\frac{1}{2}$ in.

Trucks

The elm mast-head truck from the top of a jack or ensign staff, Plate 285, N, is $13\frac{1}{2}$ in. tall by $9\frac{1}{2}$ in. diameter at base. It was dredged up from the bed of the Thames. The photograph shows the mast-head hole and the sheave through which the halyard was rove.

XIX

Scientific and Reckoning, Measuring, Calculating and Weighing

The modern versions of, or successors to some of the various devices illustrated and described in this section, could properly be described under the heading of scientific. Many of the earlier wooden examples, however, such as the treen measures of volume, some of the measuring sticks, etc. have nothing scientific about them, and are primitive and inaccurate, being based on the variable dimensions and weights of common objects. Their origins are, where feasible, briefly discussed under the following headings:

Calculating and Counting Devices
Dial Registers
Measuring Sticks and other Measuring Devices
Measures of Time (see also Dial Registers)
Measures of Volume
Machines
Optics
Tallies and Tally Boards
Weighing Appliances

CALCULATING AND COUNTING DEVICES

Abacuses

The Chinese or Japanese abacus, Plate 296, *D*, in lidded box, is one of the earliest and most widely adopted calculating devices still actively used. Believed to have originated in the Tigris-Euphrates valley, some 5,000 years ago, it was later extensively used by ancient Egyptians, Greeks, Romans, Hindus and Mexicans. It is still used for general calculations in shops and offices in China, where it is called *Suan-pan*. In many parts of Japan, Persia and Russia, businessmen carry them in pocket cases and make lightning calculations with them; in Russia, the device is called a *Stchoty*. This year, I saw well practised clerks using them most efficiently in Portuguese banks. Basically, the abacus is the familiar 'ball frame' of our nurseries, with parallel wires on which are strung movable coloured wooden beads, for teaching children to count. When used by adults for addition, subtraction, multiplication and division, the abacus usually has flattened spherical balls of uncoloured wood; some have a dividing line across, for simplifying large-scale calculations. The early 19th-century, walnut abacus, Plate 296, *C*, has brass angle plates and inlaid brass lines round the frame. It is probably Russian. *D*, in lidded pocket case, is traditional Oriental.

Chuck-rum Boards

Chuck-rums, small silver coins at one time

current in South India, were counted by shaking them over a rimmed board containing a known number of depressions, into which the coins dropped. A circular chuck-rum counting board, made of pad-auk, a dense, heavy, reddish brown timber, grown in the Andaman Islands and parts of India, is illustrated, Plate 296, *E*. Boards vary in size considerably and some, such as that illustrated, have different numbers of sinkings on each side—in this example the sinkings are 520 and 600 respectively. They may also be rectangular and provided with an open-work, scroll carved handle at one end. They are often confused with pill counting boards, but although these may have somewhat similar depressions, the majority of western European specimens which I have seen, are rimmed, triangular boards, marked out with numbered parallel lines on their base boards. These lines are arranged to bisect an angle of one corner, so that by tilting the pill towards that corner, they are automatically counted by the number of lines which they cover.

McFarlane's Calculating Cylinder

This curious and complicated, 6¼ in. high cylinder, Plate 294, *A*, was invented by McFarlane of Edinburgh, about 1840. It was so difficult and laborious to use, that understandably it was not a success. So far, I have only recorded four specimens. See also *Napier's Bones* and *Schott's Cylinders*.

Military Calculators

The boxwood slide, Plate 297, *J*, pictured on its original leather pocket case, was made by Graham and Latham. On one side are calculations for comparative ranges of rifle, field and heavy artillery fire and the reverse side is arranged for calculating march tables. It was used by staff officers during the First World War.

Napier's Bones

John Napier (1550–1617), who gave log-arithms to the world (1614), also invented Napier's rods or bones (1617), an ingenious device for calculating by means of square boxwood or bone rods, with numerical tables on each of their four sides. Original, complete sets, in good condition, are rare; a perfect specimen, made of boxwood, with its original boxwood case below, is shown, Plate 292, *N*. Pepys was much impressed by 'the mighty use of Napier's bones'; in 1667, he records his intention of buying a set. See also *Schott's Cylinders*.

Pill Counting Boards—see *Chuck-rum Boards*

Schott's Cylinders

Gaspard Schott, in 1668, substituted revolving cylinders for four-sided rods. There were a number of later variants of Napier's bones and Schott's cylinders, but none seem to have been improvements. Pepys, in 1667, referred to Sir Samuel Morland's lately invented calculating machine as 'very pretty, but not very useful'. Probably he would have made a similar remark about McFarlane's calculating cylinder—see above.

Slide Rules

The first calculating device in the form of a rule based on scientific principles and, therefore, the direct ancestor of the modern slide rule, was produced by Gunter in 1620. It consisted of a single scale and compasses were needed for calculating. The present form of two-part rule was invented six years later by Wingate. More than 2¼ centuries elapsed before Mannheim, a Frenchman, in 1850–1, added the now universal cursor. The long time lag is curious because cursors were known early in the 17th century and their advantage on slide rules was pointed out by Newton. Most slide rules are now 10 in. long, but the early ones were longer. An early specimen, 18 in. long is shown, Plate 297, *B*, with one of its three slides, *C*, beside it. As well as being a normal slide rule for multiplication, division, squares, cubes, etc., it contains numerous other scales relating specifically to vintners' and brewers' calculations. Among many headings engraved on it are:

2d. variety; Malt Wash to LW; Cyder to Couch; Divisers for Ale, Wine, etc.; Gauge Points for Ale, Wine, Malt and various other vintner's constants.

Because the rule is engraved with the name 'Owen Gill', its owner, and 'Edward Roberts of Dove Court, Old Jewry', its maker, it has proved possible to trace its history through the courtesy of the Worshipful Company of Vintners. About the year 1775, a Mr. William Gill evolved a system of ascertaining varying contents of casks and various vintner's constants by using slides and he commissioned Edward Roberts to make them. As far as can be traced, only six were made, as they were quickly proved to be inaccurate. The six were eventually used by some enterprising wine merchants, obviously including Owen Gill, who was presumably related to the inventor; these merchants are supposed to have toyed with rule and cask, in order to impress their importance upon their customers.

The more scientific excise officer's slide rule was a 17th-century invention. One of the earliest was devised by Thomas Everard in 1683; during the 18th century, J. Vero, C. Leadbetter and others, modified and improved it. By 1800 or earlier, the slide rule had become an accurate calculating instrument. It was also broader than the earlier specimens and now had four slides, but still no cursor. One made by Dring and Fage of Tooley Street, London, in the late 18th or early 19th century, is shown, Plate 297, A; another type by the same maker is illustrated, Plate 298, G. Other makers whose names occur on slide rules of the same period include Loftus of 146 Oxford Street, London; Lewis & Biggs of Bow Lane, Cheapside, and Cook, late

Wellington, of Crown Court, Soho. Plate 297, H, shows the well-known Farmar's Publican's Stocktaking Slide Rule, 'the standard for licensed victuallers'.

DIAL REGISTERS

This section excludes watches, clocks and sundials, which are discussed under *Measures of Time*.

Coaching Dials

The pair of 12 in. diameter, 18th-century, mahogany coaching dials, with heavy brass pointers, Plate 295, are rarities, in remarkably good condition after 200 years. The 'M' on one dial stands for 'Mail' and the 'P' on the other for 'Passengers' and such boards were used largely in the halls of coaching inns, to show, by setting the hand at the appropriate place on each dial, the time of departure of the next mail and passenger coach respectively. I have seen one or two much cruder specimens with two dials painted on one board, probably for use outside a building. The examples illustrated show that the use of a 24-hour dial for vehicle departure times, concerning which there has of late been so much controversy, is not entirely an innovation in this country, although another pair of 'M' and 'P' dials noted, show 12 hour markings; a third pair, marked 1 to 16, presumably denoting no night departures, might have been used at a sea port, in connection with a ferry.

Compasses

The compass is said to have been used in China 3,000 years ago and in Europe in the 12th or 13th century. Peter Peregrinus of Picardy described a pivoted compass in 1269 and Flavio Gioja of Amalfi is recorded as having made an eight-point compass in 1302; those illustrated in Plate 292 cannot claim so much antiquity. Plate 292, H, framed in boxwood, is a traditional Chinese

Fêng-Shui, or wind and water compass, made in the 19th century. *Fêng-Shui*, although literally meaning wind and water, is also the Chinese term for geomancy, which includes divining, by means of lines and figures, whether a building site would be propitious or not. In ancient China, the geomancer, with his *Fêng-Shui*, was summoned before the architect was called in. Modern governments might save millions by employing a geomancer!

The compass in circular boxwood pocket case, Plate 292, *J*, is English, 19th-century. The compass in square mahogany case, *K*, also English, can be dated by its dial and other details, to around 1700, but the same general type was still made in the 19th century. Some circular, mahogany cased compasses of 18th-century origin, without lids, are components detached from the bases of globe stands, and criss-cross marks on the underside of their cases show where they were once glued centrally on the cross rails of the stands.

Waywisers or Perambulators

The waywiser, Plate 290, was an apparatus formerly used for measuring distances. It consisted normally of a large wooden wheel with an iron tyre, to which a handle was attached, in similar manner as on a garden roller. On the handle was fixed a clock, the dial arranged upside-down, so that the person pushing it, could read the distances. Usually the clock had two hands, actuated by a simple mechanism connected to the wheel, which by measuring the revolutions of the wheel, registered on the dial, the distances traversed. The dials of 18th- and early 19th-century waywisers—and the majority of the few survivals date from that period—are normally engraved with two concentric rings, divided into yards (or links), poles, chains, furlongs and miles, or alternatively into yards, poles and miles. A few elaborate clocks have a small inner dial, like a seconds dial on a watch, with a separate hand for registering the miles.

The waywiser was essentially the product of a woodworker—more often a joiner or cabinet-maker than a wheelwright—in partnership with a clock or mathematical instrument maker. It is the latter's name which may be engraved upon the dial. The engraving of the dial and the shaping, and sometimes perforation, of the hands follow the fashion in clocks and vary from simple to elaborate, and the dials may be polished brass or silvered.

Waywisers for estate measuring are of lighter construction than those for setting up milestones on the roads. In the former, the wheels and handles are usually gracefully constructed of mahogany and polished. The latter, designed for much heavier use, are of elm, ash, or oak, or a mixture of hardwoods, and were originally varnished or painted. Most of the estate waywisers appear to have been made in London. Recorded names of London makers include Thomas Wright, No. 6 Poultry, in the City; D. Harris of Cranbourn Alley, Leicester Fields; Watkins & Smith, Charing Cross, and R. Banks of 441 Strand, who was the maker of the example illustrated, which dates from the 1790–1800 period. During the time that they were made and used, waywisers were also known as hodometers, odometers and perambulators. Perambulator was an excellent name, because, from the 16th century or earlier, to perambulate, or a perambulation, meant a ceremonial walk round a forest, manor, parish, or holding, for the purpose of recording its boundaries or extent. The Victorians, with their love of romantic misnaming, transferred the word perambulator into a name for a child's push carriage.

The earliest known reproduction of a land surveyor's carriage for measuring distances, occurs in Vitruvius' *De Architectura* of 1511. It is an elaborately ornamented, chariot-like vehicle. Additional to the two wheels on which it was drawn, it had a toothed wheel, the revolutions of which were recorded by the dropping of a pebble through a hole into a receptacle beneath, at each thousand revolutions. Some authorities state that the single wheel waywiser with clock was invented at the end of the 17th century; this is definitely incorrect; it was known at least 43 years earlier. John Evelyn recorded in his *Diary*, on August 6, 1657

> 'I went to see Col. Blount, who shewed me the application of the way-wiser to a coach, exactly measuring the miles, and shewing them by an index as we went on. It had 3 circles, one pointing to ye number of rods, another to ye miles, by 10 to 1000, with all the subdivisions of quarters; very pretty and useful'.

It may well be that Evelyn was not recording the waywiser as a new invention, but only the novelty of its application as an adjunct to a coach.

A novel type of perambulator was invented by Erasmus Darwin's friend, Richard Lovell Edgworth, in 1767. Edgworth submitted his idea to the Royal Society of Arts, who awarded him a medal. The invention, of which a drawing still exists but, so far as I know, no specimens, was a curious one. It consisted of a hub on a threaded rod. It had 11 spokes but no rim—in fact, it was a rimless wheel, measuring a pole in circumference. It had no clock, and was pushed along the road, its revolutions being recorded by means of its passage along the screw thread.

'Blind Jack of Knaresborough', John Metcalf, 1717–1810, was a famous character who made or remade many roads in the north of England, employing, it is said, up to 400 navvies. He carried out his own surveys using a waywiser, which had raised markings on its dial; his instrument is now at Knaresborough Castle. Another, reputed to have been used by him, is in the Wakeman's House, Ripon.

Dorothy Wordsworth, the poet's sister, was a well-known trundler of perambulators

and several references to her road distance measuring occur in the Pinney Papers for 1796. Other references of about the same date, show that surveying of estates and gardens was a fashionable pastime for ladies.

About 10 years ago, I met an elderly lady who remembered her father telling her that he had measured the distance from his cottage to the post office with a waywiser, because of a dispute over the charge for delivery of letters. He was able to prove that the cottage was within a mile of the post office and that he was being overcharged! This must have been prior to the penny post of 1840.

MEASURING STICKS AND OTHER MEASURING DEVICES

In early days, common objects served as measures, as we can tell from the dual meanings of such words as hand (4 in.)—the average width measured across the knuckles—foot (12 in.), etc. That such inaccurate measures led to dispute, is shown by the fact that until Tudor times, churchwardens were empowered to detain the first 20 adult males out of church, stand them barefooted in line, heel to toe, and so establish a fair average measure of 20 ft. In bad weather, it must have been a particularly disagreeable exercise. In 1101, in an effort at standardization, Henry I is said to have decreed that the length of his arm should define the yard. Presumably the nautical term 'yard-arm' survived from this. It appears that Henry defined his arm as extending from finger-tip to middle of his chest, because the fathom, 72 in., was originally the distance between the extremities of the arms, when extended. If you check these standards, you will find that Henry had the average reach of a man of the present day. Incidentally, in olden times, when building workers were often without a rule, they used the following table, based on an average 6ft. 0 in. tall man:

Fathom		= 6 ft. 0 in.
Girth or pace	= $\frac{1}{2}$ fathom	= 3 ft. 0 in.
Elbow to finger-tips	= $\frac{1}{4}$ fathom	= 1 ft. 6 in.
Foot	= $\frac{1}{6}$ fathom	= 12 in.
Span	= $\frac{1}{8}$ fathom	= 9 in.
Across the palm	= $\frac{1}{24}$ fathom	= 3 in.

Cubits, ells, palms and digits were also early anatomical units of measurement. Originally, the cubit was the length of the forearm—18 in. to 22 in.; the ancient Egyptian hieroglyphic sign for the cubit was a forearm and the Egyptian cubit was sub-divided into palms and digits. From mediaeval times onwards, ells, which were considerably longer than cubits, were sometimes called cubits in the cloth trade, which is most confusing.

Ell Rules

Until the wide adoption of the metric system on the Continent, early in the 19th century, the ell was a popular measure, particularly for cloth, both abroad and at home. The rules must have been extremely awkward however, for they varied in total length considerably in different countries, and were also inaccurate in their sub-calibrations. In England, for instance, it was officially a yard and a quarter—45 in.; in Scotland, 37·2 in., while the Flemish ell measured 26 in. to $27\frac{1}{2}$ in. To make matters worse for the researcher, some English-made ell rules, for buying continental cloth, were 26 in. to 27 in. long, whilst others, for the home trade, were 37 in. to 45 in. long. Survivals of the latter are extremely rare, probably because they were un-ornamented.

Ell rules are sometimes highly decorative and, therefore, particularly desirable to collectors; some outstanding 17th-century, continental specimens are inlaid with engraved ivory and mother-of-pearl, arranged in designs of floral scrolls, human figures and animals, in the manner of gun stocks of the period. Five 18th-century and one early 19th-century rules, which come into the 'ell category', although some of the calibrations are very odd, are shown, suspended between jumping sticks, in Plate 298; enlarged details of the handle ends are illustrated in Plate 299. A, B and C are all 18th-century and inlaid with light woods in mahogany, in the manner of work made at Tunbridge. A is inlaid with markings at $6\frac{5}{8}$ in., $13\frac{1}{4}$ in., $19\frac{3}{4}$ in. and $26\frac{1}{2}$ in. B, dated 1730, with brass inlay, has brass calibrations at $1\frac{1}{8}$ in., $3\frac{7}{8}$ in., $9\frac{3}{8}$ in., $14\frac{7}{8}$ in., $17\frac{7}{8}$ in. and $25\frac{7}{8}$ in. C has markings on one face at $6\frac{9}{16}$ in., $9\frac{13}{16}$ in., $13\frac{1}{8}$ in., $19\frac{11}{16}$ in., 23 in. and $26\frac{1}{4}$ in.; on the reverse side, the main markings are $3\frac{15}{16}$ in., $7\frac{7}{8}$ in., $11\frac{13}{16}$ in., $15\frac{3}{4}$ in., $19\frac{3}{4}$ in. and $27\frac{1}{4}$ in.; each of these main markings is divided into tenths. Allowing for obvious inaccuracies, it seems likely that these are English-made rules, calibrated for purchasing cloth in various continental countries, or possibly rules intended for export. D is an interesting Spanish mahogany continental ell rule, with a curved hand grip carved in shallow relief on all faces; the carvings depict processes of grape pressing, barrel making, etc. Inscriptions are ANNO 1797 H31· AED·RD·VRY·HVD. Calibrations are at $6\frac{3}{4}$ in., $13\frac{5}{8}$ in., $20\frac{3}{8}$ in., $23\frac{3}{4}$ in., $25\frac{1}{2}$ in. and $27\frac{1}{4}$ in. Of an unidentified wood, E is chip carved all over, with a carved rope border and inlaid with bone plaques on which are inscribed the markings and ⟨S.O S⟩. It is surmounted by one large and four small heads and is Scandinavian. It measures a $27\frac{1}{4}$ in. ell, subdivided reasonably accurately into $\frac{1}{32}$ in., $\frac{1}{16}$ in., $\frac{1}{8}$ in., $\frac{1}{4}$ in., $\frac{1}{2}$ in. and $\frac{3}{4}$ in. F, another continental, probably Scandinavian specimen, is neatly chip carved all over. It has inlaid pewter calibrations of $14\frac{1}{2}$ in., $18\frac{3}{4}$ in., $23\frac{1}{8}$ in. and $27\frac{1}{2}$ in., initials M.D. and date 1806.

Pocket quarter ell rules have rarely survived, although one would have thought such useful instruments would have been made in fair quantities. Two good, 18th-century examples, probably English, although based on the $27\frac{1}{2}$ in. Flemish ell, are pictured, Plate 297, *E* and *F*. Both are mahogany; *F* is mounted and inlaid with ivory.

Gauges
Boxwood engineering gauges, like Plate 297, *D*, were made at least from the 17th century onwards. Plain and precise instruments, like the specimen illustrated (no maker's name), are likely to date from the 18th century.

Height Measures—see *Measuring Rods*

Horse Standards—See *Measuring Rods*

Hydrometers
A typical set of 18th-century hydrometers, or proof measuring spheres—glass beads for testing proof of spirits—is illustrated, Plate 300, *D*. The beads are in their original velvet-lined mahogany case, with label of the maker, Joseph Sala of 33 High Street, Paisley (Scotland) and details of gravities for varying spirits, inside the lid.

Measuring Rods
Boxwood, on account of its density, freedom from warping and light colour, is the almost invariable selection for all the many types of wooden measuring rods. One variety is exemplified by the six-section, exciseman's measuring rod, Plate 297, *G*, shown in its original leather pocket case; each 10 in. section is mounted in brass and threaded, so that joined together they measure 5 ft. 0 in. They were made by Joseph Hughes of Queen Street, Ratcliff, London, a maker of mathematical instruments to the Excise, during the 1820–50 period. A similar specimen in the Science Museum is by

Cock of London; his name does not appear in the London Directories.

Two boxwood height measuring sticks are shown, Plate 291. That on the left is a part of the 18th-century, combined weighing and height measuring machine described under *Weighing Appliances*. On the right, the horse measuring stick, correctly described as a walking stick horse standard, was made by James H. Adams of 66 Park Lane, Liverpool, in 1872–3. On one side, the standard is calibrated in inches and one-eighth inches, and on the reverse in hands and one-eighth inches. The pivoted brass arm, which locks at the horizontal, is made to fold into the standard, which can then be slid down into the cane, when it appears to be an ordinary walking stick. For details of other walking sticks with unusual contents, see Section II, *Costume Accessories*.

Ring Measuring Sticks
The jeweller's ring measuring stick, Plate 292, *O*, is known to date from the 19th century, but how far back these devices were used in this form, I have been unable to ascertain.

Sextants—see Section XVIII, *Sailors', Sailmakers' and Fishermen's Devices*

Waist Measurers
Waist measurers of the 18th and 19th centuries, were boxwood rules with two upstanding, inward curved claws, usually of brass. One claw was fixed at one end; the other was attached to a socket with set screw, and travelled along the calibrated rod, being fixed by the set screw to show the waist measurement.

MEASURES OF TIME

Calendar, Perpetual
The rare Georgian perpetual calendar, Plate 303, was formerly in the Linn Collection. It consists of a painted board, 14 in.

by $7\frac{1}{2}$ in., with a moving pointer on the month dial and a revolving dial below for the dates of the week-days. Another kind of perpetual calendar is illustrated, Plate 302, *A*. It is a decorative, mid-18th century, rococo example, from Hinderloopen, Holland. Measuring $21\frac{1}{4}$ in. in height, the ornament, including the typical long-tailed Hinderloopen birds, is picked out in gold on a red ground. The calendar date roll in the lower window is missing, but the winding spools remain. The circular aperture above, probably housed a watch, but could have been for month cards. It is made of oak throughout.

Examination of dates on old documents is often confused by changes in the calendar at different times in various countries. In England, between the 7th and 13th centuries, the year commenced first from Christmas Day, and then from January 1. Between the 12th and 14th centuries, the legal year commenced at Lady Day, March 25, so two sets of dates were in use. Until 1752, this was not ironed out and January 1 made the official commencement of the year in the British Isles, when at the same time, the Gregorian calendar, decreed by Pope Gregory in 1582, was at last adopted. By the change from the Julian to the Gregorian calendar, October 5 became October 15; riots resulted in Great Britain, as many people thought they were being cheated out of 11 days of life, whilst leaseholders were quite certain that they were losers.

Clocks

Although wooden clock movements are usually associated with the Black Forest District of Germany, there were also makers of wooden clocks in other countries, including England and the U.S.A. John Harrison, a famous clockmaker, born in Yorkshire in 1693, revolutionized navigation by the accuracy of his marine timekeepers or chronometers, the fourth of which won the Board of Longitude's award of £20,000. He also made several interesting

clocks mainly of wood. One recently discovered at Nostell Priory, Yorkshire, bears Harrison's name and the date 1717; another, in the Science Museum, is dated 1713. Unusual features of some of his wooden clocks are that the wheels are of oak, built up in three layers (Georgian three-ply) and the pendulums of mahogany, a very early use of the wood in England. Harrison made his clock mechanisms mainly of wood so that they would need no oil. James Harrison, probably a member of the same family, was the founder of the Connecticut wooden clock industry. The wooden clock movement, Plate 294, *F*, is of the type patented by Eli Terry of Plymouth, Connecticut, in 1816.

Metronomes

The metronome is a clockwork device for indicating, by means of a pendulum and scale, and securing exact degrees of tempo in musical performance. The best known is Maelzel's patent metronome of 1816, enclosed in a pyramidal hardwood case. One of the originals, in a 9 in. high rosewood case, is shown, Plate 300, *B*. Inside the door, an embossed gilded plate announces 'Best English Make—Metronome de Maelzel, London'; later and cheaper ones have detachable doors and celluloid or ivorine scales.

Perpetual Calendars—see *Calendars, Perpetual*

Sand Glasses

The sand glass is an instrument formerly in common use for measuring intervals of time and ranging from the three- or four-minute egg timer, through quarter and half hour glasses, to the hour glass. Basically, it consists of two glass bulbs, connected by a narrow neck, so as to form a figure 8; for practical protective reasons, it was always enclosed in a wooden or metal cage, usually formed by turned balusters secured to top and bottom plates. One bulb is filled with, enough dry sand to occupy a definite period of time in flowing through the upper into the lower bulb. Sand glasses were really a more accurate follow-on of the clepsydras or water clocks of the early eastern Mediterranean civilizations, which employed falling drops of water, instead of grains of sand, to measure time.

At one time, sand glasses were a normal part of the equipment of a church pulpit and were used for measuring 'parson's sermon'. Such glasses are often handsomely mounted in batteries of two half hour, or four quarter hour, on pivoted brackets, so that they could be easily reversed. Mr. T. W. Bagshawe has a collection of 13 (originally 18) separate half hour ones, which were used by the nuns of St. Mary's Convent, York, until about 1900, when watches were first permitted there. Sand glasses were used in the Royal Navy until 1839, to count the half hours. They were also used in the home, workshops and on building sites until watches and clocks gradually superseded them.

Until early in the 18th century, the two bulbs were separate, ground true at the necks, bedded on a thin lead washer, with a carefully gauged hole in it, puttied, and bound with a lacing of narrow linen or weave of thread. From about the mid-18th century, the two bulbs were accurately blown as a single unit. A simple, English, 17th-century quarter hour glass of the two bulb type, formerly in Kingston parish church, is illustrated, Plate 300, *A*, and a German, 18th-century, pivoted, wall fixing specimen is shown, Plate 300, *C*.

Sundials

The origin of sundials, or shadow clocks, is lost in antiquity. Two Egyptian specimens, dating from the 10th and 8th centuries B.C., are in the Neues Museum, Berlin. Saxon and Norman examples are to be seen on church walls in the British Isles, scratched on the masonry; some have gnomons, others have a centre hole in which a stick could be placed. A unique, 10th-century, Saxon, silver pocket sundial, of exquisite workmanship, was unearthed in the cloister garth at Canterbury Cathedral in 1939.

A good, *circa* 1600, boxwood pocket sundial, $3\frac{3}{4}$ in. high, with folding brass gnomon, is illustrated, Plate 294, *B*. Next to it, *C*, is a 9 in. high cube sundial, adjustable on a turned beechwood stand. It is by J. G. Kleininger, a well-known maker of mathematical and scientific apparatus in the second half of the 18th century, whose work is represented in many museums. *D*, dating from the late 18th or early 19th century, is an English pocket sundial in lignum vitae case. The rare Charles II casket, *H*, *circa* 1675, inlaid on all faces with numerous dials designed to give readings in different parts of the world, also includes the floating compass and dial tray, *J*, shown alongside. It was probably made by Charles Bloud, of Dieppe.

Watches

Watches which qualify for inclusion among wooden bygones are indeed rare. The wooden watch, of normal size, Plate 293, is an amazing *tour de force*, made by the Russian Bronikov brothers, who are said to have worked at Wjatka, soon after 1800. I have records of nine of these watches by the same makers and all of them, I believe, are models of different patterns of watches. The one illustrated, Plate 293 (dial and interior views), is of burr maple, with the mechanism of boxwood and pearwood and the chain of boxwood. It has a travelling case of walnut. For details of watch stands, see Section XXVIII, *Watch Stands*.

MEASURES OF VOLUME

A mural painting in the tomb of Hesy, who was an overseer in Egypt 3000 B.C., shows a set of wooden measures for grain, and copper measures for liquids, which might have been made today. The detail of the painting is so perfect that it clearly depicts the 14 graduating wooden measures as having wooden staves and black bands. Even the wooden 'strike', for levelling off the heaped grain from the top of the measure, is of identically the same form as is in use today. Probably the same complaints were rife then, as in recent times, that the contents of the measure were not shaken down properly before using the strike.

All old English measures which I have seen, are stamped and verified, by an inspector of weights and measures, with the crown and the initials of the reigning sovereign. It is difficult to say precisely when this form of stamping originated, but it is known that by a statute of William the Conqueror, it was ordained that measures and weights should be true and stamped, in all parts of the Kingdom. In 1310, the Guild of Turners was ordered to examine measures in the City of London and in 1435, this was extended to all turnery measures. The following is an extract from *The Worshipful Company of Turners of London*, by Roland Champness, M.A., LL.M. (Cantab.), F.S.A.:

'... Early references to the Guild of Turners, before their incorporation by James I, mostly concern their responsibilities for seeing that measures for liquids were true when made and that they remained true. It must be admitted that solid turned wooden measures, although possessing the virtues of cheapness and ability to stand up to hard wear, were not ideal. Wood, being hygroscopic, changes its dimensions according to moisture content, and the tough beech, the wood usually selected, needs very careful seasoning if it is to be subjected to the severe stresses and strains imposed by alternate cycles of wetting and drying out. If "green", a wood measure would soon be false and lying, but even if well seasoned it might shrink over a period and give false measure. This is the reason why turned wood measures had to be verified and stamped periodically by a responsible authority. That if well seasoned they could and did remain true for a long time, is proved by the fact that they are sometimes found bearing the stamp of two or more successive sovereigns. ... In the *Liber Albus* of the City of London, compiled in 1419, it is laid down that wooden measures shall be sealed with the seal of the Alderman. Anyone selling by measure not sealed, was fined 40 pence for the first offence and the measure was burnt; a second offence cost half a mark, and a third twenty shillings. It was further decreed that there should be Aldermanic marking four times in the year, because some of the turned measures "... having been marked while they were green, after being used for a long time, through dryness shrink, and thereby become not so good as they ought to be ...".

From the eighteenth century, and perhaps earlier, it became the practice for an Inspector of Weights and Measures to stamp the date, crown and initials of the reigning sovereign on measures, and this continued up to the reign of Edward VII. After 1907, solid wood, as opposed to steamed bent wood measures, were no longer accepted for verification.'

Many readers will remember all these measures with their liquid sounding markings of gills, pints, quarts and gallons, in general use as measures of capacity at the greengrocer's and corn chandler's. Other odd measures occasionally to be found are those which contained a firkin of butter, or a pig of ballast, both 56 lb., or a cran of herrings, which equals $37\frac{1}{2}$ gallons.

Cubic Measures, Bentwood

A selection of the larger measures made by the cooper from thin, steamed, bent oak or ash, with inserted pine bottoms, are shown, Plate 301, *N* to *S*. They may be found in a very large range of diameters and depths. Some are banded with iron or copper and really large specimens may have projecting metal handles. *P* is branded with the William IV mark.

Cubic Measures, Turned

The wooden measures, A to L, Plate 301, are essentially the work of the turners, and A, B, C, K and L could only be turned on a pole lathe, because the reciprocal motion was necessary, in order to leave on the side handle projection, which is a part of the solid. They are all of beech and all, except L, bear the Victorian stamp. A and B are quart measures, the first brass rimmed; C is a pint measure and K a half pint. The quart measure, L, is very interesting because it bears the stamps of George III, George IV, Victoria and Edward VII; it was apparently not verified during the reign of William IV (1830–7), but this old beech measure remained 'true' for more than 80 years. Turned measures E to J are all double measures, each being divided horizontally off-centre, to provide containers of different volume; the last two types, H and J, are further discussed in Section I, *Apothecary: Measures, Double Cup Type*. M is an Oriental nest of four cane measures; the horizontal natural membranes of the cane form the bottoms of the individual measures and the lid of the nest.

MACHINES

Some early machines in which wood originally played a large part, such as the lathe, are discussed briefly in Section XXIV, *Tools of Specialist Woodworkers*, and in Section XXV, *Trade and Craft Devices*.

A remarkable working model of an engine, made almost entirely of wood, is shown, Plate 305. Measuring $12\frac{1}{2}$ in. high, it demonstrates the improvements in steam and other steering gear in ships, effected by Bremme's engine patents of 1879 and 1886. The frame and bed are of mahogany and pine, and the working parts, down to the tiny threaded nuts, are of boxwood. One would have thought it much easier to have made such a perfect model of a machine in metal.

OPTICS

Although with optics of all kinds, the lens is the most important feature, in some, wood plays, or formerly played, an important secondary part as the mounting. Some of these devices are described and illustrated here.

Magic Lanterns and Slides

The principle of the magic lantern was basically thought up by Roger Bacon in the 13th century. The projection lantern was first described by Athanasius Kircher, a German mathematician, in 1646, but he never claimed to be the inventor. The first use of condenser and projection lenses was by Robert Hooke, in 1668. Thereafter, its use was mostly scientific, until about 1820, when rather crudely hand-coloured glass slides in mahogany frames were produced commercially, and the magic lantern became a popular form of entertainment. Some slides, from the 1820s onwards, have moving parts operated by wheels, cranked handles, or sliding parts and were forerunners of the cinematograph. Typical subjects were an irate farmer soundly beating a boy stealing apples from a tree; a coloured fountain which, by the turn of a handle, played coloured jets; Punch and Judy; a dentist removing a tooth; a ship which pitched and rolled in a rough sea—and so on. Names stamped on the frames of the slides are those of the opticians selling them.

A magic lantern, dating from the 1825–35 period, in the Pinto Collection, Plate 304, comprises a mahogany box, 10 in. by 9 in. by 9 in. high, on a 17 in. long base. This well preserved specimen was obviously made very large in order to avoid the fire risk. It has doors on both sides, an iron lining, domed top and chimney. Later models were smaller, all iron, and painted. With lighting by candle or oil, they became overheated, smoky and very smelly.

Micrographs

The micrograph, Plate 292, M, in shagreen

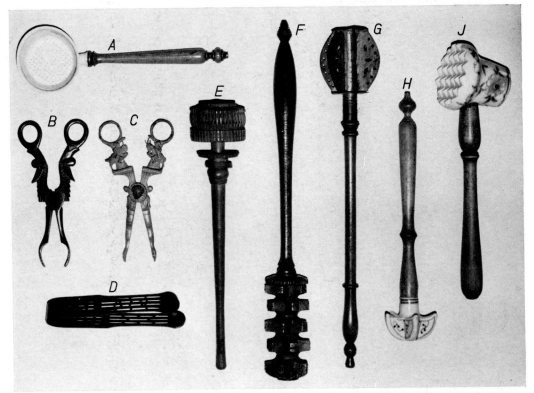

312 A, H and J, tea strainer, chocolate mill and steak beater with Dresden china terminals; B, C and D, sugar tongs, more ornamental than practical; E, F and G, chocolate mills. (*Section XX*)

313 A, Scottish teapot stand; B, C and D, tea caddies; E, coffee bean jar; F, tea urn cleaning powder box; G, *zarfs*; H, coffee pot; J, silver mounted mate tea gourd and bombilla; K and N, Victorian novelty tea caddies; L, pearwood tea cup and saucer; M, moustache cup. (*Section XX*)

314 Danish coffee stool, 18th century. *Photograph by courtesy of Dansk Folkemuseum, Copenhagen. (Section XX)*

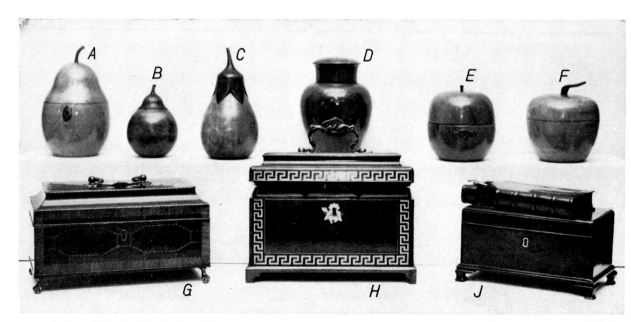

315 *A, E* and *F*, English 'fruit' caddies; *B* and *C*, Oriental 'fruit' caddies; *D*, ginger jar type caddy; *G* and *H*, inlaid mahogany caddies, *circa* 1765–70; *J*, a rare caddy, *circa* 1740–50, with caddy spoon drawer in the form of a book. (*Section XX*)

316 A superb quality, Chippendale, mahogany caddy, *circa* 1755. (*Section XX*)

317 A magnificent late 18th-century caddy. For details, see text. *Photograph by courtesy of the Tea Centre.* (*Section XX*)

318 An outstanding Scottish pen-and-ink decorated tea chest, with its three caddies, *circa* 1810; a small Sheraton mahogany caddy, and two caddies decorated with paper filigree, *circa* 1770–80. (*Section XX*)

319 LEFT AND CENTRE: Tunbridge mosaic caddies. RIGHT: an unusual geometric marquetry example, which may have been made at Tunbridge. IN FRONT: Tunbridge stickware caddy ladle. (*Section XX*)

320   Three fine quality caddies, *circa* 1780–90. *Photograph by courtesy of the Victoria and Albert Museum.* (*Section XX*)

321   The teapot, cup and saucer, *circa* 1760–5, made from Shakespeare's mulberry tree at New Place, Stratford-on-Avon. (*Section XX*) For details of the Shakespeare tobacco stopper, see *Section XXII, Tobacco Accessories: Tobacco Stoppers.*

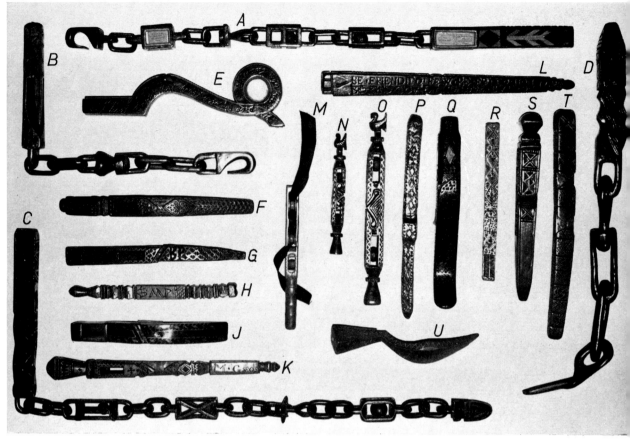

322 Knitting sheaths from the North of England and North Wales—*A*, *B*, *C* and *D* have integral carved chains and clew holders. *D*, a very early Welsh specimen is dated 1680; *L*, North of England, is dated 1688; *T*, is dated 1712. (*Section XXI*)

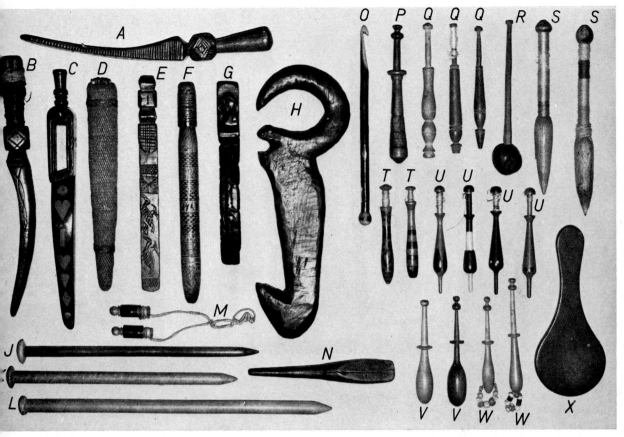

323 *A* to *G*, more English knitting sheaths—*E*, is the earliest dated specimen recorded; it may be 1615 or 1516; *H*, is a sailor's knitting stretcher; *J*, *K* and *L*, knitting needles; *M*, knitting needle guards; *N*, a knitter's broach; *O*, cherrywood crochet hook; *T*, Oxfordshire lace bobbins; *P*, *Q*, *R*, *S*, *U*, *V* and *W*, continental bobbins; *X*, a lacemaker's bat. (*Section XXI*)

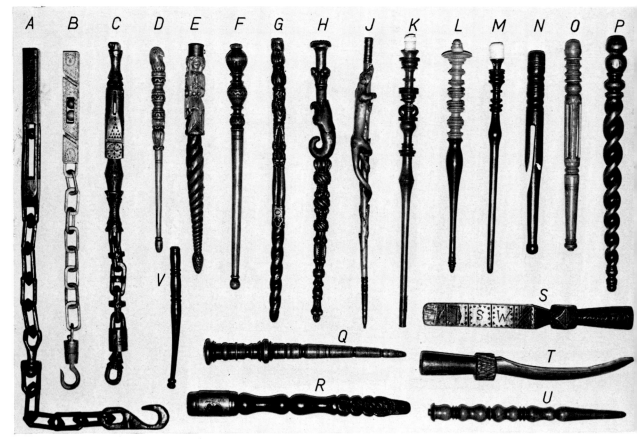

324 The knitting sheaths *A* to *C*, and *N* to *V*, are from the British Isles; *D* and *F*, are probably French; *E* and *G*, Dutch or Flemish; *H* and *J*, are Italian; *K*, *L* and *M*, Mallorcan (Spanish). (*Section XXI*)

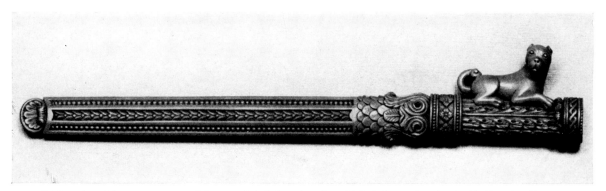

325 A French, 18th-century, carved boxwood knitting sheath, which is in a class by itself. For details, see text. (*Section XXI*)

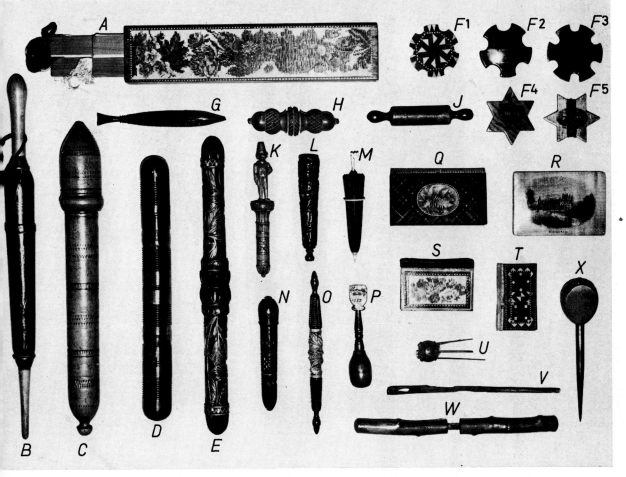

326 *A*, Tunbridge mosaic silk skein holder; *B, C, D* and *E*, knitting needle cases; *F*1 to *F*5, silk winders; *G* to *O*, needle cases; *P*, buttonhole cutter, for story—see text; *Q* to *T*, needle books; *U*, emery needle cushion; *V*, an old wooden needle; *W* and *X*, stilettos. (*Section XXI*)

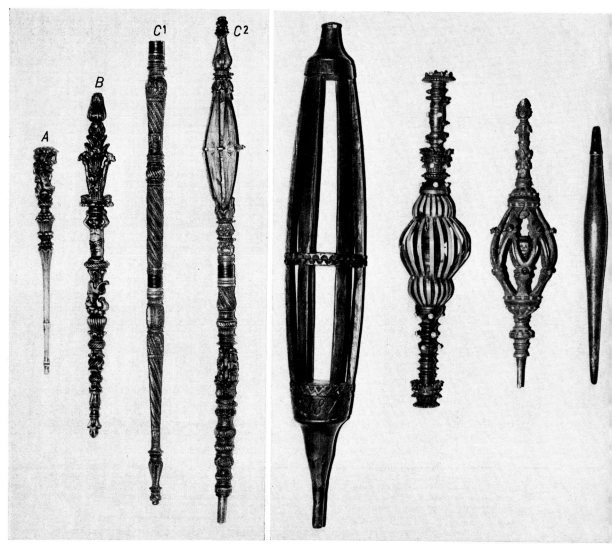

327 *A* and *B*, are finely carved, boxwood knitting sheaths, Italian, probably 17th century; *C*1 and *C*2 are two halves of a finely carved and turned boxwood distaff, probably Flemish work, 17th century. (*Section XXI*)

328 Three distaffs and a spindle. The distaff left, English, dated 1812; the two in the centre, Scandinavian, 18th century; the spindle is French. (*Section XXI*)

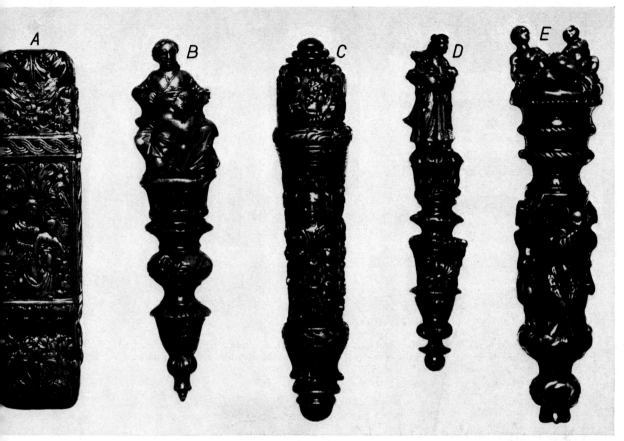

329 A selection of boxwood *etuis* in the fine art class. For details, see text. (*Section XXI*)

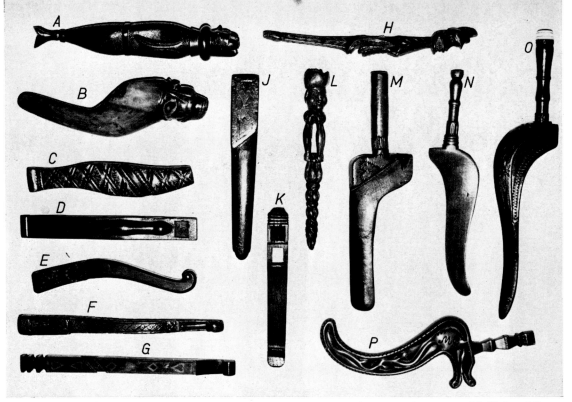

330 Further selection of North of England knitting sheaths—*A, B, C* and *D*, are 19th century; *M, N, O* and *P*, are all variants of the 'goose wing' sheaths of the North-West Yorkshire and Westmorland dales. (*Section XXI*)

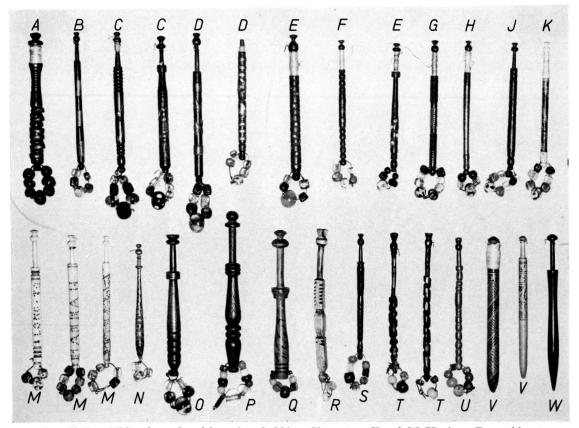

331 *A* to *T*, East Midland wood and bone lace bobbins; *U*, pewter; *V* and *W*, Honiton, Devonshire, types. (*Section XXI*)

332 The aristocrats of lace bobbins, carved and pierced individually. All except *K* and *P*, are from the East Midlands. For further details, see text. (*Section XXI*)

333 Lacemaker's pillow and stand, foot stool, and an unusually sophisticated candle and flash stool. (*Section XXI*)

334 Lace bobbin winders—*A* and *C*, English; the Welsh specimen, *B*, with wooden gear wheels instead of belt drive, is unusual. (*Section XXI*)

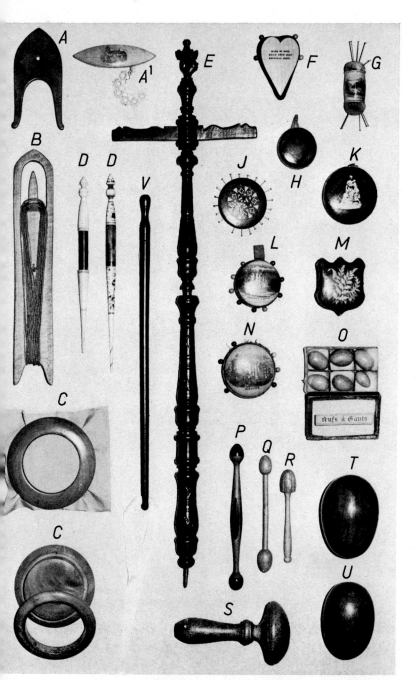

335 *A*, lucet; *A1*, tatting shuttle; *B*, single end netting needle; *C*, fabric stretching frames; *D*, probably some kind of netting implements; *E*, silk thrower—for story, see text; *F*, and *H* to *N*, disc-type pin-cushions; *G*, a double ended pin-cushion; *O*, *oeuf à gants*; *P*, *Q* and *R*, also glove darning eggs; *S*, mushroom, and *T* and *U*, egg darners; *V*, ribbon threader. (*Section XXI*)

336 Three superb, carved boxwood bobbins, believed to have been used for gold and silver lace, in the early 16th century. They may be French, Italian or Spanish. (*Section XXI*)

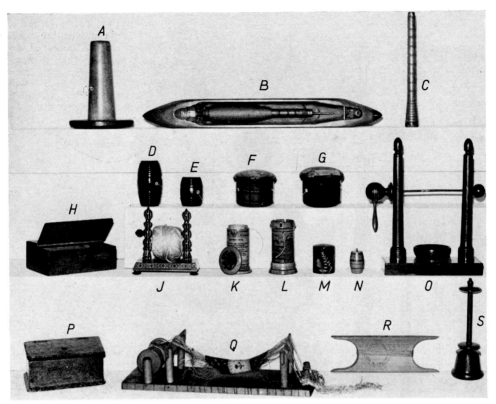

337 *A*, knitting machine cone for yarn; *B*, shuttle and pirn, and *C*, pirn; *D*, *E* and *N*, cotton barrels; *F* and *G*, triple reel or spool boxes; *K*, *L* and *M*, single cotton spool containers; *H* and *P*, lace bobbin boxes; *J*, Tunbridge, silk or thread ball holder; *O*, rare cocoon winder and *S*, silk reeling stand; *Q*, Apache bead loom; *R*, silk winder. (*Section XXI*)

338 *A* and *B*, knitting wool globes; *C*, Icelandic, and *D*, Norwegian knitting needle boxes; *E*, *F* and *K*, peg knitting devices; *G*, 19th-century wool winder; *J*, wool teasing fork; *L*, baby's shoe last; *H*, *M* and *N*, knitting wool bowls. (*Section XXI*)

case, consists of an adjustable lignum vitae enclosed eyepiece and a selection of microscopic slides. It may be roughly dated by one of these slides, which shows a Bank of England note for £1,000, dated April 28, 1859.

Microscopes

The compound microscope, for producing an enlarged image of a small object, was invented at the beginning of the 17th century, and until about 1740, all microscopes had tubes of thin wood or cardboard, usually covered with leather or shagreen. In 1742, John Cuff made the first instrument all of brass, but cheaper models followed the old construction until recent times. One of the great names associated with microscopes is Culpeper. A fine Culpeper compound microscope, *circa* 1730–40, is shown, Plate 300, *G*, with its boxwood encased specimen slides, *F*, and original oak case with drawer, *H*, alongside. The microscope, which is mainly of lignum vitae, with shagreen-covered tube and turned brass pillars, is complete with all its accessories, including eyepieces, objectives, specimen slides and glass fishplate. The boxwood microscope, Plate 300, *E*, was made at Nürnberg about 1780, by the toy turners. They were intended more for recreational purposes than scientific study.

Optiques—see *Zograscopes*

Prism Viewers

The prism viewers, Plate 292, *G*, each consist of a single prismatically ground lens, held in a turned sycamore eyepiece. By turning the eyepiece in front of the eye, the objective takes up interesting kaleidoscopic patterns. They seem to have been intended entirely for amusement. Some are of natural polished wood, some enamelled in various colours and others decorated with black and red concentric lines, in the manner of Tunbridge ware of the Regency period.

Scioptric Balls

The scioptric ball, Plate 296, *H*, is English, 18th-century; these devices are now rare. The ball is of lignum vitae, with plane glass lenses at opposite sides; it is made to pivot in any direction, being held as tightly as desired, by moulded rims, threaded on to each side of a cut-out mahogany panel. The panel was screwed on to a similarly pierced wooden window shutter and it served to concentrate solar rays on objects under a microscope, in the same manner that a water lens could be used at night (for water lenses, see Section VI, *Fire and Lighting: Candle Stands, Lacemakers'*). One of the scioptric balls in the Science Museum, London, has an adjustable plane mirror attached, as an added refinement.

Slides—see *Magic Lanterns*

Stereoscopes

The stereoscope, a binocular instrument constructed to view photographs as stereoscopic pictures, was invented by Sir Charles Wheatstone, in 1838. It soon attained great popularity all over Europe and the U.S.A., and was much diversified in form, and improved by other inventors. It was the forerunner of the modern illuminated stereolist. The mahogany cabinet stereoscope, Plate 306, is the *Achromatic*, by R. and J. Beck, of 34 Cornhill, London, and was made about 1850. The slides which go with it, cover the period 1849–62; some of them are tinted photographs. This stereoscope has angle and sight adjustments; when not in use, it fits in the bottom drawer. The cabinet is enclosed by a panelled flap, removed for photography. The burr walnut stereoscope, Plate 296, *F*, probably by Duboscq, also dates from about 1850. *G* is an inexpensive model, patented in 1901, produced both in America and England,

and based on a design by Oliver Wendell Holmes.

Telescopes

Seventeenth-century telescopes usually had cardboard tubes, covered in vellum, leather or shagreen, and with lens mounts of lignum vitae. Some mid and late 18th-century examples have mahogany tubes with brass mounts, but by this time it was more usual for the whole instrument to be of brass.

Zograscopes

Devices similar to Plate 296, *A*, which is made of mahogany, as are the majority, are usually described and sold as Georgian shaving mirrors; this, they are not; they are zograscopes, one of the more extraordinary conceits of fashionable 18th-century society, which had a second lease of life extended to the late 19th century. The zograscope, which was probably invented about 1750, was also known, during its long life, as an optical machine or an optical diagonal machine in England, and in France as an *optique*. The device was intended for viewing prints, etc., in a magnified form; at first, it was mainly used by short-sighted people who, according to the conventions of 18th-century society, would not be seen wearing spectacles in public. As copperplate engravings, on account of cost, were generally made small, the zograscope was a great boon to those who, by reason of age or other forms of nearsightedness, were otherwise debarred from enjoying them. One can only assume that in their latter days, zograscopes had become a mere amusing toy, for long after the fashionable convention had died, they were still being used, being shown by Chadburn Brothers of Sheffield and Liverpool, in the 1851 Exhibition, and appearing in trade catalogues as late as 1885.

Zograscopes have survived in such considerable quantities, that it is obvious that they must have enjoyed surprising popularity. Judging by those which I have examined, they had two phases—the first from about 1750 to 1810, when they were fashionable, and the second from about 1850 to 1890, when they were probably revived for amusement. I have seen none which, on stylistic grounds, appear to have been made between about 1810 and 1850. The example illustrated, probably dates from around 1800. It stands 27 in. high when closed, rising, by means of the telescopic stem and set-screw, a further 8 in.; it has a suspended magnifying glass in front of the pivotally adjustable mirror. When stood on a table, with the mirror correctly adjusted and the print placed on the table under the mirror, the viewer standing in front of the magnifying glass, sees the print magnified in the mirror. Moreover, there is a considerable stereoscopic effect and the ingenious and effective device undoubtedly brings out both the perspective and the detail. Special hand-coloured engravings, mostly French, were made with the titles running from right to left, for viewing through the mirrors of zograscopes. These pictures, which now often puzzle collectors, are considerably rarer than the actual zograscopes.

Makers' names seldom appear on zograscopes, but 18th-century makers who are recorded, include George Adams of Fleet Street—two generations with the same names, and Edward Nairne, the optical and mathematical instrument maker opposite the Royal Exchange, Cornhill, from 1756 to 1775; soon after 1775, Nairne took his apprentice, Blunt, into partnership and traded as Nairne and Blunt. The authority on zograscopes is Mr. J. A. Chaldecott, M.Sc., of the Science Museum, to whose research I am indebted for much of the historic background to zograscopes.

TALLIES AND TALLY BOARDS

Tallies

At first sight, there does not appear to be much connection between wooden tallies and parliament; but the 'teller' was originally the 'tallier' and tally sticks played so large a part in parliamentary recording and Exchequer accounting, that the burning of some of their accumulation in the furnaces of the Houses of Parliament overheated the flues and caused the fire which destroyed the buildings in 1834.

Until 1783, tallies were officially used in England in the Court of the Exchequer, for making receipts of money paid by and to officials, but their use lingered on in official transactions until 1824. In less literate ages, they were the universal method for recording transactions of all kinds in most European countries. They were used to record cash owed, votes cast, prayers read, hay cut, corn reaped, fish caught, goods carried, sheep sheared, work done, etc. Their use now has practically died out, although they serve still, in a small way, for hop picking and fishing catch records. Their universality in 17th-century transactions in England is exemplified by nearly 100 allusions to their use, in Pepys' Diary. On March 20th, 1665, on his appointment as Navy Treasurer, he recorded '... I am already confirmed their Treasurer, and put into a condition of striking of Tallys...'. On November 26, 1668, he was very worried at losing a tally for £1,000 and greatly relieved when it was found by a porter in Holborn, two days later.

Tallies are not decorative, but they are full of interest. The method of use was simple and proof against fraud. Notches to represent figures were cut transversely on a roughly squared stick, which was made from well seasoned hazel or other suitable local wood. The notches varied either in breadth, length, spacing or angle of cut, to denote differences between pounds, shillings and pence, or between pounds, hundredweights and tons, etc. When the particular transaction was completed, the stick was cleft down the middle with a knife and mallet, through all the notches. Thus each half tallied and one half was retained by each

of the parties until settlement was effected. Where the records involved payments, it was customary to use specially prepared tally sticks, in order to avoid any argument as to which party was the lender, and the names of the lender and borrower and the date and other details of the transaction were usually recorded in ink on the stick, which thus became a wooden account of a single transaction. Prior to the 19th century, each stick was prepared specifically for a transaction, but from about 1800 onwards, there appears to have been a commercial manufacture of tallies. These commercially prepared sticks, ready for use, were sawn through for about five-sixths of their length, the long cut nearly but not quite meeting the horizontal cut. After they had been used and the required notches representing the transaction cut transversely at intervals right across the long saw cut, and the names of the contracting parties recorded on the stick, the two 'halves' were broken apart; the long 'half', known as the 'stock' or 'tally', was retained by the lender and the short 'half', known as the 'counter-stock' or 'counter-tally', belonged to the borrower. For some time after the custom of using wooden tallies was discontinued, cheques, tickets and other documents were torn by an irregular line of separation and the 'tallying' of the torn edges was accepted as validity of claim.

The tally stick shown, Plate 297, K, is dated December 3, 1795 and records receipt from Captain Ball of the 39th Regiment for £123 off reckonings paid by Cox Greenwood, the agent for the regimental paymaster at Fort Matilda, West Indies. The tally stick, Plate 298, H, represents a transaction for more than £5,000, but there seems to have been no limit to the amount which could be recorded by tally; Pepys mentions one for more than £40,000.

Tally Boards

Tally boards differed from tally sticks not

only in their dimensions, but also in their purpose. Whereas tally sticks were permanent and unalterable records, the boards were for the temporary recording of lists, or orders, etc., for a particular trade such as laundering. Two early English laundry tallies are illustrated, Plates 309 and 310; both are believed to date from between 1650 and 1670. Both, with some variations in the spelling, record the numbers to be washed of

Handkercher. Cappes. Ruffes. Bandes. Cuffes. Bootehose. Toppes. Napkins. Shirtes. Halfshirtes.

Additionally, plate 309 includes Sheetes and Sockes. This is an oak panel, 8¾ in. by 8 in., covered in brown leather, with holes for pegs, to show the numbers of each garment to be washed. Plate 310, framed in oak, has an engraved brass record plate, on which are mounted 10 pivoted discs, each of which can be turned to expose, through an aperture in the disc, the particular number required. Both these are very rare specimens.*

Scandinavian washing tally boards are often highly decorative and usually measure between 12 in. and 15 in. in length and between 4 in. and 5 in. in width. They are sometimes confused with the longer mangling boards (for *Mangling Boards*, see Section VIII, *Laundry and Cleaning Devices*). They have plain backs, on which the list was written in chalk, and the face is usually ornamented with chip carving. A good specimen, chip carved with roundels, initials I.H.W. and date 1772, is pictured, Plate 307.

The miner's tally board, Plate 308, which is about 18 in. long, is probably a unique survival. It is an exciting piece of treen, carved with picks, mattocks and other mining tools, with holes for inserting pegs; thus, the miner below, using picture language,

* *Note:* Since writing the above, another 17th-century, English tally board has come to light. It is similar to Plate 310, except that it has 15 brass discs, arranged in three rows of five. The additional headings include Sheetes, Pillowberes (pillow cases), Tableclothes, Towells.

could make his requirements known to the man on the surface, when the board was hauled up, even if both parties were completely illiterate. It is believed to date from the 17th or 18th century and was recovered from the sump of Dark Lane Pit, one of the old 'coaleries', or rural coal mines at Murfield, Yorkshire.

WEIGHING APPLIANCES

The origin of measuring by weighing and the connections between weighing and justice are lost in antiquity. At least 11 references to weighing in the balance occur in the bible. Survivals and carved representations show that the Greeks, Romans, Egyptians and Chinese, before the Christian era, used metal scales. Complete fitted boxes of weights and scales of an almost exactly similar pattern to some used in the British Isles 200 years ago, were found in Egypt by Professor Flinders Petrie; they are of Roman workmanship and some 1,600 years old. Doubtless, the ancients also had wooden scales and balances and weighing machines like those, which up to the 19th century, were commonly used all over Europe and in many other parts of the world for weighing butter. (For *Butter Scales*, see Section V, *Farm: Dairy*.) A favourite subject for carvings and sculptures during the Middle Ages, was the Archangel Michael weighing souls on a balance.

Strictly speaking, the balance has two similar pans or saucers suspended from the ends of a centrally pivoted beam, and objects or commodities could be weighed against each other, once the weight of one object was established. Scales, similarly constructed, have two different pans—one designed specifically for weights and the other for general-purpose weighing. Generally, scales have the centre pivot supported on a standard, but balances are often made for suspension. A weighing machine is an apparatus, usually a combination of levers with weights, or a spring balance, for weighing heavy bodies. What is, perhaps, the finest collection of weighing appliances in existence, is maintained by W. & T. Avery Ltd., at their Soho Works, Birmingham, which can be viewed by appointment.

Balances, Money and Precious Stones

Specialized and ingeniously constructed scales for money and precious stones were made from mediaeval times. An outstandingly fine set is the diamond merchant's balance in the carved walnut case, Plate 311. It is probably Italian, in the fine art class, and dates from *circa* 1650. The beam, the needle and the fulcrum are steel, the standard and its base, brass, and the scale pans silver. As shown, the balance is constructed for erecting on a demountable standard in its case, and the height of the scale pans from the base is adjusted by moving forward the solid brass lion in the foreground, which pulls on a silk cord, passing over four brass pulley wheels, set in the standard. The walnut case, which has a hand-coloured engraved pastoral scene in the lid, is carved in well contrived simulation of tooled leather, fashionable at that time, when some of the boxes were shaped and carved to imitate two volumes; the exterior is illustrated, Plate 294, *G*. It measures 10 in. by 6 in. The concave slide in the front edge is designed to hold a pair of forceps.

As at the present time, gold coins were worth more than their face value in the second half of the 17th and during the 18th century, so their rate of exchange with silver coins was decided by weight. A new and ingenious folding type of coin balance, which obviated loose weights and was small enough to fit in the pocket, came into use early in the 18th century. Made of brass, except for the pins, which were of steel, this type of balance was specifically designed for a limited range of coins and was made by numerous makers. It was almost invariably fixed into a case hollowed out of a block of solid Spanish mahogany, approxi-

mately 5½ in. long by ⅞ in. by ⅝ in. Three examples, two open and one closed, are shown, Plate 302, *B*, *C* and *G*. The balances are so devised that they open automatically with the case and fold flat as the case is closed. On the opposite end of the beam to the pan, in the balance, *B*, shown open, is a pivoted weight, or 'turn' as it is described, which swings outwards to weigh a guinea and inwards to weigh a half guinea; others were designed to weigh a sovereign or half sovereign. Perfection of detail is carried to the stage that the cross pin, on to which the end of the beam drops, is covered with finely woven silk. On the other half of the beam is a travelling slide, which registers under- or over-weight coins.

The original instruction labels are usually in the boxes and bear the names of the makers. *B* and *G* are by the well-known makers H. Bell & Co. of Prescot, Lancashire, and *C* by the equally well-known Stephen Houghton & Son of Ormskirk, operating about 1770. *G*, dating from *circa* 1770, is unusual because, unlike the normal of this type, it has two pans and five weights, and the directions state that it weighs guineas and half guineas, sovereigns and half sovereigns, and seven-shilling pieces.

A simple, Turkish, pocket folding coin balance of boxwood, probably 18th-century, is shown, Plate 302, *E*. *H* is an Italian, 17th-century coin balance in walnut case; its exterior, punch decorated in simulation of leather, is illustrated, Plate 292, *L*. Very similar specimens of the same period are also found in Holland. The coin balance in mahogany case, Plate 302, *J*, measuring 7¾ in. by 3¾ in. by 1¼ in., which dates from about 1800, has an interesting label in the lid, stating that it is by Mary de Grave, widow and successor to Chas. de Grave, of 59 St. Martin Le Grand, London, and additionally

'Scales & Weights adjusted by the year. Scale maker to George III, also exporter to

East and West Indies, Turkey, Spain, Portugal, etc. Supplier of Weights & Measures for Corporations. Steelyards of all sorts.'

Bismars—see *Steelyards*

Coin Balances—see *Balances*

Diamond Merchants' Scales—see *Balances*

Scales—see introduction to *Weighing Appliances*

Steelyards and Bismars

The steelyard, also known as the Roman balance, which gives some idea of its antiquity, consists basically of a lever with unequal arms, which moves on a fulcrum. The article to be weighed is suspended by hooks and chains or cords from the shorter arm, and a counterpoise is slid along the longer arm, until equilibrium is reached. This longer arm or beam is notched at intervals, to show the weight at the point of suspension. Steelyards vary in size from pocket types to arms 20 ft. or so long, cantilevered out from buildings and powerful enough to lift and weigh a cart loaded with wool, hides, bark, or other produce. There are, or were until recently, cart weighing steelyards in the eastern counties at Woodbridge, Suffolk, Soham, near Ely,

Cambridgeshire, and King's Lynn, Norfolk. The use of these ancient weighing devices mostly died out in the British Isles during the last century, but in 1957, Mrs. Pinto photographed an itinerant greengrocer using one most dexterously, in the Isle of Ischia. A good specimen of a small, English steelyard, probably 16th- or 17th-century, is illustrated, Plate 302, *F*; the beam and pan are wood, the counterpoise brass.

A type of steelyard, in which the point of balance is moved, is called a bismar or pundlar. It was sometimes made of wood and was used in England until the 15th century, for weighing wool and silk. It lent itself to cheating to such an extent, that in 1450 the Archbishop of Canterbury decreed excommunication of anyone possessing it. The device continued in use in the Orkney and Shetland Islands until a century ago. The geographical range of usage of the bismar extended through Scandinavia and across Russia to the Far East. A Chinese bismar, in traditional 'banjo' hollowed out palmwood case, is illustrated, Plate 302, *D*; it is probably 19th-century.

Weighing Machines, Personal

A fine, English, 18th-century, personal weighing machine in mahogany, with boxwood height-measuring stick attachment, is illustrated, Plate 291. The scales pan, weights, lion paw feet and other fittings are brass. The height is 4 ft. 0 in. with platform 18 in. by $14\frac{1}{2}$ in.

XX

Tea, Coffee and Chocolate-Drinking Accessories

As tea, coffee and chocolate were all introduced into England during the Commonwealth, their background is best studied together. The Restoration really ushered in the first soft drink age, because until recently fashion, which included etiquette and manners, spread downwards in society and not until well into the reign of Charles II, did the majority in this country eschew their traditional ale or mead at breakfast, in favour of hot non-alcoholic beverages.

Whilst tea drinking commenced almost essentially as a domestic and social custom, coffee was, for a hundred years or more, a drink mainly enjoyed in the coffee houses, which sprang up in every city in the second half of the 17th and early 18th centuries. Chocolate, very much a drink of high fashion, was served both in the home and in coffee houses, and it was not long before some coffee houses also served tea as a third alternative—but they were essentially coffee houses, not chocolate or tea houses; chocolate houses were opened before the end of the 17th century, but tea houses did not assume an identity of their own until well into the 18th century.

It is difficult now to realize the importance which coffee houses attained from the reign of Charles II onwards, for at least a hundred years. They were, in all senses, sober meeting places and clubs where, at low cost, men could meet in warmth and some degree of comfort, and discuss trade, politics, wars and other news, and air their views. Some of their free speech was frightening to the government and in 1675 it issued a proclamation supressing coffee houses; but the authorities quickly found that they had gone too far and with the lesson of Charles I still close to their memory, they soon revoked the order, concluding that the coffee house safety valve was better than underground agitation, in an age which had no daily newspapers to correct rumours.

Coffee came to Oxford before London. John Evelyn relates:

> 'There came in my tyme to the Coll: (1637–40, Balliol College, Oxford) one Nathaniel Conopios out of Greece. . . . He was the first I ever saw drink coffee, wᶜʰ custom came not into England till 30 years after.'

The last part of the statement is incorrect: according to Anthony à Wood, the 17th-century, Oxford born antiquary, 'This year (1650) Jacob, a Jew, opened a coffey-house at the Angel in the parish of St. Peter, in the East Oxon.' In 1655, Arthur Tillyard, apothecary, was selling coffee at The High, Oxford.

In 1652, the first London coffee house opened at St. Michael's Abbey, Cornhill. A Greek, named according to different authorities, Pascual Rossi, Pasque Rosée and Rosa Pasquie, was the proprietor, partner or manager. Most sources describe Pascual as servant to Daniel Edwards, an English merchant trading in Smyrna, who brought him to London to brew coffee for him and his friends. The popularity of the drink was such that Edwards astutely opened a coffee house under Pascual's name. Another source gives the 'Turkey' merchant's name as Hodges, who installed his ex-coachman Bowman and his ex-Levantine servant Pascual as partners in the Cornhill venture. Whichever story is true, the coffee house was a great success and was quickly emulated. Meanwhile, for reasons now unknown, Pascual fled the country. I suggest that he may have been the Armenian named Pascal, who opened a coffee booth in Paris, at St. Germain, in 1672.

The second coffee house to open in London in 1656, was the Rainbow, on the South side of Fleet Street, and the third was Garroway's, established in 1657, in Sweeting's Rents, by the Royal Exchange. Garroway claimed to be the first coffee man to sell tea, both by weight and also for consumption on the premises. His premises destroyed by the Great Fire of 1666, Garroway reopened on the corner of Change Alley, opposite to Jonathan (Miles). Jonathan's and Garraway's were two popular city meeting places; both were particularly the haunts of stock-jobbers, just as Lloyd's, originally a coffee house in Tower Street, was the resort of seafarers, before developing into worldwide marine insurance. Other well known city coffee houses with speciality clientele, were Tom's, the Rainbow, and the Jerusalem. The last three, together with Garroway's and Jonathan's, were swept away in a fire which destroyed between 90 and 100 houses in 1748, but most of them were rebuilt. The coffee houses around Covent Garden,

particularly Button's and Will's, attracted literary men, actors and the fashionable world in general in the 17th and 18th centuries, but the St. James's Coffee House, in St. James's Street, became the great rendezvous of the Whig party.

That London coffee houses were numerous and well patronized as general meeting places and clubs by January 1660 is well established by Pepys' *Diary*, which began then. From the commencement, he makes frequent references to meeting friends at coffee houses and coffee clubs. The latter were apparently distinguished by having subscriptions and elected committees, otherwise there seems to have been little difference in their functions, which might include, as at Garraway's, 'auction by candle' (see Section VI, *Fire and Lighting*). Judging by the dates when grocers began using 'The Coffee Mill' as a trade sign, it appears likely that coffee did not become really popular in the home until after the mid-18th century.

Chocolate was introduced to England about 1652. In the *Publick Advertiser* of June 16, 1657, there was an announcement that

'In Bishopsgate Street in Queen's Head Alley, at a Frenchman's house, is an excellent West India drink called *chocolate*, to be sold, where you may have it ready at any time, and also unmade at reasonable rates.'

Chocolate drinking, therefore, commenced among people of fashion simultaneously as a home and as a chocolate or coffee house drink. On February 26, 1664, Pepys recorded drinking chocolate at home, and on November 24, 1664, he went '. . . to a Coffee-house, to drink jocolatte, very good . . .'

The Chinese say that tea drinking goes back to 2737 B.C., when Emperor Shen-Nung discovered its qualities. Whether fact or fable, the Chinese tea industry was flourishing by the 8th century A.D. and the tea drinking ritual soon spread throughout the Far East. Tea first appears in European literature about 1560; the commodity itself first reached Holland 50 years later. Full-scale invasion of Britain by the new beverage did not occur for nearly another half century.

In each country where it was introduced, tea, like tobacco, caused controversy. Britain was divided into 'pro' and 'anti' tea camps. In verbal duels, Dr. Johnson led the 'pros' and Jonas Hanway the 'antis'. By 1659 or 1660, the year in which Pepys recorded trying his first cup, Garraway advertised tea as a specific for headaches, giddiness, heaviness, stone, gravel, bleary eyes, over-eating and many other complaints. Leading designers and craftsmen quickly turned their attention to the new tea equipage required in wood, silver, porcelain, glass, pottery, etc.; this included teapots, kettles, urns, caddies, cream jugs, sugar basins, tongs, spoons, tea trays, kettle stands, cups and saucers. Cabinet-makers contributed elegant tea tables, kettle and urn stands and tea boards or trays. They also supplied the majority of tea caddies. The names of Chippendale, Hepplewhite, Sheraton and Adam are not only associated with graceful tea tables and urn stands, but also with some of the finest tea caddies.

The word 'caddy', derived from the Malay *kati*, signifying $1\frac{1}{5}$ lb. in weight, became corrupted, via katty, to caddy, a box containing that weight of tea. Our ancestors called the oblong chest which contained the tea caddies or tea boxes, a tea chest; now we interchange the word caddy for either. It is sometimes said that lead-lined caddies can always be distinguished from similarly lined tobacco jars by the locks on the former and that, owing to the costliness of early imported tea, early caddies are the smallest. Neither statement is entirely correct. Certain Sheraton period caddies are as small or smaller than those of Queen Anne's reign. Although the costly tea was certainly kept locked and served out by the lady of the house, early caddies had no locks, but were made in sets of two or three, for different varieties of tea, and were kept in a tea chest provided with a lock. Not until about 1780 did the single box with lock—really a combination of caddy and tea chest—become fashionable; it never superseded the two- or three-compartment chest which, in the late 18th and throughout the 19th century, often contained two caddies for different varieties or grades of tea for mixing, and a centrally placed glass bowl, in which mixing could take place, or sugar be kept.

CHOCOLATE ACCESSORIES

Late 17th- and 18th-century silver chocolate pots resemble coffee pots of their periods, except for one feature: they usually, but not invariably, have the spout affixed to the body, at right angles to the lid, but so do some of the early coffee pots. They differ from coffee pots, however, by always having a hole in the centre of the lid, which occasionally is covered by a swivelling finial, but more often by a smaller domed lid, rising from the main one. On most pots, both the main lid and the small upper one are hinged, but occasionally the upper has a lip fitting into the lower one, and the main lid fits in like manner to the body, both being fitted with silver safety chains, anchoring them to the body. The purpose of the aperture in the main lid was to allow the handle of the chocolate mill or stirrer to project through, so that when the upper lid was raised or removed, the mill could be rotated briskly, to keep the chocolate in suspension.

There are numerous 17th- and 18th-century references to chocolate mills. In *The Experienced English Housekeeper* (1769), Elizabeth Raffald, formerly housekeeper to Lady Elizabeth Warburton, to whom she dedicated her book, gives a recipe for making chocolate—

'Scrape four ounces of Chocolate and pour a Quart of boiling Water upon it, mill it well with a Chocolate Mill, and sweeten to your Taste, give it a boil and let it stand all Night, then mill it again very well, boil it two Minutes, then mill it till it will leave a Froth upon the Top of your Cups.'

Mrs. Raffald also advocates the use of a chocolate mill when making syllabubs—

'When you make Whips, or Syllabubs, raise your Froth with a Chocolate Mill and lay it upon a sieve to dry . . .'

A selection of chocolate mills is illustrated in Plate 312. It will be noticed that the 18th-century mill, *H*, with sycamore handle and Dresden china knop or head, is *en suite* with the tea strainer, *A*, and steak beater, *J*. The two mills from Ashburnham, Sussex, *F* and *G*, the latter 13½ in. long with metal fins and the former 14¼ in. long with a wooden cogged head, were probably used for stirring the chocolate in the pot over the fire. The mill, *H*, with china head, 10 in. long, and the one, *E*, with wooden head, fretted, reeded and fitted with loose rings, which measures 10¾ in., conforms to the normal length of mill used in a 17th- or 18th-century chocolate pot.

Certain turners, such as John Alexander, at The Elephant and Coffee Mill, Crooked Lane, London (1776–93) and Thorn at The Beehive and Patten in John Street, Oxford Market, London (1764), included chocolate and coffee mills amongst their turnery wares. The different uses of the word mill are confusing; a chocolate mill was a stirrer, the coffee mill was a grinder, and although the Georgians had some kind of chocolate breaker, they called it a chocolate machine.

COFFEE ACCESSORIES

The background to coffee will be found in the introduction to this section.

Coffee Bean Jars
Coffee bean jars of lignum vitae, harmonizing in outline with the bodies of 1760–70

coffee mills, have screw-on lids. In Plate 313, an example, *E*, is illustrated. They are not easy to find. Other types of dry store jars cannot be definitely associated with coffee beans.

Coffee Cups
Turkish *zarfs* or coffee cups of coquilla nutshell, Plate 313, *G*, are a traditional shape and may date from the 19th century or earlier.

Coffee Grinders—see Section XI, *Mortars, Grinders and Graters*

Coffee Mills—see Section XI, *Mortars, Grinders and Graters*

Coffee Pots
The small coffee pot, Plate 313, *H*, may have been intended for use, or merely as a pattern or try-out. Larger coffee pots of wood, turned out of the solid or coopered and willow bound and with inserted spouts, were formerly used in country districts in Scandinavia to a considerable extent. Whilst straight-sided vessels with spouts were the more usual for ale, and those with globular bodies were more frequently used for coffee, there is no clear definition—see Plate 48 for a Norwegian pot which may have been used for either purpose.

Coffee Stools
A practical and attractive device, found in North-west Europe, is the coffee stool for pivoting and pouring a large family coffee pot with minimum effort. The 18th-century, Danish *Kaffestol*, Plate 314, from the island of Amager, is designed so that the stool seat, pivoted in front, can be raised at the back by a winch and cord.

TEA ACCESSORIES

Caddies, Tea—see *Tea Caddies*

Maté Tea Gourds

Maté or Paraguay tea is a beverage prepared from the Brazilian holly (*ilex paraguayensis*), flavoured with lemon and burnt sugar. It is commonly sucked up through a tube, known as a bombilla, from a gourd fitted in a stand. A maté gourd in a silver stand, with a silver bombilla, is shown in Plate 313, *J*. (For further details of gourds, see Section XIII, *Nuts, Gourds, etc.*)

Moustache Cups

Presumably the only reasons for making a moustache cup in wood, Plate 313, *M*, would be either that the 19th-century inventor of the device made his preliminary try-out in wood, or else that this specimen was the *tour de force* of a woodworker.

Tea Caddies

One of the earliest shapes of English tea caddy was that based on the ginger jar with globose body, small neck and cap, and tight-fitting inner lid, which was imported by the East India Company from the Orient in the reign of Charles II. The English silversmiths copied it in silver, often elaborately repoussé or engraved, and they soon adopted the shape as elegant and appropriate for silver caddy jars; the form remained popular in the 18th century. These jars have no locks, because they were enclosed, in sets of two or three, in handsome outer tea chests, now known as tea caddies. The turners followed suit and made tea jars of similar form in pearwood, Plate 315, *D*, sometimes decorated with flowering sprays and birds in lacquer. Because none of the outer chests for the turners' jars seem to have survived, it is impossible to say whether they date from the 17th or 18th century.

In the first half of the 18th century, wooden tea chests were mostly of oblong shape and contained two lidded compartments, or two caddy boxes, metal canisters or jars, one being for green tea and one for black. Sometimes, at the back of the caddy is a long, narrow compartment for the caddy spoon; occasionally, below it, or under all the fittings, is a secret compartment, to which access is gained by sliding up one end of the chest.

A mahogany tea chest on bracket feet, dating from 1740–50, with a rare variant of the spoon compartment, is shown in Plate 315, *J*. The 'book', inlaid with amboyna and other choice veneers, laid negligently askew on the lid of the chest, is actually an integral part of it and contains a drawer for the caddy spoon. This delightful example of cabinet work is unusual also in being made of solid curl or crotch mahogany: curl mahogany is normally only used as a veneer, both on account of its value and because its nature causes it to warp badly, yet here it has stood perfectly for more than two centuries.

In using the term 'Chippendale' to describe Plate 316, no documents can be produced as proof, but a design closely resembling it is included in the *Director*, and the quality of both materials and craftsmanship are as superb as the rococo conception. The fine, crisp carving is all cut from the solid figured mahogany. The fittings are gilt bronze. It was formerly in the Fred Skull Collection.

Whilst, during their near 300 years vogue, caddies were made in a wide variety of materials, which included silver, tin, copper, pewter, glass and porcelain, it was during the second half of the 18th century that there was the greatest variety in shapes, sizes and finishes of the outer chests. It was also during this period that the term caddy came to embrace the outer as well as the inner containers; doubtless, this was because the single compartment caddy with lock came into vogue during this period and henceforth it shared popularity with the larger ones, which had separate containers or compartments within.

Caddies, using the term now in the broad sense, were made during the second half of the 18th century in such varied shapes as cubes, double cubes, rounds, ovals, octagons, and in the form of classical urns and caskets of fine quality. The majority are of wood, veneered and inlaid in the Sheraton style or with floral or Oriental designs, or painted in the style of Angelica Kauffman. They were also covered with silver, shagreen, filigree, ivory, tortoiseshell, etc.; the last two might be further embellished by etching and inlay. Some were also made by Clay of Wolverhampton, in papier mâché during this period, but the majority of papier mâché caddies are 19th-century products.

In Plate 315 are two three-compartment mahogany chests of the 1765 period, *G* and *H*. *G*, with panels of curl mahogany veneer, divided by boxwood and ebony stringings and cross banded with kingwood, is velvet lined and holds three circular caddies. *H*, with boxwood Grecian key inlay, has three removable caddies with sliding lids, which follow the concave outline of the main lid.

Plate 317 illustrates a magnificent late 18th-century, three-caddy tea chest in the collection of A. J. Wall, Esq. The caddy lids consist of oval medallions, carved and gilt; they are replicas of the motif which forms the centre of the chest lid. The same motifs are repeated in miniature on the side panels, which are enclosed in oval frames of carved pearl motifs, gilded, against a background of tortoiseshell-like veneer, arranged in quarterings. The pilasters are carved with interwoven husks, suspended from carved rams' heads; they stand on verd-antique marble plinth blocks. The frieze is decorated with carved swags of husks and oval paterae, the larger ones, gilt; the base has a border of carved and gilded guilloche ornament. The handles and claw and ball feet are silver. In contrast, centre top of Plate 318 is one of the simplest of the Sheraton mahogany, single box caddies which came into vogue in the 1780–90 period; it has boxwood lines on the angles and the typical radiating oval inlay

on the lid. Three of the more striking examples of the same period are shown in Plate 320. Oval caddies divided into two compartments, with separate lids, were particularly favoured in harewood and satinwood, inlaid *en suite* with the drawing room furniture of the period. The satinwood, two-compartment caddy, centre, with silver handles and pearl inserts round the amboyna oval inlays, is another elegant piece. The urn type of caddy, right, a miniature edition of cutlery boxes of the period, was a new shape for caddies in the late 18th century and reflects the influence of Robert Adam.

Judging by their trade cards, probably the majority of cabinetmakers made tea caddies or chests, but there were some who specialized particularly in shapely fitted boxes for cutlery, toilet, picnics, etc. Sheraton, in his *Drawing Book*, recommends John Lane, who was at 44 St. Martin's-Le-Grand, London, in 1790, for knife cases and ladies' travelling workboxes. Lane would doubtless also have made fine tea caddies. Other specialist London makers of fitted boxes were:

John Folgham	1760–1803
W. Gaimes	1802–1810
Thomas Lund	1808–1840
Medhurst	1790
Thomas Page	1817
Thomas Peake	1811–1839
Henry Robinson	1802

Between 1770 and 1815, caddies decorated with coloured paper filigree were in fashion and were made professionally, by amateurs as a hobby, and by French prisoners of war. Teachers of filigree gave lessons and also sold their own work. Specialist makers, such as John Lane, sold caddies ready prepared with plain or inlaid hardwood rims to the sunk panels, in which the patterns of coiled paper were to be inserted and glued; sometimes the sinkings were made deep enough to allow of glass enclosing the paper. Two paper filigree decorated caddies are shown in Plate 318. The colours of these particular examples are mainly blues, greens and metallic effects. The elliptical caddy, top right, has a picture, painted on silk, inserted in a window.

Caddies simulating fruits were first imported from the Orient, whether commencing in the 17th century or in the first half of the 18th century is unknown. Two, B and C, are pictured in Plate 315. Although usually described as pears, they actually represent aubergines or egg plants, a Chinese symbol of good fortune. They are extremely well made; the stalk and cluster of leaves, which form the outer cap, unscrew and disclose a tight-fitting stopper, as on the ginger jar type of caddies. Occasionally, these aubergine caddies are lightly stained green or a pinky brown, for green and black tea respectively. They have no locks and presumably were originally enclosed in tea chests.

European fruit tea caddies—pears, apples and cantaloupes—are hinged on a horizontal line about five-eighths of the way up, are fitted with a lock, have, or have had, foil linings and an inner lid; the stem is inserted as a separate component. Examples are shown in Plate 315, A, E and F. Those that have silver stop-hinges and escutcheons and good quality locks and keys were undoubtedly made in the second half of the 18th century; this covers a few well finished apples and pears, and all the cantaloupes with the segments hand carved into convexes and finished in a hard, mottled multi-coloured lacquer. But these are the minority.

During the first half of the 19th century, when most of the fruit caddies were made, quality declined rapidly. The 'fruits' were simply turnery, without any additional individual shaping, and became larger and coarser. Nineteenth-century cantaloupes little resemble that fruit; they are turned, slightly flattened spheres, with painted lines dividing segments, simulated by

staining in different colours. 'Fruits' made during the Regency period have cast brass hinges, not of the stop type, brass locks, and are french polished. Later specimens, and these are the majority, have stamped iron or steel hinges, stamped component locks, and poorly cast keys, probably of German origin, closely resembling those on mid-19th century German boxes of various types. These mid-19th century 'fruits' were originally finished with a poor varnish, which wore badly and has often been refinished. Occasionally, 19th-century fruit caddies have painted 'bloom' on their cheeks; this always seems to be the work of later 'improvers'.

Demand for fruit tea caddies has outstripped supply, with the result that prices have rocketed and, owing to indiscriminate collecting, amounts asked for poor, late specimens are often as much as for good early ones. Inevitably, where an object costing a few shillings can fetch £50 or more, reproductions are now being made. This is legitimate, but as some of the reproductions are being given a fake antique finish (not by the manufacturers), collectors should beware.

During the Regency period, the most popular shape for tea chests was the antiquarian sarcophagus, which was largely made in rosewood, walnut and mahogany. Often it had a large wood ring handle or, alternatively, brass lion mask ring handles, harmonizing with brass lion paw feet. Interiors contain two caddy boxes only, or two boxes separated by a glass sugar or mixing jar. Early Regency examples are no larger than similarly fitted late 18th-century chests, but where Regency merges into George IV and William IV fashions, tea chests become large, clumsy and coarse in detail.

In Scotland, between 1800 and 1820, some superb quality tea chests were made of sycamore, decorated with pen-and-ink and brush work, and with both the chests and the interior caddies fitted with the celebrated Scottish integral hinge. A notable example, 12 in. long, 6 in. wide and 5½ in. deep, is shown left of Plate 318, with one of its caddies open, alongside. On the outside of the lid is a good pastoral picture in black penwork. Inside the lid, roses are painted in natural colours. The exteriors of the chest and the caddies are decorated with an all-over network of fine red pen lines, in a black pen border, on the natural wood. The design, plus the remarkable accuracy of their fitting, renders the hinge lines of the caddies invisible.

In Plate 313 are three simple but unusual single box caddies. The coconut caddy, B, with silver fittings, dates from the 18th century. The Regency turned rosewood caddy, C, has a tea measure forming the lift to the lid. Of the same period is the gavel-shaped caddy, D, turned from masur birch. At the bottom are two amusing Victorian novelties. The shovel of the brass-mounted oak coal scuttle, K, or purdonium, as it was called at the time of the 1851 Exhibition, acts as the caddy spoon. The mahogany boot, N, with simulated black kid toe-cap, etc., metal 'laces' and inlaid bone diamonds, probably dates from the same period. Another popular Victorian novelty was the miniature sideboard caddy, usually of mahogany. It had a caddy in each pedestal and the glass bowl, partially concealed in a centre bridge piece.

Some good quality attractive tea chests were made at Tunbridge and decorated with the noted mosaic in the 19th century. Left of Plate 319, the rosewood tea chest, decorated with cube pattern mosaic, dates from about 1820; it contains one lidded compartment and one glass bowl. Centre, the tea casket is veneered in walnut, with 'Berlin woolwork' pattern border, and central on the lid, a cottage orné in mosaic. It dates from the 1850–60 period and contains two tea compartments and a central glass bowl. The chest on the right is not decorated with Tunbridge end-grain mosaic, but with a long-grain geometric

marquetry of rather unusual design; it was probably made about 1800 and may be a transitional Tunbridge product.

Tea Poys

Tea poys, in 19th-century parlance, were tables fitted for tea—in other words, tea chests on legs. The tables usually had rising tops, with interiors fitted with up to four caddies and one or two glass bowls. They were most frequently mounted on a centre pillar with a quadrupod base. Sometimes a tea poy was made to pair with a lady's work-table; others are combination pieces of furniture, having a needlework drawer and pleated bag below the tea compartment. The word tepoy first came into the English language in the 18th century, as a description for an eastern imported small pillar and tripod table—in Hindu, *Tepai*. It originally had no connection with tea, but fashionable English-made Georgian, small pillar and tripod tables were frequently used to place between drinkers for their tea cups and plates; thus the 18th-century tepoy became the 19th-century tea poy.

Tea Cups and Saucers and Teapots

Treen tea cups and saucers and teapots hardly rank as practical objects. The 19th-century, boxwood tea cup and saucer, Plate 313, L, thin, clean and beautifully turned and shaped, rank, however, as a fine feat of craftsmanship. So also do the paper-thickness cup and saucer and the one-piece pot, Plate 321, faithfully executed down to the vent hole in the lid and the strainer in the spout; they were made from the famous mulberry tree which Shakespeare planted at New Place, Stratford-on-Avon. The shape of the teapot suggests a date about 1760–5, which is consonant with the known fact that the irascible Rev. Francis Gastrell cut down the famous tree in 1756, and time obviously had to be allowed for seasoning it. Shakespeare died in 1616 and the house and the tree became such objects of veneration and attracted so many callers, that the Rev. Gastrell, the 18th-century owner of New Place, became increasingly incensed. As the cutting down of the tree did not decrease the number of visitors, the small-minded cleric demolished the house in 1759. Although so anti-tourist, the Rev. Gastrell had no objection to cashing in on the commercial value of the wood, which he sold to various carvers and turners, anxious to make souvenirs. The principal purchasers were Thomas Sharp, William Hurdis Harborne, William Hunt, local carvers and general wood craftsmen, and a Mr. Pierce; the last was an ivory turner and jeweller. According to documents which have been with the tea-pot, cup and saucer for many years, they were made by Pierce; their quality makes the attribution highly probable.

A number of varied objects certified by Thomas Sharp as made from the tree, have survived; most of them are elaborately carved and they include small caskets, tea caddies, toothpick cases, goblets, snuff boxes, tobacco stoppers, sugar tongs, etc.

Teapot Carriers

Enclosed teapot carriers, both of hardwood and of woven basketwork, with a hole in one side for the pot spout to project and with a quilted lining, were formerly used in China; some were exported to England, particularly in the 18th century. They may still be found with their original porcelain or pewter teapots in them. The casing insulated the teapot and acted both as tea cosy and teapot stand.

Teapot Stands

Teapot stands have been made in various materials, but probably ceramic tiles have always been the most popular. In Scotland, in Victorian times, Bell of Glasgow pro-duced a series of excellent pictorial tiles, which were mounted into moulded ma-hogany frames on castors. The stand in Plate 313, *A*, came from Scotland; the tile depicts hawking and it is probably by Bell.

Tea Strainers

An 18th- or early 19th-century strainer, with sycamore handle and Dresden china bowl, is pictured in Plate 312, *A*. A few all-wood strainers have survived and their condition shows that they have had use. They usually have two handles, shaped on similar lines to silver, and the holes are sometimes arranged in an attractive pattern. It seems doubtful whether they were ever a com-mercial proposition, and much more likely something which a turner made for his wife.

Tea Urn Powder

In Plate 313 is a small turned box, *F*, with its lid alongside. Its interior shows that it has contained some kind of silver rouge. The label on the lid, which appears to be of the Regency period, says

Superfine Urn Powder
Directions for Use

This Powder to be rubbed on dry with soft leather as soon as the urn is cold after using. It will then effectually take out all spots and stains and give a beautiful Gloss.

Unfortunately, there is no maker's name.

Tongs, Sugar

I doubt whether wooden sugar tongs can ever be regarded as objects made for serious use. The thin, springy, fret-cut pair, Plate 312, *D*, might have been a try-out for making in silver. The Swiss or Tyrolean pair, carved with knights astride goats, *C*, is a remarkable feat of skilful delicacy, but though the hands which terminate the tongs obviously belong to a 'sweetie', they could not grip sugar. The third pair, *B*, also Swiss or Tyrolean, might have served some purpose if very carefully used. For other examples, see Section X, *Love Spoons and other Love Tokens*.

Trays, Tea, etc.

Tea trays, referred to in 18th-century literature as tea boards were made in silver, wood and papier mâché. They may be oval, oblong, octagonal or circular. Wooden examples of the mid-18th century, usually of mahogany, may have solid or fret cut upstanding rims, the latter pierced in the Chippendale Chinese or Gothic taste and with hand holes cut out for lifting. Late 18th-century trays follow the Sheraton style of furniture and caddies, using the same range of woods and inlay motifs of shells, lunettes, oval fans, etc. Sometimes a mahogany tray base was used with a silver or plated rim, but such examples are more likely to be 19th-century. A large number of reproductions of 18th-century tea trays has been made.

XXI

Textile Workers' Devices

The scope of textile work is so large and varied that this section cannot describe in detail technical processes, even all those involving objects illustrated. Readers particularly interested in this aspect of the subject are advised to study books listed under *Further Reading*. Textile machinery is outside the scope of this book, and even some of the treadle forerunners, such as looms and spinning wheels, can only be briefly mentioned. Some of the specialized table looms, however, rank among smaller wooden devices of textile workers, with which this section is mainly concerned.

For the commencement of the story, we go back to Genesis III, 7, where we read that Adam and Eve '... sewed fig leaves together and made themselves aprons'. Ever since then, their daughters—and also their sons—have carried on the work, a large proportion of their output being always devoted to dress, which, according to the vagaries of fashion, has varied from the simple to elaborate, and from voluminous to almost the scantiness of the Garden of Eden. The first advance from fig leaves was probably woven bark cloth, and this, in a wide range of simple designs, some possessing a certain artistic merit, still supplies the clothing needs of the inhabitants of considerable portions of the globe. The Dyaks of Borneo, until very recently, used the bark of *Artocarpus*, the natives of

Uganda and other parts of the African continent, the bark of the *Ficus*, whilst the Sandwich, Fiji and Solomon Islanders dressed in tapa cloth, made from the bark of *Broussonetia papyrifera*. Bark cloth, too, was formerly used both in the North and South of the American continent.

With advancing civilization, the raw materials of the textile worker were at first grouped according to soil and climate— whether suitable for growing cotton, flax, mulberries for silkworms, or sheep farming for wool. The nature of the economy and the desire to protect home industries also affected developments, but as transport improved, trade gradually became international, until now all materials are available in all countries. Lastly, not only are man-made fibres increasingly taking over from natural products, but the humble wooden objects used by so many generations of hand textile workers are being rapidly superseded by plastics.

Both the antiquity of form and the conservativeness in design of many devices still commonly used by the textile worker, are strikingly illustrated in a series of engravings of the *Boyhood of Jesus*, by Hieronymus Wierix, who worked at Antwerp between 1550 and 1617. These finely delineated pictures of the Biblical story, set against a background of the 16th century, show Jesus engaged in different aspects of woodworking, whilst his mother is occupied with various branches of textile work. Six of the illustrations are included in Section XXIV, *Tools of Specialized Woodworkers*, Plates 399 to 404, and will be found of considerable interest to readers of this textile section.

Bats, Lace-makers'—see *Lace-Making Devices*

Bead Looms—see *Weaving Equipment*

Bobbin Boxes—see *Lace-Making Devices*

Bobbin Winders—see *Lace-Making Devices*

Bobbins, Lace—see *Lace-Making Devices*

Braid Looms—see *Weaving Equipment*

Broaches—see *Knitting Wool Holders*

Buttonhole Cutters
A buttonhole cutter or seam knife is like a miniature chisel, with a boxwood or ivory handle and a sharp, spade-shaped blade. A 3½ in. long specimen, with the blade engraved 'Sarah Waller 1779', is illustrated, Plate 326, *P*. This particular example may originally have been a trephination or trepanning chisel; not only is it identical to other 18th-century surgical specimens, but Sarah's husband may have been Henry Waller, who was a naval surgeon at this date. If this is so, she probably had her name engraved on the chisel to prevent her husband reclaiming it, and if she showed it to her friends and praised its new use, she may well have started the vogue which caused surgical instruments to become buttonhole cutters in work boxes.

Candle Stands, Lace-maker's—see *Lace-Making Devices*

Carding Combs—see *Spinning Devices, Cards*

Cats—see *Work Basket Stands*

Clamp Devices
It is sometimes more convenient to have such devices as wool winders, pincushions, cord making equipment, etc., screwed on to a ledge or table, rather than free standing. A large selection of such contrivances was marketed during the 19th century. They are illustrated in Plate 340 and described under their various headings. For other clamp devices, see also Section XXIII, *Toilet and Bedroom Accessories: Wig Blocks and Equipment*.

Clue Holder—see *Knitting Sheaths*

Cocoon Winder—see *Silk Devices*

Cotton and Thread Barrels and Boxes
Until early in the 19th century, cotton thread was supplied in skeins and sold by weight. In the home, it was transferred to flat wood or card winders, to barrels containing a reel and spindle, or to spools. Eighteenth- and early 19th-century barrels, usually about 1½ in. high, Plate 337, *N*, have the spindle or reel head projecting through a hole in the centre of the barrel and controlling the flow of thread through a small hole in the side. Later 19th-century barrels, supplied by the cotton manufacturer, are larger, no longer have the projecting spindle, are frequently lacquered black, and bear the maker's name or trade mark, such as Plate 337, *D*, Clark's 'Anchor' cotton, and Plate 337, *E*, 'M.E.Q.' Sewing Cotton. Although the mass-produced cotton reel had arrived in the 1820s or 1830s, barrels and decorative boxes made in Scotland, to contain three reels, were still being sold by Clark & Co. of Paisley, in the late 19th century; they were popular in tartan and transfer ware, Plate 337, *F* and *G*. Decorative single cylinders for cotton, 'fern pattern', Plate 337, *M*, 'turreted', *L*, and 'Fiery Cross', *K*, were also made until late in the 19th century; they have a notch

in the side for drawing out the thread. For significance of the Fiery Cross message, see Section X, *Miscellany: Fiery Cross Boxes*. A mid-19th-century, Tunbridge mosaic, silk, cotton or twine ball holder is pictured, Plate 337, *J*; a triple-feed barrel, clamp device of the same date, for cord making is shown, Plate 340, *D*. For spools and reels combined with needle and thimble cases, see *Needles* and *Thimbles*.

Crochet Hooks—see *Knitting Needles*

Darning Devices
Wooden darning eggs are usually impossible to date, but were probably used long before mushrooms, which are generally of sycamore, Plate 335, *S*, and appear to date from the 19th century. The majority of eggs are solid boxwood, or other close-grained hardwood, Plate 335, *U*, but some hollow, two-piece, olivewood darning eggs, Plate 335, *T*, probably imported from southern Europe, were made as combined needle and thimble holders. Eggs of glass, china and spar were made as hand coolers for needle workers, and pewter eggs, which unscrewed, were filled with hot water and carried in muffs.

Sets of boxwood miniature darning eggs, in graduated finger sizes, were made in France for darning gloves; a complete set of *Oeufs à Gants*, in original glass-topped box, is illustrated, Plate 335, *O*. Double-ended stick types are shown, *P* and *Q*; the former is of unknown provenance, the latter is English. *R*, a single-ended specimen, is Scottish.

Distaffs—see *Spinning Devices, Distaffs and Spindles*

Drizzling Boxes—see introduction to *Lace Making Devices*

Eggs, Darning—see *Darning Devices*

Ell Rules—see Section XIX, *Scientific: Measuring Sticks*

Embroidery Frames—see *Frames*

Emery Cushions—see *Needles*

Étuis—see *Needles, Needle Cases and Needle Books*

Flax Preparation Devices
The preliminary operations to the spinning of flax and the weaving into linen on the loom, yield some interesting and once common, but now rare, old-time wooden devices. After harvesting, passing through an iron fork or 'ripple' to remove the seeds needed for next year's harvest, and retting or rotting down, the flax is ready for scutching, or swingling. Scutching was carried out on a crude wooden horse, usually 4 ft or 5 ft. long, known as a flax break or brake. It has a heavy, solid, fixed top bar, inset with three parallel wooden blades or blunt knives, with a gap between them. Pivoted at one end of the bar is a rise and fall bar, fitted with two blunt knives, which on the 'fall', fit into the gap between the three lower knives. The bundle of flax was laid across the lower bar and the upper one was lowered forcibly; sometimes this upper bar was weighted at the handle end, or a mallet was used to aid the pounding. In this operation, the blunt blades broke the brittle flax straw, but without cutting or injuring the strong, flexible fibres. The flax was then beaten with a wooden scutching or swingling knife on a block, to remove the last particles of broken chaff. Old Irish, Scottish and English scutching knives are usually plain and straight bladed, but some Scandinavian specimens are of curved scimitar outline and quite elaborately ornamented with chip carving; they have holes in their handles, so that when not in use, they form cottage wall decorations. Colonial American scutching knives, like the old British ones, are usually quite plain, but may have straight or curved blades, according to the origin of the settlers.

The final operation before spinning, was hackling or hetcheling with hackels or hetchels, really iron teeth or tines set in a wood back board. A coarse hackel was used first, followed by one or more combings of the fibres with finer ones. Residue from the first combing was used in rope making.

Although flax has been grown in Ireland from early times and linen woven on a small scale, it is to the arrival of the Huguenot refugee, Samuel Louis Crommelin, in 1698, that Northern Ireland really owes its pre-eminence in linen manufacture. See also *Spinning*, and *Weaving*.

Frames

The purpose of textile frames is to hold fabric taut; in the case of tapestry and embroidery frames, it has to be in such manner that the material can be worked from both sides. The small circular frames, Plate 335, *C*, however, are designed to hold the fabric stretched over a rebated block, so as to give a firm surface for marking or drawing monograms or small designs for embroidery. They are made of boxwood, have an inside ring diameter of $2\frac{1}{4}$ in., are English, and were made by William Saunders of Devonshire Street, Mile End Road, London, in the mid-19th century.

Embroidery frames, made of a suitable steamed and bent hardwood, consist of two concentric rims, which grip the fabric between them; some are fixed to an adjustable arm, which may have a floor or table stand, or be attached to a clamp, like Plate 340, *J*, which is late 19th-century. Some of the 18th-century specimens, particularly floor-standing examples, are elegant pieces of furniture. Embroidery frames for larger work were often rectangular and identical with tapestry frames, having screw devices for tautening the fabric. An adjustable one in the Pinto Collection is very much a drawing room device, with a base veneered in curl mahogany and the pivoted threaded rods and nuts of laburnum wood. For frame knitting, see *Knitting, Frame and Peg*.

Hatchels or Hetchels—see *Flax Preparation Devices*

Knitting and Crochet Devices

Neither the date nor geographical origin of knitting is established. The earliest fragments of knitting so far discovered are, I believe, from the Syrian city of Duro-Europos, 2nd century A.D., and from Coptic 3rd century A.D. burials, but judging by the advanced technique of the finds, knitting was already an old-established craft.

Knitted silk gloves were imported into England in the 14th century. A pair worn by William of Wykeham, founder of New College, Oxford, at the opening ceremony in 1386, is still preserved, and may be Spanish. Details of other Spanish, Italian and French silk knitted garments—girdles, gloves, caps and hose particularly—are recorded in the 15th century. Henry VIII is known to have worn silk stockings on occasion, and in 1561 occurred the well-known episode when Mrs. Montague, the Queen's silkwoman, presented Elizabeth I with a pair of black silk stockings and 'thenceforth she never wore cloth hose any more'. In the 16th century, references to knitting became more numerous—Shakespeare makes several—but some are undoubtedly to the home craft in wool, which was an important part of the economy. Silk fabric was no novelty in Tudor England (see *Silk Devices*): it was the knitting of silk garments that was novel, for being a wool country, it was wool knitting which was actively encouraged by the Tudors and became well established in their time. 'Knitte hose', 'knitte petticoats', 'knitte gloves' and 'knitte sleeves' are mentioned in an Act of Parliament of Edward VI, 1552. Harrison, in his *Description of England*, referring to the period 1568–70, says

'. . . all Citizens wiues in generall, were constrayned to weare white knit Caps of wollen yarne, unlesse their husbands were of good value in the Queene's booke, or could proue themselves Gentlemen by descent. . . .'

This was not a new fashion, but a long-standing custom and was aimed at the wives of the new-rich Tudor tradesmen, who were getting above themselves and aping the nobility by wearing caps of miniver (white fur). The price of 'knitte cappes' of wool had been fixed by Act of Parliament at 2s. 8d. in 1488.

There is a tradition that knitting was introduced to England from Scotland, and that there it originated from teaching by Spanish sailors of the Armada, wrecked on the Orkneys, who taught the inhabitants the elaborate Fair Isle patterns. The Spaniards may have taught the Fair Isle pattern, but as I have shown, knitting was practised in England before this date. It is interesting, however, that St. Fiacre, son of a Scottish king, was chosen as patron saint of a guild of French stocking knitters about 1527.

The sheep grazing country of the North of England, the Yorkshire, Westmorland and Cumberland dales, and parts of Wales were the strongholds of the wool knitters from the reign of Elizabeth I until near the end of the 19th century. Knitting there was carried out not only as a cottage industry, but also in the streets and countryside, while the knitters, men and women, walked and talked. Waggoners knitted as they went with their teams, and men and women knitted as they walked to market to sell their wares. Life was hard and time was money. During the winter months, friends in the dales met at each other's cottages in turn, and held what they called a 'knitting go forth', at which the knitters sat round the fire, whilst one member of the party narrated stories, or led in the old knitting songs which 'kept the time' of the knitters. Knitting sheaths, for the collector, the most varied and interesting knitters' bygones, seldom seem to have been used in the Midlands or South of England, where knitting was not as popular. Even though knitting sheaths were not used there, the Norfolk and Suffolk sheep grazing districts were knitting centres from early times. Celia Fiennes, touring East Anglia in 1698, recorded in her diary meeting ' . . . the ordinary people knitting 4 or 5 in a company under the hedges . . .'. Robert Southey immortalized Dent in Yorkshire as the village of dreadful knitters, and Henry Brougham, during his election address at Ravensdale in 1820, remarked that the name of the place should be changed to Knittingdale.

Knitting Broaches—see *Knitting Wool Holders*

Knitting, Frame and Peg
William Lee of Woodborough, Nottinghamshire, invented the stocking frame in 1589, whilst working as a curate at Calverton. He applied to Elizabeth for a patent, which she refused on the grounds that she had too much love for her poor people who obtain their bread by knitting 'to forward an invention that will tend to their ruin'. Lee went to France and developed his invention at Rouen. He died in Paris, but his brother returned to London and sold frames there. Later, he made improvements in the frames and set up business with a partner in Nottingham. In 1657, the Framework Knitters' Company received its first charter; its second charter, under which it still flourishes, was granted by Charles II. John Evelyn, in 1661, wrote 'I went to see ye wonderfull engine for weaving silk stockings, said to have ben ye invention of an Oxford scholler 40 years since' (Lee was actually at St. John's College, Cambridge). Lee's invention increased speed from about 100 stitches per minute to 1,000 or more on the frame, and the mechanical principles which he devised remained almost unaltered until this century; but the invention did not have the effect on the popularity of hand knitting, which Elizabeth feared.

The simplest form of peg or frame knitting is the reel, with a row of tacks set in the head, used mostly by children nowadays, for making cords. In earlier times, when tubular cord making was important, a hollow wood or ivory tube, with pegs inserted or carved at one end, was employed; it was known as a 'knitting nancy'. In larger diameter, the peg device was constructed as a shallow frame, and used for making circular articles, such as girdles, caps, scarfs, bags, etc. The method of working is to tie a knot and make the first stitches by twisting the yarn once round each peg and then, by means of a hook-ended needle, each loop in turn is lifted over the working thread and slipped over the top of the peg. The number of pegs varies from three upwards, according to the size of the article being made. A circular birch peg knitting frame of traditional type is shown, Plate 338, F; it is 4½ in. in diameter, centre to centre of the pegs. Plate 338, K, is a mahogany oval variant, 10¼ in. by 3 in. to centres of pegs. A rectangular, mahogany peg frame, for making mats, one shown with it, is illustrated, Plate 338, E.

Knitting Machines

Knitting machines are outside the scope of this work, but the cones on which the yarn is wound for use on the machine, sometimes come the way of the collector, so an example is illustrated, Plate 337, A; it is 6½ in. high, with birch upstand and elm base, and so designed that the yarn readily slips off the top when pulled.

Knitting Machine Cones—see Knitting Machines

Knitting Needles and Crochet Hooks

Knitting needles have been made of wood, ivory, bone, glass, brass, steel and, more recently, plastic; they may be pointed at both ends or headed. The majority were formerly turned from hardwoods, either in one piece or with a threaded-on head of bone or ivory. They vary considerably both in length and diameter, according to the material to be used and the work to be knitted. Three, 8½ in. to 12 in. long, are pictured, Plate 323, J, K and L. They differ in no way from those used by Mary for her two ball stocking knitting in the circa 1600 engraving, Plate 404. Bow curved needles, made from wire sharpened both ends on a stone and known as pricks, were commonly used for 'bump' or coarse knitting, in conjunction with knitting sheaths.

A cherrywood crochet hook, 7½ in. long, is illustrated, Plate 323, O. Wooden specimens are comparatively rare and usually impossible to date. As early knitting needles were similarly barbed, there is no difference between a crochet hook and an early knitting needle.

Knitting Needle Cases and Boxes

Containers for knitting needles were commonly made as plain turned cylinders, which were also bought at the turners for holding netting tools, sailmakers' needles, hatpins, pencils, etc. In fact, they were general-purpose containers and all sorts of oddments may be found in them. The plain cylinders are impossible to date. A selection, including some of the more elaborate, is illustrated, Plates 326 and 338. In Plate 326, B is a Victorian umbrella novelty; C, of beech and D, of yew-wood, are probably English; E, made as a tube within a carved tube of contrasting coloured woods, is Swiss or Tyrolean, 19th-century. The two boxes, Plate 338, C and D, with sliding lids, are hollowed out of the solid and elaborately chip carved. The smaller, which holds 9½ in. needles, is Icelandic. The larger, which is sloped at the ends inside, despite its size still only holds needles 9 in. to 10½ in. long; it is Norwegian.

Knitting Needle Guards

Knitting needle guards, consisting of two small cherrywood cylinders, open one end only, and connected together by elastic, are shown, Plate 323, M. They were also formerly made in bone and ivory. I see no way of dating them; similar ones are now made of plastic.

Knitting Row Counters

Knitting row counters made of boxwood, were sold in two designs in the last quarter of the 19th century. Both types are shown, Plate 339. *E*, the single dial type, made like a games marker, with a pointer moving round, registers up to nine rows; *F*, with two revolving calibrated wheels, registers up to 99 rows.

Knitting Sheaths

Knitting sheaths average 8 in. to 9 in. in length, but vary between 3 in. and 12 in. They have a hole in the top, descending 1 in. to $2\frac{1}{2}$ in. into the wood and allowing the inserted needle a little play; sometimes the hole is lined or capped with metal, bone or ivory, to prevent wear. The sheaths were worn on the right side, in a sloping position; they held the bottom end of the needle on which the loops were formed while knitting, the top end being held by the right hand, which also manipulated the wool. Their purpose was to take the weight of the work and stop stitches slipping off the bottom of a double-ended needle.

Nearly all knitting sheaths were of wood, the majority individually made and often decorated by their makers to give as love tokens. They varied in form, partly according to the custom of the locality where they were made, but also according to how they were to be worn. The majority were tucked in the belt, rudely called a cowband, below the right arm-pit, but some have openings through which the belt could be threaded, and others are slotted to fit over the belt, or with diagonal cuts to fit over the apron strings; a few, the heart shapes particularly, are specially designed for sewing or pinning on apron or skirt. Sheaths are said to have been mainly used for 'bump' or coarse hand knitting. Those made and used in England, Wales, north of Scotland, Orkney and the Shetlands, are often peasant craft, but even so, the small diameter of some of the sheath holes show that they were also used for finer work. On the continent, where wool knitting was sometimes regarded as an elegant social pastime, knitting sheaths were sometimes costly, sophisticated and even in the fine art class, and additional to wood, might be of silver, amber, shagreen, etc.

A selection from some 80 wooden sheaths in the Pinto Collection is illustrated, Plates 322–5, 327 and 330. A few, mostly love token knitting sheaths, have initials, inscriptions and dates carved on them, but unfortunately they do not prove age of others of similar design, because rustic carvers were conservative and some patterns were used during 200 years or more. It has sometimes been stated that fine carving is early, and coarse is late; this is not true. It is a fact, however, that clumsy outlines are usually Victorian. Bearing in mind the importance of the turner in early times, I would think that some of the earliest specimens are the well-worn, simple turned ones, usually known as knitting sticks and particularly popular in the south Pennines; however, having no flat surface, they are nearly always undated. The majority of surviving knitting sheaths were made in the 19th century; 18th-century dated specimens are all quite rare and 17th-century dated specimens so rare that I only know of five additional to the three in the Pinto Collection, one of which appears to be the earliest recorded.

The peasant carver's *tour de force* of the open lantern, sometimes with loose ball, occurs mostly on the love token specimens and probably some of these are from Wales, like the love spoons which they resemble in detail (for love spoons, see Section X, *Love Spoons and other Love Tokens*). The lantern and ball is sometimes found in conjunction with another example of the carver's patience and skill, a wooden chain terminating in a hook, all carved from the one piece of wood; it is a useful adjunct, forming a clew holder for the clew, or ball of wool. Two misapprehensions must be cleared. The chain and hook were not intended for stretching the garment being knitted; a wooden chain is much too fragile for this purpose (see *Knitting Stretchers*). Nor was the hook and chain designed for hanging up the sheath when not in use.

Although the vast majority of knitting sheaths made and used in the British Isles were of wood, they were also made of ivory and bone, usually the work of sailors. Tin, brass and glass specimens were occasionally used around Sunderland. In Northumberland and the Yorkshire coast particularly, 'bundly sticks' were sometimes used; these were bundles of wooden splints encased in woven fabric. In Scotland, Orkney and the Shetlands, goose quills served the same purpose, being stitched on a cloth foundation, which was pinned on the skirt. Also in these same parts, leather-covered, horsehair pads, pierced with numerous holes for needles, were formerly used.

About 20 of the specimens illustrated were formerly in the Evan-Thomas and Linn Collections. Owing to further research, some of those from the former collection, will be found with different descriptions to those given in Evan-Thomas' book. In Plate 322, all the sheaths are English, except *D* and possibly *C*. Four sheaths with the chain and hook feature, mentioned above, are *A*, *B*, *C* and *D*. *A*, of inlaid mahogany, is 18 in. long, rectangular in section, very precisely cut and has lanterns and balls, and is unusual in having proverbs behind glazed panels; it is probably early to mid-19th-century. *B*, of fruitwood, 13 in. long, is chip carved, with initials M.R.; it is probably 18th-century. *C* is well carved with lanterns and balls, measures more than 23 in. in length, all out of one piece and has a glazed window with name, C. Elliott; it may be 18th- or early 19th-century, North of England or Welsh. *D*, a crude and early Welsh specimen, 14 in. long,

is dated 1680. *E*, a unique and original design in mahogany, inlaid with boxwood, incorporates a magnifying glass; on four sides of the scroll is engraved 'Art thou not dear unto my heart, search that heart and see, and from my bosom tear the part that beats not true to thee, but to my bosom thou art dear more dear than words can tell and if a fault be cherished there its loving thee too well. September 23. 1831'. *F* is a good quality, curved sheath, finely chip carved with lanterns, hearts, initials E.H. and apron string cross grooves; it is probably 18th-century. *G*, somewhat similar, with initials B.P., has one diagonal apron string groove. *H*, a straight stick, rather crude, with initials M.P., is probably 18th-century. *J*, a curved, mahogany sheath, inlaid with satinwood bands and stringing, has a diagonal groove and is unusual in employing such a typical 18th-century cabinet-maker technique. *K* is a curved and well carved boxwood specimen, 8½ in. long, with lantern and ball, two hearts forming the apron string diagonals, and initials M.G. and date 1805. *L*, a five-sided, tapering stick, is a very early, dated, chip carved specimen, engraved 'Be friend to few, Be fo(e) to non(e), Be kind to al(l), and love but on(e). 1688'. *M*, of boxwood, only 5 in. long, and shown needle holder downwards, appears to be an early and most unusual specimen; it has a lantern and ball, and two pulleys which control a ribbon, presumably for a clew holder.

Children began to knit at an early age, and *N* and *O* show mother's and child's matching sheaths, both chip carved, with lanterns and balls, belt slots and fantail pigeon finials, which, in use, pointed downwards. The diamond chip carved sheath with belt slot, *P*, is probably 18th-century. *Q*, a curved, mahogany sheath, with diagonal slot, chip carved and inlaid with a cross and diamonds, is 18th- or early 19th-century. *R*, a finely chip carved, boxwood stick, with needle holes at both ends and initials R.W. and R.R., is 17th- or early

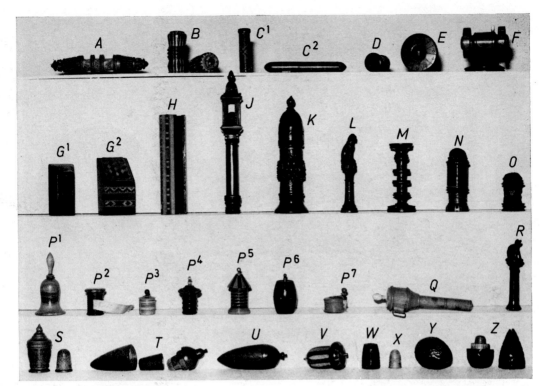

A, B, C, G, H, J, K, L and M,
...le cases, stands and holders; D,
...nd O, thread-waxers—N is com-
...d with tape measure and needle
...ion, and O, with needle cushion;
...d F, knitting row counters; P1 to
...tape measures; Q, combined tape
...sure and needle case; R, lace
...ker case; S to Z, thimbles and
...ble cases. (*Section XXI*)

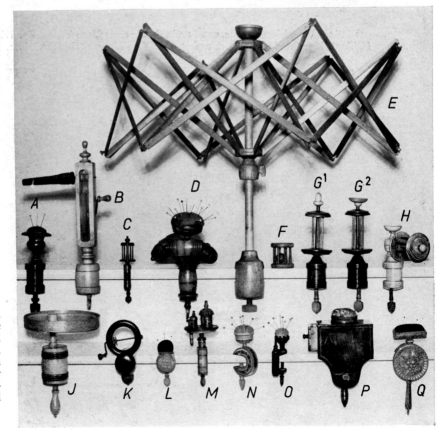

Selection of clamp devices—A,
...V, O and Q, pin-chushions; B, lace
...bin winder; C, G, H and K,
...ders; D, cord-making device; E,
...t; F, knitting wool ball foundation
...ch tinkles a bell; J, embroidery
...ne; M, needlewoman's compen-
...m; P, combination drawer and
...cushion—for story, see text.
tion XXI)

341 *A* to *G*, combined needle, spool and thimble cases; *H* to *T*, and *V* to *W*, novelty pin-cushions; *U*, Tunbridge fitted needlework casket, and *X*, miniature table work box. (*Section XXI*)

342 Selection of 19th-century reel stands, and an 18th-century spool box (with modern reels). (*Section XXI*)

343 (TOP RIGHT) A Scandinavian, 18th-century, standing distaff and two English, standing swifts or wool winders; the one in the centre is 19th century, on the right, 18th century. (*Section XXI*)

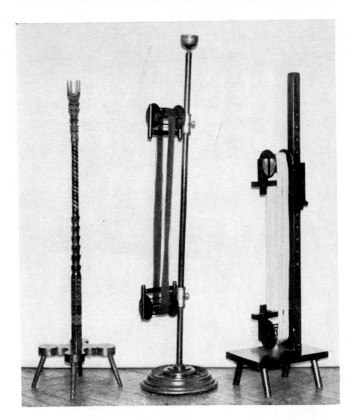

344 (LOWER LEFT) An elegant, English, late 18th-century spinning wheel of satin wood, with painted decoration. *Photograph by courtesy of the Victoria and Albert Museum.* (*Section XXI*)

345 (LOWER RIGHT) Low-type 'Irish' cottage spinning wheel, probably 18th century. (*Section XXI*)

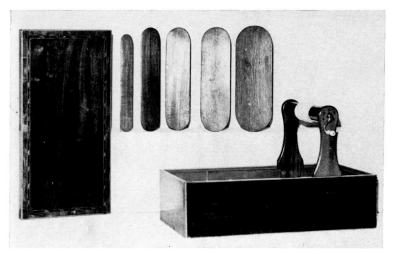

346 Inlaid mahogany netting box. English, 18th century. (*Section XXI*)

347 An unusually good quality, inlaid mahogany braid loom. English, 18th century. (*Section XXI*)

348 (LOWER LEFT) A niddy-noddy or cross-reel, from North America (*Section XXI*)

349 Two mahogany 'cats'. These wooden versions of the metal plate warmer cats were used as work basket and flower bowl stands. For story, see text. (*Section XXI*)

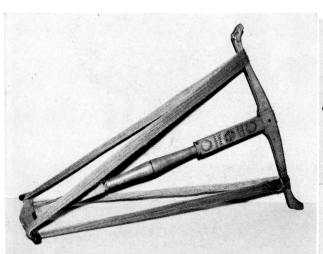

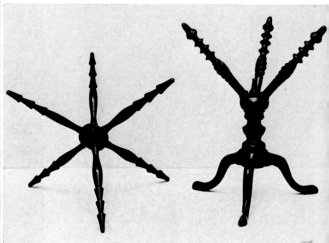

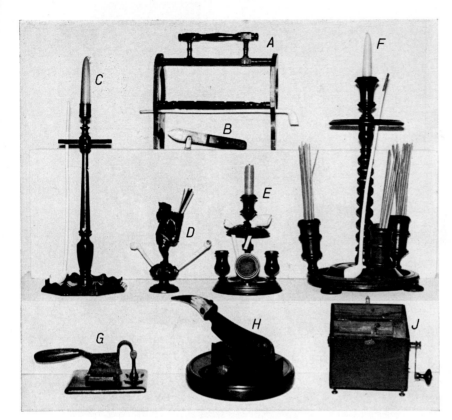

350 *A, C, D, E* and *F.* pipe racks; *B*, combined cigar box opener and closer; *G, H* and *J*, plug and cake tobacco slicers. Mostly 19th century. (*Section XXII*)

351 *A, C, E, G, J* and *L*, cigar and cheroot cases and magazines; *B*, cigar piercer; *D, F* and *H*, cheroot caskets; *M*, cigarette-making devices; *K* and *N*, smokers' compendiums. All 19th century. In front of *F*, a cigar taken off a dead Russian at the Battle of Alma in 1854. (*Section XXII*)

352 *A*, smoker's companion; *B*, cigar casket; *C*, churchwarden and cutty pipe rack; *D*, shop tobacco barrel; *E*, churchwarden cradle pipe tray; *F*, cigar mould. (*Section XXII*)

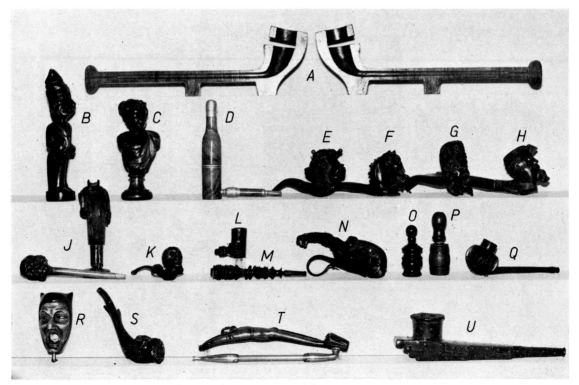

353 *A*, pipe mould; *M*, cigarette holder; *N*, pocket plug cutter; *O* and *P*, shop tobacco measures; *R*, cigar cutter. The remainder are all 19th-century pipes. (*Section XXII*)

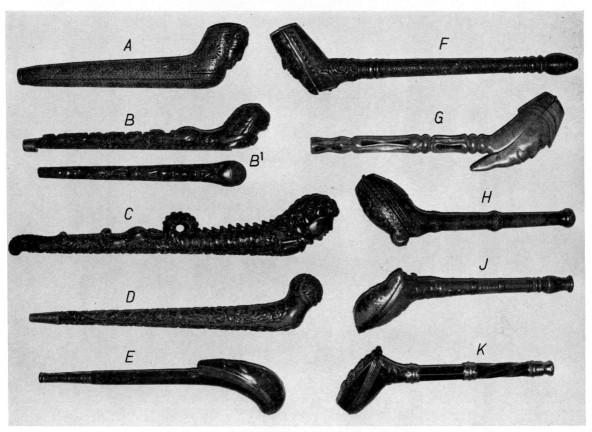

354 Selection of 17th- and 18th-century pocket cases for clay pipes. (*Section XXII*)

355 Dutch community table tobacco bowl. (*Section XXII*)

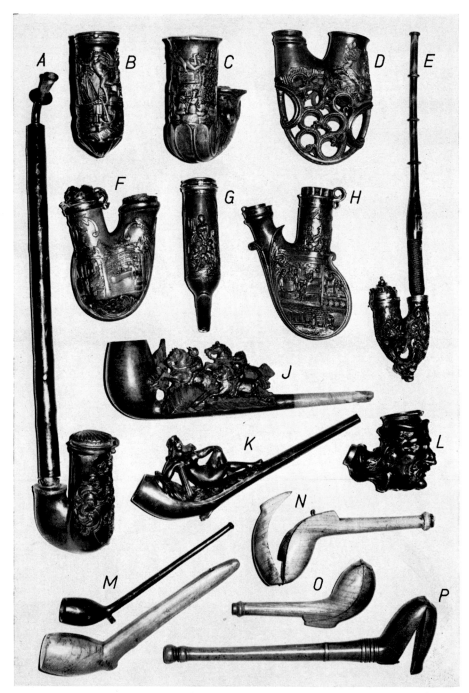

356 *A* to *L*, 18th- and 19th-century pipes; *M* to *P*, 18th- and 19th-century pipe cases. (*Section XXII*)

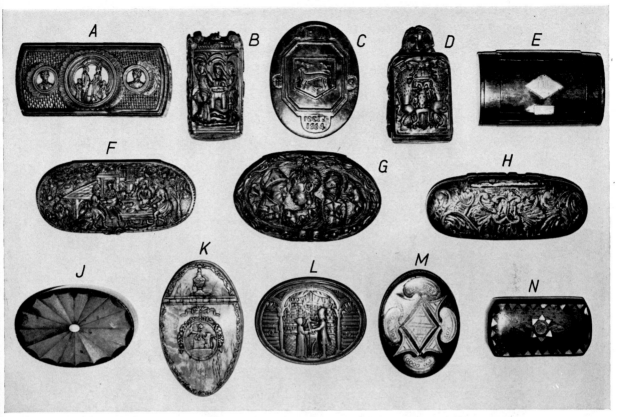

357 17th-, 18th- and 19th-century tobacco boxes. (*Section XXII*)

358 Selection of fine 17th-, 18th- and 19th-century tobacco stoppers. (*Section XXII*)

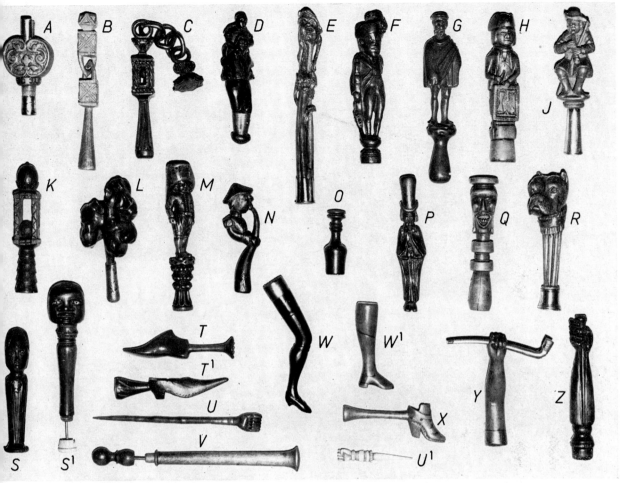

359 A further selection of fine 17th-, 18th- and 19th-century tobacco stoppers. (*Section XXII*)

360 A unique 17th-century carved boxwood snuff box of superb quality. (*Section XXII*)

361 and 362 A remarkable 16th- or 17th-century boxwood snuff box of sculptural form, in the style of Cellini. (*Section XXII*)

363 *B* to *Q*, selection of 17th-, 18th- and 19th-century tobacco jars; *A*, 19th-century pipe rack, matching tobacco jar *C*; *R*, 18th-century churchwarden pipe tray. (*Section XXII*)

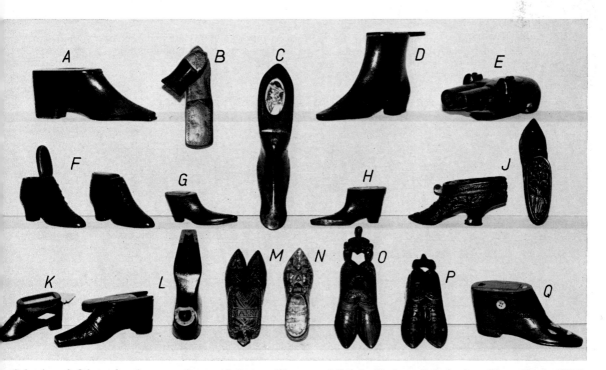

Selection of 18th- and 19th-century boot and shoe snuff boxes and *E*, a double-barrelled pistol snuff box. (*Section XXII*)

365 French pressed burr wood snuff boxes, mainly 19th century. *B* and *C* relate to phrenology. *J* and *K* are the double head type. *O* shows one from the variety of designs impressed on the bottom of these boxes. (*Section XXII*)

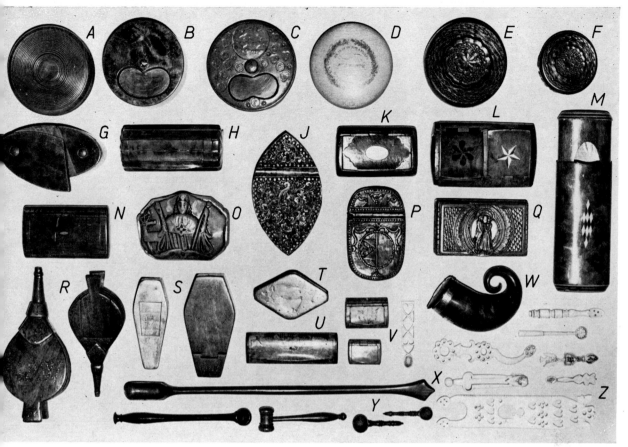

366 Selection of 17th-, 18th- and 19th-century snuff boxes, and a variety of snuff spoons; *X* was for removing snuff from bottles. (*Section XXII*)

367 Some of the infinite variety of 17th-, 18th- and 19th-century snuff boxes. (*Section XXII*)

18th-century in style. *S*, a belt-slotted, tapering stick, may be 18th- or early 19th-century. *T*, a finely chip carved, curved, tapering stick, with twin belt slots, is engraved with initials H.L. and date 1712. *U* is one of the unusual Yorkshire trowel-shaped sheaths, 5½ in. long, carved with hearts and diamonds and dated 1833.

All the sheaths in Plate 330 are from the North of England. *A*, a mahogany walrus, *B*, a walnut bulldog head sheath and *D*, a snake, are Victorian. Fish, walrus, snakes and mermaids are usually from the North-east coast and the work of sailors. *C*, which has unusual form, is charmingly decorated in red and green, on natural sycamore, and inscribed 'A Present from James Hope to Mary Newton, Disombor 12.1854'. *E*, *F*, *G* and *K* are violin scroll type sheaths and all except *F* are probably 19th-century. *E*, of mahogany, is quite plain and has initials M.C. in copper studs. *G*, of walnut, is inlaid with hearts and diamonds; both the last have diagonal belt grooves. *K*, of oak, is carved with two lanterns; the lower was probably used for threading the belt. *F*, which is 8½ in. long, is the oldest and most interesting; it is chip carved all over, with initials M.B. and date 1703, and is capped at the head with lead; it disproves the theory that all scroll types are late. *H* is crudely carved with a helmeted head at top and an alligator head forming the belt hook; it may be 18th- or 19th-century. *J*, the rare paperknife style, mahogany, inlaid with hearts, is 18th-century. *L*, of lacewood, and obviously the work of a sailor, is probably a caricature of a naval officer, *circa* 1820. *M*, *N*, *O* and *P* are all variants of the goose wing sheaths of the North-west Yorkshire and Westmorland dales; some people say they are the earliest type, but there is no proof and they are rarely dated; they were probably made over a long period. *M* and *P* are walnut; I think the former is not later than 18th-century and the latter, carved as a sea horse, is late 19th-century. *N*, also walnut, and

O, mahogany, carved, and capped with bone, are both probably 19th-century specimens; shapes such as the last two are sometimes described as scimitar types.

In Plate 323, *A* and *B*, both very crude, with faceted knops, separating downward tapering hafts from curved blades, are a well-known North-east coast, sailor-made type. *C*, of mahogany, inlaid with boxwood hearts, diamonds, etc., has a glass window enclosing the name Mary Armstrong; it is an unusual and nicely finished specimen and probably dates from *circa* 1800. *D* is a Northumberland, thread-woven 'bundly stick', filled with wood splints; it is impossible to date. Although I think that an undated North of England knitting sheath formerly in the Evan-Thomas Collection was probably made in the 16th century, *E* is the earliest dated specimen I know. It is of pine, very crudely engraved with geometric designs and birds. On each side of the square below the knop is one of the following figures—1, 6, 1 and 5. It can, therefore, be read as 1615 or 1516, but even if you accept 1615 as correct, it is still the earliest. Leicester Museum has a specimen dated 1628 and the Victoria and Albert Museum one of 1679. The other 17th-century dates recorded are 1680 and 1688 (illustrated, Plate 322, *D* and *L*), and 1684, 1686 and 1690 in other collections. *F*, a sailor's work, probably of maple, is inlaid with red and black sealing wax and dated 1753. *G*, of mahogany, is crudely carved with a bust of Nelson and the inscription 'England expects every man this day will do his duty'.

In Plate 324, only *A*, *B*, *C*, and *N* to *V*, are from the British Isles. The first three are the rare integral chain and clew holder type, like Plate 322, *A*, *B*, *C* and *D*. Plate 324, *A*, is 19 in. long, out of one piece and is engraved Thomas Osband. May. 1865. *B*, nicely chip carved and with an unusually fine chain, is also a late specimen, 1861. *C*, of boxwood, circular in section, is probably 18th-century. *N*, *O*, *P*, *Q* and *U*, are all good quality, South Pennine types, probably dating from the 18th century. *P*, and 5 in. long *V*, may be 17th- or 18th-century. *O*, is dated 1729 and *R*, which is of yew-wood, banded with lead, has had a flat surface cut on the tapering end and is inscribed B. Brooks, 1762. *S* and *T* are the North-east coast, sailor-made type, like 323, *A* and *B*.

Plate 324, *D* to *M*, are continental. *D*, of boxwood, is a good, French, 18th-century specimen, carved with a bird head. *E*, a spiral tapering sheath of boxwood, carved with the Virtues and silver mounted, and *G*, carved with musicians, may be Dutch or Flemish, 18th-century. *F*, box-wood, is probably French, 18th-century. *H* and *J*, both of boxwood and between 10 in. and 11 in. long, are Italian, probably 18th-century. *H* is carved with a dolphin, and *J* with a lizard; the latter is mounted with silver at both ends. *K*, *L* and *M*, finely turned and two of them ivory topped, are Mallorcan (Spanish), 18th- or 19th-century.

Plate 327, *A* and *B*, are two finely carved, boxwood knitting sticks. *A*, 7½ in. long, may be French or Italian, 17th-century. *B*, 11½ in. long, carved with various elaborate motifs, including a putto, supported on a dolphin, is Italian, 17th-century; its carving has points of resemblance with the spoon, left, Plate 64.

In a class by itself, is the 7½ in. long, French, early 18th-century, boxwood knitting sheath, Plate 325. It is a most superb example both of design and of small scale repetition carving. Perhaps not fully apparent in a photograph, is the almost imperceptible change of section of the sheath, from the shell at the flat end to the full circle of formal foliage between the florette and guilloche bandings, on which the beautifully modelled lynx is seated, at the needle end. The actual needle hole, which does not show in the picture, forms the centre of a florette. The leaf and berry strips, the pearl ornament borders, the

imbrication, and the scrolls, which could not be cut more perfectly by machine, are repeated on both sides. Probably because it is such a masterpiece, it shows no signs of wear and has doubtless always been treated as a showcase specimen.

Knitting Stretching Devices
As stated in the introduction to *Knitting Devices*, wooden chains and hooks on the ends of some knitting sheaths were for the clew or ball of wool and were too fragile and not intended for supporting or stretching the knitting. Various metal devices were normally used for this purpose, separately attached to the cowband. Some were hook bent wires, fixed to a clip, which fitted over the cowband; others had a chain, connecting belt clip to hook. A third alternative was a stirrup-like device, fastened to the waist belt by tape. All these contrivances could be slid round to the back of the knitter, to give the right 'pull' on the work, as the length increased. The only wooden device which I have seen, which served the same purpose, is the well-worn pine hook, Plate 323, *H*, which was used and probably made by a fisherman jersey knitter, around Lowestoft.

Knitting Wool Holders
The elusive and straying ball of wool, joy of baby, kitten and puppy, has always been the bane of the knitter; it must have been particularly trying at night, when rush, candle or firelight was the only illuminant. Clew holders on knitting sheath chains have already been described under *Knitting Sheaths*. A variant was the now very rare broach. The broach is a wooden peg or stick, on which wool was wound; about 5½ in. long and flattened at one end, it was tucked into the side of the clog or shoe. From the rare example illustrated, Plate 323, *N*, it will be seen that the flat part merges into a round section rod, which impaled the clew or ball of yarn. It should not be confused with the broderer's tool,

the wooden broche, a bobbin type device, about 8 in. long, used for laying gold thread.

The simplest and one of the most effective devices were the Georgian wool bowls, Plate 338, *H*, *M* and *N*. Made almost invariably of lignum vitae, usually between 2½ in. and 3 in. diameter, their weight kept them in position on floor or table; they are smooth, well polished and curved inside in a perfect segment, sufficiently deep to prevent the ball jumping, and with a rounded rim which allows the wool to unwind, without jamming as knitting proceeds. *N* is an unusual mahogany example, 6 in. in diameter, with a fixed peg in the middle.

In the 19th century, wool globes of wood came into vogue, Plate 338, *A* and *B*. They were made to stand, or for suspension, and had the advantage of keeping the wool clean. They were usually of sycamore, often decorated with transfers and made at Mauchline, Scotland. Others were made at Tunbridge.

Various devices were employed to give vocal warning of the whereabouts of the wool. One such was the windpipe of a goose, in which some dried peas were inserted and the pipe then bent into a circle, to act as a foundation for a clew, which betrayed itself by rattling. Another foundation for the wool was the beechwood spindle cage, Plate 340, *F*, which has a loose bell inside it.

Knotting Devices—see *Tatting and Knotting Devices*

Lace Making Devices
Pillow lace making is an ancient craft, but where it originated is unknown. It was worked in Coptic Egypt and was probably brought to Europe by the Moors. The first discovered pattern book for bobbin lace was published in Venice in 1557. Needlepoint lace, at least as ancient, is worked throughout with a needle, but in 'mixed lace' the two techniques are combined.

Names of lace, such as Brussels, Valenciennes, Mechlin, Antwerp, etc., must be regarded much more as descriptive of a type, than as strictly geographical. Most of the treen and other wooden bygones connected with lace making are or were accessories of the pillow or bobbin lacemaker.

When lace making first came to England is not established, but a few references to teaching the craft and apprenticeship occur both in the East Midlands and in Devonshire, during the last quarter of the 16th century. The allusions become frequent in the 17th century, particularly after the Huguenot persecutions began. Gold and silver lace making commenced in England at least 100 years earlier than is generally assumed. That the gold lace worn at the Stuart Court was not all imported, is amply proved by various 17th-century London indentures, to which Mr. John Chalkley has kindly drawn my attention: Amey Stephenson indentured to Elizabeth Vaughan of Steben Heath (Stepney) for seven years 'To be taught the Arte and Profession of making gould and silver lace', 9th December, 1653, is the earliest so far recorded. Other London entries for the same purpose are dated 1670, two in 1677, and two in 1679. Possibly further research will establish that the gold lace which came into fashion at Elizabeth's court was also English made. Harrison, in his *Description of England* at that time, refers to the gold lace edged handkerchiefs which the gallants had long been wearing in their hats as love tokens; buttons covered with gold and silver thread, appear to have been a new fashion about 1567.

Gold and silver lace making required specially heavy headed bobbins, and three of the earliest and finest continental specimens known are illustrated, Plate 336, and described later.

The value of the material in gold lace led to later destruction of much of it for reclamation of the gold. In France, in the late 18th century, *parfilage* or unravelling became a social and profitable pastime. Early in the 19th century, the destructive addiction came to England under the name of drizzling. According to Caroline Bauer, Prince Leopold's girl friend, the prince was an inveterate drizzler. Caroline came to dread the sight of Leopold's drizzling box and the 'ripping' sounds of his drizzling, which produced sufficient money from discarded gold lace and braid, for him to buy a silver soup tureen for the future Queen Victoria. What was a drizzling box? We do not know, but possibly it was really a netting box, similar to Plate 346, which would well serve the purpose, if any mechanical aid were needed to augment a stiletto, a knife and scissors.

Lace Bobbins

Pillow or bobbin lace was known in the 16th century, and often later, as bone lace. It is probable, therefore, that although more bobbins have been made of wood than bone, bone was used first. Every available species of close-grained hardwood was used, plum being particularly popular.

East Midland double-necked bobbins offer a greater selection of ornamental variety than is found anywhere else in the British Isles or abroad. Additional to wood and bone, a few were made of ivory, silver, brass, pewter, agate and even glass. Apart from those made from unusual materials, the most highly valued by collectors are hand-carved or inlaid wood bobbins and those of wood and bone which are individually ornamented and pierced with windows.

Bobbin making was a specialist branch of turnery and the names of a considerable number of individual turners, from the 18th century onwards, have been recorded; owing to the smallness of bobbins, few are stamped with makers' names, but Abbot of Bedford stamped his name on the shanks. The heads, necks and shanks of bobbins were usually lathe turned, but shanks could

be left blank, for ornamenting by the purchaser, as a love token gift. It is only those finished in this manner which justify the description hand or individually made and they do not include those highly decorative, straight-sided, bone ones, with inscriptions or girls' names formed out of coloured drilled dots; orders for specially inscribed bobbins were taken both by shops, and by door-to-door hawkers, who delivered the 'specials' on their next round; they were also obtained at fair booths. Inscriptions, which are much more common on bone than on wood bobbins, are not confined to girls' names and love messages, although 'Valentine' bobbins are the most numerous and varied. A girl's name and a date on a bobbin may alternatively denote a gift from a mistress to a diligent apprentice. Weddings, christenings and deaths are also frequently commemorated on bobbins; it was customary, in some parts of the East Midlands, to have a commemorative wedding bobbin made from a bone of the meat served at the wedding feast. Religious texts, royalty and coronations, M.P.s and their elections, the famous, such as Nelson and Wellington, the victories of Trafalgar and Waterloo, and the infamous were all commemorated on bobbins. A curious custom was to sell commemoration bobbins outside gaols when a murderer was hanged—thus 'Joseph Castle hung 1860' and 'Franz Muller hung 1864' are typical examples. The rarest types of inscriptions are those which show that a tradesman in another trade gave away bobbins as equivalents of trade cards.

Here are brief descriptions of the bobbins illustrated. In Plate 331, *A* to *U*, are East Midland types, with double necks for hitching the thread and glass spangles, which held the bobbins steady against the pillow when at rest. Spangles are a late 18th- and 19th-century characteristic, added to compensate for loss of weight consequent on the gradual change from the earlier, heavier based bulbous types. Spangles, if complete, consist of an uneven number, usually seven or nine beads, but more and less are known. The centre drop is generally a large Venetian or other decorative bead, but may be a coin, charm, or even a shell; some or all of the side beads are 'square cuts'; they are threaded on thin copper wire. *A* is a 'Trolly', fitted with pewter 'gingles' and used for the gimp thread—the thick, soft thread which outlines the design in point ground lace. *B* is a sectioned 'Old Maid'— that is, an extra thin bobbin which, in this example, is sectioned or spliced in contrasting colour woods, but may be wood and bone. The '*C*'s are 'bitted'—that is, inlaid in a pattern with light wood in a dark ground. The '*D*'s are 'Butterflies'— wood bobbins inlaid with winged pewter bands; if the bands are all plain, the bobbin is called a 'Tiger': the second *D*, with broken head, is really a 'Tiger Butterfly'. The '*E*'s, inlaid with pewter spots, are Bedfordshire 'Leopards'; there are other pewter inlaid designs with no specific names. *F*, *G*, *H*, *J* and *K* are wired bobbins which are decorated with continuous or intermittent bands of tightly coiled brass or copper wire. Of these, *G* is wired and beaded with turquoise beads; *H* is continuously wired, and *K*, which is bone, is coloured red, yellow and green and spirally wound to show the colours through. The '*M*'s are bone bobbins, decorated with coloured spots, which include names and inscriptions. The first states 'I long to wed'; the second belonged to Hannah and the third seems to be an acrostic. *N* is a 'mottled' bobbin. *O*, *P* and *Q* are three of the varied baluster patterns to be found amongst turned shank bobbins. Turned shanks also include reel and bead, and bobbin turned. *R* is a crude but completely hand-made wood bobbin; even the head and necks are whittled, not turned. *S* is a ring turned 'old maid'. The '*T*'s, two from a set of seven, are interesting bog oak crudities, carved in spiral ribbons and, like *R*, completely whittled by hand. *U* is a

solid 'bobbin turned' pewter. The '*V*'s are typical Honiton, Devon, single neck bobbins, probably of maple, with black and red incised ornament, and initials. The smaller has twin heart decoration, initials, and date 1804. *W*, of ebony with two red filled lines, is probably also a Honiton pattern. Honiton bobbins are always pointed, single necked and devoid of spangles, because the technique sometimes calls for them to be passed through the lace.

In Plate 332, is a fine selection of the aristocrats of wood lace bobbins, the intricately hand carved and pierced love tokens which every girl hoped to receive, and which every collector now hopes to find. Collectively, they are known as church window bobbins, but those with smaller bobbins inside the windows are described as mother-in-babe types, and those with loose balls in the openings, as lantern and ball bobbins. The most intricate feats are *B*, lantern and ball; *D*, mother-in-babe type, which is 5 in. long; *E* and *F*, which are open lanterns, finely chip carved all over their fragile framing, and the latter, diamond section on plan; and *L*, another fine and intricately carved lantern and ball example. *A*, *H*, *J*, *M*, *N* and *O*, are all mother-in-babe types. *K* and *P*, single neck types, are, I suspect, continental and the former has probably had spangles added in the East Midlands. *Q*, an unusual lantern and ball example, is sailor-made, decorated with scrimshaw work and initials W.P.

All the bobbins, Plate 323, *P* to *W*, are continental except the '*T*'s. *P*, from Bayeux, closely resembles an East Midland 'Yak'; it is 5 in. long, turned from yewwood. Yaks are large, heavy bobbins, used for worsted lace. The three '*Q*'s are Maltese. *R* is a Portuguese bobbin, 5½ in. long, with a nut forming the weighted end. The '*S*'s are crude, 6 in. to 7 in. long, Gobelin tapestry 'flutes'. The '*T*'s came from Oxfordshire; the first is mottled and inscribed January, 1818; the other is made up of light and dark wooden rings, threaded on a centre rod; some of this type take apart and have a miniature bobbin inside; they are known as 'cow-in-calf'. The '*U*'s, three from a set of unusual and all different, neatly inlaid bobbins are of unknown provenance. They give the impression that perhaps they were mounted in a special stand when filling. The inlaid glove darning egg, Plate 335, *P*, came with them. The '*V*'s and the '*W*'s are French, not very old; the '*W*'s have probably travelled to the East Midlands and been spangled there.

Plate 336 shows three superb boxwood bobbins, to which reference is also made in the introduction to *Lace-Making Devices*. Each bobbin, which is 3½ in. long, with 1½ in. diameter head, is turned from a single piece of boxwood and carved with a 'Romayne' head, surrounded by formal acanthus. They date from early in the 16th century, may be French, Italian or Spanish, and were probably used in a noble household for making gold and silver thread lace.

Lace Bobbin Boxes

Two typical, 18th-century, East Midland bobbin boxes are illustrated, Plate 337, *H* and *P*. They are very simple, measuring about 5 in. long, made of oak or other hardwood, mostly hinged with wire and secured by a hook or eye. Some are chip carved and have names or initials and dates cut into the lids. In the 19th century, when the spangled bobbins had entirely replaced the old 'dumpies', the boxes were generally about 7 in. long.

Lace Bobbin Winders

Bobbin winders on stands, some fitted with a drawer, Plate 334, were important items of equipment, but each was essentially an individual cottage-made product, sometimes very crude and assembled from all sorts of oddments of various woods. The spool holder was made larger than any bobbin and packed with soft paper or rag, which would not damage spangled speci-

mens. A grooved fly-wheel, fitted with a belt and a projection handle for turning, actuates the bobbin holder and draws the thread either from a reel holder, Plate 334, *A*, or a folding X cross-bar skein holder, provided with adjustable upstanding pegs, *C*. A Welsh variant, *B*, has wooden gear wheels instead of the usual belt drive; like the other two examples in the same illustration, it may be 18th- or early 19th-century. In Plate 340, *B* is a late 19th-century bobbin winder, made to clamp on to a piece of furniture.

Lace Prickers

Stilettos, coarse needles with sealing wax heads fitted, sharpened steel wires, and fine awls were all used for pricking the parchment lace patterns. Spring-loaded wooden cases of pencil type, sometimes hold a retractable pricker, actuated by pressure on the top. Others are contained in ornamental screw-top cases, such as Plate 339, *R*, surmounted by a seated dog. See also *Stilettos*.

Lace-makers' Bats

A lace-maker's bat, of mahogany, is shown, Plate 323, *X*. It is 6½ in. long and was used for 'setting up' after a corner was worked and when it was desired to lift and turn the cards, pins and lace complete, at right angles on the pillow. It is English, probably 18th-century, and seems more an individual than a generally recognized lace-maker's implement.

Lace-makers' Candlestands, Stools, or Flash Stools

The candlestand or flash stool, not confined to lace-makers but used for many kinds of close, fine work, was an ingenious device for concentrating light and making candles serve to the uttermost in cottages and workshops. In 18th-century England, a tax was imposed even on the cheapest candles. William Cowper, the poet, wrote 'I wish he could visit the miserable huts of our lacemakers at Olney, and see them working in the winter months by the light of a farthing candle, from four in the afternoon till midnight'. All specimens of candlestands are now very rare; the sophisticated oak example, Plate 333, on turned pillar and tripod, which dates from the first half of the 18th century, is probably unique. The majority of these candlestands are crude, have three or four peg legs, like milkmaids' stools, and holes in the perimeter of the top for 3 to 5 flashes, and a centre hole for a candle holder. In the example illustrated, the stem of the tripod is hollow, and the candle holder is spring loaded, so that it can be raised as the candle burns down. The single illuminant, refracted through the glass flashes filled with water, sends four quite bright circles of light on to the pillows of four lace-makers grouped round it. The flashes or globes shown, are modern reproductions. When not in use, flashes were kept in plaited rush baskets. For individual use, the flash was sometimes seated in a rush cushion, but more often in a stand, which resembled an ordinary candlestick with an unusually large socket, to take the neck of the flash. On the continent and in colonial America, where the device was also used, the candle holder and the flashes were sometimes suspended from the ceiling. Yet another alternative was a candlestick in the centre of a small table, with a four-sided, open frame surrounding it, and a flash suspended from the top rail on each side of the frame. See also Section VI, *Fire and Lighting: Candlestands, Lacemakers'*.

Lace-makers' Chairs and Foot Stools
Purpose-made lace-makers' chairs are straight backed for support and have seats shallow back to front, and higher than normal, tilting the sitter forward. Some of these chairs have a step for the feet; with others, the lace-maker used a stool, as shown in Plate 333, the front rail of the pillow stand, or one foot on each.

Lace-makers' Pillows and Stands
The many types and shapes of pillows and revolving pillow drums, and their method of use, are outside the scope of this book, but because of the variety, there are many types of stands. Those used in the East Midlands are usually tripods, with a bow bracketed out for the pillow, as in Plate 333, but some formed as trestles, both fixed and folding, were used both in the British Isles and abroad. Not all types of pillow lace call for a stand; in Malta and in Spain, where lace making in the open is more common than in England, a long sausage-shaped bolster is used, nearly upright, with the lower end gripped between the knees, the upper end supported against a wall, and the lace worked down the 'sausage'.

Lasts
Small lasts, similar to Plate 338, *L*, were used for making both shoes and socks for babies and dolls. The example illustrated is labelled 'This last was used to make the doll's shoes upon, for Queen Victoria, when a child'. Another, also in the Pinto Collection, is inscribed 'Socks. I.W. used this for her 9 babies'.

Lucets
Lucets were made of hardwood, ivory, bone, mother-of-pearl, etc., about $\frac{1}{8}$ in. thick, cut to the outline of a lyre, rounded on all edges, and with a small central hole. They vary from 3 in. to 6 in. in length; one, $3\frac{3}{4}$ in. long, is shown, Plate 335, *A*. The lucet was a cord-making device, popular in the 17th and 18th centuries, when hand-made cords served many purposes now taken over by other means of suspension or closure. An excellent account of how this now almost forgotten device was used is contained in Sylvia Groves' *History of Needlework Tools*. For details of other cord-making devices, see also *Knitting, Frame and Peg*.

Measures

Ell cloth rules are discussed in Section XIX, *Scientific: Measuring Sticks*. Tape measures, indispensable adjuncts of the textile worker, were formerly encased in plain or ornamental wood, ivory, silver or other cylinders, emerging from a slot in one side, and controlled either by the whole top revolving, or by means of a knob, finial or cranked handle extension of the spool, passing through the top. Until about the mid-19th century, measurements were marked on silk ribbon, not tape, and the calibrations on English ribbons are sometimes unfamiliar, the mediaeval 'nail', or $2\frac{1}{4}$ in. ($\frac{1}{16}$ yd.) cloth measure being used. Thus, a ribbon measure may be marked, 1N, 2N, 3N, $\frac{1}{4}$ yd., $\frac{1}{2}$ yd., 1 yd. Measures were sometimes combined with thread waxers, pincushions, and needle cases. A selection of these measures, some combined with other accessories, is shown, Plate 339. *N* is a Tunbridge stickware, combined pincushion, ribbon measure and thread waxer, *circa* 1820; *P1* is a transferware 'bell' measure, *circa* 1850; *P2* is a Tunbridge mosaic ribbon measure, calibrated in nails, *circa* 1820; *P3* is a Tunbridge paint decorated measure, *circa* 1810; *P4* and *P5* are *cottage orné* types, *circa* 1820—another *cottage orné* measure is included in the compendium clamp, Plate 340, *M*; *P6* and *P7*, a lignum vitae barrel and a plain boxwood case with cranked handle, probably date from about 1870; *Q*, a combined tape measure and needle case in boxwood, with an 'eye' showing views of Battle Abbey, etc., would date from about 1900.

Needles, Needle Cases and Needle Books

Reference has already been made to Adam and Eve sewing fig leaves together, and in St. Matthew, XIX, 24, Jesus is quoted as saying 'It is easier for a camel to go through the eye of a needle, than for a rich man to enter into the kingdom of God'. Survivals show that needles of wood, thorn, fish and animal bones, and ivory were used from early times. A wooden needle, found under the floor of a 17th-century cottage at Cranleigh, Surrey, is shown, Plate 326, *V*. It was probably used for pack thread; sewn hessian packaging was an important branch of industry until very recent times. Needles were made of bronze, iron, silver and even gold, before the now universal steel needle was perfected. Stow, in 1598, records that in Mary's reign (1553–8) '. . . there was a Negro (probably a Moor) made fine Spanish needles in Cheapside, but would neuer teach his Art to any'. Stow also recorded that the making of Spanish needles '. . . was first taught in Englande, by Elias Crowse (Krause) a Germaine, about the Eight yeere of Queene Elizabeth . . . (1566)'. By the 17th century, the English steel hand sewing needle industry was on a large enough scale to warrant granting of a charter to the Worshipful Company of Needlemakers (1656), and in 1669, the needle industry had become sufficiently important to be protected by the prohibition of imports. By the 18th century, Long Crendon, Buckinghamshire, had become the English centre for needle making, but it was not long before Redditch, Studley and Alcester were challenging its pre-eminence. In the 19th century. Redditch became the principal centre, which it has remained ever since.

Needles continued to be an expensive manufacture until the mechanization of the industry in the 19th century. During the 18th century, needles, as befitting their worth, were kept in cases of the finest workmanship. In accordance with what has been described as the 'French distemper' of the time—a disease which has never died out in the world of fashion—the best cases were referred to as *étuis à aiguilles*. Some of them were exquisite products of the jeweller, set with gems and made of gold, silver, gold-mounted agate, rock crystal and lapis lazuli. Others were enamelled on copper, or made of ivory, tortoiseshell, shagreen and wood. The last, although naturally including the simplest and cheapest examples, was also used on the Continent for some *étuis* which rank in the fine art class and are now eagerly sought by collectors. The best of the wooden *étuis* were made of close grained boxwood and were carved by the same highly skilled craftsmen who worked in ivory. They are cut out of the solid and usually have tight-fitting, push-on caps, to prevent rust. The avoidance of rust was very important for such expensive commodities as needles. As William Cowper, the 18th-century poet, lamented:

The needles, once a shining store,
For my sake restless heretofore,
Now rust disus'd, and shine no more,
                    My Mary!'

A small piece of emery cloth was included in *étuis* long after needles ceased to be made by hand, and emery cushions, into which needles were inserted, were normal adjuncts of the sempstress until well into Victoria's reign. A Tunbridge paint decorated example, *circa* 1810, is shown, Plate 326, *U*.

The subjects chosen for carving on 18th-century wood and ivory *étuis* were, in the main, biblical, but a few are mythological, Cupid and Psyche being a favoured subject. The most popular biblical stories carved on *étuis* are, most appropriately, Adam and Eve with the Angel holding a flaming sword. Abraham sacrificing Isaac, and the Madonna and Child also occur. The latter is the central subject on one face of the 4 in. long, French, 18th-century, rectangular, boxwood *étui*, Plate 329, *A*. The reverse face shows a saint and the sides are finely carved with guilloche ornament; the foliage swags and acanthus form two continuous horizontal bands. The 18th-century *étui*, *B*, another beautifully carved boxwood example, and probably Flemish, is the only small example of carved wood, which I have found, showing Delilah shearing the locks of the kneeling Samson. *C*, French, 16th- or 17th-century, is a su-

perbly carved boxwood example with classical heads in lozenges round the lid, and below, faces framed in foliage scrolls, and leaf and flower terminals. *D*, a Flemish (?), 17th- or 18th-century *étui*, is charmingly carved with a very naturalistic mother and child. In a scene below, Abraham is depicted with Isaac. *E*, a French or Flemish, 18th-century specimen, is surmounted by reclining figures of Cupid and Psyche, with a frieze of Pan and dancers encircling the lower part of the case.

During the second half of the 18th century, with needles becoming steadily cheaper, needle cases also tended to become inexpensive, utilitarian trifles; in fact, the simplest of them, mostly 19th-century, plain cylindrical poppets, were the containers in which the needles were sold. But if expense was much less, the variety was almost unlimited and selections, mostly 19th-century, are shown in Plates 326, 339 and 341. The carved fish, Plate 326, *G*, and *H* and *O*, are Swiss or Tyrolean, late 19th-century; *K*, also Swiss or Tyrolean, is a nice, early 19th-century specimen, carved with a boy on a pedestal. *J*, the rolling pin, *M*, the umbrella, and *N*, the simple poppet, are English, 19th-century; *L*, a much worn needlecase, probably Flemish, has a carved lantern with ball above reliefs of the Virtues, and is dated 1770.

Q, *R*, *S* and *T* are 19th-century needle books. *Q* and *R*, Scottish tartan and transfer ware respectively, date from about 1850; *S* and *T*, are Tunbridge mosaic, the former *circa* 1845, the latter *circa* 1820.

In Plate 339, *A* is Swiss, *circa* 1900; *B*, Tunbridge stickware, dated 1854, is shown open; *C1*, a needle stand and *C2*, a poppet, are both mid-19th-century Scottish tartan ware. The two 'G's are the miniature knife box type needle boxes, with sloping tops; *G1* is tartan ware and *G2*, Tunbridge mosaic of the 1830 period. *H* is a Tunbridge slatted needle folder, leather backed and with velvet leaves, probably mid-19th-century. *J* is an exceptionally nice, English,' yew-wood holder, 6 in. high, carved with a lantern and ball. *K*, *L* and *M* are all Swiss or Tyrolean, 19th-century; *L*, with the dog surmount, is a competent carving.

In the top row of Plate 341, are a number of 19th-century needle case, spool and usually thimble combinations. *A*, early 19th-century and shown open, is labelled 'A trifle from Margate'. *B*, of walnut, and *G*, of rosewood and ivory, are also English and probably date from around 1800. *C*, of boxwood, shown in three parts, is another English combination, consisting of spool, needle case and pricker. *D* is a Swiss or Tyrolean, late 19th-century needle and thimble case. *E* and *F*, 'pears', one shown open and one closed, are late 19th-century needle, thimble and reel combinations, which also act as equivalent of darning eggs.

A delightful Regency *cottage orné* compendium clamp of sycamore, made at Tunbridge, is illustrated, Plate 340, *M*. The cottages have red chimneys and green foliage painted on the walls. The four miniature cottages hold needles, thread, pincushion and tape measure.

Netting Tools

The ancient craft of netting falls under two main headings—netting used by fishermen, sailors, fowlers and hunters, the world over, and decorative or lace netting. A single-ended netting needle, 8½ in. long, is illustrated, Plate 335, *B*. For other coarse netting tools, see Section XVIII, *Sailors', Sailmakers' and Fishermen's Devices*.

An inlaid mahogany netting box, used for fancy netting about 1790, is illustrated, Plate 346. It is an exceptionally large example; they are usually about 9 in. by 5 in., but this one is 13½ in. by 7 in. and 4½ in. deep. When the lid is removed, the roller for the foundation loop, is erected on its upstands, which fit into dovetail slots in the box side. Some of the original mahogany gauges are shown behind the box. A possible further use for this device

is discussed at the end of the introduction to *Lace-Making Devices*.

The two ivory and wood implements, with spiral grooves at the pointed end, Plate 335, *D*, are continental and are believed to have been used in fine netting.

Niddy-noddies—see *Reeling Devices*

Oeuf à Gants—see *Darning Devices*

Parfilage—see introduction to *Lace-Making Devices*

Peg Knitting—see *Knitting, Frame and Peg*

Pins, Pincushions and Pin Poppets

For the early history of pins, see Section XIV, *Parcelling, Postage, Sealing, etc.* From about 1600, the pin industry was established at Stroud, Gloucestershire, afterwards spreading to Bristol and Birmingham. Descriptions of pin making in 1740 and 1815 hardly differ, and involve 18 operations. Briefly, brass wire was gauged, straightened, cut into multiple lengths of six pins, ground to a point, re-cut and the re-cut length ground, and so on. The spun wire or coil used for the individual heads was then cut, softened by heat and affixed to the blunt ends of the pins by means of hammer and anvil. The bead effect of the coiled head on old pins, can be clearly seen with a magnifying glass. The next process was tinning and then came tumbling in bran, to polish the pins. The one-piece pin making machine was developed in the U.S.A. Seth Hunt's patent of 1817 was the first, but the machine made by Wright of Massachusetts was the one generally developed, both in the U.S.A. and in England, where pins made after 1840 are all solid one-piece, with stamped heads, and may be plated brass, or steel. Simple, turned wooden cylindric containers filled with pins, known as pin poppets, sold for 1d. early in the 19th century.

Elaborate pincushions were formerly

popular gifts at christenings and were also used with the stuck pins spelling a message for other important domestic or national commemorations. Heart-shaped cushions, or wooden dolls, such as Plate 341, *H*, the 18th-century, satin dressed figure patterned in pins, might be used. The other pincushions and stands in the same picture are 19th-century productions. *J* is an early 19th-century cushion box, labelled 'I Long to See You'. *K*, *M* and *S*, and the good quality pin 'table' *V*, are Tunbridge products. *L*, designed as a miniature globe; and the lace-up boot, *N*, kettle, *O*, buckets, *P* and *Q*, cone, *R*, rosewood table, *T*, and tartan table, *W*, rank as Victorian novelties. A further selection of 19th-century pincushions, discs and pads, is illustrated, Plate 335. *F*, *G*, *L* and *N* are mid-19th-century transfer ware, *M* is fern pattern and *H* and *K* tartan ware; all these are Scottish made. *J* is Tunbridge mosaic. A 'pincushion' which appears very heavy, is probably a needle cushion, filled with emery powder.

A number of 19th-century pincushion clamps are included in Plate 340. *A*, a late example, is grained in simulation of rosewood; *L* is labelled 'A Trifle from London'. *N* is a paint decorated Tunbridge, Regency pincushion; *O*, of rosewood, has a spike alongside the pincushion, presumably used for some operation requiring a pull. *P* is a delightfully, amateurishly made needlework drawer of walnut, surmounted by a brocade covered pincushion. It is inscribed 'Maria 1853'. It is inlaid and constructed with a variety of crude experimental joints. The drawer was obviously too loose and probably ·spilt the contents rather frequently, so the ingenious and unorthodox maker devised the amusing idea of putting 'brakes' on the drawer by splitting the top edges and inserting wedges, which cause the drawer sides to bulge outwards. *Q*, a carved pincushion clamp, is Swiss or Tyrolean; all the others are English. For details of *M*, see *Needles, Needle Cases and Needle Books*.

Pirns—see *Weaving Equipment*

Prickers, Lace—see *Lace-Making Devices, Lace Prickers*

Reel Stands

The cotton reel, as we know it today, arrived in the 1820s or 1830s (see *Cotton and Thread Barrels and Boxes*), and the reel stand, known in Yorkshire as a bobbin tree, was not far behind; reel stands were made throughout Victoria's long reign. Although they differ in detail, they are alike in basic principle and some were both decorative and useful. A central stem on a circular base supports one or more revolving galleries, which may be fitted with pegs, or connected by wires, threaded through the reels. The centre stem may be surmounted by a pincushion, a cup, or a thimble holder. A selection is shown, Plate 342. They vary in height from $3\frac{1}{2}$ in. to 11 in. *A* is elm, surmounted by a pincushion, holds 14 reels, and is late 19th-century. *B*, of mahogany, a clumsy, late 19th-century design, is also surmounted by a pincushion and holds 12 reels. *C*, also of mahogany, an early 19th-century, smaller and lighter design, which holds 12 reels. *D*, of lignum vitae, a peg type, surmounted by a pincushion in a cup, dates from the Regency period and was probably intended for small refillable reels; the pegs are too close together for modern reels. *E* is walnut, surmounted by a pincushion, holds 15 reels and is mid-19th century. *F*, a very nice peg-type stand, of yew-wood, surmounted by a pincushion, holds 20 reels, and may have been intended for display in a village shop in the mid-19th century. *G*, early 19th-century, is rosewood, surmounted by a pincushion and holds five reels and a thimble. *H* is an unusual ebonised and chip carved stand, with ivory finials; it is surmounted by a pincushion in a cup, holds 10 reels and is late 19th-century. *J* is a handsome, 18th-century, walnut spool box, decorated with silver points and lined with brocade. *K*, the attractive rosewood twist stand, holds 8 of the small, Regency, refillable reels; it is surmounted by an oval cup, which may have held a thread waxer and thimble.

Reeling Devices

After yarn had been spun on a spindle or spinning wheel, it was transferred on to a wrap or clock reel, a rotary instrument which skeined and measured it. The original wrap wheel is always said to have been invented by Sir Richard Arkwright. It was copied in most parts of the world, but basically it is a six-armed star which, turning on a horizontal axis, transmits to a dial, a reading of the length of yarn wound. On the original machine, one turn of the reel equalled 1.5 yards of yarn, 80 turns equalled 120 yards or one wrap, and 7 wraps, registered by a complete revolution of the hand round the clock, equalled 840 yards or one hank. I cannot help wondering whether Sir Richard, in fact, only added the clock to an existing device, in the third quarter of the 18th century. Some of the wrap reels which I have seen, look 100 years earlier in their turnery.

The earlier device, which was in general use for the same purpose in most parts of Europe and in North America, was the cross reel, in English speaking countries almost universally known as a niddy-noddy. The Virgin is shown using one in Plate 401 and a fine specimen from North America, unusual because it is carved, is illustrated, Plate 348. The niddy-noddy is also shown in use in several 16th-century, Dutch paintings; in isolated communities, it was still used during the last century.

The niddy-noddy, which was held in one hand by the central stem, was wound with a waving motion, to the rhythm of a song, the opening line of which ran, 'Niddy-noddy, niddy-noddy, two heads and one body'. This ancient but simple skeining device is now so little known that most people, on seeing it, not only do not know its purpose, but also think that it has been assembled

incorrectly; this is because the two heads, or cross bars, rather like coat-hangers mounted centrally on opposite ends of the turned stem, are arranged so that their axes are at right angles to each other. In use, an end of the wool or twine is tied to one end of one arm and rapidly criss-crossed over the four ends of the two arms, until a skein is formed. The length of the criss-crosses of wool bear a definite relationship to an ell and so the niddy-noddy was a combined measure and skeiner; but as the length of an ell varied in different countries, so likewise did the size of a niddy-noddy. See also *Winding Devices*.

Ribbon Threaders

The ribbon threader, a round-ended, tapering rod, nearly 1 ft. long, with a large eye at the narrow end, was once a commonplace implement, although now a considerable rarity. An 11 in. long, lignum vitae example is shown, with its ribbon, Plate 335, *V*; it could be 17th- or 18th-century. In the 17th century, ribbon threaders were needed for drawing ribbons through slots or loops of fashionable garments of both sexes. In the 18th century, they were used for weaving ribbons in and out of the elaborate *coiffures* of the ladies.

Scissor Boxes and Display Stands

Some good quality, velvet-lined, hardwood boxes of tapering form, were made for scissors in the 19th century. Earlier cases were generally of leather or padded fabric, or the scissors were included with other implements in an *étui*. Scissors display stands for use in shops, are illustrated and described in Section XXV, *Trade and Craft Devices*.

Scutching or Swingling Knives—see *Flax Preparation Devices*

Sewing Machines

Sewing machines, being all metal apart from their stands and covers, are outside the scope of this book. The first patentee appears to have been Charles Weisenthal, who took out an English patent in 1775. Thomas Saint patented a model in 1790. Barthelmy Thimonier probably produced the first practical machine in Paris (1830). Newton and Archbold were other pioneers, with their English patents of 1841.

Shuttles—see *Tatting and Knotting Devices*, also *Weaving Devices*

Silk Devices
The silkworm is said to have been reared and silk spun in China for some 4,500 years; China apparently kept her secret for 3,000 years, for not until about 1,500 years ago are silkworms reputed to have been smuggled from China to India by a Chinese princess, who married the ruler of the Indian State of Khotan. Although raw silk and silk fabric had reached the Mediterranean countries by the 6th century B.C., according to most authorities it was the 16th century A.D. before silkworm breeding, travelling by way of Spain and Italy, was established in France, and not until the 17th century did it come to England, largely as a result of encouragement given by the Stuart monarchs. This is probably true so far as silkworm breeding is concerned; in fact, sericulture has never been a large-scale success in England, owing to the climate, but silk fabrics were being imported into England much earlier, and on a more magnificent scale than is generally realized. In 1242, the streets of London were covered or shaded with silk for the reception of Richard, the King's brother, on his return from the Holy Land. Matthew Paris recorded that at the marriage of Alexander III of Scotland, to Margaret, daughter of Henry III, in 1251, one thousand English knights appeared at the wedding in *cointises* of silk. How large the English silk industry was before the advent of emigrants is unknown, but to protect it against foreign competition, an English Act

of Parliament was passed in the 14th century, forbidding the importation of silken thread and manufactured goods. Its object was 'to protect certain old-established silk women against Lombards and Italians, who brought such quantities of silk threads and rebands (ribbons) into the country that the established native throwsters were impoverished'. In Elizabeth's reign, about the time that the Flemish weavers began to infiltrate, the silk weavers must have been enjoying a boom. Harrison, referring to 1568–70, says that until then

> '... there were but few silke shoppes in London, and those few were onely kept by women, and maide seruants and not by men, so now they are: At which time all the silke shoppes in London had not so much, nor so many sorts of silke, gold or siluer threed, nor sorts of silke lace, and gold and siluer lace, as is this day in diuers particular shopps in Cheapeside, and other places'.

A number of Flemish silk weavers settled in England during the struggle against Spain in the late 16th century. A further influx of French weavers occurred approximately 100 years later, after the Revocation of the Edict of Nantes. The emigrant weavers settled in East London, technically improved the industry and soon made the name of Spitalfields silk famous. Later, they spread their industry to certain districts of Norfolk and Suffolk, Braintree in Essex, Canterbury, Macclesfield, Derby, Coventry, Manchester and Paisley; all these towns or districts achieved renown for different silk products. Within 20 miles of where I write, a small silk industry developed early in the 19th century; Robson's 1838 *Directory of Hertfordshire*, records 1,200 men and women employed in throwing and winding silk.

Silk Cocoon Winders
In silk preparation, the first operation is to obtain the fine thread from the cocoon, after it has been killed by immersion in hot

water. An 18th-century, mahogany cocoon winder, used for this purpose, is illustrated, Plate 337, *O*. After removing the outside flossy covering, the operator placed the cocoons in a bowl filled with hot water in the bowl stand. The hot water removed the knub or inner covering and softened the natural gum in the silk, and allowed it to be wound off on to the spool with cranked handle, above.

Silk Reel Stands
The silk on the spool of the cocoon winder was then transferred to the lead-weighted reel stand, Plate 337, *S*, which appropriately is made of mulberry wood. What may be another silk reeling device is shown among the clamp fittings, Plate 340, *K*.

Silk Throwers
A further important stage was the silk throwing or spinning and twisting of the fine thread, carried out by the throwster. A rare, old silk thrower is shown, Plate 335, *E*. It is a Scandinavian specimen, carved and picked out in red and black, 18 in. long, made in two parts, loosely dowelling together, so that the upper can revolve in the lower stem (which has its cross bar missing). The silk threads were passed over the four notches in the cross bar; if six threads were being operated, this bar would have been replaced by one with six notches, and so on. The slot in the lower portion takes a fixed bar, probably of hardwood, which holds the device vertical, but not rigidly so; thus, if any of the silk threads became knotted and tension were exerted, there was some backward and forward play, otherwise the silken thread would have broken. The threads, after they left the arm, were twisted on a wheel. Now, the whole operation is carried out by machine.

The recent history of the silk thrower illustrated is interesting and exemplifies the unexpected thrills in collecting. In 1946, we bought a 'lot' of knitting sheaths at Sotheby's. It contained the lower half of the silk thrower which, having a hole in the top and a slot lower down, could well have been a knitting sheath with belt loop. Somehow, we did not think it was, and we put it aside in our 'dunno-what' corner. Some months later, we found the other half in an antique dealer's in the provinces!

Silk Winders and Skein Holders
Multipointed star and cog outline, flat silk winders of wood, ivory, mother-of-pearl, etc., were found in every work box until about 1850, because silk was not generally reeled until much later than cotton. A selection of 19th century winders is shown, Plate 326. *F1* is Tunbridge mosaic; *F2*, Scottish tartan; *F3*, Jerusalem olivewood; *F4* and *F5*, Scottish transfer ware. 'The Wulsilk Holder', Plate 337, *R*, Reg. No. 689112, measures 7 in. by $2\frac{1}{4}$ in. by $\frac{3}{8}$ in., has a hole through from side to side, and gives the impression that it was revolved on some kind of late 19th-century machine. The Tunbridge mosaic silk skein holder, Plate 326, *A*, was another popular mid- to late 19th-century work box adjunct. The rosewood case, open at both ends, contains a sliding, folding 'book' of aromatic cedar, which holds the skeins. See also *Winding Devices*.

Skeining Devices—see *Reeling Devices*

Spindles—see *Spinning Devices, Distaffs and Spindles*

Spinning Devices
The three primary devices used in spinning yarn were cards, distaffs, and spindles. In the late 16th century Wierix engraving, Plate 399 the Virgin is seen carding; in Plate 403, she is spinning with a distaff and spindle. Where still in use for hand spinning, none of the three devices have changed basically in the last 400 years.

Cards
Carding was the first operation. The fibres

were first cleaned and combed between two cards—brush-like instruments with wire or metal spikes inset either into wooden backs or mounted on leather, nailed to the wood. Cards set with thorns have been found at the Glastonbury prehistoric lake village. See also *Wool Teasing Fork*.

Distaffs and Spindles

After 'dressing' and folding, the roll of fibres is tied to a distaff—originally a natural stick, probably with a forked or gnarled head to grip the fibres; it was held under the left arm, leaving both hands free to draw the threads from the roll to the spindle. The first thread was attached to the neck of the spindle, which was set spinning and as it rotated, it spun the fibres. As a spindle gradually falls to the ground, it has to be raised at intervals and wound. A whorl or weight, a stone or lump of metal with a hole in it was sometimes jammed on the lower end of a spindle to keep it upright and increase the momentum. Grooves from the whorl can often be seen on spindles. An old French spindle, 7½ in. long and impossible to date, is shown, right of Plate 328. In the same picture are three distaff heads. That on the left is English, 17½ in. long and dated 1812. The two in the centre, 11¾ in. and 9 in. long respectively, are Scandinavian and, as can be seen, are highly decorative. The larger is ornamented with loose rings, and is probably 19th-century, the smaller, 18th-century; both are picked out in colour and doubtless represented a man's winter contribution to his wife's spinning.

Plate 327, *C1* and *C2*, shows two halves of a very finely carved and turned boxwood distaff with loose rings. When fitted together, it makes up a length of 31 in. Actually, each half is also in two sections, joined by boxwood pins and sockets and silver collars. Probably Flemish work of the 17th century, it was formerly in the Trapnell Collection.

The floor-standing, Scandinavian distaff, left of Plate 343, is another distinguished example of *husflid* (for *husflid*, see Introduction, *Peasant Art*). It dates from about 1800, has a lead-weighted stool and a revolving head, is 42½ in. high, competently carved and picked out in red, green, and black.

Spinning Wheels

By using a spindle horizontally and revolving it between two points by means of a wheel and driving belt, the spinning wheel was evolved; where or when it was born, is uncertain, but it had arrived in the British Isles by the 16th century. In the Wierix engraving, Plate 402, the Virgin is using an early hand-operated machine. The Horner Collection of wheels in Belfast Museum is certainly a good place to study evolution, and the numerous types. Two spinning wheels are illustrated, Plate 344 and 345. Plate 345, turned from mixed hardwoods, is a typical cottage wheel, of the so-called low Irish or Dutch type, but it was also used in England and Scotland. It is a pattern which hardly changed over the centuries; this one probably dates from the 18th century. The highly sophisticated specimen, Plate 344, which was doubtless used by a fashionable lady in some grand mansion, is English, dates from about 1785 and is an elegant and attractive example of turnery in satinwood, with painted decoration on the drawer front. Several English, late 18th-century spinning wheels of fine quality have come to light, bearing the label of John Planta at Fulneck, near Leeds. His work represents the last phase, for by 1780–90, the wheels which, spinning one thread at a time, had been a feature of so many homes, for 300 years, were falling into disuse. This was due first to Hargreave's invention of about 1757 of the 'Spinning Jenny' (named after his wife), which could spin 120 threads at once, Sir Richard Arkwright's spinning machine of 1769, and Crompton's mule spinning frame of about 1774.

His drawings leave no doubt that, about

1500, that amazing all-round genius, Leonardo da Vinci, anticipated many of the fundamentals of these inventions, when he drew out, in considerable detail, a machine for spinning with a flyer, a machine using a flyer as winding means and for a very ingenious method of automatically distributing the thread, and a cord machine with 15 spindles. Leonardo's inventions were not developed and it was left to a German wood carver, Johann Jürgen, in 1530, to work out the different and generally adopted method of effecting even distribution of the thread on the bobbin of a spinning wheel, by means of a series of hooks inserted along the arms of the flyer. Leonardo's idea of the moving flyer was vastly superior and it was this method, but substituting a moving bobbin for a moving flyer, that was re-invented by Sir Richard Arkwright, 275 years later.

Stilettos

Stilettos were an important adjunct of the old-time work box. They were made with handles of various materials, including wood, ivory and mother-of-pearl; those which were carried on the person, had protective cases, such as Plate 326, *W*, which has the handle and sheath of thorn-wood; *X*, in the same picture, has a plain handle. See also, *Lace-Making Devices, Lace Prickers*.

Swifts—see *Winding Devices*

Tape Measures—see *Measures*

Tapestry Frames—see *Frames*

Tatting and Knotting Devices

For the subtleties of the now almost forgotten crafts of tatting and knotting, one cannot do better than refer to Sylvia Grove's *History of Needlework Tools*. Miss Groves says that 'The practice of knotting thread or cord for use in embroidery was well known in this country in late medieval times, but did not become at all general until the end of the 17th century'. In knotting, oval shuttles, 4 in. to 6 in. long, were used. As it was a fashionable pastime, many of the shuttles were elaborate examples of gold or silver filigree; tortoise-shell, mother-of-pearl, and ivory shuttles were also made, but humble wooden ones exist, although they are rare. The majority of wooden shuttles now extant, are only about 2 in. long, pointed at each end, date from the 19th century and were used for tatting. Plate 335, *A1*, shows a transfer decorated example. Although the technique of tatting was similar to that of knotting, tatting produced a form of lace.

Teasing Forks—see *Wool Teasing Forks*

Textile Printing Blocks—see Section XVI, *Printing and Woodcut and Engraving Blocks*

Thimbles and Thimble Cases

The earliest type of thimble seems to have been a protective leather finger sheath, open at the top; this type, in various materials, is still used by tailors. The sailmaker's leather palm with inset thimble plate, is described in Section XVIII, *Sailors', Sailmakers' and Fishermen's Devices*. Thimbles have been made of bronze, brass, gold and silver from early times. The last two were important enough to be mentioned in 16th-century Tudor inventories, and a few have survived. From then onwards, they have been a fashionable form of gift, and many with charming poesies engraved on them, were given in presentation cases in the 17th, 18th and 19th centuries. Wooden thimbles were also made; an Irish example in bog oak and a boxwood specimen are illustrated, Plate 339, *W* and *X*. They are found particularly in 19th-century, Swiss, Tyrolean and German cases and were probably intended chiefly as tourist souvenirs. In the same row is a selection of metal thimbles with their wooden cases; all are, I think, 19th-century. *S* is boxwood; *T* and *U*, which contain needle cushions and thimbles, are mulberry wood; *V* is Tunbridge stickware; these four are all English. *Y* and *Z*, carved to represent a walnut and a pine cone respectively, are Swiss or Tyrolean. A number of combined thimble, needle and spool cases are described under *Needles, Needle Cases and Needle Books*.

Thread-waxers

Until thread was machine twisted, a thread-waxer was an important work box adjunct. It consisted either of a cake of beeswax for coarse work, or white wax for fine work, or a 1 in. length of candle was cut and fitted, sometimes on a thin rod, between two rimmed button ends of wood, bone, ivory or silver. Sometimes thread-waxers were combined with pincushions, tape measures or needle cases. Both the Tunbridge mosaic makers and the Scottish tartan ware manufacturers included thread-waxers in their 19th-century range. A tartan-ended example is shown, Plate 339, *D*, and Tunbridge specimens, *N* and *O*; the former is combined with a tape measure and a pincushion. Jane Toller, in her book, *Antique Miniature Furniture*, referring to the prevalence of ear spoons in *étuis*, says that they contain ' . . . in an unbelievably small space a thimble, pair of scissors, pair of tweezers, stiletto, bodkin and a spoon for getting the wax out of the owner's ears (which was the natural means of waxing the thread, then not already twisted as it is nowadays)'. It sounds a most unpleasant habit, but I find it perfectly credible.

Weaving Equipment

Large looms are rather outside the scope of this work, but some of the hand loom weavers' appliances are likely to come the way of the collector of wooden bygones, so are illustrated, Plate 337, *A*, *B* and *C*, and briefly described here. These three specimens came from an old mill in the Isle of Man, which closed down in 1955. The cone, *A*, is described under *Knitting Machines*. The iron-tipped shuttle, *B*, probably about 100 years old, is $17\frac{1}{2}$ in. long, but others from the same mill vary from 10 in. to 20 in. in length. The smaller ones are mostly of boxwood, but the larger examples are dogwood; large examples are also made of cornel or beech; box, although the best, is expensive and difficult to obtain for the very long shuttles, like the one illustrated. A full pirn, early 20th-century, is shown in the shuttle, and an empty one, *C*, alongside. The pirns, mostly of beech, vary in length and diameter, according to the size of the shuttles.

Bead Looms
Indian beadwork, popular in the late 18th and throughout most of the 19th century for girdles, bracelets, etc., and bands such as that round the knife stand, Plate 61, was woven on an Apache loom, as illustrated, Plate 337, *Q*; it has 5 in. long notched bars, placed $7\frac{1}{2}$ in. apart. The warp threads are attached at one end to the roller, pass over the two notched bars and are secured at the other end by three wooden pegs. The actual process of working the beads on the loom, is fully described in *The History of Needlework Tools*, by Sylvia Groves.

Braid Looms
Braid looms were used mostly during the last quarter of the 18th century and during the Regency period, for making ornamental braids and ribbons. They were superseded by the Jacquard loom. Being a fashionable occupation the braid looms themselves are usually high grade products. Nevertheless, Plate 347, is of exceptional quality. It is English, late 18th-century, of mahogany, inlaid with ivory and is lead weighted, to keep it from slipping, when in use. It measures $13\frac{1}{2}$ in. by $5\frac{1}{2}$ in., with the frame upstanding $8\frac{1}{2}$ in. high. The warp is wound on a beam, turned by a

cranked handle and checked by a ratchet and spawl.

Winding Devices

After yarn had been skeined (see *Reeling Devices*), it had to be wound into a ball. Judging by my own childhood, the most favoured device was the outstretched hands of a child, with the skein looped over four fingers and held in place by the thumbs; the child being unavailable, or on strike, the backs of two chairs, placed back to back, sufficed, unless one of the many varieties of purpose-made wool winders were available. One of the most popular of the old devices was a swift, made rather on the principle of a revolving umbrella, without its cover. It increased its diameter as the slatted frame was pushed up on the stem; it was made to stand on the floor or on a table, sometimes with a wool bowl incorporated in the base, or it was fitted to a clamp. In Plate 400, the Virgin is depicted using a 16th-century, floor-standing swift of this type, and Plate 340, *E*, shows an English, 19th-century, clamp-mounted example. Two skeleton reels, with space adjustment between them, served the same purpose. Plate 340, *G1* and *G2*, are a pair with clamp attachments; *C*, in rosewood, is one of a smaller pair, probably for silk, and *H* is a side winder, again one of a pair. In Plate 343, two English examples of the same type of swift in stand form, are shown. The 18th-century, mahogany specimen, right, has peg adjustments. The 19th-century example, centre, surmounted by a wool bowl, has screw adjustable brass collars, which travel on the stem.

Another entirely different pattern of revolving swift, with telescopic arms mounted with pegs and a wool bowl on top, is shown, Plate 338, *G*; this particular walnut specimen is unmistakably 19th-century, probably about 1840–50, but the identical device, with more elegant stem outline, is illustrated in Plate 3 of *Manuel du Tourneur*, 1792.

Wool Bowls and Globes—see *Knitting Wool Holders*

Wool Teasing Forks

The use of cards for cleaning and combing fibres, is referred to under *Spinning Devices, Cards*. When wool was being prepared, another implement that was sometimes used was the teasing fork, Plate 338, *J*. This simple device of ashwood, $23\frac{1}{2}$ in. long, with a main stem and tines bent through two cross bars, threaded on the stem, is impossible to date, and very little seems known about it.

Wool Winders—see *Winding Devices*

Work Basket Stands [Cats], Work Boxes and Work Tables

The work bag, pouch and basket have been made and used from time immemorial. Some of the so-called lace boxes (for *Lace Boxes*, see Section XXIII, *Toilet and Bedroom Accessories*), veneered in the current fashions, padded inside and silk lined, but unfitted, may really have been intended as work boxes; but the fitted work box and work table mostly date from after 1800. From then onwards, both were made in endless variety and many of the finest of the boxes or caskets were made in the Orient for the European market, and the implements fitted in here. Oriental boxes are found in carved lacquer, veneered with various exotic woods, or covered in tortoiseshell, mother-of-pearl, or engraved ivory. European novelties include miniature grand pianos and *cottages ornés*, fitted with sewing devices. The Tunbridge mosaic workers made a large variety of fitted work boxes and caskets; one in cube and vandyke pattern, dating from 1810–20, is pictured, Plate 341, *U*. The Tunbridge thimble holders, needlework books, thread-waxers, etc., now found separate, were originally fittings in such boxes. Another type of work box with a well, dating from about 1840–50, is shown, Plate 341, *X*; it is a miniature edition of a full-size work table of the same period. Many of the work tables made during the first half of the 19th century, have a pleated silk, hard-bottomed bag fixed to a frame, which slides out under the drawer or well of the table. The work tables with a well sometimes have a removable, reversible top, one side of which is inlaid to serve as a draughts or backgammon board; these were particularly a fashion of the Regency period and some of them are of the highest quality.

A novelty of the late 18th-century, was the cat or work basket stand. Cats are said to have gained their name because they always land on their feet. The true cat, like the mahogany specimen, left of Plate 349, is formed as a double tripod, with cross ringed legs or spokes radiating from a central ball, so arranged that three spokes always form legs, and three always point diagonally upwards, constituting secure ledges or holders for a circular object. Another type of cat, not reversible, right of Plate 349, has the upward radiating spokes fitting into a centre ball, which revolves on the stem of a cabriole-footed tripod; this example is also mahogany. When I wrote *Treen*, 20 years ago, I accepted the general opinion that wooden 'cats' were variants of the metal cats originally used for keeping food warm in front of the fire, now mostly employed for holding ice buckets in restaurants. These metal cats were larger versions of the iron caltrop with six-pointed spikes, which the Romans threw on the ground to hinder enemy advance by wounding the feet of men and horses. I always had some reservation about wooden cats being plate holders, and I voiced my misgivings in some later articles, pointing out that (1) it did not seem logical to place a polished wooden object near enough to a fire for it to keep food warm; (2) whilst some cats have their spokes threaded in, others are glued and the glue would gradually perish in the heat; (3) they seemed too delicate for their alleged purpose.

Cats are usually sold now to hold flower bowls or witch balls and this is practically their original purpose—one that is made clear by a contemporary account written by Sophie v. la Roche, on her visit to London in 1786. She wrote

'I will just mention the neat stands for work-baskets which have just arrived at Lady Fielding's, consisting of three smooth round legs made of mahogany, or of any other wood attractively painted, placed next to one another and fastened. The pretty embroidered work-baskets or neat flower-vases placed on them in the corner of the room form a charming decoration, and they are very convenient to carry to and fro for working purposes and take up very little space.'

Wrap Wheels—see *Reeling*

XXII

Tobacco Accessories

Tobacco, alternatively praised and reviled, smoked and sniffed, has brought into being many small wooden objects.

Probably no one will ever know where or when tobacco was first used by man, nor whether he commenced by sniffing it or smoking it. The divination of omens in smoke, expelled through a pipe or tube from the mouth, goes back to priestly ritual in ancient civilizations, but the smoke was not necessarily from tobacco: there are records of medicinal smoking of herbs in Europe before tobacco was introduced.

What is indisputable is that tobacco came to Europe from America. Columbus seems to have been the first European to report on it; he observed smoking on his first voyage to the Bahamas and West Indies in 1492, and snuff taking on his second voyage, 1494–6, but there is no record that he brought tobacco to Europe. In 1502, other Spaniards reported that the weed had been chewed in South America from time immemorial and was considered 'good medicine'. While the custom on some West Indian islands was to roll tobacco into a cigar and smoke it, the majority of natives of Central America seem to have smoked tobacco in pipes or by inhaling through their nostrils, into which were inserted the twin tubes of a Y-shaped cane, the single, long leg of which was held over the embers of a wood fire, on which tobacco

leaves were allowed to smoulder. The leaves themselves and the plant from which they came, were known by different names in various regions. The Y-shaped instrument of smoking was the tobago, and it was the supposed resemblance of the shape of the island of Tobago to a Y which, when he passed it from the South-west, caused Columbus to give it this name; the island was neither named after the plant nor vice versa.

Words have a way of changing their meaning, and not only has the name of the instrument of smoking passed to the material smoked, but the name given to the smoker has now passed to the vendor of tobacco, for in 16th- and early 17th-century literature, the smoker was known as the tobacconist and he was usually said to 'drink' tobacco and get drunk on the fumes.

As the pipe, the cigar and snuff taking were all known in America before the introduction of tobacco to Europe, all that we have added is the doubtful blessing of the cigarette.

Francisco Hernandez, who introduced the plant to Spain in 1559, may have been the first European to plant it, although the claim was disputed by Frère André Thevet, who had been in Brazil in 1555 and published a book about his travels in 1558. In this book, he described tobacco—accurately—and stated that he had brought seeds to his garden in Angoulême and was growing tobacco there. The most famous name in the story is that of Jean Nicot, French Ambassador to Portugal from 1559 to 1561, for in sending seeds of the plant to Catherine de Medici, Queen of France, he gave his name to nicotine, and for a time tobacco was known as 'The Queen's Herb'. It is interesting that tobacco's introduction to the continent of Europe was entirely on medical grounds. There is a certain grim humour in the fact that cancer was among the many diseases and disorders which tobacco was supposed to cure.

Britain introduced tobacco essentially for smoking; snuffing came 100 years later, but in Spain, Italy, Russia and Ireland, snuffing was probably established as early as smoking. Among popular rival claimants for introducing tobacco to England are Sir Walter Raleigh, Sir Francis Drake, Sir John Hawkins and Ralph Lane, Governor of Virginia. Raleigh is the most popular contender for the title, particularly because, since the 18th century, the story of the bucket of water thrown by a servant over the first smoker he had ever seen, has become associated entirely with Raleigh. Prior to the 18th century, this legend is found attached to many other persons, and the bucket of water is sometimes a flagon of wine or a tankard of ale. William Harrison, the Elizabethan chronicler, who commenced writing his description of England in the 1570s, soon after the time of the introduction of tobacco to England, says:

'Tobacco was first brought, and made knowne in England by Sir John Hawkins, about the yeere one thousand five hundred sixty five,* but not used by most englishmen in many yeers after, though at this day commonly used by most men and many women . . . .'

* In Cawdor Castle, Scotland, there is a chimney-piece dated 1510 depicting a fox smoking a pipe. How the fox obtained his tobacco at so early a date is unknown!

This seems fairly conclusive evidence in favour of Hawkins as the introducer, but in the third edition of Harrison's work, published in 1631, a footnote is added:

'Sir Walter Raleigh was the first that brought tobacco into use, when all men wondered what it meant.'

If you accept 'brought tobacco into use' as meaning popularizing it as a pleasurable smoke and a fashion, rather than as a medicine, you have, I think, the true explanation, for certainly Ralph Lane brought tobacco home to Raleigh in 1586, and by the following year he was cultivating it on his estate in Ireland. Raleigh remained a confirmed smoker until his last minutes on the scaffold in 1617.

It must be remembered, too, that James I anonymously published his *Counterblaste to Tobacco* in 1603 (he acknowledged its authorship some years later), and in it he branded Raleigh, the man he loathed and judicially murdered, as the instigator of the tobacco habit. The section of the arrogant, bombastic treatise reads:

'Now the corrupted baseness of the first use of tobacco doeth very well agree with the foolish and groundless first entry thereof into this kingdome. It is not so long since the first entry of this abuse amongst us here, as this present age can well remember both *the first* author and the form of the first introduction of it amongst us. It was neither brought in by King, great conqueror, nor learned Doctor of Physic. With the report of a *great discovery for a conquest*, some two or three savage men were brought in together with this savage custom. But the pity is the poor wild barbarous men died, but that vile barbarous custom is yet alive, yea, in fresh vigour . . . .'

James ended with:

'Surely smoke becomes a kitchen farre better than a dining chamber; and yet it makes a kitchen oftentimes in the inward parts of men, soyling and infecting with an unctuous and oyly kind of soote as hath been found in some great tobacco takers, that after death were opened. A custom loathsome to the eye, harmfull to the braine, dangerous to the lungs, and in the black stinking fume thereof, nearest resembling the horrible stygian smoke of the pit that is bottomless.'

Some may think that James 'had something' in that last sentence and that it was care for his subjects which also prompted him to raise the duty on tobacco from 2d. to the then penal figure of 6s. 10d. per lb. His record, however, shows that obtaining money interested him much more than anyone else's welfare and quite apart from the lucrative trade which he did in creating large-scale patents of nobility for cash, he also—and this instances what a humbug he was—diverted the taxation from tobacco to himself; moreover, he granted, for cash, a monopoly to the Worshipful Company of Clay Pipe Makers! The history of tobacco seems to have been a series of blasts and counterblasts.

In many European countries, during parts of the 17th century, Church and State combined to stamp out tobacco. Innocent XII excommunicated those who took snuff or tobacco in St. Peter's, Rome; at Bern, prohibition of tobacco was incorporated in the Ten Commandments; in Russia, penalties varied from slitting the lips, or amputation of the nose, to public knouting; whilst in Turkey, the penalty was death. In England, where the penalty under James I was only pecuniary—as it has been ever since—smoking increased rapidly, to the great benefit of the king's finances. By 1614, there were upwards of 7,000 shops selling tobacco in and near London. Later in the century, the use of tobacco was prescribed by doctors for its disinfectant properties and was even used in churches as incense. The plague of 1665 gave the habit further impetus, smokers and chewers being considered immune and even children being taught to smoke. Pepys records 'chawing' tobacco to take away apprehension of the

plague and it is related that a certain Etonian was whipped by his master for refusing to smoke when instructed. Smoking went on increasing until about 1700, but in the second half of the 18th century it declined rapidly in favour of snuff taking.

Snuff taking, formerly known as sternutation, came under two distinct headings—habit and fashion. The latter was naturally responsible for the finest bygones associated with snuffing. These, the elaborately carved or inlaid snuff rasps, alternatively known as *râpes à tabac*, for individual use in rasping tobacco into snuff, and some of the many varieties of snuff boxes are described and illustrated under their respective headings. Snuff taking in 16th-century western Europe originated as a supposed curative for various maladies, and continued in use for 300 years as an antidote to evil smells. On the Continent, it had by 1620 also become a social grace among a large proportion of the aristocracy, and one with a distinct etiquette of its own among nosologists, as the nose-hungry were known. Although there were also a few individual snuff takers in Britain and it was a well-established custom in Scotland early in the 17th century, it is generally accepted among historians that the exiled Court of Charles II, both men and women, brought the fashion home, as a result of their continental sojourn. It does not seem to have made great progress in challenging the supremacy of smoking, even in Court circles, until snuff taking William and Mary came to the throne in 1689. During their reigns, the vogue spread rapidly in aristocratic circles, and by the time of Anne (1702), another confirmed snuff taker, it is related that scarcely a man of rank but carried the insidious dust about him, either in an elaborate box of wood, horn, agate, tortoiseshell, enamel, gold or silver, or else in the hollow, ornamental silver head of his cane at that time as indispensable an appendage as a sword.

Throughout the 18th century, and

during the first 30 years of the 19th, snuff taking remained the fashionable addiction, gaining in popularity from the examples of the Hanoverian kings and queens. Queen Charlotte, although only 17 when she married George III, was such a confirmed snuff taker that she was known as 'Snuffy Charlotte'. The Prince Regent and his Beau Nash set of dandies continued the snuff fashion at the top level, but by this time, even in aristocratic circles, the custom of grinding one's own snuff freshly, with an elaborate continental pocket rasp, was dying rapidly. Instead, the nobility had their individually perfumed snuffs blended and prepared for them by high-grade snuff specialists, who often named the brand after the patron. At Windsor Castle, George IV had a snuff jar chamber, with a page in charge of the expensive snuffs, stored in labelled jars, bottles and canisters, on tiers of shelves. Additionally, Fribourg and Treyer, of the Haymarket, acted in an overall supervisory capacity.

Dates on some of the rasps illustrated show that they were made as late as 1775, but all those in question are continental and there is no proof that they were used in England. Hardly any individual snuff rasps seem to have been made in Britain, because the beaux who used them thought it beneath them to have anything other than the latest continental fancy, whilst lower class habitués had bought their snuff ready ground from the commencement of the 18th century.

In fact, snuff taking as a habit, among all classes in Great Britain, as opposed to a fashionable addiction of society, dates fortuitously from the introduction of ready ground snuff in 1702. In that year the fleet, under the command of Sir George Rooke, captured from the Spanish, near Cadiz, several thousand barrels of choice Spanish snuff, and near Vigo, a further cargo of Havana snuff, intended for the Spanish market. This vast quantity of sneezing powder was sold at the English seaports at a very low price, the proceeds being prize money for the benefit of sailors and officers. Thus was the general snuff habit born in Britain. At first tobacconists and apothecaries met the demand for the powder by grinding it in mills similar to those illustrated in Section XI, *Mortars, Grinders and Graters*, using mostly those with iron tipped or studded pestles. Some few were made in two parts, the upper with an iron grater base, through which the *carotte* of tobacco was rubbed into the compartment below. An alternative was a large grater tray, with a receptacle below it. After rasping the roll or *carotte* to a rough 'bran', it was then pounded in a basin mortar, with a peculiarly shaped pestle. By about 1740, snuff was being prepared wholesale, in a large grinding mill, powered by a horse or by a water wheel, and specialist snuff shops were coming into being.

In the 18th and 19th centuries, hundreds of varieties of snuff were sold, flavoured or perfumed with different scented oils. In the main, they came under eight headings—coarse and fine, dry and moist, dark and light, scented and plain. Rapee, the best-known coarse, dark snuff, derived its name from the French *râper*, to grate. It was available plain or scented and was made from Virginia tobacco. It is generally regarded as the parent of all other snuffs. Artificially coloured snuffs, finely powdered varieties, and, above all, scented snuffs, according to old accounts, lent themselves to most repulsive forms of adulteration. The fearsome additives were effectively cloaked by the perfumed oils of bergamot, orange, jasmine, violet, lily of the valley, civet, musk, cedar and various wines, in which the *carottes* of tobacco were steeped, after the leaves had been prepared by steeping in water to which various salts had been added.

The Scots had no use for these scented varieties, and Scotch snuff, made only from the stalks of tobacco, was renowned for its purity. In Ireland and Wales, a taste developed for snuff made from toasted or roasted tobacco. According to old accounts, a large tobacco warehouse was burnt down in Dublin, and one Lundy Foot, a porter at the said warehouse, purchased for a small sum a large quantity of the burnt tobacco. This he ground up into snuff, which he sold very cheaply to the poor, 'the blackguards' of Dublin. The snuff was both very pungent and very popular. Lundy Foot went on making more of it, opened a shop and became a wealthy man, selling Lundy Foot's 'Irish Blackguard'.

In the great days of fashionable snuff taking, there were teachers of the etiquette of correctly wielding a snuff box, just as there were of wielding a fan, or dancing, or fencing; there were also books explaining the rules of offering snuff to a stranger, a friend or a mistress, according to the degrees of familiarity or distance. Some users grated snuff from a rasp placed on the back of the hand and sniffed it thence; some took a pinch from a snuff box. Others used a snuff spoon. According to an 18th-century complainant

> 'To such a height with some is fashion grown
> They feed their very nostrils with a spoon'.

Snuff takers' chatelaines of silver were made. Certain elaborate ones were for ceremonial use at Scottish army mess dinners—see *Snuff Mulls*. Special snuff handkerchiefs, usually about 24 in. square, were also sold for dusting the hand and lip, or protecting the neck-cloth. For practical reasons, most of these handkerchiefs had snuff-coloured, chocolate, yellow or red backgrounds, further embellished by closely printed designs of ballads, fashionable scenes, or popular events. In 1798, Fribourg and Treyer sold them at 28s. per dozen; they still sell them.

Snuff taking, as a fashion, declined rapidly between George IV's death in 1830 and Victoria's accession in 1837. In spite of the fashionable world changing over to cigars, snuff taking never died; indeed, it is having a mild resurgence now and one firm claims to make 65 varieties. A few years ago, I read of a judge apologizing for delaying a hearing because his snuff box had come unfastened in his pocket! Until very recently the 'court' was by no means the only place where smoking was forbidden. Until the 1920s, when sprinkler systems first made smoking permissible in many woodworking factories, most woodworkers were snuff takers. I shall always remember a woodworking factory manager of 45 years ago, who from the front appeared to be wearing a snuff-coloured suit, but the back view disclosed it to be blue serge!

Like smoking, snuff taking had its enemies. Here is the anti-snuff view, expressed by *Hints on Etiquette*, 1834—

> 'As snuff-taking is merely an idle, dirty habit, practised by stupid people in the unavailing endeavour to clear their stolid intellect, and is not a custom particularly offensive to their neighbours, it may be left to each individual taste as to whether it be continued or not. An "Elegant" cannot take *much* snuff without decidedly "losing caste".'

The tobacco accessories are described alphabetically in this section under two main headings—*Smoking* and *Snuff Taking*.

SMOKING

Cigar Box Openers
The efficient cigar box opener and closer, Plate 350, *B*, was doubtless developed over a long period. The specimen illustrated, was bought about 1910. The stout knife blade is used to cut the labels and lever up the lid; the hammer on one edge of the blade, knocks in the brass pin to close the box; the nick on the opposite edge is used to remove a pin.

Cigar and Cheroot Cases
Wars and variations in excise duty have been responsible for many changes in tobacco using habits. Although a few

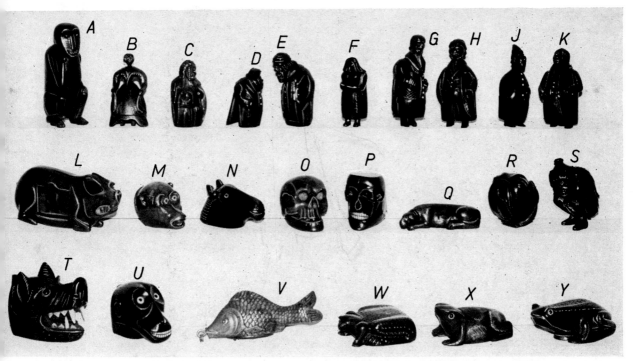

368　18th- and 19th-century human figure, animal, reptile and fish snuff boxes. (*Section XXII*)

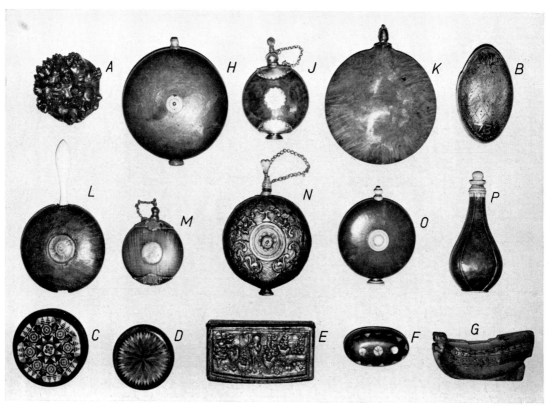

369 18th- and 19th-century snuff flasks and snuff boxes. (*Section XXII*)

370 Table snuff boxes and snuff pots. (*Section XXII*)

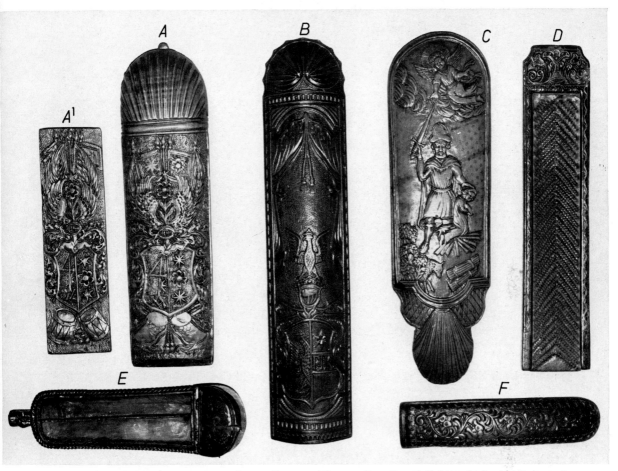

371 *A, B, C* and *D*, 18th-century, outsize snuff rasps of fine quality; *D* and *E* show the backs of rasps, the latter with the grater removed, but showing the snuff box at the end. *F*, a carved pocket rasp, curved to fit the pocket. (*Section XXII*)

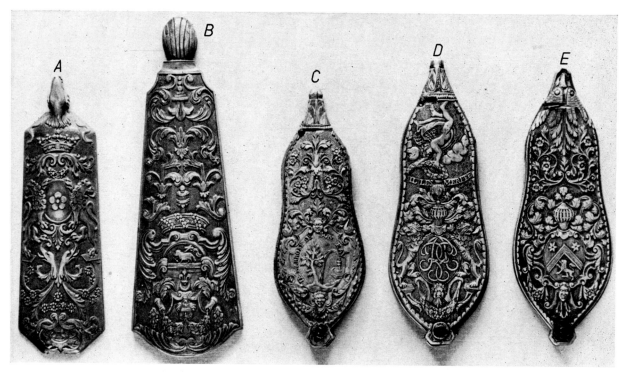

372 Five Louis XIV boxwood rasps, finely carved in the so-called Cesar Bagard style. (*Section XXII*)

373A and B An interesting Louis XIV boxwood rasp, carved with a burlesque on 17th-century methods of church preferments. (*Section XXII*)

375 A superb French 17th-century, boxwood rasp, carved with the royal French coat of arms, with bar sinister, and a trophy of arms. (*Sect. XXII*)

374A and B Another Louis XIV boxwood rasp, which is inscribed with the names both of the carver and the priest who owned it. (*Section XXII*)

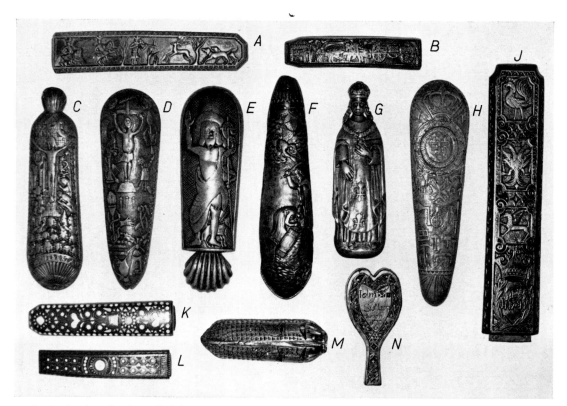

376 A selection of 17th- and 18th-century snuff rasps. *C*, *D*, *E* and *F* are characterized by religious themes in their carving. (*Section XXII*)

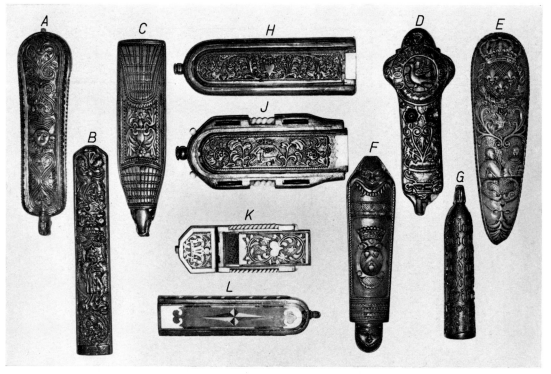

377 A further selection of 18th-century snuff rasps and *L*, a 17th-century specimen. *J*, is a very rare, early 18th-century coaster rasp on wheels, for running along a table. The back of *A* is shown, Plate 371, *E*. (*Section XXII*)

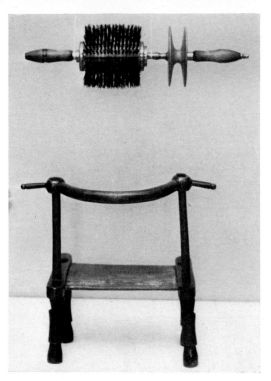

378 Barber's revolving brush, English, second half of 19th century. Below, child's barber's chair, to stand back to front on an ordinary chair; probably made by an African craftsman for an English settler. (*Section XXIII*)

379 Chamber horse—a Georgian exercise chair, almost identical with one illustrated in Sheraton's *Drawing Book*, 1793. (*Section XXIII*)

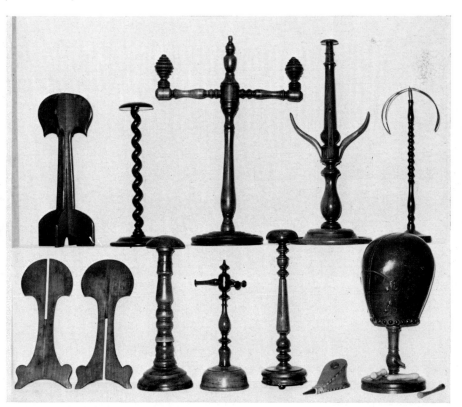

380 Wig block, wig and bonnet stands, cravat holder and wig powdering bellows. For details, see text. (*Section XXIII*)

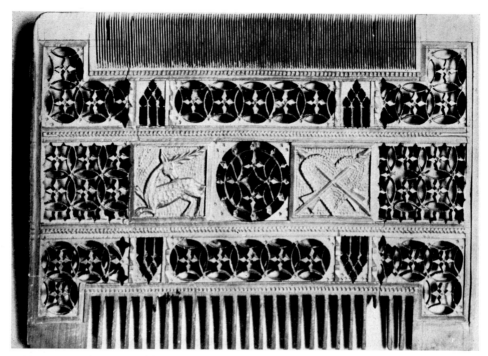

381 Boxwood H comb, French, *circa* 1500. Probably commissioned by an English gallant for his lady love; note the play on 'hart' and 'heart'. (*Section XXIII*)

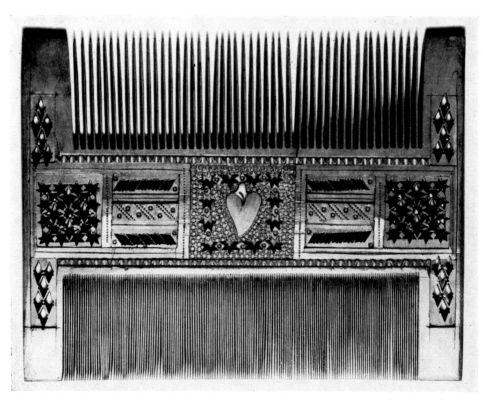

382 Another love token H comb, French, *circa* 1500. The coarse teeth may be above fine, or *vice versa*. (*Section XXIII*)

383 EXTREME LEFT, BOTH ROWS: the two spittoons are described in *Section XXII, Tobacco Accessories*. On the floor—decorative mahogany chamber pot from U.S.A. dated, 1871; children's chamber pots, one in rocking chair, both Scottish, 19th century. ABOVE: travelling chamber pot in pine case, 19th century. (*Section XXIII*)

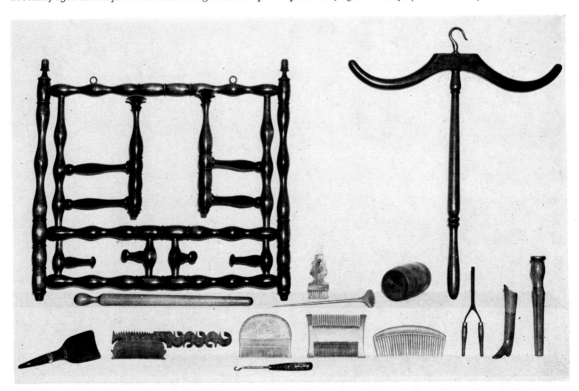

384 TOP ROW: turned, wall-type holder for wigs and cravats, or caps and scarves; ringlet curler; comb cleaner; 18th-century fop's eyebrow comb; aromatic container; early 19th-century clothes hanger. BOTTOM ROW: horn-handled, yew-wood shoe horn; selection of 19th-century boxwood combs; button hook; curling tongs; button hook 'boot'; hair puffer. (*Section XXIII*)

385 18th-century fitted dressing
case, made from a giant Scottish
chestnut tree. (*Section XXIII*)

386 RIGHT: mid-19th century lady's dressing case, veneered with calamander, inlaid with
brass, and with cut glass and silver fittings. LEFT, revolving casket of thuya wood, with gold
decorated glass bottles, etc.; for view closed, see Plate 392. (*Section XXIII*)

387 Louis XIV, carved pearwood dressing table accessories, *circa* 1685; so-called Cesar Bagard work. For further details, see text. (*Section XXIII*)

388 TOP ROW: long-haired dusting brush; two Tunbridge mosaic clothes brushes; three boxwood glove powdering flasks; a Corsican gourd scent flask. MIDDLE ROW: Valentine, heart-shaped and egg trinket boxes and selection of 'fruit' toilet boxes, BOTTOM ROW: heart-shaped trinket box; three Welsh, chip carved toilet boxes; two 17th- or 18th-century pomanders; 19th-century and early type lignum vitae glove stretchers. (*Section XXIII*)

389 TOP ROW: carved walnut bulldog and Tunbridge stickware pin-cushions, and selection of trinket stands, MIDDLE ROW: Regency revolving pin-cushion trinket stand; 18th-century tooth powder box; Victorian hair tidy; folding toilet mirror; shop counter hatpin stand. BOTTOM ROW: selection of toilet mirrors, some for travelling. (*Section XXIII*)

390 Oak tricorn hat box and wig box, both English, 17th or 18th century. (*Section XXIII*)

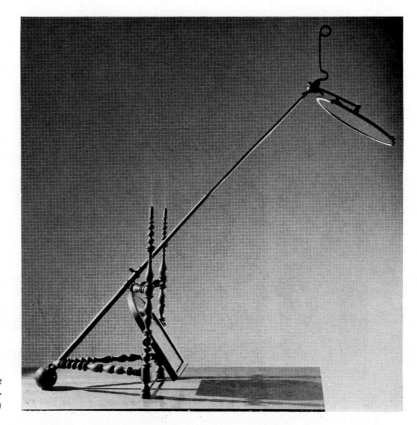

391 Heal's *Face et Nuque* mirror of 1856–7. For details, see text. (*Section XXIII*)

392   TOP ROW: Swiss or Tyrolean carved jewel casket, *circa* 1840, and exterior view of revolving casket pictured open in Plate 386. BOTTOM ROW: Italian, 15th-century jewel casket, decorated with certosina work and ivory plaques; fake Italian, 'carved' pearwood (?) casket; leather-covered jewel casket, made in Hull between 1835 and 1846. (*Section XXIII*)

393   TOP ROW: 18th-century, mahogany, wall-type wig and cravat holder, and barber's oak razor box. MIDDLE ROW: Georgian mahogany soap box; shaving cup(?); selection of razor hones; man's mahogany travelling toilet case. BOTTOM ROW: razor cases, two with strops. (*Section XXIII*)

394 James I shaving outfit dated 1606, with incised ornament similar to that on silver of the period. (*Section XXIII*)

395 Rosewood wig powdering 'carrot'. English; 18th century. (*Section XXIII*)

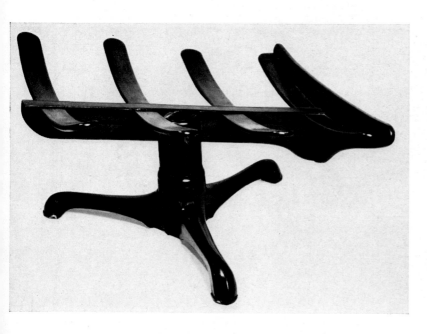

396 An unusual mid-18th-century gout stool on pillar and tripod. The curved ribs are laminated. (*Section XXIII*)

398 An early 18th-century, carved panel, probably Flemish, showing a selection of contemporary woodworking tools, etc., all cut out of the solid. (*Section XXIV*)

397 French, carved wood towel holder, finished in polychrome. (*Section XXIII*)

cigars were imported to Britain in the late 18th century, the general taste for cigars was introduced by the military, who acquired the habit in Spain, during the Peninsular war of 1808–14; but with duty on imported cigars at 18s. per lb. in 1815, when the general peace threw open our ports, nearly all cigars smoked here must have been made in this country. In 1823, only 26 lb. of manufactured cigars were recorded as imported. Then the duties were progressively reduced, until by 1830 they were halved; imports of cigars in that year went up to more than a quarter of a million pounds. By 1825, cigar consumption in London was sufficient for a Mr. Gliddon to open a 'Cigar Divan' in King Street, Covent Garden. It was really a superior coffee house and social club, for men only. Illustrations show it furnished with divans and small tables against a scenic background, purporting to represent the Middle East. Cigars, snuff, coffee, etc., were served and the latest periodicals available. It was because cigar smoking developed so much as a social custom that it dealt such a severe blow to snuffing, which, by its addicts in high society, was considered a graceful part of the design of living.

Wooden pocket cases, to hold any number from three to six cheroots or slender cigars, each in its own separate cavity, were made from about 1830. The enterprising Smith family of Mauchline, Scotland, were quick off the mark with what they described as 'magazines'. One of their beautifully made specimens, veneered with amboyna, with a gilt framed convex mother-of-pearl plaque on one face, is illustrated, Plate 351, C. It has six compartments. Inside the slide on the lid, it is stamped with the Royal Appointment to *His* Majesty, showing that it was made before 1837. The Smiths also made cheaper 'magazines', decorated with tartans, or with transfer-ware pictures.

Plate 351, A, inlaid with a spray of flowers in an ebony panel framed in olive-wood, has a gilt metal hinged outer frame and is lined with *moiré*. Although purchased in Mentone, it is probably of Italian workmanship, *circa* 1890. E, of burr walnut, with inlaid fancy banding and slide-on lid, dates from about 1870 and has no divisions. G, of figured birch or maple, is nicely carved in relief with three men in 18th-century costume; it has a wood hinged lid at the top and a single lead-lined compartment. It was probably made somewhere on the shores of the Baltic. Karelian birch cigar cases, to hold three cigars, and beautifully made from highly figured wood, with integral wood hinges, J, enjoyed quite a vogue in the first 30 years of this century. The five cheroot 'magazine', L, which simulates a book, and is veneered with rosewood banded with mahogany, is probably mid-19th-century, English.

A cigar, packed in a palm leaf for protection, is shown in front of Plate 351, F. It has its original label and bass ties on it, and was taken from the body of a Russian officer at the Battle of Alma in 1854.

Cigar and Cheroot Caskets
Some 19th-century caskets are attractively ingenious, being semi-mechanically operated. Two hexagonal examples, both about 9 in. high overall, which open by turning the knob on the top, are illustrated, Plate 351, D and H. The knob turns the centre stem, which passes through the base into a large, wooden cog wheel. This centre cog controls smaller ones, which actuate the opening and closing of the six doors of each casket. The model D, French or Swiss, 1830–40 period, is veneered with kingwood and has ebonized pivot pillars to the doors; the mounts are ormolu and include a lyre on each door. Possibly there was once a musical box under the base. Five of the doors are each fitted with gilt holders for three cheroots; the sixth has a piercer affixed, which also combines a match holder and striker. The circular model, H, to hold six cheroots, is

mahogany, ebonized externally and hand painted with flowers to harmonize with the papier mâché vogue of 1850; it is probably English. Many variants of these designs were made, including some in the Oriental taste. Being rather delicate objects, few survive in good condition. The circular rosewood casket, *F*, operates on a different principle. When closed, it is 10 in. high overall and resembles a large tobacco jar, with an outsize candle holder on top. This holder, or cup, contains a plunger; when this is operated, the top rises on a brass column and displays, umbrella-wise, 12 cheroots in gilt metal holders of leaf form. It appears to be late 19th-century and may be English or continental. A walking stick containing a central tube to hold cigars, with a similar umbrella opening match holder round it, is in the Pinto Collection. It was patented by a Mr. A. M. Clark in 1876; he may also have invented the casket.

The oak model coal truck on brass wheels, Plate 352, *B*, is a combined cigar casket and table coaster, probably dating from about 1900. The 'coal' lid is hinged and the interior contains a central match holder, striker and ashtray, with a compartment at each end for cheroots or cigars. Another in the Pinto Collection, very similarly fitted, but with a cigar cutter additional, is designed as a late Victorian trunk.

Cigar Cutters

Cigar cutters, being mostly all-metal, offer little scope to collectors of wooden bygones, but Mephistopheles, Plate 353, *R*, qualifies. He is nicely carved and polychrome finished and is probably Edwardian; he bites off cigars, inserted into his mouth, when the plunger under his chin is pressed. The turned lignum vitae pillar, Plate 351, *B*, with circular 'mouth', is a cigar piercer of about 1840, made for the torpedo-shaped cigars, formerly so popular. The bone stud on top is the head of a long pin which passes centrally through the circular aperture and into the wood below. To use the

piercer, the pin is raised clear of the aperture, the sealed end of the cigar is inserted and then the pin is stabbed down, piercing the cigar effectively from side to side, without tearing the leaf. For years it was among our 'dunno-whats'; then it was shown on television and two old gentlemen, one viewing in Yorkshire, and the other in the Isle of Wight, who remembered seeing similar piercers used in their youth, provided the answer. A test confirmed it; the side piercing gives a good 'draw' and no bits of leaf or dust get in one's mouth.

Cigar Holders—see *Cigarette Holders*

Cigar Moulds

Plate 352, *F*, shows a wooden cigar mould from Massachusetts. It moulds 20 of the torpedo-shaped cigars, still popular in the last quarter of the 19th century and the first quarter of this one. The two halves of the mould peg together. A single mould, which has a steel clip to keep it closed, has a separate base to the cavity, which facilitates removal of the cigar, and also, by variation in thickness, can be used to adjust the cigar's weight.

Cigar Piercers—see *Cigar Cutters*

Cigarette Boxes and Cases

Cigarette boxes and cases of wood, generally only vary in size, choice of material and quality. Some of the nicest are those of highly figured birch, with integral wood hinges, made in Finland.

Cigarette Holders

Cigarette holders, smaller-bore editions of cigar and cheroot holders, have been made of many materials. When of wood, cherry or briar are the most favoured, and the holders are quite plain. An exception in this last respect is Plate 353, *M*, so elaborately turned (including two loose rings) that it is impossible to identify the wood. This *tour de force* of 19th-century turnery is probably Scandinavian.

Cigarette Making Devices

Cigarette smoking did not come to Britain on a large scale until after the Crimean War of 1854–6. Even then the habit penetrated slowly. Consequently, most of the production came into the automatic machine age, whilst hand-made cigarettes virtually required no tools. Two home-cigarette-making tubes, brought out in the 1870s or 1880s, are illustrated, Plate 351, *M*. They are of rosewood and one is closed, the other open, to show the thinly turned tube, funnel and ramrod, which comprised the neat little device for making tapering, paper-covered cigarettes. Similar models of pearwood and horn were designed in France. They are stamped:

MOULE À CIGARILLES
LEMAIRE-DAIMÉ
PARIS
PROPRIÉTÉ INDIVIDUELLE DE
DESSINS
GARANTIE PAR LA LOI

A packet of the brown-coloured, thin, tapering paper tubes is shown with the gadget. The packets are also printed as above, but some are additionally worded: 'Henry Solomon & Co. sole agents for Great Britain and its colonies. London'. As the rosewood cigarille makers are not stamped, it appears likely that they are English-made versions.

It is an interesting fact that Russian cigarettes were imported in large quantities from 1866 onwards and were more mouthpiece than cigarette. They seem to have been an early attempt at a combined holder and cigarette, for the paper was cut on a spiral and tapered to a point at one end.

Jars, Tobacco—see *Tobacco Jars*

Match Dispensers—see Section VI, *Fire and Lighting*

Measures, Tobacco—see *Tobacco Measures*

Moulds, Cigar—see *Cigar Moulds*

Pipes—see *Pipe Cases and Pipes*

Pipe Cases and Pipes

During most of the time that Europeans have smoked pipes, and throughout most of Europe, the clay predominated, both for men and women; 17th-, 18th- and early 19th-century illustrations show that both sexes smoked similar shapes and sizes of pipes. Whilst pipe smoking permeated all stratas of male society, it was not general among women of fashion.

Elizabethan and James I clays had minute bowls, because of the costliness of tobacco, which at first cost 3s. per oz., coming, via Spain, from the Spanish colonies. By the 1620s, Virginia was producing half a million pounds per annum and the price of tobacco dropped to 8d. per oz.—but these figures have to be multiplied many times to find today's equivalent. By 1651, the Duke of Bedford, a very large smoker, using between ½ oz. and 1 oz. of tobacco per day, was buying Virginia tobacco for as little as 3s. 4d. per lb.; but Spanish, which he also smoked, cost him 10s. per lb. Between 1757 and 1770, Sir John Filmer, of East Sutton Park, paid 1s. 6d. per lb., but then the price gradually rose and by 1774 he was paying 2s. 4d. per lb. In 1794, Parson Woodforde paid 2s. 8d. per lb.

Clay pipes, being quickly fouled and easily broken, were used and thrown away in vast quantities. Admittedly, in inns and coffee houses, where it was customary to present customers free with clean clay pipes for smoking on the premises, the procedure was not as wasteful, because the long pipes were put, after use, into an open iron cradle, known as a pipe kiln or pipe roaster, which was suspended by a ring over a charcoal fire and pipes were roasted clean. It is doubtful, however, if such a device were considered worth using in a private house, because of the cheapness of clays. In 1651, the Duke of Bedford paid 18s. 6d. a gross for them, but by 1665 he bought them at 22s. 6d. per *twelve* gross lot; in 1695 he paid anything from 24s. to 36s. per *twelve* gross, the variation being presumably due to differences in length as well as quality. Pipe prices seemed to fluctuate in unison with tobacco, for Sir John Filmer paid 2s. 2d. per gross in 1757 and 2s. 8d. in 1774, whilst Parson Woodforde paid 3s. per gross in 1793.

Despite old clay pipes being ground and used as moth ball, for putting in woollens, etc., bowls and parts, but usually little of the stems, are continually being excavated on old inhabited sites. Consequently, their original length cannot be determined, but, from the start of smoking, engravings show that they were made in a considerable variety of lengths. Apart from individual taste, 'shorts' were necessary for the pocket and longer ones were smoked at home, or in the inn. Thus length alone will not determine age, although other factors, including dates on some specimens and makers' marks, help considerably.

As already stated, early pipes had small, short bowls, usually of barrel shape, which became larger, particularly in height, as tobacco cheapened. Early pipes had a very forward tilt, or 'lean over', on the bowl. After about 1700, fashionable bowls in England became more upright, as well as deeper, although some makers and some countries retained the forward slope later. In the 18th century, the top of the bowl was usually parallel with the stem, and after about 1690–1700 the flat heel or print, on which the maker's mark was often stamped, developed into a spur, comfortably cool to hold and particularly useful with church-wardens and other long pipes which, with their heels often resting on a table, might otherwise leave burn marks.

Because of their fragility, cases were essential for those who carried their pipes in their pockets, and the generalities about

clays, given above, help in dating cases. Raleigh had a leather pipe case, and doubtless leather was used fairly often, but the majority of pipe cases, particularly in England, seem to have been plain, hollowed out of sycamore or birch wood. Plain wooden objects, made essentially for use, when worn or old-fashioned, go on the fire. So it is with plain wooden pipe cases; I have never seen one which could be dated earlier than the 18th century and they are hard to find.

Ornamental wooden objects have a better chance of survival; in Plate 354 are included three rare and elaborate cases of late 17th- and early 18th-century design, made for pipes without spurs on the heels. They differ from later 18th-century cases in having sliding shutters and are unventilated, being blocked at both ends. Because the spurs, which later became usual on heels of pipes, would catch against sliding shutters, 18th-century cases usually have hinged lids and are open at the stem end. The three 17th-century type cases illustrated, Plate 354, B, C and D, were all intended for pipes with small, forward-sloping bowls of similar angle and although some continental 18th-century cases were made for pipes with a similar slope, all which I have seen take considerably larger pipe bowls. These cases are of such fine quality that it is possible that they were for silver pipes which Aubrey, the historian, refers to as early as 1660, and which had been made in the same shapes as clays. Very few of them, or of silver-mounted clays with quill mouthpieces, have survived, although both were made for the wealthy. B was formerly in the Moir Carnegie Collection. It was intended for a small-bowled pipe, 8 in. long, is carved walnut and silver-mounted. Although dated 1747, the rather naïve composition and form of the ornament and the shape of the case must have appeared old-fashioned at that time. The bowl compartment is carved with a stylised lion, which grasps cherub heads between its fore and hind paws. The joints of the case and shutter are carved with dog-tooth ornament and the long panels of both are carved with foliage. On the case, pierced hearts are included in the composition, while on the shutter, *B1*, shown alongside, is a shell and two girls, one dancing with a scarf and one holding a bird. *C*, of walnut, and probably late 17th-century, takes a pipe 11 in. long and is elaborately carved with a head, in heavily curled wig, which merges into an imbricated and twisted fish tail. The shutter and lower part of the case are carved with floral swags and acanthus scrolls. *D*, from Ashburnham, Sussex, is boxwood, silver mounted; carved with dogs, birds, a harpist and angels, amongst intertwined foliage. It encloses the initials E.S., and the knop, carved with stars in rope borders, suggests a maritime connection.

Plate 354, *A*, the exception to every rule, has a sliding shutter, but is inscribed An. D.C. 1800, Joseph Pont. Comparison with the other three shows that the stem of this case is much thicker and coarser, particularly where stem meets bowl; this enabled it to be grooved sufficiently deeply to allow the shutter to slide past a spur. As the bowl aperture is fairly large and is set more upright to the stem than on the other three, the pipe which it held would not have been inconsistent with the date, despite the fact that, at first sight, this appears to be a 17th- or early 18th-century type of case. Puzzling features go further, however, for this geometric carving is commonly found on Welsh and Scandinavian treen, but not on that from Latin countries, yet the use of D.C. (dopo Christi), instead of A.D., suggests Italian or at least Catholic origin.

The remainder of the pipe cases, Plate 354, are 18th-century, continental, and the pipes which they held, whilst varying considerably in angles of bowls, retained the forward tilt, usual in English pipes of the preceding century. All have metal-hinged lids, with spring catches and ventilation openings at the mouthpiece end. Five held pipes between 6½ in. and 7½ in. long, one a 10 in. Their bowls were 2 in. to 2½ in. deep overall, against the more usual 1½ in. held by 17th- and early 18th-century cases. *E* and *G*, formerly in the Bompas Collection, are both Dutch and have an acute forward slope. *E* is of well patinated pearwood, inlaid with brass. *G*, the amusing, late 18th-century bearded man, is carved from boxwood and has an unusual stem casing, pierced with three tiers of four-light lanterns. *J*, probably from the Dolomites area, is olivewood, and elaborately brass-mounted and inlaid with piqué. *F* and *H* are Austrian; *F* is carved from pearwood, and *H* from boxwood; the latter includes among its motifs a double-headed, crowned eagle, a boy skipping, a human head, and cross above a heart, which encloses the initials K.M. Engraving on the copper hinge repeats the initials K.M. and gives the date 1756. The Dutch or German specimen, *K*, is most interesting; of ebony, mounted and decorated with brass, it is fitted with a most ingenious combination dial lock, so that no one else could smoke it in its owner's absence—obviously owned by a man with ideas of cleanliness ahead of his time!

The plain cases for 'cutties', Plate 356, *N* and *O*, are English, 18th-century. *M* may be English or Flemish and dates from between 1750 and 1800; its original black clay pipe is shown alongside. *P*, of boxwood, is 18th-century, probably Dutch.

Briar pipes often have considerable artistic merit, but their origin dates back little more than a century. According to Alfred Dunhill, the discovery that briar (which incidentally has nothing to do with rose briar) was ideal for pipes occurred fortuitously: in the mid-19th century, a French pipe maker, on a pilgrimage to Napoleon's birthplace in Corsica, lost or broke his meerschaum pipe whilst there; a peasant, at his request, carved him one for temporary use, utilizing the hard, close-grained root of a tree heath or bruyère, which grows around both Mediterranean shores. The pipe was so cool smoking and generally satisfactory in wear, that the manufacturer brought away some bruyère roots and sent them to St. Claude, a small town in a valley of the Jura mountains, long noted for wood turning and carving. Soon pipe making became so important there, that it virtually ousted other branches of woodworking. Briar pipes were first made in England in 1879. Briar is no longer imported in whole roots, but in *ébauchons*— roughly shaped blocks made from roots which may be up to 200 years old.

Whilst from about 1750 both meerschaum and porcelain pipe bowls were challenging clays among the wealthy of western Europe, neither material was suitable for mouthpieces and on these *de luxe* pipes they were usually of amber or carved stag-horn, making the finished product costly.

In North-west Europe—Russia, Finland and Scandinavia—the lands of wood— wooden pipes were smoked commonly from an early date. In England, cherrywood and in America, corn cob, had some following, as they still have, but they cost more than clays, and although cooler, they fouled quickly and were not long lasting. There were, however, other pre-briar hardwood pipes, of artistic and historic merit—in fact, some with scenes carved on their bowls are documentaries in wood; they are mostly from central Europe and are of considerable interest to collectors. Although usually lumped together as 19th-century German, some of them are actually 18th-century, and their provenance includes Austria, Switzerland, Italy and Holland, as well as Germany. They are made from a variety of close-grained, hardwood roots, difficult to identify, and must have provided good, cool smoking, but none of these woods possessed the char-resisting qualities of bruyère, so the bowls, mostly of very large size, were lined with iron or silver. These pipes are almost invariably of mid-Euro-

pean shape, with bowls curving back, forming a U with the long stems; stems curve back again at the mouthpiece, so that in smoking the heavy pipe hung down, needing hand support. This shape drains well and occasionally a screw-capped outlet for tobacco juices was provided at junction of stem and bowl. Stems were usually cherrywood, said to improve the flavour of tobacco, and the mouthpieces were staghorn. Sometimes there is a junction length of woven, flexible tube between stem and tube, or between tube and mouthpiece. Most of these pipes are silver-mounted and the majority seem to have been fitted with hinged and ventilated lids, sometimes elaborately pierced and ornamented, for smoking outdoors. A selection of these attractive, carved pipes is shown in Plates 353 and 356. For convenience in grouping, most of the stems have been removed. Plate 356, *A* is a handsome, German, early 19th-century, hardwood pipe, carved with a coat of arms, with silver lid and mount and cherrywood stem; it is representative of a large group. *B* and *C* belong to another large group of late 18th- and early 19th-century pipes, all of which include 'Mercury' in their carving. *B* depicts Mercury on tip-toe, spreading his benediction over a sailing ship, alongside a bale and barrel-loaded quay. *C*, a dolphin pipe, shows Mercury in flight, holding a benediction scroll above a village, in which are peasants with casks and a beer dray; as with many pipes of this type, the dolphin grasps the pipe stem in its open mouth. *D* is a fine, Austrian, mid-18th-century, hardwood pipe, carved with a hunting scene and delicately pierced with rococo scrolls, very practical for reducing weight, and for coolness to the touch; the 2 in. deep bowl is silver-lined. *E*, the small pipe carved with flowers and foliage, is 18th-century, probably Viennese; the mounts are of brass. The Austrian pipe, *H*, with an unusual flute edged silver lid, dates from 1790–1800. The bowl is carved in the documentary manner fashionable on high quality treen around that time. It bears the name of Johann Gölner. The miniature scenes depicted, showing wine making, a wine cellar and peasants drinking in a garden, are based on the style of Teniers. *F*, is another Austrian documentary pipe, of equally high quality and perhaps with even more interesting scenes depicted. It shows, in considerable detail, merchandise landing at the quay, being carried to the warehouse, in the warehouse and being sold over the counter; it is boxwood and appears to have been carved between 1800 and 1810 and may be from the Adriatic coast. *G*, the specimen between them, also silver-lidded, probably Italian, 18th-century, portrays the Holy Family in its fine carving. *L*, an unusual and powerful sculptural head of an elderly man, with a wart on his crooked nose, glass eyes and coloured mouth, suggests a study from life. Who was the original? *J* and *K* are briars, both skilfully carved; *J*, with its jockeys, is probably near to 1900, *L*, the reclining nude, perhaps somewhat earlier.

Plate 353 includes a further selection of highly ornamental pipes, all probably made between 1860 and 1900. From about 1860, up to the present, it is curious that there has been no outstanding style in pipes. Every size, shape, style, angle of bowl, both plain and carved, seem to have been tried; but there have been a few short-lived fashions and plenty of novelties. The standing figure pipes, *B*, *C* and *J*, are mostly Swiss and Tyrolean novelties of the 1870s. They generally represent celebrities and caricatures. The bowls are in the heads and the stems go down into the bodies; Mr. Gladstone, *J*, is shown taken apart. The bust of the negress, *C*, is much more sophisticated and carefully finished than the usual production; it may be French or from French Morocco. The wooden 'bottle', *D*, was made in Germany about 1890–1900. The upper part unscrews and contains the mouthpiece, which can be used separately

as a cheroot or cigarette holder; it also fits into the hole in the front of the lower section, which is the bowl. The cap of the bottle contains a view of Port Said; this cap and the metal mounts are silver-plated copper—poor quality—and made by the firm who, about the same period, produced similarly mounted and jointed walking sticks, containing pencils, pens and inkpots, as well as pipes and cigar holders. *E* is carved as a bull head, with glass eyes and silver cover; *F* is a well carved horse head, with blinkers; *G* is a Cossack and *H*, a French *légionnaire*. In the next row, *K* is a skull; *L*, a hand grasping a bowl. *Q* is a Zulu pipe, ingeniously carved with radiating fins, which make it cool to hold; *S* is a carved dolphin pipe and *T* a Chinese 'long man' pipe, with silver mouthpiece and minute silver bowl. The pipe, when not in use, is protected between the arms and legs of the long man. These tobacco pipes are often erroneously thought to be for opium. *U*, the clumsy, iron-studded, mahogany, one-piece pipe, with iron 'candle socket' bowl, is interesting, because it is a once common (in every sense of the word), but now rare, Irish pipe, of a type which was fully documented by Hone. These extremely heavy and ill-balanced pipes were used by working men in Clonmel and Dublin between 1820 and 1830; their owners must have had good teeth! Originally they cost 6*d*. each; in 1956, this well-worn specimen was bought for £2. It is unfortunate that our possessions do not attain antique value in our own lifetimes!

Pipe Moulds

The sycamore pipe mould, Plate 353, *A*, made in two halves, is rare, because iron, not wood, moulds for pipes were normal. This example, some 150 years old, makes an 11½ in. pipe. Pipes were made in a 'flow' series of operations. Briefly, after kneading pipe clay of the right consistency into long-tailed lumps, each amply large enough for one pipe, the kneader passed them to a moulder who, with his right hand, drew the long clay tail over a fine steel rod, held in the left hand; his dexterity was such that he exactly bedded the rod in the centre of the clay and left a ball of solid clay at one end to form the bowl. Having placed the stem, with solid clay attached, in one half of the mould and closed the other half tightly on it, the mould was placed in a press and a metal cone, the size of the inside of the bowl, was driven into the clay cone by means of a lever, forcing the surplus clay upwards. This surplus of bowl wall was next removed by a knife, inserted into the cut in the mould. The rough pipe was then passed to a trimmer, usually a lad or a girl, and a certain amount of finishing operations and testing for 'draw' took place, prior to burning in the kiln. Fairholt, in 1859, relates that the average output per employee was nearly 500 pipes per day, and the price wholesale for these pipes was about 1s. 4d. per gross. They were retailed at four for a penny—theoretically a good profit, but the percentage of breakages was high.

Pipe Racks, Stands and Trays

Bowls up! Bowls down! Pipes horizontal! Which is the right way to store them? The controversy has continued for centuries and as Plates 350, 352 and 363 show, the woodworker has made pipe receptacles to meet all views.

The large, 18th-century, country-made, oak rack, Plate 352, C, to hang on the wall, was commonly found in inns and farmhouses. It holds 10 'churchwardens' horizontally, and seven shorter clays, bowls up, at the base. Additionally, it includes a useful trough for spills, etc. The churchwarden pipe box, or tray, was an 18th-century alternative; it was usually a simple, plain, mahogany object, divided into compartments, as illustrated, Plate 363, R. Occasionally a more decorative one is found, inlaid with crossed churchwarden pipes. Normally these boxes are about 26¼ in. long, including the small lidded box, for

tinder and steel, at the end; this is a common, but by no means universal, feature. Where it does not occur, the overall length is about 23 in. Widths are about 6 in., depths usually 2¾ in. Similar boxes or trays survive in silver and brass, with tobacco jars, and occasionally candlesticks, *en suite*. An alternative, but rare, 18th-century pipe tray was the mahogany cradle, 20 in. by 6 in., Plate 352, E. Perhaps unique in wood, is another kind of pipe cradle, Plate 350, A, which is of elm and fruitwood, and is simply a wooden version of the iron pipe cradle or roaster used for roasting pipes clean (see *Pipes and Pipe Cases*).

For those who preferred their churchwarden pipes stored vertically, the circular pillar stand, with candle serving both for illumination and lighting, was the ideal. The 17 in. high, mahogany pillar pipe stand, with octagonal scallop-edged base tray, Plate 350, C, shows the grace of 18th-century design. The heavy oak specimen, Plate 350, F, with three built-in spill vases, typifies the clumsy deterioration which had developed by the 1820–30 period. The smaller ebonized stand, Plate 350, E, is Irish, dates from about 1870 and is said to have been used for guests at 'wakes'. It holds a candle, 10 small clays, and a watch between the two match holders. The rather grotesque wooden figure, with spill basket on his back, standing on a 'rocky' mound pierced for five pipes, Plate 350, D, is German, mid-19th-century. The rack for pipes, bowls up, Plate 363, A, is a good example of character carving, *circa* 1900, made *en suite* with the tobacco jar, Plate 363, C. A pipe rack, bowls up, is included in Plate 352, A—for description, see *Smokers' Companions*.

Plug Cutters and Slicing Machines

The circular plug cutter of mahogany, with horn-handled knife, Plate 350, H, and the square based one, G, were probably used on a tobacconist's counter less than a century ago. The very individual pocket plug cutter, Plate 353, *N*, made in the form of a sea horse, suggests the work of a seaman in the days of sail. For shop use, a cake tobacco slicing machine, Plate 350, *J*, was developed in France in the 19th century. The cake of tobacco, D-shape in section, is placed, flat side down, on a moving carriage. When the handle is turned, the carriage, by means of a worm gear, conveys the tobacco along the slides from left to right and forces it up against a wheel formed of diagonally set cutter blades. The cutter rotates under a curved boxing at one end and the sliced tobacco drops into a drawer beneath. The cases are usually beech, grained to resemble rosewood.

Smokers' Companions

Smokers' companions, small fitted tables to stand alongside 'father's armchair', enjoyed their heyday between 1830 and 1914. The majority had a circular top, intermediate shelf, and base, supported by a central turned pillar. Equipment built into or on the shelves always included a tobacco jar and pipe rack. Early examples also had a holder for spills and usually another for pipe cleaners. Late specimens replaced spill vase by match holder and some have secondary lidded jars for cheroots and possibly cigarettes. The whole companion and its equipment are usually of wood, sometimes metal mounted. Novelty motifs were not unusual: a musician's 'companion' might have the various items of equipment designed as musical instruments, a sportsman's, with equipment based on his various sports or pastimes. Plate 352, *A*, illustrates a horseman's 'companion', *circa* 1870, each of the shelves being shaped as a horseshoe, and with the 10-hole pipe rack, match holder, tobacco jar and spill or pipe cleaner vase decorated with iron hob nails.

Smokers' Compendiums

Smokers' compendiums were smaller and usually less complete versions of companions, made to stand on a table. The smoker's compendium, Plate 351, *K*, is an amusingly busy, but none the less useful, multi-purpose object of the 1850–70 period. It is pearwood, stained and polished mahogany colour. Like many other objects of related style, such as string barrels, match containers, inkwells and penwiper buckets, made about the same time, it is heavily mounted with brass. The barrel for tobacco has a tap, which is a cigar cutter; the severed cigar ends fall into the bucket in front. At each side of the barrel is mounted another bucket, one for candle, the other for matches. On the front edge of the plinth is a match striker. Plate 351, *N*, is ebonized and has a vase-type tobacco jar with smaller ones for a candle, matches and six still smaller, either for cheroots or spills; a circular striker completes the outfit.

Smokers' Walking Sticks—see Section II, *Costume Accessories*

Spill Vases—see Section VI, *Fire and Lighting*

Spittoons

From the 17th century until at least the end of the 19th century, spittoons were normal equipment in tobacconists' shops, bars, billiard halls, etc. Old pictures show that table spittoons were used at 17th-, 18th- and early 19th-century smoking parties. The majority of table spittoons were of glazed pottery, but occasionally they were encased in wood and made with lever actuated lids; floor models were also made of glazed pottery or of metal, and sometimes encased in wood. A floor type, popular from about 1800 and continuing in vogue throughout the century, is the circular example, top left, Plate 383. The casing is mahogany, the pan and lion paw feet, brass. The tortoise, shown below, is an amusing carved wood novelty, and a forerunner of the refuse binette. Press your foot on the head, and the tail waggles and the 'shell' lifts, exposing a china pan. I think that this English example must have been the prototype for making in Britannia metal. Tortoise cuspidors of Britannia metal, lacquered in tortoiseshell colours, were made by Edward Perry and Sons, Temple Street, Wolverhampton, between 1860 and 1870; they were also made in Birmingham.

Stoppers, Tobacco—see *Tobacco Stoppers*

Tobacco Boxes

The dividing line between small tobacco jars and large tobacco boxes is thin and often non-existent between small tobacco boxes and large snuff boxes. To keep tobacco in condition, many tobacco boxes originally had lead foil linings, but frequently these have perished and the remnants have been removed. As snuff likewise must be carefully conditioned, snuff boxes were often similarly lined; lining, therefore, does not help in deciding original usage. Probably certain tight-lidded boxes were sold by tobacconists for either purpose, according to choice. If a box were good, it might, at different times during its long life, be used alternatively for snuff and pipe tobacco, and if not too large, it might be alternatively treated as table box or pocket receptacle. The worn carving on quite large boxes shows that they must have been carried in the pocket over a long period. Despite certain advantages offered by pouches, many pipe smokers, even today, prefer the protection which a rigid box gives against crushing and making tobacco dusty. It has become a convention, amongst writers on silver, copper, brass and pewter, to designate oval boxes as tobacco and round ones as snuff. There seems to be no basis for this theory, but being established, all the oval boxes in Plate 357 are described as 'tobacco'. Below are their details.

The oval maple(?)wood box, Plate 357,

C, with a dog and three birds in a centre shield, flanked by initials I.-G., must be one of the earliest dated specimens known, for its low relief carving also states EW·Fecit 1664. Even today the lid is a perfect fit. *F*, *G* and *H* are three deep, but crudely carved, Dutch boxes, all cut from the solid. *H*, showing traces of red polychrome in the background of the scrolling and dated 1792, and *F*, have integral wood hinges. The latter, carved not unskilfully with a scene after David Teniers, is date inscribed, inside the lid 'Den 17 October 1572', but this date, an instance of 'fake it' not '*fecit*', is probably 200 years before the box was made. *G* has copper hinges, a feature as common on Dutch wooden tobacco boxes as is sealing the interior with a paint lining, which two of these boxes retain. A short clay pipe was often kept with tobacco in these large boxes. The late 18th-century, oval, Sheraton box, *J*, is unusually finely made and veneered; the fan is satinwood, with a mother-of-pearl centre, the lunettes and side rims of curl mahogany; the angles are finished with a boxwood and ebony stringing. The oval box of masur birch, *K*, carved with an urn, medallion and border, is Finnish, *circa* 1800; it has the integral wood hinge, which probably originated in the Karelian Isthmus. *L*, carved and hollowed from boxwood, and well worn, is quite a documentary. It shows a haberdasher's shop, *circa* 1780, with heavy barred doors, interior fitments with pigeon-holes and shelves, bales of cloth and suspended scissors. Behind the counter, the haberdasher measures out ribbon(?) against the ell rule held by his customer. *M*, the last of the ovals, a cedar box, rimmed in horn and inlaid with bone, belongs to a small and rare English group, which all appear to have been made by one man between 1680 and 1710. They bear varied but attractive inscriptions, and dates; this one proclaims 'For you the best is not too good—1706'.

Literary references to fops' tobacco boxes go back more than 350 years. One such, penned by Henry Fitz-Geffery in 1617, mentions

> 'A spruce coxcomb . . . that never walkes without his looking-glass, in a tobacco box or diall set, that he may privately conferre with it'.

These words may well have been apposite to the original possessors of the two rare boxes, Plates 366, *Q* and 357, *A*. These handsome boxes, which date from the mid-18th century, must have been expensive productions and obviously the work of one man. The larger of the two, Plate 357, *A*, is 5½ in. long, the smaller 3 in. Both are hollowed from the solid and have integral wood hinges, which probably denotes Scottish origin. The larger box has three 'windows' cut in the lid, two each in the back and front and one in each end. These nine windows are mirror-glass backed; against the one on the lid is carved in relief, figures of a man, woman and two children, in mid-18th century costume; flanking this large window are smaller ones showing profile busts. Each window is framed by carved rays, producing a rather rococo effect. The background is infilled with a carefully composed pattern of imbrication. Inside the boxes, the lids are mirror-glass lined and the box sides and bottoms covered with lead. The small box, Plate 366, *Q*, follows the same general lines, but with only the single window, silhouetting two costume figures.

Plate 357, *B*, carved from solid boxwood, is dated 1767 and is intricately and confusedly carved all over the outside, and also inside the lid—the latter with Adam and Eve. I do not know its nationality, but there is doubtless some folk legend somewhere which links up such diverse subjects as men in Elizabethan costume, naked Red Indians(?), a man with a tail, two others with asses' heads, one of whom wears his heart outside his breast, a man with a peg leg, who holds his severed leg in his hand, a pig with a barrel round its body, and other weird and wonderful creatures, too numerous to describe here. *D*, also carved from the solid, and probably German or Austrian, has the appearance of considerable age. The box itself is grasped by a lion rampant, with Moses and Aaron, one at each side, under its paws; in front, the integral wood hinged lid is carved with a coat of arms. *E*, probably Scottish, 18th-century, is a remarkable piece of craftsmanship. It contains five separate compartments, all with integral hinges. In its length of 4¾ in. and width of 2½ in., it is quite a compendium, with receptacles for two clay pipes, tobacco, various kinds of snuff, and perhaps flint and steel. The oblong walnut box, *N*, scooped from the solid and inlaid with mother-of-pearl and brass pin points, was a specialized tourist souvenir of the isle of Rhodes in the last quarter of the 19th century. Many of these boxes were made in snuff and tobacco sizes, with some variations in design.

Tobacco Jars

Until the introduction of vacuum-lid tins, a lead container was the best method of keeping tobacco in condition. If you could afford a silver jar, it was a good alternative. Even today, domestically, a lead or lead-lined tobacco jar cannot be bettered, particularly if it has a lead weight inside, to compress and protect the tobacco from air exposure. Lead jars were probably used from the introduction of pipe smoking, but, being easily damaged and lead being reusable, the majority have been destroyed. Of those still extant, some are of 17th-century design, but no dated specimens, I believe, are earlier than 18th-century. About 1850, they were largely replaced by glazed earthenware, which had been used earlier in tobacconists' shops.

Most wooden tobacco jars originally had lead or foil liners, and being lighter than lead jars, as efficient and less easily damaged, they enjoyed great popularity. They were made in a great variety of shapes and woods for home use, but usually in the form of turned barrels for standing on the shelves in tobacconists' shops. Both because of its weight and the ease with which the metal deforms, it is doubtful if lead jars, other than those of small size, were ever used as shop containers. A large storage barrel, for shelf use, is shown, Plate 352, *D*. It measures 12½ in. in height and 11 in. in diameter. The design was used without change from the 17th to the 19th century; pole-lathe turned from an unjointed block of sycamore, it is painted red, with remains of decoration in green and other colours. Inside are traces of a lead lining.

It is sometimes difficult to distinguish between tobacco jars and certain tea caddies, but as a generality tea caddies had locks, tobacco jars did not. However, some caddies had no locks, because they fitted into outer tea chests or tea poys, which locked—See Section XX, *Tea, Coffee, and Chocolate Drinking Accessories.*

In Plate 363 is a representative selection of wooden tobacco jars, all probably English, except those otherwise described. I have never seen date-inscribed wooden tobacco jars, but design, when compared with other objects of related shape and condition, plus knowledge of fashion, make certain attributions probable. The outsize oak jar, Plate 363, *B*, 12¾ in. high over the finial, is probably not as early as it looks; I place it as a Victorian copy of a 17th-century design. *C*, decorated with carved heads, all cut from the solid, came from French Morocco about 1900 and is most skilful in its sculptural modelling of the different types of inhabitants of the country. The carving is lightly stained to give a naturalistic quality to faces and head-dresses. The pipe rack *en suite* is shown, Plate 363, *A*. *D*, the sycamore barrel, was made at Tunbridge Wells or Tonbridge early in the 19th century and the lid is decorated with the famous mosaic. The cube pattern inlaid jar, *E*, (not Tunbridge) is probably 18th-century. A nice piece of carving is the

walnut jar, *F*, cut from the solid to represent a negro market vendor, with circular discs displayed for sale on his lap. The upper part of the figure forms the lid, hinged at 'lap' level. Beside the seated negro is an empty sack and in front an empty barrel, presumably for matches and ash. It appears to be the second half of the 19th century, possibly French. The pyramidal, curl mahogany veneered jar, *G*, dates from about 1850. *H* and *J*, of yew-wood and lignum vitae respectively, are good mid-18th-century specimens. The Scottish alternate light and dark staved jar, *K*, dates from *circa* 1800; this specialized turnery, or coopering, occurred in Scotland and Holland in the 18th and 19th centuries. In both countries, designs were sometimes additionally ornamented by horizontal moulding of the built-up cylinder on a lathe or, in later work, on a spindle moulder.

L, the jar formed as a snake infested skull, was made in China, about 1900, for the European market. Inkstands, smaller versions of this unpleasant theme, were also shipped here. The lead-lined, mahogany coffin, *M*, exemplifies the kind of macabre jest which delighted our Georgian ancestors; further examples of this grim humour will be noted in the *memento mori* tobacco stopper, Plate 358, *P*, and in coffin snuff boxes, Plate 366, *S*. The cylindric ebony jar, *N*—an unusual early 18th-century specimen—retains its original lead weight. The earliest jars are *O*, *P* and *Q*, which I consider all date from the 17th century.

The very rare, Dutch, 18th-century tobacco jar-bowl, Plate 355, is hollowed out of a walnut root, handsomely mounted in brass. It is 5¾ in. deep and 12 in. in diameter, and may have been used for passing tobacco round the table at a guild or similar meeting. If, however, the engraved decoration round the brass rim of the bowl is meant to imply the letter 'S', alternating with tobacco leaves, it may have been used for conditioning tobacco leaves in various juices during the process of snuff

(Dutch *Sneuf*) making. The close-fitting lid, with its solid brass steeple, weighs 3 lb., making the bowl an efficient press, with the lid moving up and down in a 1 in. deep rebate.

Tobacco Measures

Tobacco measures, Plate 353, *O* and *P*, were used in some tobacconists' shops for parcelling up their own smoking mixtures into ¼ oz., ½ oz. and 1 oz. rolls. The measures work exactly like ejector butter prints (see Section V, *Farm*). The plunger was raised, the specially cut paper inserted, the tobacco pressed in and sealed in the paper, and the little roll ejected.

Tobacco Prickers—see *Tobacco Stoppers*

Tobacco Slicing Machines—see *Plug Cutters*

Tobacco Shop Signs—see Section XXVI, *Trade Signs, Ships' Figureheads etc.*

Tobacco Stoppers and Prickers

Every pipe smoker knows that to obtain maximum enjoyment from his smoke, he must have something to press down the tobacco in his pipe at intervals and correct the 'draw'. Admittedly, some smokers manage quite well by using a finger or thumb as a stopper, but it hardly improves the appearance of the digit so used. It is curious that tobacco stoppers have gone out of fashion, for, averaging a mere 2½ in. in length, they take little room in the pocket, are pleasant to look at and handle, and their lack causes all sorts of odd objects to be used as substitutes. Most surviving tobacco stoppers are small cast metal costume figures or busts. The majority obtainable today, particularly those of brass, are modern reproductions, some deliberately faked to look old; as they cost pence to produce, but sell for shillings or even a pound or two, they must be profitable productions.

The most interesting to collect, but difficult and expensive to obtain, are those individually carved from wood, bone, or ivory. There are numerous references to tobacco stoppers in 17th-, 18th- and 19th-century literature and they show that silver, pewter, bronze, brass, ivory, bone, mother-of-pearl and wooden tobacco stoppers were formerly made in large quantities and that the last four provided an outlet for the imagination and artistry of anyone handy with knife or chisel; probably many of the most original and skilfully carved examples were the work of amateurs. Will Wimble, one of Sir Roger de Coverley's circle in the 18th-century *Spectator*, is related by Addison to have made great quantities of tobacco stoppers during the winter ' . . . and that he made a present of one to every gentleman in the country who had good principles and smokes'. In Dickens's *Great Expectations*, Wemmick's collection of curios, in his house at Walworth, contained several tobacco stoppers carved by the 'Aged Parent'. Sir Roger de Coverley, on another occasion, when viewing the Coronation Chairs in Westminster Abbey, remarked that ' . . . if Will Wimble were with us and saw those two chairs, it would go hard but he would get a tobacco stopper out of one or t'other of them'.

Taylor, the 'Water Poet', in 1649, referring to the famous Glastonbury Thorn, said: 'I did take a dead sprigge from it, wherewith I made two or three tobacco stoppers, which I brought to London'. Many tobacco stoppers were, in fact, carved from famous woods, such as the Thorn, the Boscobel Oak, or Shakespeare's mulberry tree. A mulberry wood tobacco stopper, carved with a bust of Shakespeare, brass mounted and the mount stamped 'Sharp', is shown with the famous mulberry teapot, cup and saucer, Plate 321; Thomas Sharp, carver and turner, was one of the purchasers of the tree. Other stoppers caricatured the famous, such as the Duke of Wellington, a rabid anti-smoker—a real 'tobacco stopper'—who aroused much resentment among soldiers by forbidding smoking in barracks. Carved tobacco stoppers, mostly sold by street vendors, seem to have died out in the first half of the 19th century.

The Pinto Collection contains probably the most comprehensive collection of individually carved wooden tobacco stoppers in the world; many are unique. A selection is pictured in Plates 358 and 359.

As a generality, stoppers with small bases, $\frac{5}{16}$ in. to $\frac{3}{8}$ in. diameter, are early, to fit into the small bowled early pipes. But whilst all 17th-century stoppers probably had small bases, some 18th-century specimens, which show figures in costume of the period, or have dates carved on them, also have $\frac{3}{8}$ in. bases, but the majority are between $\frac{3}{8}$ in. and $\frac{5}{8}$ in. diameter. All kinds of hardwoods were used, sometimes protected by silver or pewter mounts, but more often unmounted and left to protect themselves with a coat of char. For the finest carvings—and some really are works of art—dense, close-grained boxwood was almost invariably preferred.

In Plate 358, *A* is an 18th-century, boxwood figure of a boy with a pack on his back. Silver and gold finger-ring stoppers exist. Some are in one piece; others have the stopper made to unscrew from the ring, which in its turn may include a signet; one silver example was a Jacobite relic of the '45. *B*, the dog stopper, is the only surviving ring type in wood which I know, *C*, a crisply carved boxwood monkey, portraying 'See, hear and speak no evil', may be 17th- or early 18th-century. *D* is a silver-mounted boxwood demon, 18th-century; the mount is chased with leaf ornament and a monogram. *E* is a finely modelled boxwood lion of the Stuart period, with paws resting on a crown. *F*, a silver-mounted boxwood figure holding a mug, probably dates from *circa* 1700. *G*, an unusual silhouette type, possibly a caricature, is carved boxwood, mounted on an ebony stem; it was probably made at Eger,

Bohemia. *H*, *J* and *K* are three versions of the popular 18th-century coursing greyhound theme, all in boxwood. *J* is silver-mounted and with silver tail. *K*, a $4\frac{5}{8}$ in. high specimen, also silver-mounted, on a plateau above leaf branches, is carved and pierced in mediaeval style and outstanding in quality.

The silver-mounted, boxwood figure of Shakespeare, above a fluted column, *L*, was the speciality of an old man named Salsbee; the standing figure of Shakespeare, with right elbow leaning on the volumes of his comedies, tragedies and histories, placed on a pedestal supported on the busts of Henry V, Richard III and Elizabeth I, is based on the statues by Peter Scheemakers (1691–1770) in Westminster Abbey and at Wilton. Despite being copies, these Shakespeare stoppers, of which I have recorded five, dating between 1765 and 1773, all have quaint variations and individuality imparted by Salsbee, who always carved his name, age and date of carving. His memory was evidently confused and sometimes slight contradictions occur in his age, compared with the date. Some Salsbee stoppers are silver-mounted, others are not, and they vary in quality. *L* is a good early specimen, dated 1765, and Salsbee gives his age as 63. The mount is engraved Thomas Stevens, Bermondsey Street; he is not recorded in the London directories of the period.

M is a silver-mounted, well-worn carving of a man's head, late 17th-century, and *N*, an even earlier and more worn figure of a man praying; the latter is pewter-mounted. *O*, a rare tobacco stopper/whistle combination, is carved with initials A.S. and date 1706. The fine, silver-mounted, boxwood *memento mori* stopper, *P*, carved with a skull, hour-glass, cross-bones, mattock and coffin, is dated 1715. *R* is a superb Flemish, late 17th or early 18th-century stopper, of intricately carved and pierced boxwood. It depicts David with the head of Goliath, around an open 'lantern', supported on a tapering leaf carved pedestal, encircled by a free revolving ring, above a lozenge carved base. *Q*, obviously by the same master, shows Abraham about to sacrifice Isaac (see also matching knife and fork handles, Plate 66). *S* is a grotesquely carved and silver-mounted vine stem stopper, engraved J.W. 1773; it is $4\frac{5}{8}$ in. high. *T* represents an 18th-century countryman, carrying two ducks; it is a miniature version of the *Gänsemännchen Brunnen* fountain in Nuremberg, behind the Frauenkirche. *U* is a delightful miniature boxwood carving of a Stuart street seller, which probably commenced life as a statuette, but the charred base shows that it has been used as a stopper. *V*, the ivory crowned mace stopper, may be 17th-century. It is a dainty piece of work, and is shown with its original lignum vitae protective case, *V1*, below it.

In Plate 359, *A*, the silver-mounted bellows, is probably 17th-century. *B* and also *C*, the ball and lantern stopper with chained signet, all cut from the solid, are probably Welsh, dating from about 1700. *D*, the man with a woman on his back—'Man with a Load of Mischief'—may be late 18th- or early 19th-century. *E* shows the reverse side of Plate 358, *S*. *F* is a miniature boxwood soldier. *G*, a well patinated boxwood stopper in 17th-century costume, is, I fancy, like *H*, the masonic figure, a 19th-century production. *J*, an extremely well carved boxwood shepherd, playing his pipe, is 18th-century and silver mounted. *K* is also 18th-century, probably Welsh. The burry root stopper, *L*, is mounted in pewter; the diameter of the stopper end, only $\frac{5}{16}$ in., denotes an early date. *M* is a good boxwood carving of a porter with a sack on his head; it is dated 1720. *N*, the hornblower and *O*, the bottle, are both unusual 18th-century designs. *P*, 19th-century, looks as though he may have been carved in the U.S.A. *Q*, a grotesque boxwood head, may be 18th- or early 19th-century, continental. *R*, the silver-mounted bulldog, could also be 18th- or early 19th-century.

Boots, shoes, legs and arms were among the most popular 17th- and 18th-century subjects for carved tobacco stoppers, *T*, *T1*, *W*, *W1*, *X*, *Y* and *Z*. They are all 18th-century except *X*, which is Stuart period. Examples of *Z*, the hand grasping a dagger, exist both in wood and ivory. The same remark also applies to *Y*, and the 'pipe' is detachable, for use as a tobacco pricker, a device which may be needed to break up caked tobacco in a pipe bowl, which brings us to *S*, *S1*, *U*, *U1* and *V*. Of 18th-century origin, but whether English or not I am uncertain, *S* and *S1* are both of horn, with bases which unscrew, disclosing metal prickers. *V*, which is $4\frac{5}{8}$ in. long, is similarly fitted, but whether this is a pricker in a stopper, or merely a 'pickwick' in a pocket case, there is no way of telling. Pickwicks were simply lengths of wire, used when necessary to uncurl a wick before cutting it off. *U* and *U1*, both with clenched fist handles, are of thornwood and ivory respectively.

SNUFF TAKING

Snuff Boxes

Snuff boxes were made in such variety of materials, shapes, sizes, styles and finishes, that they provide an assortment diverse and large enough to satisfy any collector. They are also available at prices to suit most purses, although it would not take many jewelled *bibelots* of the 18th and early 19th century to make a hole in a sizeable fortune.

Tobacco being the basis of snuff as well as smoking, many old boxes formerly used for snuff have sometimes been described as tobacco boxes. For whichever purpose they were intended—and often this is debatable—the few 17th- and very early 18th-century survivals are usually oval and either plain or engraved, or simply carved in low relief. Materials generally used appear to have been wood, silver, gold, horn, pewter, brass and ivory. Wood having to be used thicker than the other materials, wooden boxes tend to be larger than those made in other materials.

As fashionable snuff taking increased in the 18th and 19th centuries, the snuff box family proliferated. Although wooden boxes were doubtless always made in greater quantities than any other, they were largely superseded, in aristocratic circles, by Battersea and Limoges enamel, tortoiseshell, silver and gold. The last two, were sometimes further embellished by chasing, to form mounts for panels of enamel, mother-of-pearl, jade, rock crystal, agate and other semi-precious stones, or miniature paintings on ivory. Additionally, the most elaborate and expensive were encrusted with diamonds, pearls, rubies, etc. Some of the most precious of George IV's snuff boxes were melted down to form jewellery for Queen Victoria. By 1740, snuff box making merited a separate heading under silversmithing and from George I to George IV, the equivalent of 'saying it with flowers' was the gift of a snuff box to either sex. A large-scale example of the custom is recorded in the coronation accounts of George IV, which record that £8,205. 15s. 5d. was paid to Rundell & Bridge, the royal silversmiths, for snuff boxes for foreign ministers.

Throughout the snuff period, in humble circles, the principal alternatives to wood remained ivory, brass, pewter and horn, with nutshells and, in the 19th century, papier mâché additionally. A variety of papier mâché made from potatoes, was said to be particularly efficacious in keeping snuff moist.

Fine Art Snuff Boxes
Despite the tendency to lavish the most exquisite workmanship on the most expensive materials, many snuff boxes of wood come into the category of excellent design and perfect craftsmanship, a few into the fine art class. Two superlative examples are illustrated, Plates 360 to 362. Ad-

mittedly, the intricacy of their carving must have rendered both of them most unsuitable for holding 'dust'; but that also applies to all jewel-studded, chased silver and gold, and filigree boxes; this unsuitability of certain snuff boxes for purpose was commented on by early 19th-century writers. The circular box, of which both sides are shown in Plate 360, is hollowed from a single block of boxwood, and closely resembles a modern powder compact. It measures $4\frac{5}{8}$ in. in diameter, is French, probably made in the neighbourhood of Nancy approximately 300 years ago. The design is a masterly composition and the fine-scale carving, very much undercut, has the crispness denoting a master. Doubtless because it is so exquisite, it appears to have had no use, and except for the patination which it has acquired through age and waxing, it is still just as it left its maker's hands. The pictures are so clear that no account of the carving is needed; the hinge is silver.

The snuff box, Plates 361–2, is less photogenic and needs more description. It is much smaller than the last; it could be contained in a $2\frac{1}{2}$ in. diameter ball. Like the last described, it is boxwood, but there the resemblance ends, for this one is sculptural in treatment, much in the style of Cellini—and may be 16th- or 17th-century, southern French or Italian. This unique and remarkable box, which in the posture of its figures much resembles the much larger salt cellar which Cellini made for Francis I, displays the same outstanding technical skill and virtuosity, but, like Cellini's work, somewhat lacks artistic sensibility. The subject of the carving is Diana and her hound, with an infant, possibly Jupiter, holding Ganymede (in the form of an eagle), and Pan holding his pipes. They are riding on a cloud, fanned from below by cherubs. Snuff is put in through a sliding shutter under the clouds, and released through a side nozzle, concealed in a cloud swirl.

Flask Type Snuff Boxes

Snuff flasks or bottles were formerly used in aristocratic circles in several parts of the world. The wealthy aristocratic Chinese, who grew their finger nails to great length to indicate that they did no manual labour, could not, in consequence, grind their own snuff, nor take a pinch between finger and thumb. By keeping their snuff in exquisitely fashioned, carved and inlaid hardstone bottles with short necks, which had spoons fitted to their stoppers, they overcame the dilemma which they had created. With the spoons, they transferred the snuff to the back of the hand for sniffing. A similar procedure was formerly common among the wealthy in Spain and Morocco, but their bottles were usually made from small gourds and nutshells.

In the Scandinavian countries, snuff flasks were also used; some are fitted with chained silver stirrers or spoons, which form the stoppers; others have ivory stoppers. They vary considerably in size, some doubtless for table, others for pocket use. Bodies of flasks are usually hollowed out of maple or birch burrs; the actual scooping is done from the centre of each side, where the ornamental silver or ivory disc is then inserted. Flasks were filled, presumably with a small funnel, through the hole at the base and the snuff removed through the spout at the top. A selection of Scandinavian snuff flasks is illustrated in Plate 369, *H* to *P*. *N* may be Norwegian; the others are Swedish; all are 18th-century. For convenience of photographing, *L*, with handle, is shown upside down. Though inscriptions, which sometimes occur on them, make their purpose abundantly clear, these snuff flasks are often confused with and described as gunpowder flasks. In Plate 367, *U* is another Swedish burr wood snuff flask; it has bone studs, like the double cup and jug, illustrated in Plate 48, *E* and *F*.

French Pressed Burr Snuff Boxes

Amongst circular wooden snuff boxes is a well-known French group, Plate 365, usually described as Napoleonic, although the themes depicted are wider than that title suggests. They are all made from maple or birch burr, to a universally high standard, with linings of tortoiseshell. Judging by their subjects, of which there are 100 or more, the majority were made between 1800 and 1810. They usually measure between $3\frac{1}{4}$ in. and $3\frac{1}{2}$ in. in diameter. A few boxes of similar type, but only about 3 in. in diameter, appear to date from the second half of the 18th century; their subjects include some in the Chinese taste, such as *D*, and also one, at least, showing Prince Charles Edward. All these boxes were made in the same manner: first 'turned' to a solid block of the required diameter and thickness, they were then submitted to steam treatment and, whilst relatively soft, scenes or subjects were impressed on the tops with medal dies. Sometimes another die, simulating engine turning, was impressed on the bottom. There are a wide variety of 'bottom' impressions; an elaborate one is shown, *O*. After hardening up, a fine horizontal saw-cut was made through the block and the two layers were recessed to form box and lid, and then lined with tortoiseshell. A few of these boxes have secret compartments concealed in the base; these may contain a profile of Napoleon or an erotic picture. Below are details of some of the more interesting examples illustrated.

B shows the lid and the bottom of a box depicting the principles of craniology. The lid is impressed with three views of a skull, with the 'bumps' numbered; on the bottom of the box is a key to the 'bumps'. *C* shows events in the life of Dr. Gall, founder of craniology. *G* is a satire on England, entitled '*Allegorie sur la bataille des 3 Empereurs*' (Austerlitz). Round the border is the inscription '*Il a vu sans effroi leur violens efforts*'. The scene, illuminated by a garlanded sunhead, shows a crowned French eagle, perched on a prostrate double-headed German eagle; the French eagle has seized a

Russian double-headed eagle by one claw, has knocked off his crown and is proceeding to pull the feathers out of his wings. On the left, a Prussian lion is slinking off, tail between legs. Across the channel, England, in the form of a complacent bulldog, sits watching, with fleet before and the Tower of London behind him. There is a Napoleonic secret compartment in the base of this box and also of *W*, a rather fanciful portrayal of a scene at Napoleon's grave in St. Helena.

J and *K* are the rare 'double head' types. Turn the pictures round and you will see entirely different faces. The man, *K*, turns into a horse. *J* shows a smiling face which, when the box is turned round, becomes a picture of misery. Occasionally, when these pressed boxes show simply the head of a notability in profile, such as the philosopher, *A*, Apollo, *S*, and George IV as Prince of Wales, *F*, the pressing has been sharpened up by a slight amount of carving. Cardinal Mazarin, *T* and Ferdinand VII of Spain, *E*, are left straight off the dies. Instead of having reliefs impressed on their lids, a few boxes of this type have ivory relief carving or gilt commemoration medallions enclosed by convex glass panels. The equestrian figure of Henri IV, *L*, is a particularly fine impression. *R* is a Flemish peasant scene after Teniers. *V* shows children tying grandma's bonnet on the dog. *Q* depicts the several different ways of enjoying tobacco. *P* is the legend of the lion of Florence; probably 18th-century, *U*, the only oblong box which I have seen in this series, portrays Diana turning Actaeon into a stag.

Miscellaneous Snuff Boxes

The top row of Plate 366 shows various other types of circular snuff boxes. *A*, probably 18th-century, is a trick box, which opens by pressing the centre. *B* and *C*, of the same period, pivot round for taking a pinch twixt finger and thumb. *D*, a Regency box, probably made at Tunbridge, announces

'He that is not a friend at a pinch, is not worth a snuff'. *E* and *F* are fine and rare 17th-century, lignum vitae, engine-turned boxes. *G* is an oval trick box, of which quite a few were made. When the pivoted lid is swung round, another lid is found beneath it; the puzzle is how to open the second lid. *J* and *P* have several points in common. Both date from *circa* 1800; both are cut from a solid burr of birch or something closely resembling it—burrs are notoriously difficult to identify. Both have the integral wood hinge, usually associated with Scotland and Scandinavia—especially Finland. Both are curved to fit the pocket, a feature common enough in metal, but difficult and, therefore, costly in time, to make in wood. The pointed box, *J*, with its all-over scrolled acanthus ornament, could easily be Scandinavian or Scottish. *P*, which seems to bear something in the nature of an armorial device, would, I expect, if identified, turn out to be Scottish. *H*, *K*, *L*, *N*, *U* and *V* are also Scottish. All have the integral wood hinge, are tortoiseshell lined, and each is hollowed out of a block of amboyna. *L* has two compartments, with separate lids. *K*, *N* and *U* are the well-known cushion types, which were also produced as miniature boxes, like *V*, an inch or less in length, but complete with tortoiseshell linings. *H* is a reeded cylindric box. These Scottish boxes are so well made that many of them serve as 'shag' tobacco boxes today, although made anything from 100 to 160 years ago. In the Moot Hall, Aldeburgh, is an amboyna cushion box which belonged to the poet George Crabbe, 1754–1832.

O is a Scandinavian, early 18th-century box. *Q* is probably Scottish, mid-18th-century. A larger version of this box, obviously by the same carver, is illustrated, Plate 357, *A*, and described under *Tobacco Boxes*. *M* is a sliding variant of *B* and *C*, more likely intended for shag than snuff, which would have clogged it. Bellows, *R*, also occur in tobacco stoppers and even in pipes, and one can see the implication of blowing up the embers. With bellows snuff boxes, presumably the allusion is to blowing away the dust.

Coffin snuff boxes seem to have been made in the 18th and 19th centuries; some have facetious inscriptions on them, such as 'Sacred to the dust of Virginia', but the left-hand coffin box, *S*, appears to be a genuine *memento mori*. It is hollowed out of kingwood and has a bronze lid, neatly engraved 'Mr. Charles Russell Wyatt died 13th May, 1825. Aged 34 years'.

The well worn diamond-shaped box, *T*, is inlaid with a punch bowl, goblets and clay pipe. *W* is a typical 18th-century horn mull; its silver band is engraved 'A grand refreshment'. The Scots pronounce mill as mull, and the original Scottish mulls were grinders, but the name mull became transferred to the Scottish receptacle for the snuff, usually a horn with a point curled. In the National Museum of Antiquities, Edinburgh, is a conical horn box for snuff, tapering to a straight point. My guess is that such boxes were used to hold *carottes* and may have had graters under their lids. When snuff was purchased ready ground, and a pocket box was needed, it would be logical to curl the horn to prevent it making a hole in the pocket.

A group of boxes said to have been particularly popular with students and bibliophiles, are 'books', Plate 367, *A* to *F*. Except where dates are inscribed on them, it is impossible to gauge their age accurately, but they appear to have enjoyed popularity both in the 18th and 19th centuries. They are almost invariably carved out of a solid block and much work went into simulating the book binding. Some are charming, with inlaid or chip carved covers and gilt or boxwood 'leaves'. Sometimes the owner's name, or initial, is substituted for the title of the volume and a heart is inlaid on the spine. Most of the geometric chip carved boxes, such as *E*, are Welsh. The majority of book boxes have sliding lids, but occasionally they are pivoted. They vary from crude

to fine quality. One of the crudest, *C*, has a slot screwed spine, which locks the sliding lid.

The large burr box, *G*, contains a silver lined receptacle, with hinged silver lid engraved 'A knot of oak from Cowper's Tree, Yardley Chase 1840'. Then follows an extract from one of Cowper's poems, referring to the oak. *H*, *N* and *O*, present a choice of snuffy headgear. *H* is a tortoiseshell lined, Napoleonic hat, early 19th-century, and *N*, a peaked cap, later still, and made from figured birch. The well-patinated helmet, *O*, is much earlier. It is Italian and may be 17th- or 18th-century; it is inlaid with various woods and tortoiseshell, with brass piqué lines between the inlays. *J* is a crude but rare 17th-century box, and *K* is carved with inscriptions and scenes relating to the devil taking off snuffers. *L* and *M* are two of our snuffy ancestors' macabre jokes: the first represents a tomb with headstone, the second, a boot, and they must have provided many shocks, for when the lids are slid back, a most realistic green snake, with metal eyes, pops out. If it emerged from a cloud of snuff, it must have appeared horrific enough to startle the most iron-nerved nosologist.

P is unusual in its D shape and in having an architectural frieze running round and ending in free standing pillars. The 'hands', *Q*, *R* and *S*, taking a pinch 'twixt finger and thumb, are rare. The boxwood example, *R*, has a hinged thumb; the rosewood specimen has its lid at the wrist line; *S* opens round the 'heart' in the hand.

The two planes, *T* and *Z*, were probably woodworkers' charming fancies. As mentioned earlier, woodworkers, because of fire hazards, were notorious snuff takers until recently. The planes are the type known as Bismarks, or German planes, about 100 years ago; it does not follow that the boxes were necessarily German, for these planes were used in England too. The wedge in front of the 'plane box' lifts out of a dovetail groove and then the lid, with the 'iron' and wedge on it, slides forward.

Reference has already been made to *U* being a Swedish snuff flask (see *Flask Type Snuff Boxes*). The next two boxes, *V* and *W*, although almost devoid of ornament, are absolutely in the top grade and show that perfect simplicity and good proportion which require great skill to attain. Each is made from carefully selected burr maple, with particularly handsome markings. Both have silver hinges; that on the circular box is scrolled and connected to a silver rim which encircles the lid and encases the thumbpiece. The oblong box, with the bombé sides, hollow canted corners, and shallow domed lid, with incorporated thumb lift, exactly follows the outline of certain mid-18th-century boxes made in enamel, gold and silver. Both were probably made about that time. *X* and *Y* are probably two of the earliest Scottish mulls or snuff boxes extant. Both are of lignum vitae, silver-mounted. *X* is engraved with initials I.K. and date 1684. *Y*, undated, but similar, has the silver band engraved 'Richard Burrell, Newcastle'.

In Plate 368 is included a selection of coquilla nutshell snuff boxes, *C* to *K* (for coquilla nuts see Section XIII.) Most are German or Dutch, the majority early 19th, a few late 18th-century. The hinged flaps to the boxes are behind the figures; the bodies use a whole nut each; the heads and feet are dowelled on.

The remainder of the human and animal snuff boxes, Plate 368, much sought by collectors, are of carved wood. *A*, an ape squatting on its haunches, has a sliding panel at the back. *B* is a charming little 18th-century lady; *L*, a large boxwood pig; *M*, a monkey head; *N*, a horse head; *O* and *P*, boxwood skulls; *Q*, a reclining dog; *R*, a good, but not photogenic, silver-mounted bulldog head and *S*, a little hunchback. *T*, a boar's head and *U*, an ape head, are ebony. *V* is a well carved boxwood fish; *W*, a tortoise; *X* and *Y*, two excellently modelled frogs. Most of these are 18th-century.

In Plate 369, *A* is made from a Scottish elm burr; the lid, at the back, has the noted integral hinge. *B* is a rare oval Scottish box with laced rim; the lid, chip carved with hearts and diamonds, is inlaid in brass with 'W.D. 1739'. *C* and *D* are early 19th-century Tunbridge mosaic rosewood boxes. *F*, inlaid with mother-of-pearl, is a speciality of the island of Rhodes. *G*, a miniature carved boxwood man-of-war, inlaid with silver, dates from the early 19th century; rather similar models were made in coquilla nutshell.

In Plate 364, the novel walnut snuff box shaped as a twin-barrelled pistol, *E*, is based on an early 19th-century joke about a nosologist who is alleged to have invented such a weapon so that he could prime both nostrils simultaneously.

Shoe Snuff Boxes

Shoes represent one of the largest groups among wooden snuff boxes. A selection is shown in Plate 364 and literally hundreds of varied specimens may be collected without including materials other than wood.

Carved shoes cover, in their styles, every period from mediaeval times (as exemplified by *C*) to the end of the 19th century. As snuff was not known in Europe in mediaeval times and as, moreover, the few dated specimens usually show dates in the 1880s, many people dismiss all boot and shoe snuff boxes as Victorian romantic revival work. This, however, is wrong as regards shoes because Fairholt, writing in 1859 about quaint forms of snuff boxes, says 'One favourite in the last century was *A Ladies Shoe*' and he illustrates one similar to the pair, *J*. It looks, therefore, as though shoes had at least two phases of popularity —one in the 18th century and another in the late 19th, and that probably they were out of fashion in the mid-19th century, when Fairholt was writing.

It has been said that shoe snuff boxes were made as 'passing-out' pieces by cobbler apprentices; this is probably true of accurately produced models, particularly those studded with brass tacks and having steel sole and heel tips. Woodworking formerly was an essential part of the cobbler's trade, and miniature 'lasts' were an apprentice's recognised passing-out piece.

The association of shoes with love and marriage goes back to the bible. Silver shoes on wedding cakes, the ancient Yorkshire custom of 'trashing'—throwing old footwear after brides and bridegrooms, as they leave the church—and the old shoe tied behind the bridal vehicle still continue the connection. Heart motifs frequently found, inlaid with ivory and mother-of-pearl, on shoe snuff boxes, suggest that this type was particularly regarded as love tokens. This is further substantiated by dated examples made in pairs and having different initials on each shoe and also by the rather rare twin joined pairs, which proclaim 'We two are one'. The two chip carved, twin joined pairs, O and P, are Scandinavian; each contains two separate cavities. The twin pair, M, has hearts carved on the toes and MARRY on the lid; it has a single snuff cavity and is Welsh. The pair of button boots, F, dated 1884, and the pair of rosewood shoes, L, are probably apprentices' pieces. B, shown upside down, is a boot, the heel of which pivots round, to disclose the snuff cavity in the sole; this is the only instance I know of this treatment. All the other boxes shown, open from the top; the majority have sliding lids, but a few are hinged and some have lift-off lids. A, D, G, H, K and Q are all good quality, Victorian, mahogany specimens, brass studded and mostly inlaid with ivory or mother-of-pearl.

Table and Counter Snuff Boxes and Snuff Pots
Although special snuff waistcoats were formerly worn, with capacious flap pockets in them for snuff boxes, many boxes, probably including some of those already described, must have been too large, or too elaborate and delicate for the pocket. They were, in fact, intended for table use in the home, for passing along the table at convivial functions, or, in the case of the more robust specimens, for a free dip on the counter of a tobacconist's shop or at an inn. In such establishments, snuff was rasped daily and a large circular box was provided, usually about 6 in. in diameter. One made from figured mahogany is shown, Plate 370, A, and another, of yew-wood, C, is carved in spirited fashion, with a demon playing a drum. G, a satinwood box, inlaid with ebony, J, stained in imitation of Sheraton inlay, and L, made from oak of old London Bridge, with a silver plaque, engraved with the City Arms and date 1176, are all domestic, table snuff boxes. The making of snuff boxes from famous trees, or timber and metal from famous buildings, was formerly quite a mania and, according to a writer 100 years ago, boxes made from Shakespeare's mulberry tree would have cubed up sufficient wood to build a warship. This may be somewhat of an exaggeration, because you can make a great many snuff boxes out of a fair sized branch.

E, a 6 in. long, rosewood book, with pivoted lid, also ranks as a domestic table snuff box; B, D and F come into the community or ceremonial class. The first is not treen, but a handsomely silver-mounted, ceremonial Scottish mull of ram's horn. These decorative mulls were used at dinners of Scottish regiments and societies and passed or slid along the table. B, made between 1870 and 1880, has a cairngorm forming the knob of the silver lid of the box and a silver elk head mount; a silver elk foot supports the silver tipped horn. On silver chains, suspended from the mount, are the traditional ivory and silver mallet, rake, snuff spoons, etc. As these ceremonial Scottish mulls go, this is not a particularly large nor elaborate one; sometimes they have a whole head in silver, plentifully studded with cairngorms, between a pair of silver-tipped horns. The much more sober specimen, D, is an English, 18th-century, turned yew-wood snuff box, mounted on a matching tobacco box and probably similarly used at functions. *F* is a mahogany table snuff pot with handle, for passing round; it could be 18th-century or early 19th-century. *H* is a Rhodesian, native-made snuff pot. *K* is an English, laburnum, snuff mixing pot. Keeping snuff in condition and moistening when necessary, usually with salt water, was very important to the majority, who liked moist rather than dry snuffs. Small wooden snuff pots, such as *K*, which also acted as miniature mortars, or, more correctly, mixing pots, for stirring while adjusting the moisture content, were sold by snuff shops in the 18th and early 19th centuries. The spoon and pestle or stirrer, are attached to opposite sides of the lid.

Snuff Flasks—see *Snuff Boxes, Flask Type*

Snuff Mallets—see *Snuff Spoons*

Snuff Pots—see *Table and Counter Snuff Boxes and Snuff Pots*

Snuff Rasps

The most common shop device for converting tobacco into snuff was probably an outsize rasp, a foot or more in length, tapering in width from about 6 in. to 4 in. It was usually a plain board of bat-like form, rebated out, so that a wood rim was left round the flush grater, which was nailed in, and consisted of a sheet of iron, crudely punched with a close pattern of perforations. The snuff fell into a cavity beneath the grater and an opening at one end allowed for pouring into a jar or canister. In Fribourg and Treyer's snuff shop, whose early Georgian bow windows still grace the Haymarket, one of these graters still survives. Their account books go back to 1764 (with a reference to an earlier one). From these books, which read like pages out of *Debrett*, it is apparent that even by

1764 the individual rasp, for home use, was passing out of fashion. Some customers were still buying *carottes* unrasped until the end of the 18th century, but the generation which did so was rapidly dying out. The following entries show different ways of buying snuff.

1764
　Sir John Chapman paid for rasping　　1.0.
1764. Jan. 16
　Mr. Rakes.
　　1 carrote Mont^{n,}　　　　　　　18.0.
May 20, 1765.
　　1 lb. rappee　　　　　　　　　5.0.
　　Lead Cannister　　　　　　　　6.
1765. Aug. 22
　Lord Spencer
　　1 Paris carrote　　　　　　　1.1.0.
　　Rasping　　　　　　　　　　1.0.
　　Cannister　　　　　　　　　　6.
1766. April 26
　Walter Smythe
　　8-lb. Paris Rappee Carrote　　2.8.0.
　　Jar and Basket　　　　　　　2.0.
1774. December
　5 Snuff spoon　　　　　　　　6.

The canisters to which reference is made were of lead; some still survive; so also do the alternative glazed pottery jars; both are circular and probably hold no more than 1 lb. Square glass jars, shouldered to a wide circular neck, seem to have been used for larger quantities and were protected by basketware, as many foreign wine bottles still are. References to these glass jars in baskets seem most common round about 1750. Additional to being packed in glass jars for dispatch from the snuff shop, some of the most expensive foreign snuffs were imported from abroad in long-necked glass bottles, exactly like wine bottles. To remove snuff from these bottles, long lignum vitae scoops, such as the rare survival, Plate 366, *X*, were employed.

Martinique, or King's Martinique as it was also called, from George IV favouring it, was in particular vogue between 1830 and 1840 and was the last of the expensive fashionable snuffs to be imported in long-necked bottles. Martinique, prepared in the island of the same name, by a Madame Grandmaison, retailed at 21s. per lb., compared with the normal price range which varied from 6s. to 11s. at that time. In the 18th century, most snuffs were sold in the 3s. 6d. to 7s. per lb. range, but some imported and perfumed grades, used largely as 'essences' for extending other mixtures, were much more expensive. Spanish Bran, favoured by the Prince Regent, cost £3 per lb.

The Fribourg and Treyer accounts give a good idea of amounts of snuff used by fashionable addicts. Half an ounce per day seems to have been slightly below average. Beau Brummel, a customer from 1799 to 1815, who appears to have introduced the Prince Regent to the firm, used considerably less. With snuff taking both expensive and a major occupation and social grace of the fashionable, it becomes easy to see why the beaux of the hundred years from 1660 onwards, demanded elegant, continental snuff rasps. Fashionable ones were mostly of silver, ivory and wood. The wood chosen for the finest carved rasps was usually box, which is close grained, even textured and hard. In its qualities it closely resembles ivory and the same craftsmen usually worked both materials. Although one refers to snuff rasps as being of these materials, the actual graters are of perforated iron, set either behind or between two faces of these materials. Most of the iron graters are missing now, but to collectors this makes no appreciable difference in value. Generally, snuff rasps measure about 8 in. in length, but they actually vary between 5 in. and 14 in., and divide into three principal groups: open backed rasps, with exposed metal graters, which were kept in leather cases; rasps with sliding shutters; rasps with pivoted shutters.

Silver snuff rasps, quite often, are long snuff boxes with a grater covering one side, and a hinged outer cover enclosing it; the box part is large enough to hold a small *carotte* for grating. Ivory rasps frequently incorporate a small snuff box at one end; with wood rasps, the small snuff box is a rarity. With both wood and ivory rasps which include a snuff box, it is never large enough to hold even a small *carotte*. Presumably, therefore, those who carried a wood or ivory rasp in the pocket, had a separate box, or perhaps a leather roll, for the *carotte*. I can find no literature which throws any light on this. Although some rasps, judging by their wear, were carried in the pocket, and others are curved to fit the pocket, it is possible that wood and ivory rasps were not carried as extensively as is thought. Perhaps most of them were kept at home, to fill the pocket box or boxes daily, for different snuffs and different boxes were used by fops at different times of the day.

Wood and ivory rasps follow the same patterns in their mechanics. Plate 371, *D*, shows the back of a rasp with the iron grater covering a cavity. This is divided longitudinally by a centre rib, as shown in Plate 371, *E*, which has the grater removed. The rib prevents the grater sagging and also, by diverting the snuff into two channels, prevents it clogging. At the narrow end of the rasp is usually a spout, through which snuff may be poured into a separate box, or on to the back of the hand. If a snuff box is incorporated, as in *E*, it is in the wide end. There seems to be no significance, regarding date or country of origin, in the wide or narrow end occurring at top or bottom of the design.

The five Louis XIV boxwood rasps, Plate 372, are fine art and excellent examples of the so-called Cesar Bagard work, said to have been executed at Nancy in the last quarter of the 17th century. Like most of the finest *râpes à tabac*, they were individually commissioned and exquisitely carved with coats of arms and mottoes of their noble owners, against a small-scale background of flowers, formal foliage and arabesques. *A* and *B* are open type, with exposed graters at the back. The other three have pivoted shutters and are equally finely carved on both faces. *E* has a *risqué* and amusing carving on the back. *B* and *C* give me particular pleasure because I bought them as a boy, some 50 years ago, in the Caledonian Market and they cost me less in shillings than some do in pounds today.

In Plates 373 and 374 are back and front views of two further outstanding examples of Louis XIV, 17th-century, boxwood *râpes*, with pivoted shutters. Plate 373, which was formerly one of the prizes in the Evan-Thomas Collection, is fully described in his book. Briefly, the subject of this highly skilled and cleverly composed carving, appears to be a burlesque on methods of church preferments of the period. Plate 374, following the same late 17th-century outline, is less sophisticated in its carving, but extremely interesting as a documentary. It is the only rasp I have seen which records both its carver's name and its owner's name and profession. On the front, below stylised acanthus leaves, are carved twin flaming hearts, in an oval inscribed *L'amour nous unit*. Below, are the Emblems of the Passion. At the back, above a coat of arms, is the inscription *Je suis a Claude de Cabaza, prestre.* Beneath the carving of the Ascension is inscribed *Faite par F. Castel.* The snuff flows out through a hole in the priest's tonsure. This is obviously an example of a secular object which did belong to a priest; but although records show that snuff taking was very prevalent among the clergy, I do not share the common belief that all snuff rasps and other secular objects carved or engraved with the sacred initials, religious texts, or biblical episodes, were originally owned by priests, made by ecclesiastical craftsmen or intended for priestly or church use. So many homely objects were decorated in this manner—even trade tools—that I think one must assume that the main purposes were usually to remind people that

religion was a part of their daily life, and to please the devout with emblems of their faith.

One of the finest carved boxwood rasps extant is the $11\frac{1}{2}$ in. long, French, 17th-century specimen, Plate 375, formerly in the Trapnell Collection. The royal French coat of arms, above the trophy of arms, armour and standards, shows the bar sinister between the fleur-de-lis. The design is masterly, well matched by the skilled execution.

The 18th-century rasp, Plate 376, *A*, either English or more probably German, is an open backed, curved type for the pocket; it is unusual in two respects—portraying a hunting scene, and in having it arranged to view horizontally. It was formerly in the Carnegie Collection. Also curved for the pocket and arranged for horizontal viewing is *B*, a rare and unusual Italian, 17th-century rasp, inlaid with brass piqué, and depicting, rather naïvely, a four-horse chariot approaching a house. More usual Italian, 17th-century patterns are *K* and *L*, also curved to fit the pocket and inlaid with brass piqué and mother-of-pearl; they were formerly in the Evan-Thomas Collection and, before that, in the Hilton Price and Drane Collections. *C*, *D*, *E*, *F* and *G* show a selection of late 17th- and early 18th-century carved wood rasps, mostly French and Italian and characterized by religious themes in their carving. The majority were formerly in the Evan-Thomas Collection. *C* and *D* are both carved from boxwood, with the Crucifixion and Emblems of the Passion. *D* is dated 1741. *C* includes an Adoration, heads of angels, etc., and, although very worn, is much the finer composition and carving; it is inscribed Florent Bertaut. *E*, the John the Baptist rasp, is inscribed at the back that it belongs to Jean Baptiste Gimier, living at Aviltaneus, 1749. *F* shows a rather naïve rendering of Abraham being restrained by the angel from sacrificing Isaac. *G* is an early 17th-century, boxwood rasp, portraying St. Louis crowned;

Animose finde. Pater,   *Est laborum consolator*
Animosa perge Mater   *Mundi puer fabricator*
     Fila trahens linea.   *Frusta legens lignea.*

Hieronymus Wierx fecit et excud. Cum Gratia et Priuilegio. Buschere.

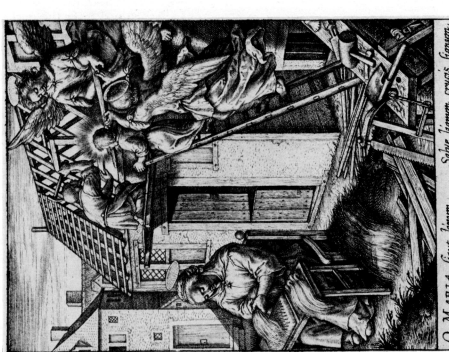

O MARIA sicut bonam,   *Sabæ lignum crucis lignum.*
Munda cordis nostri sinum,   *Qui fert paruum puer tignum.*
     Peccatis innumeris: *Crucem feret humeris.*

Hieronymus Wierx fecit et excud. Cum Gratia et Priuilegio. Buschere.

399–404 Six of the Holy Family engravings of Hieronymus Wierix, *circa* 1600, which show woodworking tools and constructional techniques of the period and also textile working devices. (*Section XXIV*)

Ecce, Mater, cum labore   Nonne dicis mente tota?
Largo vultus cum sudore   Curre linum, curre rota.
     Serrantem filiolum;   Cito da Strophiolum.

Hieronymus wierx fecit et excud.   *Cum Gratia et Privilegio. Bussinere.*

Ferro trabes vult ſecare,   Mater fuſo voluit lina,
Puer, terras, cælum, mare,   Angelorum quæ regina.
    Qui pugillo continet.   Supra cælos eminet.

Hieronymus Wierx fecit et excud.   Cum. Gratia et Privilegio. Byſchere.

Fruſtra pater nauem dabit,   Quando volet nauigare
Fruſtra caligas parabit   Ambulabit ſuper mare.
    Texens Mater filio;   Nullius auxilio.

Hieronymus Wierx fecit et excud.   Cum. Gratia et Privilegio. Byſchere.

406 An 18th-century, treadle jig-saw, used by one of the Tunbridge marquetry manufacturers. Most of the machine is wood. (*Section XXIV*)

405 The Dolling, late 18th-century, inlaid mahogany tool chest. For details, see introduction to this section. (*Section XXIV*)

407 Illustration from John Evelyn's *Sylva*, 1664. TOP: a multiple band-saw, water powered; BOTTOM: the method of drilling out elm water pipes. (*Section XXIV*)

408 Elm water pipes excavated by Wilkinson Sword Co. from a farm at Colnbrook, showing the method of making a right-angle junction. (*Section XXIV*)

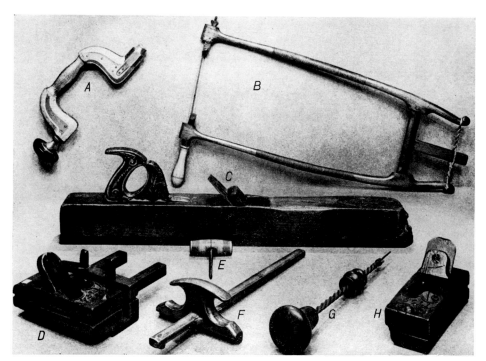

409 *A*, English, 19th-century brace; *B*, English, 18th-century fret saw; *C*, European, 17th- or early 18th-century, carved tryplane with handle offset centre; *D*, Dutch, 18th-century, carved fillister plane, dated 1764; *E*, English, 18th- or early 19th-century gimlet; *F*, English, early 19th-century marking gauge; *G*, mid-19th century Archimedean drill; *H*, Dutch, carved skew-mouthed side-moulding plane, dated 1729. (*Section XXIV*)

410 18th-century woodworking tools in the Victoria and Albert Museum. For details, see text. *Photograph by courtesy of the museum.* (*Section XXIV*)

411 Examples of mid- and late 19th-century ornamental turnery. (*Section XXIV*)

412 Examples of mid- and late 19th-century ornamental turnery. (*Section XXIV*)

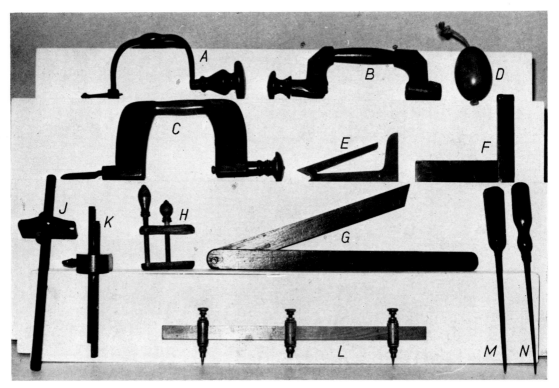

413 *A, B* and *C*, braces; *D*, plumb-bob; *E* and *G*, bevels; *F*, square; *J* and *K*, marking gauges; *H*, cramp; *L*, trammel; *M* and *N*, steels. For further details, see text. (*Section XXIV*)

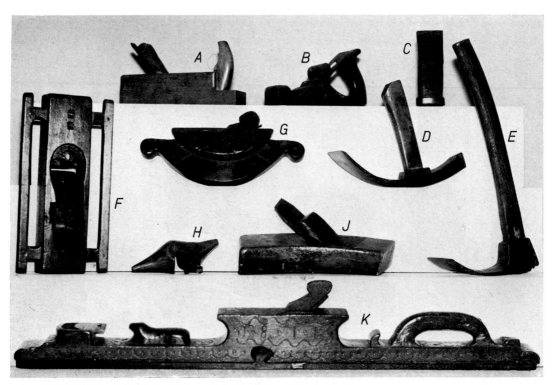

414 *A, B, F, G, J* and *K*, planes; *C*, cooper's wedge and *D* and *E*, adzes; *H*, a nogg or rounding plane. All except *F* and *K*, English. For further details, see text. (*Section XXIV*)

415 Top and bottom view of a rare spelk plane, dated 1776. Probably Dutch. (*Section XXIV*)

416 Two views of a fine croze, probably dating from the 17th century. (*Section XXIV*)

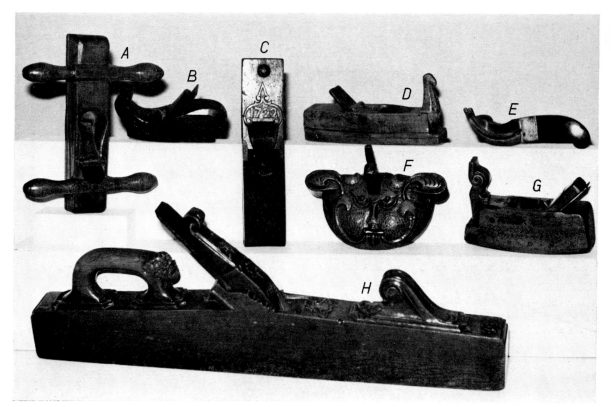

417 Selection of continental planes, mostly 18th-century, and *E*, an English, 18th-century, curved scratch-stock. For details, see text. (*Section XXIV*)

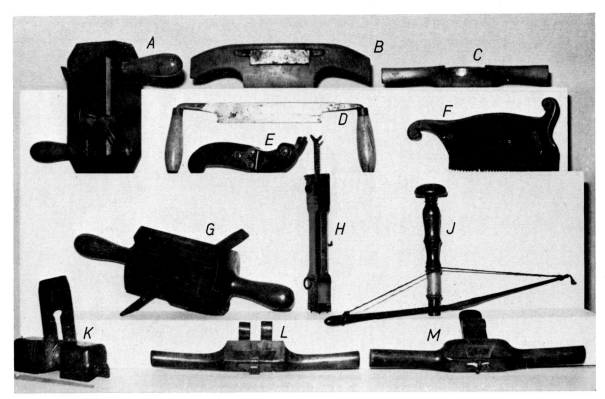

418 *A* and *G*, witchets or rounding and tapering planes; *B*, *C* and *D*, shaves—the last is more often known as a draw-knife; *E*, reverse view of scratch-stock shown Plate 417; *F*, Italian or Austrian, 18th-century, coffin saw; *H*, lifting jack, 17th or 18th century; *J*, bow-drill, 17th or 18th century; *K*, spill plane; *L* and *M*, coachmaker's rounders. (*Section XXIV*)

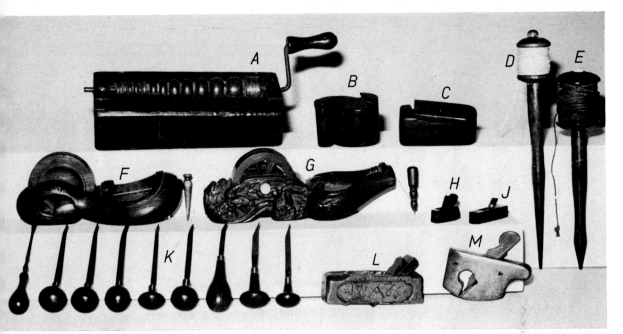

419 *A*, gouge and chisel burr remover; *B* and *C*, grease boxes; *D* and *E*, chalk line winders; *F* and *G*, sumi tsubos; *H* and *J̄*, model maker's planes; *K*, wood block engraver's burins; *L*, small smoothing plane, dated 1766; *M*, miniature bullnose plane. (*Section XXIV*)

420 French, early 18th-century treadle lathe with many of its original tools. Wood parts of the machine are mostly of Spanish mahogany. (*Section XXIV*)

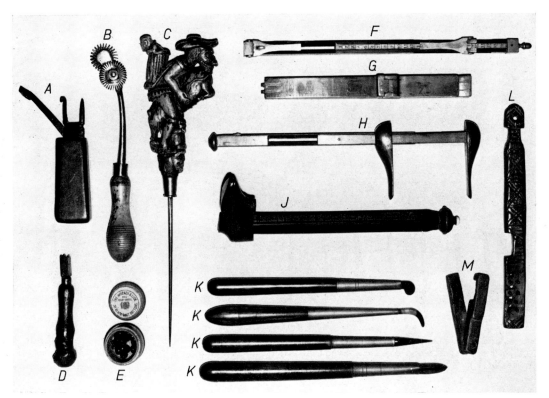

421 *A*, saddler's race; *B*, leatherworker's prick wheel; *C*, leatherworker's awl; *D*, cobbler's edge setting iron; *E*, 'penny barrel' of boot buttons; *F* to *J*, 18th- and 19th-century size sticks; *K*, agate burnishers; *L* and *M*, spinet wire stretchers. (*Section XXV*)

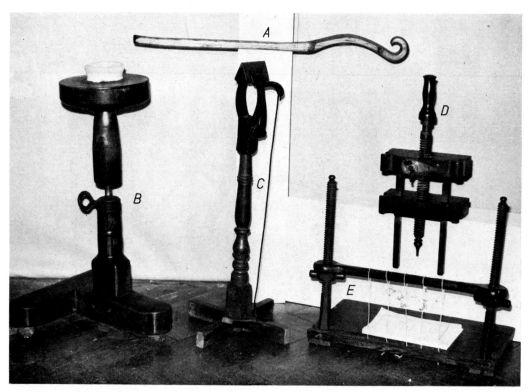

422 *A*, pedlar's pack stick; *B*, potter's wheel; *C*, glovemaker's donkey; *D*, bookbinder's hand trimmer press; *E*, bookbinder's sewing frame. (*Section XXV*)

423 Brewhouse and brewers' devices: *A*, malt shovel; *B*, beer drayman's sink; *C*, beer funnel; *D*, malt fork; *E*, mash stirrer; *F*, beer bowl. (*Section XXV*)

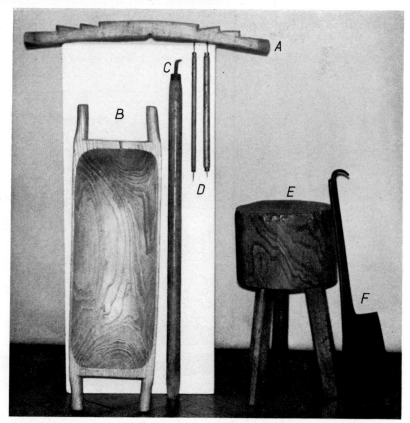

24 Butcher's devices: *A*, gambrel; , shoulder tray; *C*, britcher; *D*, arcase back stretchers; *E*, butcher's lock with cleaver, *F*, alongside. *Section XXV*)

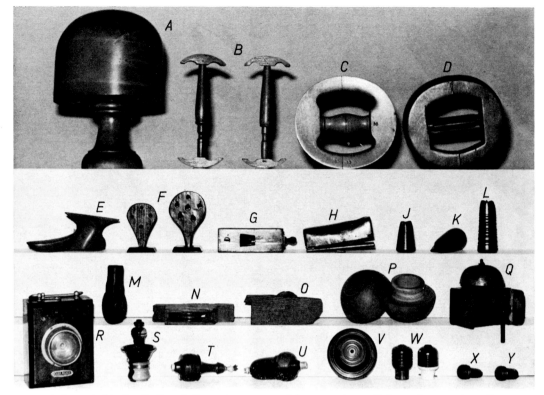

425 *A*, hatter's block; *B*, *C* and *D*, various types of hat stretchers, *E*, hatter's smoother; *F*, straw splitters; *G* and *H*, osier shaves; *J*, *K* and *L*, osier cleavers and splitters; *M*, oak pulley wheel; *N* and *O*, oak encased, boxwood sash pulleys; *P*, Lamson Paragon boxwood cash ball; *Q*, Victorian shop door bell; *R*, oak encased, Ever Ready electric torch; *S*, Victorian speaking tube mouthpiece and whistle of lignum vitae; *T* and *U*, Victorian bell pushes; *V*, rose; *W*, lamp socket plugs; *X* and *Y*, blind cord acorns of boxwood and coquilla nut respectively. (*Section XXV*)

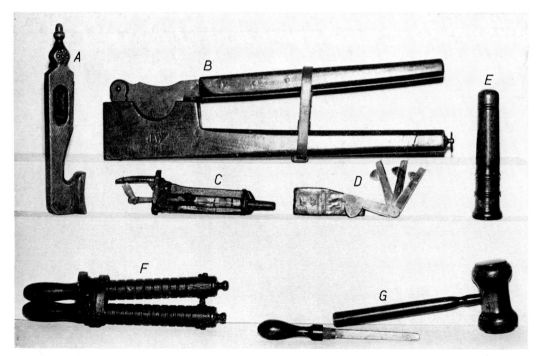

426 *A*, *Hüfscharfen* (hoof-parer); *B*, tail docker; *C*, syringe, veterinary(?); *D*, folding fleam; *E*, balling gun; *F*, Rutters patent horse twitch; *G*, fleam and mallet. (*Section XXV*)

427   *A*, harness rack; *B*, stable logs; *C*, Scandinavian harness saddle; *D*, Edwardian shop display leg and shoe; *E*, straw plait mill; *F*, straw or reed combing fork; *G*, possibly a thatching device; *H*, leggat; *J*, hoof-parer; *K*, horse tooth rasp; *L*, shop window long-arm. (*Section XXV*)

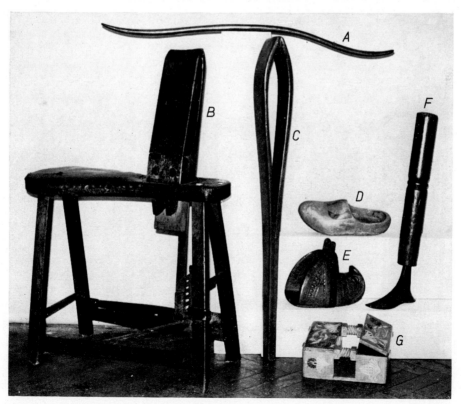

428   *A*, pedlar's pack stick; *B*, saddler's clamp stool, *C*, cobbler's clam; *D*, sabot; *F*, cobbler's last; *G*, Russian shoe cleaning box. (*Section XXV*); *E*, foot muff. (*Section XV*)

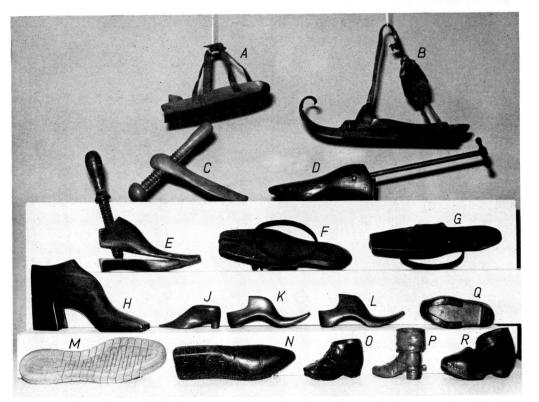

429 *A* and *B*, ice skates; *C*, Watt's patent shoe tree; *D*, adjustable last; *E*, instep stretcher; *F* and *G*, under and upper views of pattens; *H* and *J*, hardwood block shoes, probably for display; *K* and *L*, miniature lasts, probably also for display; *M*, flexible beechwood sole; *N*, Scandinavian last, dated 1796; *O* and *P*, miniature shoe and spurred jack-boot containers; *Q* and *R*, sole and upper views of child's clog-soled boots. (*Section XXV*)

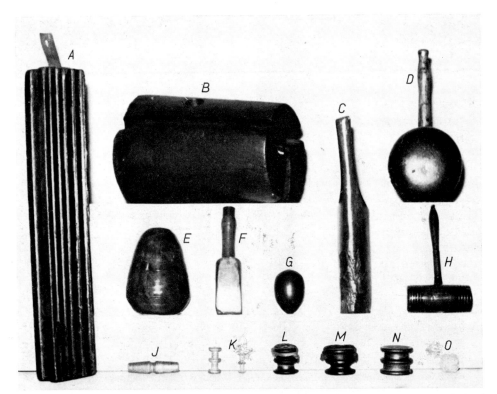

430 *A*, rope layer's gauge; *B*, rope layer's top (diagram showing usage in text); *C*, lead dresser; *D*, saddler's maul; *E* and *G* plumbers' turnpins; *F*, plumber's chase wedge or glut; *H*, plumber's mallet, also used in other trades; *J*, commando's toggle; *K* to *N*, whorls; *O*, pre-war ½*d*. ball of string. (*Section XXV*)

I have seen other examples of this subject in ivory, but not in wood. *H*, a boxwood rasp, dated 1724, French, and carved with a coat of arms and an order, is interesting because of the selection of woodworking tools carved in relief in the lower half. A very similar rasp, obviously by the same maker, dated 1723, but without most of the tools, is also in the Pinto Collection. The 11 in. long rasp, *J*, is a rare, rather outsize specimen, dated 1745, probably Hungarian. It is of dark, heavy wood, inlaid with contrasting panels, carved with armorials and bordered with silver piqué; its back is shown in Plate 371, *D*. The chip carved crudity, *M*, a very deep rasp, which bears some resemblance to a fish, and *N*, are the only domestic specimens which I have ever seen which are likely to have been made in the British Isles. I believe *M* to be Welsh, 18th-century. *N*, the possibly unique heart-shaped specimen, with chip carved border, is engraved John Suttun·June 11·1706.

In Plate 377, *A* is dated 1733 and bears initials G.Q. and B.I. Presumably the centre motif, between the hearts, may represent *le roi soleil*, although he was dead by that date. It is unusual in shape and, more so, in having a snuff box at the back, fed by a hole in the right half of the divided receptacle behind the grater, whilst the left half feeds the spout. The back of this rasp, with its grater removed, is shown in Plate 371, *E*. *B*, dated 1743, is a rather ambitious, but not very skilled, composition of interlocked biblical scenes and religious motifs. *C* is unusual in its face decoration. Back view, it shows a boar's head forming the spout, and four acorns. Its nationality is doubtful, but it may be French provincial, 18th-century. *D*, which has a pivoted shutter, is 17th-century, probably Italian; it is carved with the name Joseph Lanti. *E* and *F* are French, early 18th-century; the former is unusual in being carved with relief portraits, additional to the royal arms. *G* is a finely lettered, German, 18th-century rasp of unusual type, so deep inside that it

could have held a small *carotte*. Its shutter continues the lettering. The inscription translates:

> 'I will in lowly state remain
> And not for high position strain'.

How happy for the world had Hitler been the owner!

The Dutch rasp, *H*, with sliding shutter, is inlaid on the edges with bone, has a border of brass piqué and includes among its low relief carved motifs a heart, double-headed arrow and the initials I.S. On the back is carved Rechd. V Baschin and date 1725.

Although there are not many survivals now, coaster snuff boxes, for passing along the table after a dinner or other social function, were not unusual; neither were wine coasters on wheels, but the coaster snuff rasp on four wheels, *J*, must always have been a rarity. It was obviously made by the same man who fashioned *H*, and may also be dated around 1725.

K, an attractive and unusual Dutch specimen, is of pearwood, only $5\frac{1}{2}$ in. long, carved in low relief on both sides with tulip scrolls and inlaid with bone or ivory. It has a sliding shutter over the grater, and the cavity beneath connects by holes to the hinged snuff box, which is lined with red lacquer. It is dated 1740, on the back of the case. Like two others in this picture, it includes a heart motif in its decoration and was doubtless a love token. *L* is a German, 17th-century rasp, belonging to a well defined group, all inlaid with engraved ivory and some dark wood; it has a sliding shutter and hinged brass nozzle.

Three outsize rasps, but of such fine quality that they could not have been intended for shop use, are portrayed in Plate 371, *A*, *B* and *C*. They could hardly have been carried in the pocket, however, as they measure respectively $11\frac{1}{2}$ in. by $3\frac{3}{8}$ in., $13\frac{7}{8}$ in. by 3 in., and 12 in. by $3\frac{3}{4}$ in. Curiously, the largest, *B*, is the curved type, which one usually regards as shaped to the pocket. This one is probably from one of the

18th-century German, Austrian or Hungarian Archduchies; its carving is inlaid with brass piqué. The rasp, *A*, 18th-century, possibly Austrian, has a sliding shutter and hinged snuff box at the back; the shutter is shown, *A1*. The interesting armorial designs on the two sides are not identical, but both include a merchant's mark. The open back rasp, *C*, an Italian, 17th-century conception of the sacrifice of Isaac, is a competent carving, flattened by wear.

Snuff Shop Signs—see Section XXVI, *Trade Signs, Ships' Figureheads etc.*

Snuff Spoons
Small spoons of bone, ivory, hardwood and silver were used by snuff addicts; some sniffed direct from the spoon, others used it to transfer snuff from the box to the back of the hand for sniffing. Sometimes snuff spoons are an integral part of a snuff pot, or chained to a ceremonial snuff mull (for snuff pots and snuff mulls, see *Table and Counter Snuff Boxes and Snuff Pots*). In Plate 366, *Y* shows a selection of lignum vitae snuff spoons and a miniature mallet for dislodging moist snuff from the box rim. *X* is a long-handled spoon for removing snuff from a snuff jar. *Z* comprises a good variety of English, Scottish and bone snuff spoons, including one to serve both nostrils simultaneously.

Snuff Walking Sticks—see Section II, *Costume Accessories*

XXIII

Toilet and Bedroom Accessories

This section mainly covers toilet items used in the bedroom, or applied or supplied by the barber or *perruquier*, also various devices and containers needed in the bedroom for apparel and jewels. Most of the objects are explained under their alphabetical headings, but wigs were (and are again now) such a peculiar fashion or social custom, that they require some explanatory introduction.

· Wigs were worn by the ancient Egyptians and by both sexes in Greece and Rome in the time of the Emperors. Elizabeth I had exotic tastes in attire and hairdressing. From about 1580, she favoured saffron or red dyed wigs and many ladies of her court followed suit, varying the colour of their hair to complement their costume. Nevertheless, it is problematical whether this particular wig phase originated as pure fashion, or how much it was an attempt to remedy or disguise the passing of the years. As opposed to wigs, an addition of false hair has been common among women from time immemorial and might take the form of curls, plaits, borders, bullheads, buns, etc., according to the dictates of fashion. Men of fashion are said to have commenced wearing periwigs in France in 1529. The fashion did not spread to England until the return of the court of Charles II from their continental sojourn, in 1660. Even then, wearing of wigs

spread slowly downwards through male society.

Between 1640 and 1650, differences in hairdressing and clothing had characterized 'parties'. Cavaliers originally were exaggeratedly long curled and overdressed, their opponents crop headed and severely garbed. Although the Roundheads triumphed militarily, they were conquered sartorially and in hairdressing. Before the Restoration, all except the most bigoted had adopted modified Cavalier fashions. Most men had returned to beribboned lovelocks by 1650; in 1654, John Evelyn's *Diary* tells of women painting themselves again. In 1659, Pepys makes several references to his own and his wife's gay clothes.

At the 1660 Restoration, fashions went to extremes of extravagance. Women's headdressing rose steadily and by the century's end was mounted on two or three storey wire cages, known as 'commodes'. The male popinjays of Charles II's court wore jewelled and feathered tricorn hats over periwigs, elaborately embroidered waistcoats and gaily coloured, long, full skirted coats, decorated with more embroidery and ornamental gold buttons. Yards of lace and ribbons were worn at neck, shoulders, wrists and knees, with sometimes additional bows on sword hilts. Silk stockings, red tongued and high heeled shoes, with elaborate buckles, gold fringed gauntlet gloves and a lace *mouchoir*, hanging negligently from coat pocket, completed this amazing ensemble.

Fashionable gentlemen of the Charles II period well exemplified the theory that people grow to resemble their pets. With enormous and top-heavy curled periwigs raised in two tufts or ears over the temples, they resembled nothing so much as outsize King Charles spaniels.

The wig fashion was particularly useful in that it enabled any close cropped Round-heads still remaining at the Restoration, to become Cavaliers overnight. The fashion also originated the expression 'to pull the wool over one's eyes', it being a favourite trick of highwaymen to approach their victim from behind and push his wig over his eyes, whilst they relieved him of his money.

The real reason for wearing wigs was the introduction of the French fashion of powdering; the inevitable sequence to that step is neatly told in the diary of Samuel Pepys:

> May 31, 1662 'Had Sarah to comb my head clean, which I found so foul with powdering and other troubles, that I am resolved to try how I can keep my head dry without powder . . . .'

A year later Pepys was still fighting against fashion—

> May 9, 1663 ' . . . at Mr. Jervas's, my old barber, I did try two or three borders and perriwiggs, meaning to wear one; and yet I have no stomach [for it,] but that the pains of keeping my hair clean is so great.'

Three months later, Pepys was faltering—

> Aug. 29, 1663 ' . . . to Jervas the barber's, and there was trimmed, and did deliver back a periwigg, which he brought by my desire the other day to show me, having some thoughts, though no great desire or resolution yet to wear one, and so I put it off for a while.'

On October 30th, he capitulated and bought his first periwig; on November 3rd, he took the plunge and decided to wear it—

> 'By and by comes Chapman, the periwigg-maker and upon my liking it, without more ado I went up, and there he cut off my haire, which went a little to my heart at present to part with it; but, it being over, and my periwigg on, I paid him £3 for it; and away went he with my owne haire to make up another of, and I by and by, after I had caused all my mayds to look upon it; and they conclude it do become me . . . .'

Next day he bought a case for the wig from the trunk makers. Four days later, he went to church in his new periwig and appears rather disappointed that it caused no stir—

> Nov. 8 'I found that my coming in a perri-wigg did not prove so strange to the world as I was afeard it would, for I thought that all the church would presently have cast their eyes all upon me, but I found no such thing.'

In 1665, the Great Plague impeded the fashion, through fear, as Pepys relates, that hair for wigs might have been ' . . . cut off the heads of people dead of the plague'. The plague was no permanent deterrent to fashion, for by 1680 powdering was so firmly established that the larger and better planned houses, built after the Great Fire, had powdering closets leading from bedrooms. In 18th-century houses, an additional one was sometimes provided on half landings, where visiting gallants, with the aid of a mirror and a three-legged basin and powdering stand (sometimes erroneously described as a wig stand), could repair the ravages of their journey.

During the basic powdering, ladies and gentlemen, wearing dust cloaks and sometimes holding stiff paper cones, like dunces' caps, over their faces, sat while their wigs were pomaded, perfumed and powdered. Bewigged men of fashion were luckier than women; their heads were shaven and when at home and not entertaining, they wore nightcaps or turbans. The unfortunate ladies sat long hours while their own hair, interwoven with artificial additions, was dressed over cushions of tow, which advanced in height and complexity with the years of the century. Finally, these mountains, of which the most exaggerated had pinnacles crowned by artificial flowers, fruits, feathers, ribbons, birds in nests and even miniature windmills, ships and carriages, reached such a pitch that they necessitated the powderer using a pair of steps, whilst women had to travel in sedan chairs with open roofs, and sleep upright in bed! The structures were so expensive and tedious to erect that they were left undisturbed for weeks and it is understandable that the fashionable carried elegant tapering head scratchers—for *Head Scratchers*, see Section II, *Costume Accessories*.

After 1765, powdering declined among young men of fashion and the periwig makers vainly petitioned the king, complaining that 'men will wear their own hair'. By 1789, the change of fashion had spread to the old and Parson Woodforde recorded 'I did not know Mr. Dalton at first as he now wears his hair.' The lingering fashion died soon after 1795, when a tax of one guinea per 'head' was levied on powdered hair. Thereafter, apart from menservants, only lawyers, Members of Parliament and the clergy, who had most violently attacked the fashion in its early stages, continued wearing wigs; they became known as guinea-pigs. Now only the legal profession wear wigs as a professional badge, but at the height of the wig wearing craze, every profession and trade had a specific wig of office; for instance, naval, military, ecclesiastical, medical and coachmen's wigs were all different. In general, the higher the position, the larger and more elaborate was the wig—hence the term 'bigwig'.

Barber's Chair, Child's

Probably the old-time barber's shop usually contained a child's high chair, with protec-

tive bar in front, but some may well have had an ancillary chair, like Plate 378, for placing on an ordinary chair, so that the child could sit with his feet dangling between the uprights and his hands grasping the horns of the guard rail. The design and construction of the specimen illustrated are both unusual and suggest that it was made by a native African craftsman, to the order of a white settler, some time in the last century.

Bonnet Stands—see *Wig Stands*

Bottle Cases

Bottle cases of boxwood, ebony, etc., used in the bedroom and at the barber's, were the same as those illustrated and described in Section I, *Apothecary*.

Brushes, Clothes and Dusting

Clothes and dusting brushes are seldom allowed to outlast their useful life, unless the handles or backs are made of a more valuable material than wood, or unless the wood is ornamented in some way. Of the two with backs faced with Tunbridge wood mosaic, Plate 388, the cube pattern probably dates from *circa* 1820 and the floral from *circa* 1840. The long-haired dusting brush alongside has a handle of an outline used both in the 18th and 19th centuries. A French, late 17th-century dusting brush, with a finely carved pearwood handle, in the so-called Cesar Bagard style, is shown in Plate 387—for Cesar Bagard, see *Dressing Table Sets*.

Brushes, Hair, Revolving

The barber's revolving hair brush, Plate 378, is said to have been exhibited first at the 1851 Exhibition. It remained in general use until about 1914. Originally, a boy turned the handle of a large wheel which, by means of a countershaft and belt, revolved the main shaft, which was suspended from the ceiling over the line of chairs. In the first decade of this century, electricity took the place of the boy. Over each chair dangled a continuous loop of circular section belting. The brushes, stored one above another in a rack on the wall when not in use, were each fitted with an oak pulley wheel, which engaged the belt. The brush and pulley are hollow and revolve together on a spindle, independently of the fixed wooden handle at each end. The barber grasped the two hardwood handles and pressed the revolving brush downwards on to the head of the customer. It provided a pleasurably tingling climax to the 4*d.* haircut of my boyhood, but was not so good for the barber, who had the loose hair blown in his face. The brush illustrated was used until 1964 by Mr. George Thomas, hairdresser, of St. James's Street, Piccadilly, who on his retirement at the age of 85, presented it to the Pinto Collection.

Button Hooks and Shoe Horns

Examples are shown in Plate 384, dating from the 19th century. The majority of button hooks, made in their millions in the last century, when boots, shoes and gloves all buttoned tightly, were metal throughout, but a few have wood handles. Shoe horns were mostly of horn or metal, but a few were all wood, or had wood blades with horn handles. Combined button hook/shoe horns were made, one forming the handle to the other, but being all-metal, are outside the scope of this book.

Cesar Bagard—see *Dressing Table Sets*

Chamber Horses

Henry Marsh, of Clement's Inn Passage, Clare Market, advertised in the *London Daily Post and General Advertiser*, 1739/40, that he was the inventor of the 'Chamber Horse'. Later, it was sometimes described as a dandy horse or exercise chair. Exercise in the bedroom was its main function— probably a very necessary one in the case of some of our over eating and drinking Geor-

gian ancestors. The 18th-century 'horse' illustrated, Plate 379, is in good working order and simulates the up and down motion of horse riding, shakes up the liver, and doubtless helps to reduce weight.

Thomas Sheraton gives a clear description of the construction in the 1793 edition of his *Drawing Book*; here is an abridged version—

'... the inside when the leather is off, consists of five wainscot inch boards, clamped at the ends; to which are fixed strong wire twisted round a block in regular graduation, so that when the wire is compressed by the weight of those who exercise, each turn of it may clear itself and fall within each other. The top board is stuffed with hair as a chair seat and the leather at each end is cut in slits to give vent to the air, which would otherwise resist the motion downwards. The workman should also observe, that a wooden or iron pin is fixed at each end of the middle board, for the purpose of guiding the whole seat as it plays up and down. This pin runs between the two upright pieces which are framed into the arms at each end, as the design shews. The length of the horse is twenty-nine inches, the width twenty, its height thirty-two. To the top of the foot board is eight inches, and to the board whereon the seat is fixed is thirteen.'

The pull-out step is an essential feature, because when the springs are depressed, it forces the knees upwards, inducing a crouching position, which vigorously exercises the abdominal muscles of the 'rider'. The example shown in Plate 379 is almost identical with the illustration in the *Drawing Book*.

Additional to dealing with adiposity, some variety of chamber horse was used for juvenile amusement—perhaps an alternative to the rocking horse, or for teaching children the rudiments of horse riding. In the *Great Wardrobe Bills* for the quarter ending Lady Day 1768, John Bradburn, William Vile's successor as royal cabinet-maker to George III and Queen Charlotte, is recorded as maker of such a chair for the royal children, for use in the nursery of the Queen's House (later to be enlarged into Buckingham Palace), in St. James's Park. The entry is as follows:

> 'For a neat chamber horse to carry four children at onne with a mahogany frame and spring seats covered all round with Morroca Leather the top lined with fine green cloth and brass nails with 4 handles to hold by, 2 of them supported with iron brackets finely pollished and made to turn on a swivell and 4 foot boards made to fall down occasionally for the convenience of carrying it through any doorway, etc ... £10/15/-.'

Neither the original drawings nor the chamber horse seem to have survived, but one which appears very similar to the description was given by George III to the Countess of Egremont, for her children, and is now owned by her descendant, Lord Polwarth.

It is interesting that coil springs were originally introduced into seat furniture, not to increase comfort, but purely for exercising purposes. The modern method of using coil springing did not follow for a long time—not, in fact, until someone thought of removing the 'wainscot oak boards' and substituting webbing. Spring-upholstered chairs did not come into prominent use until the reign of William IV and general acceptance was delayed until the beginning of the Victorian era. There were, however, evolutionary stages in the application of springs to upholstery. The first appears to have been a patent of 1826 by Samuel Pratt of New Bond Street. Pratt's reason for including of springs in upholstery was ' ... preventing the unpleasant effects of seasickness'. Chair springing must very soon have spread beyond this limited use, however, for two years later Pratt was granted a further patent (No. 5668) for 'Certain improvements on elastic beds, cushions, seats, pads and other articles of that kind'. The improvement was the omission of the hard edges of wood framing and substituting for them, cane or whalebone instead.

By 1833, J. C. Loudon's *Encyclopaedia* devoted a section to spring upholstery. This section concluded by saying—

> 'The effect of spiral springs as stuffing has long been known to men of science; but so little to upholsterers, that a patent for using them in stuffing was taken out, some years ago, as a new invention. Beds and seats of this description are now, however, made by upholsters generally, and the springs may be had from Birmingham by the hundred-weight.'

Roughly 100 years elapsed, therefore, between the time when Marsh thought of taking the stuffing out of people by bouncing them on springs, and Pratt thought of putting it back again by enticing them to loll comfortably on stuffed sprung upholstery.

Chamber Pots

Chamber pots, like most other domestic objects, formerly had their social gradings. Silver, porcelain, pewter, earthenware and wood were all used. Wooden chamber pots, being virtually unbreakable, were particularly favoured for children and were used in rural districts of Scotland at least until the end of last century. These bowls, inward curving towards the wide, slightly convex rim, were usually turned from sycamore, and made in various sizes. Their use is now so far forgotten, that they often puzzle collectors. The specimen illustrated, Plate 383, is 8 in. diameter outside rim, and 5½ in. inside. The child's rocking chair with chamber pot, in the same plate, was another Scottish product of the 18th or early 19th century.

The mahogany chamber pot with gilt and painted decoration, comes from the U.S.A. Inside the pot is initial M on an ornamental five-point star. Under the base is inscribed 'Presented by Geo. A. Morse January 1st 1871'. The story behind this curious object is unknown.

The china travelling chamber pot in pine case, painted black externally and fitted with leather straps and carrying handle, was a common object in days of coach travel and before long distance corridor trains. The early 19th-century example illustrated, came from Penrhyn.

Clothes Hangers

Throughout the 19th century, hanging wardrobes were commonly 7 ft. or more in height. This necessitated clothes hangers being made with stem handles which could be grasped at a convenient height. Some hangers had downward curved shoulders, but others, for use for *decolleté* dresses, had an upward tilt at each end of the curve, to prevent the dresses slipping off. Early 19th-century specimens are usually of mahogany and quite plain, Plate 384. Those made in the debased taste of the 1870s have turned wood hand grips and the hanger itself is sometimes of ornamental cast brass, with china knob terminals.

Combs

The H form was the logical outline for a comb before the advent of suitable man-made materials in the 19th century. The hitherto most commonly used materials, boxwood, bone and ivory, all have similar characteristics and limitations. In all three materials, plenty of length is available, but width is limited, and the greatest strength lies in the direction of the grain. The teeth, in order to have sufficient strength for their purpose, could only be cut in the direction of the grain, so once the advantage of incorporating coarse and fine teeth in a single comb was appreciated, the limited width of material made it logical and expedient to place fine teeth above or below coarse. The nature of the materials also made it necessary that the H should act as a structural stiffener, with a deep cross-bar between upper and lower teeth, and with sturdy 'legs'.

The double-sided or H outline comb has great antiquity. In 1951, a large fragment of an ivory H comb of the period 883–859 B.C. was excavated from the ruins of the palace of King Assur-Nasir-Pal II in Nimrud, the ancient Assyrian 'Calah'. Several fragmentary Persian H combs of the 5th century B.C. have also been recorded. The fact that in the Middle East, H combs are still manufactured of the same materials and in the same traditional manner, makes it impossible to date the simpler ones with any degree of accuracy. With the finest specimens of South European H combs of the mediaeval period, however, one is usually on firmer ground, for they are highly ornamented, of magnificent workmanship and the character of designs usually provides clues both to their period and country of origin.

A curious error has arisen of describing all ornamental mediaeval H combs as liturgical combs. Little study of the subjects depicted on the vast majority of them, is sufficient to dispel this fallacy. Liturgical H combs were used both in the ceremony of the consecration of bishops and in the coronation of kings, but descriptions of them, where they exist, show, as one would expect, that they were carved with biblical stories, such as scenes from the life of Christ. Liturgical combs must always have represented an infinitesimal proportion of the ornamental H comb output and, as with many church treasures, their rate of destruction has been unusually high. The majority of surviving H combs were obviously made for secular use and are carved with mythological subjects, pagan stories, hunting or battle scenes, or, most commonly of all, with love motifs. This last is not surprising, because throughout the mediaeval period, ornamental H combs were a recognized and highly valued European love gift from a gallant to his lady. The ornamental combs were carved *en suite* with mirror cases and *gravoirs* and formed part of the fittings of the *trousses* or dressing cases used by royalty and the nobility. They are frequently mentioned in inventories. M. Koechlin, in *Les Ivoires Gothiques Français*, records names of a number of comb-makers and merchants, as well as the prices paid and the names of some of the purchasers, frequently members of the French royal family. Most of the fashionable mediaeval H combs which have survived, appear to have come from France or Italy. A Guild of Comb-Makers existed in Venice as early as the middle of the 13th century, but in England the comb-makers did not receive their first charter as a Livery Company until 1635, and they seem to have concentrated their manufacture on simple, utilitarian combs.

A late 15th- or early 16th-century, French, boxwood H comb, measuring 7½ in. by 5¼ in., Plate 381, doubtless commissioned by an Englishman, includes in its pierced and fretted decoration, two carved relief panels, one depicting an arrow-pierced heart and the other 'punning' with a carved hart. Another boxwood specimen, of the same period, decorated with pierced and fretted ivory panels, backed with its original pink and green silk, includes a carved panel depicting a man's arm, with his hand grasping an arrow, about to pierce a heart; to ensure that his message should not be misunderstood, he also wears his heart upon his sleeve. Another French boxwood comb, 7½ in. by 5¼ in., 15th- or early 16th-century, in absolute mint condition, is illustrated in Plate 382.

These incredibly lacy wooden combs were always made from carefully selected boxwood, which was the only known hardwood with sufficiently dense, interlocked straight grain to allow the fine cutting of the teeth. This operation was performed with an ingenious twin-bladed saw, known as a *stadda*. The fine-toothed blades were separated by a distance-piece, corresponding to the width of the teeth of the comb. The first saw projected further than the second, so that as one tooth of the comb was cut, a notch or slight groove was made, to

position the next one. The fine teeth usually run approximately 32 to the inch.

Mediaeval ivory H combs, although following the same outline as boxwood, usually tell their story more as a 'strip cartoon', with a rather limited range of tales, mostly devoted to love making. One of the most popular themes was the storming of the castle of love. One side of the comb usually depicts the attack on the castle; the reverse side shows the victor kneeling before the lady, at whom Cupid discharges a dart.

Mediaeval tapestries and carvings frequently show both mermaids and harlots using mirrors and combing their tresses with H combs. Several paintings of great ladies at their toilets have also survived and include ornamental H combs in their portraiture.

One cannot tell the relative proportions of ivory and boxwood H combs which were made in mediaeval times, but many more of ivory have survived, doubtless because the boxwood are so much more fragile.

The manufacture of fine art H combs declined in Europe in the 16th century, but in Jamaica they were made in tortoiseshell, with very distinctive incised ornament, between 1671 and 1690. Jamaican combs usually have leather cases, lined with velvet, with embroidered floral patterns in silver wire; they are dated, very similar in design and appear to be the work of one craftsman, who was probably a Dutchman, or under Dutch influence. Incised tulips appear on nearly all these combs, although the other ornament used is predominantly West Indian. The engraving used for the incised ornament, which is filled with white pigment, bears some resemblance to tha on 17th-century Dutch tobacco boxes.

Plain H combs of boxwood and all the other materials mentioned, were made in Europe at least until the end of the last century and some of wood, studded with imitation gems, are still made in the Middle

East, India, Burma and the Far East. Examples of some of these later combs are shown in Plate 384, where is also illustrated a small boxwood, 18th-century comb on the end of a slender handle. Its use is best described by a critic of male dandies, in the *Connoisseur* of April 24, 1755—

> 'I could not but observe a number of boxes of different sizes, I had the curiosity to examine the contents of several, in one I found a lip-salve, in another a roll of pig-tail, in the middle stood a bottle of *Eau de Luce* and a roll of perfumed pomatum, almond pastes and powder puffs. But I could not conceive for what use a small ivory comb could be designed, till the valet informed me it was a comb for the eyebrows.'

An article of mine describing hand-made combs at greater length and with 17 illustrations, appeared in the *Connoisseur*, December, 1952.

In the bottom row, the crude boxwood comb with fretted handle, ornamented with badly spaced incised circles, is possibly Egyptian. Next to it, the D-shaped, boxwood, fine comb, engraved on one side with tropical birds and on reverse with a tiger, is late 17th- or early 18th-century and may be English, or Jamaican made for the English market. The boxwood H comb is an 18th-century type barber's comb, used on wigs after the coarse or 'rake' comb. The curved back, boxwood comb, is a *chignon* comb, for combing the hair on the nape of the neck. It may be English or French, 18th-century.

Comb Cleaners

The comb cleaner, Plate 384, is a Victorian device, made of mahogany, with a bristle brush at one end and seven retractable steel blades at the other end; the blades are withdrawn into the sheath by pressing a button and sliding it along the groove.

Cravat Holders—see *Wig Stands*

Curling Sticks, Tongs, etc.

The traditional ringlet curling stick, about 12 in. long, resembles a ring measuring stick without the calibrations (for *Ring Measuring Sticks*, see Section XIX, *Scientific*). In Plate 384, a ringlet curling stick is shown, together with a 'Sanitary Hair Puffer' and 19th-century fringe tongs. The hair puffer, for curling and puffing hair, extreme right, bottom row, is a hollow, tapering, wooden tube, with grooves in the side for slipping in hair pins. The pins, when not in use, are kept in the cavity, which is stoppered by a metal topped cork. On this cap, is the patent number of John Adams Davis of Chicago, dated 1908. The fringe tongs, of traditional form, have hardwood handles. They were generally heated over a folding spirit stove.

Dressing and Toilet Cases

It is difficult to draw a line with dressing and toilet cases, because so many were designed as travelling compendia, which might include not only toilet accessories and jewel cases, but also picnic sets and writing cabinets; in some instances, the fittings for the last two purposes occupy most of the space. The cases chosen to illustrate this section are essentially dressing and toilet cases.

In Plate 385 is shown a remarkable 18th-century, chestnut dressing case, with its mahogany interior fitment removed and placed in front of it, showing a secret drawer. The general style of the inlay, with satinwood veneered box lids, cross-banded with kingwood, etc., and a shell within an oval in the lid (not shown), suggests a date about 1780 for the making. The top of the lid pictures the giant Scottish chestnut tree from which the box is made. A parchment label inside the box records—

> 'This box is made of the Chestnut Tree which grew in the parish of Finhaven in the County of Forfar. The Dimensions of the Tree as measured by two Justices of the

peace, are, the Circumferance of the smalest grain is 13 ft.-2⅜ in.—the Circumferance of the largest grain is 23 ft.-9 in.—the Circumferance of the smalest part of the trunk is 30 ft.-7 in.—the Circumferance of the top of the Trunk where the grains branch out is 35 ft.-9 in.—the Circumferance of the root end of the trunk half a foot above the ground is 42 ft.-8½ in.

Measured at Finhaven the 29th Aprile, 1745.'

This dressing case was formerly in the collection of the Earl of Glenesk.

Plate 386 shows, on the right, a good quality lady's dressing case of a type popular in the mid-19th century. One of this pattern was awarded a gold medal in the 1851 Exhibition. The example illustrated measures 12 in. by 9 in. by 7¼ in. high and would originally have had an outer leather travelling case. The exterior is veneered with calamander, inlaid with brass and a mother-of-pearl plaque on the lid is engraved 'G.E. to J.E.E. January, 1855'. The interior is lined with gold-tooled cerise leather and matching velvet and satin. The fittings are of cut glass with engraved silver mounts and lids. The velvet cushioned panel in the lid is reversible and the reverse side has a mirror, in tooled leather frame; it forms the lid of a recess to hold papers. There are two concealed drawers, controlled by springs; one opens at the side, the other, fitted for jewellery, pulls out in front. Basically similar cases, plain veneered and with plated fittings, were made in large quantities.

The gentleman's toilet case of mahogany, Plate 393, a neat cylinder, 8½ in. long by 2⅜ in. diameter, was made in the first quarter of the 19th century. It is a clever design, which holds a surprising amount. A mirror in the lid conceals a well (original contents unknown). A tray, shown alongside, holds two razors, with a recess under them for scissors. Below the tray are compartments for a shaving brush, tooth and ear picks, tweezers, corkscrew and tooth brush and, at the end, a circular pewter box for tooth powder.

Made about 1830, the hexagonal revolving casket of thuya wood, with ebonized mountings and gilt mounts, shown open left of Plate 386 and closed at right of Plate 392, holds, on four of its doors, glass bottles decorated with gilt stars and lines, in pierced gilt metal holders of Gothic outline; there are blue *moiré* silk pads, with pockets for various small implements, on the other two. The knob on the top, connected to a central spindle, actuates wooden cog-wheels in the base, which control the opening and closing. Caskets of this type were made with fitments for various purposes, particularly for holding cheroots (see Section XXII, *Tobacco Accessories*). Some of the caskets have musical boxes in their bases.

Dressing Table Sets

Plate 387 illustrates a selection of seven Louis XIV toilet objects of carved pearwood, *circa* 1685. These are not all from one set; but judging by complete sets of the period which exist in silver, both Charles II, English and Louis XIV, French, there would have been between 15 and 18 pieces. These almost invariably included a toilet mirror, supported by a strut, a pair of candlesticks, one or two dusting brushes, one or two pin or trinket trays, two scent flasks, several rectangular and some circular boxes, and a pincushion, often mounted on a box. Sometimes a small oval pocket mirror in case is *en suite*. In Louis XV silver, 1715–74, and English equivalents of the same period, the sets became gradually larger, rising to as many as 35 pieces, which include a greater selection of trays, boxes and bottles, an ewer and basin, a caudle cup and jug, a clothes brush, a funnel, an inkstand, and snuffers and tray. So far as I know, there are no equivalents of these 18th-century silver sets in wood, but in the 19th century, simple dressing table sets were frequently made in ebony.

The elaborate and minutely carved woodware shown in Plate 387 has, I think quite erroneously, become associated with the name of Cesar Bagard of Nancy. Whether museums, dealers, fine art auctioneers, or collectors commenced the attribution, I know not; it is, however, well established now and it conjures up a mental picture of what the work is like. Occasionally, instead of the confident attribution of 'Work of Cesar Bagard', some small, finely carved object is described as 'School of Cesar Bagard'. This is a slightly more reasonable description, because even if Bagard designed or carved any of the work, which is extremely unlikely, he could neither have carved the quantity nor the wide range of qualities, varying from mediocre to superb, which are credited to him.

What is the truth about Cesar Bagard? He was born at Nancy in April, 1620 and was the fourth child of the sculptor Nicolas Bagard; he was a pupil of the sculptor Jacuin, and specialized in the sculpturing of colossal statues—figures on a grand scale, mostly intended for churches or public places. He was nicknamed 'Le Grand Cesar' and his output of work was large; unfortunately, the majority of it was destroyed in the French Revolution.

The fine-scale carving which is now associated with his name, closely resembles the carving on some stone pedestals for his statues, but there is no reason to suppose that he had anything to do with these pedestals. In fact, the so-called Cesar Bagard woodware is essentially Louis XIV design, of the last part of the reign, and it is a good translation of the silver of the period into terms of wood carving, bearing the same motifs and following the same outlines as silver, made approximately between 1660 and 1700.

In the main, the objects, mostly carved in pearwood, but occasionally in boxwood, cover the wide range of toilet accessories which are also found in silver. They include dressing table mirror frames, with shapely heads, both for wall hanging and strut support, a large selection of toilet boxes and jewel caskets—square, oblong, circular and hexagonal, also some with truncated domed lids—trinket trays, bottle stands, clothes brushes (backs) and candlesticks. The last are usually on octagonal bases, which are sometimes pierced, and have inverted pear-shaped knops on the turned stems and the deep, small diameter, straight-sided cups associated with William and Mary silver. The elaborately carved miniature table illustrated, was presumably intended for trinkets and may be regarded as an alternative to a trinket tray or stand. Fine quality back scratchers, snuff rasps and snuff boxes were also made in the same style.

The carving is invariably shallow and small in scale, set against a punched, stippled background. Most of the objects must have been commissioned specially by the French nobility, for often the main ornamentation of individual pieces, or toilet sets, is centred on a coat of arms, or a monogram with a ducal coronet above. Occasionally, a depiction of a fable or an allegory forms the centrepiece and when lettering is included, it is invariably executed beautifully, but rather large in scale.

The general designs of the carvings, mostly flowers, leaf trails appropriate to the flowers, or acanthus leaves, together with birds, vary from naturalistic to formal Renaissance scrolls. The most favoured motif is a forget-me-not like flower, with six or more petals. On boxes with hinged lids, six-petalled flowers are repeated in silver, to form the heads of the hinge rivets. Such metal fittings as there are on boxes, mirror struts, etc., are, if original, of silver. Sometimes the forget-me-nots have naturalistic leaves and foliage, and stylized birds and grotesque masks in character are included in the compositions; at other times, the forget-me-nots form the terminals to Renaissance scrolls. Formal laurel wreaths and branches, tied with lovers knots, are also found framing monograms and are bordered by vines, with long-legged birds pecking the grapes.

Rectangular 'Cesar Bagard' boxes were badly constructed and have not stood the test of time well. Bottoms of the boxes, of solid wood, were glued under the framed sides and ends, with a carved rim projecting all round; no allowance in the construction having been made for width shrinkage of the bottoms, they have usually split and the same has occurred with lids, when grooved on the underside, to fit over the box.

The co-called Cesar Bagard work is most decorative, and highly prized today, but, as mentioned previously, it varies enormously in quality. It is worth noting that the low grade, coarse work was originally varnished, but sometimes the varnish has been removed later and the carving wax polished, to try and make it pass for the better work.

Fruit Boxes—see *Powder and Other Toilet Boxes*

Glove Accessories—Powdering Flasks, Stretchers

Gloves have great antiquity and in former times played nearly as important a part in social custom and, in some instances, had the same connotations that pertained to footwear (see Section XXV, *Trade Devices, Footwear*). The throwing down of a glove in mediaeval times was the recognized form of challenge. The gift of a glove was a love token from a lady to her knight. In reverse, jasmine or other sweetly perfumed gloves, preferably from France, were a welcome gift from a gentleman to any lady, including Queen Elizabeth I. In Shakespeare's *Winter's Tale*, Autolycus offers 'gloves as sweet as damask roses'. In the 17th century, Samuel Pepys several times refers to buying gloves for his Valentines, and in January, 1669, he was somewhat annoyed with his wife over perfumed gloves. A friend had returned from France and ' . . . brought a great many gloves perfumed, of several sorts; but all too big by half for her, and yet she will have two or three dozen of them, which vexed me, and made me angry. So she, at last, to please me, did come to take what alone I thought fit, which pleased me.'

In the East, the transfer of a glove from seller to purchaser, sealed a transfer of property. In the Dutch East Indies in the 17th century, Dutch nutmeg planters sent to the Mother Country for brides. The prospective bride might be someone the planter had known in Holland, or someone chosen for him by the Dutch East India Company. To present his suit, the planter sent a letter of proposal, a marriage contract and a glove. The girl, before sailing for the East Indies, went through a church ceremony involving the glove and known as a 'Glove Marriage'. When she arrived and met the planter, she was regarded as already married to him.

Glove powdering flasks were only needed when tight gloves were worn. I have seen a few among the French, 17th-century, pearwood toilet accessories known as Cesar Bagard (see *Dressing Table Sets*). The majority of flasks are, however, simple turned ones of boxwood, top shelf, Plate 388, made in Queen Victoria's reign, when long, tight-fitting gloves were in fashion; the powdering flasks were used in glove shops and in the bedroom. The same names are found stamped on them as on bottle cases (see Section I, *Apothecary*). When there is a screw cap to fit over the perforated nozzle, the flask was made for travelling.

The 12 in. long type of glove stretchers, pivoting on a wooden ball and with a spring between the handles, one from right, Plate 388, was made in large quantities, in a selection of hardwoods and in ivory, from the beginning of Victoria's reign; it is not generally recognized that the separate turned lignum vitae rods, $19\frac{1}{2}$ in. long, shown extreme right, usually tied together loosely in pairs, with a piece of string which passes through a hole in the handle end of each, were their predecessors. They were used by inserting the thin ends of two sticks in the finger of a glove and pivoting the bulge of one stick against the other. They were excellent for long gloves and continued in use in a few country glove shops up to about 1900. Their use is now so far forgotten, that when found in pairs, they are usually described as diavolo sticks, or if only one has survived, it is often thought to be a head scratcher.

Gout Stools

Hippocrates described gout about 350 B.C. Some 300 years later, the philosopher, Seneca, drew attention to the evil effects of luxurious living, remarking that 'even women had become gouty, thus setting at naught the authority of physicians which had asserted their little likelihood to gout'. Certainly, gout is more frequently a man's than a woman's complaint and most pathetic of all where inherited, and when the sufferer has enjoyed none of the pleasure which should precede it. Although sufferers from gout seem to have occurred in most countries, throughout many centuries, the 18th and early 19th centuries might well be described as the vintage years. Port at 3s. per bottle and the general addiction to hard drinking of red wines and over-eating of rich foods undoubtedly made gout an occupational hazard of the well-to-do Georgian. Even when not prepared to forswear the probable cause, the sufferer, naturally, determined to mitigate his agony with as much comfort as possible and a well padded stool, adjusted to the correct angle, was an essential.

In Hepplewhite's *Cabinet-Maker and Upholsterer's Guide*, 1794, is illustrated the fashionable 'Gouty Stool' of the period, '... the construction of which being so easily raised or lowered at either end, is particularly useful to the afflicted'. The illustration shows an oblong stool frame on square tapered legs, with concave upholstered seat, which is raised or lowered and adjustable in angle, by means of an inter-

mediate hinged frame, with ratchets at each end. The mechanism is identical with that used on architects' tables of the period. A somewhat similar illustration is shown in *The Prices of Cabinet Work*, 1797 edition, and Sheraton illustrates another version of the same type of stool, with the addition of a protective end-piece, in the 1802 edition of his *Drawing Book*. Probably many more of these gouty stools have survived than is easily apparent. The height and angle adjustment mechanism was comparatively fragile, and after a time was usually broken and discarded. When this occurred, the top was fixed to, or made to fit into the frame, converting this specialized piece of furniture into an ordinary stool. Sometimes, when re-upholstering an old stool, the hinge marks of the ratchet rail will be found in the top edge of the seat rail.

An unusual mid-18th-century mahogany example, employing a different principle, is shown in Plate 396. This stool, which would have been used with a loose cushion, is supported on a typical Georgian turned centre pedestal and tripod claws and the 'cradle' is made to revolve and has a pivot and screw adjustment of angle which can be fixed to suit the user's comfort. To the student of construction, the most interesting feature of this particular example is that the graceful, curved ribs, which are slotted through the 'back-bone', are of laminated mahogany, with a central glue line in each. For further Georgian uses of plywood, see Section IV, *Eating: Cheese Coasters*, Section II, *Costume: Buckles* and Section III, *Drinking: Carriers, Coasters, Drinking Ancilliaries*.

Hair Puffers—see *Curling Sticks*

Hair Tidies

The hair tidy was a component of many 19th-century dressing sets. It was usually a 2½ in. to 3½ in. diameter bowl or pot, with a tight-fitting lid, which had a hole of about ¾ in. diameter for poking in the hair. Such tidies were made in china, glass, tortoise-shell, ebony, etc., often with silver lids. The Regency, ornamentally turned, $3\frac{1}{2}$ in. diameter, fruitwood specimen, Plate 389, is unusual. Another type of tidy, shaped as a cornet, heart, or miniature satchel of wood or card, sometimes covered with fabric, was made to hang from the upright post of a dressing table mirror, suspended by a ribbon loop.

Hat Boxes

Hat boxes of thin steamed bent wood have been included among the large range of multi-purpose round and oval spelk boxes, made in many countries by specialist makers of spelk boxes, trugs, grain measures and sieves, over a period of 300 years or more. The thin wood or spelk used for the box and lid rims was usually oak, ash or beech, riven or prepared with a spelk plane, steamed, bent round and nailed into the edges of a pine bottom and lid. The junction of the two ends of the spelk were tapered and either riveted together, laced, or interwoven, sometimes in an ornamental pattern. English specimens are usually quite plain, but those from Scandinavia are sometimes decorated with chip carving or poker work and enlivened by painting. Some of the boxes of this type formerly made by the Shakers in the U.S.A., are particularly well finished. Specimens of spelk boxes are illustrated in Plate 138, *F* to *M*, Section VII, *Kitchen*.

The triangular, country-made, oak hat box, Plate 390, measuring 17 in. on each side by $5\frac{1}{4}$ in. deep, has twisted wire hinges and a peg fastener. It was used by an 18th-century Sussex farmer for his churchgoing tricorn hat and it remained in his family until it joined the Pinto Collection recently.

Hatpin Stands

Hatpin stands, straight-sided cylindric vases, were often included in 19th-century ebony dressing table sets and are indistinguishable from spill vases. The $7\frac{1}{2}$ in.

mahogany hatpin stand, with brass ring lift, Plate 389, holds more than 120 hatpins and was doubtless a display stand for the counter of a 19th-century shop.

Hones, Razor—see *Razor Boxes*

Jewel Caskets

Elaborate jewel caskets have survived from ancient Greece, Rome, Egyptian and other Middle East civilizations, also from mediaeval times in other parts of Europe. They are found in bronze, wrought iron, ivory, bone and wood, overlaid or decorated with other materials.

The truncated wood casket, 6 in. wide, bottom left, Plate 392, is inlaid with certosina work and, like others of its type, incorporates re-used ivory and bone plaques of various dates and different countries of origin. It was probably assembled in Italy in the 15th century. The carved wood (probably pearwood) casket next to it, $7\frac{1}{2}$ in. wide, is in a very fragile state, due to worm and rot. At first sight, it appears to have been made in Italy, between the 8th and 10th century. It also appears to have had triangular uprights in the corners, left slightly upstanding, to position the lid; these one would assume to have been removed in the 19th century, to fit a lock and hinges. A sad mutilation? No, not really, because careful examination shows that the much worn 'carved' warriors in the sunk panels of the top, front, back and ends, are of two designs only and each one, of each design, is *absolutely identical*, as are also the rosettes. So this must be regarded as a clever fake, not, I think, machine carved, but with the ornament made by a steaming and die-stamping process, and the wood aged by burial or submersion, and introduction of worm, perhaps deliberate. Bearing in mind the cost of 'tooling up' and the need for a 'run' to make it pay, it is surprising that no similar examples have been recorded.

The leather-covered travelling casket, on

the right, bears the label of Thomas Free, trunk and casket maker of Queen Street, Hull; he worked there between 1835 and 1846. The rather crude Swiss or Tyrolean casket, top left, has swing out trays and a lower compartment padded and fitted for a watch and jewellery. It belonged to one of my maternal great-grandmothers, Diamante Foligno, and was made about 1840–5.

Some containers for an individual gift of jewellery are shown in Plate 388. Left, middle and bottom row, the heart-shaped boxes tell their own stories of being love gifts. The marbled egg, next to the smaller heart box, was for a Valentine trinket; it was one of the specialities of W. H. Cremer Jnr., of 210 Regent Street, London, an importer of foreign toys and novelties in the second half of the 19th century.

Lace Boxes

Lace boxes, to stand on chests of drawers and probably made *en suite* with each other, enjoyed their greatest popularity during the second half of the 17th century and during Queen Anne's reign. Seventeenth-century boxes were veneered with various oyster-shell effects, or floral and seaweed marquetry, arranged in similar designs to those on chests of their period. In course of time, chests and boxes have become separated, and it is unusual to find an exactly matching pair. Those of the Queen Anne period are usually veneered with quartered figured or burr walnut, with herring-bone cross banding. Lace boxes vary in size from about 12 in. by 10 in., to 20 in. by 15 in., and 3 in. to 4 in. in depth. Interiors may have quilted or padded silk or other fabric linings, or fancy paper. It is quite likely that some of the carved oak boxes of earlier times, now usually lumped together indiscriminately as Bible or desk boxes, were really lace boxes.

Mirrors, Toilet

What we call mirrors, our ancestors called looking glasses, or simply glasses. The change of nomenclature did not become general until between 1900 and 1930. Dressing table mirrors, as furniture, are outside the scope of this book, but Heal's *Face et Nuque* mirror of 1856–7, was so ingenious that it merits description here and illustration in Plate 391. The design, which is remarkably delicate for its period, consists of a clever arrangement of two adjustable mirrors, which can be used on any existing table. The mirror to see the face is quite small—6 in. wide by 8 in. high. It is pivoted between two bobbin turned uprights, which are reminiscent of 17th-century design. Rising from the weighted back point of the triangular stand, and projecting forward at an angle of about 55°, is a telescopic brass tube, on the end of which is mounted a 6½ in. diameter circular mirror, on a ball joint, adjustable to any angle. The telescopic arm passes over the head of the lady seated at her toilette and the back mirror, reflecting in the front one, enables her to see her *nuque*—in fact, by adjustment of mirror and arm, she can see the front, top, back and sides of her head. Several versions of the mirror are shown in Heal's 1856–7 catalogue, but I have only seen the one complete *Face et Nuque*. The mirror stands do, however, turn up from time to time, without the rather fragile telescopic arm and back mirror; one in this condition, which had doubtless acquired respectable patination in its hundred years of existence, was advertised a few years ago, in an American journal, as a Jacobean dressing mirror!

Smaller mirrors, particularly for travelling or pocket use, are shown in Plate 389. The example on the middle shelf, which folds flat and pivots into an easel position, was popular in the last quarter of the 19th century; it was made with case and frame of any suitable hardwood. The two with pivoted shutters, left of bottom row, are framed in mahogany and probably made about 1790. The banjo type, with removable mahogany lid, may be some 20 years later. The two chip carved examples, with sliding shutters, are Welsh, late 18th- or early 19th-century; the one on the left, inlaid with coloured wax, is probably sailor work. The small round and oval mirrors with handles, for pocket use, were also made in much larger sizes for the dressing table. Some of the Sheraton inlaid mahogany examples were probably made in the last 20 years of the 18th century, but the basic design has not changed to this day. All examples illustrated are English, apart from the two Welsh ones.

Pincushions—see *Trinket Holders*; also Section XXI, *Textile Workers' Devices*

Pomanders
Pomander, literally a translation of apple of amber, was from mediaeval times onwards, a ball of aromatic substances carried in the pomander case, which we now call the pomander. Pomanders were used by the wealthy and fastidious as a safeguard against infection and to protect their noses against the evil stenches which assailed them so frequently. In the broadest sense, a pomander was a small container with a lid for carrying, or a larger one with a perforated top for scenting rooms, clothes closets, etc. Pomanders for carrying were of gold, silver, ivory and occasionally hardwood, mostly for wearing on the person by means of a chain, cord or ribbon, but sometimes incorporated in the hollow knob of a walking stick. Jewelled pomanders occur in Tudor inventories and are shown in portraits of the period. Two 17th- or early 18th-century, lignum vitae specimens, the left-hand one finely engine turned, are illustrated at the bottom of Plate 388. A 19th-century, barrel-shaped, boxwood aromatic container, for hanging in a wardrobe, is in Plate 384.

Powder and Other Toilet Boxes
I have not identified English powder boxes of earlier date than 1780. Dated specimens

are rare, but two made between 1780 and 1800 are plain cylindric boxes, with projecting base and screw-lid rims, painted externally with coloured stripes on a white ground; one has a ring stand on the lid. Some Regency boxes, also painted, are of skippet outline, like the hair tidy, Plate 389, and have mirrors inside the lids. Victorian powder boxes are mostly quite plain, of boxwood or ebony, and have convex screw-on lids with projecting rims; they were made in a considerable range of sizes. Some of the more decorative powder and other toilet boxes are shown in Plate 388. The 'fruit' boxes, all 19th-century, are particularly popular with collectors. Commencing 5th from left, middle shelf, are apple, orange, apple, pear, plum, pear. Below, are three 18th- or early 19th-century, Welsh toilet boxes of mahogany, chip carved; one simulates three book volumes, with a mirror in the spine; it has a sliding lid, as have also the oval box, with mirror in the slide, and the shoe.

Powdering Flasks, Glove—see *Glove Accessories*

Razor Boxes, Cases, Hones and Strops
The finest and earliest English wooden shaving case I know, is the James I outfit, Plate 394. It is of double bass shape, $11\frac{7}{8}$ in. long and probably made of pearwood, but age, discoloration, and decoration make it difficult to be certain. It is dated 1606 and the incised ornament, which resembles that on James I silver, includes on the lid, the sacred initials, a lion, flowers and foliage. On one end is inscribed MARIA and on the sides, a fox and stags, among foliage. The lid pivots and slides in two layers, with the trick fastening sometimes found on snuff boxes. The main lid discloses two compartments, one for razors and one for soap. The upper lid forms a protective shutter for a small mirror.

On the top shelf of Plate 393, is an 18th-century, barber's oak razor box, with sliding lid, inlaid with an open razor. The box is divided into three compartments.

On the centre shelf is a lignum vitae cup with a 'cut out'; it is one of a pair. Their purpose is unknown, but they may have been used when shaving. Alongside, are three hones. That on the left, inset in mahogany, is 18th- or 19th-century. The rare example centre, inset in walnut, has the much worn handle carved with a woman's head, having stylized acanthus tresses; it is Italian and probably 17th-century. The smaller one, right, dates from 1870.

Bottom left, is an elegant Georgian razor box of macassar ebony, with pivoted lid, inset with a hone; its original gold-tooled red leather case is alongside. Next, is a crude, fan-shaped, 17th-century razor box, with incised decoration, and on the right is a chip carved razor box, with sliding lid and strop, dated 1830. It was formerly in the Evan-Thomas and Bussell Collections.

Shaving brushes are reputed to have been introduced to England from France in 1756. Prior to that date, barbers—and there were women as well as men—lathered their customers with their fingers, as many continued to do into this century.

Ribbon Threaders

Ribbon threaders, used for weaving ribbons in and out of elaborate head-dresses and costume, were used during several periods of fashion in the 17th and 18th centuries. They are described and illustrated in Section XXI, *Textile Workers' Devices*.

Ringlet Curling Sticks—see *Curling Sticks*

Ring Stands—see *Trinket Stands*

Salve Pots

Egyptian wooden salve pots have survived for over 3,000 years; but in our much shorter civilization it is difficult to find any wooden survivals, definitely identifiable as salve pots, which are earlier than 1800. Salve pots of similar shape to the fourth from left, centre shelf, Plate 388, were made at Tunbridge throughout the Regency period and probably later. They are usually turned from rosewood; some are plain, others have geometric mosaic on their lids, which usually screw on; if complete, they have glass or china liners.

Scent Flasks

Flasks of various shapes and sizes made from gourds, are to be found in most parts where gourds grow. In Elba, silver-mounted gourd scent flasks, engraved with portraits of Napoleon, have been tourist attractions for 100 years; one is shown right of top shelf, Plate 388. In Whitby, Yorks, a hundred years ago, scent flasks were nicely carved from jet, which was then particularly fashionable for mourning jewellery. For further details of gourds and of jet, see Section XIII, *Nuts, Gourds, Fruit Stone, Jet and Bog Oak Jewellery*.

Hardwood scent flasks are mostly confined to close-grained boxwood and pear, are in the fine art class and are rarities. A French, 17th-century, pearwood specimen, with ivory cap and rings on the neck, is shown in Plate 387. Another three are included with the chrism bottles and other fine art objects in Plate 171. *D* is a superb French, boxwood flask, 4½ in. high, *circa* 1700; the stopper is in the form of a pierced crown and both sides of the flask are carved with classical heads in lozenges set in foliage. *E* is another French, *circa* 1700, boxwood flask, 4 in. high, the design simulating stitched leather, carved with figures in acanthus scrolls. *J* is an interesting and fine quality boxwood flask, shaped as a bellows; acanthus scrolls descend from the spout and enfold circular panels on both faces, carved with scenes in relief. The scrolled and pierced handle encloses a classical head in an oval lozenge. It is 4 in. long, Italian, 17th-century. It was formerly in the Evan-Thomas Collection.

Shoe Horns—see *Button Hooks*

Soap Boxes

It seems probable that before the 18th century, an ordinary pole-lathe turned bowl was used for soap, when the container was a wooden one. Wooden soap bowls continued in use in laundries and bathrooms until well within living memory. Although the mid-18th-century Georgians had washstands with soap bowls built in, they also had specially designed spherical and ovoid toilet containers, usually of mahogany, provided with a ventilating hole in the lid; one is pictured on the middle shelf, Plate 393. Sometimes these soap containers (or alternatively powder boxes, which had no hole in the lid) are fixtures above the middle shelf of the three-legged basin stands, to which reference is made in the general introduction to this section.

Stretchers, Glove—see *Glove Accessories*

Strops, Razor—see *Razor Cases*

Toilet Cases—see *Dressing Cases*

Tooth Powder Boxes

One from the left, middle shelf, Plate 389, is a turned lignum vitae box, which may be equally correctly described as a tooth powder or snuff box. It was used for Spanish Sabillia, a brick red snuff, much esteemed about 1800 as a tooth powder. It cost 16s. per lb. and was reputed to keep the gums healthy. Tooth brushes were used in France in the mid-17th century, but their acceptance in England was slow. Even early in the 18th century, they were regarded by many with suspicion. Sir John Philipps of Picton Castle, Pembrokeshire, wrote to his wife in 1721 ' . . . that using a brush to ye Teeth and Gums (as you constantly do) will certainly prove in time injurious to them Both, and especially to ye Last which will be quite worn away by it; and I beg of ye for ye future to use a Sponge in its room' (quoted by Mark Girouard in an article in *Country Life*, Jan. 14, 1960).

It was, I think, in the 1790s that a silver-handled tooth brush was first included in a travelling toilet set, together with a tooth brush box and a tongue scraper, both of silver. Joseph Taylor of Birmingham and William Pitts of London were makers of these sets. Itinerant vendors of tooth powder, wash balls and tooth picks are recorded in 17th-century England, but the powder may have been for rubbing on the gums and teeth. Recipes for mouth washes and instructions for massaging the gums with a cloth occur in 15th-century literature. False teeth go back much further and some are said to have been of wood, but all those surviving appear to be of ivory. The Etruscans made ivory false teeth, fastened to neighbouring teeth by gold wire or bands. In the preface to Blagrave's *Mathematical Jewel* (1585), the author mentions that his nephew, who had all his teeth drawn, ' . . . afterwards had a sett of ivory teeth in agayn.' These, like 17th- and 18th-century false teeth, of which there are numerous mentions, were probably for appearance only and had to be removed for eating.

Towel Holders

Mediaeval European towel holders were sometimes made as highly decorative carved figures, gripping the rail between their hands. The figure might be a monk, a jester, a girl in period costume, etc. Unfortunately, more drawings of them than actual examples survive. There was a revival in the 18th and first half of the 19th century and most of the figures still extant, date from then, including the delightful polychrome finished, Brittany peasant girl in 16th-century costume, Plate 397.

Trinket Stands and Pincushions

The majority of ring and trinket stands, top shelf, Plate 389, which have survived, are Victorian. The walnut 'twist' stand, however, appears to date from the Charles II period; compare it with a wig stand in Plate 380. The 19th-century tree and shell pattern trinket stand is Swiss or Tyrolean, the others, English.

Pincushions are detailed more fully in Section XXI, *Textile Workers' Devices*, but on the shelf with the trinket stands in Plate 389 is a carved walnut bulldog with pincushion inserted in his back, English, probably 18th-century, and an early 19th-century, Tunbridge stickware cushion alongside. On the shelf below, is a Regency revolving trinket stand, with a pincushion finial, and on the stand a pincushion box, *circa* 1800.

Wig Blocks and Equipment

Wig blocks were constructed as solid wooden heads, as malleable cork blocks, canvas covered, or as a hollow leather head, Plate 380, bottom right. The last were favoured by travelling wig-makers, as the trap-door in the block enabled the use of the hollow interior as a tool chest. Wig blocks, in every head size, were made to stand or clamp on a table and as floor-standing models. Use of wig blocks was not confined to *perruquiers* for making the mounts of wigs; they were also found in bedrooms, for use by their owners or valets and lady's maids in hairdressing. On the stand of the wig block illustrated, are two fire-clay wig curlers, and on the right, one of turned wood.

Apart from various combs, the only other wooden equipment used in wig making, which the collector is likely to encounter, are weaving sticks. They are upright, turned sticks, mounted on clamps and the sticks project about 8½ in. above the clamps which, in use, were set 2 ft. to 3 ft. apart. The right-hand stick has three equidistant grooves running round it; the left-hand one has none. Three silk threads are tied round the grooves in the right-hand stick, drawn taut, and meet together in an eyelet or hole, halfway up the left-hand stick. The hair was woven in and out of the silk threads. The operation is fully described in *The Art and Craft of Hairdressing*, New Era Publishing Co., 1958. For further details of wigs, see the general introduction to this section.

Wig Boxes

Few survive, but they appear to have been made in a wide range of styles and qualities. They range from elaborate specimens in mahogany and satinwood, to the simple country-made, oak specimen, Plate 390, which may be 17th- or 18th-century. Probably the majority of wig boxes for travelling were of leather (see introduction to this section).

Wig Powdering Bellows

Neat wooden wig powdering bellows, with leather gussets and brass nozzles, as shown in Plate 380, were used largely in the 18th century, and later in the theatrical profession.

Wig Powdering Carrots

Wig powdering carrots, Plate 395, are now great rarities. They are the aristocrats of 18th-century wig powdering devices. The example illustrated, of turned rosewood, is 11½ in. over the spout or ejector, which is horn; the three smallest rings are flexibly mounted on leather, so that the horn nozzle may be directed at any angle. The beautifully made tube was filled with powder by unscrewing the cap at the wide end. On the 'stalk' at this end, there must originally have been some kind of squeeze bulb, perhaps of soft leather, but unfortunately none seem to have survived. Satirical prints of aristocratic 18th-century hairdressing, clearly show the powderer at work, squeezing something at the stalk end of his carrot and blowing a cloud of powder over his victim.

Wig and Bonnet Stands and Cravat Holders

The most general type for a 17th- or 18th-century wig stand is a single column, mounted on a circular base and finished at the top with a mushroom cap of 3 in. to 3¾ in. diameter. Any stand with a mushroom over 4 in. diameter, is likely to be a 19th-century millinery display stand, especially if it is over 14 in. in height and french, not wax, polished. Generally, 18th-century wig stands vary from 10 in. to 14 in.; 17th-century examples are so rare that no average height can be given. The Charles II, walnut, 'twist' wig stand, top shelf, Plate 380, is one of a pair and 13 in. high. The 18th-century, 'pack-flat', mahogany wig stand, one shown complete on the left, and in parts below, is exactly like modern travelling millinery stands. Centre, top row, is a mahogany stand with twin arms, terminating in reeded knobs, and next to it, another mahogany stand, with a 1½ in. diameter button top and four curved branching prongs. Both of these appear to date from the early 19th century and they may be wig or bonnet and cravat stands, or they may have served some other purpose. Extreme right, and probably made about 1790, is one of a pair of unusual, simulated rosewood, wig stands, with brass wire tops. In the bottom row, the three-arm cravat

holder probably dates from 1790–1800; the yew-wood wig stand on the left, one of a pair, is Welsh, 18th-century; the one on the right, unusual because it is on ball feet, is laburnum, probably 1780–90.

It must be pointed out that basically there is no difference between a wig and a bonnet or nightcap stand, nor between a cravat and a scarf holder and this becomes more apparent when considering the wall types of holders. There is no reason to doubt that the plain and simple, 18th-century, mahogany, wall hanging holder, Plate 393, with two swing-out gates and four pivoted pegs, was intended for two wigs and four cravats. But when one comes to the early 19th-century, bobbin turned example of the same device, Plate 384, one must consider the possibility of it being for nightcaps and scarves, although it is known that this pattern was also used in theatrical dressing rooms. It does not end there, however, for in the mid or late 19th century, a clumsy version of the same thing was still being made, usually ebonized and complete with china knobs, instead of mushroom tops, on the gates and china buttons on the end of the pegs.

XXIV

Tools, Devices, Techniques and Some Products of Specialized Woodworkers

Mr. W. L. Goodman's *A History of Wood-working Tools* (G. Bell & Sons, 1964) so fully lives up to its title, that no attempt need be made here to duplicate it by tracing the general evolution of the principal woodworking tools. Moreover, some being all or nearly all of metal, are outside the scope of this work.

As will be seen from the six Wierix engravings reproduced here, Plates 399–404, many tools in use today are virtually unchanged since the end of the 16th century. The majority of those shown in the panel, Plate 398, never changed, although some are hardly used today; this polychrome painted panel, signed with initials F.T. and name du Buf, is probably of Flemish origin and may have been a guild sign or trophy, of the early 18th century; its frame has painted decoration. The panel itself is noteworthy as a wood carving, and also for its design and technical execution, much of which is free standing, and exceptionally accurate in depiction. The motifs include love birds in a beribboned wreath, and sprays of oak and laurel. The tools comprise a rule hung with a chain, a framed saw with cord and toggle, auger with spoon bit, axe, claw hammer, mallet, chisel, drawknife and pincers—all carved wood. Incidentally, a hammer and pincers may be noted among the Emblems of the Passion, relief carved on the snuff rasp, Plate 376, *D*, dated 1741 and, in the same plate, a larger selection of tools appears on *H*, dated 1724.

This section may be regarded mainly as supplementary to Goodman's excellent and comprehensive work, and concentrates on such speciality tools as the lathe, whilst also including descriptions and illustrations of some less well known tools and devices, and some of the more ornamental tools, devices and other objects in the Pinto Collection, which have survived mainly because of their ornament or intricacy and now rank as wooden bygones. Among these, pride of place goes to the woodworker's tool chest, which with its contents was often, in the past, almost the craftsman's sole asset. It was not only the repository of his valuable kit, some of which was made by him; it was also the most impressive proof of his own skill as a woodworker, and as such, the interior had to be designed and executed not only to hold his tools safely and without damage in transit or in the workshop, but also to impress a prospective employer with his prowess. Until a man could give proof of his workmanship in employment, his past references, his tools and his chest, were his best spokesmen. The miniature furniture, so often described as 'apprentices' passing-out pieces' is, I think, entirely a myth, as I have explained in Section XV, *Pastimes: Models and Miniature Furniture*.

Tool chests reached their zenith of size, elaboration and craftsmanship when woodwork attained its apex of quality in the 18th century. They are plain externally, strong and heavily built of pine, dovetailed at all angles, weathered, and well protected with paint, made to withstand rough travel by wagon and ship, and in workshop usage. Interiors, however, are sometimes quite different—lined with mahogany, fitted with tool racks and nests of drawers, and occasionally as elaborately veneered and inlaid as the finest furniture. One of the most splendid examples is in the Victoria and Albert Museum. Another excellent specimen of the 1780–90 period, known as the Dolling Chest, is illustrated, Plate 405, with some of its interior fitments and tool contents shown in front. The chest, with its contents, was purchased by us from Mr. C. V. Dolling of Beccles, Suffolk, in 1957. The interior fitments are oak and pine veneered with Spanish mahogany and inlaid with ebony, satinwood, tulipwood, sycamore, etc., in the Sheraton style of 1790; drawer handles are ivory. A *tour de force* is the laminated rule-joint dust bead in the hinge line of the lid. When filled, the chest weighs $4\frac{1}{2}$ cwt. It stands on its original travelling trolley. A considerable number of the tools are stamped C. Dolling and many are stamped J. Puzey; some bear both marks. A few are stamped H. Loader. They vary considerably in age, and generally represent a cross section from about 1780 to 1930. The curious lack of balance between one type of tool and another, gives the impression that the chest must have been owned and used by men in several different branches of the woodworking industry during its long years of active service. Some of the tools are hand-made, others are by well-known makers; some would be appropriate to a shipwright, others to a house carpenter; some would have been used by a joiner, others by a cabinet-maker. There is no doubt that many must have worn out and others have probably been duplicated, through one man buying the whole of a dead mate's kit. Out of a total of 55 planes, the number of moulding planes, 44, is somewhat exceptional for any branch of the trade. There are 39 chisels, 9 marking gauges, and no less than 24 bradawls. Contrariwise, there is only one screwdriver, except for special ones for undoing saw blades; nor is there a toothing plane, although it would be almost a necessity for the man who veneered the chest. The complete list comprises 345 items.

The tool chest either stayed in the workshop or went with the woodworker on journeys, where he was likely to be based on a site or in a building for a length of time. For daily journeys, he carried either a basket or the familiar long, stout fabric bag with handle, or hold-all fitted with pockets, which is still sometimes used.

The carpenter's bench, as opposed to the horse or trestle, was probably evolved at the same time as the plane—early Roman times—when the necessity for the bench stop, holdfast and some sort of vice must immediately have arisen. The Roman type of bench with splayed legs, morticed right through a heavy top, continued in use throughout the Middle Ages. The straight, square-legged bench, with heavy underframing and legs dowelled into a detachable top, seems to have developed in the 17th century. Before the end of the 18th century, the sunk back-tray was added, and the general form had become the same as it was in the early years of this century.

There seems to be a widespread and erroneous belief that all furniture and other woodwork was hand-made until the end of the Regency period (1820); that between then and 1837, when Victoria ascended the throne, all the machinery was invented, and that Victoria pressed a button and set it going. Actually, woodworkers have used machines to cut down unnecessary heavy labour, and to obtain certain effects, from early times. The origin of the pole lathe (see *Lathes*) is lost in antiquity and, in general, progress of machines was slowed much more by limitations of metallurgy and by inadequacy and irregularity of water, wind, animal and human power, than by lack of inventiveness. Leonardo da Vinci designed practical and ingenious screw-threading, drilling, and punching machines before the end of the 15th century and also invented or improved a machine for boring wooden water pipes (see *Boring Tools*). A variant of this last, together with a multiple band-saw (see *Saws*), both powered by water, are illustrated by John Evelyn in the 1664 edition of *Sylva* and reproduced in Plate 407. Treadle operated jig-saws were probably used in the 17th century and certainly in the 18th—see Plate 406.

In 1779, Sir Samuel Bentham invented and patented the first practical wood-planing machine, powered by wind, water, steam or animal strength. Another type of planing machine was invented by Joseph Bramah in 1802. These early woodworking machines had heavy wood frames and in his brother Jeremy's house in Queen's Square Place, Westminster, in 1791, Sir Samuel Bentham set up the first factory for making a range of planing, moulding, rebating, grooving and sawing machines. In 1793, he obtained an inclusive patent, No. 1838, which covered the basic elements of nearly every modern woodworking machine.

Between 1801 and 1805, Sir Marc Isambard Brunel invented the famous block-making machines, which were made by Henry Maudslay, 'engineer and mechanist' of 78 Margaret Street, London. These machines for making small elm blocks, of which some 1,000, each previously made by hand, were needed for each fully rigged frigate of the line, were installed in the Block Mills Workshop of H.M. Dock-yard, Portsmouth, in 1804. They were used as late as 1946, and are still in working order. Brunel and the Benthams jointly improved the circular saw out of all recognition, between 1805 and 1810.

Adzes and Axes

Both the axe and the adze go back to the Stone Age, developed during the Copper and Bronze Ages and by the Middle Ages were probably the most widely used tools in the woodworker's kit. By the 18th century, both had proliferated into large families, with different outlines and sharpening bevels for varying purposes. The different types of both these tools are superbly illustrated in Eric Sloane's *A Museum of Early American Tools*. As a broad generalization, and it is a very broad one, the axe is primarily a felling or cleaving tool—an alternative to a saw; the adze is primarily a face surfacing or texturing tool, partially a substitute for a plane (see also *Planes*). Nevertheless, the chisel-edged broad axe was used mainly for hewing or shaping round logs into square beams, in the same manner that the carpenter uses its small brother, the hewing hatchet; the gutter or spout adze, and its much smaller brother, the one-hand cooper's adze, were not for producing flat surfaces, but as their names imply, for hollowing out. The cooper's adze has a much more curved blade and shorter handle than the carpenter's tool, because he has to swing it within the radius of a cask. The Wierix engravings, like most mediaeval and later pictures of woodworkers at work, show the important axe in nearly every illustration. In Plates 399 and 401, there is one on the trestle; in Plate 400 Joseph is wielding it. In Plates 402 and 403 there are axes in the foreground. Curiously, the axe head in the 18th-century carving, Plate 398, is even more mediaeval in type than the earlier portrayals. The adze appears less frequently in old pictures; one is shown on the upturned boat in Wierix engraving, Plate 404. A 19th-century

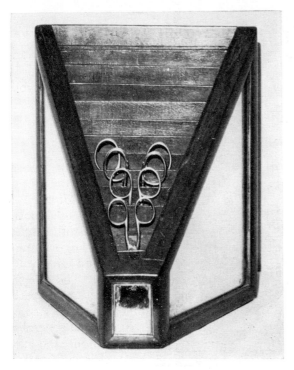

431 Mahogany and mirror panelled, scissors display stand. English, 18th century. (*Section XXV*)

432 Interior of fine straw work casket, with straw marquetry picture of Forde Abbey, Dorset. Early 19th century. (*Section XXV*)

434 English milk pram, *circa* 1900. (*Section XXV*)

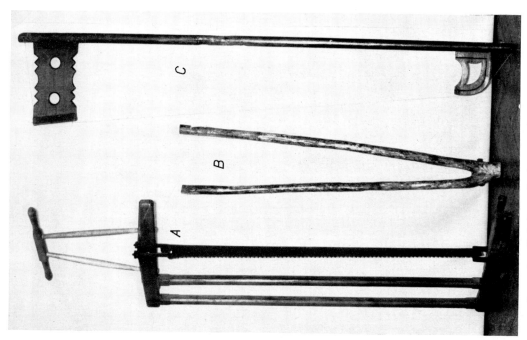

433 *A*, two-handled, framed, pit or trestle saw (*Section XXIV*). *B*, thatcher's yoke; *C*, hatter's bow, a great rarity. (*Section XXV*)

435 Victorian scissors-to-mend-and-knives-to-grind machine, used by the Glenholmes family of Carlisle about 1900. The machine was tipped on the wheel for trundling through the streets. (*Section XXV*)

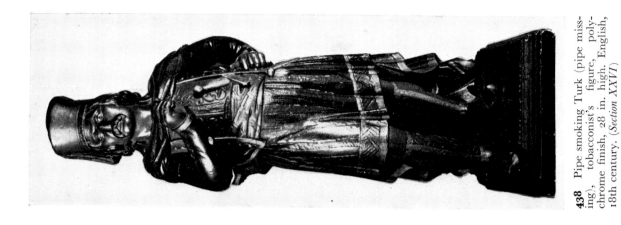

438 Pipe smoking Turk (pipe missing), tobacconist's figure, polychrome finish, 28 in. high, English, 18th century. (*Section XXVI*)

437 American cigar store Red Indian, polychrome finish, 7 ft. 3 in. high. Late 19th century. *By courtesy of Henry Ford Museum, Dearborn, Michigan.* (*Section XXVI*)

436 Blackamoor figure, with crown and 'kilt' of tobacco leaves, polychrome finish, 26 in. high, English. 17th century. (*Section XXVI*)

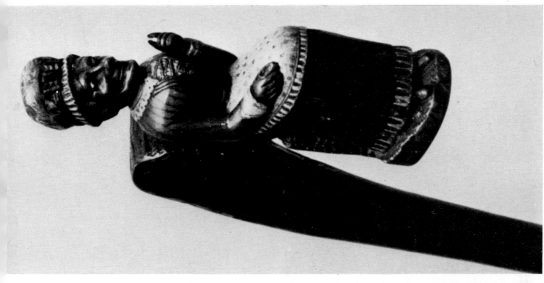

441 Unique snuff pedlar's staff shop sign. Polychrome finish, total height of staff 5 ft. 10 in. English. *Circa* 1815. (*Section XXVI*)

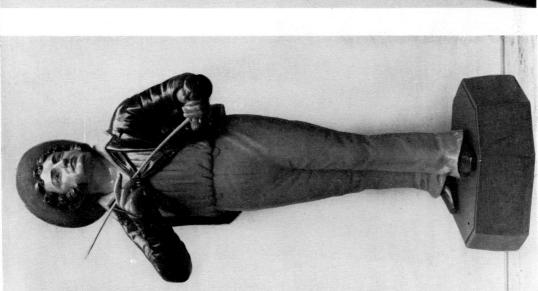

440 Carved figure of a sailor, with churchwarden and pouch. Seaport tobacconist's sign. Polychrome finish, 54 in. high. English or Scottish. Early 19th century. *Charles Rattray Collection.* (*Section XXVI*)

439 Highlander snuff shop figure taking a pinch from his mull. Polychrome finish, 36 in. high. Scottish. 19th century. (*Section XXVI*)

442 Ship's figurehead, probably from a ship named *Swallow*. Polychrome finish. English. Mid-19th-century. (*Section XXVI*)

443 A little admiral. Sign of a ship's instrument maker. Polychrome finish, 33 in. high. English. 18th century. *Collection of Mr. and Mrs. Christopher Sykes. (Section XXVI)*

444 Carved roundabout horse. Polychrome finish. English. 19th century. *Collection of Mr. and Mrs. Christopher Sykes. (Section XXVI)*

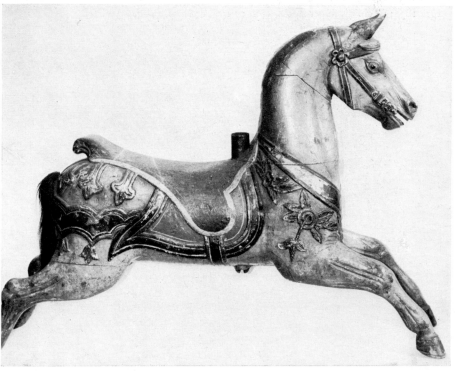

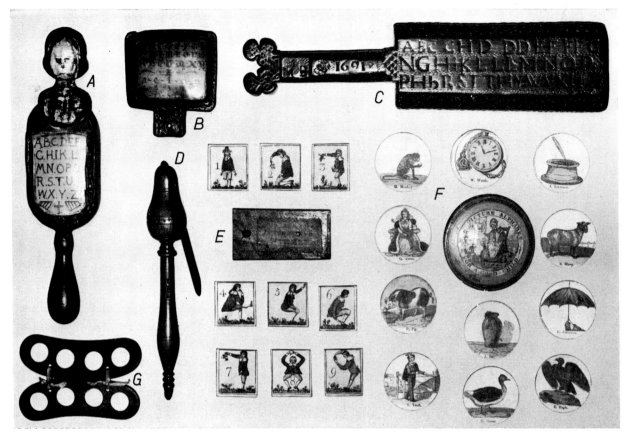

445 *A*, rare 18th-century doll-horn-book-rattle; *B*, leather horn-book; *C*, Welsh horn-book bat, dated 1691; *D*, dame school clicket; *E*, an instructive puzzle aid to teaching the numerals, dated 1789; *F*, picture alphabet, *circa* 1830; *G*, child's finger stocks, 18th or 19th century. (*Section XXVII*)

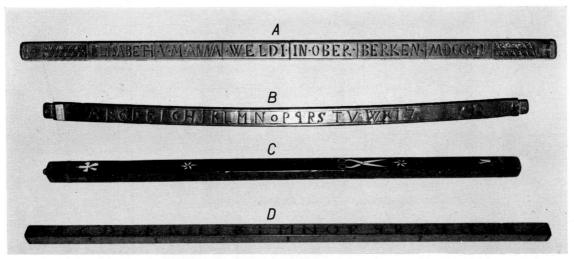

446   Alphabet sticks, probably Baltic region, early 19th century. (*Section XXVII*)

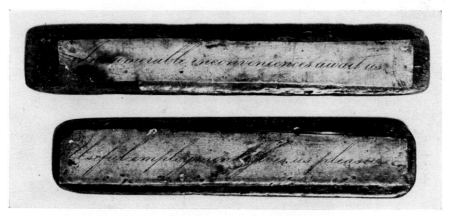

447   Copying sticks, English, *circa* 1860. (*Section XXVII*)

448   Deportment boards, English, third quarter of the 19th century. (*Section XXVII*)

449 *A*, Butter's Tangible Arithmetic cubes; *B*, the direction book for same, 1852; *C*, Wallis's Revolving Alphabet, *circa* 1830. (*Section XXVII*)

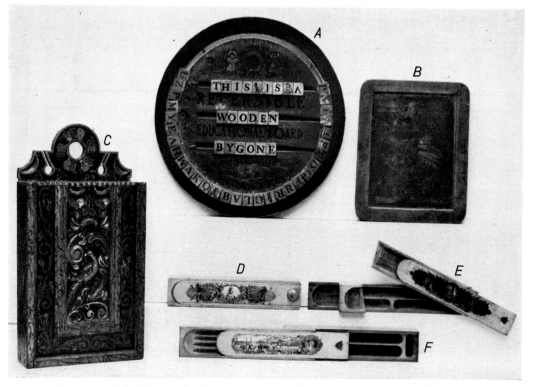

450 *A*, The Reversible Educational Board, *circa* 1915; *B*, the traditional slate; *C*, school box from Hindeloopen, Holland, 17th century; *D*, *E* and *F*, Bavarian pencil boxes, made for the English market, *circa* 1900. (*Section XXVII*)

451 *The School*, by Jan Steen (1626–79). *In the Collection of His Grace the Duke of Sutherland.* Several school boxes of the type shown in Plate 450, *C*, are to be seen in this picture. (*Section XXVII*)

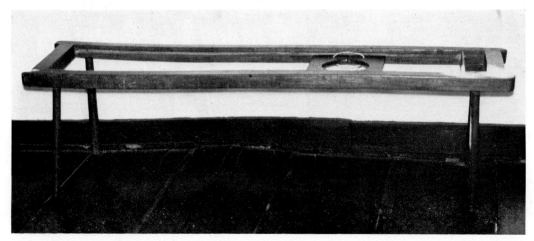

452 Baby minder with sliding carriage, English, 17th or 18th century. *In Strangers' Hall Museum, Norwich.* (*Section XXVII*)

454 Baby minder, English, 17th century. (*Section XXVII*)

455 The Chautauqua Kindergarten Drawing Board and Writing Desk, made for the English market about 1901. (*Section XXVII*)

456 A selection of bedside watch stands, some made to fold for travelling. For details, see text. (*Section XXVIII*)

457 BOTTOM ROW: from left, the second and third are bedside watch stands, as are also the two extreme right. The remainder are mantelshelf specimens. For details, see text. (*Section XXVIII*)

458 Three rococo, mantelshelf watch stands. LEFT: the figure depicts a Louis Quinze man of fashion; CENTRE: the superstructure supported Atlas style; RIGHT: Death, pointing at the time, awakens the sleeper. (*Section XXVIII*)

459 A gruesome, mantelshelf watch stand, carved with a multitude of drowned corpses and wrecked ships; 19th century, probably sailor's work. (*Section XXVIII*)

460 Father Time, the whole stand carved from a single block of pearwood; German, 17th or 18th century, English under German influence. (*Section XXVIII*)

THE AUTHOR

joiner's adze, with 16½ in. handle, is illustrated, Plate 414, *E*, and a cooper's adze of the same period, with 8 in. handle, Plate 414, *D*.

Augers—see *Boring Tools*

Awls
The awl, a pointed, tapering, round steel blade with a tang inserted into a wooden handle and sometimes called a pricker or scratch awl, was both a piercing tool and the predecessor of the marking knife; at some period it also became a recognized tool for putting a 'burr' or edge on a scraper. A bradawl, also formerly known as a nail-passer, bevelled from two sides of the round and sharpened to form a small blade, is a boring tool which is twisted to open the wood fibres; it may also be used as a driver for small screws.

Axes—see *Adze*

Bevels—see *Levels*

Boring Tools
The principal boring tools are, or have been, the auger, bow-drill, brace, bradawl (see *Awl*), gimlet, and later the Archimedean drill and wheel brace. The bow-drill appears in some of the earliest Egyptian reliefs, but being a somewhat complicated instrument, it is unlikely that it was really the first boring tool; some kind of bradawl seems a more likely candidate for the honour. Since Roman times, the bow-drill has rarely figured in the woodworker's kit in western Europe, although still used by jewellers and other fine workers. In the Middle East, however, it still has wider application. Old survivals are rare; one probably dating from the 17th or 18th century and of English or continental origin, with mahogany and boxwood stock, is illustrated, Plate 418, *J*. It may have been used by a woodworker, but more likely by a

sculptor. The movement was reciprocal, and the bow was usually held horizontally in the right hand and pushed backwards and forwards with the string or rawhide wound round the drill, held vertically by the left hand, grasping the top disc. Sometimes the positions were reversed, the bow being used with the drill horizontal and its disc pressed against the breast of the operator.

The auger family, the smaller members of which include gimlets or wimbles (a late 18th- or early 19th-century specimen is shown, Plate 409, *E*), are T-shaped tools, consisting of drills of many different types, permanently or detachably fitted into a cross-bar handle. They appear frequently in mediaeval and later illustrations, sometimes with crutch-head shaped handles, but survivals earlier than the 19th century are rare. A good specimen, with boxwood handle and a large selection of bits, is included in the Dolling chest, Plate 405. Jesus is depicted using one in Wierix engraving, Plate 401. Another, with spoon bit, is included among the tools carved in the du Buf panel, Plate 398. During the mediaeval period, the breast auger was evolved; this gave much more power for heavy drilling; the cross-bar being morticed through the stock about halfway down, pressure was exerted by the operator's chest against the revolving head or breast-plate of the stock, whilst the cross-bar was turned in the normal way with both hands.

Where or, indeed, exactly when the cranked drill or brace originated is unknown, but that it was used in mediaeval Europe is clearly attested by the painting of Joseph using one, in the Maitre de Flémalle's well-known Annunciation triptych of 1483. Although Goodman shows an all-metal German brace of 1505, it is fair to say that it was normally a wooden tool until the late 19th century. It is rather hard to see why the all-metal brace took so long to gain acceptance, because it was so much stronger and could be cranked so much more than one shaped from wood. The answer doubtless was price, because the steel brace was expensive and had to be purchased by the woodworker, who could make his own of wood. What I take to be a steel brace with square pad, is illustrated in Plate 4, *H*, of the 1703 edition of Moxon's *Mechanick Exercises*. Another very similar, is shown in Plate XXI, *E*, of Bergeron's 1792 edition of *Manuel du Tourneur*. An actual steel brace, but probably 19th-century, English, is shown, Plate 413, *A*. Apart from price, woodworkers are notoriously conservative. Even as late as 1914, when I bought my first full-size kit of tools, I was offered the choice of the modern steel brace with ratchet, or the old wood type strengthened with brass plates, as shown, Plate 409, *A*.

The simple, early wooden shape, with only slight cranking, is clearly shown, lying on the boat, in Wierix engraving, Plate 404. This primitive pattern, made by the user, persisted among chair bodgers, working in the woods around High Wycombe, Buckinghamshire, until the end of the 19th century. An example made of the traditional beech wood and believed to date from about the mid-19th century, is shown, Plate 413, *C*. An earlier type of brace, impossible to date accurately, but almost an exact facsimile of that used on the Novaya Zemyla Expedition of 1596, now in the Rijksmuseum, Amsterdam, is illustrated, Plate 413, *B*. It came from the Italian border of Switzerland. Soon after 1800, the wooden brace was commercially produced with a wider crank and a spring button controlled chuck. Gradually, as the century advanced, the crank was reinforced by ever longer brass, and later, steel strengthening plates, until the change over to the all-steel modern brace, with its various refinements, became the logical step.

Although the name Archimedean drill suggests antiquity, the tool, Plate 409, *G*, only appeared about the mid-19th century. It was later followed by its more robust brother, the 'Yankee', which, acting as a screwdriver or drill, did not attain much popularity in England until the 1914–18 War. The more complex French brace or breast drill, came into the English woodworker's tool chest just before 1900, but it was illustrated in Bergeron more than 100 years earlier.

American, 19th-century, drilling or boring machines, with angle adjustments, are strong and effective machines. Some are still giving good service in country workshops, after what appears to be a full century of hard work; but this could be misleading, for the same design has been made now, without any material alteration, for more than 100 years.

A 17th-century, horizontal boring machine for boring a hole, up to 6 in. in diameter, through an elm water pipe 6 ft. long, is illustrated, lower half of Plate 407, taken from a plate in John Evelyn's *Sylva*, 1664. The log was clamped on to a bed, sliding on wheels between runners, and was pushed by the workman against the end of a giant auger, like the three shown in the foreground. The auger was powered by water, transmitted by a wheel and a cog with 36 or more teeth, to a pinion with 6 teeth. Considerable skill was needed to keep the bore to the centre of the log. After drilling, one end of the log was shaped into a cone, as shown on the log in the background; this engaged into a reverse shaped socket in the next log; to make the joint watertight, tallow was used. Logs were driven end-on into each other with a sledge hammer—hence the term 'driving a main'. The method of making a right-angle turn, or a T junction, is shown in Plate 408, where the tapered short section is driven into a cone socket in the side of the longer length of elm pipe. These specimens were excavated from an ancient water supply on a farm at Colnbrook, Buckinghamshire, belonging to the Wilkinson Sword Co.

Bow Drills—see *Boring Tools*

Braces—see *Boring Tools*

Bradawls—see *Awls*

Breast Augers—see *Boring Tools*

Chalk Line Winders

The chalk line is simply a long string, coated with chalk, or other colouring matter, drawn taut, and 'twanged', so that it strikes a marking line on a flat surface. The most usual winders are either the wooden skeleton frames, as used for kites, or the reel revolving on the end of a pointed stick, as shown, Plate 419, *D* and *E*. These particular specimens are probably 18th- or 19th-century, but are not readily datable. The type has considerable antiquity and the advantage that, for outdoor work, the stick can be stuck in the ground. Marking by means of a coloured cord was known to the Egyptians, and marking with a line is referred to in *Isaiah* in the Old Testament. One of the earliest European illustrations is a fresco by Christofano Buffalmacco at Pisa, painted about 1350. In the Far East, the sumi tsubo, Plate 419, *F* and *G*, has, for many centuries, taken the place of the chalk line. It is a hollowed-out hardwood boat, 7 in. to 9 in. long, filled with liquid pigment. The cord, fastened to a peg, is wound on a grooved wheel provided with a cranked handle, at the stern of the boat; it passes through the pigment and out of a hole, sometimes carved as a face with an open mouth, in the bows. In some instances, a sumi tsubo may be carved to represent a dragon. Some, such as Plate 419, *G*, have considerable artistic merit.

Chests—see introduction to this section.

Chisels and Gouges

Chisels of sharpened flint, copper and bronze were, in due course, followed by iron and steel. As with more modern specimens, the Romans made iron chisels with tangs to fit into wooden handles, and with iron sockets into which the wooden handles fitted; they also used chisels with iron handles and blades in one. By mediaeval times, bevel edge paring chisels, firmer chisels and mortise chisels all appear in illustrations, in a variety of widths, and some, but not all, appear to have ferrules to handles. For firmer chisels, the splayed blade, widening out towards the cutting edge, seems to have originated in the Middle Ages and did not die out until the 19th century. In the British Isles, boxwood, ash and beech appear always to have been the most favoured woods for handles, which may be turned and straight, turned in barrel outline, or octagonal in section. A firmer chisel may be seen in use in Wierix engraving, Plate 401 and two in Plate 404. One of the splay-bladed type is among the carved tools in panel, Plate 398 and an actual mid-18th century chisel, with carved handle, is illustrated, top left, Plate 410.

Gouges, a form of chisel with curved cutting edges, used for carving and shaping, have been available from early times. The basic types are—bent for carving; firmer for paring or scribing, and socket for turning. They are, and have long been, made in a wide variety of depths and diameters (sizes) of curves and with sharpening bevels inside and outside of their curved profiles. Mid-18th-century gouges with carved handles are shown each side of the plane, at top of Plate 410. See also *Sharpening Devices*.

Cramps

Wooden cramps, the general run of both G cramps and sash cramps, are too familiar to need any special description, but the miniature boxwood cramp, Plate 413, *H*, is so exceptionally well finished as to merit illustration. It is English and may be 18th- or 19th-century.

Crozes—see *Planes*

Draw Bore Tools—see *Steels*

Draw-knives—see *Shaves and Jiggers*

Drills—see *Boring Tools*

Gauges, Marking

Until recent years, the marking gauge was usually made by the woodworker during his apprentice days. Whilst, therefore, possessing individuality, the principle was always the same and has remained unchanged for at least 300 years. The gauge consists of two parts, the stem and the fence or block. The stem is pierced through at a right angle, near one end, and a narrow blade, or sharpened point, is inserted in the hole. This point is the marker, which is adjustable in depth, sometimes by means of a wedge, like a miniature plane iron. The stem slides through a mortise in the block or fence, which may be square, round, or oval in outline, or, in 18th-century or early 19th-century specimens, such as Plate 409, *F*, and 413, *J*, of an ornamental outline. The fence, which sets the distance for the marking point from the edge of the wood, is sometimes rebated on old specimens, such as Plate 409, *F*, and is adjusted and fixed where desired, by means of a side wedge; modern specimens have a set screw. The gauge was so cheap and simple to make that a woodworker often had several in his kit, set for different line-marking distances from the fence. Some joiners, who did a lot of mortise and tenon work, fitted two marking points at fixed distances on one stem, to mark simultaneously the thickness of a tenon or its mortise. An alternative was a gauge with twin stems, Plate 413, *K*, which allowed one stem to be slid out beyond the other, so that the marking points provided two parallel lines.

Grease Boxes

A grease box, used for greasing the sole of a plane, the end of a screw, or numerous other purposes, is an adjunct which a woodworker has always made for himself. Basically, it consists of a block of hardwood, hollowed out for the grease, and provided with a lid, pivoting on a screw or hardwood dowel. Examples are shown, Plate 419, *B* and *C*.

Hammers and Mallets

Basically, the only difference between a hammer and a mallet is that the first has a metal head and is used for striking metal, whilst the latter has a head of wood, leather, or felt, and is used for striking wood or other resilient materials. In detail, the differences go much further, for both tools are used not only in all branches of woodworking, but in many other trades and professions as well. In consequence, they vary in size, weight, shape and materials of both heads and handles, and include such widely different implements as the medical percussion hammers, jeweller's hammers, chairman's or auctioneer's gavels, right through the range to the sledge-hammer. Hammer heads, from early times, have frequently been combined with axes and adzes, and the claw hammer, which also has great antiquity, combines, in some measure, the function of pincers. The most important thing to the worker, is not only a grip, but that the balance should be right. A striking tool should fall with its own rhythmic momentum and almost without effort on the part of the wielder. A badly balanced hammer or mallet is not only exhausting, it never gives good work. The last remark also applies to the use of the wrong type or weight of the tool used for a particular job. Hammers and mallets, *circa* 1600, are shown in Wierix engraving Plates 399, 401, 403, 404, and among the carved tools, Plate 398. A well balanced and highly ornamental, 18th-century hammer is included in Plate 410.

Jacks

The very rare, 9 in. high lifting-jack, Plate 418, *H*, is almost identical with the one illustrated in Moxon's *Mechanick Exercises* of 1696, where it is described as 'An

Engine used for the removing and commodious placing of great Timber'.

Jiggers—see *Shaves*

Lathes
The lathe and the potter's wheel may be considered together, because they perform exactly the same function—that of rotating material, so that the turner or the potter can profile the work in the desired manner. The potter's wheel rotates the clay on a vertical axis; the lathe rotates the wood, ivory, or other material, horizontally. Both are essential aids to the operator and, ignoring modern automatic machines, with both, the co-ordinated brain, eye and skill of the operator remain paramount. Although the potter's wheel was probably invented before the lathe, the latter may be considered as the earliest and for ornament the most important mechanical aid of the woodworker. In more recent years, it has become the machine on which the smooth or threaded cylindric parts of all other machine components are made.

The long familiar phrase, 'The ancient art and mystery (it should actually be mistery, or craft) of the turner', is appropriate, for it remains a mystery as to when and where the art commenced. A fragment of an Etruscan bowl, *circa* 700 B.C., from a tomb at Corneto, is possibly the earliest definitely turned object still in existence. Other remains of turned vessels have been found in 7th century B.C. graves in Asia Minor. Complete examples of turned ornaments, beads, etc. have been found in fair quantities in 6th century B.C. Etruscan excavations and a Celtic bowl of the same period has been found at Uffing in Upper Bavaria; but we know nothing of the lathes on which they were turned, nor whether the idea of the lathe developed simultaneously in several parts of the world.

The earliest lathe illustration occurs as an out of perspective and much damaged low relief carving on the stone wall of an Egyptian tomb of about 300 B.C. It shows the workpiece mounted between centres; the turner is using a long-handled tool, while his assistant keeps the work in rotation by means of a two-hand cord or strap drive. Incidentally, a strap drive is still used both in Egyptian and Indian bazaars.

The lathe appears to have been introduced to England at least as early as 200 B.C., by the Iron Age Celtic peoples. Large bowls and wheel hubs of that period have been preserved in the peat of the Glastonbury Lake Village. The treadle pole lathe came into being in the Middle Ages and has remained in use ever since; but again, where and when it was born, we do not know.

The principal disadvantage of all strap, cord and pole driven lathes is their reciprocal movement, involving an idle return stroke and one is amazed at the fineness of some of the work which was executed on such primitive machines. An advantage which they had, was that they made it possible to part-turn wooden measures and wood vessels for drinking, etc., leaving a block of wood projecting from the cylinder at one place, to be shaped into a handle—see Section III, *Drinking*, Plate 44, Irish lámhógs and methers and Section XIX, *Scientific*, Plate 301, measures.

The continuous drive first appeared round about 1500 A.D. Leonardo da Vinci illustrated one which he probably invented and which was driven by a treadle acting on a crankshaft and flywheel, connected directly to the mandrel. The machine also had an alternative hand crank. Although the continuous treadle lathe came into being at the end of the Middle Ages, the pole lathe has still survived as a woodland turner's machine up to the present day, and an elm bowl was turned for me in 1954 by 85 year old Mr. G. W. Lailey, on a pole lathe in a hut on Bucklersbury Common. It is not possible to trace here the full progress of the lathe, but during the 17th century it became a heavily built machine and some of the reasons for these developments are described in the introduction to Section III, *Drinking*, under the heading *Lignum Vitae*. What the lathe looked like in the first quarter of the 18th century, may be seen in Plate 420, a fully operative French lathe, still capable of turning out fine work and complete with many of its original tools. The bed and other principal wood parts of the machine are of Spanish mahogany.

It is needless to describe here the varied small works of the plain turner—nearly every page and illustration in this volume pays tribute to his skill—but brief mention should be made of his larger work. From the dawn of furniture making, the turner, except during brief periods when his work was unfashionable, has been an important furniture craftsman; it made no difference whether the carpenter, the joiner or the cabinet-maker was the basic furniture maker—he still needed the turner to lighten, refine and embellish his work, and provide an almost unlimited variety of balusters and columns, ranging in outline from bobbin, vase, reel and bead, etc., to twist turnings. The turner was and still is the man who gives grace to table and chair legs, rails, and chair spindles. He provided an important part of the attractiveness of four-poster beds, torchères and columns for clock cases and chimneypieces. Until the 17th century, turned parts in furniture were structural and to some degree functional. Unfortunately, early 17th-century furniture joiners used split turnings as applied decoration to oak furniture, a lapse which, whilst bringing considerable work to him at the time, harmed him long term. Turners were possibly the earliest craftsmen in western Europe to make the rare and important chairs or thrones used in palaces and for church dignitaries. One of the best portrayals of a 12th-century 'thrown' chair is shown by a 12th-century stone carving in Chartres Cathedral. The turners' essay at making a triangular seated 'thrown' chair,

although undeniably a *tour de force* and both ingenious and quaint, was hardly a success, as it was one of the most impractical and uncomfortable seats ever devised. Nevertheless, these three-sided chairs were made, probably in very small quantities, from quite early times until the 17th century, and they may well have been the basic reason why the turners were allowed to exercise so much control over the quality of chair making up to the mid-17th century. Probably the most satisfactory chair in which the turner has played the major part, is the Windsor, for it is and always has been essentially a chair with parts designed for making on a lathe. Its soundness and functional and aesthetic appeal have already ensured its popularity for some 250 years and today it is in greater demand than ever.

In building joinery, the turner has made important contributions over many centuries, particularly by providing the turned balusters of staircases, landings, balconies, roof lanterns and parapets, and church screens. Turners also provided similar balusters for the poops and sterns of 16th- and 17th-century ships, as well as pulleys and many other wood components used on sailing vessels.

Before referring to some specialized lathe work, brief mention should be made of the turner's contribution to Noah's Ark toy animals—for details, see Section XV, *Pastimes* and Plates 226 and 227.

Rose engine turning, of which several examples are illustrated in Section III, *Drinking*, is a specialized and early type of ornamental turnery, executed on a rose engine lathe, or a rose engine chuck adapted to an ordinary lathe. With other ornamental turnery, a special type of lathe may be used, or comparatively simple attachments may be made to an ordinary lathe. The basic difference between plain and ornamental turnery is that with the first, the work revolves while it is being profiled and the type of cutting tool and its angle are varied; ornamental turnery is a secondary operation, and it is the tool which revolves, cutting a surface pattern on the already profiled work, which may be varied in its position as desired. This is an over simplification, but the whole story requires a book; several books, Plumier and Northcott particularly, are mentioned under *Further Reading*.

Although Jacques Besson, the French engineer, constructed an ornamental turning lathe in 1578 and Charles Plumier published the first full-scale treatise on ornamental lathes in 1701 (Moxon gave some brief details in 1696), it was Charles Holtzapffel who, with his *Turning and Mechanical Manipulation*, Vol. III, 1856, really made ornamental turning into a popular hobby. Some of the effects which the ornamental turner obtained, mostly in the second half of the 19th century, are shown in Plates 411 and 412. The facility with which ornament could be cut into plain turnery, unfortunately resulted in over ornamentation, as many of the objects illustrated clearly show. The temptation to use a small object as an exercise ground for as many patterns as possible, leaving no plain space to rest the eye, ruins many examples of ornamental turnery. Examples of twist turning are shown in Section VI, *Fire and Lighting*, candlesticks, Plates 121 and 124. Two 3¼ in. diameter plaques turned on a copying lathe are illustrated, Plate 292, *P* and *Q*; they are heads of Octavius and Vespasian, turned in boxwood. Such work is normally executed on the *end grain* of a dense hardwood, as otherwise the angles of the cutter are liable to tear out the grain. It is a point worth noting that several collections contain what are believed to be fine original relief carvings, but they are actually copying lathe, end-grain reproductions of originals which were carved in the normal manner.

Levels, Plumbs [or Plumb-bobs], Bevels and Squares

Although Hadley had attached a spirit level to a sextant as early as 1733 and it was also used on surveying telescopes and other scientific instruments in the 18th century, this important device did not enter the woodworker's and builder's tool kit as a separate entity until the first quarter of the 19th century. A square, shaped like a letter A, with a plumb-bob descending from the apex, had been used from Egyptian times, continuing virtually unchanged and uninterruptedly through the Roman civilization and the Middle Ages. As an alternative to a metal bob, the heavy lignum vitae plumb-bob, Plate 413, *D*, virtually superseded all other woods for bobs in the 17th century. Traditional bevels, *E* and *G*, and a try square, *F*, are shown in the same plate.

Machinery, Woodworking—see introduction to this section

Mallets—see *Hammers*

Marking Gauges—see *Gauges*

Ornamental Turnery—see *Lathes*

Planes

The plane, one of the most essential tools in a woodworker's kit, is, in its simplest form, a chisel wedged at an angle in the mortise of a solid block of wood, in such manner that the cutting edge projects forward and slightly through the sole of the block. It has a long but interrupted history, virtually two histories—pre- and post-mediaeval, with a hiatus between. The earliest planes to come to light so far, are those from Pompeii, but altogether the remains, in some instances the irons only, of more than 50 have been excavated from various Roman occupied parts of Europe, including several in Great Britain. Judging by those in the most complete condition, they were advanced tools, which probably had several centuries of evolutionary progress behind them, prior to the destruction of Pompeii in 79 A.D. There is, however, no evidence so far to support the theory that the Greeks were the original inventors, as has sometimes been claimed. Nearly all these excavated planes were composite, having wood bodies with iron soles, some with attached side plates; in fact, they were ancestors of the 19th-century, Spiers type of planes, in both jack and smoothing sizes. Surviving woodwork at Pompeii and Herculaneum also suggests, as Goodman points out, that Roman joiners had moulding, plough and rebate planes in their kits. In his scholarly research, he has brought to light a tenuous but continuous line of rather specialized planes between the Roman and early mediaeval periods, but has been unable to discover any actual planes made between about 800 A.D. and 1596–7, the date of the plane which survived from the Nova Zemlya expedition. Nevertheless, whilst pictures prove that the plane did not die out all over Europe for 800 years, it is probable that in many parts, and during most of the time, the average woodworker never saw, nor used one. Certainly there is no pictorial evidence nor, I think, any indication from surviving woodwork, that the plane was used in Great Britain during the Middle Ages up to about 1400 A.D., for furniture, joinery or carpentry; there is, however, plenty of evidence of adze surface finishing. I except from this sweeping generalization, fine specialized work, such as musical instrument making, for which small planes were probably used. Moulding planes were probably introduced or re-introduced to England early in the 15th century by Flemish craftsmen, working on linenfold panels.

When I wrote *Treen*, 20 years ago, speaking of planes, I said 'I cannot accept the general contention that they were invariably made by the craftsmen who used them: in my opinion, there was probably an eighteenth-century commercial undertaking which made planes'. This was then regarded as a very contentious theory, but time and research have proved it correct. The 18th-century moulding plane, top centre, Plate 410, is stamped Michael Saxby and F.C., 1756, and research by Goodman has already brought to light other Saxby planes, as well as about 150 18th-century planes made by Gabriel & Sons of 32 Banner Street, off Old Street, London. This street was and until very recently has remained in the heart of the cabinet-making district of London and was a natural place to find tool makers and cabinet brass founders congregating. After the Gabriel family left 32 Banner Street in 1815, the business of plane making was taken over by the Ponder family at the same address. Goodman has also found a plane stamped Casebourne; he was a plane maker at 14 Banner Street, from some time in the 1790s until 1824. As late as 1838, these same premises were occupied by Seth Lazenby, another plane maker. Incidentally, 'Plane Makers' justified a heading in Pigot's *London and Provincial Commercial Directory* as early as 1823–4, when 10 were listed. The Sheffield directory entries show that plane, brace and bit, auger and file making were well established in the 18th century, but it is possible, indeed probable, that in some instances only the plane irons were made there, and that the plane stocks and the wooden parts of other tools were made in London and elsewhere, both by specialist firms and individual craftsmen. It is also highly probable that many of the firms listed in 18th-century directories as ironmongers, were later listed as tool makers. Support to these contentions is given by the U.S.A. research of Charles F. Hummel of the Henry Francis du Pont Winterthur Museum, who published his most interesting findings in *Winterthur Portfolio* II, 1965, under the heading of *English Tools in America—The Evidence of the Dominys*. Three generations of the Dominys, working at East Hampton, Long Island, in the 18th and early 19th centuries, were, like other American wood craftsmen of the period, considerable importers of

English tools. One of the largest exporters of all kinds of English woodworking tools to America, throughout the 18th century, from the first decade onwards, was Sir Ambrose Crowley and his descendants; Sir Ambrose was a Knight and Alderman of the City of London, with premises in Thames Street and his firm is always described as an ironmongers. Incidentally, Hummel's research shows that English plane irons are often found in American-made beech plane stocks, which is quite logical, because it would have been waste of valuable shipping space to import anything more than the superior English steel cutters. A clearly defined group of Dutch, 18th-century planes with scrolls and dates carved on them, also suggests commercial production in Holland, and it is probable that many of them emanated from the same plane manufactory but, so far as I know, no maker has been traced.

Planes may be grouped roughly under seven principal headings—planes for smoothing; planes for roughing; planes for truing; planes for moulding; planes for grooving and rebating; planes for rounding or tapering; and planes, such as spelk or spill, for producing a particular type of residue or shaving. The variety of names for these planes is very considerable and, even excluding most of the alternative names for the same species and various proprietary types such as Bailey, Norris, Preston, Sargent, Spiers and Stanley, includes the following: badger; bead; Bismark; block; bullnose; chamfer; chariot; coachmaker's; compass; croze; dado; dovetail; edge; fillester; forkstaff; hollows; gutter; jack; jointer; matching; mitre; moulding—in great variety; ogee; old woman's tooth; ovolo; panel; plough; rebate; reed; roughing; rounds; router; scraper; scrub; scurfing; shave; shoulder; side rebate; smoothing; spelk; spill; spokeshave; sun; toothing; trenching; try; turning plane or witchet, and Universal plane. It is not possible to illustrate and describe all these

different types here, but some of the more ornamental or unusual planes in the Pinto and other collections are illustrated.

A 26 in. beech long plane, with carved closed handle, set off-centre behind the mouth, and the front carved with a grotesque face, composed of leaf scrolls is shown, Plate 409, C. It is almost certainly western European, 17th- or early 18th-century, but closer than that in identification, I will not venture. The handle over to the right is quite a common feature on 18th-century planes, but I think that much more research is required before planes can be authoritatively dated and their regions of origin settled by reference to the types and positions of handles. Goodman is never dogmatic, but some other writers, with much less experience, have sometimes made most questionable attributions. Some of the difficulties may be realized by a few of the broader facts. Some 17th- and 18th-century planes have no handles and have never had any; some fairly early 17th-century planes have the so-called 18th-century, closed type 'saw' handles, whilst late 18th-century, country-made planes have the early type of open handle; some 19th-century planes have late 17th-century type 'loop' handles; some 18th- and 19th-century planes have handles fore and aft, others have the more normal single handle, which may be central or off-centre behind the mouth. Whether a handle is open or closed, is more often decided by the length and purpose, than by the age of the plane, and many 'draw' planes with two or four turned, horizontal side handles, described as Chinese or Korean, are actually European.

Reverting to Plate 409, D and H are two of the now well-known, Dutch, 18th-century group, of which 100 or more are recorded, with carved dates covering the whole century. The dates are carved in ornamental scrolls in front of the mouths, as on the adjustable fillister plane, D, dated 1764, and the skew-mouthed side moulding plane, *H*, dated 1729. It will be noted that when the plane iron wedges are original, as they are on these two planes, they are carved with a whorl. The long jointer plane, shown at bottom of Plate 410, with fore and aft handles, is dated 1771 and seems related to the last two, but not by the same maker. The same remark applies to Plate 417, *C*, a convex soled moulding plane of beech, dated 1722, used for rounding the insides of wooden gutters; this type of plane was also known as a forkstaff or hollowing plane.

In Plate 414, *A*, a mid-19th-century Bismark roughing off plane is shown; this type, which has considerable antiquity on the continent, is characterized by the up-standing 'horn' or hand trip on the forward extending sole plate. Some 19th-century Bismarks were made with sole slightly rounded in section, to give a textured surface in simulation of adze finish. *B* is a mahogany-infilled, steel-soled smoothing plane, *circa* 1860, of the type originated by Stewart Spiers of Ayr, about 1840. *F*, an Italian, 18th-century *Ketschobel* or roughing plane with side handles, which can be pushed or pulled, is a type which appears to have been used in southern Europe for more than 700 years. Goodman tells me that one is illustrated in the *Serajevo Haggadah*, a manuscript of the Jewish Passover service, with the picture painted in northern Spain, about 1350. The illustration depicts Noah directing operations in the building of the Ark. *G* is an English, 18th-century cooper's chiv, for cutting a broad, shallow channel, about 2 in. below the top of the staves of a barrel. The channel itself is properly called a howell, but the tool is often known as a howell plane or howell. *H* is a nogg, a specialized rounding plane for working a taper on ladder rungs or dowels. *J* is a cooper's sun or topping plane, for planing in a 'sweep' on barrel heads, to provide a flat surface on which the fences of the chiv and croze can travel. *K* is an extremely curious long plane,

made of walnut, decorated with a punched design, including initials I.L.N. and date 1811; it measures $35\frac{1}{2}$ in. in length. The sole is 2 in. wide, with a $\frac{5}{8}$ in. wide fence running down the middle, and wedged cutters each side (one is missing). An unusual feature is the grease box incorporated near the front of the stock. Probably of Scandinavian origin, it appears to have been designed for a repetition operation which involved rebating two fillets to form an exact pair.

Reference has already been made to that highly specialized type of plane, the cooper's croze; two views of an unusually ornamental, Italian, walnut example, probably dating from the 17th century, are shown, Plate 416. The croze is used for ploughing out the groove for the barrel head; it is a 'follow on' tool to the chiv. The upper picture shows the saw-tooth cutter, and the enclosed finger grip, which is an early and unusual feature; the lower picture shows the decorative nature of this particular specimen. Some crozes have a router type of cutter.

Plate 415 shows top and bottom views of a curious draw plane, dated 1776, and probably Dutch. The sole is grooved out to a depth of $\frac{1}{2}$ in. between solid fences $2\frac{1}{2}$ in. apart and it is believed to have been used for making hazel, poplar, or willow slats for woven spelk baskets. It would never have been used for English spelk baskets of tough oak and, indeed, no plane figures in the English spelk basketmaker's kit, as his spelk was boiled and riven. Even for comparatively soft timbers, this plane must have needed tremendous force to drive it, as the three side, and one upright handle at the rear indicate. The iron can be set to various depths and the mouth at the rear, through which the spelk emerges, measures $2\frac{1}{2}$ in. by $\frac{5}{8}$ in.

Plate 417, *A*, is a two-man *Ketschobel* or draw plane, 11 in. long, which closely resembles one shown in a painting of the Holy Family by Bartolomeo Schidone

(1560–1616) in the Palazzo Reale, Naples. The actual example, Plate 417, *A*, probably dates from the 18th or even early 19th century, showing the persistence of this type, which is still used in central and southern Europe. It is this variety of *Ketschobel* which is usually erroneously described as a Chinese or Korean plane. Most of the European specimens have the two pairs of grips, but if they have only one, it is behind the iron; Oriental planes with one pair of grips, have them in front of the mouth. *B* is a *Schaaf* type of smoothing plane, 17th- or 18th- century, punch decorated, probably from the region of the Baltic, but they are found all over Europe and are characterized by their boat-like, graceful two-way curved sides rising behind the iron, descending in front, narrowing on plan and rising again to form a scrolled hand grip. Many are much more elaborate than this specimen. They sometimes occur in the range of scroll-decorated, 18th-century, Dutch planes, and also as compass and moulding planes. *C* has already been described among Dutch, dated planes. *D* is a 10½ in. long, carved and punch decorated, walnut smoothing plane from the German region of Switzerland. The carved 'prow' gives it a Scandinavian look, but the forward projection of the sole (re-soled) shows its common ancestry with the Bismark. Plate 417, *E*, is an exceptionally fine, English, carved walnut scratchstock, with steel cutter, wedge and face plate. It was used for cutting grooves in circular work, probably in either an 18th-century ship-yard or coachbuilder's establishment. The view of the reverse side is shown, Plate 418, *E*.

Plate 417, *F*, is an 'old woman's tooth', a router plane of French walnut, probably 16th- or 17th-century. Usually, such tools are essentially plain and utilitarian, but during the last 50 years I have seen three of this mediaeval style, with the shavings emerging from the old woman's mouth and it makes one wonder whether design in-

spired name or vice versa. *G*, of walnut, is a compass plane for smoothing inside curved work; it is carved and punch decorated with initials I.W. and dated 1775, is 8¼ in. long and probably South German or Austrian. Modern examples have adjustable steel soles. Apart from the cooper's 6ft. 0 in. long jointer plane, which is regarded as a fixture and used upside down, like a planing machine, the jointer plane, *H*, is the heaviest for size which I have met. It is 28½ in. long, made of oak and weighs 11½ lb. It is competently and elaborately carved, and dated 1810. Its style suggests one of the shores of the Baltic. It bears a label stating 'This carpenter's plane was purchased by me in Egypt in the year 1855 and I now present it to my grandson John Henry Leech 1877' (signature indecipherable), which only goes to show that place of purchase is not necessarily related to place of manufacture.

In Plate 418, *A* and *G* may be considered together, because both are different versions of the same tool, known as a stail-engine, witchet, or rounding and tapering plane; the last describes the purpose. The stocks are of beech and both are operated with both hands, although *A*, has one cutter and *G*, two. I assume these two specimens to be English, 19th-century, but they are the traditional tools of rake makers and other craftsmen needing to round and taper handles. The nogg, Plate 414, *H*, already described, is a smaller and earlier version of these devices. *K* is a spill plane, modern, but of a traditional type; one of the tightly curled spills it makes, is shown in front of it. *L* and *M* are twin- and single-bladed coachmakers' rounders, with stocks of hickory, both English, 19th-century.

In Plate 419, *H* and *J*, although only 1⅝ in. and 2½ in. long respectively, are not toys, but model maker's planes. *L*, a 4¾ in. long smoothing plane of beech, has the sacred initials in a sunk panel on one side and the date 1766 on the reverse; the sacred initials and crosses occur on other woodworking tools and some writers have suggested that such tools were used for church work, but it seems more likely to me that the association of woodworking with religion goes back to Jesus of Nazareth. Among the delightful drawings in Eric Sloane's *Museum of Early American Tools*, what appears to be the same plane, with the same date, is illustrated; I do not know if Eric Sloane has an identical one, or if he sketched this one on a visit to the Pinto Collection. *M* is a miniature steel-soled, 19th-century, bullnose compass plane, formerly owned by J. T. Baily, the Quaker craftsman. A plane, not illustrated, the toothing plane, looks like an ordinary smoothing plane with the iron nearly vertical and grooved on the back to provide a serrated cutting edge; it is used for roughing and increasing the area and the 'keying' of groundwork for veneering.

At the time of writing, W. L. Goodman's book, *British Plane Makers from 1700* (G. Bell & Sons, Ltd.) has not yet appeared*; it will obviously be a 'must' for all interested in old planes.

Plumbs, or Plumb-bobs—see *Levels*

Rules—see Section XIX, *Scientific: Measuring Sticks and other Measuring Devices*

Saws

The so-called hand saw (all saws are 'hand' if they are not machine saws) and the tenon saw, being all-metal tools apart from their hand grips, are outside the scope of this encyclopaedia; but in passing, it was undoubtedly the difficulty and, therefore, the costliness of the making, and the slowness and inefficiency in use and short life of early saws which led to axe-cleaved and adze-dressed timber being used wherever possible, in preference to sawn. A useful type of wood backed saw, with handles of varying shapes incorporated in the back or stiffening piece, has long been used on the continent for making cuts or grooves across

* This book has now been published.

a plank. An Italian or Austrian, 18th-century example, with scrolled walnut stiffener, is shown, Plate 418, *F*. The Germans call these tools 'edge saws', the French 'tail saws'; in England, so far as I can learn, they were usually known as coffin saws, because they were only used regularly by coffin makers, for making the grooves across the inside of coffin sides, for curving them at the head end.

The frame saw family, which includes all sizes from the two-man, framed, trestle or pit-saw down to the jig or fret saw, was, until very recently, a saw blade tensioned by one means or another in a wooden frame. Various sizes and types of saws in this category are shown in Plate 398, 399, 403, 405, 406, 407, 409 and 433. A two-handed trestle or pit-saw, *circa* 1600, is clearly shown in Plate 403, with Jesus as top sawyer and Joseph as bottom sawyer. As Roman vase paintings and frescoes of the 1st century A.D. show similar framed, trestle saws in use, the type was already 1,600 years old when Wierix engraved it, yet Goodman found Arab sawyers in Cairo with identical framed saws and using the same methods in 1961.

A two-handled, framed, pit or trestle saw of early type, which came from Lincolnshire and is probably 150 to 200 years old, is illustrated, Plate 433, *A*. It is 5 ft. 10 in. long and has the long ash-wood top handle and 'tiller' type bottom handle (showing behind the bottom cross bar) but the tensioning of the saw is different: instead of the saw exerting a central pull on the head and bottom rails of a rectangular frame, the frame, in this example of pine, is made up as a cantilever. The Wierix engraving, Plate 399, shows the end of a framed saw which in its shaping, is almost a bow-saw; but the true bow-saw of antiquity had the tension provided by a piece of springy wood, such as ash bent into a half hoop and fixed to the two ends of the saw blade, so that the whole implement formed a D outline. The tubular steel cross-cut of today is the direct lineal descendant. The carved representation of a framed saw in the early 18th-century panel, Plate 398, shows very clearly the tensioning of the broad-saw blade by means of the twisted cord and toggle stick. Goodman has demonstrated conclusively that this method of tensioning goes back to Roman times, whilst illustrations show that the basic outlines of the whole tool have varied but slightly over the centuries. In Plate 405, a framed saw for finer work is shown on the tool chest. In Plate 407, is shown the multiple, frame band-saw of the 17th century, driven by water power and capable of deeping heavy timbers. The fret saw, Plate 409, *B*, of mahogany with box-wood handle, and of 18th-century date, is not merely a thing of grace which is a joy to the eye, but is also one of the best balanced tools I have ever handled; it has the exceptional reach from saw to cross-bar of 20 in. The treadle-operated, vertical jig-saw, Plate 406, has its return action assisted by a powerful spring in the wooden cylinder casing above the frame. It was made and used in the 18th century by one of the Tunbridge marquetry manufacturers who, in the 19th century, produced some of the finest of the famous Tunbridge wood mosaic. The machine is built as far as is practical of wood, is in full working order and is a rare and interesting example of its period.

Sharpening Devices

Grindstones, oilstones, saw wrests and files are outside the scope of wooden bygones, but one device, which may be unique and for which I can give no better name than a burr remover, is pictured, Plate 419, *A*. It consists of a block of wood, 10 in. by 4 in. by 2¼ in., hollowed out to receive a reeded lead or soft pewter 'carrot', which revolves by means of a cranked handle. By pressing a woodcarving gouge at the correct angle against the appropriate size reed, the 'burr' on the edge, which always occurs in sharpening, is effectively removed. The

largest diameter band, at the handle end, is flat, for use with chisels. See also *Steels*.

Shaves, Jiggers and Draw-knives

The origin of the draw-knife or shave, Plate 418, *D*, has never been traced, but being a simple device and very much a follow-on tool after the axe or adze, it probably has great antiquity. Goodman has traced one form of it back to about 1000 A.D.; certainly it was widely used from the mediaeval period onwards. It was called a drawing knife in earlier times, because you draw it towards you with both hands grasping the two upstanding wooden handles. The blade, sharpened on one edge, may be straight—the cooper's or shingler's draw-knife, or hollow—the hollow shave, or straight each end and hollow in the middle—the coach-maker's draw-knife, or straight at one end, running into a hollow at the other—the jigger. How far back in history the spoke-shaves go is unknown, but they are quite a considerable family, in many sizes, both straight and in a wide variety of curves. They are smaller relatives of the draw-knife, extremely versatile and have many more uses than shaving spokes. Two of the interesting shapes which had developed by the 19th century, are shown, Plate 418, *B* and *C*; they have beech handles, *B*, 14 in. and *C*, 12½ in. long.

Spokeshaves—see *Shaves*

Spirit Levels—see *Levels*

Squares—see *Levels*

Steels

The wood-handled, tapering steel tools, Plate 413, *M* and *N*, have different names and serve diverse purposes in various trades. Woodworkers use them as sharpening steels for scrapers, and formerly they were used as draw bore tools for pegged mortise and tenon joints. Butchers used them as sharpening steels, leather-workers for punching out or opening holes in leather, and to ice merchants they are ice picks.

Sumi Tsubos—see *Chalk Lines*

Toggle Sticks—see *Saws*

Tool Chests and Tool Kits—see introduction to this section.

Trammels
A boxwood trammel for drawing elliptical curves is pictured, Plate 413, *L*. The points are set on the rod where desired, by means of their boxwood screws, and the device may be used with one pointer as centre pivot and the other scoring the wood, or one pointer may be removed and replaced by the centre fitting, which holds a pencil. This example was made about 1890, by a fine old craftsman in the Isle of Wight.

Turnery—see *Lathe*

Wooden Water Pipes—see *Boring Tools*

Woodworking Machinery—see introduction to this section.

XXV

Trade and Craft Devices, Miscellaneous

Trade and craft devices illustrated and described here, include many wooden objects formerly used in workshops, outdoor crafts, and for maintenance or sale in shops. They are arranged under the following main headings, some with a brief introduction.

Bookbinding devices
Brewhouse devices
Butchery devices
Electrical and communication devices
Hatters' devices
Horse care devices and horse equipment
—Blacksmith, farrier, harness room, stable
Itinerant traders' devices
Leather workers' devices and footwear—
Boot and shoe maker, cobbler, saddler, gauntlet and glove maker, etc.
Plumbers' devices
Osier workers' tools
Pottery devices
Rope, cordage and string devices
Shops and shop display devices
Thatching, straw and reed work devices
Trade tools—miscellaneous
Watchmakers' and jewellers' devices

BOOKBINDING DEVICES

Agate Burnishers
Burnishers with various shaped blades of agate set in hardwood handles, like the four early 19th-century examples, Plate 421, *K*, were and are used for applying and burnishing gold leaf on book fore-edges.

Bookbinder's Hand Trimmer Presses
The beechwood hand trimmer press, Plate 422, *D*, was made or sold by Hampson and Bettridge, of 35–37 Cloth Fair, London, in the third quarter of the 19th century.

Bookbinder's Mallets
A bookbinder's traditional form of mallet is pictured, Plate 430, *H*. See also *Plumbers' Tools*.

Bookbinder's Sewing Frames
The bookbinder's hand sewing frame, Plate 422, *E*, the predecessor of the book-sewing machine, remained virtually unaltered from the 16th to the 19th century. This traditional English specimen is impossible to date accurately.

BREWHOUSE DEVICES

Although ale houses and commercial breweries have existed from the earliest times, the home brewing of ale and beer and the making of local country wines remained a normal part of country household life at least until last century; it will probably never die out completely. In small houses, the bakehouse and brewery were sometimes combined, but larger ones had their separate brewhouse, where ale and beer were brewed at intervals, and speciality drinks, such as cider, perry and mead, or gooseberry, mulberry, raisin, dandelion wines, etc., were made according to season, locality and availability of ingredients. Our ancestors were thirsty people; the amount of drink they consumed was gargantuan. Food, heavily spiced to disguise contamination, and heavy manual labour, added to thirst, and water was little drunk owing to the danger from contaminated wells and streams. It was lucky, therefore, that in Tudor times 'penny beer', the most common beverage, cost only 1d. a quart. 'Double beer', costing 1½d. a quart, contained double the amount of hops. Until after the Restoration, when tea, coffee and chocolate became available and gradually worked their way downwards through the social structures, ale or beer was the normal English beverage for adults and children, even at breakfast. The preparation of all brewed drinks involved the use of large numbers of wooden containers and utensils, such as casks, vats, mash tubs, shallow coopered vessels known as keelers, and presses. Some of the now less familiar English brewing ancillaries are illustrated, Plate 423, and described here.

Beer Bowls

Beer bowls, such as Plate 423, F, turned on a pole lathe, with the handle worked out of the solid, varied in size but averaged about 9 in. in diameter. Normally of beech, they were unchanging in design and are impossible to date.

Beer Drayman's Sinks

The coopered iron-bound, open, oak vessel, tapering inwards at the top, Plate 423, B, is a beer drayman's sink. It was formerly carried on the dray and used for placing under the taps of large casks, to catch the overflow, when filling smaller casks; it is fitted with a bung and iron downpipe for returning beer to the cask. The traditional type of specimen illustrated is 8 in. tall, 10 in. in diameter at the top, and 12 in. at the base.

Beer Funnels

The one-piece beer funnel of beech, Plate 423, C, blackened by many brewings, measures 9¾ in. in diameter, about the average. This, like most of the brewer's equipment, remained unchanged over centuries; it was sometimes known as a tunnel.

Malt or Barley Shovels

The traditional one-piece, 14 in. broad-bladed malt shovel of beech, Plate 423, A, which is much warped, came from the 16th-century Easthorpe Mill, Battisford, but the shovel itself is probably not more than 100 years old.

Malt Forks

The 19th-century malt fork, Plate 423, D, is of ash, with a beech handle connected by a bolted iron socket. It is 38 in. tall and 13 in. wide.

Mash Stirrers

The traditional mash stirrer, Plate 423, E, was an important brewing implement, used for stirring the mash of malt and water, particularly in preparing the second brew, known as small beer. It is 50 in. tall, with the paddle 11 in. by 8 in. at the top, tapering to 7 in. at the bottom.

BUTCHERY DEVICES

A travelling butcher, usually following some other trade additionally, was formerly to be found in every village, where the cottagers kept a pig or two, largely fed from scraps in the swill tub. The travelling butcher carried most of his own tools with him, but the hog pole or gibbet and the hog-stool, a heavy oak or elm bench, some 5 ft. long and 18 in. high, supported on splayed legs, with a top about 2 in. thick, had to be provided. Some cottagers had these useful multi-purpose benches, others borrowed from neighbours. Some of the wooden devices used by butchers in various branches of the trade are illustrated, Plate 424, and described below.

Blocks

The simple elm butcher's block, Plate 424, *E*, with cleaver *F* alongside, is 23 in. high, with a diameter of 12 in. Elm and beech were the most commonly used woods and diameters were sometimes considerably larger.

Britchers

The britcher, Plate 424, *C*, is an iron-shod pole, 36 in. to 40 in. long by approximately 2 in. diameter. The specimen illustrated is pine, but it may be found in elm or other suitable hardwood. One end terminates in a straight spike; the spike at the other end is angled. The britcher is used for propping up the carcase of a bullock, etc., during the skinning process.

Carcase Back Stretchers

A pair of butcher's carcase back stretchers of beech, with iron spike ends, is shown, Plate 424, *D*. This type, in varying lengths, has been used probably for many centuries for holding open the carcases of sheep, pigs, etc.

Gambrels

The gambrel, Plate 424, *A*, is a curved bar for stretching the carcase of a hog or calf. It varies in length, usually between 30 in. and 34 in. and is generally of elm or ash. The commonest type is notched, as shown, but some specimens, particularly in the U.S.A., instead of being notched, have cross dowels inserted, forming pegs each side of the spine at intervals, as illustrated in Plate 86, *A*.

Shoulder Trays

Butchers' shoulder trays, like Plate 424, *B*, were known alternatively as 'butchers'

barrows' and 'boater boards' in the not long distant past, when the butcher and his 'boy' still wore the traditional straw boater and blue striped apron. Trays of this outline, suggestive of an animal carcase, were used without change of design over many centuries. They were made of elm as illustrated, or of ash or beech. The tray part of this example is $27\frac{1}{2}$ in. by 10 in., 35 in. over the handles. They vary considerably in size, downwards from these dimensions.

ELECTRICAL AND COMMUNICATION DEVICES

Until as recently as the end of the First World War, wood was used very largely in the provision of indoor cable ducts, circular mounting blocks for electric fittings and casings or boxings for bells and fuses. From the viewpoint of future collectors of treen, the most interesting objects are the small electric fittings, now entirely obsolete, which were made wholly or partially of wood. A few of these are detailed below.

Electric Fittings

Two different patterns of late 19th-century, lignum vitae encased bell pushes are shown, Plate 425, *T* and *U*, a matching lignum vitae bell-rose, *V*, and two matching lamp socket plugs, *W*. Similar lignum vitae or other close grained hardwood lamp holders, and covers for two-pin plugs were also made *en suite*. About the beginning of this century, with the trend to cheapen, all these fittings were made in turned beech, birch or sycamore, which was white enamelled, or stained and varnished a walnut or mahogany colour, or ebonized, in the case of bell pushes. The Ever Ready electric torch, *R*, in oak case, is believed to have been made about 1914.

Lamson Paragon Cash Ball

The Lamson Paragon boxwood cash ball, Plate 425, *P*, is through-dowelled in all directions to prevent breaking out of grain, due to friction while running on the shop railway. The system was invented by William Stickney Lamson for his store in Lowell, Mass., U.S.A. In 1888 he formed the Lamson Store Service Co. Ltd., and from then until about 1934, the system was operated extensively in many parts of the world, including the United Kingdom. The overhead metal railway along which the balls travelled, conveying cash and bills to an elevated cash desk, and receipts back to customers, was to be seen in most of the large drapery establishments before the First World War. In the later stages of development, the ball system became increasingly ingenious. Lifts were used to give the height to allow a gravity run over the required distance and this permitted two or more floors to be served. There were even different sized balls travelling along the same tracks, for different destinations, with a 'loading gauge' over the track, which triggered off points when a ball of the right size passed by. The Lamson ball system was already largely superseded in England by the Lamson Engineering Company's pneumatic tube system before 1934, when a fire in the factory destroyed much of the ball equipment.

Shop Door Bells—see *Shops and Shop Display*

Speaking Tube Whistles
The lignum vitae, combined mouthpiece and whistle, Plate 425, *S*, was a commonplace in large Victorian houses, shops, warehouses, etc. With its long length of tube attachment, it was the forerunner of the house telephone system, and in the home was used particularly to communicate with the staff in the dungeon-like basement. In a large house, there were often a number of different 'call' points—such as the dining-room, library and various landings—each with a separate tube to the basement, where the whistle outlets were placed in a row.

The method of call was to blow down the tube; this caused a shrill blast on the whistle at the other end. When the call was answered, you could speak into or hear through the tube. It was still in common use prior to the First World War.

HATTERS' DEVICES

The evolution of the hat industry from a hand craft to machine manufacture was slowly accomplished during the 19th century, but some of the wooden devices employed in the past are still used. Those connected with straw plaiting are described under the heading *Thatching and Straw Work*, the remainder, below.

Hatter's Blocks
The hatter's block, Plate 425, *A*, *circa* 1900, is made of sycamore and is of a type still being made in various sizes.

Hatter's Bows
The hatter's bow, Plate 433, *C*, is a great rarity. It measures 6 ft. 10 in. long and is made of a pine pole 1¾ in. in diameter. It was used horizontally above the felting table.

The late Charles Freeman in *Luton and The Hat Industry* wrote

'Felt is produced by the inherent property of certain animal fibres, unlike vegetable fibres, to knit with each other to form a homogeneous material. Before the mechanization of the industry both wool and fur were separated by means of a bow and catgut, like a violin bow but about 7 ft. long, which was plucked by a bow-pin and by its vibrations could be made to scatter the fibres in a thin regular layer'.

Hatter's Smoothers
The curiously shaped boxwood object, Plate 425, *E*, is a smoother for inside the curly brims of silk hats (toppers). It was made about 1892 by Anthony Runacres,

hatter's trimming and tool makers, of Union Street, London, S.E. Modern ones are made of brass.

Hat Stretchers

The hat stretchers, Plate 425, *B*, were used in the Luton straw hat industry. They are adjustable in length and were used both length-wise and breadth-wise in hats. Types *C* and *D* were made in various sizes and used for stretching both hard and soft felt hats; they open out by means of left- and right-hand screws; *C* is a 19th-century, all sycamore specimen, whilst *D*, probably about 50 years old, has a brass screw action.

HORSE CARE DEVICES AND HORSE EQUIPMENT

Saddlery devices are included under the separate heading of *Leather Worker* in this section. Wooden objects connected with riding, hunting, etc., will be found in Section XV, *Pastimes*. Some used by black-smiths, farriers and in the harness room and stable are illustrated and described here. The large items, such as the black-smith's wood and leather bellows, and the trave are omitted. The trave, travel or travise was a heavily built wooden post-and-rail cage, used during many centuries for shoeing horses in many countries. Whilst the French name trave was commonly used in the British Isles for the shoeing cage, and still survives in the Wensleydale as a frame on which cheeses are stood, the more usual description in England was horse-stocks. At Oakham, the capital of Rutland, Eng-land's smallest county, an interesting and ancient custom still pertains. For many centuries, every peer passing through Oakham has been required to leave a shoe of his or her horse, or the money to have one made, for mounting on a wall in the castle. Among the goodly array of horse-shoes are specimens presented by Queen Elizabeth I and Queen Elizabeth II.

Balling Guns

The balling gun, Plate 426, *E*, is a turned wooden tube, through which it is said the administrator blew the pill into the horse's mouth. Older readers may remember an early Charlie Chaplin film in which, whilst using a gun of this type, the horse blew first! Some balling guns were provided with a wooden plunger, which ejected the pill like a cork from a pop-gun.

Fleams and Mallets

Two types of fleams, for bleeding horses, are illustrated, Plate 426, *D* and *G*. Shown with its leather case behind it, *D* is the more ordinary 19th-century pattern, made like a folding penknife with three notched blades of varying sizes. The pointed projection was placed against the vein and smartly tapped with a mallet, the blood flow being controlled by a tourniquet. *G*, which is Welsh, probably early 19th-century, con-sists of a fleam which screws into the hollow wooden handle of the mallet when not in use; it may be 18th- or 19th-century.

Harness Pegs and Racks

A harness peg may consist of a large, up-ward-turned peg, mortised into a wooden back plate, a natural fork of a tree, or, in the second half of the 19th century, it was commonly a cast iron hook and back plate made in one piece. But there are no clear lines of demarcation on dates, because even today, wooden pegs and backplates are sometimes made on site. One of the most efficiently designed and attractive harness racks, Plate 427, *A*, was the patent of Musgrave of Belfast and was popular about 1900. The frame is of malleable iron, to which the hardwood split-turnings are screwed.

Harness Saddles

Scandinavian harness saddles, stirrups and horse collars are most decorative. The early 19th-century harness saddle, Plate 427, *C*;

is carved and painted, but ranks as a comparatively simple specimen, some additionally being elaborately pierced. These harness saddles, which fit on the necks of horses, are not seats, but guides for the reins. In some, the reins pass through loops; in others, such as the example illustrated, the carved heads serve the same purpose. The metal plates at the ends, originally had bells suspended from them.

Hoof Parers

The traditional English searcher or hoof parer, Plate 427, *J*, is a simple, thin, curved blade, set in a wood handle. The Swiss version, the *Hufschärfen*, Plate 426, *A*, is more elaborate. It is made like a spokeshave, with an adjustable blade, and the wood, of ornamental profile, is surface etched and decorated with brass studs. This specimen is believed to have been made about 1845.

Horse Standards—see Section XIX, *Scientific: Measuring Rods*

Stable Logs

The two stable logs, Plate 427, *B*, are made of weighty lignum vitae and cocus wood respectively. They have been used on the end of a halter rope, from time immemorial, to prevent the horse straying too far, whilst not restricting movement unnecessarily. They are also known as horse tethering rings, and halter weights.

Syringes, Veterinary

The extremely crude wood and glass syringe, Plate 426, *C*, is probably an early type of veterinary syringe, but this is not definitely established. Its age and provenance are also unknown.

Tail Dockers

An early 19th-century horse-tail docker, with hardwood handles, is illustrated, Plate 426, *B*. The purpose for which it was used is now, happily, illegal.

Tooth Rasps

A typical example of a wood-handled tooth rasp, 25 in. long, is shown, Plate 427, *K*. It was probably made during the last 100 years.

Twitches

Twitches were generally used to hold shut the mouths of fractious or fidgety horses during clipping, shoeing, or other attention. Rutter's Patent horse twitch, Plate 426, *F*, of oak, with leather straps, was in common use around 1900. It could be used to keep the horse's mouth shut, or gagged open, while attending to teeth, etc.

ITINERANT TRADERS' DEVICES

The wheeled vehicles and other wooden apparatus which itinerant traders used for carrying their stock up to 50 or 60 years ago, are now but a memory. The muffin man's and kerb-side toy seller's tray, the specialized hot potato, chestnut and pie barrows, the chair mender's wheeled stool, the street musician's hurdy-gurdy or piano organ, and the scissors to mend and knives to grind machine, Plate 435, the front wheel of which became the driving wheel, when the cart was tipped up at rest for grinding, have all disappeared. So also, has the clattering milk pram, a *circa* 1900 specimen of which is illustrated, Plate 434. The water carrier's yoke has already been described under milk-maid's yoke, but the once commonest 'carrier' of all, the pedlar's pack stick, is now so distant in memory in most parts of the United Kingdom that when one comes to light, its purpose is usually unknown.

Pedlar's Pack Sticks

Two types are illustrated here, Plates 422, *A* and 428, *A*. The steamed and bent ash pedlar's or packman's stick, Plate 428, *A*, which is 37 in. long by 1¾ in. wide and ¾ in. thick in the centre, figures in 16th-century 'Street Cries', and even then probably had great antiquity; there is no way of dating such a specimen, which was carried across one shoulder with packs on both ends. The single-ended ash stick with scroll handle, Plate 422, *A*, figures mostly in 18th- and 19th-century illustrations. This particular example, 30 in. long, dating from about 1840, is stamped with the owner's or maker's name, Wellbourn. A variant of Plate 428, *A*, but considerably longer, leather-covered and with a sharp upturn at each end, is still used in some southern countries. I saw milk sellers and onion sellers both using these traditional pack sticks in Madeira this year (1968).

LEATHER WORKERS' DEVICES AND FOOTWEAR

In this section are grouped some of the tools and devices of boot and shoe makers and cobblers, saddlers, gauntlet and glove makers, etc. A number of the tools and devices are common to several of the leather working trades. They are, therefore, described under this general heading in alphabetical order.

Awls, Leather Workers'
In the main, leather workers' awls are plain, strictly utilitarian stilettos, set in wooden handles. A particularly interesting and ornamental specimen is illustrated, Plate 421, *C*. It is believed to be German, of the 16th or 17th century. Polychrome finished, it is carved to represent a man in the costume of the period, astride a sow, with his chin resting on the sow's stern end. He has a baby in a basket slung on his back. It probably depicts some old German legend.

Boots—see *Model Lasts and Shoes*

Boot Button Boxes
'The Wreath and Lion Big Penny Barrel', Plate 421, *E*, containing 50 black boot buttons, is a reminder that although wages were low in Victorian times, a penny really bought something.

Clams
The clam, Plate 428, *C*, really a clamp, was held upright between the knees of a seated cobbler. It is 40 in. long, made of ash, riveted at the lower end, and the springy jaws held a shoe under repair or in course of manufacture. This particular London specimen is known to be well over 100 years old.

Clamp Stools or Stitching Horses
The saddler's stitching horse, Plate 428, *B*, is a more sophisticated version of the cobbler's clam, which incidentally is also used by the saddler. The leather-topped stool is 22 in. high and 26 in. long. The jaws of the ash clamp are foot operated. It was used for holding parts of harness, etc., whilst sewing. This traditional English specimen may be 18th- or 19th-century.

Clogs and Sabots
Although in Great Britain we often refer to an all-wood shoe, like Plate 428, *D*, as a clog, it is correctly described as a sabot. The specimen illustrated is Dutch, but sabots were normal footwear in the mills of Lancashire and other parts of the country and in foundries, at least until the First World War.

Oliver Goldsmith, in *Distress of a Common Soldier*, has a character who says 'I hate the French because they are all slaves and wear wooden shoes'. Wooden shoes, however, have been worn during different periods in most parts of the world and sometimes have been connected with revolt *against* slavery: one Frenchman, a textile worker and wearer of wooden shoes, far from being a slave, during a strike in 1890, hurled one of his sabots into a loom and, in so doing, gave us the word 'sabotage'. We in Britain in the 1940s, reverted to wearing wooden-soled shoes as a necessary part of our import restrictions, designed to defeat Hitler's threat to our liberty.

Willow, alder and poplar, all light and springy woods, were widely used in bygone days for making clogs in many parts of the world. In London, the patten and clog makers formed a large and sufficiently important industry to merit a trade guild of its own. In the district of Eastcheap, where their workshops were mostly congregated, the parish church in Rood Lane is still known as St. Margaret Pattens and two pairs of pattens still hangs in the church—see *Pattens*. On the continent, clogs are worn even today in country districts, and in Holland there still pertains a delightful Christmas custom among children, who leave apples and carrots in their sabots, to reward Santa's reindeer for bringing them gifts. Continental clogs are often decorated with low relief carving or etching, sometimes picked out in colour, but English specimens are plain.

Clogs are the wooden soles, sometimes incorporating heels, of boots or shoes with leather uppers. A pair of Lancashire, child's 19th-century, clog-soled shoes, is illustrated, Plate 429, *Q* and *R*. In Northampton Museum is preserved an early 17th-century lady's white leather shoe with a clog or platform sole forming the base of an open arch by bridging from under the toe to under the high but narrow based heel. It might be an idea to revive the fashion to nullify the pernicious effects of stiletto heels on floor surfaces and carpets. See also *Soles* and *Pattens*.

Donkeys, Glove Maker's

The 28 in. high, glove maker's donkey, Plate 422, *C*, is a foot operated clamp, with toothed brass jaws. It was used for holding handmade gloves, etc., during stitching. This specimen is probably 18th-century.

Edge Setting or Shoemaker's Glazing Irons

The shoemaker's glazing iron, Plate 421, *D*,

of which there are many shapes, is a piece of steel with a convex edge, set in a wood handle; it is the traditional tool used by cobblers for smoothing and slightly rounding the edges of soles. This specimen probably dates from the 18th century.

Lasts

The typical cobbler's last of iron, set in a turned willow post, is shown upside down, Plate 428, *F*; it is impossible to date. Individual English lasts are strictly utilitarian feet, in a range of sizes, made of hardwood and used for fitting boots and shoes. Some lasts, used by makers of handsewn boots and shoes, such as Plate 429, *D*, are adjustable in width and provided with holes for pegging on protuberances, to allow for bunions or other abnormalities; it dates from the mid-19th century. A Scandinavian, chip carved last, painted black and red and dated 1796 is illustrated, Plate 429, *N*. It may have been used for making slippers or for sock making. Babies' sock lasts are illustrated and mentioned in Section XXI, *Textile Workers' Devices*. See also *Model Lasts and Shoes*.

Mauls, Saddlers' and Harness Makers'

The saddler's and harness maker's mallet, known as a maul, Plate 430, *D*, probably 18th-century, has a 6 in. diameter lignum vitae head and ash handle. Mauls were known by their weight, 7 lb. maul, 10 lb. maul, etc. They had many uses, such as evening out the straw used for padding leather horse collars.

Model Lasts and Shoes

The purpose of miniature hardwood lasts, such as Plate 429, *K* and *L*, 3 in. or 4 in. long, is very uncertain. They are always beautifully made, usually in pairs, and were probably intended for shop display, although one cannot altogether rule out the apprentice's passing-out piece. The same remarks apply to the solid hardwood block shoes, *H* and *J*. The miniature shoe, *O*, and the spurred jack boot, *P*, representative of but not made in the mid-17th century, were probably intended as ornamental containers. For other 'shoe' containers see Section XXII, *Tobacco Accessories: Shoe Snuff Boxes*.

Pattens

Pattens, although often described as overshoes, or a kind of clog, were never such. They were undershoes or supports for leather footwear, worn particularly by women *below* their shoes, to protect them from the damp. They were in constant demand by servants in the wash-house and by all classes out of doors, where muddy paths and unmade or cobbled roads, strewn with refuse, were more the rule than the exception in days gone by.

A pair of these now rare pattens is shown, Plate 429, *F* and *G*. Each consists of a stout wooden sole, to the underside of which is screwed an oval hoop of iron, which lifts the wooden sole an inch above the ground. To the edges of each sole is nailed a pair of leather straps with laces, which tie together across the shoe of the wearer. A view of the underside of a patten is on the left, and the top view on the right.

Comments on the effeminate habits of young dandies are a commonplace in 18th-century literature and this satirical one, relating to pattens, appeared in *The Female Tatler* of December 12, 1709:

'The young gentleman, that for fear of the rain, borrowed the umbrella at Will's Coffee House in Cornhill ... is herby advertised that to be dry from head to foot on the like occasion, he shall be welcome to the maid's pattens'.

John Thorn, who traded at *The Beehive and Patten* in John Street, Oxford Market, about 1764, showed a patten on his trade card and described his premises as *Thorn's Cricket Bat, Turnery and Patten Warehouse*. Joseph Patterson of *The Crown* in New Bond Street, advertised in 1730, 'Pattens and Clogs Made and Sold'. At least six churches in England still display old notices in their porches, asking ladies to remove their pattens before entering. The famous Van Eyck painting (1434) 'Arnolfini and his Wife', shows early use of pattens.

Prick Wheels, Leather Workers'

The leather worker's prick wheel may have a single wheel, or twin serrated revolving wheels, like the 19th-century specimen, Plate 421, *B*. The tool is designed for marking a single or double line of stitches; the number of teeth varies according to the number of stitches required to the inch.

Races, Saddlers'

The saddler's race or race knife, Plate 421, *A*, used for marking leather, is the same tool that is also used by coopers, lumbermen, and carpenters to mark or scribe logs or timber sections, or to register tallies. The example illustrated, formerly in the Evan-Thomas Collection, is English, probably 18th-century.

Sabots—see *Clogs*

Shoe Boxes

Shoe boxes, for use in the home or by the street shoe-black, are not usually attractive acquisitions for the collector. The Russian shoe box, Plate 428, *G*, *circa* 1900, is the exception. It is made of birch, well designed, crisply chip carved and painted on all faces.

Shoe Stretchers

The English, adjustable instep stretcher, Plate 429, *E*, is made of beech, *circa* 1800.

Shoe Trees

Shoe and boot trees were formerly all wood, made in many designs and usually of beech. The simple effective type, Plate 429, *C*, is one of a pair of Watt's Patent, *circa* 1880, lady's size 8.

Size Sticks

The adjustable foot measurer, used by the boot and shoe maker, Plate 421, *F* to *J*, was known as a size stick. If it folded flat for carrying in a leather case in the pocket, *F* and *G*, it was a pocket size stick. All the specimens illustrated are English. *F* is a particularly fine quality, ebony and brass, telescopic pocket size stick, *circa* 1800. *G*, of boxwood, is the normal 18th- and 19th-century, elbow jointed, folding pattern. *H* is a boxwood, telescopic specimen, 18th-century or earlier, formerly in the Evan-Thomas Collection. *J* is the rarest specimen; of boxwood, telescopic, with pewter calibrations and date 1776, it is so designed that when the fixed and sliding stops or distance pieces are brought together, they form an 18th-century shoe; it was formerly in the Marshall Collection.

Skates—see Section XV, *Pastimes*

Soles, Flexible

The beechwood sole, Plate 429, *M*, multiple saw cut to give flexibility, was used in occupied France to overcome the shortage of leather during the last war.

PLUMBERS' DEVICES

With the changeover from lead to copper and plastic piping, many of the plumber's ancient skills and traditional tools are fast becoming relics of the past. Some of the old tools are described below, and illustrated.

Bobbins—see *Turnpins*

Chase Wedges

The plumber's chase wedge, also known as a plumber's glut, Plate 430, *F*, is an iron collared, boxwood wedge, used for drawing sheet lead into angle. A similar tool was used by the woodman for opening up splits in logs.

Lead Dressers

The 14 in. long, roughly shaped lignum vitae club, Plate 430, *C*, flattened on one face, was the plumber's and other lead worker's conventional lead dresser or beater. If it had a V-shaped face, it was known as a setting-in-stick. When egg-shaped in section, it was known as a bossing stick.

Mallets

Plate 430, *H*, is a plumber's traditional mallet. Similar mallets were used in many other trades. See *Bookbinding*.

Turnpins

The solid hardwood eggs or cones, Plate 430, *E* and *G*, are plumbers' turnpins, used for opening up ends of lead pipes. If they had holes through them, they would not be termed turnpins: *E* would then be a plumber's taper bobbin, and *G* would be a bobbin. Bobbins were used to remove dents from the bore of lead piping. A cord was passed through the bobbins and tied to an iron weight, known as a follower. The cord was pulled, so that the follower struck the bobbin and forced it along the pipe.

OSIER WORKERS' TOOLS

The origin of making baskets from osiers goes back to the dawn of history and the craft is found in all parts of the world beside river banks, wherever the various kinds of osiers grow. The method is unchanging and tools required are few; apart from various knives and bodkins with wooden handles, those of interest to collectors of wooden bygones are osier splitters or cleavers and two different kinds of shaves.

Osier Cleavers

Three osier cleavers or splitters are illustrated, Plate 425, *J*, *K* and *L*. Cleavers are used to divide osiers into sections known as *skeins* for fine work. After making a cut in the butt of the rod, the 3 in. to 4 in.

long cleaver, which is provided with three or four sharp, radiating fins at one end and rounded at the reverse end, to fit into the palm of the hand, is pressed into the osier, dividing it neatly into three or four sections. *J* and *K* are of lignum vitae, *L*, of boxwood, tipped with brass. Such simple and unchanging tools are undatable, except for the rarities with dates engraved on them.

Osier Shaves

Osier shaves, Plate 425, *G* and *H*, are special purpose planes about 4 in. long, shaped like the cleavers to fit in the palm of the hand. *G*, shown on its side with its twin adjustable blades towards the camera, is an upright shave. Skeins are passed between the blades to reduce them to parallel width throughout their length. The distance between blades is adjusted by the set screw in the end. *H* is an osier thicknessing shave with a metal sole and an adjustably bolted steel blade; the skein is passed between the metal sole and the cutter, which is set to give the desired thickness. This tool is really a small variant of the spelk plane illustrated and described in Section XXIV, *Woodworking Tools, Planes*. These two English osier shaves appear to have been made as a pair; both have walnut stocks and may be 18th- or early 19th-century.

POTTERY DEVICES

Potter's Wheel

The potter's wheel and the turner's lathe, the two oldest machines in the world, perform the same function of rotating materials so that the skill of the operator can form them into the desired shapes. The potter revolves his wheel or table horizontally on a vertical axis, the turner does the reverse. The turner's lathe is still used as a follow-on machine for trimming the clay after shaping on the wheel. The potter's wheel is the simpler and basically the more primitive of the two machines, not only because any circular table revolving smoothly on a centre can be used as a wheel, but also because in the simplest work no hand tools are required other than the potter's own fingers. Early potteries are always found in close proximity to local beds of clay because of the difficulties of transport of materials. The English wheel illustrated, Plate 422, *B*, is 26 in. high, of traditional form and is found made of any suitable hardwood. This particular specimen may be 18th- or early 19th-century. See also, Section XXIV, *Tools of Specialized Woodworkers: Lathes*.

ROPE, CORDAGE AND STRING DEVICES

Most of the paraphernalia of rope, cordage and string making nowadays is of metal, but because the craft is one of the oldest in the world, long antedating the Iron Age, it was formerly of wood and some of the old wooden devices are still used in small scale manufacture. Until recently, all the raw materials were natural vegetable fibres decorticated on a primitive machine. Internationally, since early in the 19th century, the most important fibres have been sisal, hemp, cotton, flax and jute. In earlier times, man made do with local materials and these have included ling or heather (gad rope) and the fibres of the common stinging nettle. Strippers, decorticators, balling machines, and waisters for making a waist round a ball of string for winding the last length to make a tie, are somewhat outside the scope of wooden bygones, although some of the machines of 100 years or more ago, are partially of wood. The ball of string, Plate 430, *O*, shows what could be bought for a $\frac{1}{4}d$. before the last war.

Blind Cord Acorns

Blind cord acorns, now mostly of plastic, were until recently usually of hardwood, boxwood preferred, or coquilla nut. One of each material is illustrated, Plate 425,

X and *Y*. They are of the best quality, which was made in two parts threaded together, so that the cord, when passed through the 'cup' and knotted, was then concealed in the base.

Gauges, Rope Layer's

The rope layer's gauge, Plate 430, *A*, was a block made from any suitable hardwood and moulded into grooves of different diameters on all faces. The English specimen illustrated, probably 18th-century, has eight different diameter gauges and measures $21\frac{1}{2}$ in. by 4 in. by $2\frac{1}{2}$ in.

Lopers

Whilst the cabinet-maker knows a loper as a sliding support for a bureau fall flap, to a rope-maker, it is a swivel, now usually of metal, upon which yarns are hooked at one end whilst being twisted into cordage.

Pulley Wheels

It has often been stated that sliding sash windows were introduced into the British Isles in the 18th century. This is incorrect; they were possibly introduced from Holland by Sir William Bruce of Kinross in 1672. A number of houses built soon after the great Fire of London, 1666, had this new feature. The boxwood pulleys in oak casings, Plate 425, *N* and *O*, came from the original sash windows of houses erected in the Minories, London, between 1666 and 1690. They were presented to the Pinto Collection by the architect responsible for the restoration of the houses following bomb damage in the Second World War. *M* is an oak suspension pulley probably of about the same date; it could have been used in a wooden clock or for some other purpose involving the raising and lowering of a weight.

Rope Tops—see *Tops*

Toggles

A modern beechwood toggle, as used by commandos during the last war, for joining individual climbing ropes, is shown, Plate 430, *J*.

Tops

The rope layer's elm top, Plate 430, *B*, which is 14 in. long and tapering between $9\frac{1}{2}$ in. and $7\frac{3}{4}$ in. in diameter, is probably about 100 years old; one of the most important devices formerly used in rope making, its use is explained in the diagram. Briefly, its purpose was to twist three hemp yarn strands into rope, in one of the stages of rope making. In making large cordage, some 15 or 20 yarns are formed into a strand and three or more strands are combined into a rope. The twist of the strand is in the opposite direction to that of the yarn. To make a rope, the three strands were attached to three twist hooks in a fixed post and, at the other end, to one main hook in the 'traveller'. The 'rope-top', supported on a bar on the 'cart', fed the twisted strands through its grooves, forming it into rope. The length of the rope walk limited the length of the rope and some rope walks were as much as 600 ft. long, although 300 ft. was more usual. See diag. opposite.

Square section ropes were made by forcing rope through square holes cut in a board; before the days of asbestos packing, they were used for making water-tight linings for engines.

Whorls

The five beech whorls of various diameters, Plate 430, *K* to *N*, were used in making chalk lines and fishing lines; the two smallest are modern.

SHOPS AND SHOP DISPLAY DEVICES

In the days when shops were individually owned, mostly small, kept to their own trades, offered service with a smile, welcomed their customers and gave real value; there were no gift coupons, large plate

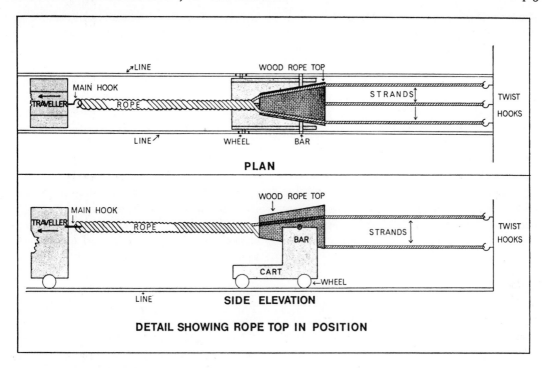

glass windows nor cash registers. They did not call themselves, centres, boutiques, supermarkets or chain stores; they were mainly plain and rather drably fitted, overcrowded with merchandise, lacking in display and badly lit, but you were welcome. Drapers' shops still had counters with brass rules inserted, reminders of the origin of the word; and change was given from a till drawer, one of the fitted boxes which preceded the cash register, or the Lamson pneumatic ball already described under *Electrical and Communication Devices*. The lignum vitae shop counter string barrel is illustrated in Section XIV, *Parcelling, Postage, Sealing, etc.* Some of the other wooden devices from that not long past age are described below.

Display Objects

Many wooden objects puzzle collectors because they are apparently useless. Some of them undoubtedly were meant for display, and because windows were small, such display objects were often in miniature.

This probably accounts not only for some miniature furniture (see Section XV, *Pastimes*), but also for some of the miniature coaches, ships, boots and shoes, millinery heads, etc. Some of the wooden objects for display, later superseded by papier mâché, wax and plastic, were full size: these included wooden arms and hands for displaying gloves, bracelets and rings, and legs and feet. An interesting Edwardian display leg and foot, entirely carved from a single block of sycamore, including the shoe and garter and mounted on a block, is shown, Plate 427, *D*.

Display Stands

For millinery display stands, see Section II, *Costume Accessories*; for hat-pin stands, see Section XXIII, *Toilet Accessories;* for shop counter reel stands, see Section XXI, *Textile Workers' Devices*. Various platforms on pillars which are often regarded as pillar candle stands lacking height adjustment, are really old, general-purpose window display stands. Among the rarest special-purpose display stands of which only a few have survived, are Georgian shop counter, scissors display stands, like Plate 431. Of mahogany throughout, with mirror insert panels in the sides and front, it follows somewhat the outline of 18th-century cutlery boxes; it has 15 compartments, numbered on the side slopes, and each graduated from back to front as well as from side to side. No. 15 at the top is $7\frac{1}{2}$ in. wide by $\frac{1}{2}$ in. back to front and No. 1 at the bottom, $\frac{7}{8}$ in. by $\frac{3}{16}$ in. For years, this stand was one of our 'dunnowhats', until an antique dealer friend came across another still containing some of its complement of rusty, 18th-century scissors.

Door Bells

A Victorian, box enclosed, shop door bell, wound by clockwork and actuated by the opening of the shop door is illustrated. Plate 425, *Q*. It was made about 1870, and is of a type popular with the keepers of small shops, who it called from parlours or workshops behind the shop, when customers entered.

Long-arms

The trigger action, long-arm hook, Plate 427, *L*, for removing objects from crowded windows, was a useful and necessary device in Victorian times, when customers were given their choice from over-crowded windows. It is still made in modified form, to assist invalids in picking up objects which are otherwise out of reach.

Scissors Display Stands—see *Display Stands*

THATCHING, STRAW AND REED WORK DEVICES

Straw work falls under two main headings, agricultural uses and straw manufactures. The first heading includes straw thatching, straw ropes, corn dollies, etc. Straw manufactures are divided between plaited straw constructions, such as hats and baskets, and decorative applied facings—straw work caskets, boxes, pictures, etc. Tools and devices of straw work are accordingly grouped under the two sub-headings (1) Thatching and other Agricultural Reed Devices; (2) Straw Manufacturing Devices.

Thatching and other Agricultural Straw and Reed Devices

Among the common tools and devices traditionally used by thatching and other agricultural straw and reed workers are wimbles, yokes, leggats, reed holders and various rakes or combing forks.

Combing Forks

The thatcher's straw or reed combing fork or rake, Plate 427, *F*, varies in shape in different parts of the British Isles. It may have anything from 6 to 10 tines, and instead of the handle being at right angles, it may be an extension of the batten in which the tines are embedded.

Leggats

The leggat, legget or reed bat, Plate 427, *H*, of oak with iron hook at the back, is used for patting or beating reeds into position. This is a short-handled leggat; some are long-handled, made of various hardwoods and are without grooves, but studded on the face of the blade with holes, iron pegs, or horseshoe nails.

Reed Holders

The reed holder (not illustrated) is a D-shaped device for holding a bundle of reed. It consists of a straight batten, pierced near each end by a bent hazel, thus forming a bow. The batten is provided centrally with an iron hook, which hooks into the roof.

Wimbles or Straw Splitters—see Section V, *Farm, Agricultural*

Yokes

A yoke, jack, knave or bow, is simply a natural forked branch, usually of hazel, like Plate 433, *B*, some 3 ft. to 4 ft. long, used for carrying bundles or yealms of straw up to the roof.

Plate 427, *G*, is said to be a thatching device and came to us with other thatching tools, but I have been unable to obtain any information as to its name or use.

Straw Manufacturing Devices

The plaiting of straw and grasses into hats, baskets, etc., goes back to the earliest civilizations. The late Charles Freeman, in *Luton and the Hat Industry*, quoted references to English straw hats in the late 14th century. The industry was well established in Bedfordshire, Buckinghamshire and Hertfordshire early in the 17th century and although Ware, Tring, Watford, St. Albans, Hitchin, Dunstable and Luton were all early centres, the last gradually became pre-eminent. Whilst hat making developed into a factory product in the 19th century, the making of the actual plaits remained a cottage industry, carried out mainly by women and children, but also by men as a secondary occupation, or in old age. The principal wooden devices of the straw worker were the straw sorter, straw splitters and splint and plait mills.

Mills

The splint-mill, which had plain, narrow rollers, was a mangling device, through which straw or plaits were passed for flattening. The plait-mill, of similar construction, but with wider, ribbed rollers, Plate 427, *E*, was used for flattening the finished plaits and making them more pliable. Both were used in the Luton hat industry between 1807 and 1870 and were usually of beech with boxwood rollers, like the specimen illustrated. They were generally screwed on the doors or door posts

of cottages and the cranked handles worked by children.

Plait-mills—see *Mills*

Splint-mills—see *Mills*

Straw Sorters

The straw sorter was a crude, hand-made, table-like frame, with two or more circular mouths in the top, fitted with various meshed sieves, down which the straws were jolted and out through sloping troughs into boxes below. The straws, after sorting, were bundled for sale to the plaiters.

Straw Splitters

Straw splitters, first devised about 1800, in succession to knives used hitherto, were initially points with radiating fins or cutters, mounted on the ends of sticks. About 1815, an improved standing straw splitter of battledore shape was produced, Plate 425, *F*. All the specimens which I have examined are of mahogany and they are pierced with a number of circular windows, in which are inserted a plurality of wheels with radiating spoke blades, which divide the straws neatly into anything from 4 to 16 even sized 'splints'. Some of these straw splitters have makers' names stamped on them.

Straw Twisters or Wimbles—see Section V, *Farm: Agricultural*

Straw Marquetry

Straw marquetry work in England goes back at least to the 17th century, but the majority of that available today is attributable to Napoleonic French prisoners-of-war in England. The delicate nature of the decoration mostly limited its use to pictures, work and dressing boxes, tea caddies, spectacle cases, trinket and other small boxes, silk holders, hand screens, fans, etc. Furniture was sometimes similarly embellished but understandably, little has survived in good condition.

A considerable amount of straw marquetry, showing great technical and artistic proficiency, was executed by prisoners-of-war at Norman Cross depot, Huntingdonshire, between 1793 and 1815, where the number of prisoners confined usually averaged about 6,000. The core work used by prisoners for the various boxes, panels, etc., will be found to be deal, probably from packing cases; but it must have been well seasoned, for it hardly ever shows signs of movement. The straws used for decoration were cut into lengths of up to 8 in., free of defects, and then split into segments on straw splitters, which divided them in sixteenths, twelfths, eighths, quarters, or halves, according to the fineness of the pattern or picture desired. For certain background effects, straws were damped, opened out and used full width. For the next stages of the prisoner-of-war process, some writers have stated that the straws were dyed by immersion in weak tea, saved by the prisoners, and then pasted on the wood. Some research, together with examination of damaged prisoner-of-war work, disproves this. The hard siliceous surface of straw makes it impermeable to dyes without thorough scouring, softening, sometimes at boiling point, and then bleaching. After this, it has to be dyed with basic or acid dyes. The colours used for prisoner-of-war work cover a wide range, from delicate shades of pink to vermilion and purple, and another range through vivid greens to blue, these being contrasted by the natural cream to brown straw. How these colours could have been obtained by immersion in tea, I cannot imagine! Moreover, as the prison records show, tea was not included in prisoners' rations! Actually, the prisoners did not attempt the difficult and complicated dye process: they used some of the money which they made from the sale of their various work and employed readily available tinted varnishes for surfaces of straw strips. Examination of damaged work confirms that there is no penetration of colour through the straw in prisoner-of-war work.

Having formed their palette of coloured straw strips of various widths, they next glued them on thin paper, on which they had already drawn their designs. They used animal glue, made from bones of their meat meals. The deal boxes and other objects had previously been covered with a glued-on layer of thick, unsized, brown paper; the thinner paper backing of the straw marquetry was then glued to it. The finished work, occasionally woven in straw, shows exceedingly deft finger work and that some of these men must have been brilliant and very original pattern designers; others were considerable artists, although most of the landscapes and buildings are copies of engravings and paintings. In some instances, the resemblance to the best of Tunbridge wood mosaic is so close, that careful examination is necessary. The illustration, Plate 432, shows a straw marquetry view of Forde Abbey, Dorset, from a drawing by Prideaux. This marquetry panel, the inside of the lid of a superb casket, is unsigned.

TRADE TOOLS—MISCELLANEOUS

Spinet Wire Stretchers
The pocket type, folding hardwood spinet wire stretcher with iron pegs inserted, Plate 421, *M*, was formerly in the Evan-Thomas Collection and may date from the 17th century. *L*, alongside, is a non-folding type, probably as old.

Upholsterer's Dwangs
A wooden device shaped like a hand-mirror, about 11 in. long and ¾ in. thick, with a rectangular slot, bevelled on the two long edges, cut out of the blade, is an upholsterer's 'dwang' or webbing stretcher. It should have a wood block attached to it by a leather strap, the block being made to fit

into the aperture and wedge the webbing, while it is being stretched tight over a chair frame for tacking.

WATCHMAKERS' AND JEWELLERS' DEVICES

The wooden devices of the watchmaker and repairer, and the jeweller, were mostly devoted to the safe keeping and handling of precious stones and small parts. A selection is shown in Plate 292, *A* to *F*.

Boxes, Watchmakers' and Jewellers'

Plate 292, *A*, shows the lid and three compartments of a boxwood nest of boxes used by British watch repairers in the 18th and 19th centuries, for storing the component parts of dismantled watches during cleaning or repair. Each compartment has a tight fitting steel disc lid and the compartments nest into each other. A complete box assembly is shown, *B*.

Eye-glasses, Watchmakers' and Jewellers'

The turned wooden case for an eye glass and the boxwood rimmed glass alongside, Plate 292, *C*, may be 18th- or 19th-century.

Glass-Topped Boxes

Three 18th- or 19th-century, small, turned boxwood boxes for jewels are shown, Plate 292, *E*.

Tweezers

Tweezers of mahogany for picking up hair springs and other small parts without damage, are illustrated, Plate 292, *D*. They are impossible to date.

Vices

The jeweller and watchmaker's hand vice, Plate 292, *F*, probably dates from the 18th century.

XXVI

Trade Signs, Ships' Figureheads, Fairground Steeds, etc.

Carved and painted wooden trade signs, ships' figureheads and other carvings, fairground steeds and other roundabout figures, Punch and Judy and other puppets, carved decoration on canal boats, processional figures, and carved and gilded vehicles, such as Coronation and Mayoral coaches and State barges, all served different primary purposes, but there was a secondary aim common to them all. This was to provide colour and gaiety and, in many instances, a spirit of carnival and pageantry, for the multitude. It applied as much to religious figures paraded in church processions, as to legendary giants and monsters in secular pageants; in fact, all were manifestations of popular art in carved and painted wood, and doubtless many of them were the work of the same artificers.

TRADE SIGNS

The primary purpose of projecting, swinging trade signs was to provide easy pictorial identification of business premises and inns, in an age when the majority were illiterate. Swinging signs made streets picturesque and colourful, but were noisy and particularly dangerous in gales. They were frequently dilapidated and insecurely fixed and traders competed in making them ever

larger, heavier and more elaborate, resulting in their falling and killing or injuring passers-by, or being hit by passing traffic. By the mid-18th century, their nuisance had reached such a climax and their usefulness had so lessened, owing to increased literacy, that in 1762, a proclamation was issued in London ordering their removal. In 1765, street numbering was decreed and by 1770 this was virtually completed and the creaking of swing signs became rare. Trade labels on London goods sold between 1765 and 1770, are sometimes printed with the old shop sign, with the street number added in ink—see Section XVII, *Reading, Writing, Copying, Drawing etc.: Pantographers*. Inn signs escaped the ban and have survived, but some of them, like those remaining shop signs, are trade devices or symbols recessed in, or securely fixed on outer walls, or above lettered and numbered fascia boards.

Judging by 18th-century engravings, the majority of hanging signs were ornamentally shaped and painted flat boards; some, on inns especially, are said to have been painted by well-known artists, in return for hospitality. A considerable number, however, were made up of one or more carved symbols, sometimes included with a painted board, suspended from an iron bracket and enclosed in an ornamental frame. In course of time, the carved symbols often became separated from each other, were treated as ornaments, incorrectly painted, and now present an intriguing but almost impossible to solve puzzle for collectors. Even if the sometimes utterly incongruous carvings were still together, it would not always be possible to relate them to their correct trade, in the absence of documentary evidence. This is because a tradesman taking over a shop with a well-known sign, might retain it, even though his own trade were different; alternatively, he might add a symbol of his own trade to the existing one. Several changes of trade must have occurred to account for signs such as 'The Naked Boy and Three Crowns' as the sign of a nursery-man; a naked boy, with or without a coffin (or coffins) was usually associated with undertakers, whilst three crowns occur indiscriminately; a crowned artichoke or pineapple was a more usual sign for a nurseryman. 'The Civet Cat and Three Herrings' was the sign of a particular chemist; the civet cat part is understand-able, because 'The Civet Cat' or 'The Civet' was a well-known perfumer's sign, but the smell of musk and herrings hardly seem compatible! How did 'The Hog and Porridge Pot' come to be the trade sign of a tinman and lamplighter, a trade more often represented by 'The Lamp and Crown'? A giant coffee mill was sometimes used as an 18th-century wood turner's sign, but the turner's sign of 'The Coffee Mill and Nimble Ninepence' is curious. The unmilled silver ninepence was common un-til 1690, when it was called in. The pliable or nimble ninepence was often bent and given as a love token.

Some wooden signs are easy to identify, such as the pawnbroker's three golden balls and the apothecary's and chemist's outsize pestle and mortar, but the latter also used a unicorn, or various unrelated golden emblems. Old carved busts may also be trade signs of apothecaries and chemists, who frequently used busts of Glauber or Galen—'The Glauber's Head' or 'The Galen's Head'. Booksellers also used appropriate busts as trade signs, trading at 'The Shakespeare's Head', or at the head of Ben Johnson, Erasmus, Sir Isaac Newton, Pope, Homer, Virgil, Dry-den, etc., as well as under the sign of a bible or other book. Stationers also used a bible or other book, or a large ink bottle. Hosiers frequently suspended a carved wood leg, unshod; bootmakers, a shod one. Glovers hung out a wooden hand or glove, hatters a beaver or a hat; stick and parasol makers displayed an outsize example of their craft. Saddlers rather favoured a white or golden horse, but such a carving is just as likely to have been an inn sign. Gold-smiths naturally used gilded emblems, a 'Golden Cup' or 'Golden Crown' being among the most popular, but golden in-signia were used by all and sundry. A carved golden sun was the almost invariable trade sign of the pinmakers, but it was also used by other trades and by a Fire Office. Barbers hung out a red and white striped pole (see Section XXIII, *Toilet Accessories*). Chimneysweeps used a golden pole. Coopers sometimes traded at the sign of 'The Bath Tub' (a coopered one). Public baths and shampooers used a Turk's Head sign. Iron-mongers and locksmiths used a statue of St. Peter with his keys, or a golden key or padlock, usually of wood. A pair of scales, or statue of Justice, or an angel holding scales, may also be a scalemaker's sign. 'The Case of Knives' (see Section IV, *Eating*), or 'The Flaming Sword' were popular signs of cutlers.

Oilmen used a giant oil jar above the fascia; some are still *in situ*. Spectacle makers suspended outsize spectacle frames and playing card manufacturers, a depic-tion on wood of a painted court card. Mercers and woollen drapers hung out a carved lamb or ram and designated them-selves at the sign of the lamb or the golden fleece; the former also used 'The Blacka-moor's Head' or 'The Indian Queen', to show that they imported Eastern textiles. Watch and clock makers congregated at 'The Dial and Crown', 'The Dial', or 'The Clock Case', but the most popular sign was a carved and gilded watch. A variant was Father Time striking the hours on a bell. A bell or peel of bells was naturally the sign of a bell founder. A globe, orrery, quadrant, or Sir Isaac Newton's head, often drew attention to a scientific instrument maker. A sports equipment manufacturer might display a giant wooden fish, fishing rod and creel, or other speciality equipment, such as an outsize cricket bat with stumps, bail and ball, or a tennis racquet. Confectioners and pastrycooks seem to have been rather partial to 'The Pineapple', 'Golden Pheasant', or 'Sugar Loaf', but the last, more often described as 'The Sugar Cone', was a favourite sign of the grocer and tea-man, who also used such delightful carved wooden signs as a black wooden ham, a carved Chinese mandarin, a tea canister, a teapot, or a grasshopper, the crest of Sir Thomas Gresham, the merchant grocer and builder of the first Royal Exchange; this, although rebuilt twice, still has a grass-hopper on its weathervane.

The tobacconist has provided the collector of shop signs with some of the most attractive carved figures and other items. Some tobacco figures are larger than life, or life size; others were small enough to stand on the counter or in the shop window. The oldest of these is the black boy. 'At the Sign of the Black Boy', or 'At the Sign of the Blackamoor', has been a popular address for a tobacconist since the early 17th century. The black boy figure was originally supposed to represent a rather 'pot bellied native of Guinea with de-formed feet', and 17th-century tobacconists' figures, like Plate 436, which is only 26 in. high and a very rare survival, were so depicted. In the 18th century, the black boy became more refined, better proportioned and virtually a blackened European com-edian, always, however, retaining his

crown and 'kilt', both consisting of tobacco leaves, usually painted red, green and gold in sequence. Under his left arm is tradi-tionally a plug of tobacco and his right hand holds to his mouth either a clay pipe, or a cigar, shaped like a cornucopia.

Latterly, the Blackamoor has often been erroneously termed a Red Indian and his headdress and kilt referred to as feathers. This is confusion: the Red Indian is the much handsomer, proud looking figure, traditional as the sign of the cigar store or tobacconist in North America, Plate 437. This particular example is 7 ft. 3 in. tall, and is a vigorous carving of high indi-viduality, executed by Arnold and Peter Ruef, of Tiffin, Ohio, about 1880. His hands and face are painted the traditional copper colour, and he wears a brown coat and leggings, trimmed with red, yellow and green; his hair and mocassins are black and the brown rifle has a black barrel. Note the bundle of cigars in his right hand.

In Scotland, the kilted Highlander, with plumed bonnet, Plate 439, taking a pinch of snuff from his ram's horn mull, has long been welcoming those who partake of *sneesh* (Scotch snuff). The figure illustrated dates from about 1810. David Wishart, tobac-conist, of Haymarket, Edinburgh, placed a 6 ft. carved Highlander outside his shop in 1720. Wishart's figure wore flat cap, jacket and trews, carried broadsword and targe and had no tobacco emblem. It denoted to Jacobite sympathizers that a smoking parlour rendezvous existed behind the shop. Wishart's imitators converted flat cap into plumed bonnet, substituted kilt for trews, and snuff mull for sword and targe. Usually such figures are dressed in Peninsular War period fashion, 1808–14. The long gap between Wishart's figures and later ones was due to 'Butcher' Cumber-land's proscription of Highland costume, after the 1745 rising, not being rescinded until 1786. Occasionally, although rarely, a Highlander figure holds a clay pipe.

Formerly, a sailor, holding a clay pipe

and tobacco pouch, like the delightful carving illustrated, Plate 440, was sometimes found in seaports. This figure wears a dark blue jacket with gold buttons, light blue blouse, red kerchief with white spots, white trousers, black shoes and straw hat; his tobacco pouch is brown. Not all sailor figures were tobacconists' signs; some advertised pawnbrokers and slop sellers.

The Turk, Plate 438, with flowing robes, who should be smoking a long pipe (it is broken off) was a rather rare, 18th-century, English tobacconist's alternative form of welcome. In the 19th century, the Turk sometimes smoked a cigar.

Many tobacconists formerly hung outside their premises a cylinder of wood or metal, with horizontal reeds or ropes running round it, painted in various colours. It represented a tobacco roll and denoted that strong flavoured rope tobacco, sweetened with treacle and intended for smoking or chewing, was on sale within. Early 19th-century writers refer to hanging signs shaped to represent gigantic snuff rasps as being normal outside snuff shops. Have any survived? I have never seen one.

What may well be a unique snuff shop sign is the so-called snuff pedlar's staff, Plate 441. Although snuff pedlars undoubtedly did a thriving trade in the 18th and early 19th centuries and probably some carried a staff, I feel it unlikely that they used anything as long, heavy or beautifully finished to brave the elements, when tramping the streets or countryside. This remarkable specimen, 5 ft. 10 in. high and all cut from one piece (actually an inverted 'fork' from a tree), shows an old woman seated, with open snuff box on knee, taking a 'pinch' between finger and thumb. The carving is full of character; the colouring, which appears to be contemporary with the date of the costume (1810–20), is extremely natural.

It is probable that a number of carvers of trade signs worked at seaports, combining ships' figureheads and possibly roundabout and other figures in their output; their names, unfortunately, never seem to be recorded. A late London carver of signs, William Puckridge, of 26 Hosier Lane, West Smithfield, recorded in Sir Ambrose Heal's *London Furniture Makers*, was working between 1760 and 1809 and stated that he 'Makes all Sorts of Signs in Elm and Mahogany'. Where I have been able to examine the wood of signs, nearly all are elm.

SHIPS' FIGUREHEADS

The custom of painting or carving eyes on the bows of ships and boats, so that they could see their way, is lost in antiquity, but still survives on Mediterranean and South Atlantic fishing boats. It is probable that this *oculus* originally derived from the eye of Horus, hawk-headed sun god of Egypt, whose hawk eye was a look-out for the mariner. It is easy to see how, via the Viking long boat, with snake or dragon head carved on the prow and sometimes with the tail on the stern post, the fully fledged, elaborate ships' figureheads developed, and remained a prominent feature until wooden ships were superseded by metal. From the reign of Elizabeth I, until 1796, ships of the Royal Navy, except first class battleships, had lion figureheads. The first class had figureheads which included a historical or mythological tableau of figures, linked up to other elaborate carving, extending from stem to stern. From the early 19th century, ships of the line had figureheads emblematic of their names. The figureheads of merchantmen reflected the whims of their owners and are often delightful carvings, portraying their wives or daughters. Some of those which portray their actual Victorian owners, in frock coats and even top hats, appear quite ridiculous. Very horizontally designed figureheads are usually off clippers.

A gracefully designed girl off a mid-19th-century ship, either a merchantman or a small warship, is illustrated, Plate 442. The name was probably 'Swallow', as a swallow is carved in the scroll each side. Seven vessels bearing this name, appear in the 1850 Lloyd's Register.

One of the oldest ships' figureheads in existence must be the lion off the 'Vasa', a Swedish warship of 1,400 tons, which sank in 1628. In a miracle of salvage, she was brought to the surface 333 years later, on May 4, 1961 and is now in process of preservation and restoration at Stockholm.

Nelson's 'Victory' at Portsmouth and 'Cutty Sark' at Greenwich are wonderful ships to visit and get the whole atmosphere of the wooden walls. Collections of ships' figureheads are preserved at most of the naval dockyards, in the grounds of Tresco Abbey, Scilly Isles, that graveyard of ships, at the National Maritime museum and on board 'Cutty Sark' at Greenwich. Individual ones may be seen in coastal gardens and acting as trade signs for ships' chandlers, inns and antique dealers.

One type of shop sign which emphasizes the link with ships' figureheads, is that of the carved and painted naval figure, formerly used by ships' instrument makers. A delightful 18th-century example, 33 in. high, is illustrated, Plate 443. See also, Section XVIII, *Sailors', Sailmakers' and Fishermen's Devices.*

ROUNDABOUT AND PAGEANT FIGURES

The gorgeously exuberant carved figures encasing the mechanical core of Victorian and later roundabouts and the brightly painted horses, such as Plate 444, the pigs, ostriches and fabulous beasties, which acted as steeds before the days of cars, probably helped to provide a living for figurehead carvers, when their trade was dying. Early processional or pageant figures are unlikely to come the way of collectors. The majority have perished; the remainder are usually cherished in museums. Generally, they only had carved wooden heads, with canework bodies, covered in fabric. They had to be light structures, to accommodate the man inside. As he, when impersonating a giant, also had to walk on stilts, bringing his total height up to 14 or even 20 feet, he needed stamina as well as balance. The oldest English surviving carnival giant is probably the Salisbury giant. The head, which is believed to date back to 1496, is in Salisbury Museum. Redressed from time to time, he still occasionally appears in the streets on festive occasions, accompanied by his companion 'Hob Nob', the frisky hobby-horse dragon, with snapping jaws. 'Hob Nob' is ancient, his age uncertain, but the Norwich dragon, 'Old Snap', is believed to date back to 1451. The Chester and Coventry giants have perished, but on the continent a number of giant saints and fabulous beasts still perambulate the streets on festive occasions. London's own two giants, Gog and Magog, were originally figures of wickerwork and pasteboard, manipulated by men on stilts in each Lord Mayor's Show and resting between times in Guildhall. In 1707, they were replaced by 14½ ft. high, permanent wooden figures in Guildhall, by the eminent carver, Richard Saunders of King Street, Cheapside, a captain in the trained band, who was paid £70 for the two. Captain Saunders' work lasted until December 29, 1940, when Gog and Magog were burnt to ashes in the great German incendiary bomb raid. Their successors have a somewhat oriental look and are smaller. Readers of Harrison Ainsworth's *Tower of London* will remember Gog and Magog as the giant warders of the Tower in Tudor times, but according to legend, one giant was Gogmagog, a Cornish giant, and the other Corinaeus, a Trojan; the original processional giants mentioned above, were known by these names.

STATE VEHICLES

The voluptuously curved, carved and gilded State coach, which weighs 4 tons, is now only used at Coronations. It is as gaudy, gorgeous and eyecatching as anything ever thought up for a fairground or a fairy tale illustration. It was designed by Sir William Chambers, the panels were painted by Cipriani and the wood sculpture was by Joseph Wilton; it was delivered in 1760. Many admire it; see it for yourself in the Royal Mews. London's other 18th-century 'gingerbread coach', the Lord Mayor's, also has panels by Cipriani.

XXVII

Tuition

It is difficult to draw a clear line of demarcation between tuition and amusement. Many early games and puzzles had an educational motive; they will be found in Section XV, *Pastimes*. Under *Tuition*, are only assembled those old wooden devices with a primary educational objective. These include some connected with reading, writing, arithmetic, learning to walk, deportment and discipline.

The varied contrivances for teaching the alphabet are grouped together under *Alphabet Teaching* and, as far as possible, those for arithmetic under *Arithmetic Teaching*, but there is an overlap, because some of the contrivances were intended to teach both subjects. Moreover, systems and devices such as horn-books and sand tables could be used for elementary teaching of reading, writing and counting.

Abacus

The abacus, consisting of coloured wooden beads threaded on parallel wires, within a wooden frame, was used in the nursery until very recent times. It was sometimes incorporated in a toddler's play-pen, or as a high chair attachment. It not only helped to keep a child amused, but could also be used to teach distinguishing of colours and elementary arithmetic—see also Section XIX, *Scientific, Abacus*.

Alphabet Teaching

Horn-books, battledore-books and criss-cross-books are one and the same—tablets designed primarily for teaching children the alphabet in bygone days. They probably came into fashion about 1450, contemporaneously with printing. As the second name suggests, they were sometimes shaped like a shuttlecock bat, but more often were wider than long, with a handle extension at the bottom. The third alternative name originated because the heading of the tablet was often a Cross, to remind the child to commence his lesson by crossing himself. Additional to the alphabet, was usually the Lord's Prayer, or a verse reading,

> 'Christe's Cross be my speede
> In all virtue to proceede'.

Numerals 1 to 10, and sometimes vowel combinations were included. The last occur mostly on 18th-century specimens. Frequently there is a hole pierced near the end of the horn-book handle, to take a cord or ribbon, by means of which, as old pictures show, the horn-book was suspended upside down from the child's waist or neck. The child's primer seems to have finally superseded the horn-book early in the 19th century. But to the public, horn-book had so generally come to mean an alphabet tablet, whether horn entered into its composition or not, that the term was often given erroneously to the later 'A, B, C' book or child's primer which succeeded it.

The majority of horn-books are of wood, on which is pasted paper or parchment, protected by a thin sheet of horn, secured by a strip metal frame, nailed on. A considerable number were made from a sandwich of stiff leather, with the back and the back half of the handle in one piece, Plate 445, *B*. This was faced with the lettered parchment, and covered with a sheet of horn; these were enclosed by a leather frame incorporating the front half of the handle; the two layers of leather were then stitched together, leaving the parchment and horn as the meat in the sandwich. Some horn-books had no horn: they were metal, usually pewter tablets with letters cast or moulded out of the solid. A few, in the luxury class, were ivory, with black and red engraved letters. An Elizabethan specimen with silver filigree backed by red silk on the handle and back, still survives. Some were sold for a penny, and several references to them occur in *London Cries* of the 16th and 17th centuries, but now they are rare and valuable, and consequently the faker has been busy. It is no exaggeration to say that there are many more fakes than genuine antique horn-books about today. This applies to wooden ones, to leather specimens, often ingeniously made from old harness leather, and to metal ones, which I suspect are still being made from old moulds. Additionally, there are 19th-century reproductions which have now attained respectable age and add to the collector's difficulties. These last mainly came into being innocently. Andrew Tuer, after considerable research, produced *The Horn Book* in two enormous volumes; it was dedicated to Queen Victoria and published in 1896. Probably never before nor since, has so much been written or produced so elaborately about so little. To add to the interest, Tuer had made a quantity of horn-books of different types, which were included in pockets in the covers of the volumes. These have now usually left their original nests and entered collections as genuine antiques.

Some horn-books only had the horn secured by metal strips on the two long sides and at the bottom, so that new and more advanced teachings could be slid down behind the horn, as the child's knowledge increased. Such an example is the probably unique, 18th-century, combined doll-rattle-horn-book, Plate 445, *A*. Its lettered sheet is not original.

Other interesting horn-book variations were those made of gingerbread, with the raised letters gilded (taking the gilt off the gingerbread—see Section XII, *Moulds*). The idea was to teach the child its letters by means of a reward for the tummy. Moulds for turning out gingerbread horn-books occur with alphabets in English, Welsh, German, etc. Sometimes one wood block is carved with several repeats, which turn out a quantity of horn-books simultaneously. Gingerbread horn-book moulds are illustrated in Plate 187.

A rare Welsh horn-book variant made as a child's bat, rather like a miniature yew-wood cricket bat, 13 in. long, chip carved and deeply incised with the alphabet and date 1691, is shown, Plate 445, *C*. Although the grouping of letters is typically Welsh, it must be assumed that the child was having a bilingual education, because X and Z, included here, do not occur any more than does Q in the Welsh alphabet.

Alphabet building cubes, both solid and hollow ones in graduated sizes, which nested into each other, were made of wood until well into this century. They were covered with paper showing letters of the alphabet and sometimes additionally with pictures of objects which began with the letter depicted.

Picture alphabet cards were common in the 18th and 19th centuries, but seldom survive complete. A complete set, *The Picture Alphabet for a Good Child, circa* 1830, is illustrated, Plate 445, *F*. The lid of the original sycamore box, in colour, enclosed in red and black lines, is shown with some of the hand coloured cards grouped round it. The designation letters are on the backs of the cards. It originally sold for 1*s*., complete.

J. & E. Wallis of 42 Skinner Street, Snow Hill, London, made a novel 'Revolving Alphabet' between 1818 and 1820, Plate 449, *C*. It comprised an ornamental coloured picture of a Regency interior, mounted on cedar. Behind a pierced gilt 'eagle' mirror frame on the wall, is a revolving wooden disc which, by turning, exposes each letter in turn in the frame. John Wallis was established as a bookseller in Ludgate Street, London, by 1777. He moved several times between 1808 and 1811, when he went to Skinner Street and set up the Juvenile Depository. In 1821, Edward Wallis took over the business, opening additional premises in Islington in 1827. He continued at both premises at least until 1840, by which time he described himself as 'Dissected map manufacturer and publisher'. A dissection was an early name for an educational jigsaw puzzle—see Section XV, *Pastimes: Puzzles*.

'Crandall's Building Slabs', patented by H. Jewitt & Co. of Leighton Road, N.W. in 1867, are end 'combed' wooden rectangles, each printed with one letter; they can be joined together to form words.

Alphabet rods, 18 in. to 24 in. long, of rectangular or triangular section, were also used as horn-book alternatives. Like the latter, they vary greatly in quality, but each is an individual production. They are usually dated and their heyday was apparently the first quarter of the 19th century. They all include the alphabet, usually the child's name, and some have engraved or inlaid, on one or other of their sides, the sacred monogram, the sun, moon and numerals. Four are illustrated, Plate 446; judging by their inscriptions, they appear to have been made or used near the shores of the Baltic, but I have been unable to obtain any corroborative evidence. The details are:

A. Boxwood; rectangular section; length 23 in.; chip carved and pewter capped each end, with pewter inlaid crosses on each face.

Face 1—Pot of flowers, sun, moon and other insignia, sacred initials and initials C.M.B.

Face 2—IN.DER.F | ASTEN | AN.S. FR. | IdOLINS | TAG.VI | MERZ

Face 3—The alphabet (no J, and I instead of Y).

Face 4—ELIZABETI | V.M.ANNA | WELDI | IN.OBER | BERKEN | MDCCCIV

B. Yew-wood; triangular section; length 21½ in.

Face 1—ANA GETZ 1804

Face 2—Divisions.

Face 3—The alphabet (no J, and I instead of Y).

C. Dark hardwood; triangular section; length 21 in.; inlaid with brass, ivory, ebony and pewter.

Face 1—Stars, hearts, scissors, carnation and tulip, initials MG and date 1817.

Face 2—The alphabet, with Y between H and K, and no V, all carved in relief.

Face 3—Blank.

D. Sycamore; triangular section; length 23½ in.; capped with ebony.

Face 1—Date 1845. Initials M$ (T and S intertwined). Divided into three compartments approximately 7⅞ in. long, by ebony inlaid strips.

Face 2—Alphabet (no J, V or Y).

Face 3—Divided into four compartments by ebony strips.

A late, but interesting device for teaching word making, is 'The Cress Reversible Educational Board', patented 1912, 1915,

1916. A circular board, 14 in. in diameter, Plate 450, *A*, has captive wooden rectangles of H section which travel along a cut-out railway running round the board, and for word making are diverted on to straight lines running across it. On one side of the rectangles are letters, on the reverse are numerals and the various mathematical symbols. The side of the board illustrated is used for word making, the reverse side for sums. See also *Sand Tables* and *Chautauqua*.

Arithmetic Teaching

The 'Cress Reversible Educational Board', referred to above, was one of many devices intended for teaching both reading and arithmetic. The abacus, sand table and even the horn-book had, as one of their purposes, the basic recognition and elementary use of numerals. A device, primarily for teaching arithmetic, but also having secondary purposes of amusement in building and word making, was Butter's *Tangible Arithmetic and Geometry for Children*, 4th edition, published 1852, at 3*s*. The basic idea was good; the box of 144 oak cubes, Plate 449, *A*, was accompanied by the book of instructions, *B*, with numerous diagrams showing how to use the cubes for addition, subtraction, multiplication, division, fractions, proportions, geometry, etc. The teacher had to be well educated to understand Butter's use of long and unusual words such as parallelopipeds. If not completely stunned, he could order the "appropriate sequels" Butter's *Dissected Trinomial Cube*, Butter's *Etymological Spelling Book and Expositor*, and Butter's *Graduations in Reading and Spelling*, which were recommended as 'excellent Birth-Day or Christmas Presents'!

A more entertaining way of teaching a child to recognize the numerals and to count was *An Instructive Puzzle*, dated 1789, in a mahogany box, 3¾ in. by 2 in., Plate 445, *E*. There should be 10 cards 0 to 9, but 0 is missing. The hand-coloured cards, pasted on mahogany, portray human figures in postures of numerals.

Baby Cages

Bridging the stage from crawling to walking must have presented problems to mothers, ever since the first baby was born. During the toddling stage, there are the twin problems of keeping the baby out of mischief and danger, and teaching it to walk. The former has probably always been attempted by means of some kind of playpen or enclosure; the latter was solved in many homes, at least as early as the Middle Ages, by means of a variety of babyminders, known alternatively as baby cages, baby walkers, baby trotters, toddlers' go-carts, walking cradles, or teach-to-walk.

The earliest type of which illustrations survive, was the continental go-cart—a low, moving table of rectangular or oblong form, with a tray top provided with a central circular aperture, in which the infant was held upright, so that the 'ring' gripped at waist height of its voluminous clothing, leaving its arms free. This ring, probably padded, was hinged at each end to the frame and the two half circles were clipped together. The tray afforded a place for toys—until they were thrown overboard. The legs of the go-cart were splayed outwards to provide a wide base, which could not be overturned; it was provided with non-pivoted wheels or rollers, allowing it to move in one direction only. A go-cart is illustrated in a German woodcut of the early 15th century, in the British Museum, and another is shown in the painting of 'The Holy Family' (1520) by Vincienzio Briago, in the Dresden Gallery. There, Joseph is depicted trying to persuade the Infant Jesus to leave the comfort of his Mother's knee for the adventure of the go-cart. Go-carts are said to have originated in Italy and to have been introduced to England via the Low Countries at the beginning of the 17th century. One is shown in 'A Family Group', by the Flemish artist Gonzalez Coques in 1640, now in the National Gallery.

Additional to the wheeled go-cart, a

different type of baby minder was used in England in the 17th century, Plate 454. Basically, it consists of a pole, out of the side of which projects horizontally, at the height of an infant's waist line, what might be described as a gigantic screw-eye, arranged so that the circle of the 'eye' is open on plan. The pole runs from floor to ceiling, is tapered at each end and is fitted with pivot pins, passing into the floor and ceiling joists, enabling it to revolve easily. The cross-bar is mortised into the pole and wedged, and fitted at its outer end with the ring to hold the child. In some examples, the ring is of iron. It is hinged, so that it can be opened, and is secured by a hook and eye, or other suitable device. Although most of the few specimens still extant have lost their upholstery, it is known that the rings were covered with padded leather, or velvet. It was probably an effective device for teaching a child to walk and keeping it out of mischief, but it is rather reminiscent of the old donkey wheel used for drawing water from a well, or operating a cider press.

Another crude type of baby-minder used in England and in North America in the 18th century and probably in the 17th century as well, consisted of an oblong, open frame, about 5½ ft. to 6 ft. long, mounted on four legs, which were fixed to the floor, Plate 452. In grooves in the long side rails of the upper frame was mounted the baby ring, so arranged that it would slide from end to end of the frame. To entice the child to operate it, abacus type coloured beads on wires, or toy trays, were provided at either end of some specimens.

In *Nollekens and His Times* (1828), J. T. Smith relates that, when he was a boy, the varied baby-minder devices were sold by toy shops all over London, but in the greatest abundance in the famous turners shops of Spinning-Wheel Alley, Moorfields. The major contribution of the 18th-century turner to the making of go-carts is clearly shown by the specimen illustrated, Plate 453. As can be seen, it was much less limited in the range of activity it allowed, than were earlier specimens. It was, in fact, as humane, practical and ornamental a device as anyone could desire.

Back Boards—see *Deportment Boards*

Butter's Tangible Arithmetic—see *Arithmetic Teaching*

Chautauqua

The Chautauqua Kindergarten Drawing Board and Writing Desk, Plate 455, is 44 in. high, 22½ in. wide and made to fold flat. When opened out as shown, it provides a writing surface and compartments for paper, crayons, etc. When closed, the back of the writing surface is vertical and forms a blackboard. The roller-controlled scroll, with diagrams printed white on black, provides the various instruction sheets for copying or teaching. There are 27 different views, ranging from elementary to quite difficult subjects. These include the alphabet in seven different forms of lettering; numerals, mathematical symbols and simple sums; simple geometric figures and ornaments; elements of building, houses, furniture and other objects connected with domestic living; outline drawings of humans, animals, birds and fish; fruit, flowers and insects; music lines and notes; shorthand symbols; pronunciation and rules of grammar, punctuation, abbreviations and symbols; line drawings of a dynamo, a train, ships, landscapes and public buildings; famous personages. As the last mentioned show outline drawings of Queen Victoria, King Edward VII, Queen Alexandra, the Marquis of Salisbury and W. E. Gladstone, this particular outfit must have been designed for the British market about 1901–2.

The Chautauqua Institution was established in 1874 on the shores of Lake Chautauqua, New York. It was founded by the Methodists as a residential summer vacation school for Sunday school teachers.

It has since become non-sectarian and has had considerable influence on education. A graphic and humourous description of the discomforts of a short stay at Chautauqua, in the 1880s, is contained in a collection of odds and ends by Rudyard Kipling, entitled *Abaft The Funnel*, (New York, 1909). Chautauqua is still going strong and now provides all up-to-date amenities for study and recreation.

Clicket

The dame school clicker, usually known as a clicket or snapper, was used for calling the inattentive to order. Pressure and quick release of the trigger produces a sharp resonant click. Clickets were usually made of boxwood or lignum vitae. Early specimens have the trigger held to the 'head' by a gut loop. Later specimens, like Plate 445, *D*, have pivoted, spring-loaded triggers, for which a 19th-century patent was taken out.

Copying Sticks

Copying sticks consisted of a line of copperplate handwriting on paper, glued on each side of a thin strip of wood, usually 7 in. to 8 in. long and 1 in. to 1¼ in. wide, and varnished over. The wording formed an 'improving text', and served the dual purposes of teaching copperplate handwriting and acting as a model for lines. Copying sticks appear to have been used in all schools at least until the mid-19th century, but survivals are now very rare. The two much worn examples Plate 447, which were used in the village school at Shepley, near Huddersfield, Yorkshire, in the 1860s, are inscribed—

'Faith dwells with simplicity'.
'Silent waters are seldom shallow'.
'Innumerable inconveniences await us'.
'Useful employment gives us pleasure'.

Deportment Boards

Deportment boards, Plate 448, sometimes called back-boards, were a 'must' for Victorian and Georgian children, who had to stand for a certain time each day with a board held horizontally behind the back; the handles were looped through the child's crooked elbows, holding the shoulders well back. The 38 in. long, oak board is believed to date from 1870. The 36 in. long, pine board, dated 1864, was used by the young ladies of Ashburnham, Sussex; what they scribbled on it would have surprised their parents!

Another type of deportment board, for correcting curvature of the spine, was devised for lying on full length and had a hole cut in it to fit the head; the board was slightly raised above the floor, so that the head was forced well back, keeping the back straight.

Education Games and Puzzles—see Section XV, *Pastimes*

Fescues

The pointer used for teaching children their letters, particularly in a dame's school, was known as a fescue. An attractively carved and pierced specimen, English or Welsh, and possibly dating from the 17th century, is shown, Plate 266, *D*.

Finger Pillories

Finger pillories, heavy boards hinged together, one above the other, with grooves gouged out for the fingers, half of the groove being made in each board, are said to have been used to punish unruly behaviour in church. One such pillory surviving in Ashby-de-la-Zouch Church, Leicestershire, has 13 unevenly spaced holes of different sizes. I am not convinced that finger pillory is the correct explanation.

Finger Stocks

The mahogany finger stocks, Plate 445, *G*, were used as a form of punishment in the 18th and 19th centuries. They are described, among other devices, in *The Penrose Method*, a description of the theory and practice of education at the academy kept by Dr. and Mrs. Penrose in Victoria's reign. The guiding principle was 'Happiness for the Obedient—Discipline for the Wayward—Knowledge for All'. Most of the discipline involved keeping the wayward immobile in a position which varied in its degree of discomfort according to the seriousness of the misdemeanour. Additional to mahogany finger stocks, the somewhat sadistic Penroses also used (1) wooden gags; (2) wrist or arm stocks; (3) polished wooden discs of various diameters, placed in twos between the knees or calves and the ankles, so that the discs clattered to the floor if the offender moved; (4) bags to go over the head during punishment; (5) various types of strap and wood restraining harnesses.

In a book entitled *Bygone Punishments* by William Andrews, originally published in 1899 and reprinted 1931 (Philip Allan and Co.), these finger stocks are illustrated and described as used in dames' schools and in manorial halls for general punishment. Fingers were inserted in the holes, with hands back to back behind the body. With shoulders well thrown back, the child had to stand before the dame, to repeat the lesson in which it had failed.

Horn-books and Horn-book Devices—
see *Alphabet Teaching*

Kindergarten—see *Chautauqua*

Numerical Human Figures—see *Arithmetic Teaching*

Pencil Boxes
The Bavarian manufacturers of children's pencil boxes certainly knew how to bring joy to the hearts of late-Victorian and Edwardian school boys and girls. They seem to have exported their intriguing beechwood boxes to many parts of the world and their enterprise included brightly coloured transfer pictures on the lids, which depicted scenes or events of topical interest in the countries concerned. So far as I can recall, the boxes cost 4*d*. to 6*d*., varying according to whether there were only two trays with multitudinous divisions, one pivoted above the other, or whether there was a third sliding tray beneath. The slide lid locked the whole box, which usually measured $9\frac{1}{2}$ in. by 2 in. wide and $1\frac{1}{2}$ in. to $1\frac{7}{8}$ in. deep. Three examples are shown in Plate 450: a two-tier box, *D*, and a three-tier one, *E*, commemorate Queen Victoria's 1897 diamond jubilee, and *F*, an England versus Scotland football match at the Crystal Palace. The predecessors of these specialized boxes were turned wooden cylindric boxes, which were also used for knitting needles, crochet hooks, and sailors' netting tools; if plain, they retailed at 1*d*. in Victorian times, but some were ornamentally carved and might cost several pence. Examples of these general-purpose cylindric boxes are described and illustrated in Section XXI, *Textile Workers' Devices*. Two Oriental cylindric pencil boxes are illustrated Plate 267, *J* and *N*. The first, a crude, 19th-century portrayal of a mandarin, was probably in the penny or twopenny class, but *N*, even allowing for low labour rates, must have been expensive. It is made of cane, the natural cross membranes forming the ends, and it is finely and skilfully engraved all over in great detail, with a panorama of an eastern seaport, probably *circa* 1800. It was formerly in the Evan-Thomas Collection.

The carved and painted oak school box, Plate 450, *C*, dates from the 17th century and was made at Hindeloopen, Holland. Although usually known as a satchel box, this was not really the equivalent of a satchel which a child carried between home and school, but was the forerunner of the well in the purpose-made school desk, and each child had one of these boxes which hung on the wall in the schoolroom during term-time. Quill pens, horn-books and several similar boxes can be seen on the wall, and with children using them on the floor in the well-known painting of a school-room, Plate 451, by Jan Steen (1626–79). The rare box illustrated, measures 11½ in. by 8¼ in. by 3 in., plus the shaped pediment with hole for hanging on the wall. Inside, is a small till, with pivoted lid, for pencils and pens; the rest of the space is for books, etc. The exterior, painted in red and blue with marbled borders, has tulips and other flowers, with birds on the sides, and the typical Hindeloopen long-tailed bird carved and painted on the sliding lid. In general design and construction, these school boxes resemble candle boxes—see Section VI, *Fire and Lighting*.

Picture Alphabets—see *Alphabet Teaching*

Reversible Educational Board—see *Alphabet Teaching*

Sand Tables
Forming symbols and patterns in sand, with a stick or the finger, is probably the oldest form of writing and drawing in the world. The sand table is a very ancient device and may be referred to by Isaiah 'Now go,

write it before them in a table'. Basically, a sand table is any ordinary table with a flange or rim running round and projecting ¾ in. or more above the top, so as to form a trough for about ½ in. depth of sand. One or more rectangular smoothing boards, each provided with an upstanding wooden handle on the upper face, were used for smoothing the sand after writing. The sand writing table was used for teaching reading, writing, counting, etc. Examples survive in Dennington Church, Suffolk and Barton Turf Church, Norfolk. It is probable that many more, which have lost their rims, are now regarded as ordinary antique tables of various periods.

Satchel Boxes—see *Pencil Boxes*

Slates—see Section XVII, *Reading, Writing, Copying, Drawing, etc.*

Snappers—see *Clickets*

Wallis's Revolving Alphabet—see *Alphabet Teaching*

XXVIII

Watch Stands

☆   ☆   ☆

There are two kinds of watch stands—the bedside and the mantelshelf types. Most of the former are 19th-century examples, but among the latter are some handsome 18th-century specimens.

Bedside Watch Stands

These are usually quite small, intended as a receptacle by night for the man's pocket watch and the woman's brooch or chain necklet watch; sometimes they incorporate a trinket tray. Quite often they were made to fold for travelling, and as such they were the precursors of and were superseded by the travelling clock, which in its early form was a large watch, permanently fitted in a travelling case. A variant of the bedside watch stand is the hook for a watch, fitted to an ornamental safety pin, for hanging the watch on the bed curtains; its purpose is often now unrecognised.

A selection of bedside watch stands is shown in Plate 456. On the top shelf are two pairs, made for grandmother's and grandfather's watch. Both pairs are typically late Victorian examples of the pillar and saucer type. At the end, is a plain mahogany block, recessed for a watch, with a hook for the key at the side; it may be 18th- or early 19th-century. In the bottom row are four travelling watch stands and a Swiss watch stand, designed as a bear holding a hoop; all are 19th-century. The

two Swiss or Tyrolean, pearwood, folding watch stands on the left, one shown open and the other closed, are of a type which was formerly made in large quantities. One is carved with fruit and flowers, the other with a rustic design. They have velvet-lined recesses for the watches, and integrally carved wood hinges; they open to form miniature easels. Centre, is a variant which has the recessed watch block made to slide forward out of its wooden sheath, and then tip back. The same pattern, usually of olivewood, sometimes inlaid with figures in coloured veneers, was made in Italy in the 19th century. The next example, of walnut, formed as a hinged album, ornamented with brass mounts and studs and provided with a magnifying glass to the watch enclosure, is English, dating from about 1870. Another English type made particularly for children, is carved to represent a model of the coronation chair and has a seat cushion which lifts, exposing a slot to a money-box in the base; the watch hangs on a hook on the back of the chair.

In the 18th century, a few mahogany bedside watch stands were designed like miniature pillar and tripod claw tables, with the watch recess 'top' permanently set at 45° to hold the watch; such specimens are now very rare. An early 19th-century type, designed as a circular well-head, with twin pillars and a half circular arch with hook,

424

for suspending the watch like a bucket, and others with three pillars and domed tops, like miniature garden temples, are delightful and sometimes come to light. Examples of both the miniature table and twin pillar types are shown bottom right of Plate 457. In the same row, one from left, is an English, mid-19th-century, oak, double watch stand for mother's and father's watches. It has a trinket tray behind. Although somewhat 'busy', the carved and pierced design of floral scrolls in a rope border is pleasant. Next to it is a much more ambitious piece of oak carving, with the watch holder and trinket tray behind all hollowed out of the same block. It appears to be late 18th-century, English, and the carving includes heraldic lions, scrolls, shells, English banners and the motto *Porro Est Necessarium*.

Mantelshelf Watch Stands

The appearance and purpose of the mantelshelf watch stand were entirely different from the bedside. It had to be made to look important, for it was intended to convert into a clock, a watch, still doubtless reliable as a timepiece, too valuable to discard entirely, but now outmoded. Although mantelshelf watch stands were made in great variety throughout the 18th and 19th centuries, it is probable that the periods of strongly marked designs coincide either with technical improvements, or fashion changes which rendered expensive pocket watches outmoded. There were, for instance, outbreaks of rococo watch stands in the 1750–60 period, and of exaggeratedly large architectural designs in the 1780–1800 Sheraton style. The carved wood rococo designs, sometimes gilded or painted in natural colours, are often so akin to Louis XV, that it is difficult to distinguish English from French examples. They are usually between 9 in. and 12 in. high, the actual watch surround being carved like a miniature rococo mirror frame, supported by a carved figure or figures, above a moulded

plateau. In Plate 458, the example left, portrays a Louis Quinze man of fashion, right, a macabre figure of Death pointing to the time and awakening a sleeper, and centre a single figure, Atlas style, supporting the superstructure. Other supporters used were Father Time, and Gog and Magog. An attractive and unusual variant is the case on four twist pillars, one from right, top shelf Plate 457; it is entirely cut out of a single block of hardwood and unlike the others, only the ornament and not the outline of the case follows rococo principles.

The Sheraton period façades are usually of mahogany, inlaid with other lighter woods and represent the fronts of imaginary or real buildings of importance, usually of several storeys, with a front entrance approached by a flight of steps, many windows set in inlaid 'brick' or 'stone' veneers and the watch looking very insignificant in a clock tower, anything from 12 in. to 18 in. above the plinth.

Two very distinctive types of mantel watch stands are the miniature grandfather clock, bottom left, Plate 457, and the bracket clock case, fourth from left. Both types vary from country-made to sophisticated cabinet models. The clock case example illustrated, French or Flemish, dated 1796, is a good country-made specimen, at least 50 years later than its style suggests.

There is also another group which may, perhaps, be described collectively as Welsh rustic love token types, with a medley of pierced heart motifs, chip carving and bobbin turning; a good representative example, 18th- or 19th-century, $11\frac{1}{2}$ in. high, is shown, top right, Plate 457.

There are also many which cannot be classified. Among these is the castellated wooden castle, painted in natural colours, complete with ivy, which looks like a Rockingham castle, top left, Plate 457. The watch goes above the doorway between two drum towers, which can be used as spill vases. Another, unusual and most gruesome, carved with a multitude of drowned corpses and wrecked ships, perhaps portrays 'the sea gives up its dead'. It is 11 in. high and is shown in Plate 459. It consists of two heavy blocks of Spanish mahogany, screwed together one above the other and is deeply and elaborately carved, on all four faces, with an irregular and rather crude composition, comprising mainly naked human figures with bone eyes and, additionally, skulls, skeletons and a lion mask. Judging by the continuous marine dado and the style of the storm-tossed and wrecked ships, lighthouse, etc., it is the work of an early 19th-century sailor. The watch slides down a shaft, cut centrally in the upper block. The vigorously carved Father Time, leaning against an ivy-clad tree stump, in

Plate 460, is cut from a single block of pearwood. It may be 17th-century, German, or 18th-century, English work under German influence.

Cases such as the last two described, where insertion and removal of the watch is quite laborious, raise the question as to how the watch was wound daily; the answer is presumably that they were used for watches with key slots in their faces.

Watch stands designed as miniature dressing table mirrors, pivoted between uprights, were made in England in the 19th century, in both mantelshelf and bedside sizes. One of the former type, 10½ in. high, is one from left, top shelf, Plate 457. It is entirely an example of turnery in fruitwood and laburnum.

Why the Pinto Collection has gone to Birmingham

During the 11 summers that the Pinto Collection was open to the public, attendances rose from 1,239 visitors in 1955, to 23,249 in 1965. At first, it was only open four afternoons per week for six months of the year, but soon it became necessary to open in the mornings (except Sunday mornings), and most of the other afternoons for booked parties. Even so, there was often serious congestion in the house, which was no stately home; by the end of 1963, when nearly 15,000 visitors came, it was obvious that some drastic reorganization must be urgently undertaken.

Apart from the fact that the collection, and its display, had completely outgrown the available accommodation, there were other serious problems. Like most museums, this one lost money; there was no subsidy, and the loss had to be met out of our taxed income. To keep the loss down, we managed with part-time receptionists and a part-time secretary, and no other staff; we ourselves carried out the whole of the administration, ordering, catering, arranging and re-arranging of display, labelling, writing of brochures, advertising and publicity, booking of parties, repairing and cleaning of treen, etc., and answering a vast number of telephone calls and a mass of correspondence. The running of the museum on a shoe-string was becoming too onerous to us both as we grew older, and as I had to retire from business in 1964, owing to serious ill-health, both the labour and the financial burden had to be eased quickly.

We tried to solve both problems by making application to the local council for permission to erect a block of flats and a museum extension in the spacious grounds; the income from the flats would have paid for the proper staffing of the museum. The application for the flats was turned down on the grounds that the site is in the Metropolitan Green Belt; we understood, however, that the museum extension would be permitted. An appeal to the Minister of Housing and Local Government met with the same negative result. In his report to the Minister, the Inspector said that while recognizing as he does 'the unselfish motives' of Mr. Pinto 'in trying to ensure the retention of his remarkable collection* for the nation, on planning grounds the end does not justify the means'.

The flats were intended as a source of revenue during our lifetime, so that at our deaths, the whole collection, the buildings and the grounds could be handed over to the nation with an endowment. Without the flats, it was unfortunately impossible for us to build the much needed museum extension.

Following the shattering of our hopes of

* Actually, the collection was the joint property of Mrs. Pinto and myself.

what seemed to us the ideal project, we issued a press statement in July, 1964, from which the following is an extract:

'The collection of 6,000 to 7,000 objects, ranging in size from a carved peach stone to a wooden fire engine, which has been assembled discriminately over nearly fifty years, is valued at £50,000 upwards. Although our efforts at self-help, in order to continue the mission we have set ourselves, have now failed, we are still willing to give half the value of the collection to the nation, if someone will come forward with £25,000 to cover the other half. More than that we cannot do, because the collection represents too high a proportion of our total capital.

Unless some private individual or some institution now comes forward with an offer of financial help, it is inevitable that the collection will eventually be closed to the public, and that it will be dispersed; it is probable that the bulk of it will go abroad. However, none of this will happen immediately and we have not lost hope. We plan to open as usual next year; in fact, we are not attempting to fix a final closing date at this juncture. There is still hope that some public spirited individual or organisation may provide a solution to the problem.'

Two museums wrote to us on July 23, but a postal strike delayed the letters and Birmingham Museum and Art Gallery's Director, John Lowe, won by a day, because he telephoned us on July 24. That Birmingham lost no time is proved by the fact that the Director and the Chairman of the Museum Committee came to view the collection on July 31, and on August 7 the Birmingham Corporation were able to make the following press announcement:

'Mr. and Mrs. Edward Pinto recently announced that they wished to find a suitable permanent home for their well-known collection of wooden bygones which since 1955 has been shown to the public in the private museum at their home, Oxhey Woods House, Northwood, Middlesex. They said that they would be prepared to sell the collection to a Museum in this country for the nominal sum of £25,000.

The Birmingham Corporation have now asked Mr. and Mrs. Pinto if they would consider selling the collection to the City for inclusion in the collections of the Museum and Art Gallery and the Pintos have welcomed the idea that the Collection should find its permanent home in Birmingham. The Collection contains well over 6,000 objects, and has been conservatively valued at £50,000. Mr. and Mrs. Pinto are making a great personal sacrifice to keep their unique collection together and permanently available to the public in this country.

The Museum and Art Gallery Committee, at a special meeting on Friday 7th August, considered the generous offer of Mr. and Mrs. Pinto and decided that they would make every effort to acquire the Collection for the Museum. A substantial part of the purchase price will be paid by the City, but it may be necessary to obtain some part of the money from outside sources. The purchase will not be made until next year and the Collection will be taken over by the Museum during the next three years. The Collection will be shown to the public next year as usual at Oxhey Woods House, but will be closed in 1966 when the transfer to Birmingham will begin. The Committee felt that the Collection would be of particular fascination to a city that exists by a tradition of craft skills and would also be of great interest and educational value to children in the city.

Neither the description *Wooden Bygones*, nor the more technical word *treen* conjure up the extraordinary fascination of the Pinto Collection. Over a period of many years Mr. and Mrs. Pinto have assembled a collection of wooden objects which not only show every side of the woodworker's craft from the Middle Ages to the present day, but which create an intimate picture of social life and customs throughout that period from the humble activities of the farm kitchen to the sophisticated fashions of elegant society. Many objects of fine quality show the highest skill of the European carver and turner and other woodworking craftsmen. Others of humbler origin reveal many almost forgotten corners of domestic life and usage. The Pinto Collection, which provides one of the most scholarly and revealing pictures of European social history ever assembled is the life work of Mr. and Mrs. Pinto who are recognised as the leading experts in this field. Already at Oxhey Woods House, the Collection has been seen by nearly one hundred thousand visitors from all over the world. It is the hope of the Pintos, through their public-spirited gesture, that in its new home in Birmingham the Collection will reach a new and wider public. The acquisition of this Collection will be one of the most important developments in the history of the Birmingham Museum and Art Gallery, and its illustration of craft, social history and folklore will add a new dimension to the museum which will be of great interest to all the people of Birmingham and an attraction to foreign visitors.'

It must be emphasized that the arrangement which we made was deliberately minimum part sale and maximum part gift. Our primary object was to preserve the collection intact, in this country, permanently on view and in a large city easily accessible to a wide public; Birmingham met this objective admirably. If we had been able to afford to do so, we would have given the whole collection to the nation. We could not, but we related our price to our basic need, £25,000, not to the worth of the collection, which was then valued by Messrs. Sotheby at over £63,000 (recently, sales of treen and bygones at Sotheby's show that such a collection would now fetch more than £100,000).

The collection commenced its move to Birmingham in 1966 and was phased for completion at the end of September, 1967. The arrangement was made to suit both Birmingham and ourselves. They had virtually to rebuild and entirely refit a gallery to display the majority of the collection; we wanted to dismantle it slowly, section by section, so that Mrs. Pinto could photograph and I could write this encyclopaedia with the objects still to hand. The programme has worked well; Birmingham has just completed its gallery for the greater part of the collection, and work is in hand at recently acquired Sarehole Mill, where some of the larger objects will be displayed; the collection should be on display again by Spring of 1969.

Mrs. Pinto completed her photography last year; I have just finished my manuscript (March, 1968). Allowing for typing, correction, production, etc., publication should be in 1969.

A Selection of Formerly Normal Uses of the Word Treen

☆　　　☆　　　☆

1. 'Throwing (turning) of treyn vessel'.
   —*The Promptorium.* 15th century.

2. 'The third thing they tell of, is the exchange of (vessell, as of) treene platters into pewter, and woodden spoones into siluer or tin. For so common were all sorts of treen stuffe in old time, that a man should hardlie find foure peeces of pewter (of which one was peraduenture a salt) in a good farmers house, and yet for all this frugalitie (if it may so be justly called), they were scarse able to liue and paie theur rents at their daies without selling a cow, or an horse, or more, although they paid but foure pounds at the utter-most by the yeare.'
   —Harrison's *Description of England* between the years 1577–87.

3. 'The wanton loues of false Fidessa fayre,
   Bought with the blood of van-guisht Paynim bold;
   The wretched payre transformed to treen mould . . .'
   —Edmund Spenser's (1522?–1599) *The Faerie Queene.*

*4. *Thomas Garner* of Mollington　1578
   'the trene dishes with the spoones
   ・・・・・IVᵈ'

—Oxfordshire Probate Inventories, 1559–90.

*5. *Richard Sparkes* of Mollington　1578
   'all kynde of treyne ware・・・・・・
   VIIIˢ'
   —ibid.

*6. *Elinor Pare* of St. Michaels, Oxford 1582–3
   'a Cubbord with Treen vessell・・・・・・
   IIˢ'
   —ibid.

*7. *Thomas Taylor* of Witney　1583
   '6 Treen dishes'
   —ibid.

*8. *John Bodie* of Checkendon　1582–3
   '1 Kever together with the bowles tubbes & tryne platters・・・・・・Xˢ'
   —ibid.

*9. *Richard Bendeforde* of Holton　1594
   'for Trine dissies (dishes) sponnes (spoons) & transiorrs (trenchers) ・・・・・・XIIᵈ'
   —ibid.

*10. *John Culles* of Henley-on-Thames 1587
   '4 Tren dishes'
   —ibd.

*11. *Margery Penny* of Benson　1588
   'a cherne heresive (hair sieve) three

buckettes trenchers twoe dosen treene dishes with the lumber in the kitchen······VIˢ'
—ibid.

*12. *Christopher Gold* of Banbury 1588–9
'2 little tubbes 2 payles one kyver one pen twoe treene platters 5 woodden disshes one dossen of trenchers······IIˢ VIIIᵈ'
—ibid.

*13. *Nicholas Hill* of Witney 1589–90
'2 Treen platters'
—ibid.

**Note*—References 4 to 13, from the Oxfordshire Probate Inventories, 1559–1590, have been kindly supplied to me by Mrs. Kate Havinden.

Some unusual, early uses of the word treen, are referred to in the *Introduction*.

Rhyming List of Wares

ASHLEY,
Umbrella and Parasol Maker,
No. 11, Bottom of Old Bond-Street, Bath.

———

With your request I now comply,
Resolved again my Muse to try
To reckon up my wares in rhyme,
But 'tis unwise to lose much time;
For wit I've by experience bought,
And that's the best of wit, 'tis thought
Therefore I promise nothing new
But just my former rhymes review.
My Friends or those who deign to stop
To purchase Goods at ASHLEY'S Shop,
Could save much time if they'd decide
Themselves with "Tokens" to provide,
"Change" being scarce and 'tis well known
The Guineas are to France all flown,
Or somewhere else I cannot tell,
Good local "Notes" I like as well.
WHITCHURCH and DORE much praise do
  merit,
They act in truth like men of spirit,
Deserve the very best of thanks
Of high and low and middle ranks;
Much to their credit be it spoken,
For issuing the silver token.
I hope you'll pardon the digression,
Next come my wares in quick succession;
Choice Umbrellas for the Rain,
Parasols, Chinese and plain,
Every sort made to your order,
Silk, (fast color) fringed or border,
Repaired, new covered, neatly made,
And "Cheap" as any in the trade;
Hat Cases, Hoods, and Bathing Caps,
Riding Aprons, Razor Straps,

Backgammon tables very good,
Chessmen, ivory, bone or wood,
Chess and Draft Boards, wood or leather,
Neatly made to fold together;
Ivory Combs shell, horn, and box,
Best Rackets, Battledores, and Cocks,
Corkscrews, Butt'ners, and boot-hooks,
Bone Rattles, totums, Pocket Books,
Penknives, Curling-tongs, Nut-cracks,
Jointed Tongs called Lazy-Backs,
Dolls drest, undrest, wood and leather,
Children's Balls light as a feather,
Also Dolls of wax and paper,
Figures like Vestris, made to caper,
Backboards & Stocks, first brought from
  France
Now used by those who learn to dance;
A pretty art I must confess,
And quite as needful as to dress.
Black-lead Pencils, Ivory rules,
Crimping Boards and neat Foot Stools,
Thread Cases, Pin-cushions, Boot-jacks,
And Ivory Hands for scratching backs.
Pope Joan Boards, and Bagatelles,
Fox and Goose, and Coronells
Tin Toys, wood, plain and painted Carts,
Cribbage Boards of various sorts,
Hay-forks, Rakes, and iron Spades,
Guns and Swords with iron blades,
Oxford Balls, Cuckows, Whips,
Sloops, Cutters, Boats, wood and toy Ships.
Comfit boxes, Shoeing Horns,
Neat Clasp Knives for cutting corns,
Boxes, Brushes, Shaving Cases,
Ugly Masks for pretty faces,
Artificial Chins and Noses,
Otto genuine of Roses.
Cities, Camps, Sheep-folds in boxes,

Lions, Bears, Dogs, Wolves, and Foxes.
Furnish'd Kitchen Brooms and Mops,
Purses neat with spring clasp tops,
Netting and Knitting Needles good,
Of steel or ivory, bone or wood,
Nests of Drawers, Dolls' Arms and Cradles,
Sugar bruisers and Punch Ladles,
Nail Nippers, Nested Fruit, Ruffsticks,
Fifes, Bandeleurs and Box with bricks.
Garden Rollers, Barking Dogs,
Lambs, Stilettos, Leaping Frogs,
Toy Watches, Cricket Balls and Bats,
Skipping Ropes and Sticks for Hats.
Pocket Bottles, very good,
In Leather Cases, also wood,
Strainers, Funnels, Butter Pats,
Apple-scoops, and Dolls' Straw Hats.
Alphabets, Bone Cups and balls,
Powder Boxes, and Dog-Calls,
Fish and Counters, Chamber Bellows,
Wrestlers, Hobbies, Punchinellos,
Syringes of every size,
Hand-screens to preserve the Eyes.
Brushes of all sorts for Cloth,
If often used destroy the moth,
Shoe Brushes of the best I sell,
For Boot-tops, Hat, and Flesh as well,
Tooth Brushes, wax'd and silver wire,
Of every sort you can desire,
Also for Hair, Comb, Nail, and Shaving,
To buy of me, you'll find a saving.
Card Cases, Scissars Sheaths, Dolls' Shoes,
China Boxes with Bath Views,
Shoe Traps, Bats, and Dogs on Wheels,
Gig Mills, Windmills, and Silk Reels.
Spectacle Cases, Lemon Squeezers,

Bodkins, Toothpicks, and Steel Tweezers,
Tea-urns, Tea-sets, Provision Dishes,
Conjuring Toys, and Magic Fishes;
Drums, Trumpets, Rattles, Noah's Arks,
Watchmen's Rattles, Knives and Forks,
Brass Cannon, Fifes, and Leather Purses,
Suckling Horns for careful nurses,
Salt and Mustard Spoons I sell,
Egg and Marrow, polished well.
Saucepans, Kettles, Tankards, Cans,
Vice-cushions, Humming-tops, and Fans,
Lanterns, Dominos, and Arrows,
Bows for Youth to shoot at Sparrows.
Hoops and Hoop-sticks, Kites and Twine,
Scissars polished very fine,
Cases to put in Notes, or Cash,
Or any kind of trifling Trash.
Dice Boxes, Devils with Two Sticks,
And other entertaining Tricks;
Corals with Bells, and ivory Rings,
Sword-Sticks, Canes, and choice of Strings,
Sticks plain and mounted, large and small,
It is my wish to oblige you all;
I've either sort that you may lack,
Blackthorn, Hazle, Supple Jack,
Crab, Beech, Cherry, or Wangees,
To suit my Friends of all degrees.
My Customers both great and small,
I've Obligations to you all,
Return you Thanks for Favors past,
And trust your Friendship to the last.
Let Ridicule not judge too rashly,
Of your Obedient

W. Ashley

Bath.
1811.

For Further Reading

In compiling this encyclopaedia, many hundred of books have been consulted and articles read; but mostly they were primarily works on other subjects, which only contained a few sentences or paragraphs relevant to wooden bygones.

Much of the information included here is derived from interviews with old craftsmen, research on patents, inventories, directories, manufacturing treatises, trade encyclopaedias, mediaeval and later books on teaching, manners, customs, etc., diaries, histories, old account books, registers, Acts, and other documents, and comparison and checking of thousands of objects and their uses, combined with nearly half a century of study of wood and practical experience of construction and techniques of woodworking.

For these reasons, it is impracticable to include a bibliography, but the selective list of books which follows, will be found of general interest, or in some instances of particular interest to readers of specific parts of this volume. They are set out under appropriate group headings but, with few exceptions, omit the basic source books and documents referred to above.

TREEN AND WOODEN BYGONES
Treen or Small Woodware—Edward H. Pinto (1949)
Domestic Utensils of Wood—Owen Evan-Thomas (1932)
Early American Wooden Ware—Mary Earle Gould (U.S.A., 1942)

FORESTRY, TREES, TIMBER, WOOD PESTS AND WOOD PRESERVATION
Timbers of the World—Alexander Howard (1920 and reprints)
Timber—Bryan Latham (1957)
Sylva—John Evelyn (1664)
The Insect Factor in Wood Decay—Norman Hickin (1963)
The Care of Woodwork in the Home—Edward H. and Eva R. Pinto (1955)
Various publications of Forest Products Research Laboratories, Princes Risborough
Various publications of Timber Research and Development Association, Hughenden Valley, High Wycombe.

WOODLAND, COUNTRY AND FARM CRAFTS
Woodland Crafts in Britain—H. L. Edlin (1949)
Traditional Country Craftsmen—J. Geraint Jenkins (1965)
The Craftsman in Wood—Edward H. Pinto (1962)
Household and Country Crafts—Alan Jobson (1953)
Made in England—Dorothy Hartley (1939)
The Village Carpenter—Walter Rose (1937)
The Wheelwright's Shop—G. Sturt (1934)
The Thatcher's Craft—Rural Industries Bureau (1961)
The Story of Cheese Making in Britain—Val Cheke (1959)
Milking and Dairying—R. U. Sayce, M.A., M.Sc. (Reprinted from the Montgomeryshire Collections, Vol. LII, Part II 1952)
Woodwork—W. L. Goodman (1962)
Plywoods of the World—A. D. Wood (Revised, 1963)
Raking and Handling Lowbush Blueberries—Dennis A. Abdalla (Bulletin 497, University of Maine, U.S.A.)

SOCIAL HISTORY, DOMESTIC BACKGROUNDS AND RECIPES OF BYGONE DAYS
The Diary and Correspondence of John Evelyn
The Diary of Samuel Pepys
Parson Woodforde's Diary

The Journeys of Celia Fiennes

The Housekeeping Book of Susanna Whatman

The Verney Papers

Farm and Cottage Inventories of mid-Essex—edited by Francis W. Steer, F.R.Hist.S. (1950)

The English Mediaeval House—Margaret Wood (1965)

The Flowering of the Middle Ages—edited by Joan Evans (1966)

A Baronial Household of the Thirteenth Century—Margaret Wade Labarge (1965)

English Home Life—Christina Hole (1947)

The English Townsman—Thomas Burke (1946)

Housekeeping in the Eighteenth Century—Rosamond Bayne-Powell (1956)

The English Countrywoman—G. E. and K. R. Fussell (1953)

Georgian England—R. E. Richardson (1931)

Life in a Noble Household, 1641–1700—Gladys Scott Thomson (1937)

The Russells in Bloomsbury, 1669–1771—Gladys Scott Thomson (1940)

Family Background—Gladys Scott Thomson (1949)

Mayhew's London—edited by Peter Quennel (1949)

Elizabethan Life in Town and Country—M. St. Clare Byrne (1925)

Tudor Family Portrait—Barbara Winchester (1955)

The Elizabethans at Home—Elizabeth Burton and Feliz Kelly (1958)

Tudor Renaissance—James Lees-Milne (1951)

Hints on Etiquette (1834, reprinted 1955)

Delightes for Ladies—Sir Hugh Plat (1609, reprinted 1948)

The English Hous-wife—Gervase Markham (1656)

Tudor Food and Pastimes, Life at Ingatestone Hall—F. G. Emmison (1964)

Shops and Shopping 1800–1914—Alison Aldburgham (1964)

Home Life in Colonial Days—Alice Morse Earle (U.S.A., 1898)

WOODWORKING TOOLS

A History of Woodworking Tools—W. L. Goodman (1964)

Plane Makers from 1700—W. L. Goodman (1968)

Ancient Carpenters' Tools—Henry C. Mercer, Sc.D. (U.S.A., 1929, revised 1951)

Story of the Saw—P. d'A. Jones and E. N. Simons (1960)

A Museum of Early American Tools—Eric Sloane (U.S.A., 1965)

The Traditional Tools of the Carpenter (booklet)—Philip Walker (1966)

Winterthur Portfolio II, English Tools in America (U.S.A., 1965)

The Portsmouth Blockmaking Machinery—K. R. Gilbert (a Science Museum Monograph, 1965)

TURNING AND TURNERY

L'Art de Tourner—Le P. C. Plumier (French, 1st ed. 1701)

Manuel du Tourneur—Bergeron (French, 1st ed. 1780)

History of the Lathe to 1850—Robert S. Woodbury (U.S.A., 1961)

The Practical Wood Turner—F. Pain (1957)

Woodturning—Design and Practice—Gerald T. James (1958)

Introductory Notes to Ornamental Turning (booklet)—A. W. Jones (1958)

The Worshipful Company of Turners of London—Roland Champness, M.A. (1966)

Lathes and Turning—Henry Northcott (1868)

Turning and Mechanical Manipulation, Vol. II—Chas. Holtzapffel (1856)

WOOD CARVING, WOOD SCULPTURE, WOOD ENGRAVING AND WOOD PRINTING BLOCKS

Practical Woodcarving and Gilding—Wheeler and Hayward (1963)

Wood Carving—Alan Durst (1938, revised 1948)

Wood Sculpture—Alfred Maskell (1911)

The Art of Drawing and Engraving on Wood—G. W. Marx (1881)

A Student's Guide to Wood Engraving—W. Gregson (1953)

The Book of Wallpaper—E. A. Entwistle (1954)

Albrecht Dürer—T. D. Barlow (1948)

Wood Engravings by Thomas Bewick—John Rayner (1947)

FIRE AND LIGHTING

London's Fire Brigades—W. Eric Jackson (1966)

Bryant and May Museum of Fire-Making Appliances Catalogue, and Supplement (1926 and 1928)

Flickering Flames—Leroy Thwing (U.S.A., 1958)

Early Lighting in New England—Helen Brigham Hebard (U.S.A., 1964)

BACKGROUND TO CHILDHOOD, PASTIMES AND TUITION

Hoyle's Games (many editions)

Teaching Toys in the Norwich Museums Collection (booklet)—Rachel M. R. Young, M.A. (1966)

Children's Toys Throughout The Ages—Leslie Daiken (1953)

World of Toys—Leslie Daiken (1963)

History of Toys—Antonia Fraser (1966)

Table Games of Georgian and Victorian Days—F. R. B. Whitehouse (1951)

Toys and Games—London Museum Picture Book

A Book of Toys—Gwen White (1946)

Dolls of the World—Gwen White (1962)

English Dolls Houses—Vivien Green (1955)

Model Soldiers—John G. Garratt

Antique Miniature Furniture—Jane Toller (1966)

The Georgian Child—F. Gordon Roe (1961)

The Elizabethan Home—M. St. Clare Byrne (1924, 1935, 1949)

Dolls' Houses—Victoria and Albert Museum Small Picture Book No. 51

Queen Mary's Dolls' House—Windsor Castle Souvenir booklet

Period Dolls' Houses from Many Lands—House of Bewlay Exhibition Catalogue 1955–56

Knur and Spell and Allied Games—Frank Atkinson (reprinted from *Folk Life*, Vol. I, 1963)

TOBACCO

Tobacco, Its History and Associations—F. W. Fairholt (1859)

Wooden Bygones of Smoking and Snuff Taking—Edward H. Pinto (1961)

Nicotiana Tabacum—Georg A. Brongers (Holland, 1964)

European and American Snuff Boxes—C. le Corbeiller (1966)

Sublime Tobacco—Compton Mackenzie (1958)

TEXTILES AND STRAW WORK

The History of Needlework Tools and Stitchery—Sylvia Groves (1966)

The Craftsman in Textiles—Leslie J. Clarke (1968)

The Old Hand Knitters of the Dales—Marie Hartley and Joan Ingilby (1951)

Pillow Lace in the East Midlands—Charles Freeman (Luton Museum booklet, 1958)

A History of Hand-Made Lace—F. N. Jackson (1900)

The Romance of the Lace Pillow—F. Wright (1919)

Knitting Through the Ages—James Norbury (1955)

Tools and Toys of Stitchery—Gertrude Whiting (U.S.A., 1928)

Romance of the Straw Hat—Charles Freeman (Luton Museum booklet, 1933)

Luton and the Hat Industry—Charles Freeman (Luton Museum booklet, 1953)

Spinning Wheels—Belfast Museum Bulletin, Vol. I, No. 5

Textile Machinery—Catalogue of the Collection in the Science Museum

Upper Canada Village (guide book)—spinning and weaving

TRADE SIGNS AND CARVED FIGURES

History of Signboards—Larwood and Hotton (many 19th century editions)

Signboards of Old London Shops—Sir Ambrose Heal (1907)

English Popular Art—Margaret Lambert and Enid Marx (1951)

NAUTICAL

Manual of Seamanship, Vol. 1 (1937)

Steel's Elements of Mastmaking, Sailmaking and Rigging—arranged from the 1794 edition by Claude S. Gill (1932)

Decorative Arts of the Mariner—edited by Gervais Frere-Cook (1966)

CYCLES

Cycles, History and Development, Parts 1 and 2—Science Museum (1955)

The Velocipede—H. S. Vaughan (1869)

LEATHERCRAFT

Leather Craftmanship—J. W. Waterer (1968)

Glossary

This is a short glossary of terms used in the text, which may not be familiar to all readers. The explanation given here to terms are essentially associated with their relation to wood or woodworking and they may have additional or different meanings in other connotations.

Acanthus Leaf Ornament: a conventionalized arrangement of the leaves of the Bear's Breech plant. Used in Corinthian and Composite capitals, and extensively for Renaissance ornament, it was also much favoured by late 17th- and 18th-century carvers for the classical ornament and mouldings of furniture, panelling, etc.

Annual Ring: the concentric ring of wood which an exogenous tree adds to its growth annually in temperate zones; in tropical

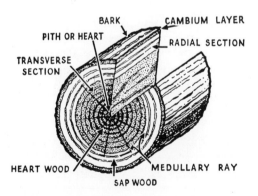

Simplified detail of the structure of a tree and natural lines of cleavage along the medullary rays.

climates, trees grow continuously, but not necessarily by means of annual rings. Certain trees such as palms are endogenous,

making their growth in the interior of the stem. In temperate climate trees, where the annual ring is easily distinguishable on the end grain of most species, the ring is seen as a 'double'—a light coloured ring of spring wood, formed when the sap is rising, and a darker autumn ring, when the sap is descending. The latest outer ring under the protective bark is the cambium layer, in which the growth occurs. Injury to the cambium layer prevents growth of new cells and if severe will kill the tree.

Hardwood trees, such as oak, ash, sycamore, walnut, mahogany, etc., have more complex structures than softwoods, such as pines, yew, etc. Hardwoods and softwoods are traditional and well recognized terms of convenience, but are not necessarily descriptive of the nature of the wood. Various other terms are used, such as evergreen (softwood) and deciduous (hardwood), or broad-leaved (hardwood) and coniferous or needled (softwood). But no description is entirely satisfactory because nature provides exceptions to all these generalizations. Balsa, a broad-leafed tree, ranks as a hardwood, but is one of the lightest and softest known. Laurel is a hardwood, but an evergreen. Pitch pine and yew are softwoods, but hard and heavy, whilst larch is a softwood but sheds its needles annually.

Anthemion: a formal, basically Greek arrangement of honeysuckle flower, much favoured in classical architecture, furniture, and ironwork during the late 18th century and in the Regency period. The term anthemion is also alternated with palmette for an Egyptian arrangement of the date palm leaf.

Astragal: in cabinet work, the term may mean a small, raised moulding, used as a cover joint for a pair of doors, or a basically T section glazing bar. In both usages, the astragal may be plain, ornamentally moulded, or carved.

Bandings: see Veneers and Veneering

Blister Figure: see Fiddleback

Bog Wood: dark brown or blackened wood of trees submerged and compressed for centuries in peat bogs. The chemical changes harden as well as darken the wood. Many species of trees are found in bogs, including oak, elm, birch, hazel, willow, alder and pine, but they are usually all described as bog oak. The wood is sometimes difficult to work, but is much esteemed.

Burrs: comparatively shallow excrescences, sometimes of large circumference, which occur on many trees, most commonly at the junction of the trunk with the ground or root, or at the junctions of branches. They are caused by a number of small shoots which are unable, or not allowed to break out, and then form an interwoven, contorted, but unusually stable mass. They can also be induced artificially by stooling (see Stooling). Burrs of certain species are highly ornamental, and greatly valued for veneers, snuff boxes, shallow drinking vessels, etc. See also Veneers and Veneering.

Cambium Layer: see Annual Ring

Carving: a method of surface decoration of wood and other materials by means of chisels and gouges. It may be conveniently described under three headings—chip carving, low relief and high relief. The first is the simplest and usually consists of chipping out a pattern, generally geometrical, from a flat surface. When completed, a 'straight edge' placed on the surface will slide smoothly over it, touching all the unchipped

surface. With low and high relief carving, much of the surface is cut away leaving the decoration in various degrees of projection. The value of the work varies according to the skill of the designer and carver, and the fineness of the work, not the depth of the carving. There is no hard and fast distinction between low and high relief carving, but generally, high relief is at least half way to 'in the round sculpture', sometimes with some of the work free standing.

Conversion: the act of sawing timber into smaller sections or into veneers. A log may be converted in various ways to give different effects and provide different qualities in use. Flat sawing in parallel slices cut

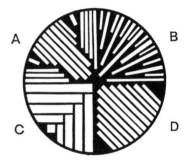

Log section, showing different methods of cutting to give figured oak. A and B give good figure but the latter creates more waste. C and D give mixed quality of figure.

through the log is the most economical, but with some woods it loses much of the figure; it also results in more shrinkage of some boards than occurs with quarter sawing. Quarter or rift sawing, which means cutting boards radially from the log, is naturally most wasteful, produces 'silver grain' in oak (the best figure) and in all woods makes boards with minimum shrinkage and less inclination to warp than flat sawn.

Coopering: the craft of building up staved vessels which are bound with hoops of various steamed woods, or suitable metal.

Cross Banding: see Veneers and Veneering

Crotch, Curl, Feather or Flame Veneers: veneers cut from just below where a tree trunk branches or forks into a U. Owing to the swaying of the tree in the wind, there are great stresses in this beautifully marked wood and it may be split in the grain to some extent below the point where the fork apparently begins. These fractures of the grain, which is always congested at this point, therefore take place in the crotch itself, which makes it unstable and difficult to convert and lay without subsequent movement and cracking, which shows through the polish. Our ancestors, who had no choice, cut their crotch veneers with a saw, and this is much more satisfactory in results than the modern and more economically knife cut veneer, which is apt to be 'distressed'—that is, torn on one side. This is particularly apparent when crotches are turned over into pairs to form a double width and give the much admired feather or flame effect. See also VENEERS AND VENEERING.

Dovetails: see JOINTS

Dowel: a wooden 'pin'; a length of wooden rod. See also JOINTS.

End Grain: see GRAIN

Feathering: this may mean (1) the insertion of a thin strip of wood used as a tongue on an angle joint; it was particularly used to strengthen mitre joints in the sides of thin boxes of various types. Or (2), the term is applied to the skilful cutting and interlocking of feathered edges of adjoining staves in Scottish quaichs, where a moisture tight joint was essential. See also JOINTS.

Fiddleback: a horizontal ripple effect, which conveys an appearance of undulation to a smooth surface. It occurs in some logs of sycamore, maple, mahogany, satinwood, etc. and is prized particularly for veneers. The same trees also yield *blister* or *pommele* marked veneers, in which the simulated undulations are more oval than in fiddleback. The same reason governs both types of marking—unevenness in the annual rings which are cut through when slicing by saw or knife.

Figure: see GRAIN; also VENEERS AND VENEERING

Grain: technically this is the direction of the fibres relative to the axis of the tree. Thus long grain shows on the surface of a board, and end grain, showing annual rings or parts of them, is apparent on the end of a board or log. Straight grain is best for strength and ease of working. Irregular grain, interlocked grain, and wavy grain in trees create ornamental grain, which when converted is known as figure. Generally, highly figured woods, which may occur in nearly all varieties of hardwood, are difficult to work to a smooth finish, but are esteemed for their beauty and particularly prized for veneers. See also VENEERS AND VENEERING.

Halved Joints: see JOINTS

Hardwood: see ANNUAL RING

Herring Bone Banding: see VENEERS AND VENEERING

Imbrication: fish scale pattern ornament.

Incised Surface Decoration: the working of a pattern into the surface of the wood by means of a sharp pointed instrument. Where the work was done by old-time sailors on wood, whalebone or walrus ivory (the subjects were mainly marine), it was known as scrimshaw work. Patterns made with a heated steel point are known as pokerwork; if the work is fine and used to create a hot etched picture, it is termed pyrography.

Inlay: see VENEERS AND VENEERING

Intarsia: see VENEERS AND VENEERING

Joints: the commonest woodworking joints used in the objects described in this volume, all of which are normally glued to secure or 'lock' the joints, are—pin and socket; dowel and socket; halved joints; mitred joints; mortise and tenon; dovetail. All of them have many variations.

Pin and socket joints consist of boring a

hole or socket in one member to be jointed and 'shouldering' a wooden 'pin' on the end of the other member, to fit the socket; the pin and the socket are sometimes threaded, so that the two members screw together.

Dowel and socket joints are similar to the last except that both the members to be joined have ends drilled out and a length of dowel or wooden rod is inserted into each, to form the connection.

Halved joints are the simplest form of cross joints. Half the material is removed from each member, so that when brought together, the surface is flush; the joint is rather weak and not used for highly stressed, or good quality, exposed work.

Mortise and tenon joints are the normal joints for junctions of door and other framing; the mortise is the slot cut in the side of the stile or outer vertical member, to receive the tenon or shouldered ends of the rails. A muntin or intermediate vertical member may be tenoned into the horizontal rails.

Mitres are the equal intersecting angles of two pieces of timber to form a junction. Mitre joints were formerly much used for joining box sides and for the junctions of back and sides of small stationery drawers, etc. Being a comparatively weak joint, they were frequently strengthened by diagonal feathering.

Better practice for the junction of drawer backs and side is to *dovetail* the angles, or set the back slightly forward and groove it into the sides. Dovetail joints are used for the best drawer and carcase work. The dovetail pins in a drawer side fit into the dovetail sockets in the drawer front. A neat and close fitting dovetail joint is a test of a woodworker's skill. The common dovetail joint, showing the joint in both angles and never used on drawer fronts, is the easiest to make. The lapped dovetail, used for junctions of most drawer fronts and sides, is more difficult to make. The secret dovetail, in which the joint is concealed within a mitre, requires considerable skill.

Knop: A small rounded protuberance or knob. It is frequently found on turned stems of standing cups, candle and wig stands, etc., or on the finials on covers of standing cups.

Long Grain: see GRAIN

Marquetry: see VENEERS AND VENEERING

Mitred Joints: see JOINTS

Mortise and Tenon Joints: see JOINTS

Oyster Pieces: obtained by cutting end grain slices of veneer from small trunks or branches of dense hardwood trees, particularly those which have contrasting colour heart and sapwood. The oysters are then fitted together to form oyster pattern, which is glued on the core. In the second half of the 17th century, furniture veneered with lignum vitae, olive, and laburnum oysters was popular. End grain wood is the most porous and difficult to glue, therefore branches for oysters were more often cut at 45° to 60°, rather than 90°, across the grain and this automatically produced the oval oyster effect rather than the circle, which results from cutting the branch at right angles. The oysters were then profiled into octagons, for fitting together. See also VENEERS AND VENEERING.

Pin and Socket Joints: see JOINTS

Poker Work: see INCISED SURFACE DECORATION

Pollarding: see STOOLING

Pommele Figure: see FIDDLEBACK

Pyrography: see INCISED SURFACE DECORATION

Rebate or Rabbet: a recess or step cut into the edge of a piece of material, to receive another piece; thus, in a pair of doors, the meeting edge of one may be rebated over the other

Scrimshaw Work: see INCISED SURFACE DECORATION

Seasoning of Wood: the process of reducing the moisture content of wood to a suitable proportion for the purpose intended. Unseasoned timber, when used indoors, shrinks unduly, splits, warps and is much more prone to decay than seasoned wood. When dried to the correct moisture content, it is relatively stable, but being a hygroscopic material, it changes its moisture content according to the atmosphere in which it is placed. Timber was formerly air dried; now it is usually dried in scientifically controlled drying kilns. Central heating is bad for all woodwork, but much damage can be obviated by the use of humidifiers.

Short Grain: see GRAIN

Softwood: see ANNUAL RING

Stooling: when a tree is cut down but not killed, it sends out a secondary growth of new shoots; this development is known as stooling. Osiers for basket making are induced by stooling willows at regular intervals. With some trees, stooling is practised in order to encourage burrs; in this process, more commonly known as pollarding, the young shoots or knurls are 'rubbed off' before they can develop into branches. Pollard oak or pollarded oak is a misnomer: the brown colour of such oak is not due to pollarding, but to the effects of the beef-steak fungus.

Stringings: see VENEERS AND VENEERING

Tenons: see JOINTS

Transfer Decoration: transfers, printed from engraved metal plates, were applied to woodwork from the second quarter of the 19th century. The work was particularly applied to small objects such as snuff boxes, tea caddies, blotters, etc., constructed from sycamore and made in Scotland. The transfer and the wood surface was subsequently protected by varnish or polish.

Tunbridge Wood Mosaic: a process of wood mosaic developed and largely practised at Tonbridge and Tunbridge Wells throughout the 19th century. Bundles of profiled sticks of various coloured timbers were arranged to form geometric and floral designs, landscape scenes, etc., *on the end grain*; the design thus ran right through the bundle, as on seaside lettered peppermint rock. The bundles comprising the pattern or picture were glued together and then cut across the grain into thin slices of end grain mosaic; they were then glued on to the objects to be decorated and polished or varnished.

Turnery: any object made on a lathe.

Veneers and Veneering: Veneering is the craft of covering a sound, mild, stable, but comparatively uninteresting wood, usually described as the core, with a thin layer of decorative and rarer wood, which is glued and pressed on. It is not, as many people think, a method of covering over something cheap and nasty. Frequently, the rarer and more attractive veneer, quite apart from being semi-precious—something too expensive to waste as solid timber—is, by reason of the contorted grain which gives it its beauty, unstable or even constructionally unsound. Veneering, in good practice, is carried out on both sides of the core, to equalize the 'pull', but the backing veneer is of a cheaper type.

In the past, all veneers were saw cut, which was wasteful, both because the veneers had to be thicker than when knife cut, and also because so much was lost in sawdust. Modern machines slice the veneer off the log with a straight, horizontal or vertical knife cut; alternatively, veneers are rotary cut, which means the log is virtually unpeeled. Mostly, the best veneers are straight cut, but for plywood, rotary cutting is generally employed; it is also used for certain face veneers where a bold, flowery grain is desired, due to the knife slicing through the irregularly formed annual rings.

Veneers may be laid with straight, matched joints, so that they look like solid wood. Alternatively, they may be laid in geometrical or symmetrical patterns by turning over consecutive leaves into pairs, described as halving; if they are turned again, it is quartering, and so on. Further decorative effects may be obtained by introducing burr veneer (see BURRS), or oyster pieces (see OYSTER PIECES), or crotch or curl veneers (see CROTCH, CURL ETC.) as centrepieces.

Patterns may be framed or divided by stringings or bandings. *Stringings* is the term usually applied to a narrow—about $\frac{1}{16}$ in. to $\frac{1}{8}$ in. wide—strip of contrasting veneer. A *banding* is made up of two or more stringings enclosing a wider strip of cross veneer, known as a cross banding, or a centre strip arranged herring-bone fashion; the border stringings are sometimes omitted from a banding. Composite bandings may consist of numerous bandings and stringings.

Marquetry is a pattern of contrasting veneers cut flush into a background of veneer; thus there is floral, seaweed, figure marquetry, etc. Occasionally, particularly on Dutch work, marquetry was sometimes cut into solid timber.

Inlay is the flush insertion into veneer or solid wood of bandings, stringings, etc. of contrasting veneers, prepared motifs, such as shells, lunettes, etc., or other materials such as mother-of-pearl, ivory, brass, etc.

Intarsia is the formation of flush *perspective* pictures, landscape, architectural, etc., using veneers of various colours, grains and figure as the palette.

Index

Numerals in italic refer to plate numbers

Abacus 272, 416, *296*
Acanthus leaf ornament 437
Adzes 378, *404, 414*
Aeolian harps 165, *174*
Agate burnishers, bookbinders'
    393, *421*
Agricultural devices—general
    introduction 90
Ainsworth, Harrison 414
Airers 149, *152*
Ale bowls 59
Alegoose 57, *48*
Alphabet bats 417, *445*
    building cubes and slabs
        417, 418
    picture cards 417, *445*
    rods 418, *446*
    Wallis's Revolving 418, *449*
Amadou—see *Tinder*
Anaesthetist's gags 15, *8*
Anderl, Georg 174
Andrews, William 422
Animal toys 205, *214, 217,
    218, 226*
Annual ring 437
Anointing spoons 172, *64*
Anthemion 437
Apothecary—general introduc-
    tion 11
Apothecary cabinets 11, *3*
    jars 12, *4*
    mortars 182, *178*
Apple parers 90, *86*
    scoops 83, *80*
Apprentices' indenture boxes
    165, *165*
Archery 235
Archimedean drills 380, *409*
Armorial decorated cups 34–7,
    55–8
Articulated toys 206, *214*
Artificial limbs 12, *5*
Artists' dark mirrors—see
    Claude Lorraine glasses

Ashley, Umbrella Maker 27,
    432
Astragal 438
Atkinson, Frank 141
Aubrey, John 334
Auction by candle 114
Augers 379, 380, *401, 407*
Automata—see *Moving-Part and
    Mechanical Toys*
Awls 379, 399, *421*
Axes 378, *398–402*

Babla pins 199, *213*
Baby cages 419, *452–4*
    houses—see *Dolls' Houses*
    minders—see *Baby Cages*
Back boards—see *Deportment
    Boards*
Back boards, skiff 270
Backgammon 216, *228*
Back scratchers 25, *14*
Back stretchers, carcase 395,
    424
Bacon racks 132, *131*
Bacon, Roger 262, 282
Bagard, Cesar 120, 122, 353,
    359, 366, 367
Bagatelle 216, *232*
Balances, diamond merchants'
    287, *294, 311*
    money 287, *292, 294, 302,
    311*
Balancing toys 206, *217*
Balling guns 397, *426*
Ballot boxes 165, *166*
Bandage winders 13, *6*
Bandalores—see *Yo-Yos*
Band boxes 136
Bandings—see *Veneers and
    Veneering*
Barbers' bowls 13, *6*
    chairs, child's 359, *378*
    poles 14

Barker, H. 5
Barley shovels 394, *423*
Barrels, cotton and thread
    300, 337
    flour 136, *144*
    tobacco 342, *352*
    wine 52, 64, *42, 54*
Basting sticks 133, *133*
Bath chairs 176
Bats, alphabet 417, *445*
    cricket 230, *234*
    lacemakers' 312, *323*
    reed 406, *427*
    washing 149, *149, 150*
Bead looms 323, *337*
Beakers 34, *20*
Bedroom accessories—general
    introduction 357
Bed smoothers 170, *167*
    wagons 124, *127*
    warmers 124
Beekeepers' bellows 167, *170*
Beer bowls 394, *423*
    coasters 62
    drayman's sink 394, *423*
    funnels 394, *423*
    pulls 59, *50*
Beetles, washing 150, *149*
Belaying pins 265, *285*
Bellows 108, 150, 167, 374,
    *112, 113, 151, 170, 380,
    395*
Bell pulls 167, *167*
Bells and calls, birds, cattle, etc.
    90, 237, *85, 245*
Bells, shop door 406, *425*
Belt buckles 21, *15*
Benediction horn 98, *95*
Bentwood boxes 135, 202, *138*
    cubic measures 281, *301*
Bergeron 380
Berry's patent boxes 109, 254,
    114, 264
Bevels 385, *413*

Bewick, Thomas 246, 247
Bibers 42, *20*, *39*
Bickers 53, *46*
Bicycle handle-bar grips 167, *165*
Bicycles 177, *176*
Bilboquets 229, *241*
Billiard accessories 216, *232*
Bird cages 236, *245*
   calls—see *Calls*
   clappers 236, *245*
   decoys 238, *247*
   scarers 236, *245, 246*
Biscuit prickers 140, 189, *141, 193*
Bismars 288, *302*
Bisschop, Cornelius 125
Bitter cups—see *Quassia Goblets*
Blacksmiths' bellows 108
Blagrave 373
Blanket pegs 153, *156*
Bleeding bowls 13, *6*
Bligh, Hon. Ivo 230
Blind cord acorns 403, *430*
Blister figure—see *Fiddleback*
Britchers 395, *424*
Blocks, butchers' 395, *424*
   engraving 246, *261, 262*
   hatters' 396, *425*
   printing 243, *252–257*
   pulley 269, *285*
   reeving 266, *285*
   wig 374, *380*
   woodcut 246, *258–260*
Blood-letting and cupping outfit 14, *6*
Blotter cases 250
Blotting paper 250
Blow tubes 109
Blueberry rakes 91, *86*
Boards, back—see *Deportment
   Boards*
   breeches 150, *151*
   butter—see *Butter Hands*
   carving 72, *68*
   chess 217, *228–230, 235*
   chopping 18, 95, *6, 105*
   chuck-rum 272, *296*
   Cress Reversible Educational
     418, 419, *450*
   crimping 150, *156*
   deportment 421, *448*
   draughts—see *Chess Boards*
   gathering 150, *156*
   griddle—see *Riddleboards*
   haver—see *Riddleboards*
   ironing 151, *152*

knife 151
mangling 153, *153*
pastry 133
pill counting—see *Chuck-rum
   Boards*
Pope Joan 224, *233*
riddle 141, *144*
scrubbing 155, *152*
tally 285, *307–310*
traverse 270, *289*
Boat puzzles 226, *240*
Bobbins, lace 310, *323, 331, 332, 336*
   plumbers 402
Bobbin trees—see *Reel Stands*
Bog oak jewellery 192, *15*
Bog wood 438
Bonnet stands 374, *380, 384, 393*
Bookbinding devices 393, *421, 422, 430*
Bookcases, travelling 250, *266, 272, 273*
Book covers 250, *284*
   markers 251
   rests 251, *265, 267, 281, 282*
Boot button boxes 399, *421*
Boot jacks and lifts 236, *246*
Boring tools 379, *401, 404, 407, 409, 413, 418*
Bossing sticks—see *Lead Dres-
   sers*
Bottle cases 14, 359, *7*
   corkers 60, *49*
   cork pressers 60, *49*
   corks 59
   cranes 60, *49*
   openers 62, *50*
   pourers 63, *52*
   sealers 60, *49*
Bottles, chrism 172, 196, *171, 207*
   coopered 64, *54*
Bow-drills 379, *418*
Bowl stirrers and scrapers—
   see *Spatulas and Spurtles*
Bowls (game) 230
Bowls, barbers' bleeding 13, *6*
   beer 394, *423*
   bread, fruit, etc. 70, 193, *61, 199*
   butter 99, *96*
   dairy 98, *95, 97*
   drinking, lignum vitae 34, *39*

   eating 89, *84*
   general purpose 133, 191, *135, 136, 199*
   marriage—see *Ale Bowls*
   mazer 43–47, 58, *22–26, 48*
   sheep salve 96, *105*
   sweetmeat 87, *61*
   wassail 48–52, *26, 29, 31–37*
   wine strainer 66, *50*
   witches' brew 19, *8*
   wool 309, *338*
Bows, hatters' 396, *433*
Boxes, apprentices' indenture
   165, *165*
   ballot 165, *166*
   bentwood 135, 202, *138*
   boot button 399, *421*
   candle 115, 117, *121*
   cigarette 332
   collecting 167, *168*
   cotton and thread 300, *337*
   cutlery 144, *147*
   document storage—see *Skip-
     pets*
   dominoes 219, *233*
   drizzling 310, *346*
   écarté 220
   egg 94, *105*
   fiery cross 170, 300, *165, 337*
   games counter 218, *233*
   grease 382, 388, *414, 419*
   hat 369, *390*
   hone 93, *85*
   jewel 369, *388, 392*
   knife—see *Spoon Racks* and
     Cutlery Boxes
   knitting needle 304, *338*
   lace 370
   lace bobbin 312, *337*
   match 110, 114, *115*—also
     see *Instantaneous Light Con-
     trivances*
   money 167, 211, *168, 225*
   netting 316, *346*
   offertory 167, *168*
   paint 256, *278–280*
   pencil 422, *267, 450*
   pill 17, *8*
   playing card 223, *233*
   poor's 168
   posting 199, *210*
   pounce 261, *264*
   powder 371, *388*
   propellor 172, *170*
   razor 371, *393, 394*

Boxes, (contd.)
roundel 79, *30, 61, 76, 77*
rush-light 123, *117*
salt 142, *143*
school or satchel 422, *450, 451*
scissor 318
seal 200, *213*
Shaker 136, 369, *138*
shoe cleaning 401, *428*
snuff 163, 181, 195, 196, 345, *162, 178, 206, 207, 360–362, 364–370*
soap 373, *393*
spice 65, 143, 181, *26, 53, 141, 178*
spool 317, *342*
stamp 202, *213*
string 203, *211, 212*
taper 112, *117*
tea urn powder 297, *313*
tinder 112, 115, 116, *115, 117, 125*
tobacco 340, *357, 366*
toilet 371, *388*
tooth powder 373, *389*
wafer 172, 196, *171, 207*
watchmakers' and jewellers' 409, *292*
wig 374, *390*
work 324, *341*
Braces 379, *404, 409, 413*
Bradawls—see *Boring Tools*
Braided fusees 109, *115*
Braid looms 323, *347*
Branding irons 96, *105*
Brand, John 50
Brazil nuts 193, *199*
Bread bowls 70, *61*
Bread-crumb graters 179, *177*
Bread oven doors 134, *132*
Bread prints or stamps 134, 187, *132, 186*
slicers 134, *134*
Breast augurs—see *Boring Tools*
Breast ploughs 91, *92*
Breeches boards 150, *151*
Breughel the Elder 89
Brewhouse devices 393, *423*
Briago, Vincienzio 419
Brighton buns 116, *125*
Broaches, knitting 308, *323*
Broches, broderers' 309
Brushes, clothes 359, *387, 388*
dusting 359, *387, 388*
hair 359, *378*
tennis ball 156, *151*

tooth 373
Buckets 64, 94, 98, *86*
Buckles 21, *13, 15*
Bucks 147, 148
Building cubes and slabs, alphabet 417
Bundly sticks 306, 307, *323*
Burney, Fanny 260
Burnishers, bookbinders' 393, *421*
Burr remover 391, *419*
Burrs 438
Busks, stay 22, *10, 11*
Butchery devices 394, *86, 424*
Butter bowls 99, *96*
cups 99, *95*
curls and cutters 99, *95*
hands 99, *96*
kegs 99, *98*
pouncers—see *Butter Workers*
prints 100, *99, 100, 102*
moulds 99, 100, 101, *86, 95, 100, 101, 102*
scoops 101, *95*
slicers 99, *95*
scales 101, *101*
workers 101, *96, 111*
Butter's Tangible Arithmetic and Geometry 419, *449*
Button hooks 360, *384*
Buttonhole cutters 300, *326*
Buttons 24, 193, *15*
Button sticks 150, *151*

Cabbage pressers 134, *135*
Cabinets, apothecary 11, *3*
stationery 263, *268, 276*
Cachet machines 15, *8*
Caddies, tea 293, 313, 315–*320*
Caddy ladles 319
Cages, baby 419, *452, 453, 454*
bird 236, *245*
cricket 191, 237, *199, 245*
mouse 236, *245*
Calculating and counting devices 272, 292, 294, 296–*298*
Calendars, perpetual 178, *302, 303*
Callot, Jacques 86
Calls, bird 237, *245*
cow 90, *85*
Cambium layer—see *Annual Ring*

Cammann, Schuyler 191
Campbell, R. 244
Camphor containers 15, 7
Canarium nut jewellery 192
Candelabra—see *Chandeliers*
Candle arms 121, *120*
Candle, auctions by 114
Candle-beams 115
Candle boxes 115, *117, 121*
extinguishers 115, *122*
holders 115, 123, *118, 120, 125*
moulds 116, *116, 119, 120*
screens or shields 117, *117*
stands 117, 312, *121, 333*
Candles and candle making 113, 116
Candlesticks 118, *121–124*
Cap crown smoothers 150
Caramel rollers 142, *142*
Carcase back stretchers 395, *424*
Cards, alphabet picture 417, *445*
Mentor's 223, *233*
spinning 320, *399*
Carpenters' benches 377
Carpet bowls 230
Carriers, egg 72, *68*
game 239, *246*
teapot 297
visiting card 177
wine 62
Cartridge devices 237, *245*
Cartwright, Rev. Edmund 177
Carving 438
Carving boards 72, *68*
Carving, intaglio 184, *182, 183*
Cases, blotter 250
bottle 14, 359, *7*
camphor 15, *7*
cheroot and cigar 330, *351*
cigarette 332
dressing 364, *385, 386*
funnel 16, *9*
knife 71
needle 196, 268, 314, *206, 286, 326, 329, 339, 340, 341*
pipe 334, *354, 356*
spectacle 262, *266, 267, 269*
surgeons' instrument 19, *9*
syringe—see *Bottle Cases*
thermometer—see *Bottle Cases*
thimble 322, *339*

Cases (contd.)
toothpick 26, *15*
toilet 364, *385, 386,* 392, *393*
tumbler—see *Bottle Cases*
visiting card 28, *14*
wax tablet 263, *266*
Cases for silver 70, *61*
Cash ball, Lamson Paragon 395, *425*
Caskets, jewel 369, *392*
revolving 331, 365, *351, 386, 392*
Casters—see *Sifters*
Cat-o-nine-tails 171, *170*
Cats 324, *349*
Celebrano, Francesco 174
Cellini, Benvenuto 346
Ceremonial tools 167, *165, 170*
Chains, wooden 162, 268, *163, 286*
Chairs, bath 176
child's barbers' 359, *378*
exercise—see *Chamber Horses*
lacemakers' 313
sedan 176
Chalk line winders 381, *419*
Chamber horses 360, *379*
Chamber pots 361, *383*
Champness, Roland 281
Chandeliers 121, *124*
Chase wedges, plumbers' 402, *430*
Chaucer 237
Chautauqua 420, *455*
Cheese coasters or cradles 70, *63*
moulds—see *Cheese Vats*
planes—71, *65*
plateaux 79, *61*
presses 102, *107*
prints 102, *103, 104*
scoops 83, *80*
vats 102, *97*
Cheeses (skittles) 233, *234*
Chess boards 217, *228–230, 235*
Chessels—see *Cheese Vats*
Chessmen 217, *235*
Chests, tool 377, *405*
Chisels 167, 381, *165, 401, 404, 410*—see also *Button-hole Cutters*
Chocolate drinking—general introduction 289
Chocolate mills 291, *312*

Choppers, kitchen 134, *134*
Chopping boards 18, 95, *6, 105*
Chrism bottles 172, 196, *171, 207*
spoons 172, *171*
Christmas boxes 168
Chuck-rum boards 272, *296*
Churns 103, 105, *98, 106, 110*
Cigar box openers 331, *350*
Cigar, cheroot and cigarette cases and boxes 330, 332, *351*
Cigar and cheroot caskets 331, *351, 352*
Cigar cutters 332, *351, 353*
holders—see *Cigarette Holders*
lighters 109, *115*
moulds 332, *352*
piercers 332, *351*
Cigarette holders 332, *353*
Cigarette making devices 333, *351*
Cigarren-Zünders 109, *115*
Cipriani, Giambattista 415
Clamp devices 300, 374, *340*
Clamp stools 399, *428*
Clams 399, *428*
Claude Lorraine glasses 251
Cleaning devices—general introduction 147
Cleavers, osier 402, *425*
Clew holders 306, 307, 308, *322–324*
Clickets 421, *445*
Clocks 279, *294*
Clogs 399, *429*
Clothes brushes 362, *387, 388*
hangers 362, *384*
pegs 153, *156*
Cluckets—see *Bells and Calls*
Coaching dials 274, *295*
Coaching horn rack 242, *250*
Coasters 61, 70, *50, 51, 60, 61, 63*
Coconuts 193, *202–204*
Cockamaroo—see *Bagatelle*
Codd bottle openers 61, *50*
Coffee drinking—general introduction 289
Coffee bean jars 292, *313*
cups 292, *313*
grinders—see *Coffee Mills*
mills 180, *177, 180*
pots or jugs 58, 292, *48, 313*
stools 292, *314*

Coggies or cogs 54
Coin balances 287, *292, 302*
Collecting boxes 167, *168*
Comb cleaners 364, *384*
Comb-Makers, Worshipful Company of 363
Combing forks, thatchers' 406, *427*
Combs, curry 91, *105*
toilet 362, *381, 382, 384*
Compasses 274, *292*
Compo moulds 184, 185, 190, *196–198*
Condiments—see *Salts*
Cone or conic section 252, *294*
Cones, dinghy plug 266, *285*
knitting machine 304, *337*
Conversion, timber 438
Coopering 438
Copying—general introduction 248
Copying lathe work 385, *292*
Copying machines—see *Hectographs*
Copying sticks 421, *447*
Coques, Gonzalez 419
Coquilla nuts 194, 350, *15, 205–207, 368*
Cordage devices—see *Rope Devices*
Cork objects 265, *286*
Corks, bottle 59
Corkscrews 59, *49, 50*
Corn shauls and strikes 91, *87*
Corn stook binders—see *Wimbels*
Cornucopia 169, *165*
Coronas—see *Candle-beams*
Coryat, Thomas 69
Costrels—see *Kegs*
Costume accessories—general introduction 21
Cotton barrels and boxes 300, *337*
Counterblaste to Tobacco, James I's 327
Counter boxes and counters, games 218, *233*
Counters, knitting row 305, *339*
Cow calls—see *Bells and Calls*
Cowper, William 312, 315, *349*
Cradles, cheese 70, *63*
pipe 338, *350, 352*

Craft devices—general introduction 393
Cramps 381, *413*
Crandall's patents 206, *214*
Crane, J. 186
Cranes, bottle 60, *49*
Cratches—see *Bacon Racks*
Cravat holders 374, *380, 384, 393*
Crayons 252, *267*
Cream stirrers 103, *95*
Creels 266, *286*
Cress Reversible Educational Boards 418, 419, *450*
Cribbage boards 218, *233*
Cricket bats 230, *234*
Cricket cages 191, 237, *199, 245*
Crimping boards 150, *156*
Cripps, W. J. 43
Crochet hooks 304, *323*
Crooks, shepherds' 96, *93*
Croquet 231, *232*
Cross banding 438
Crotch veneers 439
Crozes—see *Planes, Woodworkers'*
Cruet stands—see *Salts and Condiments*
Crutches, wine 169
Cubic measures 281, *301*
Cucumber slicers 146, *134*
Culinary moulds 94, 139, 184, *86, 136, 184–193.* See also *Butter Prints, Bread Prints, Cheese Prints*
Cullen of Ashbourne wassailing suite 52, *35–37*
Cup and ball game—see *Bilboquets*
Cups, armorial decorated 34, *55–58*
  bitter—see *Cups, Quassia*
  butter 99, *95*
  coffee 292, *313*
  dice 219, *233*
  dipper 37, *21*
  egg 73, *68*
  engine turned standing 38, *26*
  eye 16, *9*
  feeding—see *Pap Boats*
  goblets 38, 39, 193, *20, 26, 202*
  loving 39, *26*
  milkmaid 39
  moustache 293, *313*

nest of 40, *27*
ornamental 169, *169*
pledging 163
posset 40, *21, 30, 61*
quassia 39, *20*
seed 95, *105*
shaving 372, *393*
standing 34–37, 38, 58, *26, 28, 55–58*
stirrup 41, *39*
tea 296, *313, 321*
travelling 41, *39*
vendageur 41, *39*
whistling 41, *38*
wine tasting 42, *20*
Curl veneers 439
Curling sticks, hair 364, *384*
Curry combs 91, *105*
Curtain rings 170
Cutlery boxes 144, *147*
  cases 71
  stands 71, *61*
Cylinders, McFarlane's Calculating 273, *294*
  Schott's 273

Daiken, Leslie 206
Dairy—general introduction 97
Dairy bowls 98, *95, 97*
  scales—see *Butter Scales*
  stools—see *Milking Stools*
  thermometers 104, *96*
Dairymaid yokes 105, *110*
Dame school clicket 421, *445*
Darning eggs and mushrooms 301, *335*
Dart, Raymond 83
Darts 231
Dating of treen 4
Dead eyes 266, *285*
Decanters 42, *53*
Decanter stands 81, *50*
Decorators' moulds—see *Compo Moulds*
Decoy birds 238, *247*
Deed racks 199, *209*
Defoe, Daniel 26, 216
Dental keys 15, *8*
Dentists' gags 15, *8*
Deportment boards 421, *448*
Desks, portable 252, *274–277*
Dial registers 274, *290, 292, 295*

Diamond merchants' balances 287, *294, 311*
Diavolo or diabolo 231, *241*
Dice and dice cups 219, *233, 238, 239*
Dicing machines 219, *238, 239*
Dickens, Charles 265, 343
Dinghy plugs 266, *285*
Dinner mats 72
Dipper cups 37, *21*
Dish slopes 72, *62*
Dishes 6, 72, 89, 142, *2, 62, 68, 84, 139*
Display devices, shop 202, 203, 369, 375, 404, *209, 212, 389, 425, 427, 431*
Dissected puzzles—see *Jig-saw Puzzles*
Distaffs 321, *327, 328, 343*
Document storage boxes—see *Skippets*
Dog tongs 92, *94*
  wheels 105, 134, *106, 146*
  whistles 28, 90, 237, *16, 85, 245*
Dollies, washing 150, 151, *152, 156*
Dolls 296, 417, *215–217, 220, 445*
Dolls' furniture—see *Models and Miniature Furniture*
  houses 207
Dominoes and domino boxes 219, *233*
Donkeys, glove makers' 400, *422*
Door bells, shop 406, *425*
  porters 170, *170*
Double cup measures 17, *6*
Dovetails—see *Joints*
Dowels 439
Dowel and socket—see *Joints*
Draughts 219, 231, *233*
Draughts boards—see *Chess Boards*
Draw bore tools—see *Steels*
Drawing—general introduction 248
Draw-knives 391, *418*
Dredgers 143, *141*
Drenchers 93
Dressing cases 364, *385, 386*
Dressing table sets 365, *387*
Drills—see *Boring Tools*
Drink measures 63, *6, 49*
Drinking ancillaries 59, *49–54*

Drinking—general introduction 30

Drinking vessels 31, *8, 20–36, 38–48, 55–58*

Drizzling boxes 310, *346*

Drug jars 12, *4*

Dry store jars 135, *135*

Dumb-bells 232, *234*

Dust bellows 150, *151*

Dusting brushes 359, *387, 388*

Dwangs, upholsters' 408

Ear trumpets 16, *9*

Eating—general introduction 67

Eating bowls 89, *84*

Écarté boxes 220

Eck, Adam 221

Edge setting irons, shoemakers' 400, *421*

Eger work 220, *228–231*

Egg boxes 94, *105*
  carriers 72, *68*
  cups 73, *68*
  stands 73, 136, *68, 136*
  timers 137, *136*

Eggs, coquilla, 195
  darning 301, *335*

Electrical devices 395, *425*

Electric torches 395, *425*

Ell rules 277, *297–299*

Embroidery frames 302, *335, 340*

Emery cushions 315, *326*

Emmison, F. G. *132*

End grain—see *Grain*

Engine, model 282, *305*

Engraving blocks 246, *261, 262*

Equilibrists 206, *217*

Etiquette, snuff taking 330
  table 68

Étuis 196, 314, *206, 326, 329, 339*

Evan-Thomas, Owen 43, *50*

Evelyn, John 3, 44, 75, 112, 129, 238, 276, 289, 303, 357, 378, 380

Eye cups 16, *9*
  glasses, watchmakers' and jewellers' 409, *292*
  testers 16, *9*

Exercise chairs—see *Chamber Horses*

Fairground figures—see *Roundabout and Pageant Figures*
  swing boats model 211, *224*

Fairholt, F. W. 338, 350

Fairings 185, 187, 188, *187, 189, 190*

Fans 24, *14*

Feather bed smoothers 170, *167*

Feather veneers 439

Feathering 439

Feeding cups—see *Pap Boats*

Fen overshoes—see *Horse Mud Shoes*

Fenders, boat 266, *285*

Fescues 421, *266*

Fiddleback 439

Fids 266, *285*

Fiennes, Celia, 216, 303

Fiery Cross boxes 170, 300, *165, 337*

Figure, wood—see *Grain*, also *Veneers and Veneering*

Figureheads 413, *442*

Finger pillories 421
  protectors 92, *85*
  stocks 421, *445*

Fire buckets 126
  engines 126, *129, 130*
  escape model 211, *234*
  fighting—general introduction 126
  making and maintenance—general introduction 107
  pistons 109, *116*
  services 127

Firkins—see *Kegs*

Fischer, Hans Georg 221

Fishermen's companions 267, *286*
  devices—general introduction 265
  floats 267, *287*
  gaffs 267, *287*
  reels 269, *286*
  rods 267

Fitz-Geffery, Henry 341

Flails 92, *87*

Flame veneers 439

Flashes—see *Lacemakers' Candlestands*

Flasks 64, 163, 191, 194, 196, 241, 347, 367, 372, *53, 162, 171, 203, 204, 206, 207, 245, 369, 387, 388*

Flax preparation devices 301

Fleams 397, *426*

Floats, fishermen's 267, *287*

Flour barrels 136, *144*
  scoops—see *Scoops*

Flower pickers 171, *167*

Flummery 187

Folk art—background to 7

Followers—see *Cheese Prints*

Food warmers 124, *117, 121*

Foot warmers 125, *126*

Forks, agricultural 92, *87*
  eating—see *Knives and Forks*
  love token 161, *161*
  malt 394, *423*
  thatchers' combing 406, *427*
  wool teasing 324, *338*

Forts, toy 208

Fox and geese 221, *240*

Frame knitting 303, *338*

Frames, bookbinders' sewing 393, *422*
  textile work 302, 303, *335, 338, 340*

Fraser, Lady Antonia 206, 232

Freedom scroll containers 267, *289*

Freeman, Charles 396, 407

Friction matches 110

Fruit bowls 70, *61*
  pulpers 137, *138*

Funnels and funnel cases 16, 137, 394, *9, 136, 423*

Furniture, miniature—see *Models and Miniature Objects*

Fusee matches 109, *115*

Gaffs, fishermen's 267, *287*

Gags, anaesthetists' and dentists' 15, *8*

Gambrels 395, *86, 424*

Game carriers 239, *246*

Games markers 221, *233*—see also *Cribbage Markers*

Gaming laws—see *Archery*

Garnishing moulds 137, *142*
  skewers 84, *80*

Gas turn-keys 112, *118*

Gasogene 17

Gathering boards 150, *156*

Gauges, engineers' 278, *297*
  marking 382, *409, 413*
  rope layers' 404, *430*

Gavels 171, *165*

Georgian plywood 21, 61, 71, 368, *13, 60, 63, 396*

Gimlets 379, *409*

Gingerbread 185, 186, 187, 188, 189, *187*, *189*, *190*, *195*

Ginger sifters 143, *141*

Ginner, Charles 247

Girandoles—see *Chandeliers*

Girdles 25, *12*

Girouard, Mark 373

Glass-Sellers, Worshipful Company of 168

Glazing irons, shoemakers' 400, *421*

Globe puzzles 227, *241*

Globes, wool 309, *338*

Glove hands 151, *151*
 powdering flasks 367, *388*
 symbolism 367
 stretchers 367, *388*

Glove-makers' donkeys 400, *422*

Gluts, plumbers' 402, *430*

Goblets 38, 39, 193, *20*, *26*, *202*

Go-carts—see *Baby Cages*

Goffering machines 154, *156*
 stacks 154, *156*

Goldsmith, Oliver 50, 247, 254, 399

Goldsmiths, Worshipful Company of 52

Golf and golf clubs 232

Goodman, W. L. 376, 379, 386, 387, 388, 390, 391

Gori, Guiseppe 174

Gouges 381, *410*

Gourds 191, 293, *199*, *313*, *388*

Gout stools 368, *396*

Grain scoops—see *Scoops*
 shovels—see *Shovels and Spades*

Grain, wood 439

Gratchov 85

Graters 179, 195, *177*, *178*, *181*, *205*—see also *Snuff Rasps*

Gravers 246, *419*

Gray, Thomas 108

Grease boxes 382, 388, *414*, *419*

Griddle boards—see *Riddle-boards*

Grinders 180, *177*, *180*

Grocers, Worshipful Company of 51

Groves, Sylvia 313, 322, 323

Gun periscopes 239, *245*

H combs 362, *381*, *382*, *384*

Haberstumpf, Johann Karl 221

Hair brushes, revolving 359, *378*
 curling tongs 364, *384*
 puffer 364, *384*
 sieves 97, *86*
 tidies 368, *389*
 weaving sticks 374

Halma 222

Halter weights—see *Stable Logs*

Halved joints—see *Joints*

Hammers 382, *404*, *410*

Hanaps and Hanapers 32

Handles 27, 173, *17*, *66*

Hands, butter 99, *96*
 glove 151, *151*

Hanks 267, *285*

Hanway, Jonas 26, 254, 291

Hardwood—see *Annual Ring*

Harness pegs and racks 397, *427*
 saddles 397, *427*

Harrison, William 24, 67, 147, 154, 199, 249, 302, 309, 319, 327, 430

Hassall, Joan 243, 247

Hat boxes 369, *390*

Hatchels or hetchels 302

Hat pegs 171, *170*

Hatpin stands 369, *389*

Hatters' devices 396, *425*, *433*

Haver boards—see *Riddle-boards*

Havinden, Kate 431

Hay forks 92, *87*
 rakes—see *Rakes*

Hazard—see *Dice and Dice Cups*

Head scratchers 25, *14*

Heal, Sir Ambrose 413

Hectographs 253, *263*, *268*

Height measurers 278, *291*

Herrick, Robert 49, 50

Herring bone banding—see *Veneers and Veneering*

Heywood, Thomas 30

Hobby-horses 232, 234

Hobs 137, *135*

Hockey 232

Hogarth 185, 257

Holders, candle 115, 123, *118*, *120*, *125*
 cravat 374, *380*, *384*, *393*
 kettle and iron 138, *141*
 night-light 122, *117*

reed 406

rush-light—see *Rush-Light Nips*

silk skein 320, *326*

skewer 143, *139*

towel 373, *397*

tumbler 58, 65, 82, *20*, *45*, *78*

whip 242, *246*, *250*

Holtzapffel, Charles 385

Hone, William 337

Hone boxes 93, *85*

Hones 372, *393*

Honeycomb rollers 142, *142*

Hoof parers 398, *426*, *427*

Hoops and minders 209

Hoppity 222

Horn-books 185, 186, 187, 189, 416, 417, *187*, *445*

Horns, benediction 98, *95*
 drinking 42, 59, *48*
 grease—see *Hone Boxes*
 powder 241, *245*

Horse care devices and horse equipment—general introduction 397

Horse mud shoes 93, *86*
 standards 278, *291*
 tethering rings—see *Stable Logs*
 tooth rasps 398, *427*
 twitches 298, *426*

Hour glasses—see *Sand Glasses*

How, Com. G. E. P. 46

Howe, F. J. 40

Howes, Dr. F. N. 194

Howlett, Robert 217

Hughes, G. Bernard 38, 237

Hummel, Charles F. 390

Husflid 9, 153, 321

Hutten, Ulrich von 32

Hydrometers 278, *300*

Ice buckets 64
 picks 171

Icing guns 137, *139*

Imbrication 439

Incised surface decoration 439

Indian clubs 233

Inkpots 253, 254, *263*, *264*

Inkstands 253, 254, *263–265*, *268*

Inlay—see *Veneers and Veneering*

Instantaneous light contrivances 109, *114*

Intaglio carving 184, *182*, *183*

Intarsia—see *Veneers and Veneering*
Iodoform sprinklers 14, *7*
Iron holders 138, *141*
Ironing boards 151, *152*
Itinerant traders' devices 398, *422, 428, 434, 435*

Jack-in-the-boxes 209
Jack straws 228, *244*
Jacks, boot 236, *246*
  lifting 382, *418*
  tankard 65, *49*
Jars 12, 135, 292, 341, *4, 135, 313, 363*
Jelly mould stands 138, *139*
Jesters' baubles 209, *218*
Jet jewellery 192, *15*
Jewel, John 3
Jewel boxes and caskets 369, *388, 392*
Jewellers' devices 409, *292*
Jewellery 192, 196, *15, 200, 201*
Jiggers, pastry making 140, *142*
  woodworking 391
Jig-saw puzzles 224, 236, 237
Jig-saws, treadle operated 391, *406*
Johnson, Ben 185
Johnson, Dr. 224, 254, 291
Joints 439
Jugs 42, 43, 58, 138, *41, 48, 136*
Jumping jacks 212, *218*
Jumping sticks 233, *298*

Kasas 57, *47, 48*
Keelers 54, 156, *151, 152*
Kegs 64, 99, *50, 54, 98*
Kelchins 121, *128*
Kettle holders 138, *141*
Key indicators 93, *105*
Keys 161, *161*
Kindergarten—see *Chautauqua*
Kipling, Rudyard 421
Kitchen—general introduction 129
Kites 209
Kneeling mats 94, *87*
Knife boards 151
  boxes—see *Spoon Racks* and *Cutlery Boxes*
  cases 71

cleaning machines 151, *151*
grinders' machine 398, *435*
stands 71, *61*
Knitting and crochet—general introduction 302
Knitting broaches 308, *323*
  machine cones 304, *337*
  nancy 304
  needle containers 304, *326, 338*
  needle guards 304, *323*
  needles 304, *323*
  row counters 305, *339*
  sheaths 305, *322–325, 327, 330*
  stretchers 308, *323*
  wool ball foundation 309, *340*
  wool holders 308, *323, 338*
Knitting, frame and peg 303, *338*
Knives and forks 73, *64, 66, 67, 81*
Knives, paper 257, *266, 267, 269*
  pen 259, *67, 266*
  scriveners' 259, *270*
  scutching 301
Knop 440
Knotting shuttles 322
Knur and spell 233, *234*
Koechlin, M. 363

Labarge, Margaret Wade 148
Lace making—general introduction 309
Lace bobbins 310, *323, 331, 332, 336*
  bobbin boxes 312, *337*
  bobbin winders 312, *334, 340*
  boxes 370
  presses 155, *156*
  prickers 312, *339*
  tongs 152, *156*
  washing dollies 151, *156*
Lacemakers' bats 312, *323*
  candle-stands 118, 312, *333*
  chairs 313
  foot stools 313, *333*
  pillows and stands 313, *333*
Ladles 58, 74, 86, 140, 144, *21, 45, 62, 82, 137, 141, 319*
Laennec, René 18
Lambs-wool bowls 50

Lámhógs 55, *44*
Lamson Paragon cash ball 395, *425*
Lanterns or Lanthorns 122, *118, 122*
Lard squeezers 138, *137*
Lark lures 239, *248, 249*
Lasts 313, 400, *338, 428, 429*
Lathes 33, 383, *1, 420*
Laundry—general introduction 147
Laundry tally boards 285, *307, 309, 310*
  troughs 156
Lay figures 255, *283*
Lazy Susans 79
Lead dressers 402, *430*
Leather workers' devices 151, 399, *151, 421, 422, 428, 429*
Leggats 406, *427*
Lemon squeezers, scoops and pressers 138, *49, 140*
Letter boxes 199, *210*
  scales 200
Levels 385
Library steps and ladders 255, *271*
Life preservers 171, *170*
Lighting—general introduction 112
Lignum vitae, history of early uses of 32
Lignum vitae sawdust and shavings 12, 32
Limners' easels 256, *282*
Linen presses 154, *148*
  smoothers 155, *156*
Liners, music 256, *266*
  sailmakers' 269, *288*
Line winders, washing 157, *156*
Liotard, Jean-Etienne 125
Little Bedlam Club 37
Lockyer, Lionel 17
Long-arms 406, *427*
Long grain—see *Grain*
Looms, bead and braid 323, *337, 347*
Lopers, rope makers' 404
Loriners, Worshipful Company of 60
Lotto 222, *240*
Loudon, J. C. 361
Love spoons and other love tokens 158, *158–164*—see also, *H Combs; Stay Busks;*

Love spoons and other love
  tokens (*contd.*)
  *Lace Bobbins; Knitting
  Sheaths; Washing Bats;
  Mangling Boards; Snuff
  Spoons; Snuff Boxes;
  Money Boxes; Feather
  Bed Smoothers; Ell Rules;
  Marriage Bowls*
Loving Cups 39, *26*
Lucets 313, *335*
Lucifers 110
Luggies 54, *46*
Lures, lark 239, *248, 249*

McFarlane's calculating cylin-
  der 273, *294*
Machinery,   woodworking
  377, *407*
Macquoid, Percy 256
Magic lanterns 282, *304*
Magnus, Olaus 57, 170
Mahogany, early uses of, in
  England 115, 279
Mallets, bookbinders' 393, *430*
  ceremonial 167, *165*
  gavels 171, *165*
  plumbers 402, *430*
  snuff 356, *366*
  veterinary 397, *426*
  woodworkers' 382,   *398,*
  399, 401, 403, 404
Malt forks 394, *423*
  shovels 394, *423*
Manchets 88
Mangles 153, *154*
Mangling boards and rollers
  153, *153*
Maple sap buckets and spouts
  94, *86*
Maple sugar moulds 94, *86*
Marchpanes 186
Marionettes—see *Puppets*
Markers, sailmakers'—see *Sail-
  makers' Liners*
Markham, Gervase 240
Marking gauges 382, *409, 413*
Marmalade feeders—see *Pod-
  gers*
Marquetry—see *Veneers and
  Veneering*
Marriage bowls 59
  customs 74, 85, 141, 163
Mash stirrers 394, *423*
Mashers, potato 141, *135, 141*
Massage balls 16, *6*

roulettes 16, *6*
Match boxes and containers
  110, *114*, 115—see also
  *Instantaneous Light Contri-
  vances*
  dispensers 120, *116*
Matches, friction 110
  fusee 109, *115*
  sulphur tipped 108, *115*
Maté tea gourds 293, *313*
Mats, dinner 72
  kneeling 94, *87*
Mauls, saddlers' and harness
  makers' 400, *430*
Mazers 43, 58, *22–26, 48*
Mealey begs—see *Butter Bowls*
Measures, cubic 280, *301*
  double cup 17, *6*
  drink 63, *6, 49*
  height 278, *291*
  tape 314, *339, 340*
  time 278, *293, 294, 300,
  302, 303*
  tobacco 343, *353*
Measurers, waist 278
Measuring   devices—general
  introduction 276
Measuring rods 278, *291, 297*
  see also *Ell Rules*
  spheres, proof—see *Hydro-
  meters*
  sticks, ring 278, *292*
Mechanical toys 212
Melon pip purses 192, *15*
Mentor's cards 223, *233*
Mercers, Worshipful Company
  of 62
Mercury droppers 14, *7*
Merels 222, *240*
Methers 55, *44*
Metronomes 279, *300*
Micrographs 282, *292*
Microscopes 283, *300*
Military calculators 273, *297*
Milk prams 398, *434*
Milk sieves—see *Benediction
  Horns*
  skimmers 104, *96*
  vessels 104, *110*
Milking stools 104, *110*
Milkmaid cups 39
Millinery display stands—see
  Wig Stands
Mills, chocolate 291, *312*
  coffee 180, *177, 180*
  plait 407, *427*
  splint 407

Mincers 139
Miners' tally boards 286, *308*
Miniature objects—see *Models
  and Miniature Objects*
Mirrors, artists' dark—see
  Claude Lorraine Glasses
  toilet 370, *389, 391*
Missal stands 251, *281*
Mitres—see *Veneers and Veneer-
  ing*
Modelling stands or stools
  256, *283*
Models and miniature objects
  168, 207, 208, 209–211,
  270, 305, 400, *168, 215,
  216, 219, 221, 222, 224,
  234, 282, 286, 429*
Mole traps 175, *175*
Money balances 287, *292,
  294, 302, 311*
  boxes 167, 211, *168, 225*
Monteiths 65, *59*
Mortars 51, 182, *33, 178,
  179*
Mortise and tenon joints—see
  Joints
Moulds—general introduction
  183, *182, 183, 261*
Moulds, butter 99, 100, 101,
  86, 95, 100–102
  candle 116, *116, 119, 120*
  cheese—see *Cheese Vats*
  cigar 332, *352*
  compo 184, 185, 190, *196–
  198*
  culinary 94, 137, 139, 184,
  86, 136, 142, 184–195—see
  also *Butter Prints, Bread
  Prints, Cheese Prints*
  pie 141, *136*
  pipe 337, *353*
  spoon 144, *136*
Mouse cages 236, *245*
  traps 175, *175*
Moustache cups 293, *313*
Moving-part toys 211, *218*
Moxon, Joseph 38, 380, 382,
  385
Mud shoes, horse 93, *86*
  spades or scuppits 96, *93*
Muffin ladles 140, *141*
  prickers 140, *141*
Muffineers—see *Salts and Condiments*
Mulls, snuff 349, 350, 351,
  366, 367, 370
Munthe, Axel 240

Music liners 256, *266*
Musical boxes 212, 331, 365
Muzzles, ox 94, *108*

Napier's bones 273, *292*
Napkin presses 154
Nativity figures 173, *172, 173*
Needle books and cases 196,
    268, 314, *206, 286, 326,*
    329, 339–341
Needlemakers,   Worshipful
    Company of 314
Needles 314, *326*
Nesting toys 211, *216*
Netting boxes 316, *346*
    tools 268, 316, *287, 335*
Newbery, John 224
Newspaper rests—see *Book*
    Rests
Niall, Ian 268
Niddy-noddies 318, *348, 401*
Night-light holders 122, *117*
    lanterns 122, *122*
Nine-men's-morris—see *Merels*
Nine-pins 233, 234, *241*
Noah's Arks 212, *226, 227*
Nocturnals 268
Noddy—see *Cribbage*
Northcott, Henry 385
North-west European treen,
    characteristics of 7
Numeral human figure cards—
    see *Arithmetic Teaching*
Nutcrackers 75, 84, *70–75, 80*
Nutmeg graters 180, 195, *181,*
    205
Nut picks 78, *73*
Nuts, Brazil 193, *199*
    canarium 192
    coconuts 193, *202–204*
    coquilla 194, 350, *15, 205–*
    207, 368

Oatbread or oatcake slices—
    see *Riddleboards*
Oatmeal rollers 142, *142*
Oeufs a gants 301, *335*
Offertory boxes 167, *168*
Operation pegs 17, *9*
Optics 282, *292, 296, 300,*
    304, 306
Optiques—see *Zograscopes*
Ornamental cups 169, *169*
    turnery 385, *411, 412*
Osier workers' tools 402, *425*

Otters 268
Oven peels 140, *144*
Ox muzzles 94, *108*
    yokes 94, *88–91*
Oyster measurer 140
    opener 140
Oyster pieces 440

Pageant figures 414
Paint boxes 256, *278–280*
Palettes, artists' 257
Palmer, H. E. 235
Palms, sailmakers' 268, *287*
Pantographers 257, *270*
Pap boats 78, *62*
Paper knives 257, *266, 267,*
    269
    weights 258, *268, 269*
Parasols—see *Umbrellas*
Parfilage 310
Paris, Matthew 319
Pastimes—general introduction
    204
Pastimes, indoor 205, *214–*
    233, 235–244, 251
    outdoor 229, *218, 232, 234,*
    241, 245–250, 299, 428,
    429
Pastry boards 133
    markers 140, *142*
    servers 79, *62*
Peach stone jewellery 192,
    200, 201
Peasant art—see *Folk Art*
Peat cutters 94
Pedlars' pack sticks 398, *422,*
    428
Peels 140, *144*
Peggy sticks—see *Washing Dol-*
    lies
Peg knitting 303, *338*
    tankards 47
Pegs, harness 397
    hat 171, *170*
    laundry 153, *156*
    operation 17, *9*
Peithynens 258, *265*
Pell-Mell 231
Pencil boxes 422, *267, 450*
Pencils 259, *266*
Pen cutters 260, *266*
    knives 259, *67, 266*
Penrose, Dr. and Mrs. 422
Pens 259, 260
Pen stands 260, *263*
    trays 260, *269*

wipers 261, *263*
Pepper mills 181, *181*
Pepperers, Guild of 132
Peppers—see *Salts and Condi-*
    ments
Pepys, Samuel 33, 50, 61, 69,
    114, 131, 168, 216, 231,
    257, 273, 285, 290, 291,
    328, 358, 367
Perambulators—see *Waywisers*
Periscopes, gun 239, *245*
Perpetual calendars 278, *302,*
    303
Petrified wood 196, *208*
Phlebotomization outfit 14, *6*
Pickling dishes 142, *139*
Picks, ice 171
    nut 78, *73*
Pickwicks 345
Picnic outfits 79, *62*
Picture alphabets—see *Alpha-*
    bet Teaching
Pie crimpers 140, *142*
    moulds 141, *136*
    peels 140, *144*
Pigeon ringing devices 241,
    246
Piggins 47, 104, *50, 95*
Pigs-in-clover 226, *241*
Pill boxes 17, *8*
    counting boards—see *Chuck-*
    Rum Boards
    making machines 17, *8*
    rounders 17, *8*
    silverers 18, *8*
Pin and socket joints—see
    Joints
Pincushions 268, 316, 374,
    287, 335, 340, 341, 389
Pin poppets 316
Pins 199, 316, *213*
Pin tables—see *Bagatelle*
Pinto Collection, history of
    1, 427
Pipe Makers, Worshipful Com-
    pany of 328
Pipe moulds 337, *353*
    racks 338, *350, 352, 363*
    stands 338, *350*
    trays, boxes or cradles 338,
    350, 352, 363
Pipes and pipe cases 196, 333,
    207, 353, 354, 356
Pipes, pitch 172, *165*
    wooden water 380, *407,*
    408
Pirns 323, *337*

Plait mills 407, *427*
Planes, cheese 71, *65*
  woodworkers' 111, 385, *116*, *409*, *410*, *414–419*
Plassen, Mistress van der 154
Plateau 79, *20*
Plat, Sir Hugh 138, 240, 261
Platters—see *Trenchers*
Playing card boxes 223, *233*
  presses 223, *233*
  stands 223
  woodcut blocks 247, *260*
Playing cards 223, *233*
Playing Cards, Worshipful Company of 223
Pledging cups 163
Ploughs, breast 91, *92*
Plug cutters, tobacco 338, *350*, *353*
Plugs, dinghy 266, *285*
Plumbers' devices 402, *430*
Plumbs or plumb-bobs 385, *413*
Plumier, Charles 38, 52, 385
Plywood, Georgian 21, 61, 71, 368, *13*, *60*, *63*, *396*
Podgers 141, *136*
Poker work—see *Incised Surface Decoration*
Poking sticks 154
Pole ladders 255, *271*
Poles, barbers' 14
Police rattles—see *Bird Scarers*
Pollarding—see *Stooling*
Pomanders 371, *384*, *388*
Pommele figure—see *Fiddleback*
Poor's boxes 168
Pope Joan 224, *233*
Poppets, needle—see *Needle-cases*
  pin 316
Pork pie rammers 141, *136*
Porridge bowls 54
Poss sticks—see *Washing Dollies*
Posset cups 40, *21*, *30*, *53*
Postal service, evolution of 198
Posting boxes 199, *210*
Potato ball makers 141, *142*
  mashers 141, *135*, *141*
Pots, chamber 361, *383*
  coffee 58, 292, *48*, *313*
  salve 372, *388*
  snuff 352, *370*
  tea 296, *313*, *321*
Potters' wheels 403, *422*
  also see *Lathes*

Pounce boxes 261, *264*
Powder boxes 371, *388*
  horns or flasks 241, *245*
Powdering flasks, glove 367, *388*
Presepio figures 173, *172*, *173*
Pressed wood 347
Pressers, bottle cork 60, *49*
  cabbage 134, *135*
  lemon—see *Lemon Squeezers*
Presses, bookbinders' hand trimmer 393, *422*
  cheese 102, *107*
  lace 155, *156*
  linen and napkin 155, *145*
  playing card 223, *233*
  sailmakers' 269, *288*
  stocking 155, *149*
Prick wheels, leather workers' 401, *421*
Prickers, biscuit 140, 189, *141*, *193*
  lace 312, *339*
  muffin 140, *141*
  tobacco 345, *359*
Priests, fishermens' 269, *287*
Printing blocks—general introduction 243
Printing blocks, textile and wallpaper 243, *252–257*
Prints, bread 134, 187, *132*, *186*
  butter 100, *99*, *100*, *102*
  cheese 102, *103*, *104*
Prior, Matthew 186
Prism viewers 283, *292*
Proof testing spheres—see *Hydrometers*
Propellor boxes *172*, *170*
Püchler-Muskau, Prince 62
Puirmans 123, *120*
Pulley blocks 269, *285*
  wheels 404, *425*
Pulls, beer 59, *50*
  bell 167, *167*
Pulverizers—general introduction 179
Puppets 213
Purses 25, 192, 196, *15*
Puttenham, George 80
Puzzles, jig-saw and dissected 224, *236*, *237*
  miscellaneous 226, *419*, *240*, *241*, *445*
Pyrography—see *Incised Surface Decoration*

Quaichs 54, *46*
Quassia cups 39, *20*
Querns 181
Quill pen cutters 260, *266*
Quoits 227, *232*, *251*

Race horse game 227, *242*
Races, saddlers' 401, *421*
Racks, bacon 132, *131*
  coaching horn 342, *250*
  deed 199, *209*
  harness 397, *427*
  pipe 338, *350*, *352*, *363*
  spoon 144, *147*
  sulphur tipped matches 108, *118*
Radio carbon dating 5
Raffald, Elizabeth 187, *291*
Rakes 91, 95, *86*
Rammers, pork pie 141, *136*
Rasps, horses tooth 398, 427
  snuff 352, *371–377*
Rat traps 175, *175*
Rattles, bird scarer 236, *245*
  children's 214, *218*
  police—see *Bird Scarers*
Razor boxes 371, *393*, *394*
  hones and strops 372, *393*
Reading—general introduction 248
Rebate or rabbet 440
Reed bat 406, *427*
  holders 406
Reel stands 317, *342*
Reeling devices 318, *348*, *401*
Reels, fishermen's 269, *286*
Reeving blocks 266, *285*
Relief marquetry—see *Eger Work*
Religious objects, non-secular 172, *64*, *66*, *171–173*, *192*, *207*
Reversible educational boards —see *Alphabet Teaching*
Revolving caskets 331, 365, *351*, *386*, *392*
Reynolds, Sir Joshua 257
Ribbon threaders 318, 372, *335*
Riddleboards 141, *144*
Ring measuring sticks 278, *292*
  stands—see *Trinket Stands*
Ringlet curling sticks 364, *384*
Ringolette 227, *251*

Rings, curtain 170
   serviette 84, *62*
Roche, Sophie v. la 76, 124, 325
Rocking horses 214
Rodent traps 175, *175*
Rods, alphabet 418, *446*
   fishing 267
   measuring 278, *291, 297*
Roller prints—see *Butter Prints*
Rollers 142, 150, 153, *142, 153, 156*
Rolling pins 141, *135, 137*
Root cutting boards 18, 95, *6, 105*
Rope devices 403, *425, 430*
Rosary coquilla eggs 195
Rose engine turning 384, *21, 26, 35–37, 264*
Roulette 227
Roundabout figures 414, *444*
Roundels and roundel boxes 79, *30, 61, 76, 77*
Roundelays 80
Royal Game of Nine Holes 223, *240*
Rubbers, sailmakers'—see *Sailmakers' Liners*
Rulers 200, 262, 267, 269
Rules, ell 277, *297–299*
   slide 273, *297, 298*
Rush-lights 123
Rush-light boxes 123, *117*
   nips 123, *120*
Ruskin, John 252
Russell, John 46, 68, 70, 240

Sabots 399, *428*
Saddlers, Worshipful Company of 166
Sailmakers' devices—general introduction 265
Sailmakers' liners 269, *288*
   needle cases 268, *286*
   palms 268, *287*
   rubbers—see *Sailmakers' Liners*
   smoothers—see *Sailmakers' Liners*
   spools 170, *286*
Sailors' devices—general introduction 265
St. Fond, Faujas de 84
St. John Hope, W. H. 43
Salad servers 81, *62, 81*
Saladiers 146, *134*

Salamanders 142, *144*
Salt boxes 142, *143*
Salting dishes 142, *139*
Salts and condiments 81, *78, 79*
Salve pots 371, *388*
Sammartino, Giuseppe 174
Sand glasses 18, 137, 279, *9, 136, 300*
Sand tables 423
Satchel boxes 422, *450, 451*
Sauce bottle stands 83, *62*
Save-alls 123
Saws 95, 390, *93, 398, 399, 403, 405–407, 409, 418, 433*
Saw sticks 95, *93*
Scales 101, 200, 287, *101, 292, 294, 302, 311*
Scent flasks 191, 196, 366, 372, *171, 207, 387, 388*
Scheemakers, Peter 344
Schidone, Bartolomeo 388
Schoenhut patents 214, *217*
Schott's cylinders 273
Scientific—general introduction 272
Scioptric balls 283, *296*
Scissor boxes 318
   display stands 405, *431*
Scoops, apothecary 18, *8*
   apple 83, *80*
   butter 101, *95*
   cheese 83, *80*
   flour 143, *137*
   general purpose 95, *87, 137*
   lemon 139, *140*
Score boards—see *Games Markers*
Scott Thomson, Gladys 59, 148
Scratchers, back 25, *14*
   head 25, *14*
Scrimshaw work 269—see also *Incised Surface Decoration*
Scriveners' knives 259, *270*
Scrubbing boards 155, *152*
Scuppits—see *Apple* and *Cheese Scoops*, also *Shovels and Spades*
Scutching knives 301
Seal boxes 200, *213*
Sealing wax outfits 200, *209, 267*
Searces 18, *6*
Searchers—see *Hoof Parers*

Seasoning wood 440
Seat sticks 175, *167*
Sedan chairs 176
Seed cups 95, 105
   lips 95, *87*
Serviette rings 84, *62*
Serving mallets, sailmakers' 269, *288*
Sewing frames, bookbinders' 393, *422*
   machines 318
Sextants 270, *289*
Shaker boxes 136, 369, *138*
Shakespeare and Shakespeare's mulberry tree 147, 222, 228, 296, 302, 343, 351, 367
Sharpening devices 391, *419*
Shauls, corn 91, *87*
Shaves, osier 403, *425*
   woodworkers' 391, *418*
Shaving cups 372, *393*
Sheaths, knife 73, 74, *64, 81*
   knitting 305, *322–325, 327, 330*
Sheep bells—see *Bells and Calls*
   branding irons 96, *105*
   dipping troughs 96, *109*
   salve bowls 96, *105*
Shepherds' crooks 96, *93*
   whistles—see *Bells and Calls*
Sherry barrels 64, *54*
Ship models 269, *286*
Ships' figureheads 213, *442*
   instrument makers' sign 414, *443*
Shoe buckles 21, *13, 15*
   cleaning boxes 401, *428*
   horns 360, *384*
   stretchers 401, *429*
   symbolism 351
   trees 401, *429*
Shoe shaped boxes and containers 163, 261, 296, 317, 349, 350, 400, *115, 162, 263, 313, 341, 364, 367, 384, 429*
Shoemakers' devices—see *Leather Workers' Devices*
Shoe-trap—see *Trap Ball*
Shoes, horse mud 93, *86*
   marriage 163, *162*
   model 400, *429*
Shop door bells 406, *425*
   display devices 202, 203, 369, 375, 404, *209, 212, 389, 425, 427, 431*

Shop signs—see *Trade Signs*

Shops, model—see *Models and Miniature Objects*

Short grain—see *Grain*

Shot pourers 241, *245*

Shoulder trays, butchers' 395, *424*

Shove Ha'penny 228, *232*

Shovels 96, 394, *93, 423*

Shuttles 322, 323, *335, 337*

Sidney, Sir Philip 229

Sieves 18, 97, *6, 86*

Sifters 143, *141*

Signets 200, *213*

Silk cocoon winders 319, *337*

   reel stands 320, *337, 340*

   skein holders 320, *326*

   throwers 320, *335*

   winders 320, *326, 337*

Sin-eaters 46

Sinkers—*see Cheese Prints*

Size sticks, shoemakers' 402, *421*

Skates 241, *429*

Skeining devices—see *Reeling Devices*

Skewer holders 143, *139*

Skewers, garnishing 84, *80*

Skiff back boards 270

Skimmers, milk 104, *96*

Skippets 202, *209*

Skittles 233, *234, 241*

Slailing shovels—see *Shovels*

Slates 262, *450*

Sledges 177

Slicers, bread 134, *134*

   butter 99, *95*

   cucumber 146, *134*

   vegetable 146, *134*

Slickenstones 155, *156*

Slide rules 273, *297, 298*

Slides—see *Magic Lanterns*

Sloane, Eric 378, 390

Slöjd (sloyd) 9

Smith, J. T. 420

Smokers' companions 339, *352*

   compendiums 339, *351*

   walking sticks—see *Sticks, Dual Purpose*

Smoking accessories 196, 330, *207, 350–359, 363*

Smoothers, cap crown 150

   feather bed 170, *167*

   hatters 396, *425*

   linen 155, *156*

sailmakers'—see *Sailmakers' Liners*

Snappers—see *Clickets*

Snow spades 96, *93*

Snuff accessories 163, 181, 195, 196, 345, *162, 178, 206, 207, 360–362, 364–377*

   boxes 163, 181, 195, 196, 345, *162, 178, 206, 207, 360–362, 364–370*

   flasks 163, 347, *162, 367, 369*

   graters 181, *178*

   mallets 356, *366*

   mulls 349, 350, 351, *366, 367, 370*

   pedlars' staff 413, *441*

   pots 352, *370*

   rasps 352, *371–377*

   spoons 356, *366*

   walking sticks—see *Dual Purpose Walking Sticks*

Snuffer trays 123, *122*

Scap boxes 373, *393*

Soft grain—see *Grain*

Softwood—see *Annual Ring*

Soldiers 214

Soles, flexible shoe 402, *429*

Solitaire 228, *240*

Southey, Robert 303

Spades 96, 234, *93*

Spathes 144, *138*

Spatulas 143, *142*

Speaking tube whistle 396, *425*

Spectacle cases 262, 266, 267, *269*

Spectacle Makers, Worshipful Company of 262

Spellicans 228, *244*

Spenser, Edmund 430

Spice boxes 65, 143, 181, *26, 53, 141, 178*

Spice graters 180, 181, *178, 181*

Spigots 65, *50, 54*

Spill planes 111, *116*

   vases 111, *116*

Spills 111, *116*

Spindles 321, *328*

Spinet wire stretchers 408, *421*

Spinning devices—general introduction 320

Spinning wheels 321, *344, 345, 402*

Spirit levels—see *Levels*

Spirit proof measurers—see *Hydrometers*

Spits 130, 134, *146*

Spittles 141

Spittoons 339, *383*

Splint mills 407

Spokeshaves—see *Shaves*

Spool boxes 317, *342*

Spools, sailmakers' 270, *286*

Spoon moulds 144, *136*

Spoon racks 144, *147*

Spoons 58, 85, 101, 144, *45, 81–83, 135, 137, 138, 147*

Spoons, anointing 172, *64*

   chrism 172, *171*

   love, 158, *158–164*

   snuff 356, *366*

Spurs stands 241, *250*

Spurtles 143, *142*

Squails 228, *240*

Squares 385, *413*

Squeezers, lard 138, *137*

   lemon 138, *49, 137*

Stable logs 398, *427*

Staffs, running footmen's 28

Stalker and Parker 33

Stamp boxes 202, *213*

   dispensers 202, *209*

   perforators 203, *209*

Standing cups 34, 38, 58, *26, 28, 55–58*

Standishes—see *Inkstands*

Stands, bonnet 374, 380, 384, *393*

   bottle 81, *50*

   candle 117, 121, *333*

   cheese 102, *97*

   cruet 82, *78, 79*

   cutlery 71, *61*

   decanter 81, *50*

   egg 73, 136, *68, 136*

   hatpin 369, *389*

   jelly mould 138, *139*

   knife 71, *61*

   lacemakers' pillow 313, *333*

   millinery display—see *Wig Stands*

   missal 251, *281*

   modelling 256, *282*

   pen 260, *263*

   pipe 338, *350*

   playing card 223

   reel 317, *342*

   ring—see *Trinket Stands*

   sauce bottle 83, *62*

Stands (*contd.*)
  scissor display 405, *431*
  silk reel 320, *337, 340*
  spurs 241, *250*
  teapot 297, *313*
  trinket 373, *389*
  watch 424, *456–460*
  wig 374, *380, 384, 393*
  work basket 324, *349*
State vehicles 414
Stationery cabinets 263, *268, 276*
Stay busks 22, *10, 11*
Steak beaters 145, *136, 312*
Steels 391, *413*
Steelyards 288, *302*
Steen, Jan *423*
Stereoscopes 283, *296, 306*
Stethoscopes 18, *9*
Sticks, basting 133, *133*
  button 150, *151*
  copying 421, *447*
  dual purpose walking 28, 175, 332, *16, 93, 167, 291*
  hair curling 364, *384*
  hair weaving 374
  knitting—see *Knitting Sheaths*
  pedlar's pack 398, *422, 428*
  poking 154
  seat 175, *167*
  shoemakers' size 402, *421*
  shooting—see *Seat Sticks*
  tally 285, *297, 298*
  walking 28, 95, *16–19, 93, 167, 171, 291*
Stilettos 322, *326*
Stirrup cups 41, *39*
Stirrups 242, *428*
Stitching horses, saddlers' 399 *428*
Stocking airers 149, *152*
  presses 155, *149*
Stocks, finger 421, *445*
Stooling 441
Stools, clamp 399, *428*
  coffee 292, *314*
  gout 368, *396*
  lacemakers' foot 313, *333*
  milking 104, *110*
  toasting 145, *145*
Stoppers, apothecary jar 19, *8*
  tobacco 343, *358, 359*
Stow, John 154, 314
Strainers 66, 145, 297, *50, 313*
Strainer spoons and ladles 144, *135, 137, 138, 142*

Straw manufacturing devices 407, *427*
Straw marquetry 407, *432*
Straw sorters 407
  splitters 407, *425*
  twisters 97, *85*
Stretchers, carcase 395, *424*
  glove 367, *388*
  hat 397, *425*
  knitting 308, *323*
  shoe 401, *429*
  spinet wire 408, *421*
Strickles 93, *85*
Strikes, corn 91, *87*
String boxes 203, *211, 212*
Stringings—see *Veneers and Veneering*
Suckling, John 218
Suction cleaners 156, *151*
Sugar nippers 145, *139*
  tongs 163, 297, *162, 312*
Sulphur tipped matches 108, *115*
Sulphur tipped matches racks 108, *115*
Sulpice, Jean 68
Sumi tsubos 381, *419*
Sundials 280, *294*
Surgeons' instrument cases 19, *9*
Sweetmeat bowls 87, *61*
Swift, Jonathan 113
Swifts 324, *338, 340, 400*
Swizzling sticks 65, *50*
Syllabubs 292
Syringe cases—see *Bottle Cases*
Syringes, veterinary 398, *426*

Table croquet—see *Croquet*
Tables 216
Tail dockers, horse 398, *426*
Tallies 284, *297, 298*
Tally boards 285, *308–310*
Tankard bearers 47
  jacks 65, *49*
Tankards 47, 57, *26, 45, 48*
Tape measures 314, *339, 340*
Taper boxes 112, *117*
Tapestry frames 302
Tatting shuttles 322, *335*
Taylor, John 343
Tazzas—see *Bowls, Bread, Fruit, etc.*
Tea caddies 293, 313, *315–320*
  cups and saucers 296, *313, 321*

poys 296
strainers 297, *313*
trays 297
urn powder box 297, *313*
Tea drinking—general introduction 289
Teapot carriers 297
Teapots 296, *313, 321*
Teapot stands 297, *313*
Teeth extractors 15, *8*
Teetotums 229, *233*
Telescopes 284
Teniers, David 340, *348*
Tennis ball brushes 156, *151*
Tenons—see *Joints*
Textile frames 302
  printing blocks 243, *252–257*
Textile work—general introduction 299
Thatch hooks 127
Thatching devices 406, *427, 433*
Theatres, toy 214
Thermometer cases—see *Bottle Cases*
Thermometers, dairy 104, *96*
Thevet André 326
Thievals—see *Spatulas and Spirtles*
Thimbles and thimble cases 322, *339*
Thonet, Michael 175
Thraa-crooks or throw hooks 97, *85*
Thread barrels and boxes 300, *337*
  waxers 323, *339*
Three-pins 234
Tilting hobs 137, *135*
Tinder 112
Tinder boxes 112, 115, 116, *115, 117, 125*
  pistols 112, *116*
Tip-cat 234, *218*
Toad-in-the-hole 229, *243*
Toasting dogs or stools 145, *145*
Tobacco—general introduction 326
  James I's Counterblaste to 327
Tobacco boxes 340, 357, *366*
  cutters 338, *350, 353*
  jars and barrels 341, *352, 355, 363*
  measures 343, *353*